Destination Marketing

Destination Marketing offers the reader an integrated and comprehensive overview of the key challenges and constraints facing destination marketing organisations (DMOs) and how destination marketing can be planned, implemented and evaluated to achieve successful destination competitiveness.

This second edition has been revised and updated to include:

- a slimline 15-chapter structure
- new chapters on Destination Competitiveness and Technology
- new and updated case studies throughout, including emerging markets
- new content on social media marketing in destination marketing organisations and sustainable destination marketing
- additional online resources for lecturers and students including PowerPoint slides, test bank and video links.

It is written in an engaging style and applies theory to a range of tourism destinations at the consumer, business, national and international level by using topical examples.

Steven Pike is Associate Professor of Marketing at Queensland University of Technology, Australia. Steven spent 20 years working in the tourism industry before completing his PhD in destination marketing in 2002 and is a regular speaker at international tourism conferences.

Destination Marketing Essentials

Second edition

Steven Pike

Routledge
Taylor & Francis Group

LONDON AND NEW YORK

First published 2016
by Routledge
2 Park Square, Milton Park, Abingdon, Oxon OX14 4RN

and by Routledge
711 Third Avenue, New York, NY 10017

Routledge is an imprint of the Taylor & Francis Group, an informa business

British Library Cataloguing in Publication Data
A catalogue record for this book is available from the British Library

Library of Congress Cataloging in Publication Data
Names: Pike, Steven, author.
Title: Destination marketing / Steven Pike.
Description: Second edition. | New York, NY : Routledge, 2015. |
    Includes bibliographical references and index.
Identifiers: LCCN 2015025370 | ISBN 9781138912915 (hdk) |
    ISBN 9781138912908 (pbk) | ISBN 9781315691701 (ebk)
Subjects: LCSH: Tourism—Marketing.
Classification: LCC G155.A1 .P544 2015 | DDC 910.68/8—dc23LC
    record available at http://lccn.loc.gov/2015025370

ISBN: 978-1-138-91291-5 (hbk)
ISBN: 978-1-138-91290-8 (pbk)
ISBN: 978-1-315-69170-1 (ebk)

Typeset in Iowan Old Style
by Swales & Willis Ltd, Exeter, Devon, UK
Printed in Great Britain by Ashford Colour Press Ltd.

Contents

Figures

Tables

Case studies

In practice

Research snapshots

Preface

The rise and fall . . . and rise of a resort destination

The first destination marketing organisations (DMOs) predate the start of the tourism destination marketing academic literature by over a century. For example, Switzerland's first regional tourism organisation (RTO) was established at Saint Moritz in 1864 (Läesser, 2000), while the first destination marketing journal articles were published in the early 1970s (see Matejka, 1973; Gearing *et al.*, 1974; Hunt, 1975; Riley and Palmer, 1975). The ensuing 40 years of published research in our field now represents a rich resource that is valuable in enhancing academic understanding of how marketing principles may or may not apply in the context of tourism destinations. It is hoped this literature is also a valuable reference for tourism industry decision makers and stakeholders. However, little has been reported about the extent to which tourism academic research models, findings and recommendations have been adopted in practice. For the first published review of this first 40 years of the destination marketing literature, see Pike and Page (2014).

Destination Marketing: Essentials is underpinned by my 40 years' experience in tourism, the first 20 as a travel industry practitioner and the time since as an academic researcher and teacher. Readers should therefore be aware that, while this brings the benefits of first-hand involvement observing how marketing principles apply in real world settings, personal experience also brings with it inherent biases. It is not my intent to portray myself here as an expert in destination marketing, but rather as someone offering a reasonably long-term experience-based perspective. I am not the only academic with hands-on experience of working for, or providing consulting to, DMOs, and I have enjoyed exchanging ideas with some of the others who have had similar roles including Noel Scott in Australia, Nigel Morgan and Stephen Page in the UK, and Jonathon Day, Bill Baker, Rich Harrill and Bob Ford in the USA. Whether we are destination marketers, tourism business managers, local taxpayers, academics or students, we will see the same situation from different perspectives, sometimes resulting in opposing opinions. Therefore, not everyone will agree with all of my views, as evidenced in published critical reviews of my previous books, for example. That is healthy. This field of ours is not an exact science. There is so much we do not understand, and so we need to be open-minded about alternative perspectives. As French philosopher, Voltaire, wrote in a letter to Frederick the Great in 1770: 'Doubt is not a pleasant condition. But certainty is an absurd one' (see Levene, 2013: 109). This is particularly so in 2015, when the rise in influence of user-generated content on social media is leading to a revolution in internet democracy. We are on the cusp of a new digital age of destination marketing that will see new models of DMO structure and implementation of place promotion, and no one knows for sure yet how this will manifest.

I am fortunate to have had hands-on experience of some of the *political* and *marketing* challenges (these two terms are inseparable in the context of DMOs) involved in promoting destinations at both a national tourism office (NTO) level, working for the predecessor of Tourism New Zealand (www.tourismnewzealand.com), and at an RTO level establishing and managing Tourism Rotorua (www.rotoruanz.com). As a result, I have been exposed to the political tensions, not only inside the DMO and between the DMO and stakeholders but also in the NTO/RTO relationship. Little has been reported about these tensions in the academic literature from an emic (inside) perspective, mainly because of the difficulty in gaining unfettered access to the boardroom. Blumer (1962, in Jennings, 2001: 128) described what I am referring to here as 'being obliged to enter the social setting and become one of the social actors in that social setting', in terms of being part of the discourse rather than merely surveying the participants. I believe strongly that a discussion about *industry politics* warrants inclusion in the tourism/travel/hospitality curriculum, so that graduates are at least aware of its existence. Also, I am hopeful that the future will see more written on the topic in the literature, in the form of ethnographic case studies and practitioner-academic collaborations.

The world's first NTO destination management organisation

The New Zealand Department of Tourist and Health Resorts, established in February 1901, represented the world's first NTO (NZTPD, 1976). This was visionary thinking for a small, fledgling, far-flung South Pacific colony at the edge of the world. To put this into perspective, consider that neighbouring Australia had only become an independent nation the month before. New Zealand was also the first country to introduce government tourist bureaus (Coventry, 2001), within the first few years of the NTO's existence, which were a vertical integration of overseas sales and promotion offices, tour wholesale and coach tour operators, retail travel agents and visitor information centres. The first domestic Government Tourist Bureau was built in Rotorua in 1903 and still stands on the southern end of the city's current visitor information centre. The office was funded and operated by the NTO for almost 90 years. It was in this historic building that I began my career as a cadet with the department in the 1970s.

The NTO's first overseas sales mission was a visit to the 1904 St Louis Exposition in the USA, and in 1906 the first overseas bureau was opened in Sydney, Australia (NZTPD, 1976). By 1910 honorary agents had been appointed in England, USA, Canada and South Africa (TNZ, 2001). Interestingly, it would be another 50 years before a national umbrella association of private sector tourism interests was formed in New Zealand (Staniford and Cheyne, 1994), now known as the Tourism Industry Association of New Zealand (www.tianz.org.nz).

Rotorua was New Zealand's first tourism resort destination, rising to prominence 100 years ago on the back of the government's vision for a South Pacific spa to rival those of Europe. The township of Rotorua was officially created in 1881, as part of the New Zealand parliament's legislative Thermal Springs Districts Act, which made indigenous Maori land available for settlement by Europeans for the first time (Stafford, 1986). This was in response to recognition by the government that the undeveloped natural geothermal features in the area were becoming an established part of the European gentry's grand tour of the colonies (see Savage, 1986), and that they were attracting increasing numbers of invalids from Auckland seeking the supposed curative powers of the many and varied natural hot springs (Stafford, 1986). While entrepreneurs were drawn to this activity, it was the New Zealand government that was responsible for developing, *managing* and promoting the new township as a resort area for the best part of a century.

Initially, the government commissioned the development of a number of bath houses and gardens in the 1880s (Stafford, 1986) and a rail link to Auckland in 1894 (Steele, 1980).

In 1902 English balneologist, Dr Wohlmann, following a tour of European spas, convinced the New Zealand government of the value of the sanatorium concept (Stafford, 1988). Wohlmann persuaded the government to invest all available resources in the development of one spa, at Rotorua, rather than spread limited resources thinly around the fledgling nation. The New Zealand Minister of Finance was attributed with picking up Wohlmann's spa vision:

> *The history of the establishment and development of mineral hot water spas in New Zealand is a tribute to the vision and statesmanship of one man – Sir Joseph Ward, Minister of Finance in the Liberal Ministry in 1902 and Prime Minister of New Zealand in 1906.*
> *(Rotorua Public Relations Office, 1963: 44)*

The flagship tudor-style sanatorium, which opened in 1908, remains one of the most photographed buildings in New Zealand and now houses the Rotorua Museum (www.rotoruamuseum.co.nz).

The New Zealand government funded almost everything in the development and management of Rotorua: 'No other town in the country enjoyed such support from public funds' (Stafford, 1986: 36). Indeed, it has even been claimed Rotorua was the only town in the British Empire to have been completely controlled by central government (Braynart Group, 1980). This included development and management of: the airport, drainage, water supply, roads, parks and gardens, railways, hotel development, spa facilities, electricity, visitor information, swimming pools, lake boat cruises, deer and possum release for hunting, administration of Maori villages, licensing of tourist guides, geothermal tourist attractions and development of the town's most popular attraction, the New Zealand Maori Arts & Crafts Institute.

The reliance on government resources was such that Rotorua did not have an independent local government until 1950 (Stafford, 1988; Tapsell, 1972), and the town's visitor information centre was operated by the department for 90 years. Rotorua was essentially managed by the NTO, which was clearly representative of a destination *management* organisation. This is a term that I will critique in Chapter 1 as one that is incorrectly used by many as a blanket descriptor for organisations that are actually only involved in marketing or promotion of a destination and are not responsible for the actual *management* of resources (see also Pike and Page, 2014).

The New Zealand government's decision to invest so heavily in one town was courageous and not a populist strategy, given that there were many other regions with geothermal resources or other geographic features with potential tourist appeal, which were lobbying for support. Ironically, this level of government support would ultimately be responsible for causing a crisis in Rotorua, which as I have previously reported (with the benefit of hindsight) seemed largely self-inflicted by the local community (see Pike, 2007).

By the 1950s the New Zealand government had dispensed with the Rotorua sanatorium spa plan (Stafford, 1988). Forty year later, Rotorua District Council (1992) attributed the concept's failure to: the long distances from major markets and lengthy travel times; slow internal travel options within New Zealand; high plant maintenance costs in the sulphuric acid environment; too few people actually using the facilities; and a relatively strong medical (sanatorium) focus that fell from vogue in the 1920s as modern medicinal practices evolved. While the local government gradually assumed control of managing the town's infrastructure from the 1950s, the NTO still remained the largest active stakeholder in Rotorua's tourism industry. Rotorua's decline took place gradually over the next 30 years.

When I joined the NZ Government Tourist Bureau (NZGTB) in Rotorua as a cadet in the 1970s, my first role was in the accounts section. One of my roles was the weekly delivery of cash-filled wage envelopes to the dozens of department employees. These included the NZGTB staff, boat masters, pool attendants, tour guides, fishing advisor and an army of gardeners. Separate NZ government departments also operated key facilities such as Rotorua's airport, local bus service, forest parks, the largest hotel and the most visited tourist attraction. However, this was also the beginning of the era of government withdrawal from Rotorua (New Zealand's NTO is now a destination *marketing* organisation), which would eventually create a massive void in terms of *management* of key resources and promotion. The region was simply not strategically prepared for the looming cessation of government subsidisation. As an aside, I recall many parts of the Rotorua NZGTB building were unchanged from the early 1900s and, on one occasion when work was being undertaken to replace floorboards, a horse skeleton was uncovered, a reminder of the dominant mode of tourism transport at the turn of the twentieth century when the office opened.

I spent much of the 1980s working for the New Zealand NTO in Australia. This was the decade when Rotorua's decline as a leading destination became pronounced. Devolvement of the government's role in the management of the Rotorua tourism industry also coincided with major shifts in New Zealand travel patterns. These included the demise of traditional passive coach tours and the rise of independent self-drive travel options. Major coach tour operators collapsed and tour wholesalers had declining influence over the touring routes, which saw a rise in the competitiveness of other destinations such as Queenstown and Taupo.

Rotorua's increasingly forced independence from central government from the 1950s onwards coincided with a steady decline in destination image, due to a lack of infrastructure maintenance by local government. Examples of negative publicity included (Pike, 2002):

- In 1965 the president of the Travel Agents Association of New Zealand described Rotorua to the national media as 'the most squalid place in the country'.
- The government had developed the town's rubbish tip on the Lake Rotorua foreshore, adjacent to the central business district, and released sewerage into the lake after only partial treatment. An overseas scientist gained national media coverage when he publicly labelled the lake an 'unflushed toilet' in the 1970s.
- The 200 people attending a national tourism conference in 1978 reached a consensus that Rotorua was 'losing its oomph' against other destinations.
- In 1986 a major newspaper and national television network described the situation as the death of a tourist town.

A number of attempts to develop a private sector destination promotion organisation ultimately failed due to infighting and a lack of funding. A crisis point was reached during the 1980s when tourism stakeholders and the local council recognised the destination was losing ground to unheralded competition. The year 1988 proved to be a watershed in the evolution of destination marketing by Rotorua, with the failure of an experiment of having an industry cooperative known as the Rotorua Promotions Society (RPS) undertake campaigns with the support of a small Rotorua District Council grant. Out of frustration over its ineffectiveness due to the poor budget, the RPS board resigned en masse and abdicated its Rotorua District Council agreement, abruptly forcing the council to act. One of the RPS's last acts was to commission an Auckland consultancy to develop a situation analysis, which found that (PA Hotels and Tourism, 1987, in Pike, 2002):

- Rotorua did not communicate itself well, and the visitor base was eroding due to the superior marketing by competing destinations.

- Local and national media were biased in their negative publicity, using sensationalism rather than facts.

- Rotorua was developing into a town that was not particularly attractive, and living on its reputation.

- The Mayor and local councillors were not seen to be supporting tourism.

- Rotorua's destination image was tarnished.

- Rotorua needed professional help.

Rotorua's first RTO

Ultimately, the 1988 crisis would lead to Rotorua's rise again as a destination. Finally acknowledging a tourism crisis, the local council agreed to take responsibility for destination marketing. The council's financial commitment to proactive tourism promotions, an economic development unit and a much needed NZ$30 million infrastructure redevelopment saw Rotorua rekindle the interest of entrepreneurs, hotel developers and travel intermediaries. In January of 1989 I was allocated a desk and a phone in a quiet second floor corner of the council headquarters. I was employed, at the age of 28, to establish Rotorua's first RTO. Tourism Rotorua, the RTO, undertook local pride campaigns and extensive television advertising in the domestic market, organised coordinated marketing opportunities for local tourism businesses and established stronger links with the NTO, other RTOs and key wholesalers in international markets.

Rugged individuals

My experience in establishing and managing the RTO was never dull, due to local and national tourism industry politics and the challenges of marketing a multidimensional destination in a dynamic and heterogeneous market place. While the marketing challenges were exciting, the politics were frankly frustrating and tedious. However, the two issues of marketing and politics are inextricably linked for DMOs. Then Rotorua Mayor, the late John Keaney, counselled me that tourism operators were like farmers, of which he was one, because they were *rugged individuals* with strong opinions. I recall one particularly vocal businessman, who seemed to enjoy being an agitator at any tourism forum, often declaring: 'I'm not here to make friends . . . I'm here to make money!' From my experience I learnt that tourism operators are more than happy to be led at a destination cooperative level during a crisis, but they will demand increasing involvement in decision making when progress is being made and the budget is increasing. The more operators are involved in destination marketing planning, the more they must be empowered in RTO decision making. However, the more they are empowered, the more bureaucratic the process becomes and the slower the decision making. A fast-moving entrepreneurial approach during a crisis (see Ateljevic and Doorne, 2000) can evolve into a politically correct bureaucracy. This can in turn be a source of frustration for entrepreneurial RTO staff and the rugged individual tourism operators alike.

The challenge

It would be an understatement to suggest that the task of establishing the Rotorua RTO was recognised as representing a significant challenge. An airline CEO commented at the time: 'If you can turn Rotorua around you will be able to write your own ticket!' With the benefit of hindsight, Wahab *et al.*'s (1976: 92) reflections on negative images were certainly appropriate in Rotorua's case: 'It is easy to downgrade a product or allow it to deteriorate; but it is the devil's own work to upgrade a low-image product'.

Once-proud Rotorua was suffering serious image problems, not only in the market place but also within the host community, with local pride at an all-time low. For example, during my first week back in Rotorua, one local businessman asked me: 'Why have you come back to this Godforsaken hole?' Aspects of the history leading to this crisis point had been reported previously (see, for example, Ateljevic, 1998; Ateljevic and Doorne, 2000; Horn *et al.*, 2000; Pike, 2002, 2007; Pike *et al.*, 2011). One of the problems I encountered during my initial meetings with local industry groups was the disparate nature of the tourism community. In particular, there was a strong feeling that Rotorua Promotion Society activities had only focused on the larger tourism businesses, which were referred to as *the fat cats*. The larger operators explained to me that since they contributed the majority of the funding, it was only fair to expect they receive more promotional exposure. It was also implied that any future destination promotions should continue to feature their products. Ironically, one of these businesses was from outside the district's political boundary and therefore not a contributor to the local authority rates (tax), which funded the new RTO. Another offered to provide a fund of NZ$1,000 every month to our office to ensure their product featured in all destination advertising. I learnt from countless discussions with counterparts in New Zealand and overseas that this was certainly not a situation unique to Rotorua.

Some of the types of political tensions I experienced included:

- pressure from tourism businesses to promote the destination in a way that best suited their interests. Informal groups were formed to gain strength in their direct lobbying to the RTO and *back door lobbying* with the Mayor and other local government officials;
- pressure from local residents who were unhappy the local government was *subsidising* the tourism industry;
- pressure from local businesses to gain better exposure in NTO promotions, and expectations the RTO would be the attack dog on their behalf;
- return pressure from the NTO to quell the Rotorua tourism dissidents;
- pressure from local, elected government representatives to consider initiatives that would best suit their constituents;

- pressure from the local members of the national parliament to help their publicity, particularly close to election time. One gained publicity slamming the effort of the RTO in comparison to rival destination Queenstown, where his brother was the Mayor;

- pressure from local media to publicly discuss negative issues associated with local tourism.

Rotorua has always been a tourist town, and most locals have an opinion on how tourism works, what the opportunities are and how they should be delivered to the community. The range of RTO stakeholders is not therefore limited to those directly involved in the tourism industry. Everyone in Rotorua knows someone in the tourism industry. In my case my late mother, Pearl, worked at Rainbow Springs wildlife sanctuary for 30 years and my late father-in-law, Ben Hona, was the Kaumatua (elder) at the New Zealand Maori Arts & Crafts Institute for over a decade. I therefore felt it important to include this Preface case to acknowledge the perspective from which I approached *Destination Marketing: Essentials*. I enjoyed almost 20 years as a tourism practitioner, in Australia and New Zealand, and participated in cooperative destination promotions in North America, Australasia, the Pacific, Asia and Europe. I have attempted to provide an objective analysis in each chapter, but acknowledge that I have brought to the discussion my own experiences and biases, as with my previous books (see Pike, 2004, 2008, 2010).

Easier said than done

While academic theory provides a wealth of possibilities for tourism practitioners, implementation for DMOs responsible for coordinating a diverse range of stakeholders in multiple markets is problematic. From those very first studies published in the academic literature in the 1970s, destination marketing research has been undertaken by academics with an interest in applied studies that address practical challenges faced by DMOs (Pike and Page, 2014). In this regard, we academics need to take particular care when writing up the conclusions of our research. Any recommendation to industry should be carefully considered, with the explicit acknowledgement that it is often *easier said than done*, when applying academic theory to real world practice.

REVIEW QUESTION

The suggestion is made, with the benefit of hindsight, that the Rotorua crisis was self-inflicted, even though the city's tourism stakeholders had no control over the New Zealand government's withdrawal of resources. Search for the story of the *boiling frog* and relate this as a metaphor to explain why Rotorua tourism stakeholders allowed a crisis to manifest and how this serves as a lesson for other destinations.

REFERENCES

Ateljevic, I. (1998). *Circuits of Tourism: (Re)Producing the Place of Rotorua, New Zealand*. Unpublished PhD Thesis. University of Auckland, NZ. Hard copy only.

Ateljevic, I. and Doorne, S. (2000). Local government and tourism development: Issues and constraints of public sector entrepreneurship. *New Zealand Geographer* 56(2): 25–31.

Braynart Group. (1980). *100 Years of Rotorua*. Rotorua, NZ.

Coventry, N. (2001). *Inside Tourism*. 332. 3 May.

Gearing, C. E., Swart, W. W. and Var, T. (1974). Establishing a measure of touristic attractiveness. *Journal of Travel Research* 12(4): 1–8.

Horn, C., Fairweather, J. R. and Simmons, D. C. (2000). *Evolving Community Response to Tourism and Change in Rotorua*. Rotorua Case Study Report No. 14. Christchurch, NZ: Lincoln University.

Hunt, J. D. (1975). Image as a factor in tourism development. *Journal of Travel Research* 13(3): 1–7.

Jennings, G. (2001). *Tourism Research*. Milton, QLD: John Wiley & Sons.

Läesser, C. (2000). Implementing destination-structures: Experiences with Swiss cases. In Manete, M. and Cerato, M. (eds) *From Destination to Destination Marketing and Management*. Venice, Italy: CISET, pp. 111–126.

Levene, L. (2013). *I Think, Therefore I Am*. London: Michael O'Mara Books.

Matejka, J. K. (1973). Critical factors in vacation area selection. *Arkansas Business and Economic Review* 6: 17–19.

NZTPD. (1976). *75 Years of Tourism*. Wellington, NZ: New Zealand Tourist & Publicity Department.

PA Hotels and Tourism. (1987). *Rotorua Promotions and Development Society: Development of a Marketing Strategy*. Auckland, NZ.

Pike, S. (2002). *Positioning as a Source of Competitive Advantage: Benchmarking Rotorua's Position as a Domestic Short Break Holiday Destination*. PhD Thesis. University of Waikato. November. Hard copy only.

Pike, S. (2004). *Destination Marketing Organisations*. Oxford: Elsevier Science.

Pike, S. (2007). A cautionary tale of a resort destination's self-inflicted crisis. *Journal of Travel & Tourism Marketing* 23(2/3/4): 73–82.

Pike, S. (2008). *Destination Marketing: An Integrated Marketing Communication Approach*. Burlington, MA: Butterworth-Heinemann.

Pike, S. (2010). *Marketing Turistickog Odredista*. Zagreb, Croatia: Turizmoteka.

Pike, S. and Page, S. (2014). Destination marketing organizations and destination marketing: A narrative analysis of the literature. *Tourism Management* 41: 202–227.

Pike, S., May, T. and Bolton, R. (2011). RTO governance: Reflections from a former marketing team. *Journal of Travel & Tourism Research* Fall: 117–133.

Riley, S. and Palmer, J. (1975). Of attitudes and latitudes: A repertory grid study of perceptions of seaside resorts. *Journal of the Market Research Society* 17(2): 74–89.

Rotorua District Council. (1992). *So, You Want to Be a Spa City!!* Rotorua, NZ: Economic Development Section. December.

Rotorua Public Relations Office. (1963). *Your Future's in Rotorua*. Rotorua, NZ.

Savage, P. (1986). In the shadow of the mountain. In Rotorua District Council (eds) *Tarawera Eruption Centennial*. Rotorua, NZ: Rotorua District Council.

Stafford, D. (1986). *The Founding Years in Rotorua: A History of Events to 1900*. Auckland, NZ: Ray Richards.

Stafford, D. (1988). *The New Century in Rotorua*. Auckland, NZ: Ray Richards.

Staniford, T. and Cheyne, J. (1994). The search for the perfect organisation: A New Zealand case study. *Tourism Down-Under: A Tourism Research Conference Proceedings*. Palmerston North, NZ: Massey University.

Steele, R. (1980). Tourism. In Stafford, D., Steele, R. and Boyd, J. (eds) *Rotorua: 1880–1980*. Rotorua, NZ: Rotorua and District Historical Society.

Tapsell, E. (1972). *A History of Rotorua*. Rotorua, NZ: Published by the author.

TNZ. (2001). *100 Years Pure Progress*. Wellington, NZ: Tourism New Zealand.

Wahab, S., Crampon, L. J. and Rothfield, L. M. (1976). *Tourism Marketing*. London: Tourism International Press.

Acknowledgements

With thanks to my 'inspirators' . . .

- my dad Don . . . one of life's true gentlemen

- my children Jesse and Alexandra . . . arohanui (big love)

- my wingman Lacey . . . anni, amanti e bicchieri di vino non sono da contare

- my surreal conference buddy Faye . . . next welcome, what to do?

- my angel Lene . . . diet coke!

- my time thief Jacinta . . . everyone needs one when flying London/Dubai

- my mates Le Cobbler and Fran . . . profitez de votre séjour français 2016

- destinations . . . this manuscript was written between December 2014 and June 2015 . . . at a number of destinations . . . in order of visitation . . . Brisbane, Macau, Gold Coast, Byron Bay, Las Vegas, Miami Beach, Fort Lauderdale, Cozumel, Nassau, Dallas, Singapore, London, Southampton, Leeds, Glasgow and Dubai

Chapter **1**

The study of destination marketing

AIMS

To enhance understanding of:

- the rationale for the study of destination marketing;
- the extent of academic literature relating to destination marketing;
- the divide between tourism academics and practitioners.

ABSTRACT

The politics, challenges and constraints inherent in marketing a tourism destination are very different to those faced by individual tourism service businesses. Destination marketers must somehow create and manage a compelling and focused market position for their multi-attributed place, in multiple geographic markets, in a dynamic macro environment. The complexity of this is magnified by the active interest in the process and results by a diverse, dispersed and eclectic range of individual, corporate and political stakeholders who have a vested interest in the attraction of visitors to the area. Therefore, an understanding of destination marketing is *essential* for anyone working in, or contemplating, a managerial or entrepreneurial career in tourism, travel or hospitality. The success of individual tourism-related businesses is reliant to some extent on the competitiveness of the destination in which they are either located in, or supply services to. A major contributing factor to destination competitiveness is being effectively organised, in the form of a well-resourced and well-managed destination *marketing* organisation (DMO) that has strong collaborative relationships with government, media, local businesses, travel intermediaries and host communities. Understanding the DMO perspective can better equip entrepreneurs to take advantage of opportunities in promotion, distribution and product development, thereby enhancing their own success, which in turn contributes to the competitiveness of the destination. Also, it is in the interests of destination marketing practitioners to appreciate the increasingly rich depth of relevant published tourism research that has developed since the 1970s. At the same time it is also necessary that academics and students appreciate the complex realities of destination marketing practice that often render the blanket application of theory and research recommendations as *easier said than done*.

Introduction

Following my three previous destination marketing books (see Pike, 2004, 2008, 2010), the principle aim of *Destination Marketing: Essentials* is to provide a synthesis of how marketing principles might be applied by practitioners to enhance the competitiveness of tourism destinations. This is an overview of the study of destination marketing from the perspective of the DMO and is global in outlook, since the theory and case study examples highlight the commonality of challenges, constraints and opportunities facing DMO management everywhere, whether in Lima, Peru; Southampton, England; or Macau, China. Destinations have become the biggest brands in the travel industry (Morgan *et al.*, 2002), and most countries, states and cities now fund a DMO to attract visitors to their distinctive place (Pike and Page, 2014). Therefore, the destination and destination marketing have emerged as a central element of tourism research (Wang and Pizam, 2011; Fyall *et al.*, 2012) and perhaps even 'the fundamental unit of analysis in tourism' (UN World Tourism Organization (UNWTO), 2002), since most tourism activity takes place at destinations (Leiper, 1979). For any given travel situation, consumers are spoilt for choice of destinations, all of which compete for attention in markets cluttered with the promotional messages of substitute products and services as well as rival places. The focus of the book is the *raison d'etre* and mission of DMOs as being to enhance the competitiveness of their geographic space as a visitor destination.

Readership

Destination Marketing: Essentials is primarily designed for use by undergraduate students undertaking a degree or diploma in tourism, travel, leisure, recreation or hospitality. The rationale is that an understanding of the nature of DMO operations, challenges and constraints is not only a prerequisite for those seeking a career in destination marketing but should also be regarded as essential for those who will become active stakeholders, such as managers of hotels, attractions, adventure operations and airlines, as well as entrepreneurs, financiers, advertising agencies, consultants, local government politicians and policy makers. As future tourism industry managers, students will almost certainly interact with DMOs at national, state and/or local levels during their career. Opportunities exist for even the smallest of tourism-related businesses to participate in, benefit from and contribute to DMO planning and operations in some way. All DMOs around the world share a common range of political and resource-based challenges not faced by private sector tourism businesses. Understanding these will be of benefit to those who will be dealing with DMOs. Without this knowledge, initial encounters with DMO staff can be frustrating, which can then inhibit a long-term relationship with the organisation that is marketing their region. Private sector tourism managers must understand that the principles guiding staff in public sector and non-profit organisations, such as in DMOs, are often quite different to their own and that by considering these they will be able to collaborate more effectively for mutual benefit.

A destination represents an amalgam of a diverse and eclectic range of businesses and people, who might or might not have a vested interest in the prosperity of their destination community (Pike and Page, 2014). For example, some research has found that not all small business owners are necessarily interested in the viability of the destination, when their own objective for operating a business is lifestyle (Thomas *et al.*, 2011). The aim should be to develop relationships that both create opportunities to further their own business interests more effectively, and contribute positively to the competitiveness of the destination. After all, the success of these individual tourism businesses will ultimately be reliant to a large extent on the competitiveness of their destination (Pike, 2004), just as the success of the destination will be reliant on the competitiveness of individual tourism businesses. Recent research testing this proposition includes SMEs' dependence on DMO resources in Finland (Seppala-Esser *et al.*, 2009) and hotel performance in Spain (Molina-Azorin *et al.*, 2010). At one extreme, the very viability of tourism enterprises at destinations in crisis caused by a diversity of exogenous events, as has been the case with Cyclone Pam in Vanuatu in 2015; military coups d'état in 1998 and 2006 in Fiji; devastating earthquakes in Christchurch, New Zealand in 2011; and terrorist bombings in 2002 and 2005 in Bali, Indonesia, for example, have rendered the destination uncompetitive overnight. Clearly, hotel managers cannot stop a cyclone or military coup. What they can do is work with the DMO to prepare a disaster contingency marketing plan, for example, to mitigate the effects of such a disaster turning into a longer-term crisis.

Another audience of interest is students in business schools and creative arts schools, where tourism, hospitality or travel is not their degree or diploma major. Many students destined for careers with advertising agencies, public relations firms, business consultancies, financial services and branding agencies will likely engage with tourism clients, given the sheer scale of the tourism industry. Likewise, those heading for roles promoting special events, art galleries, museums and orchestras will engage with their DMO. It is hoped the style of the book will prove a useful reference resource for those seeking to understand the idiosyncrasies and pressures inherent in destination marketing. Working for a DMO can seem like life in a fishbowl, where every move is observed. This is particularly the case in regional communities where DMO staff will regularly run into their stakeholders in the street, shopping centre and pub!

Learning outcomes

Two clear themes underpin the discussion throughout *Destination Marketing: Essentials*. The first, involving both the demand-side and supply-side perspectives of marketing, is concerned with the challenges involved in promoting multi-attributed destinations in dynamic and heterogeneous markets. The second theme concerns the need to provide more effective bridges linking academic theory and research outputs with real world DMO practice. The key learning outcomes of the book are to enhance the understanding of the:

- rationale for the establishment of DMOs;
- application of marketing principles in a tourism destination context;
- differences between the concepts of destination marketing, destination management and place marketing;
- complexities of marketing multi-attributed destinations as distinctive tourism brands;
- multidimensional nature of destination competitiveness;
- rise in influence of user-generated content (UGC) on destination image formation and consumer engagement;
- structure, goals and roles of DMOs;
- key opportunities, challenges, constraints and pressures facing DMOs;
- politics in destination marketing decision making;
- design, implementation and monitoring of effective destination marketing communication strategies;
- necessity of disaster response planning;
- importance of marketing research and effective destination marketing performance measures.

Nomenclature and definitions

Since the mid-1960s, marketing practice has been structured around the four Ps framework, originally promoted by Harvard University Professor Neil Borden (see Borden, 1964), featuring **p**roduct, **p**rice, **p**romotion and **p**lace (distribution). In the tourism and hospitality fields this has been expanded to the seven Ps and eight Ps, with the inclusion of partnerships, people, programming and packaging (see, for example, Shoemaker and Shaw, 2008; Morrison, 2010). DMOs have limited influence over the practices of their destination's service suppliers and external travel intermediaries in relation to all but one of the four or more Ps, and that is promotion. Therefore, a premise of *Destination Marketing: Essentials* is that the core focus of DMO activities is promotion, leading the development and implementation of collaborative marketing communication strategies that match internal (destination) resources with macro environment (market) opportunities. Destination marketing is as simple and as complicated as that.

Destination management

It is the premise above about promotion that motivates my criticism of the use of the term destination *management* organisation as an incorrect blanket descriptor for all DMOs. The vast majority of DMOs simply do not have the mandate or the resources to control the management of their destination's resources, as was the case with the New Zealand Department of Tourist and Health Resorts discussed in the Preface. This early national tourism office (NTO) controlled and managed the tourism resources of the resort district of Rotorua since the mid-1960s. These days the role and activities of New Zealand's NTO and Rotorua's regional tourism organisation (RTO) are limited to destination marketing. Like most DMOs around the world, neither of these could be classified as a destination *management* organisation, since they do not have control over the resources they promote.

There has been a lack of research related to destination management (Jenkins *et al.*, 2011). This book is concerned with destination *marketing* organisations and not destination *management* organisations. As Fyall (2011: 345) argued: 'unless all elements are owned by the same body, then the ability to control and influence the direction, quality and development of the destination pose very real challenges'. Therefore the destination management organisation nomenclature is inappropriate and misleading, since *management* implies control and few if any DMOs have the mandate or resources to *manage* their locality. Following Pike and Page (2014: 204–205), there are a number of key constraints facing DMOs in this regard:

- **DMOs cannot change the official name or geographic boundary of the place they represent, to better appeal to the market.** For example, in a private meeting with the Mayor of Rotorua I was involved in, a Japanese delegation of leading travel wholesalers suggested very strongly the city should consider changing the city's indigenous Maori place name to an English sounding name such as Kingstown, in an effort to appeal to Japanese travellers who were increasingly drawn to the competing NZ resort area of Queenstown. For cultural sensitivity issues this suggestion was never seriously contemplated. As discussed in Chapter 11, an alternative strategy for places with unusual or unattractive place names is to adapt or create a term that is synonymous with the area's tourism promotion, but does not necessarily officially appear on a map.

- **DMOs have no control over visitor arrival levels relative to carrying capacity.** This can involve an over-supply of visitors, particularly during peak periods at famous hotspots such as Venice's Piazza San Marco (St Mark's Square), resulting in calls for de-marketing to reduce overcrowding. Conversely an under-supply of visitors during the off season is a common challenge. I have previously reported an extreme example of this caused by powerful offshore intermediaries that controlled visitor levels to Alanya in Turkey (see Pike, 2008: 11–12). The area's hotels were forced to close for three months during the off season when European tour wholesalers directed group travel to warmer destinations, creating a serious impact on the local economy. In this regard, probably the most neglected area of DMO performance measurement has been in relation to destination marketing and its impact on seasonality (Pike and Page, 2014). While seasonality is a well-documented theme in the literature (see Baum and Lundtorp, 2001; Jang, 2004), with a long history of development in the economic modelling of tourism (Bar-on, 1975), particularly in peripheral areas (Commons and Page, 2001), the role of public sector interventions to address seasonality has received limited attention, especially from the DMO perspective (see, for example, Spencer and Holecek, 2007).

- **DMOs have little if any control over the quality of the actual visitor experience, relative to the promise made in marketing communications.** The state tourism office (STO) for Queensland in Australia once offered a money back guarantee for sunny weather during a holiday to support the then brand slogan 'Beautiful one day, perfect the next', which ultimately proved unrealistic. See Harris *et al.* (2005) for a case highlighting the lack of control over service quality delivery by another Australian STO. Of paramount importance are the quality service standards of individual tourism and non-tourism businesses. At the time of writing, this issue was becoming critical for Macau, where the number of hospitality service staff was expected to double from 27,000 in 2014 to 54,000 in 2015 due to increasing casino developments generating an additional 42,000 hotel rooms. Other factors include: overcrowding and traffic congestion during peak periods, graffiti, litter, crime, host community attitudes and even the weather.

- **DMOs have little if any contact with the visitors they might have had some responsibility in attracting to the destination.** As a result of this the opportunity for continued meaningful engagement with previous visitors in the pursuit of repeat patronage is lost, even though relationship marketing represents an efficient means to stimulate more business. While Web 2.0 technologies and social media represent the best ever opportunity to engage with consumers, most DMOs are currently only experimenting in an *ad hoc* manner, with a definitive practical model yet to emerge.

- **DMOs have little control over the host community's acceptance of, and attitude towards, visitors.** This aspect is exemplified in *Bye Bye Barcelona*, an online documentary freely available on YouTube, which exposes the potential negative effects of mass tourism on the host community, as spoken by local residents.

- **DMOs have no control over stakeholders' product development.** Destination marketers can only suggest new product development opportunities to meet the wants of the market. For example, the decline in the number of visitors to outback Australia since the late 1990s has been attributed to the failure by destinations to adapt to changing market trends by way of rejuvenation of existing services and development of new products (Schmallegger *et al.*, 2011).

- **DMOs are at the mercy of political masters and stakeholders for continuity of funding.** DMOs are not usually commercial businesses and so have no direct income. Most can only operate effectively with government funding, and governments and their policies change regularly. Page and Connell (2009), for example, provided a detailed outline of the restructuring of the DMO structure in the UK, where many faced major public funding cuts while others were abolished. Public sector funding cuts have also recently affected all the Greek municipal DMOs (see Trihas *et al.*, 2013a, 2013b).

- **DMOs are reliant on a small set of powerful intermediaries for packaging and distribution.** Destination marketers do not directly distribute the tourism services they represent. Rather, DMOs act as information brokers in the tourism distribution system. Again, the case of Alanya, Turkey (see Pike, 2008: 11–12) highlights the potential severity of this issue facing some destinations. As discussed in Chapter 9, developing a strong brand image in the market place is increasingly seen as an effective strategy to counter intermediary power, albeit complicated by the democratisation of the internet through social media.

- DMOs have little control over access issues such as bilateral airline agreements and development of airport, port, rail and road transport infrastructure.

- DMOs have little influence over the management of the natural environment, the development/ maintenance of land use zoning, infrastructure such as local transport networks and superstructure.

- DMOs have no control over stakeholders' pricing or marketing communications apart from when joint promotions are undertaken.

Therefore it is misleading to stakeholders at a destination to suggest that the DMO is concerned with destination resource *management* issues if they are not. Yes, it could be argued the DMO manages destination promotion and attempts to manage the stakeholder network collaboration. However, while this labelling issue is probably not a problem during boom times, the term has the potential to raise expectations of the DMO's role and capabilities during periods of crisis or declining visitor numbers (Pike and Page, 2014). Interestingly, in a consensus building session on this issue at the second Biennial Forum on Advances in Destination Management in 2014, there were calls from some delegates to re-label DMOs as destination *communication* organisations (see Reinhold *et al.*, 2015). At the time of writing, the world's largest association of DMOs still used the term destination *marketing* organisation, which is reflected in the name Destination Marketing Association International (see http://www.destinationmarketing.org).

Place marketing

This book does not deal with the literature or practice related to *place marketing*, where tourism is just one of a wide range of sectors including export trade, education, public policy and diplomacy, and economic development. There are, of course, overlaps between the fields of destination marketing and place marketing, as is highlighted in case study 1.1, and an important research gap is the lack of understanding about the extent to which the reputation of a country, province or city influences tourism destination brand perceptions, as well as the reverse (see Martinez and Alvarez, 2010). Readers interested in the wider field of place marketing are referred to the journal *Place Branding and Public Diplomacy* that was launched in 2004, the *Journal of Place Management and Development* that started in 2008, a special issue of the *Journal of Brand Management* (9(4)) on 'nation branding', the online newsletter *The Place Brand Observer* (www.placebrandobserver. com), and a number of scholarly books (Ashworth and Voogd, 1990; Kotler *et al.*, 1993; Ward and Gold, 1994; Anholt, 2003, 2007, 2010; Broudehoux, 2004; Greenberg, 2008; Govers and Go, 2009; Ashworth and Kavaratzis, 2010; Dinnie, 2011; Colomb, 2012; Go and Govers, 2012; Zavattaro, 2013, 2014; Karavatzis *et al.*, 2015).

CASE STUDY

1.1 Destination and place brands – Collaboration, coexistence and common goals: The case of Orlando, Florida

Professor Alan Fyall
Rosen College of Hospitality Management
University of Central Florida, USA

With over 62 million visitors in 2014, contributing an estimated economic impact of around US$55 billion, Orlando in Central Florida is one of the leading tourist destinations in the world. From its humble citrus fruit economic origins in the early 1900s, the arrival of Walt Disney World in 1971 served as the catalyst for an incredible journey of destination development which continues to this day. Its world-class theme parks and attractions, hotels and restaurants, retail malls and convention space continue to attract visitors from all over the globe with significant further investment planned long into the future. Less well-known, however, is that Orlando is the 26th largest metropolitan area in the United States with a population of 2.3 million, boasting a gross domestic product in excess of US$100 billion. With an expanding non-tourism economy that boasts national and international leaders in aerospace and defence, life sciences and biotechnology, modelling, simulation and training and digital media, Orlando offers far more than large mice and roller coasters! Further evidence of Orlando's growing diversity is its Medical City, a life-science cluster that is projected to create 30,000 jobs with a US$7.6 billion economic impact within 10 years, while Orlando is also home to the nation's second largest university, the University of Central Florida.

Not wishing to stand still, Orlando continues to grow with its non-tourism economy central to its ambitions. Despite its many successes, however, Orlando remains relatively unknown outside of the tourism world with even its local residents not fully aware of its non-tourist allure. To counter this imbalance of perceptions and economic activity, Orlando's Economic Development Commission has recently launched a new 'place' brand – *Orlando. You Don't Know the Half of It* – with the strategic intention of enhancing significantly its identity as an attractive place for economic development and inward investment. With Orlando benefiting from a cost of living equivalent to the national average and significantly less than competing destinations, which include the likes of New York and Boston in the East and San Francisco and San Diego in the West, its irresistible lifestyle options are a central tenet to its future 'place' positioning in the eyes of future investors, residents and students. As such, and with an underpinning desire to showcase Orlando as an excellent place to live and work, this new regional 'place' branding initiative runs parallel to Orlando's more prominent 'destination' brand identity – *Orlando Makes Me Smile* – as it seeks to encourage business leaders in the US and internationally to take Orlando seriously as a place in which to invest.

With each brand offering a distinct message and desired outcome, as well as being targeted at very different audiences, both the 'place' and 'destination' brands happily coexist with the greater good of the wider region central to both branding propositions. Supported by a broad spectrum of industry, political and public sector stakeholders that span education, health and the third sector, Orlando represents an unusual and refreshing case study where all relevant stakeholders understand the benefits to be achieved through collaboration and grasp the advantages to be achieved through effective, enduring and appealing 'place' and 'destination' brands. Unlike many destinations where the 'place' and 'destination' brands represent uncomfortable bedfellows, Orlando represents an oasis of 'common sense' where both brands are a reflection of the political maturity, business foresight and common goals shared by all stakeholders that seek to expand the destination's appeal as a place to both live and visit.

Useful web links

VisitOrlando: http://www.visitorlando.com
Orlando Economic Development Commission:
http://www.orlandoedc.com/Why-Orlando/You-Dont-Know-the-Half-of-It.aspx

Discussion question

What is the rationale for a destination to develop a branding theme that goes beyond the realm of tourism attributes?

Since the focus of this book relates to the activities of tourism DMOs, some thoughts on defining these key terms are necessary.

Tourism

It must be recognised that tourism is a relatively new academic discipline, and research in the field has drawn extensively from theories developed in other disciplines such as geography, marketing, economics, sociology, political science, history, psychology, management and anthropology. With no theories of its own, tourism has been the subject of disdain in academic circles (Hall, 2013; Leiper, 1979: 392): 'The study of tourism as a focal subject has sometimes been treated with derision in academic circles, perhaps because of its novelty, perhaps because of its superficial fragmentation, perhaps because it cuts across established disciplines'.

The fragmentation alluded to by Leiper is also a cause for ambiguity about what constitutes the *tourism industry* (Vanhove, 2005; Ermen and Gnoth, 2006), given the term subsumes hospitality (broken down further into accommodation, wining/dining, gaming, etc.), travel, tour operations, entertainment, recreation and leisure: 'All tourism involves travel, yet not all travel is tourism. All vacation travel involves recreation, yet not all tourism is recreation. All tourism occurs during leisure time, but not all leisure time is spent on tourism activities' (Mill and Morrison, 2002: 1).

An industry is generally viewed as a group of firms engaged in the same kind of business activities. However, in terms of being organised to compete in the market place, by getting all vested interests to work together, it is far more difficult for a tourism destination than other industry cooperatives such as a cluster of winemakers or primary producers such as cheesemakers. Drive around Champagne in France, Napa Valley in California, the Barossa Valley in Australia or Marlborough in New Zealand and you will easily spot who is in the wine making industry. At a destination, many businesses in other services sectors, such as convenience stores, entertainment (e.g. movie theatres), sports (e.g. football stadiums) and transportation (e.g. local rail), would not generally be classified as *tourism* firms, even though these businesses will service visitors as well as local residents. Further complicating the matter is the range of other secondary beneficiaries of indirect and induced employment created when local businesses and residents spend money earned from tourism (see, for example, Page and Connell, 2009).

So, to date there is no universally accepted definition of *tourism*, and it has even been suggested that such a definition is conceptually impossible (see Smith, 1988; Holloway, 1994). As has been pointed out by leading tourism academics such as Leiper (1995), Hall (1998) and Page and Connell (2009), most tourism textbooks offer a different definition. The definition used will also depend on the purpose for which it is to be applied, which most commonly is to define markets and analyse visitor impacts and statistics. For DMOs these include, for example, reports that seek to:

- promote the economic, social and cultural benefits of tourism to a community in a bid to enlist government funds for destination promotion;

- promote the scale and growth of tourism in a business investment prospectus;

- highlight potentially negative environmental impacts at a proposed development site.

Following Buck's (1978) assertion that tourism scholarship was organised across two distinctive streams, economic development and tourism impacts, Leiper (1979) sought to develop a general framework for tourism that would bridge the two. In reviewing previous attempts at defining tourism, Leiper

(1979) identified three approaches. The first was economic, where definitions only recognised business and economic aspects, such as: 'Tourism is an identifiable nationally important industry. The industry involves a wide cross section of component activities including the provision of transportation, accommodation, recreation, food, and related services' (Australia Department of Tourism and Recreation, 1975, in Leiper, 1979: 392).

Leiper criticised this approach for the lack of a number of elements, the most important being the human dimension. The second approach was technical, where the interest was in monitoring the characteristics of tourism markets, such as describing tourists, travel purpose, distance travelled and length of time away. For example, the first of these was that adopted by the League of Nations Statistical Committee in 1937, which defined an international tourist as someone who 'visits a country other than that in which he habitually lives for a period of at least twenty-four hours' (OECD, 1974, in Leiper, 1979: 393). Most definitions have used this approach, usually as a basis for collection of comparable statistics. The third approach was holistic, where the attempt was made to capture the whole essence of tourism, such as: 'Tourism is the study of man away from his usual habitat, of the industry which responds to his needs, and of the impacts that both he and the industry have on the host's socio-cultural, economic and physical environments' (Jafari, 1977, in Leiper, 1979: 394).

Many historians (see, for example, Shaffer, 2001: 11) have cited the *Oxford English Dictionary* explanation of the origin of the word *tour* originating from the Latin *tornus*, which came from the Greek word for a 'tool describing a circle'. This is representative of a circular journey away from home, from site to site, and then returning home, as shown for example in Leiper's outline of the geographical elements of tourism in Figure 1.1.

Shaffer (2001) suggested the verb *tour* first emerged in the English language during the seventeenth century, while Sigaux's (1966: 6) overview of the history of tourism suggested the first definition appeared in the nineteenth century. Sigaux cited the *Grand dictionnaire universel du XIXe siècle* of 1876, which defined tourists as 'people who travel for the pleasure of travelling, out of curiosity and because they have nothing better to do'. Curiously, Sigaux (1966: 92) also limited the scope of tourism to preclude domestic travel: 'One can almost say that national tourism, at home in one's own country, hardly counts as tourism'.

Tourism has traditionally been viewed from the demand perspective as being hedonic (pleasure seeking). However, such a perspective does not encompass all categories of temporary visitors to a destination, who would otherwise still contribute to the coffers of businesses whose managers consider they are in the tourism industry. Other than travel for general pleasure, many other types of tourism, for example, which

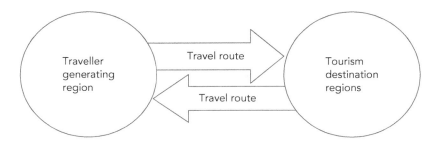

Figure 1.1 Geographic elements of tourism
Source: Adapted from Leiper (1979).

may or may not fit the category of a *holiday*, have been documented. These include travel for: medical procedures, business, conferences, exhibitions, sport, visiting friends or relatives, sex and romance, gambling, educational field trips, gastronomy, art and spiritual pilgrimages. For example, Canada attracts an estimated 3 million wine tourism visitors worth CAD$1.2 billion (see TravelandTourWorld.com, 2015a). Also, recently entering the tourism lexicon are: *adoption tourism*, involving couples travelling for the purpose of adopting an orphan child; *health tourism*, the phenomenon of people travelling to another country for health treatment, because it is either not available in their own country, or the waiting list is too long or they are unable to afford the treatment in their own country (see *The Guardian*, 2013); *fertility tourism*, where Dubai in particular has developed specialist IVF procedures for visitors; *slum tourism* (see 2015 special issue in the journal *Tourism Analysis* 18(4)); *astro tourism*, where visitors are attracted to sites of astronomical observatories (see TravelandTourWorld.com, 2015b); and *suicide tourism*, in which individuals travel to places where euthanasia is possible.

Tourism then is concerned with the activities and interactions of people as they visit different places. Importantly, people not only include travellers but also the travel trade at the place of origin, along the transit route and at destinations, as well as residents of the host communities. This book is interested in tourism as representative of: 'The activities and interactions of people, other than regular commuters, and the resultant economic, socio-cultural and environmental impacts, while travelling to temporarily visit places away from home'.

Thus, it is helpful to consider DMOs are in the *visitor* industry, rather than the *tourism* industry. After all, would you not prefer to be referred to as a visitor, rather than a *tourist*, a term often used in a derogatory way?

Destinations

Currently, there is no widely accepted definition of the term *destination* (Pike and Page, 2014; Reinhold *et al.*, 2015). For an in-depth review of the literature relating to the challenges regarding the conceptualisation of *destination*, see Saraniemi and Kylanen (2011). From the DMO supply perspective, the destination is commonly defined by a political boundary, ranging from a continent, a country, a state or a province, to a city or town. The reason for this is entirely logical, given a DMO's main funding source is a government that levies taxes on landowners and/or businesses and/or workers within the geographic constituency. However, a *destination* might be perceived quite differently from the demand perspective (Ryan, 1991), such as a geographic space in which a cluster of tourism resources exist. Other terms for clusters identified in a literature review by McDonnell and Darcy (1998) include: precinct, recreational business district, peripheral tourism area, tourism destination zone, enclave, integrated beach-resort development, tourism shopping village and tourist district.

A tourism cluster has been defined as 'an accumulation of tourist resources and attractions, infrastructures, equipments, service providers, other support sectors and administrative organisms whose integrated and coordinated activities provide customers with the experiences they expected from the destination they chose to visit' (Rubies, 2001: 39).

From this perspective a tourism cluster might or might not be representative of a political boundary. Dredge (1999) suggested that any conceptualisation of *destination* must therefore be flexible in a hierarchical structure that is adapted to suit different locations and markets. Some clusters exist as a subsection of a political boundary, others are a political boundary, while others cross political boundaries. Examples of these are shown in Table 1.1.

Table 1.1 Examples of different types of destination clusters

A subsection of a political boundary	A political boundary	Across political boundaries
• Cotai entertainment precinct, Macau • The Surfers Paradise precinct within the city of Gold Coast, Australia • The French Quarter, New Orleans • Fisherman's Wharf precinct, San Francisco	• The city of Southampton, England • The state of California, USA • South Africa	• The Algarve, Portugal • Latin America • The Mediterranean • The South Pacific • Scandinavia • The Middle East

From the demand perspective, destinations are places that attract visitors for a temporary stay and range from continents to countries to states and provinces to cities to villages to purpose built resort areas to uninhabited islands. Some of these places have no DMO or tourism infrastructure. Consider Antarctica, a continent that has even attracted visitors to its airspace only through sightseeing flights from Australia and New Zealand, paid for with consumers' discretionary spending and therefore competition for destinations with DMOs. On a smaller scale, consider the case of Peel Island. Accessible only by private boat, this sub-tropical island off the coast of Brisbane in Australia's Moreton Bay is a year-round retreat featuring a beautiful beach, bush walks, snorkelling, fishing and wildlife such as eagles, dolphins, stingrays, sharks and dugong (sea cow). Once housing a leper colony in the nineteenth century, the island is now uninhabited and is protected by government from commercial development. The only facility on the island is an eco-toilet. So, even though there is no opportunity to spend money as a visitor here, the island is seen as taking potential visitors from neighbouring islands and beach areas. Since the focus of this text is the DMO, a tourism destination can be defined as 'a geographic area represented by a DMO at which visitors, other than regular commuters, temporarily base themselves for whatever purpose'.

Marketing

Marketing is essentially a negotiation and exchange between two forces: a supply side and a demand side. The supply side is the travel and visitor industry, which seeks to stimulate demand for products and services. The demand side represents consumer-travellers, who seek travel products and services to satisfy wants: 'Marketing is a social and managerial process by which individuals and groups obtain what they need through creating and exchanging products and value with others' (Kotler *et al.*, 1999: 12).

What is not explicit in many definitions of marketing is whether it is a strategy, a series of processes or a philosophy. Ideally, marketing should be viewed as an organisational philosophy, not the sole responsibility of the marketing department. After all if a firm fails to sell its wares, there will not be any need for accountants or human resource managers, except to close the business. On this basis could it be argued that marketing is the most important function of an organisation? A *marketing orientation* should pervade the entire organisation. This approach is based on the principle of making all decisions with the customer's needs in mind: 'A marketing orientation is a philosophy that recognizes the achievement of organizational goals, requires an understanding of the needs and wants of the target market, and then delivering satisfaction more effectively than rivals' (Kotler *et al.*, 2003).

This represents the third stage in the evolution of marketing. Medlik and Middleton (1973) proposed tourism was following the traditional three-stage process towards a marketing orientation, which had been experienced by other industries. The three stages were identified as:

1. **Production orientation**. This stage is characterised by a shortage of available goods and services that are in demand and is therefore a seller's market. The main problem is to increase output, and most tourism was at this stage until the 1950s.

2. **Selling orientation**. This occurs when technological progress enables mass production, leading to increased imitation and competition, lower prices and a supply in excess of demand. This is therefore a buyer's market with a sales orientation from the producer to sell the increased output. In the case of tourism, the introduction of wide-bodied jet aircraft and large hotels in the 1960s and 1970s stimulated the start of this stage in which many of the world's tourism businesses and DMOs operate.

3. **Marketing orientation**. Increased competition and sophistication of buyers in an affluent society leads to the recognition of the necessity to identify consumer needs. Selling will not be sufficient since consumer needs become the starting point for what is produced. 'Modern marketing is designed to achieve optimal satisfaction of the consumer and to do so at an appropriate return to the producer' (Medlik and Middleton, 1973: 34). Tourism has been slow to evolve to this stage.

An emerging fourth level to this hierarchy is the *societal marketing orientation*, which dictates a market orientation, but operationalised in a way that also altruistically considers the wellbeing of the wider society and environment. DMOs, as representatives of a host community and natural environment as well as commercial tourism services, have such a wider societal obligation. For DMOs, marketing may be considered as representing 'the process of matching destination resources with external macro environment opportunities, with the wider interests of society and the environment in mind'.

DMO

At a country and state level there can be three quite distinctive types of *tourism* organisations, with interests in aspects of destination *management*. One is a DMO responsible for marketing, another is a government ministry providing policy advice to government, while the third is an umbrella industry association of predominantly private sector businesses that champion the interests of the industry. This book is concerned with DMOs at different levels:

- **Macro region tourism organisation (MTO).** An MTO is a collaboration between DMOs for marketing and/or networking and information sharing purposes, and can be at a country level, such as the Scandinavian Tourist Board (www.goscandivaia.com), or at a regional level, such as, for example, RTO New Zealand (www.rtonz.org.nz).

- **National tourism office/organisation (NTO).** The UNWTO (1979: ii) introduced the term national tourism administration (NTA) as 'the authorities in the central state administration, or other official organization, in charge of tourism development at the national level'. The term NTA was used to distinguish from national tourist organisation and national tourist office. For consistency in the book, the term NTO is used.

- **State tourism office/organisation (STO).** An STO assumes overall responsibility for marketing a state (e.g. Hawaii Visitors and Convention Bureau, USA), a province (e.g. The Tourism Bureau of Sichuan Province, China) or territory (e.g. Tourism Northern Territory, Australia) as a tourism destination, in a country that has a federal political system.

- **Regional tourism organisation (RTO).** The term region has a number of different meanings, ranging in geographic scope from a trans-national area, such as South East Asia, to a local area. For the purposes of the text, the term is used to represent 'concentrated tourism areas' (Prosser *et al.*, 2000: 4), such as cities, towns, villages, coastal resort areas, islands and rural areas. This level of DMO is also known by other titles in various parts of the world, such as convention and visitor bureau (CVB), regional tourism partnership (RTP), regional tourism board (RTB) and area tourism board (ATB), for example. The vast majority of the world's destinations are essentially communities based on local government boundaries. With regard to the multidimensional nature of destinations, it has been suggested that the smaller the destination region, the greater the likelihood of internal homogeneity (Kelly and Nankervis, 2001). Intuitively, this appears logical since a town or city would likely be more compact and less geographically diverse than an entire country. However, a diversity of natural features and tourism facilities also represents both a strength and a challenge for many smaller regions. In reality, the political operating environment is usually a microcosm of that faced by NTOs.

- **Local tourism administration/Local tourism association (LTA).** Not all local tourism areas, as defined by a local authority boundary, have a standalone RTO. Instead they might have an LTA, which is a term used to represent both a local tourism administration and a local tourism association. The former may be the local government authority, while the latter is a form of cooperative association of tourism businesses. An LTA is more common at smaller geographic places such as villages or precincts within an RTO area.

The destination marketing literature

The destination marketing academic literature commenced in 1973 and has become an established field with many academic institutions offering courses on the topic. Key milestones within the field of destination marketing have included:

1973   the first journal article (see Matejka, 1973)

1988   the first book (see Gartrell, 1988)

1990   the first academic conference (see Table 1.4)

1992   the first book on DMOs (see Pearce, 1992)

1997   the first destination branding conference session (see Gnoth, 1998)

1998   the first destination branding journal articles (see Dosen *et al.*,1998; Pritchard and Morgan, 1998)

1999   the first journal special issue, in the *Journal of Vacation Marketing*

2002   the first book on destination branding (see Morgan *et al.*, 2002)

2005   the first destination branding academic conference (see Table 1.4)

2007   the first journal special issue on destination branding, in *Tourism Analysis*

2009   the first review of the destination branding literature (see Pike, 2009)

2014   the first review of the destination marketing literature (see Pike and Page, 2014)

Following the suggestion of Fyall *et al.* (2012) that a critical analysis mapping out the field was due, Pike and Page (2014) presented the first narrative analysis of the first 40 years of destination marketing research. Pike and Page (2014) argued that much of the initial stimulus for the destination marketing research emerged from the germane area of tourism marketing, the evolution of which was well synthesised by Gilbert (1989). A later review by Ritchie (1996) noted tourism marketing research had been undertaken by those with a market orientation. Similarly, destination marketing research has been dominated by applied studies addressing operational challenges faced by practitioners (Pike, 2004). Pike and Page (2014) argued that the destination marketing field has been characterised by a 'fragmented applied research approach rather than theory building' (Pike and Page, 2014: 203). Knight (1999) observed the same in the services marketing field and proposed that this was characteristic in the early development of many academic fields.

Jafari (1993) claimed few other sectors had evolved as quickly as tourism had in a few decades. Certainly, it is astonishing how many changes have occurred within the travel industry since the destination marketing literature began in 1973 and which have had significant practical implications. Transformations, which have stimulated research on the implications for destinations, have included the following, for example (Pike and Page, 2014):

- the introduction of jet aircraft;
- the demise of communism;
- privatisation and the outsourcing of government services;
- global recognition of sustainability issues;
- multiplication of media channels;
- globalisation;
- disintermediation and online distribution;
- the internet, digital technologies, information communications technologies (ICT), computer reservation systems (CRS), Web 2.0 and social media;
- the decline of the traditional passive all-inclusive coach tour and the rise of independent travellers and travel packages;
- the rise of short break holidays, backpackers, adventure travellers, medical travel and ecotourism;
- the emergence of low-cost carriers and dynamic pricing;
- the resurgence of cruising, dark tourism and medical tourism;
- global terrorism.

Destination marketing journal articles

Goeldner (2011) estimated that there are 150 English language tourism-related journals in existence, as well as countless non-tourism journals in which tourism research has been published. He traced the earliest academic tourism journals to be: *Tourism Review* (1946), *Turizam* (1956), *The Cornell Hotel and Restaurant Administration Quarterly* (1960), *Journal of Leisure Research* (1968), *World Leisure Journal* (1968), *Journal of Travel Research* (1972) and *Annals of Tourism Research* (1973).

The establishment of the first DMOs preceded the academic field of destination marketing research by at least 100 years, with the first English language journal articles written by Matejka (1973), Gearing *et al.* (1974), Hunt (1975) and Riley and Palmer (1975). Pike and Page (2014) found the reference lists in these papers did not cite any earlier studies and noted that it was not known whether the German and French language journals, such as *The Tourist Review* (first published in 1946 and now known as *Tourism Review*), contained any previous articles. The journal *Place Branding and Public Diplomacy* was first published in 2004, and the first dedicated to destination marketing, the *Journal of Destination Marketing and Management*, was launched in 2012. At the time of writing, the newest journal is the *International Journal of Tourism Cities*, which was launched in 2015.

As summarised in Table 1.2, there have been at least 14 journal special issues on aspects of destination marketing, the first of which was published in 1999 by the *Journal of Vacation Marketing*. There have also been a number of related special issue topics that have featured destination marketing articles:

Table 1.2 Academic journals' special issues on destination marketing

Year	Journal	Issue(s)	Theme
2016	Journal of Destination Marketing & Management	In press	Marketing and branding of conflict-ridden destinations
2014	Journal of Destination Marketing & Management	3(1)	Destination branding
2013	Tourism Tribune	28(1)	Tourism destination branding and marketing
2013	Anatolia	24(1)	Destination marketing – Tourists and places: A cross cultural research agenda (Graduate research)
2012	Journal of Travel and Tourism Research	Spring	Destination management
2011	International Journal of Tourism Research	13(4)	Marketing innovations for sustainable destinations
2010	Tourism Review	65(4)	Destination governance
2008	Tourism Review	63(2)	Destination management and marketing
2007	Journal of Travel Research	46(1)	Destination promotion
2007	Tourism Analysis	12(5/6)	Destination branding
2007	Journal of Travel & Tourism Marketing	22(3/4)	Marketing national capital cities
2005	Journal of Travel & Tourism Marketing	19(2/3)	Destination crisis marketing
2000	Tourism Management	21(1)	The competitive destination
1999	Journal of Vacation Marketing	5(3)	Destination branding

Source: Adapted from Pike and Page (2014).

- The *International Journal of Contemporary Hospitality Management*'s 2016 special issue on 'Contemporary issues in events, festivals and destination management';
- *Tourism Review*'s two 2014 special issues (69(1/3)) on 'Destination leadership';
- The *Journal of Hospitality Marketing and Management*'s 2011 special issue (20(7)) on 'Website evaluation';
- *Tourism Economics*' 2005 special issue (11(1)) on 'Tourism competitiveness';
- The *Journal of Travel and Tourism Marketing*'s 2005 special issue (19(2/3)) on 'Tourism crises and disasters';
- The *Journal of Brand Management*'s 2002 special issue (9(4)) on 'Nation branding';
- The *Journal of Travel Research*'s 1999 special issue (38(1)) on 'War, terrorism, tourism'.

Destination marketing books

The first destination marketing text to be published was by Gartrell (1988). Table 1.3 highlights the range of related books that have appeared in the time since, in order of topic popularity.

Academic destination marketing conferences

The first academic conference on destination marketing was convened in 1990 in Reading, UK. Since then there have been at least 13 further such meetings as shown in Table 1.4. For a summary of the main insights gleaned from participants of the second Biennial Forum on Advances in Destination Management, held in St Gallen in 2014, see Reinhold *et al.* (2015). At the time of writing, the third Biennial Forum was expected to be held in Colorado, USA, in June 2016.

Table 1.3 Books related to destination marketing

Theme	Author(s)
Destination marketing	Gartrell (1988), Ashworth and Goodall (1990), Goodall and Ashworth (1990), Heath and Wall (1992), Nykiel and Jascolt (1998), Pike (2008, 2010), Fyall *et al.* (2009), Kozak *et al.* (2009), Wang and Pizam (2011), Hawn (2011)
Destination branding	Morgan *et al.* (2002, 2004, 2011), Baker (2007, 2012), Donald and Gammack (2007), Cai *et al.* (2009), Moilanen and Rainisto (2009)
Destination marketing organisations	Pearce (1992), Pike (2004), Harrill (2005a, 2005b), Lennon *et al.* (2006), Ford and Peeper (2008)
History of destinations	Walton (1983), Stafford (1986, 1988), Shaffer (2001), Cross and Walton (2005)
Selling destinations	Ashworth and Voogd (1990), Ward and Gold (1994), Mancini (2008)
Destination conference/ events marketing	Gartrell (1994), Davidson and Rogers (2006), Kolb (2006)
Destination crisis marketing	Beirman (2003), Avraham and Ketter (2008)
Island destination marketing	Lewis-Cameron and Roberts (2010)
Destination marketing performance measurement	Woodside (2010)

Source: Adapted from Pike and Page (2014).

Table 1.4 Academic conferences on destination marketing

Year	Conference title	Organisation
2015	Re-branding Serbia	Contemporary Trends in Tourism and Hospitality
2014	Fifth International Conference on Destination Branding and Marketing, Macau	IFT Tourism Research Centre, Macau; University of South Carolina; Welsh Centre for Tourism Research; University of Surrey

2014	Second Biannual Forum: Advances in Destination Management, St Gallen	Institute for Systemic Management and Public Governance at the University of St Gallen, Switzerland
2012	First Biannual Forum: Advances in Destination Management, St Gallen	Institute for Systemic Management and Public Governance at the University of St Gallen, Switzerland
2012	Fourth International Conference on Destination Branding and Marketing, Cardiff	Cardiff Metropolitan University
2009	Third International Conference on Destination Branding and Marketing, Macau	IFT Macau and Perdue University
2007	Second International Conference on Destination Branding and Marketing, Macau	IFT Macau and Perdue University
2005	First International Conference on Destination Branding and Marketing, Macau	IFT Macau and Perdue University
1999	Tourism Destination Marketing: Gaining the Competitive Edge, Dublin	TTRA Europe
1999	Destination Marketing and Management Conference, Venice	Centro Internazionale di Studi Économia Turitica (CISET)
1998	Destination Marketing: Scopes and Limitations, St Gallen	International Association of Scientific Experts in Tourism (AIEST)
1996	Second International Forum on Tourism: The Future of Traditional Tourist Destinations	Fundacion Cavanilles for Advanced Studies in Tourism
1993	The competitiveness of long haul destinations, St Gallen	Association Internationale d'Experts Scientific du Tourisme (AIEST)
1990	Selling tourism destinations	Geographical Institutes of the University of Groningen and the University of Reading

Source: Adapted from Pike and Page (2014).

The divide between destination marketing academics and practitioners

Information that has a limited audience is bound by formal considerations. Scientific information appears in scholarly monographs; political information in speeches, pamphlets, editorials and wall posters; commercial information in advertisements and catalogues; news in reports. Each special informational format presupposes a set of methods and has its own version of reliability, validity and completeness. Becoming a scientist or a politician means, in part, learning and adhering to, even 'believing in', the standards and techniques of one's profession.

(MacCannell, 1976: 135)

This statement, from MacCannell's seminal work *The Tourist*, suggested the process of becoming a tourist is akin to the learning process involved in becoming a member of a profession. The proposition also highlights one of the themes underpinning the book, which is the divide between tourism academics and destination marketers. In an ideal world the academic literature would inform industry, while DMO best practice would inform the literature, in a mutually beneficial cycle. However, separate conferences are held for tourism practitioners and academics, with generally little overlap in attendance. The UNWTO's 2002 think tank on destination competitiveness was the first time practitioners and academics had met in a UNWTO forum on destination management (UNWTO, 2002). The UNWTO has since held a series of these forums.

Academics must publish to gain recognition from peers, in an environment of *publish or perish*. Some are rewarded for level of output rather than level of contribution to either theory or practice. Even though numerous studies in the tourism literature have practical implications, the vast majority of practitioners have probably never actually read the academic papers relevant to their business operations. Academics gain credibility by being published in peer reviewed academic journals, textbooks and academic conference proceedings. Increasingly, due to government funding policies and the proliferation of publishing opportunities, papers must be seen to be in the right journals. Many parts of the world are adopting a tiered system of journal rankings and academic rewards, such as the Australian Business Deans Council ranking system (see http://www.abdc.edu.au/pages/abdc-journal-quality-list-2013.html). Some Australian universities reward academics with cash research funds for an article published in the four Tier A* tourism journals: *Tourism Management*, *Journal of Travel Research*, *Annals of Tourism Research* and *Journal of Sustainable Tourism*, while others offer the reward of a reduced teaching load. At the time of writing, the SCImago Journal & Country Rank (SJR) journal rankings system was beginning to be adopted by universities (see http://www.scimagojr.com/journalrank.php).

There has been little if any incentive to convert academic research into practitioner-friendly, open access research summaries. This is part of a much wider debate now occurring in many countries about the impact of research and its reach and significance (Higher Education Funding Council (HEFC), 2012), and is further evidence of the divide between destination marketers and academic researchers, which has been raised many times since the destination marketing literature commenced (see, for example, Riley and Palmer, 1975; Jafari, 1984; Taylor *et al.*, 1994; Baker *et al.*, 1994; Selby and Morgan, 1996; Hall, 1998; Jenkins, 1999; Ryan, 2002; Pike and Schultz, 2009). Important, but as yet unanswered, questions warranting research attention include:

- To what extent is academic research relating to practical DMO challenges actually read by those practitioners who might benefit?
- To what extent is academic research impacting on current DMO best practice?
- What is the extent of engaged scholarship?

While some academics do engage with DMOs as research consultants, their output is usually not publishable. This is either because of the confidentiality of the findings and recommendations, or because the research was of a descriptive nature and non-theoretical. In their review of the destination marketing literature, Pike and Page (2014) lamented the relative lack of case studies, which would guide both practitioners as well as academics, including analyses of historical destination developments and given that the first DMOs predate the destination marketing literature by over a century. They also suggested the need for more practitioner insights and academic/practitioner collaborations, such as those by Crockett and Wood (1999), Frisby (2002), Morgan *et al.* (2002, 2003, 2004, 2011, 2012), Pride (2002), Beirman (2003), Fyall *et al.* (2003), Leigh and Harrill (2005), Yeoman *et al.* (2005), Pike and Mason (2011) and Pike *et al.* (2011). However, there should be anticipation that the value of the literature will be more widely accepted by the next generation of tourism managers, as a higher percentage will have had exposure to tourism marketing principles through participation in the tourism and hospitality degree courses that have only emerged since the 1990s.

Last word

These words from tourism research pioneer, Richard Butler, in his recent reflection on the evolution of tourism research, which, while referring to tourism in general, should be heeded by destination marketing researchers seeking to make a *real world* contribution:

> *If tourism research is to contribute seriously to knowledge, even if only about tourism, it should return to a more factual approach, examining tourism in the context of the world in which it exists with an emphasis on the topic as a whole, rather than trying to develop new niches for further personal aggrandisement resulting in fragmentation of effort and interest. The present polarity between highly personal subjective interpretation, often using tiny non-representational samples or advanced statistical analysis . . . producing significant (in the statistical sense) but completely irrelevant findings needs to change if tourism research is to be taken seriously and the results to have real meaning . . . The necessity amongst almost all scholars to publish to survive means that the present scale of production of manuscripts heavily outweighs their value. Tourism research, like so many other fields, is becoming dominated by a combination of 'so what?' and 'the emperor has no clothes' writings.*
>
> *(Butler, 2015: 25)*

CHAPTER SUMMARY

Key point 1: The rationale for the study of destination marketing

Understanding the complexity of challenges, opportunities, pressures and constraints facing DMOs is as important to the management of individual tourism businesses as it is to those seeking a career in destination marketing. An understanding of such issues enables stakeholders to take advantage of opportunities in promotion, distribution and new product development, thereby enhancing their own prospects of success as well as contributing to the effectiveness of their destination's competitiveness.

Key point 2: The extent of academic literature related to destination marketing

The first academic journal articles related to destination marketing appeared in the early 1970s. In the 40 years since, the field has increased exponentially in line with recognition of the central role played by destinations in the tourism system. For a narrative analysis of the first four decades of destination marketing research see Pike and Page (2014). The majority of destination marketing research has been undertaken by academics with a practical marketing orientation and the result is a wealth of research of relevance to practitioners.

Key point 3: The divide between tourism academics and practitioners

Ideally, best practice should inform theory, and theory should inform practice, in a symbiotic cycle. However, practitioners and academics alike acknowledge the general divide between theory and practice. More collaboration and information dissemination forums are required for mutual benefit.

REVIEW QUESTIONS

1. To what extent do you believe your nearest DMO is a destination *marketing* organisation or a destination *management* organisation? Explain why.

2. Why it is important for the general manager of a major hotel to have an understanding of the opportunities, challenges and constraints facing DMOs?

3. What initiatives do you think could be developed to stimulate more engagement between academics and practitioners for mutual benefit?

REFERENCES

Anholt, S. (2003). *Brand New Justice: The Upside of Global Branding*. Oxford, UK: Butterworth-Heinemann.

Anholt, S. (2007). *Competitive Identity: The New Brand Management for Nations, Cities and Regions*. Basingstoke, UK: Palgrave Macmillan.

Anholt, S. (2010). *Places: Identity, Image and Reputation*. Basingstoke, UK: Macmillan.

Ashworth, G. J. and Goodall, B. (1990). *Marketing Tourism Places*. New York: Routledge.

Ashworth, G. J. and Voogd, H. (1990). *Selling the City: Marketing Approaches in Public Sector Urban Planning*. London: Belhaven Press.

Ashworth, G. and Kavaratzis, M. (2010). *Towards Effective Place Brand Management: Branding European Cities and Regions*. Cheltenham, UK: Edward Elgar Publishing Ltd.

Avraham, E. and Ketter, F. (2008). *Media Strategies for Marketing Places in Crisis: Improving the Image of Cities, Countries and Tourist Destinations*. Burlington, MA and Oxford, UK: Butterworth-Heinemann.

Baker, B. (2007). *Destination Branding for Small Cities: The Essentials for Successful Place Branding*. Portland, OR: Creative Leap Books.

Baker, B. (2012). *Destination Branding for Small Cities: The Essentials for Successful Place Branding* (2nd edition). Portland, OR: Creative Leap Books.

Baker, K. G., Hozier, G. C. Jr and Rogers, R. D. (1994). Marketing research theory and methodology and the tourism industry: A nontechnical discussion. *Journal of Travel Research* 32(3): 3–7.

Bar-on, R. R. (1975) *Seasonality in Tourism: A Guide to the Analysis of Seasonality and Trends for Policy Making*. London: Technical Series No. 2, The Economist Intelligence Unit Ltd.

Baum, T. and Lundtorp, S. (2001). *Seasonality in Tourism*. Oxford: Elsevier.

Beirman, D. (2003). *Restoring Destinations in Crisis*. Crows Nest, NSW: Allen & Unwin.

Borden, N. (1964). The concept of the marketing mix. *Journal of Advertising Research* 4(1): 2–7.

Broudehoux, A. M. (2004). *The Making and Selling of Post-Mao Beijing*. London: Routledge.

Buck, R. C. (1978). Towards a synthesis in tourism theory. *Annals of Tourism Research* 5(1): 110–111.

Butler, R. (2015). The evolution of tourism and tourism research. *Tourism Recreation Research* 40(1): 16–27.

Cai, L. A., Gartner, W. C. and Munar, A. M. (eds) (2009). *Tourism Branding: Communities in Action*. Bingley, UK: Emerald.

Colomb, C. (2012). *Staging the New Berlin: Place Marketing and the Politics of Urban Reinvention Post-1989*. London: Routledge.

Commons, J. and Page, S. J. (2001). Managing seasonality in peripheral tourism regions. In Baum, T. and Lundtorp, S. (eds) *Seasonality in Tourism*. Oxford: Elsevier, pp. 153–172.

Crockett, S. R. and Wood, L. J. (1999). Brand Western Australia: A totally integrated approach to destination branding. *Journal of Vacation Marketing* 5(3): 276–289.

Cross, G. S., and Walton, J. K. (2005). *The Playful Crowd: Pleasure Places in the Twentieth Century*. New York: Columbia University Press.

Davidson, R. and Rogers, T. (2006). *Marketing Destinations & Venues for Conferences, Conventions and Business Events*. Oxford: Elsevier.

Dinnie, K. (ed.) (2011). *City Branding: Theory and Cases*. Basingstoke, UK: Palgrave Macmillan.

Donald, S. H. and Gammack, J. G. (2007). *Tourism and the Branded City: Film and Identity on the Pacific Rim*. Aldershot, UK: Ashgate.

Dosen, D. O., Vranesevic, T. and Prebezac, D. (1998). The importance of branding in the development of marketing strategy of Croatia as tourist destination. *Acta Turistica* 10(2): 93–182.

Dredge, D. (1999). Destination place planning and design. *Annals of Tourism Research* 26(4): 772–791.

Ermen, D. and Gnoth, J. (2006). A reclassification of tourism industries to identify the focal actors. In Kozak, M. and Andreu, L. (eds) *Progress in Tourism Marketing*. Oxford: Elsevier.

Ford, R. C. and Peeper, W.C. (2008). *Managing Destination Marketing Organizations*. Orlando, FL: ForPer Publications.

Frisby, E. (2002). Communicating in a crisis: The British Tourist Authority's responses to the foot-and-mouth outbreak and 11th September, 2001. *Journal of Vacation Marketing* 9(1): 89–100.

Fyall, A. (2011). Destination management: Challenges and opportunities. In Wang, Y. and Pizam, A. (eds) *Destination Marketing and Management: Theories and Applications*. Wallingford, UK: CABI, pp. 340–358.

Fyall, A., Callod, C. and Edwards, B. (2003). Relationship marketing: The challenge for destination. *Annals of Tourism Research* 30(3): 644–659.

Fyall, A., Kozak, M., Andreu, L., Gnoth, J. and Lebe, S. S. (2009). *Marketing Innovations for Sustainable Destinations*. Oxford: Goodfellow Publishers.

Fyall, A., Garrod, B. and Wang, Y. (2012). Editorial. *Journal of Destination Marketing and Management* 1(1–2): 1–3.

Gartrell, R. B. (1988). *Destination Marketing for Convention and Visitor Bureaus*. Dubuque, IA: Kendall/Hunt.

Gartrell, R. B. (1994). *Destination Marketing for Convention and Visitor Bureaus*. Dubuque, IA: Kendall/Hunt.

Gearing, C. E., Swart, W. W. and Var, T. (1974). Establishing a measure of touristic attractiveness. *Journal of Travel Research* 12(4): 1–8.

Gilbert, D. (1989). Tourism marketing: Its emergence and establishment. In Cooper, C. (ed.) *Progress in Tourism, Recreation and Hospitality Management Volume One*. London: Belhaven, pp. 77–90.

Gnoth, G. (1998). Branding tourism destinations: Conference report. *Annals of Tourism Research* 25(3): 758–760.

Go, F. and Govers, R. (2012). *International Place Branding Yearbook 2012: Managing Smart Growth and Sustainability*. Basingstoke, UK: Palgrave Macmillan.

Goeldner, C. R. (2011). Reflecting on 50 years of the *Journal of Travel Research*. *Journal of Travel Research* 50(6): 583–586.

Goodall, B. and Ashworth, G. (eds) (1990). *Marketing in the Tourism Industry: The Promotion of Destination Regions*. London: Routledge.

Govers, R. and Go, F. (2009). *Place Branding: Glocal, Virtual and Physical Identities, Constructed, Imagined and Experienced*. Basingstoke, UK: Palgrave Macmillan.

Greenberg, M. (2008). *Branding New York: How a City in Crisis Was Sold to the World*. New York: Routledge.

Hall, C. M. (1998). *Introduction to Tourism: Development, Dimensions and Issues* (3rd edition). Sydney, Australia: Pearson Education Australia.

Hall, C. M. (2013). Through a glass darkly: The future of tourism is personal. In Leigh, J., Webster, C. and Ivanov, S. (eds) *Future Tourism: Political, Social and Economic Challenges*. London: Routledge, pp. 103–120.

Harrill, R. (2005a). *Fundamentals of Destination Management and Marketing*. Washington, DC: IACVB.

Harrill, R. (2005b). *Guide to Best Practises in Tourism and Destination Management: Volume 2*. Lansing, MI: EIAHLA.

Harris, R., Jago, L. and King, B. (2005). *Case Studies in Tourism & Hospitality Marketing*. Frenchs Forest, NSW: Pearson.

Hawn, C. A. (2011). *Destination Success: The Official Guide in How to Develop Winning Marketing Strategies*. USA: Ameriguard Communications LLC.

Heath, E. and Wall, G. (1992). *Marketing Tourism Destinations: A Strategic Planning Approach*. New York: John Wiley & Sons.

HEFC. (2012). *Panel Criteria and Working Methods*. Bristol, UK: Higher Education Funding Council.

Holloway, J. C. (1994). *The Business of Tourism*. Harlow, UK: Longman.

Hunt, J. D. (1975). Image as a factor in tourism development. *Journal of Travel Research* 13(3): 1–7.

Jafari, J. (1984). Industry, academe and the national tourist organizations. *Tourism Management* 5(2): 155–156.

Jafari, J. (1993). Anchoring tourism projects on a scientific foundation. In Bar-on, R. R. and Even-Zahav, M. (eds) *The First International Conference on Investments and Financing in the Tourism Industry: Conference Proceedings*. Jerusalem, Israel: Ministry of Tourism.

Jang, S. (2004). Mitigating tourism seasonality: A quantitative approach. *Annals of Tourism Research* 31(4): 819–836.

Jenkins, C. L. (1999). Tourism academics and tourism practitioners: Bridging the great divide. In Pearce, D. G. and Butler, R. W. (eds) *Contemporary Issues in Tourism Development*. London: Routledge, pp. 52–64.

Jenkins, J., Dredge, D. and Taplin, J. (2011). Destination planning and policy: Process and practice. In Wang, Y. and Pizam, A. (eds) *Destination Marketing and Management: Theories and Applications*. Wallingford, UK: CABI, pp. 21–38.

Karavatzis, M., Warnaby, G. and Ashworth, G. (eds) (2015). *Rethinking Place Branding: Comprehensive Brand Development for Cities and Regions*. New York: Springer.

Kelly, I. and Nankervis, K. (2001). *Visitor Destinations*. Milton, QLD: John Wiley & Sons.

Knight, G. (1999). International services marketing: Review of research, 1980–1998. *The Journal of Services Marketing* 13(4/5): 347–360.

Kolb, B. N. (2006). *Tourism Marketing for Cities and Towns: Using Branding and Events to Attract Tourists*. Oxford: Elsevier.

Kotler, P., Haider, D. H. and Rein, I. (1993). *Marketing Places*. New York: The Free Press.

Kotler, P., Bowen, J. and Makens, J. (1999). *Marketing for Hospitality and Tourism* (2nd edition). Upper Saddle River, NJ: Prentice Hall.

Kotler, P., Adam, S., Brown, L. and Armstrong, G. (2003). *Principles of Marketing* (2nd edition). Sydney, Australia: Prentice Hall.

Kozac, M., Gnoth, J. and Andreu, L. (eds) (2009). *Advances in Tourism Destination Marketing: Managing Networks*. London: Routledge.

Leigh, J. and Harrill, R. (2005). *Fundamentals of Destination Management and Marketing*. Washington, DC: IACVB.

Leiper, N. (1979). The framework of tourism. *Annals of Tourism Research* 6(4): 390–407.

Leiper, N. (1995). *Tourism Management*. Collingwood, VIC: TAFE Publications.

Lennon, J. J., Smith, H., Cockerell, N. and Trew, J. (2006). *Benchmarking National Tourism Organisations and Agencies: Understanding Best Practice*. Oxford: Elsevier.

Lewis-Cameron, A. and Roberts, S. (2010). *Marketing Island Destinations: Concepts and Cases*. Oxford: Elsevier.

MacCannell, D. (1976). *The Tourist*. New York: Schocken Books.

Mancini, M. (2008). *Selling Destinations* (5th edition). Clifton Park, NJ: Cengage.

Martinez, S. C. and Alvarez, M. D. (2010). Country versus destination image in a developing country. *Journal of Travel & Tourism Marketing* 27(7): 748–764.

Matejka, J. K. (1973). Critical factors in vacation area selection. *Arkansas Business and Economic Review* 6(1): 17–19.

McDonnell, I. and Darcy, S. (1998). Tourism precincts: A factor in Bali's rise and Fiji's fall from favour – An Australian perspective. *Journal of Vacation Marketing* 4(4): 353–367.

Medlik, S. and Middleton, V. T. C. (1973). The tourist product and its marketing implications. *International Tourism Quarterly* 3(1): 28–35.

Mill, R. C. and Morrison, A. M. (2002). *The Tourism System*. Dubuque, IA: Kendal/Hunt.

Moilanen, T. and Rainisto, S. (2009). *How to Brand Nations, Cities and Destinations: A Planning Book for Place Branding*. Basingstoke, UK: Palgrave Macmillan.

Molina-Azorin, J., Pereira-Moliner, J. and Claver-Cortes, E. (2010). The importance of the firm and destination effects to explain firm performance. *Tourism Management* 31(1): 22–28.

Morgan, N. J., Pritchard, A. and Pride, R. (2002). *Destination Branding: Creating the Unique Destination Proposition*. Oxford: Butterworth-Heinemann.

Morgan, N. J., Pritchard, A. and Piggott, R. (2003). Destination branding and the role of stakeholders: The case of New Zealand. *Journal of Vacation Marketing* 9(3): 285–299.

Morgan, N. J., Pritchard, A. and Pride, R. (2004). *Destination Branding: Creating the Unique Destination Proposition* (2nd edition). Oxford: Butterworth-Heinemann.

Morgan, N. J., Pritchard, A. and Pride, R. (2011). *Destination Brands: Managing Place Reputation* (3rd edition). Oxford: Butterworth-Heinemann.

Morgan, N. J., Hastings, E. and Pritchard, A. (2012). Developing a new DMO evaluation framework: The case of Visit Wales. *Journal of Vacation Marketing* 18(1): 73–89.

Morrison, A. M. (2010). *Hospitality and Travel Marketing* (4th edition). Clifton Park, NY: Delmar.

Nykiel, R. A., and Jascolt, E. (1998). *Marketing Your City, USA*. New York: The Haworth Hospitality Press.

Page, S. J. and Connell, J. (2009). *Tourism: A Modern Synthesis* (3rd edition). Andover, UK: Cengage Learning.

Pearce, D. (1992). *Tourist Organizations*. Harlow, UK: Longman.

Pike, S. (2004). *Destination Marketing Organisations*. Oxford: Elsevier Science.

Pike, S. (2008). *Destination Marketing: An Integrated Marketing Communication Approach*. Burlington, MA: Butterworth-Heinemann.

Pike, S. (2009). Destination brand positions of a competitive set of near-home destinations. *Tourism Management* 30(6): 857–866.

Pike, S. (2010). *Marketing Turistickog Odredista*. Zagreb, Croatia: Turizmoteka.

Pike, S. and Mason, R. (2011). Destination competitiveness through the lens of brand positioning. *Current Issues in Tourism* 14(2): 169–182.

Pike, S. and Page, S. (2014). Destination marketing organizations and destination marketing: A narrative analysis of the literature. *Tourism Management* 41: 202–227.

Pike, S. and Schultz, D. E. (2009). Tourism research: How is it relevant? *Tourism Recreation Research* 34(3): 326–328.

Pike, S., May, T. and Bolton, R. (2011). RTO governance: Reflections from a former marketing team. *Journal of Travel & Tourism Research* Fall: 117–133.

Pride, R. (2002). Brand Wales: 'natural revival'. In Morgan, N., Prichard, A. and Pride, R. (eds) *Destination Branding*. Oxford: Butterworth-Heinemann, pp. 109–123.

Pritchard, A. and Morgan, N. (1998). Mood marketing – The new destination branding strategy: A case of Wales the brand. *Journal of Vacation Marketing* 4(3): 215–229.

Prosser, G., Hunt, S., Braithwaite, D. and Rosemann, I. (2000). *The Significance of Regional Tourism: A Preliminary Report*. Lismore, NSW: Centre for Regional Tourism Research.

Reinhold, S., Läesser, C. and Beritelli, P. (2015). 2014 St. Gallen consensus on destination management. *Journal of Destination Marketing & Management* (in press).

Riley, S. and Palmer, J. (1975). Of attitudes and latitudes: A repertory grid study of perceptions of seaside resorts. *Journal of the Market Research Society* 17(2): 74–89.

Ritchie, J. R. B. (1996). Beacons of light in an expanding universe: An assessment of the state-of-the-art in tourism marketing/marketing research. *Journal of Travel & Tourism Marketing* 5(4): 49–84.

Rubies, E. B. (2001). Improving public-private sectors cooperation in tourism: A new paradigm for destinations. *Tourism Review* 56(3/4): 38–41.

Ryan, C. (1991). *Recreational Tourism: A Social Science Perspective*. London: Routledge.

Ryan, C. (2002). Academia-industry tourism research links: States of confusion. *Pacific Tourism Review* 5(3/4): 83–97.

Saraniemi, S. and Kylanen, M. (2011). Problemizing the concept of tourism destination: An analysis of different theoretical approaches. *Journal of Travel Research* 50(2): 133–143.

Schmallegger, D., Taylor, A. and Carson, D. (2011). Rejuvenating outback tourism through market diversification: The case of the Flinders Ranges in South Australia. *International Journal of Tourism Research* 13: 384–399.

Selby, M. and Morgan, N. J. (1996). Reconstruing place image: A case study of its role in destination market research. *Tourism Management* 17(4): 287–294.

Seppala-Esser, R., Airey, D. and Szivas, E. (2009). The dependence of tourism SMEs on NTOs. *Journal of Travel Research* 48(2): 177–190.

Shaffer, M. S. (2001). *See America First: Tourism and National Identity, 1880–1940*. Washington, DC: Smithsonian Institution Press.

Shoemaker, S. and Shaw, M. (2008). *Marketing Essentials in Hospitality and Tourism: Foundations and Practices*. Upper Saddle River, NJ: Pearson.

Sigaux, G. (1966). *History of Tourism*. London: Leisure Arts Ltd.

Smith, S. L. J. (1988) Defining tourism: A supply-side view. *Annals of Tourism Research* 15(2): 179–190.

Spencer, D. M. and Holecek, D. F. (2007). Basic characteristics of the fall tourism market. *Tourism Management* 28(2): 491–504.

Stafford, D. (1986). *The Founding Years in Rotorua: A History of Events to 1900*. Auckland, NZ: Ray Richards.

Stafford, D. (1988). *The New Century in Rotorua*. Auckland, NZ: Ray Richards.

Taylor, G. D., Rogers, J. and Stanton, B. (1994). Bridging the gap between industry and researchers. *Journal of Travel Research* Spring: 9–12.

The Guardian. (2013). Available at: http://www.theguardian.com/society/2013/oct/24/medical-tourism-generates-millions-nhs-health

Thomas, R., Shaw, G. and Page, S. J. (2011). Understanding small firms in tourism: A perspective on research trends and challenges. *Tourism Management* 32(5): 963–976.

TravelandTourWorld.com (2015a). *Wine Tourism Attracts 3 Million Visitors to Canada.* 28 May. Available at: http://www.travelandtourworld.com/news/article/wine-tourism-attracts-3-million-visitors-canada

TravelandTourWorld.com (2015b). *Chile Emerges as a New Astro-Tourism Destination.* 4 June. Available at: http://www.travelandtourworld.com/news/article/chile-emerges-new-astro-tourism-destination

Trihas, N., Perakakis, E., Venitourakis, M., Mastorakis, G. and Kopanakis, I. (2013a). Social media as a marketing tool for tourism destinations: The case of Greek municipalities. *Journal of Marketing Vistas* 3(2): 38–48.

Trihas, N., Perakakis, E., Venitourakis, M., Mastorakis, G. and Kopanakis, I. (2013b). Destination marketing using multiple social media: The case of 'Visit Ierapetra'. *Tourism Today* Fall: 114–126.

UNWTO. (1979). *Tourist Images.* Madrid, Spain: UNWTO.

UNWTO. (2002). *Thinktank.* World Tourism Organization. Available at: http://www.world-tourism.org/education/menu.html

Vanhove, N. (2005). *The Economics of Tourism Destinations.* Oxford: Elsevier.

Walton, J. K. (1983). *The English Seaside Resort: A Social History 1750–1914.* Leicester, UK: Leicester University Press.

Wang, Y. and Pizam, A. (eds) (2011). *Destination Marketing and Management: Theories and Applications.* CABI International. Available at: www.cabi.org

Ward, S. V. and Gold, J. R. (1994). *The Use of Publicity and Marketing to Sell Towns and Regions.* Chichester, UK: John Wiley & Sons Ltd.

Woodside, A. G. (ed.) (2010). *Tourism-Marketing Performance Metrics and Usefulness Auditing of Destination Websites: Volume 4.* Bingley, UK: Emerald.

Yeoman, I., Durie, A., McMahon-Beattie, U. and Palmer, A. (2005). Capturing the essence of a brand from its history: The case of Scottish tourism marketing. *Journal of Brand Management* 13(2): 134–147.

Zavattaro, S. M. (2013). *Cities for Sale: Municipalities as Public Relations and Marketing Firms.* State University of New York.

Zavattaro, S. M. (2014). *Place Branding through Phases of the Image: Balancing Image and Substance.* Basingstoke, UK: Palgrave Macmillan.

Chapter **2**

The destination marketing organisation (DMO) and destination competitiveness

AIMS

To enhance understanding of:

- the history of DMO development;
- destination competitiveness as the fundamental DMO mission;
- the key goals of DMOs in the pursuit of destination competitiveness.

ABSTRACT

A destination marketing organisation (DMO) is formed as a consequence of a community seeking to become formally organised to attract visitors. While the literature relating to the history of destination marketing development is sparse, it is evident the early DMOs were predominantly promotion orientated, driven by short-term economic boosterism. Nowadays, it is widely recognised that a more holistic approach is required, where the mission of the DMO will be focused on enhancing the long-term competitiveness of the destination. The sustainability of natural and human resources is fundamental and, consequently, tensions are increasing between entrepreneurs, conservationists, local residents and governments. Destination competitiveness is a complex multidimensional construct and is a relatively new field of academic research, with attempts to model and measure destination competitiveness emerging in the 1990s. DMOs are not only competing for attention in fiercely competitive tourism markets for travellers spoilt for choice by available destinations but also a global market place where travel for pleasure is discretionary spending, which means additional competition with giant corporate brands such as Apple and BMW, the marketing budgets of which see even the largest of DMOs pale into insignificance. Essentially, a competitive destination is one that features a balance between nine critical success factors, for which DMOs design their goals.

DMO history

Recognition by communities of the need to become organised and to achieve success as a tourism destination has led to a proliferation of DMOs since the 1980s, particularly at the regional tourism organisation (RTO) level. The DMO mission/vision for the destination to be competitive must subsume all other goals and objectives, since, for any given travel situation, consumers are now spoilt for choice by available destinations (Pike and Page, 2014). In the USA alone, there are 20,000 cities, 3,400 counties, 126 America's Byways and 12,800 National Historical Districts competing for visitors (Baker, 2007: 16). From UN World Tourism Organization (UNWTO) (2014) data, it is apparent that the world's top ten most visited countries in 2012, as listed in Table 2.1, accounted for almost half (44 per cent) of all 1.035 billion international visitor arrivals. Therefore the other 95 per cent of UNWTO member national tourism offices (NTOs) compete for the remaining 56 per cent of travellers. The forecast top ten most visited cities in 2015 are listed in Table 2.2.

People have always travelled, although it is not clear when the first communities became organised to attract visitors. As early as the eighth century BC in ancient Greece travellers visited places such as: Olympia for the games, Delphi for the oracle and the island of Delos to visit the Sanctuary of Apollo, to name but a few. We also know travel to festivals was an important part of life for first-century Galileans (Harland, 2011). There are also detailed records of tourism in first-century BC Augustan Rome in the form of guidebooks, museums, resorts full of drunken holidaymakers, restaurants, spas, souvenir shops, boring tour guides and even postcards (Lomine, 2005). Latin terms in use at this time included *peregrinator*, meaning 'to go abroad, to travel'; *otium*, meaning 'spare time for doing something of leisure rather than business'; and *hospitum*, meaning a 'kindness in welcoming guests'. Lomine (2005: 75) pointed out the Augustan Grand Tour of 2,000 years ago

Table 2.1 Top ten most visited countries in 2012

Country	International visitor arrivals (millions)
France	83.0
USA	66.7
Spain	57.5
China	57.7
Italy	46.4
Turkey	35.7
Germany	30.4
UK	29.3
Russia	25.7
Thailand	22.4

Source: UNWTO (2014).

Table 2.2 Forecast most visited cities in 2015

Ranking	City	Visitor arrivals (millions)
1	London	18.82
2	Bangkok	18.24
3	Paris	16.06
4	Dubai	14.26
5	Istanbul	12.56
6	New York	12.27
7	Singapore	11.88
8	Kuala Lumpur	11.12
9	Seoul	10.35
10	Hong Kong	8.66

Source: Adapted from TravelandTourWorld.com (2015).

significantly predated the more famous European Grand Tour of British aristocrats, with five of the Seven Wonders of the World being obligatory inclusions, all notably man-made rather than natural attractions:

- Pyramids at Giza;
- Phidias statue of Zeus at Olympia;
- Temple of Artemis at Ephesus;
- Mausoleum at Halicarnassus;
- Lighthouse at Alexandria.

In the Middle Ages there is evidence that printed travel guides were in use in France in the 1500s (see Sigaux, 1966). Prior to this, however, was the first reported existence of sports tourism in France in the form of an international jousting tournament in 1389, where knights and supporters travelled from England (McClelland, 2013). The earliest places to have formal promotion agencies were probably at a local community level (Pike, 2004), with perhaps the first RTO to be established at St Moritz, Switzerland in 1864 (Läesser, 2000). The first NTO was launched in New Zealand in 1901 (NZTPD, 1976; McClure, 2004), and in 1903 Hawaii established the first state tourism office (STO) (Choy, 1993). The number of DMOs grew considerably in the period following the Second World War, with many establishing their core marketing role in the 1960s and 1970s alongside the rise of the package holiday and the introduction of jet aircraft. The 1980s and 1990s continued to witness the creation of many new DMOs as more and more communities recognised the value of a coordinated approach to destination promotion (Pike and Page, 2014).

There has been a paucity of historical analyses of DMOs in the tourism literature. However, the lack of historical analyses in the wider tourism literature has been lamented by Walton (2005: 6): 'A problem in tourism studies has been a prevailing present-mindedness and superficiality, refusing deep, grounded or sustained historical analysis'.

Examinations of the evolution of DMOs have commonly appeared as chapters within historical reviews of tourism in different countries (Pike and Page, 2014). Examples of these have included New Zealand (Cushman, 1990; McClure, 2004), Great Britain (Middleton and Lickorish, 2005) and Ireland (Furlong, 2008; Zuelow, 2009). Pike and Page noted only a limited number of individual destination studies referred to the role of DMOs, such as by Brown (1985), Stafford (1986), Russell and Faulkner (1999), McClure (2004) and Adamczyk (2005). The 2009 launch of a specialist tourism history journal, the *Journal of Tourism History*, will hopefully result in increased research and case studies related to the historical successes and failures of destinations and DMOs, to serve as a resource for students and staff working with newer organisations. For example, the establishment of the first NTO for Oman was as recent as 2004, only a year after the USA had an active DMO at the national level. There is an emerging body of books interpreting the development of tourism, a selection of which is shown in Table 2.3. The next section provides a brief history of the establishment of DMOs around the world, from the limited historical publications accessible at the time of writing.

Table 2.3 Books on tourism history

Author	Topic	Country
Sigaux (1966)	History of tourism	France
Walton (1983)	Seaside resorts in the eighteenth and nineteenth centuries	UK
Stafford (1986, 1988)	Development of a resort area in the nineteenth and twentieth centuries	New Zealand
Sears (1989)	Tourist attractions in the nineteenth century	USA
Black (1992)	The Grand Tour of the eighteenth century	UK
Aron (1999)	History of vacations	USA
Richardson (1999)	A history of Australian travel and tourism	Australia
Walton (2000)	Seaside holidays in the twentieth century	UK
Davidson and Spearritt (2000)	Tourism in Australia since 1870	Australia
Shaffer (2001)	Tourism and national identity, 1880–1940	USA
Walton (2005)	Tourism development	British Empire, UK, Japan, Spain, Austria, Nazi Germany, ancient Rome
Cross and Walton (2006)	Pleasure places in the twentieth century	UK, USA
Berger (2006)	Development of Mexico's tourism industry	Mexico

Stokes (2007)	Myrtle Beach, 1900–1980	USA
Morgan (2008)	English–Canadian travel, 1870–1930	United Kingdom, Europe
Gassan (2008)	The birth of American tourism, 1790–1830	USA
Ward (2008)	Development of package holidays in the Spanish Caribbean	Latin America
Hollis (2008)	Florida tourism advertising	USA
Laderman (2009)	USA tourism in Vietnam	Vietnam
Zuelow (2009)	Tourism and national identify in Ireland, from the 1920s	Ireland
Kosta-Thefaine (2009)	Travel in the Middle Ages	Various
Vickers (2010)	The role of Cypress Gardens in the development of Florida tourism	USA
Revels (2011)	Florida tourism since the 1820s	USA
Harland (2011)	Travel and religion in antiquity	Europe, Middle East
Borsay and Walton (2011)	Seaside resort and port towns since 1700	Europe
Cox (2012)	Historical development of tourism in the American South.	USA
Jackson (2012)	History of the rise and decline of the Florida–Alabama Coast	USA
Gottfried (2013)	History of travel guidebooks	USA
Thomas (2014)	History of desire and disaster in New Orleans	USA
Moranda (2014)	Relationship between tourism, conservation and dictatorship in the German Democratic Republic	East Germany

NTOs

As suggested in the Preface, the establishment of the New Zealand Department of Tourist and Health Resorts in 1901 represented not only the world's first NTO but also the first destination *management* organisation at a national level. Many nations did not establish an NTO until decades after New Zealand. For example, of the key neighbouring South Pacific competitors to New Zealand in European markets, Australia's federal government did not provide NTO funding until 1929, with the formation of the Australian National Tourist Authority (Carroll, 1991), while the Samoa Visitors Bureau was not established until 1986.

In Europe the French NTO was established in 1910 (Sigaux, 1966). By 1919, when the Italian NTO was established, the Alliance Internationale du Tourisme had been formed in Brussels, bringing together

30 European NTOs. In Britain the government provided financial support for the 1929 establishment of the Travel Association of Great Britain and Ireland (Elliott, 1997). However, the organisation was no more than embryonic until after the Second World War when the publicly supported British Tourism and Holiday Board was formed in 1947 (Jeffries, 1989). Predating this was the English Channel island state of Jersey, where a tourism committee was empowered to promote the destination in 1937. With unfortunate timing, both the Irish Tourism Board and Belgium General Commission for Tourism were established in 1939 (UNWTO, 1979), just prior to the outbreak of the Second World War. The Northern Ireland tourist board was established through the Development of Tourism Act of 1948 (Davidson and Maitland, 1997). The first statutory legislation in Britain did not occur until the Development of Tourism Act of 1969 (English, 2000), which paved the way for the national tourist boards of Scotland, Wales and England, as well as the British Tourist Authority. It has been suggested that in Scotland, tourism had not been seriously addressed until this time (Kerr and Wood, 2000). The first official NTO for Sweden was not established until 1976 (Pearce, 1996a).

Following the Second World War the International Union of Official Tourism Organizations, the predecessor of the UNWTO, had around 100 member NTOs in 1946 (Vellas and Bécherel, 1995). In Asia the Hong Kong Tourism Association was established in 1957 (Gartrell, 1994), Japan and Thailand established NTOs in 1959 and Singapore in 1964 (Choy, 1993). Regarding communist countries in Asia, the Vietnam Tourism Corporation was formed in 1960, while China did not become active in inbound tourism until after the Reform and Opening Up Policy of 1978. In Africa the Ghana Tourist Board and Ivory Coast Ministry of Tourism were established in 1960, and the Nigerian Tourist Association was formed in 1962 (UNWTO, 1979).

In the Americas, the Mexican Federal Government created the Mixed Pro-Tourism Commission in 1928, which brought together representatives from government ministries and the private sector, to develop a tourism industry (Berger, 2006). The Cuban National Tourism Commission was also formed in the 1920s (Berger, 2006), while the Canadian Bureau of Tourism was established in 1934 (Go, 1987; Jenkins, 1995). Argentina's first attempt at setting up an NTO was the short-lived National Tourism Directorate in 1942 (Piglia, 2011). It has been suggested the government of the USA did not become seriously involved in international tourism promotion until 1961 when the International Travel Act was passed by Congress (Mill and Morrison, 1985), although Dawson (2011) argued a USA Travel Bureau was opened in 1937. The 1961 Act led to the establishment of the United States Travel Service as a division of the Department of Commerce, which would later be changed to the US Travel and Tourism Administration (USTTA). The USTTA folded in 1996 due to a lack of funding (Brewton and Witham, 1998). Morrison *et al.* (1998) observed convention and visitors bureaus (CVBs) such as Las Vegas had larger budgets than the fledgling NTO. Congress then established the National Tourism Organization, a smaller NTO to encourage public–private sector cooperation, which was in turn scrapped (Blalock, 2000). The USA became actively involved at a national level again in 2003 with the formation of the fledgling Tourism and Travel Promotion Advisory Board (Hoover, 2003). In 2010 the federal government's Travel Promotion Act in 2010 led to the creation of Brand USA as the NTO. Brand USA's short-term future was confirmed with the US Congress passing a bill to renew the organisation in December 2014 for a further five years (Travelindustrywire.com, 2014).

In the Caribbean, the Barbados Tourism Board was formed in 1958 (Scantlebury, 2008). By 2015, UNWTO membership comprised 156 member NTOs (see www2.unwto.org/member/states).

STOs

The Hawaii Visitors Bureau was established in 1903, following tourism promotional visits to the US mainland in 1901 and 1902 by the Honolulu Chamber of Commerce and Merchants Association (Choy, 1993). Most other American state tourism marketing did not occur until much later. For example, the

Progress Association, established in 1937, was the first government tourism promotional agency for the state of Washington, with a similar initiative by neighbouring Oregon a year later (Dawson, 2011). Doering (1979) suggested some STOs were established during the 1940s in anticipation of a post-war surge in domestic tourism. Of the then 48 states, 26 had become involved in tourism promotion by 1946. It would not be until the 1970s that all states had an STO. In Canada the Bureau of Industrial and Tourist Development was established in the province of British Columbia in 1935.

The state government of Tasmania in Australia initiated the Tasmanian Tourist Association in 1893 (Davidson and Spearritt, 2000), although little has been reported about its activities. Tasmania at the time was not officially a state as Australia had not achieved independence from Great Britain. Spurred on by the success of the Tasmanian group in creating a tourism profile, the Governor of the state of New South Wales convened a conference of government officials in 1905 to initiate the establishment of a tourism division that was curiously called the Intelligence Department. The states of South Australia and Victoria followed in 1908. However, the first STOs to be formed as distinct government agencies, rather than as part of other departments did not occur in Australia until 1919 in New South Wales, 1921 in Western Australia and 1934 in Tasmania.

While little has been reported in the literature about the history of destination development in India, the STO for Goa was established during the 1960s (Michael and Kotsi, 2015).

Provincial tourism organisations

Some countries with a federal system of government have provinces instead of, or as well as, states and so operate provincial tourism organisations. However, for ease of consistency these are referred to as STOs in this text. The best known of this type of DMO are in Canada (e.g. Tourism Ontario), Australia (e.g. Tourism Northern Territory), China (e.g. The Tourism Bureau of Sichuan Province) and South Africa (e.g. Eastern Cape Tourism Board).

RTOs

The reported history of regional tourism promotion significantly predates that for NTOs and STOs. For example, the first guidebooks in England were printed for Scarborough in 1734 (Brodie, 2012) and Cambridge in 1758 (Davidson and Maitland, 1997). In Switzerland the first RTO was established at St Moritz in 1864 (Läesser, 2000). In 1879 the Blackpool Municipal Corporation obtained British government authority to levy a local property tax for advertising the destination's attractions (Walton, 1991, in Cross and Walton, 2005). This was a unique privilege as competing British resort areas only obtained lesser powers four decades later when the Local Authorities (Publicity) Act (1931) legislated for local government to be given the opportunity to engage in destination promotion (Lavery, 1990). In Germany the first promotion association for the Black Forest region was formed in 1906. Viipuri, in the Finnish/Russian Karelian Isthmus, had an active tourism board by 1912 (see Kostianen, 2011). Following the establishment of the English Tourist Board (ETB) in 1969, 12 English regional tourist boards were created, jointly funded by the ETB, local government and the private sector (Davidson and Maitland, 1997). Old industrial cities such as Bradford, Sheffield, Birmingham and Manchester did not establish DMOs until the 1980s (Bramwell and Rawding, 1996). Ireland formed an initial eight RTOs in the 1960s (see http://www.failteireland.ie/Footer/What-We-Do/Our-History.aspx). The establishment of RTOs in Spain occurred only slowly from the 1980s (Pearce, 1996b).

In New Zealand most RTOs were established in the 1980s when local government became more proactive in economic development; although there had been various other forms of destination promotion since the 1880s (Pike, 2004). In Australia Dredge (2001) suggested New South Wales local governments were given legislative powers to develop leisure and recreation facilities as early as 1858, at a time when demand was increasing for such facilities by excursionists and holidaymakers, and by 1908 were given powers to stimulate tourism through advertising. However, for a number of reasons, including a legacy of paternalistic and centralised state government, there had been, in general, a 'timid approach' towards direct involvement in tourism development initiatives.

CVBs

Even though infrastructure developments enabled regional tourism in the north-eastern USA during the late 1700s and early 1800s (Shaffer, 2001; Gassan, 2008), the development of place promotion organisations did not occur for another century. Interestingly, at Coney Island, which had attracted visitors since the early 1800s, there was no attempt to collectively advertise the destination until 1902 when a Board of Trade was formed (Cross and Walton, 2005). In the interim, travel advertising in many parts of the USA was organised by *boosters* and the railways. The CVB format emanated in the USA, where the first were established in Milwaukee and Des Moines in 1888 (Ford and Peeper, 2008). The next CVBs to be established were in Detroit in 1896 (Gartrell, 1992), Atlantic City in 1908, Denver in 1909 and Atlanta in 1913 (see www.iacvb.org, in Pike, 2008). Well-known cities to set up CVBs much later include New York in 1934, Chicago in 1943, Las Vegas in 1955, Anaheim in 1961 and Orlando and Orange County in 1984. While Sheehan and Ritchie's (1997) survey of 134 North American CVBs identified 15 that had been in existence for over 50 years, the average at that time was only 23 years.

Macro region marketing organisations (MMOs)

In many regions there has been recognition of the opportunities to benefit from working with contiguous competitors for mutual benefits. In terms of geographic scale then, the largest DMOs are those that have been established to market the tourism interests of a group of countries. In this regard, there have been calls for increased cooperation between countries in many parts of the world, including, for example: Scandinavia (Flagestad and Hope, 2001), Central and Eastern Europe (Davidson and Maitland, 1997; Hall, 1998), East Africa (Beirman, 2003) and Australasia (Tourelle, 2003). Examples of marketing cooperatives at an inter-country level include:

- The European Travel Commission (ETC) (see http://www.etc-corporate.org) was established in 1948 and is the Brussels-based headquarters for 33 European member NTOs. The roles of the ETC are to market Europe as a tourism destination and to provide advice to member NTOs. A key aspect of the organisation's structure has been the formation of *Operations Groups* of member NTOs in North America, Japan and Latin America.

- The Confederación de Organizaciones Turísticas de la America Latina was formed in 1957 (see www.cotal.org.ar).

- The ASEAN tourism association was formed in 1971 (see www.aseanta.org).

- The Caribbean Tourism Organization (CTO) (see www.onecaribbean.org) was formed in 1989 as a cooperative to marketing the region's small island nations. The CTO comprises over 30 member countries and has offices in New York and London. An earlier attempt was the Caribbean Travel Association, which was established in 1951.

- The South Pacific Tourism Organisation (SPTO) (see www.tourismsouthpacific.com) was formed in the 1980s to promote tourism to the region. SPTO represents 14 Pacific Island NTOs and, interestingly, the People's Republic of China.

- During 2003 the Irish government established a new national tourism development authority, Fáilte Ireland (see www.failteireland.ie), to replace Bord Fáilte and CERT. Previously the countries of Ireland and Northern Ireland operated separate NTOs.

- VisitBritain was also established in 2003 to replace the British Tourist Authority (BTA) and English Tourism Commission. VisitBritain represents England, Scotland, Northern Ireland and Wales.

- The Scandinavian Tourist Board is a collaboration between the NTOs of Denmark, Sweden, Finland and Norway (see http://www.goscandinavia.com/scandinavia/go-scandinavia).

- The Tourism Promotion Organization for Asia Pacific Cities (see www.aptpo.org) was formed to provide networking opportunities and inter-city cooperation.

- In late 2014 the European National Convention Bureaux was launched, as an initial alliance of the convention bureaus of 17 nations.

Similar cooperatives have been formed at the regional level, including:

- Destination Marketing Association International (see http://www.destinationmarketing.org) is the world's largest association of DMOs, with over 600 members. Membership is predominantly CVBs in North America. The organisation was formerly known as the International Association of Convention and Visitor Bureaus from 1975 to 2005 (see http://www.iacvb.org).

- In the USA many states now have cooperatives of CVBs. The Destination Marketing Association of North Carolina (see http://www.destinationmarketingnc.com/about-us), established in 1976, and the Florida Association of Destination Marketing Organizations (see http://www.fadmo.org), formed in 1996, seek to enhance the effectiveness of member organisations through educational initiatives and networking opportunities. The Northern Indiana Tourism Development Commission was also established in 1996 as a marketing collective representing nine counties (Wang, 2008).

- The Association of Australian Convention Bureaux (www.aacb.org.au) is a collaboration between 15 city and regional CVBs.

- Regional Tourism Organisations New Zealand (RTONZ) (www.rtonz.org.nz) is a member-based organisation that represents the interests of all 30 of New Zealand's RTOs. The role of RTONZ is summarised in case study 2.1.

CASE STUDY

2.1 Regional Tourism Organisations New Zealand (RTONZ)

Charlie Ives
Executive Director, RTONZ

RTONZ is an unincorporated collective of 30 existing RTOs (see www.rtonz.org.nz). The collective was established as a Charitable Trust in 2005, to represent the interests of the collective RTO sector in New Zealand. RTONZ has regular formal meetings and a Board of Trustees of six (three North Island, three South Island), including an elected chairperson. RTONZ activities on behalf of all RTOs are administered through a full-time Executive Officer, based in Wellington.

As the peak body for RTOs, RTONZ aims to encourage better coordination among RTOs, as well as ensuring collective RTOs are engaged and consulted with on issues critical to the development of the regional tourism sector in New Zealand. Key activities of RTONZ include:

- developing RTONZ submissions on issues and draft plans that impact the collective;
- providing advice and assistance to members;
- developing and maintaining ongoing relationships with stakeholder agencies;
- negotiation and execution of project-based funding contracts;
- managing and implementation of projects on behalf of RTONZ;
- coordination of media enquiries;
- advocacy of the RTO sector and the important role it plays in the New Zealand tourism landscape.

RTONZ vision

RTOs are acknowledged and respected as the key regional agencies responsible for fostering and promoting sustainable regional tourism development.

Key issues

As with all tourism trade associations, resourcing is a constant challenge. Funding comes solely from member subscriptions and contributions towards project work, which mainly covers the cost of maintaining the secretariat and the employment of one full-time Executive Officer. There is currently no central government funding scheme available to assist sector associations to support their members. RTONZ subscriptions are tiered, whereby the six largest organisations pay significantly more than the smallest regions. As RTOs are funded primarily by local councils (average 83 per cent of RTO income comes from these sources), they are constantly required to provide their stakeholders with evaluations on the value of their expenditures.

Broadly, larger RTOs are more interested in engaging with RTONZ on high-level planning and advocacy matters, while small RTOs are more likely to require upskill training and individual support for specific regional issues, such as funding submissions to council stakeholders. This wide spectrum of needs, of providing value to larger members versus supporting a disproportionate number of smaller RTOs to a higher degree, is always a balancing act.

RTO structures are constantly changing, and currently there is a phase occurring whereby many RTOs are being subsumed into Economic Development Agency (EDA) frameworks. It is estimated that by the end of 2016 approximately 18 of the 30 RTOs will be housed within an EDA. The stimulus for this shift has been the formation of a *supercity* amalgamation of six Auckland councils into one and the creation of its economic development arm, Auckland Tourism, Events and Economic Development (ATEED). This initiative created a huge pool of funds (approximately NZ$700 million) for regional marketing and business attraction and development.

While Auckland, with its large population base and resource capability, is a unique entity, other regions see that through bringing together all of a region's economic sectors (farming, industry, sciences, tourism, etc.) under one roof there are synergies created and economies of scale achieved through greater investment and profile. This presents opportunities as well as concerns.

From the aspect of tourism, which is often regarded as the *shop window* to a region's economic investment opportunities, there can be some worry that the industry voice and influence might be diluted in competition with other sectors for scare resourcing.

Many RTOs are marketers, with little experience in the specialist area of economic development. RTONZ has had to step up a capability programme for members to help them understand the EDA environment and be strong and confident advocates around the negotiating table for the sector.

Discussion question

What initiatives could RTONZ take to help members transition smoothly into EDAs?

Boosterism

Boosterism is a term used to describe 'a simplistic attitude that tourism development is inherently good and of automatic benefit to the hosts' (Hall, 1998: 248). Getz (1987, in Hall, 1998) argued boosterism is practised by two groups: politicians seeking economic development and those benefiting financially from tourism. In boosterism, little planning consideration is given to the wider issues of potential negative economic, social and environmental impacts. The first major booster campaign in the USA was probably the 1906 *See America First* concept, which originated in Salt Lake City (see Shaffer, 2001). The campaign attempted to convince Americans to see the West of the USA instead of travelling to Europe, which was in vogue at the time. The idea was for the formation of an alliance of railways, governments and businesses to advertise the West's tourist attractions, as well as develop infrastructure. While a lack of funding quickly derailed the original plans, the *See America First* theme continued to be used for many years by various Western booster groups.

Many of the early DMOs would have adopted a booster approach, representative of the promotion or selling orientation in marketing evolution, which has been observed in Spain as recently as the 1970s (see Bueno, 1999), the 1980s in Denmark (see Halkier, 2014) and Mexico at the turn of the twenty-first century (see Cerda, 2005). Nowadays, it is widely recognised that a more holistic approach is needed, where the mission of the DMO will be focused on enhancing the long-term competitiveness of the destination, in which sustainability of resources is fundamental. As posited by Ritchie and Crouch (2003: 9), pioneers in this new field of destination competitiveness research: 'competitiveness without sustainability is illusory'. Increasing tensions between entrepreneurs, conservationists, local residents and governments requires a partnership approach to resource-based tourism. See, for example, Department of Industry, Tourism and Resources (2003) for insights into 18 case studies of partnerships between tourism and conservation in Australia. Examples of mission statements from different levels of DMOs, which exemplify this philosophy, are highlighted in Table 2.4.

Destination competitiveness

For many destinations, maintaining competitiveness is now a major challenge (WTTC, 2001, in Australian Department of Industry, Tourism and Resources, 2003). Competition has intensified due to maturing tourism growth rates, increasing numbers of DMOs and increasing budgets of NTOs (Ritchie and Crouch, 2000a). However, it is not only rival destinations that DMOs must compete with. It is widely recognised that travel for the purpose of pleasure is representative of discretionary spending for many people, rather

Table 2.4 DMO mission statements highlighting a holistic approach

DMO	Mission	Source
NTO St Vincent and The Grenadines	To advance the positioning of St Vincent and The Grenadines as a diverse, globally competitive tourism destination through effective planning, development, management, marketing and sustainable use of the natural resources and heritage sites and attractions of the country	http://www.discoversvg.com/index.php/es/contact/about-us
STO Hawaii Tourism Authority	Honor Hawaii's people and heritage; value and perpetuate Hawaii's natural and cultural resources; engender mutual respect among all stakeholders; support a vital and sustainable economy; and provide a unique, memorable and enriching visitor experience	http://www.hawaiitourismauthority.org/default/assets/File/about/tsp2005_2015_final.pdf
RTO Discovery Coast, Queensland, Australia	Promoting and developing sustainable tourism and economic development within the town of 1770/Agnes Water and the region known as Discovery Coast for the benefit of all businesses and the wider community	http://www.dctc.com.au/extensions/mission-statement
CVB Regional Office of Sustainable Tourism, Lake Placid	To enrich the lives of visitors and residents alike by engineering a tourism economy which will sustain itself over time economically, socially, and environmentally	http://www.roostadk.com/wp-content/uploads/2014/08/2014-Sales-Marketing-Plan.pdf

than a necessity, which means it can be postponed if other priorities emerge (see, for example, Biederman, 2007). Destinations, therefore, are also forced to compete with substitute products and services, against global corporate brands, such as BMW and Sony, for example, which have marketing budgets that are higher than even the best-funded NTOs (Pike, 2004).

The destination lifecycle

In considering long-term competitiveness it is helpful to recognise that destinations usually evolve through a lifecycle, with positive and negative interventions influencing progress. The destination lifecycle model (see Plog, 1974; Butler, 1980) plots a destination's evolution through the phases of exploration (discovery), involvement, development (growth) and stagnation, which will then ultimately lead to either decline or rejuvenation. Destinations will progress through the cycle at different timeframes and also through different catalysts. For example, Russell and Faulkner's (1999) analysis of the development of Australia's Gold Coast noted the instigators of change were the contributions of a few individual entrepreneurs. Each was responsible for an innovation that stimulated a sequence of changes, resulting in a major shift in the structure of tourism at the destination. However, as discussed in the Preface, in the case of Rotorua it was the initiatives of central and local government that shaped the destination's rise and fall and rise most noticeably. Regardless, Butler (1980) supported Plog's (1974: 58) assertion that the evolution of destinations can change or obliterate the nature of attractions responsible for the area's popularity: 'Destination areas carry with them the potential seeds of their own destruction, as they allow themselves to become more commercialised and lose their qualities which originally attracted tourists'.

Progressing through the development phase to achieve competitiveness can be difficult to achieve and maintain, as has been shown in developing countries such as in Cambodia (see case study 2.2), Eastern Europe (Hall, 1999), sub-Saharan Africa (Brown, 1998; Kadel *et al.*, 2011), Ethiopia (Shanka and Frost, 1999), Jordan (Schneider and Sonmez, 1999; Hazbun, 2000), Turkey (Okumus and Karamustafa, 2005; Martinez and Alvarez, 2010) and Cameroon (Kimbu, 2011). A number of destinations at the decline or stagnation stages have also been reported in the academic literature. The global nature of this phenomenon is highlighted, by country, in Table 2.5. The problem has been such that the European Commission (2004) published the guide *Early Warning System for Identifying Declining Tourist Destinations and Preventative Best Practice*. However, there are limited examples of destinations that have positively reversed a decline in their fortunes, such as Las Vegas, Torbay and the Calvia Municipality in Mallorca (see Pritchard and Morgan, 1998; Buhalis, 2000; Gilmore, 2002), by innovating, developing new products and refurbishing the accommodation and attraction base (Baidal *et al.*, 2013).

Table 2.5 Analyses of destinations in the decline or stagnations stage of the lifecycle

Europe

Hamm, Germany (Buckley and Witt (1985); Majorca, Spain (Morgan, 1991); Valencia, Spain (Amor *et al.*, 1994); Amsterdam, The Netherlands (Dahles, 1998); Spain (Bueno, 1999); Croatia (Meler and Ruzic, 1999); European Commission (2004); Malaga, Spain (Barke *et al.*, 2010); northern coastal resorts, Spain (Larrinaga, 2005); Bugibba, Malta (Chapman and Speake, 2011); Vichy, France (Gordon, 2012); Portoroz, Slovenia (Rudez *et al.*, 2013)

North America

Canada (Go, 1987); USA (Ahmed and Krohn, 1990); Bermuda (Conlin, 1995); Cleveland, Lancaster Country, Pennsylvania (Hovinen, 2002); Atlantic City, New Jersey and Coney Island, New York (Cross and Walton, 2005); Florida (Revels, 2011); Florida-Alabama Coast (Jackson, 2012)

United Kingdom

Northern Ireland (Leslie, 1999); English seaside resort towns (English, 2000; Agarwal, 2002); Blackpool (Clarke 2008, in Pike 2008); Irish seaside resorts (Cusack, 2010)

Australasia and the South Pacific

Rotorua, New Zealand (NZTB, 1992; Rotorua District Council, 1992; Ateljevic and Doorne, 2000; Pike, 2007; Pike *et al.*, 2011); Fiji (McDonnell and Darcy, 1998); The Gold Coast, Australia (Russell and Faulkner, 1999; Faulkner, 2002); outback Australia (Schmallegger *et al.*, 2011)

Scandinavia

Denmark (Halkier, 2014)

Middle East

Lebanon (Rowbotham, 2008)

CASE STUDY

2.2 Cambodia, an *add-on* destination

Dr Pagna Pich (Royal University of Phnom Penh, Cambodia)
Dr Puthika Cheab (Royal University of Phnom Penh, Cambodia)
Dr Marady Phoeun (Royal University of Phnom Penh, Cambodia)
Dr Phyra Sok (Queensland University of Technology, Australia)

Traumatised by a genocidal regime and decades of civil wars, Cambodia has evolved to become a political, social and economically stable country. In developing countries such as Cambodia, travel and tourism development is largely regarded as a source of foreign exchange and forms part of the government poverty reduction strategy (Chen *et al.*, 2008; Reimer and Walter, 2013). Tourism has become the third largest sector in Cambodia, after the agricultural and garment industries, in generating the government's revenue. According to the data obtained from the Ministry of Tourism of Cambodia, in 2000 total international tourist arrivals were 466,365; and in just over a decade had increased to 3,584,307 in 2012, 4,210,165 in 2013 and 4,502,775 in 2014. Cambodia is well-known for its nature and cultural heritage. In particular, Angkor Wat, the UNESCO world heritage site, alone attracted more than 2 million international visitors in 2014. Aside from Angkor Wat, Cambodia has other potential tourist sites that are mostly natural. Kampot, Sihanouk Ville and Koh Kong in the southwest of the country are leisure sites for tourists who seek relaxation. In north-eastern Cambodia lie the protected forests popular for their ecotourism, where tourists can experience indigenous life and see some of the world's rarest animals. Historical sites like the Royal Palace, the Khmer Rouge Killing Field, the National Museum and similar can also be found in Phnom Penh, the capital city of Cambodia.

There is an estimate that international arrivals will undergo an upsurge of 25 per cent to Southeast Asian countries and reach 86,700,000 by 2015. However, Cambodia is not a nation that can enjoy the significant benefits from this large increase. Cambodia possesses wonderful treasures other countries do not have. The treasures notwithstanding, Cambodia is not the first destination for most international arrivals. The main ten source markets for visitors to Cambodia, however, subsume Vietnam, China, Laos PDR, South Korea, Thailand, Japan, the United States, Malaysia, France and the UK. Although Cambodia was able to attract a significant number of international tourists in 2014, the country was not really their first destination of choice. Holidays were planned for countries such as Thailand, Malaysia, Vietnam or Singapore; yet Cambodia was an *add-on* destination among many travellers after their visits to neighbouring countries. Thailand, Malaysia and Singapore have much bigger markets for international tourists coming from Southeast Asian countries. Thailand and Malaysia currently attract more than five times, with Singapore attracting more than three times as many tourists as Cambodia. Cambodia accounted for less than 5 per cent of the total amount of tourists in Southeast Asia, while Thailand accounted for up to 30 per cent and Malaysia 27 per cent in 2012.

Further reading

Dong, P. and Siu, N. Y. M. (2013).
Chen, Y. C. *et al.* (2008).
Reimer, J. K. and Walter, P. (2013).

Discussion question

Why is Cambodia still an *add-on* destination for international visitors?

Since different stages of the destination lifecycle attract different types of visitors (see Pike, 2002), the model will clearly be of use in strategic planning. For example, Kozak and Martin (2012) promoted the combination of the model with customer pyramid theory to make recommendations that would help Turkey's Mediterranean resort destinations avoid reaching the maturation stage. Also, McKercher (1995) combined the destination lifecycle model with the growth-share matrix to create the destination–market matrix, which is presented in Chapter 11. Other planning applications of the lifecycle model have included Pacific Island destinations (Choy, 1992), the Catalan Coast, Spain (Priestly and Mundet, 1998), the Island of Tenerife, Spain (Rodriguez *et al.*, 2008) and Zhangjiajie, China (Zhong *et al.*, 2008).

Key competitiveness factors

Destination competitiveness has been described as 'tourism's holy grail' (Ritchie and Crouch, 2000a), and yet this field of academic research only emerged during the 1990s. A special issue on tourism and travel competitiveness in *Tourism* (see 47(4), 1999) featured three papers at the destination level. *Tourism Management* then devoted a special issue to 'The Competitive Destination' (*Tourism Management*, 2000). The range of topics covered in this issue highlights the multidimensional nature of destination competitiveness:

* sustainable competitiveness (Ritchie and Crouch, 2000b);
* price competitiveness (Dwyer *et al.*, 2000);
* managed destinations (d'Hauteserre, 2000);
* responding to competition (Kim *et al.*, 2000);
* the destination product and its impact on traveller perceptions (Murphy *et al.*, 2000);
* the role of public transport in destination development (Prideaux, 2000);
* environmental management (Mihali, 2000);
* integrated quality management (Go and Govers, 2000);
* regional positioning (Uysal *et al.*, 2000);
* marketing the competitive destination of the future (Buhalis, 2000).

From these works, along with a review of the literature, it is clear that while there is not yet a widely accepted causal model of destination competitiveness, there is agreement that the construct comprises economic, social, cultural and environmental dimensions (see Ahmed and Krohn, 1990; Poon, 1993; Smeral, 1996, 2004; Faulkner *et al.*, 1999; Crouch and Ritchie, 1999; Kozak and Rimmington, 1999; Buhalis, 2000; Goeldner *et al.*, 2000; Ritchie *et al.*, 2000; Rubies, 2001; Smeral and Witt, 2002; Kozak, 2002; Fayos-Solà, 2002; Ritchie and Crouch, 2003, 2011; Heath, 2003; March, 2003; Melian-Gonzalez and Garcia-Falcon, 2003; Dwyer *et al.*, 2003, 2004; Enright and Newton, 2004, 2005; Vanhove, 2005; Paskaleva-Shapira, 2007; Mazanec *et al.*, 2007; Gomezelj and Mihalic, 2008; Baker and Cameron, 2008; Botti *et al.*, 2009; Lee and King, 2009; Crouch, 2011; Chen *et al.*, 2011; Pike and Mason, 2011; Hallmann *et al.*, 2012; Pike and Page, 2014; Webster and Ivanov, 2014). In synthesising this literature, a competitive destination is one that features a balance between nine critical success factors. These are listed in Table 2.6, with examples of DMO goals for each.

Table 2.6 DMO goals reflecting the nine critical factors for destination competitiveness

1. **Effective market position**
   - Hold or grow market share in key markets (Tourism Australia)
   - Strengthen external positioning through new marketing strategies and branding (New Orleans CVB, USA)

2. **Profitable tourism businesses**
   - We will provide support and advice to businesses, with the goal of improving the quality and sustainability of the tourism sector (Visit Scotland)
   - Increase the average room nights and spend to equal national averages (Tourism Rotorua Destination Marketing, New Zealand)

3. **Ease of access**
   - The New Zealand Tourism Industry offers booking services that are easy to use (Tourism New Zealand)
   - Partner with airports to support aviation route development and increase route capacity (Tourism and Events Queensland, Australia)

4. **Attractive physical environment**
   - Enhancing destination attractiveness (Singapore Tourism Board)
   - The city's environment should be protected (Visit Brighton, England)

5. **Positive visitor experiences**
   - To facilitate greater engagement between the visitor and the experience (Visit England)
   - To ensure a positive visitor experience by providing the most detailed information and the ultimate customer service (Paducah CVB, USA)

6. **Ongoing investments in new product development**
   - Provide favourable conditions for investment and expansion by the private sector (Visit Brazil)
   - Encourage more retail development in the city centre and independent retail across the city (Belfast Tourism, Northern Ireland)

7. **Cooperative tourism community**
   - Develop and implement an annual integrated strategic marketing plan that provides direction and focus for industry to collaborate, participate and contribute (City of Yarra, VIC, Australia)
   - Stronger engagement between the tourism industry and non-tourism community groups (Northland Tourism, New Zealand)

8. **Supportive local residents**
   - Support the government in promoting to the community the importance of tourism (Hong Kong Tourism Board)
   - Creating jobs and opportunity for local residents (Las Vegas CVB, USA)

9. **Effective DMO organisation**
   - Successfully deliver the fourth year of our match funded £100 million marketing programme, and implement a new partnership strategy to secure high levels of return (VisitBritain)
   - Secure adequate funding for all strategic plan initiatives (Michigan Tourism, Canada)

Table 2.7 WTTC competitive indices for Australia and China

Index	Australia index value	China index value	Australia rank	China rank
Price competitiveness	35 (red)	89 (green)	95	3
Human tourism	32 (red)	9 (red)	68	107
Infrastructure	100 (green)	34 (red)	1	93
Environment	60 (orange)	38 (orange)	42	133
Technology	100 (green)	51 (orange)	24	93
Human resources	100 (green)	50 (orange)	1	82
Openness	56 (orange)	35 (red)	89	127
Social	96 (green)	53 (green)	6	93

Indices of place competitiveness

There is no widely accepted causal model of destination competitiveness, which is to be expected given the newness of research and the complexity involved. In addition to the literature listed previously, there have been a number of destination competitive indices developed in recent years by academics and by private sector consultancies. For example, in 2004 the WTTC developed a destination competitiveness index (WTTC, 2004), in conjunction with the Christel de Haan Tourism and Travel Research Institute at the University of Nottingham. The index tracked the extent to which each of over 200 countries provided a competitive environment for travel and tourism development. The data was summarised through a traffic light colour coded system for each country across eight indices. These provided a measure out of 100 that was relative to the other countries. Green, amber and red lights indicate above average, average and below average performance. For example, the assessments for Australia and China across the eight measures are compared in Table 2.7. Australia was judged a world leader in terms of infrastructure, technology, human resources and social, but lagged in a number of areas such as price competitiveness and openness. China, on the other hand, was regarded as a leader in price competitiveness, but fell short in areas such as environment, openness and human tourism.

Other *place* competitive indices, which have been published annually, include:

- The World Economic Forum's *Global Competitiveness Report* (see WEF, 2014);
- Anholt GFK Roper Nations Brands Index (www.simonanholt.com);
- Govers Good Country Index (www.goodcountry.com);
- MasterCard Global Destinations Cities Index (www.insights.mastercard.com).

CHAPTER SUMMARY

Key point 1: The history of DMO development

DMOs predate the academic literature relating to destination marketing by over a century. The first RTO was established in the nineteenth century and the first NTO and STO at the beginning of the twentieth century. Many DMOs, however, have only been established relatively recently as communities have recognised the need to become organised for a coordinated approach to destination promotion. Recognition of the positive impacts of tourism, and the need for a coordinated destination promotion effort, has led to a proliferation of DMOs worldwide.

Key point 2: Destination competitiveness as the fundamental DMO mission

The rationale for the development of DMOs at all levels has been as a means of enhancing destination competitiveness. Given the multidimensional nature of destination competitiveness, it is doubtful in today's competitive travel market place that a destination could sustain, even attain, competitiveness, without effective organisation. Therefore, destination competitiveness is the DMO's raison d'être and mission.

Key point 3: Key goals of DMOs in the pursuit of destination competitiveness

A competitive destination is one that features a balance between nine critical success factors, for which DMOs design their goals: an effective market position, profitable tourism businesses, ease of access, attractive physical environment, positive visitor experiences, ongoing investments in new product development, a cooperative tourism community, supportive local residents and effective DMO organisation.

REVIEW QUESTIONS

1. If there were no DMO at your destination, what would be the likely impacts on the local tourism industry?

2. What is a market orientation? To what extent does your DMO demonstrate a marketing orientation?

3. For your favourite destination, what type of cluster does it represent?

REFERENCES

Adamczyk, B. (2005). The national tourism organisation of Poland, the Czech Republic, Slovakia and Hungary. *Tourism* 53(3): 247–248.

Agarwal, S. (2002) Restructuring seaside tourism: The resort lifecycle. *Annals of Tourism Research* 29(1): 25–55.

Ahmed, Z. and Krohn, F. B. (1990). Reversing the United States' declining competitiveness in the marketing of international tourism: A perspective on future policy. *Journal of Travel Research* 29(2): 23–29.

Amor, F., Calabug, C., Abellan, J. and Montfort, V. R. (1994). Barriers found in repositioning a Mediterranean 'sun and beach' product: The Valencian case. In Seaton, A. V., Jenkins, C. L., Wood, R. C., Dieke, P. U. C., Bennett, M. M., MacLellan, L. R. and Smith, R. (eds) *Tourism: The State of the Art*. Chichester, UK: John Wiley & Sons Ltd.

Aron, C. S. (1999). *Working at Play: A History of Vacations in the United States*. New York: Oxford.

Ateljevic, I. and Doorne, S. (2000). Local government and tourism development: Issues and constraints of public sector entrepreneurship. *New Zealand Geographer* 56(2): 25–31.

Australian Department of Industry, Tourism and Resources. (2003). *Destination Competitiveness: Development of a Model with Application to Australia and the Republic of Korea*. Canberra, Australia: Industry Tourism Resources Division.

Baidal, J., Sanchez, I. and Rebello, J. (2013). The evolution of mass tourism destinations: New approaches beyond deterministic models in Benidorm, Spain. *Tourism Management* 34(1): 184–195.

Baker, B. (2007). *Destination Branding for Small Cities: The Essentials for Successful Place Branding*. Portland, OR: Creative Leap Books.

Baker, M. J. and Cameron, E. (2008). Critical success factors in destination marketing. *Tourism and Hospitality Research* 8(2): 79–97.

Barke, M., Mowl, G. and Shields, G. (2010). Malaga: A failed resort of the early twentieth century? *Journal of Tourism History* 2(3): 187–212.

Beirman, D. (2003). *Restoring Destinations in Crisis*. Crows Nest, NSW: Allen & Unwin.

Berger, D. (2006). *The Development of Mexico's Tourism Industry: Pyramids by Day, Martinis by Night*. New York: Palgrave Macmillan.

Biederman, P. S. (2007). *Travel and Tourism: An Industry Primer*. Upper Saddle River, NJ: Pearson.

Black, J. (1992). *The British Abroad: The Grand Tour in the Eighteenth Century*. New York: St Martin's Press.

Blalock, C. (2000). Slow, steady approach might win funds for tourism promotion. *Hotel and Motel Management* 215(11): 10.

Borsay, P. and Walton, J. K. (eds) (2011). *Resorts and Ports: European Seaside Towns since 1700*. Buffalo, NY: Channel View Publications.

Botti, L., Peypoch, N., Robinot, E. and Solonadrasana, B. (2009). Tourism destination competitiveness: The French Regions case. *European Journal of Tourism Research* 2(1): 5–24.

Bramwell, B. and Rawding, L. (1996). Tourism marketing images of industrial cities. *Annals of Tourism Research* 23(1): 201–221.

Brewton, C. and Withiam, G. (1998). United States tourism policy: Alive, but not well. *Cornell Hotel and Restaurant Administration Quarterly* 39(1): 50–59.

Brodie, A. (2012). Scarborough in the 1730s: Spa, sea and sex. *Journal of Tourism History* 4(2): 125–153.

Brown, B. J. H. (1985). Personal perception and community speculation: A British resort in the 19th century. *Annals of Tourism Research* 12(3): 355–369.

Brown, D. O. (1998). German and British tourists' perceptions of Africa, Latin American and Caribbean travel destinations. *Journal of Vacation Marketing* 4(3): 298–310.

Buckley, P. J. and Witt, S. F. (1985). Tourism in difficult areas: Case studies of Bradford, Bristol, Glasgow and Hamm. *Tourism Management* September: 205–213.

Bueno, A. P. (1999). Competitiveness in the tourist industry and the role of the Spanish public administrations. *Turizam* 47(4): 316–331.

Buhalis, D. (2000). Marketing the competitive destination of the future. *Tourism Management* 21(1): 97–116.

Butler, R. W. (1980). The concept of a tourist area cycle of evolution: Implications for management of resources. *Canadian Geographer* 24(1): 5–12.

Carroll, P. (1991). Policy issues and tourism. In Carroll, P., Donohue, K., McGovern, M. and McMillen, J. (eds) *Tourism in Australia*. Sydney, Australia: Harcourt Brace Jovanovich, pp. 20–43.

Cerda, E. L. (2005). Destination management in Mexico. In Harrill, R. (ed.) *Fundamentals of Destination Management and Marketing*. Washington, DC: IACVB, pp. 259–272.

Chapman, A. and Speake, J. (2011). Regeneration in a mass-tourism market: The changing fortunes of Bugibba, Malta. *Tourism Management* 32: 482–491.

Chen, C. M., Chen, S. H. and Lee, H. T. (2011). The destination competitiveness of Kinmen's tourism industry: Exploring the interrelationships between tourist perceptions, service performance, customer satisfaction and sustainable tourism. *Journal of Sustainable Tourism* 19(2): 247–264.

Chen, Y. C., Sok, P. and Sok, K. M. (2008). Evaluating the competitiveness of tourism industry in Cambodia: Using self-assessment from professionals. *Asia Pacific Journal of Tourism Research* 13(1): 41–66.

Choy, D. J. L. (1992). Life cycle models for Pacific Island destinations. *Journal of Travel Research* 30(3): 26–31.

Choy, D. J. L. (1993). Alternative roles of national tourism organizations. *Tourism Management* 14(5): 357–365.

Conlin, M. V. (1995). Rejuvenation planning for island tourism: The Bermuda example. In Conlin, M. V. and Baum, T. (eds) *Island Tourism: Management Principles and Practice*. Chichester, UK: John Wiley & Sons Ltd.

Cox, K. L. (2012). *Destination Dixie: Tourism and Southern History*. Gainesville, FL: University of Florida Press.

Cross, G. S. and Walton, J. K. (2005). *The Playful Crowd: Pleasure Places in the Twentieth Century*. New York: Columbia University Press.

Crouch, G. I. (2011). Destination competitiveness: An analysis of determinant attributes. *Journal of Travel Research* 50(1): 27–45.

Crouch, G. I. and Ritchie, J. R. B. (1999). Tourism, competitiveness, and societal prosperity. *Journal of Business Research* 44(3): 137–152.

Cusack, T. (2010). 'Enlightened Protestants': The improved shorescape, order and liminality at early seaside resorts in Victorian Ireland. *Journal of Tourism History* 2(3): 165–185.

Cushman, G. (1990). Tourism in New Zealand. *World Leisure and Recreation* 32(1): 12–16.

Dahles, H. (1998). Redefining Amsterdam as a tourist destination. *Annals of Tourism Research* 25(1): 55–69.

Davidson, R. and Maitland, R. (1997). *Tourism Destinations*. London: Hodder & Stoughton.

Davidson, J. and Spearritt, P. (2000). *Holiday Business: Tourism in Australia since 1870*. Carlton South, VIC: Melbourne University Press.

Dawson, M. (2011). Travel strengthens America? Tourism promotion in the United States during the Second World War. *Journal of Tourism History* 3(3): 217–236.

Department of Industry, Tourism and Resources. (2003). *Pursuing Common Goals: Opportunities for Tourism and Conservation*. Canberra, Australia.

D'Hauteserre, A-M. (2000). Lessons in managed destination competitiveness: The case of Foxwoods Casino Resort. *Tourism Management* 21(1): 23–32.

Doering, T. R. (1979). Geographical aspects of state travel marketing in the USA. *Annals of Tourism Research* 6(3): 307–317.

Dong, P. and Siu, N. Y. M. (2013). Servicescape elements, customer predispositions and service experience: The case of theme park visitors. *Tourism Management* 36: 541–551.

Dredge, D. (2001). Local government tourism planning and policy-making in New South Wales: Institutional development and historical legacies. *Current Issues in Tourism* 4(2/4): 355–380.

Dwyer, L., Forsyth, P. and Rao, P. (2000). The price competitiveness of travel and tourism: A comparison of 19 destinations. *Tourism Management* 21(1): 9–22.

Dwyer, L., Livaic, Z. and Mellor, R. (2003). Competitiveness of Australia as a tourist destination. *Journal of Hospitality and Tourism Management* 10(1): 60–78.

Dwyer, L., Mellor, R., Livaic, Z., Edwards, D. and Kim, C. (2004). Attributes of destination competitiveness: A factor analysis. *Tourism Analysis* 9(1): 91–101.

Elliott, J. (1997). *Tourism: Politics and Public Sector Management*. London: Routledge.

English, G. (2000). Government intervention in tourism: Case study of an English seaside resort. In Robinson, M., Evans, N., Long, P., Sharpley, R. and Swarbrooke, J. (eds) *Management, Marketing and the Political Economy of Travel and Tourism*. Sunderland, UK: The Centre for Travel and Tourism, pp. 86–101.

Enright, M. J. and Newton, J. (2004). Tourism destination competitiveness: A quantitative approach. *Tourism Management* 25(6): 777–788.

Enright, M. J. and Newton, J. (2005). Determinants of tourism destination competitiveness in Asia Pacific: Comprehensiveness and universality. *Journal of Travel Research* 43: 339–350.

European Commission. (2004). *Early Warning System for Identifying Declining Tourist Destination, and Preventative Best Practices*. Delft, The Netherlands. Hard copy report.

Faulkner, B., Oppermann, M. and Fredline, E. (1999). Destination competitiveness: An exploratory examination of South Australia's core attractions. *Journal of Vacation Marketing* 5(2): 125–139.

Fayos-Solà, E. (2002). Globalization, tourism policy and tourism education. *Acta Turistica* 14(1): 5–12.

Flagestad, A. and Hope, C. A. (2001). 'Scandinavian winter': Antecedents, concepts and empirical observations underlying a destination umbrella branding model. *Tourism Review* 56(1/2): 5–12.

Ford, R. C. and Peeper, W. C. (2008). *Managing Destination Marketing Organizations*. Orlando, FL: ForPer Publications.

Furlong, I. (2008). *Irish Tourism 1880–1980*. Dublin, Ireland: Irish Academic Press.

Gartrell, R. B. (1992). Convention and visitor bureau: Current issues in management and marketing. *Journal of Travel & Tourism Marketing* 1(2): 71–78.

Gartrell, R. B. (1994). *Destination Marketing for Convention and Visitor Bureaus*. Dubuque, IA: Kendall/Hunt.

Gassan, R. H. (2008). *The Birth of American Tourism: New York, the Hudson Valley, and American Culture, 1790–1830*. Amherst, MA: University of Massachusetts.

Gilmore, F. (2002). Branding for success. In Morgan, N., Pritchard, A. and Pride, R. (eds) *Destination Branding: Creating the Unique Destination Proposition*. Oxford: Butterworth-Heinemann, pp. 57–65.

Go, F. M. (1987). Selling Canada. *Travel & Tourism Analyst* Dec: 17–29.

Go, F. M. and Govers, R. (2000). Integrated quality management for tourist destinations: A European perspective on achieving competitiveness. *Tourism Management* 21(1): 79–88.

Goeldner, R. C., Ritchie, J. R. B. and McIntosh, R. W. (2000). *Tourism: Principles, Practices, Philosophies* (8th edition). New York: John Wiley & Sons.

Gomezelj, D. O. and Mihalic, T. (2008). Destination competitiveness: Applying different models, the case of Slovenia. *Tourism Management* 29(2): 294–307.

Gordon, B. M. (2012). Reinventions of a spa town: The unique case of Vichy. *Journal of Tourism History* 4(1): 35–55.

Gottfried, H. (2013). *Landscape in American Guides and View Books: Visual History of Tourism and Travel.* New York: Lexington Books.

Halkier, H. (2014). Innovation and destination governance in Denmark: Tourism, policy networks and spatial development. *European Planning Studies* 22(8): 1659–1670.

Hall, C. M. (1998). *Introduction to Tourism: Development, Dimensions and Issues* (3rd edition). Sydney, Australia: Pearson Education Australia.

Hall, C. M. (1999). Rethinking collaboration and partnership: A public policy perspective. *Journal of Sustainable Tourism* 7(3/4): 274–289.

Hallmann, K., Muller, S., Feiler, S., Breuer, C. and Roth, R. (2012). Suppliers' perception of destination competitiveness in a winter sport resort. *Tourism Review* 67(2): 12–21.

Harland, P. A. (2011). *Travel and Religion in Antiquity.* Waterloo, ON: Wilfred Laurier University Press.

Hazbun, W. (2000). Enclave orientalism: The state, tourism, and the politics of post-national development in the Arab world. In Robinson, M., Evans, N., Long, P., Sharpley, R. and Swarbrooke, J. (eds) *Management, Marketing and the Political Economy of Travel and Tourism.* Sunderland, UK: The Centre for Travel & Tourism, pp. 191–205.

Heath, E. (2003). Towards a model to enhance destination competitiveness: A South African perspective. *CAUTHE Conference.* Coffs Harbour, NSW: Southern Cross University.

Hollis, T. (2008). *Selling the Sunshine State: A Celebration of Florida Tourism Advertising.* Florida, FL: University of Florida Press.

Hoover (2003). Industry execs appointed to new tourism board. www.bizjournals.com. 11 August.

Hovinen, G. (2002). Revisiting the destination life-cycle model. *Annals of Tourism Research* 29(1): 209–230.

Jackson, H. H. (2012). *The Rise and Decline of the Redneck Riviera: An Insider's History of the Florida-Alabama Coast.* Athens, GA: University of Georgia Press.

Jeffries, D. (1989). Selling Britain: A case for privatisation? *Travel & Tourism Analyst* 1(1): 69–81.

Jenkins, J. (1995). A comparative study of tourist organisations in Australia and Canada. *Australia–Canada Studies* 13(1): 73–108.

Kadel, R., Rodl, M. and Wollenzien, T. (2011). Tourism tackles poverty: A case study of Africa. In Conrady, R. and Muck, M. (eds) *Trends and Issues in Global Tourism 2011.* Heidelberg, Germany: Springer-Verlag.

Kerr, B. and Wood, R. C. (2000). Tourism policy and politics in a devolved Scotland. In Robinson, M., Evans, N., Long, P., Sharpley, R. and Swarbrooke, J. (eds) *Management, Marketing and the Political Economy of Travel and Tourism.* Sunderland, UK: The Centre for Travel & Tourism, pp. 284–296.

Kim, S., Crompton, J. L. and Botha, C. (2000). Responding to competition: A strategy for Sun/Lost City, South Africa. *Tourism Management* 21(1): 33–41.

Kimbu, A. N. (2011). The challenges of marketing tourism destinations in the Central African subregion: The Cameroon example. *International Journal of Tourism Research* 13(4): 324–336.

Kosta-Thefaine, J. F. (2009). *Travels and Travelogues in the Middle Ages* No. 28. New York: AMS Press Inc.

Kostianen, A. (2011). Tourism and political change in Northern European borderlands: The Karelian Isthmus, c. 1870–1940. *Journal of Tourism History* 3(2): 129–145.

Kozak, M. (2002). Destination benchmarking. *Annals of Tourism Research* 29(2): 497–519.

Kozak, M. and Martin, D. (2012). Tourism life cycle and sustainability analysis: Profit-focused strategies for mature destinations. *Tourism Management* 33: 188–194.

Kozak, M. and Rimmington, M. (1999). Measuring destination competitiveness: Conceptual considerations and empirical findings. *Hospitality Management* 18(3): 273–283.

Laderman, S. (2009). *Tours of Vietnam: War, Travel Guides, and Memory.* Durham, NC: Duke University Press.

Läesser, C. (2000). Implementing destination-structures: Experiences with Swiss cases. In Manete, M. and Cerato, M. (eds) *From Destination to Destination Marketing and Management.* Venice, Italy: CISET, pp. 111–126.

Larrinaga, C. (2005). A century of tourism in northern Spain: The development of high-quality provision between 1815 and 1914. In Walton, J. (ed.) *Histories of Tourism: Representation, Identity and Conflict.* Clevedon, UK: Channel View Publications, pp. 88–103.

Lavery, P. (1990). *Travel and Tourism*. Huntington, UK: ELM Publications.

Lee, C. F. and King, B. (2009). A determination of destination competitiveness for Taiwan's hot springs tourism sector using the Delphi technique. *Journal of Vacation Marketing* 15(3): 243–257.

Leslie, D. (1999). Terrorism and tourism: The Northern Ireland situation – A look behind the veil of certainty. *Journal of Travel Research* 38(1): 37–40.

Lomine, L. (2005). Tourism in Augustan society (44 BC–AD 69). In Walton, J (ed.) *Histories of Tourism: Representation, Identity and Conflict*. Clevedon, UK: Channel View Publications, pp. 69–87.

March, R. (2003). A marketing-oriented model of national competitiveness in tourism. *CAUTHE Conference*. Coffs Harbour, NSW: Southern Cross University.

Martinez, S. C. and Alvarez, M. D. (2010). Country versus destination image in a developing country. *Journal of Travel & Tourism Marketing* 27(7): 748–764.

Mazanec, J. A., Wober, K. and Zins, A.H. (2007). Tourism destination competitiveness: From definition to explanation? *Journal of Travel Research* 46(1): 86–95.

McClelland, J. (2013). The accidental sports tourist: Travelling and spectating in Medieval and Renaissance Europe. *Journal of Tourism History* 5(2): 161–171.

McClure, M. (2004). *The Wonder Country: Making New Zealand Tourism*. Auckland, NZ: Auckland University Press.

McDonnell, I. and Darcy, S. (1998). Tourism precincts: A factor in Bali's rise and Fiji's fall from favour – An Australian perspective. *Journal of Vacation Marketing* 4(4): 353–367.

McKercher, B. (1995). The destination–market matrix: A tourism market portfolio analysis model. *Journal of Travel & Tourism Marketing* 4(2): 23–40.

Meler, M. and Ruzic, D. (1999). Marketing identity of the tourist product of the Republic of Croatia. *Tourism Management* 20(1): 635–643.

Melian-Gonzalez, A. and Garcia-Falcon, J. M. (2003). Competitive potential of tourism in destinations. *Annals of Tourism Research* 30(3): 720–740.

Michael, I. and Kotsi, F. (2015). Re-branding the state of Goa, India: The 'Kenna' campaign. *International Interdisciplinary Business-Economics Advancement Conference Proceedings*. Fort Lauderdale, FL. March/April.

Middleton, V. and Lickorish, L. (2005*). British Tourism: The Remarkable Story of Growth*. Oxford: Butterworth-Heinemann.

Mihali, T. (2000). Environmental management of a tourist destination: A factor of tourism competitiveness. *Tourism Management* 21(1): 65–78.

Mill, R. C. and Morrison, A. M. (1985). *The Tourism System: An Introductory Text*. Englewood Cliffs, NJ: Prentice Hall.

Moranda, S. (2014). *The People's Own Landscape: Nature, Tourism and Dictatorship in East Germany*. Ann Arbor, MI: University of Michigan Press.

Morgan, C. (2008). *'A Happy Holiday': English Canadians and Transatlantic Tourism, 1870–1930*. Toronto, ON: University of Toronto Press.

Morgan, M. (1991). Dressing up to survive: Marketing Majorca anew. *Tourism Management* March: 15–20.

Morrison, A. M., Bruen, S. M. and Anderson, D. J. (1998). Convention and visitor bureaus in the USA: A profile of bureaus, bureau executives, and budgets. *Journal of Travel & Tourism Marketing* 7(1): 1–19.

Murphy, P., Pritchard, M. P. and Smith, B. (2000). The destination product and its impact on traveller perceptions. *Tourism Management* 21(1): 43–52.

NZTB. (1992). *A Review of Rotorua's Tourism Infrastructure*. Wellington, NZ: Policy Planning and Investment Division, New Zealand Tourism Board.

NZTPD. (1976). *75 Years of Tourism*. Wellington, NZ: New Zealand Tourist & Publicity Department.

Okumus, F. and Karamustafa, K. (2005). Impact of an economic crisis: Evidence from Turkey. *Annals of Tourism Research* 32(4): 942–961.

Paskaleva-Shapira, K. A. (2007). New paradigms in city tourism management: Redefining destination promotion. *Journal of Travel Research* 46(1): 108–114.

Pearce, D. G. (1996a). Tourist organizations in Sweden. *Tourism Management* 17(6): 413–424.

Pearce, D. G. (1996b). Regional tourist organizations in Spain: Emergence, policies and consequences. *Tourism Economics* 2(2): 119–136.

Piglia, M. (2011). The awakening of tourism: The origins of tourism policy in Argentina, 1930–1943. *Journal of Tourism History* 3(1): 57–74.

Pike, S. (2002). *Positioning as a Source of Competitive Advantage: Benchmarking Rotorua's Position as a Domestic Short Break Holiday Destination*. PhD Thesis. University of Waikato. November. Hard copy only.

Pike, S. (2004). *Destination Marketing Organisations*. Oxford: Elsevier Science.

Pike, S. (2007). A cautionary tale of a resort destination's self-inflicted crisis. *Journal of Travel & Tourism Marketing* 23(2/3/4): 73–82.

Pike, S. (2008). *Destination Marketing: An Integrated Marketing Communication Approach*. Burlington, MA: Butterworth-Heinemann.

Pike, S. and Page, S. (2014). Destination marketing organizations and destination marketing: A narrative analysis of the literature. *Tourism Management* 41: 202–227.

Pike, S., May, T. and Bolton, R. (2011). RTO governance: Reflections from a former marketing team. *Journal of Travel & Tourism Research* Fall: 117–133.

Plog, S. T. (1974). Why destination areas rise and fall in popularity. *The Cornell HRA Quarterly* 14(4): 55–58.

Poon, A. (1993). *Tourism, Technology and Competitive Strategies*. Oxford: CAB International.

Prideaux, B. (2000). The role of the transport system in destination development. *Tourism Management* 21(1): 53–63.

Priestly, G. and Mundet, L. (1998). The post-stagnation phase of the resort cycle. *Annals of Tourism Research* 25(1): 85–111.

Pritchard, A. and Morgan, N. (1998). Mood marketing: The new destination branding strategy: A case of Wales the brand. *Journal of Vacation Marketing* 4(3): 215–229.

Reimer, J. K. and Walter, P. (2013). How do you know it when you see it? Community-based ecotourism in the Cardamom Mountains of southwestern Cambodia. *Tourism Management* 34: 122–132.

Revels, T. J. (2011). *Sunshine Paradise: A History of Florida Tourism*. Florida, FL: University of Florida Press.

Richardson, J. I. (1999). *A History of Australian Travel and Tourism*. Elsternwick, VIC: Hospitality Press.

Ritchie, J. R. B. and Crouch, G. I. (2000a). Are destination stars born or made: Must a competitive destination have star genes? *Lights, Camera, Action: 31st Annual Conference Proceedings*. San Fernando Valley, CA: Travel and Tourism Research Association.

Ritchie, J. R. B. and Crouch, G. I. (2000b). The competitive destination: A sustainability perspective. *Tourism Management* 21: 1–7.

Ritchie, J. R. B. and Crouch, G. I. (2003). *The Competitive Destination: A Sustainable Tourism Perspective*. Oxford: CABI Publishing.

Ritchie, J. R. B. and Crouch, G. I. (2011). A model of destination competitiveness and sustainability. In Wang, Y. and Pizam, A. (eds) *Destination Marketing and Management: Theories and Applications*. CABI International, pp. 326–339.

Ritchie, J. R. B., Crouch, G. I. and Hudson, S. (2000). Assessing the role of consumers in the measurement of destination competitiveness and sustainability. *Tourism Analysis* 5(1): 69–76.

Rodriguez, J. R. O., Parra-Lopez, E. and Yanes-Estevez, V. (2008). The sustainability of island destinations: Tourism area life cycle and teleological perspectives. The case of Tenerife. *Tourism Management* 29: 53–65.

Rotorua District Council. (1992). *So, You Want to Be a Spa City!!* Rotorua, NZ: Economic Development Section.

Rowbotham, J. (2008). 'Sand and foam': The changing identity of Lebanese tourism. *Journal of Tourism History* 2(1): 39–53.

Rubies, E. B. (2001). Improving public-private sectors cooperation in tourism: A new paradigm for destinations. *Tourism Review* 56(3/4): 38–41.

Rudez, H. N., Sedmak, G. and Bojnec, S. (2013). Benefit segmentation of seaside destination in the phase of market repositioning: The case of Portoroz. *International Journal of Tourism Research* 15(2): 138–151.

Russell, R. and Faulkner, B. (1999). Movers and shakers: Chaos makers in tourism development. *Tourism Management* 20(4): 411–423.

Scantlebury, M. (2008). Barbados Tourism Authority: The challenge of inclusion. In Pike, S. (ed.) *Destination Marketing*. Burlington, MA: Butterworth-Heinemann.

Schmallegger, D., Taylor, A. and Carson, D. (2011). Rejuvenating outback tourism through market diversification: The case of the Flinders Ranges in South Australia. *International Journal of Tourism Research* 13: 384–399.

Schneider, I. and Sonmez, S. (1999). Exploring the touristic image of Jordan. *Tourism Management* 20(4): 538–542.

Sears, J. (1989). *Sacred Places: American Tourist Attractions in the Nineteenth Century*. New York: Oxford.

Shaffer, M. S. (2001). *See America First: Tourism and National Identity, 1880–1940*. Washington, DC: Smithsonian Institution Press.

Shanka, T. and Frost, F. A. (1999). The perception of Ethiopia as a tourist destination: An Australian perspective. *Asia Pacific Journal of Tourism Research* 4(1): 1–11.

Sheehan, L. R. and Ritchie, J. R. B. (1997). Financial management in tourism: A destination perspective. *Tourism Economics* 3(2): 93–118.

Sigaux, G. (1966). *History of Tourism*. London: Leisure Arts Ltd.

Smeral, E. (1996). Globalisation and changes in the competitiveness of tourism destinations. *AIEST Conference*. Rotorua, NZ: Waiariki Polytechnic.

Smeral, E. (2004). Evaluating leisure time travel source markets: An innovative guide for national tourist organizations for future competitiveness. *Leisure-Futures Conference*. Bolzano, Italy.

Smeral, E. and Witt, S. F. (2002). Destination country portfolio analysis: The evaluation of national tourism destination marketing programs revisited. *Journal of Travel Research* 40(3): 287–294.

Stafford, D. (1986). *The Founding Years in Rotorua: A History of Events to 1900*. Auckland, NZ: Ray Richards.

Stafford, D. (1988). *The New Century in Rotorua*. Auckland, NZ: Ray Richards.

Stokes, B. F. (2007). *Myrtle Beach: A History, 1900–1980*. Columbia, SC: The University of South Carolina Press.

Thomas, L. (2014). *Desire and Disaster in New Orleans: Tourism, Race and Historical Memory*. Durham, NC: Duke University Press.

Tourelle, G. (2003). United tourism market mooted. *The New Zealand Herald*. 29 July. Hard copy.

Tourism Management. (2000). Available at: http://www.sciencedirect.com/science/journal/02615177/21/1

TravelandTourWorld.com. (2015). *London Remains on Top of Travel Destination in 2015 Mastercard Global Destination Cities Index*. 5 June. Available at: http://www.travelandtourworld.com/news/article/london-remains-top-travel-destination-2015-mastercard-global-destinations-cities-index

Travelindustrywire.com. (2014). *Travel Leaders Applaud Bipartisan Effort to Extend Travel Promotion Program in Omnibus Bill*. Available at: http://www.travelindustrywire.com/article81260.html

UNWTO. (1979). *Tourist Images*. Madrid, Spain: UNWTO. Hard copy report.

UNWTO. (2014). *UNWTO Tourism Highlights: 2014 Edition*. Geneva, Switzerland: UNWTO. Available at: http://www.e-unwto.org/doi/pdf/10.18111/9789284416226

Uysal, M., Chen, J. S. and Williams, D. R. (2000). Increasing state market share through a regional positioning. *Tourism Management* 21(1): 89–96.

Vanhove, N. (2005). *The Economics of Tourism Destinations*. Oxford: Elsevier.

Vellas, F. and Bécherel, L. (1995). *International Tourism: An Economic Perspective*. Basingstoke, UK: Macmillan Business.

Vickers, L. (2010). *Cypress Gardens: How Dick Pope Invented Florida*. Florida, FL: University of Florida Press.

Walton, J. K. (1983). *The English Seaside Resort: A Social History 1750–1914*. Leicester, UK: Leicester University Press.

Walton, J. K. (2000). *The British Seaside: Holidays and Resorts in the Twentieth Century*. Manchester, UK: Manchester University Press.

Walton, J. K. (ed.) (2005). *Histories of Tourism: Representation, Identity and Conflict*. Clevedon, UK: Channel View Publications.

Wang, Y. (2008). Collaborative destination marketing: Roles and strategies of convention and visitors bureaus. *Journal of Vacation Marketing* 14(3): 191–209.

Ward, E. R. (2008). *Packaged Vacations: Tourism Development in the Spanish Caribbean*. Gainesville, FL: University Press of Florida.

Webster, C. and Ivanov, S. (2014). Transforming competitiveness into economic benefits: Does tourism stimulate economic growth in more competitive destinations? *Tourism Management* 40: 137–140.

WEF. (2014) *The Global Competitiveness Report 2014–2015*. Geneva, Switzerland: World Economic Forum. Available at: http://www3.weforum.org/docs/WEF_GlobalCompetitivenessReport_2014-15.pdf

WTTC. (2004). Available at: http://www.wttc.org

Zhong, L., Deng, J. and Xiang, B. (2008). Tourism development and the tourism area life-cycle model: A case study of Zhangjiajie National Forest Park, China. *Tourism Management* 29: 841–856.

Zuelow, E. G. E. (2009). *Making Ireland Irish: Tourism and National Identity since the Irish Civil War*. Syracuse, NY: Syracuse University Press.

Chapter **3**

The role of government in destination competitiveness

AIMS

To enhance understanding of:

- the importance of government support for sustained destination competitiveness;
- the rationale for long-term government funding of destination marketing;
- the opposing view that governments should not *subsidise* the tourism industry.

ABSTRACT

It is axiomatic that sustained destination competitiveness requires government support. In the history of tourism development it is clear the majority of destination marketing organisations (DMOs), including those cooperatives established by the private sector, would not have succeeded without government resources. Indeed, reported cases of government withdrawal of funding have demonstrated major negative impacts on destinations. The two key arguments for government involvement are the economic and socio-cultural benefits from visitor spending and the risk of market failure from a free market approach. However, the issue of whether governments should or should not use public funds to support the tourism industry will likely always be contentious with some in the community, particularly in times of economic uncertainty. 'Why should taxpayers *subsidise* tourism businesses?' is a question often asked by outside observers. Therefore, it behoves anyone with an interest in a career in tourism management to be able to clearly articulate the rationale for the existence of publicly funded DMOs and understand the key arguments for and against government support of sustainable tourism development.

DMO funding

A DMO cannot be effective without long-term funding certainty. Fundraising has been a perennial and challenging chore for many DMOs, as it is time consuming and diverts scarce financial and human resources away from activities in the market place. For example, the Hawaii Visitors Bureau was forced to spend up to US$500,000 to generate US$2 million in membership dues (Rees, 1995, in Bonham and Mak, 1996). This is a common problem for smaller RTOs in particular, many of which have abandoned attempts to generate membership subscriptions due to low returns relative to costs incurred in the enlistment process. The majority of DMOs, at all levels, and regardless of how they are structured, rely to a large extent on government support. Government funding is commonly provided in the form of annual grants or through some form of levy on visitors or businesses. The overreliance on government funding has been of concern to many DMOs, given the often long-term uncertainty of political commitment towards tourism. For example, in 2014 Brand US received legislative support only a further five years until 2020, at which time the Travel Promotion Act might or might not be re-enacted (see Travelindustrywire. com, 2014). Another example is in New Zealand where RTOs are funded primarily by local government, accounting for an average 83 per cent of their income. Governments and their policies change periodically, and so there is no guarantee that current levels of support will continue forever. Many governments are faced with the escalating essential services challenges, such as planning for the demographic test of providing for the retirement and healthcare costs for the aging baby boomer population bubble. In times of economic uncertainty, destination marketing might not be seen as an essential service.

The Preface indicated how the fortunes of one resort destination have risen and fallen and risen in line with government intervention and investment. The case of Rotorua can be used to highlight, on the one hand, the difficulty in stimulating an effective cooperative approach to destination promotion without government support, and on the other hand the damage that can take place when stakeholders become complacent through an overreliance on a paternalistic government (see also Ateljevic and Doorne, 2000; Horn et al., 2000; Pike, 2004, 2007, 2008; Pike et al., 2011). More research into alternative forms of funding is required, particularly after austerity measures imposed by many governments in the wake of the 2008 global financial crisis impacted greatly on the budgets of many DMOs.

Threats to funding

A state government referendum in 1993 resulted in the abolition of a tax that funded the Colorado Tourism Board (CTB). Without such government funding the CTB was closed (Bonham and Mak, 1996). Colorado became the only state in the USA that did not have an STO. At the time, tourism was the state's second largest industry, worth an estimated US$6.4 billion annually (La Page, 1995). The effects in the market place were significant, with estimates that Colorado slipped from 3rd to 17th in terms of traveller recognition of state destinations, and that pleasure travellers decreased by up to 10 per cent (Donnelly and Vaske, 1997). McGehee et al. (2006) cited a report indicating Colorado's share of domestic pleasure travel declined by 30 per cent between 1993 and 1997.

In 2003 the then governor of California proposed the state tourism office be closed as a cost saving measure. The STO had a US$7.5 million budget and at the time the California government faced a US$35 billion shortfall (Inbound, 13 January 2003: 1). However, in 2015 the budget for Visit California doubled from US$50 million to US$100 million, as a result of a lengthy process known as Dream Big Dividend (Shankman, 2015). The process culminated in 75 per cent of 9,500 participating businesses agreeing to an increase in levies on hotels, restaurants, rental cars and attractions.

In 2004 the Illinois governor's office proposed a 54 per cent cut in tourism funding to help offset the state deficit (Bolson, 2005). This was successfully opposed in an aggressive campaign by the tourism industry, led by the state's convention and visitor bureau (CVB) association. In 2006 Tourism Waikato, one of New Zealand's RTOs, had its budget unexpectedly cut in half by the local government (see Coventry, 2006: 1). Tourism Waikato's Chief Executive Officer lamented: 'It's a very gut wrenching situation. Marketing of the whole Waikato will be suspended until funding regenerates'.

Recent political changes in England have thrown regional tourism interests into a destabilised situation of complexity and in some cases even chaos. For in-depth analyses on the way in which the existing structure of tourism promotion has been abruptly redefined by the government, see Coles *et al.* (2014). Many regional tourism boards (RTBs) abolished or had their funding cut as part of public sector austerity measures imposed by the incoming 2010 British Conservative government. The government was forced to implement the cuts due to inheriting a public debt level equivalent to 62 per cent of national GDP from the previous administration. Local Economic Partnerships (LEP) replaced the RTBs, formerly funded by the Regional Development Agencies that were dismantled. Now tourism is subsumed under a wider economic development agenda, as a partnership between local authorities and businesses, and it is their responsibility if they wish to assume any of the former DMO functions:

> *In this respect, tourism as an economic driver of the economy has been downgraded from its former priority status under the RDAs to a position where it is effectively in limbo and destination marketing is an ad hoc activity determined by each LEP (or local authority) if they choose to assume this role.*

> *(Pike and Page, 2014)*

In addition to the cuts in funding to regional tourism groups, the NTO Visit England's budget had been slashed by 34 per cent by 2014–2015 (Coles *et al.*, 2014). Coles *et al.* found that since the government was the main source of funding for all the regions, over half had been forced to cut staff, with claims the sector was facing a brain drain of management experience. VisitBritain's government funding was slashed by a third in 2010, resulting in 70 job losses and the closure of 14 overseas offices (Johnson, 2011, in Hays *et al.*, 2013). Other funding cuts reported in the academic literature have included Maine, USA (Doering, 1979), Portugal (see Oliveira and Panyik, 2015), Greece (Trihas *et al.*, 2013) and Italy (Reinhold *et al.*, 2015). Case study 3.1 briefly summarises how one small community has been forced to adapt to government austerity measures in the UK.

CASE STUDY

3.1 Community destination marketing: The Pitlochry Partnership, Scotland

Dr Samantha Murdy and Dr Matthew Alexander
University of Strathclyde, Scotland

For DMOs to compete in a context of global competition they rely on their destination image as a way to position themselves and resonate with prospective visitors. DMOs are responsible for the promotion and management of the brand, generally using a top-down approach. That is, many of the decisions made are from external or detached perspectives. However, in many smaller communities in the United Kingdom the lack of funding, and in some cases the withdrawal of government affiliated DMOs, has contributed to the neglect of destination marketing.

Pitlochry is a small town located on the River Tummel within the county of Perth and Kinross in Scotland, with a population of only a few thousand. The region first gained popularity after a visit by Queen Victoria in 1842. Given her favourable opinion of the region and ability to transform the fortune of a destination with a single mention, the town became increasingly popular, and a train station was built in 1863 enhancing the levels of tourism.

Pitlochry is an interesting case in which residents of the community have taken it upon themselves to promote the town as a tourism destination. The Pitlochry Partnership was developed in 2007 to assist in the promotion of not only the town as a whole but also businesses, by allowing them to join as members. Community-based tourism activity includes: *Pitlochry in Bloom*, a group that organises floral displays, flower beds, hanging baskets and litter pickups around the town; *The Pitlochry Station Bookshop*, which serves the many visitors to the town, raises money for charity and is run by volunteers; and *The Enchanted Forest*, an autumn festival where a local area of woodland is transformed through lighting, sound and visual effects.

One of the key benefits of the partnership is the development of promotion to encourage visitors to travel to Pitlochry. Many of the members of the partnership own and manage small accommodation services and other businesses within the town, and the enhancement of tourism is beneficial to their organisations. Other benefits of this bottom-up approach include the engagement of the community, as they have taken ownership of the activities to enhance their town and, in turn, tourism. Many of the volunteers (and residents) feel that social engagement is enhanced, leading to satisfaction based on their contributions.

There have been setbacks to this kind of bottom-up approach. Primarily, funding is an issue that is prevalent within the community. Much of the contribution to community-based activities and enhancement of the town is reliant on volunteers, the submission of grants and fundraising (e.g. morning teas or selling strawberries). Another is the dedication of key members of these voluntary groups. While having enthusiastic and devoted members is a positive, the reliance on a few means that succession planning is something that must occur, but rarely does. The notion of free-riders, or those who reap the benefits of others who volunteer but do not have any input themselves, also occurs within the community. Finally, the partnership has become a lot like a surrogate council (local government). Given council cutbacks, members of the community contact the partnership to address additional issues within the town, which should have been addressed by the local authority, such as cutting of public grass.

Figure 3.1 Pitlochry, Scotland

Discussion question

How might this form of community ownership be facilitated and supported by national tourism organisations?

High fixed costs

Destination marketing is labour intensive. A key management challenge for DMOs is finding the optimal balance between fixed costs and promotional spend. For NTOs with budgets of between US$20 million and US$50 million, the average was 64 per cent. In the USA IACVB (1993, in Morrison *et al.*, 1998) estimated that of all room taxes collected, approximately 27 per cent is used for the convention centre construction, debt servicing and operations; 25 per cent for CVB marketing; and 48 per cent for *non-visitor uses*. McKercher and Ritchie's (1997) study of local government tourism units in New South Wales and Victoria, which identified a median operating budget of AUD$215,000, found over half of average budgets were allocated to staffing, with the median marketing allocation being only AUD$70,000.

Small budgets

Funding is a critical issue for DMOs. In fact, for any marketing organisation without products or services of its own to gain sales revenue, it is arguably the most important consideration. Non-business organisations usually cannot cover costs through sales and often devote ongoing efforts to generate new tax revenues, sponsorships and/or contributions from members. The marketing of destinations in a dynamic environment requires significant financial and management resources. However, DMO budgets pale into insignificance in the global market place in comparison to leading consumer goods brands such as Sony and Apple. DMOs compete with such brands for a share of voice in discretionary spending categories.

The high reliance on government funding leaves many DMOs at the mercy of political masters. A key exception is in places where a bed tax regime operates, such as North America, where increased accommodation revenue can lead to an increased budget for CVBs. Of course the reverse also applies, as in the 9/11 aftermath when accommodation revenue decreased in many places. For example, in Las Vegas, a 10 per cent decrease in visitors following 9/11 resulted in a similar decrease in the CVB's US$250 million annual budget.

While Vallee (2005) reported Canada's largest CVBs, such as Montreal, Toronto and Vancouver, had budgets ranging from CAD$10 million to CAD$25 million, many DMOs have been forced to operate with very limited budgets. For example, Rogers (2005) found only one in five British CVBs had a budget greater than £100,000. Relative to RTOs in other major cities, the London Tourist Board (LTB) had been poorly funded by government (Hopper, 2002). In 2015 the LTB received only £1.85 million from central government and £241,000 from local authorities annually; and yet, as discussed in Chapter 2 (see Table 2.2), the city is the most visited in the world. The remainder of the £6 million annual budget was contributed by the private sector through subscriptions, partnership marketing and sponsorships.

The problem is global. RTO budgets in Australia have generally been modest, and in New South Wales many have struggled to survive (Jenkins, 2000). Carson *et al.* (2003) found local authority budget contributions to tourism in the state of Victoria, Australia, ranged from AUD$2,000 to AUD$6.5 million, with a median of AUD$232,000. They found 40 per cent of councils surveyed indicated a tourism budget of less than AUD$150,000. In Scotland, Kerr and Wood (2000) reported on the financial difficulty, including near bankruptcy, for some ATBs due to reduced levels of local government funding. They cited the example of the Dumfries and Galloway Tourist Board, which was £1.2 million in debt in 1998. One of the problems was that the ATB areas did not match local government boundaries, and so ATBs were forced to lobby several councils for funding support. This cross-boundary issue is a problem in England as a result of the new LEP structure implemented by the British government in 2010.

IN PRACTICE

3.1 The Pikes Peak region lobby

In 2015 the Colorado Springs CVB in the USA was lobbying for an increase to the city's lodgers and auto rental tax, on the back of a consultant's study commissioned by a consortium of 26 municipalities and businesses in the Pikes Peak region. The US$40,000 study suggested forming a three-county, tax supported, marketing region and that increasing the current budget of US$2.8 million to US$8.2 million would generate an additional US$250 million in visitor spending annually and lead to the creation of 2,700 new jobs. It was suggested the increased budget could come from raising the local visitor taxes. For example, one of the municipalities, Colorado Springs, funds its CVB through a lodgers and auto rental tax (LART), which has never been increased since its introduction 35 years ago. The LART involves a 2 per cent levy on hotel rooms and a 1 per cent levy on rental vehicles. The study suggested that by increasing both portions to 4 per cent and including a levy on visitor attractions, this would generate US$6.8 million a year, and that implementing the same regime in nearby counties would increase it to US$8.2 million. The study was part of a plan to initiate community-wide discussions on the benefits of enhanced marketing efforts, since raising taxes requires a public ballot and forming a new marketing district needs approval from the Colorado General Assembly.

Source

Laden, R. (2015).

There is no common model for determining the appropriate level of funding for a DMO. In an examination of government policy of European Community member countries, Akehurst *et al.* (1993) found little correlation between central government tourism expenditure and international receipts on a per capita basis. For example, Greece, which had the highest government spend per capita, was at the lower end of international tourism receipts per capita. Comparisons can be made between DMO budgets from different regions using many different measures, including:

• host population size;

• number of commercial accommodation beds/rooms;

• number of taxpayers/ratepayers;

• visitor numbers;

• visitor spending.

Ultimately the funding decision process will depend on the local situation, with influences including:

• local politics;

• community acceptance of tourism;

- destination lifecycle stage and industry maturity;
- economic size and importance of tourism relative to other industries;
- DMO history and current structure;
- the lobbying power of stakeholders;
- the global/national economic situation.

Other than government grants, sources of revenue for DMOs include: accommodation tax, tax on business, member subscriptions, commercial activities and joint venture campaigns.

Accommodation tax

Key advantages of accommodation taxes are that they directly target visitors and can generate large amounts of revenue for a relatively low cost. Visitor taxes are a way for governments to shift the financial burden of funding DMOs and infrastructure from local taxpayers. Room taxes, which are additional to any other local, state or national general sales taxes, have existed in the USA since at least the 1940s (Migdal, 1991, in Morrison *et al.*, 1998). A survey of IACVB members (IACVB, 2001, in Fenich, 2005) found the average city hotel tax was 11.6 per cent, with an average of 56 per cent of the tax collected dedicated to funding the CVB. Sheehan and Ritchie's (1997) survey of USA CVBs found the largest source of revenue was hotel room taxes, generating an average 72 per cent of total revenue. The next level of funding sources was modest by comparison: membership fees (7 per cent – the highest was 58 per cent), government grants (6 per cent – highest 90 per cent), local authority taxes (2.6 per cent – highest 100 per cent), cooperative programmes (2 per cent – highest 41 per cent) and restaurant taxes (2 per cent – highest 60 per cent). Other sources, representing an average of 8 per cent included: convention centre grants, merchandising, advertising sales, county tax, events, admissions, in-kind services and a provincial or state tax. In Mexico federal government legislation in 1996 enabled the states to levy hotel room tax of up to 5 per cent (Cerda, 2005). Just over half of Mexico's CVBs are now funded by room taxes. In Europe Vienna introduced a bed tax of 2.8 per cent in 1987. A variation of this, reported by *The News Mail* (2003: 3) was used in Queensland's Wide Bay region. Around AUD$80,000 was collected from a visitor levy during the 2002 whale watch season, which was being used on an advertising campaign to promote the 2003 season.

However, the hotel room tax is far from universally lauded. A major challenge here though is the power and influence of major hotels, within the politics of DMO decision making, as the major collector of these funds. Also, accommodation taxes are viewed as an extra tax on businesses and an additional layer of bureaucracy, and make the destination more expensive for visitors. For example, the repeal of the 5 per cent bed tax in the state of New York was hailed by some in the tourism industry as the removal of an inhibitor to destination marketing (see Cahn, 1994 in Pike, 2004). The tax, which was introduced in 1990, was the subject of strong criticism from industry, with one executive likening it to *economic suicide* for the meetings sector. There were reports New York lost US$2 in related taxes for every US$1 in tax revenue (McMahon and Sophister, 1998, in Davidson and Rogers, 2006). Similarly, in a survey of delegates attending the 1999 Scottish Hospitality Industry Congress, Kerr and Wood (2000) found a resounding 93 per cent of participants were against the concept of a bed tax, although 35 per cent did indicate possible support if all the revenues were devoted to the tourism industry. In early 2015, the Bahamas Ministries of Finance and Tourism reported the repeal of a 10 per cent hotel tax, to be replaced by a 7.5 per cent value added tax. Tourism Minister Obie Wilchcombe said the 2.5 per cent tax saving was indicative of a determination among government officials to make the Bahamas a value for money destination (www. breakingtravelnews.com, 5 January 2015).

In India Goa reduced the luxury hotel tax from 15 per cent to 8 per cent during the peak season and 4 per cent during the low season, which ironically resulted in an increase of 23 per cent in tax revenue. In Ireland an estimated 10 per cent of hotels closed following the 1980s value added tax (VAT) on hotel rooms increasing to 23 per cent. Lobbying by hotels resulted in a decrease in 1985 to 12.5 per cent (see McMahon and Sophister, 1998, in Davidson and Rogers, 2006).

Tax on business

Another taxation option for destinations is a levy on local businesses, based on either turnover or capital value. This can be used as an effective means of raising revenue for RTOs and an alternative to funding from the general household tax or rates base, or through member subscriptions. The political challenge is of course to convince businesses that do not receive direct spending from visitors of the efficacy of such a levy. This approach has been demonstrated in smaller resort areas where tourism has a high profile, such as at the New Zealand resort destinations of Lake Taupo and Queenstown. These local governments charge a levy to all local businesses, thereby avoiding the challenge of defining tourism businesses, at a percentage rate of each business's capital value. The mechanism provides the main source of funds for the RTOs in both areas. Other examples are Monaco and Macau, two countries that have no personal income tax system due to the reliance on levies on casinos' revenue.

Bonham and Mak (1996) reported the Oklahoma Tourism Promotion Act (1991) levied a tourism promotion tax of 0.1 per cent of gross turnover of accommodation, rental car and restaurant and bar operations. The intent was for the state government to collect the tax from the tourism industry, to be used solely by the industry, for which the state would charge a 3 per cent collection fee. Prior to its demise in 1993, the Colorado STO had a similar tax of 0.2 per cent (Bonham and Mak, 1996). A downside of this approach is a reduction in funding during periods of crisis when visitation levels have fallen, even though such periods demand more marketing funds. For example, in Canada, the *Calgary Herald* reported a fall in the Banff/ Lake Louise Tourism Bureau's 2003 revenue was likely to result in a reduction in marketing spend of CAD$168,000, which would directly impair the organisation's ability to promote Banff in their traditional secondary markets such as New Zealand and Australia.

IN PRACTICE

3.2 From US$7.5 million to US$100 million in 12 years

In 2003 the budget for California's STO was US$7.5 million. In 2015 Visit California's CEO, Caroline Beteta, announced the STO would double its annual budget from US$50 million to US$100 million as a result of increased levies on tourism businesses. The increase was the culmination of a three-year process known as the *Dream Big Dividend*. In 2012 the board of directors worked with Oxford Economics, which is a business venture of the UK's Oxford University, to work out the optimum budget for the state to effectively compete internationally. The optimum figure of US$100 million was set and three years later this was achieved through increasing assessments levied on hotels, restaurants, rental cars and attractions. Assessments are a percentage of transactions. In December 2014 75 per cent of 9,500 participating businesses voted in favour of increasing their assessment rates (per US$1 million in transactions) as follows:

- accommodation increased from US$650 to US$1,950;
- attractions increased from US$650 to US$975;
- restaurants and retail increased from US$650 to US$975.

Source

Shankman, S. (2015).

Member subscriptions

In the UK 58 per cent of CVBs receive funding from membership fees (Rogers, 2005). The IACVB (1993, in Morrison *et al.*, 1998) found that while half of their member CVBs received membership subscription fees, for those responding to a survey, the level of subscriptions was only 5 per cent of their collective budgets, while Sheehan and Ritchie (1997) found an average of 7 per cent. Bonham and Mak (1996) noted only Alaska, Hawaii and Washington, DC received significant private sector contributions such as through membership subscriptions.

The Hawaii Visitors Bureau (HVB), which has one of the longest histories of private membership, has offered a range of incentives to financial members including: monthly newsletters, HVB posters and brochures, reduced fees for HVB meetings, participation in trade promotion and cooperative advertising, listings in information guides and a copy of the annual report. In its early years the organisation received more in private sector contributions than from government. However, by 1988 only an estimated seven per cent of all businesses were financial members of the HVB, and by 1994 private sector contributions represented less than 10 per cent of the annual budget. One of the reasons offered by Bonham and Mak (1996) was extensive *free riding* by tourism operators. They cited Mok's PhD thesis, which estimated HVB memberships representing 78 per cent of airlines, 66 per cent of hotels, 32 per cent of banks, 24 per cent of restaurants and only 4 per cent of retail outlets.

A survey of IACVB members (IACVB, 2001, in Fenich, 2005) found half of the CVBs were membership-based organisations, with an average of 663 members. Membership fees can be based on tiered sponsor categories, a standard arbitrary amount, tiered based on organisation turnover level, number of employees, or per number of rooms for accommodation establishments. Donnelly and Vaske (1997) investigated the factors influencing membership of the voluntary organisation, the Colorado Travel and Tourism Authority (CTTA), established to replace the previously state funded DMO. The CTTA targeted businesses that directly benefited from tourism, such as hotels, restaurants and attractions. Their review of the literature relating to voluntary organisations identified two participative incentive themes: instrumental and expressive. Instrumental incentives are those public goods, such as promotion of the destination, which are obtained by both members and non-members. Expressive incentives are resultant benefits that will only be obtained by membership, such as access to a database of consumers who have requested tourism information from the DMO. For example, Pritchard (1982) reported an innovative approach used by Alaska to stimulate industry contributions to the STO budget. For every (US) dollar contributed by an individual business, the STO would provide one name and address from the consumer database for direct marketing. The database was tailored to provide contacts from segments of interest to the contributing tourism business. Donnelly and Vaske (1997: 51) suggested the value placed on expressive incentives to join a DMO will depend on an individual's:

- financial ability to pay membership dues;

- beliefs about tourism and destination marketing;

- level of perceived importance about the costs and benefits of membership.

IN PRACTICE

3.3 'We are not in the tourism industry'

The following story was relayed to me a number of years ago by a member of an RTO membership subscriptions committee who was frustrated by the lack of support from businesses in a tourism resort area. Two RTO directors were attempting to enlist the modest financial support of one of the region's busiest petrol stations. They were told, very bluntly, by the business owner that he was not in the tourism industry and therefore refused to subscribe to the RTO. Standing directly behind the owner were two 40-seat sightseeing buses, filling up with diesel fuel.

Commercial activities

Some DMOs have developed an income stream from their own activities to fund destination marketing. For example, in the USA iconic brands such as *Virginia is for Lovers* are a source of merchandising licence revenue for the STO. In the UK 63 per cent of CVBs receive some funding from commercial activities (Rogers, 2005). In some cases, however, legal issues can prevent some types of DMOs from maximising their earning potential. In the USA most CVBs have been structured as non-profit associations, qualifying for tax-exempt status. These organisations promote the business interests of their members, but are not permitted to engage in regular profit making business activities.

Marks (2004) reported entrepreneurial alliances with non-traditional partners as well as tourism businesses. The San Francisco CVB, for example, has partnered with a diverse range of companies such as Visa, See's Candies, Colavita Olive Oil, Buick and the San Francisco Giants. Similarly, New York City and Company has partnered with American Express, Coca-Cola and the National Football League to leverage budgets (Nicholas, 2004). *Marketing News* (1997) reported the new logo developed by Florida's STO in 1997 would be used to generate royalties of 6 per cent of the wholesale price of items featuring the logo. In Australia Tourism Queensland licensed the STO's wholesale travel division, Sunlover Holidays, to a private sector firm, earning what outgoing CEO, Ian Mitchell, described in 2007 as 'millions of dollars new income through licensing fees for the purposes of international marketing'.

It is also not uncommon for DMOs to earn commissions from their member hotels for bookings emanating from conferences secured by the CVB department. However, this approach can lead to the DMO focusing on conference promotion, business travel and short break hotel packages to the exclusion of other destination products (Bramwell and Rawding, 1996).

Other RTOs earn commissions through subsidiary visitor information centre (VIC) sales. Net returns are often modest, even with a substantial turnover, if there is an absence of big-ticket items. In New Zealand local government regulations prohibited many local authority-owned VICs to trade commercially, other than sales of sightseeing tickets and postcards. However, the greater empowering provisions of the Local Government Act (2002) have enabled enhanced trading opportunities. VICs are labour intensive and, as their title suggests, a large component of visitors are there seeking *information* only and are therefore generally low yield overall. Even with a multi-million dollar turnover, it is difficult for VICs to generate a profit when relying on sightseeing sales paying on average 5 to 10 per cent commission. However, many of these VICs could be profitable if they adopted private sector practices used by travel agencies such as *preferred supplier* agreements. This might involve, for example, one operator per service category, receiving preferential treatment and in return providing higher commissions of up to 25 or 30 per cent. A tiered system of commissions might be used to rank providers in terms of preference levels and prominence of brochures on display. For example, in Canada, travel agents represent on average only four preferred tour wholesalers (Statistics Canada, 1999, in Hashimoto and Telfer, 2001). However, it would be hypocritical for an RTO that receives government funding for the purpose of developing tourism in the region to then preclude the majority of suppliers from receiving VIC bookings in a preferential system. In some parts of the world this type of activity would leave the DMO open to litigation from disadvantaged businesses. Many local authorities understand the need for a trade-off and provide an operating grant for the VIC on the basis that the contribution is for the wider public good.

Cooperative and joint venture (JV) campaigns

Cooperative campaigns managed by the DMO can be an effective vehicle for demonstrating to government the level of industry contributions. In this regard, the government grant is seen as seeding funding to attract private sector contributions. Cooperative campaigns include a diverse range of initiatives, such as sales missions, travel exhibitions participation, media advertising features and visiting media programmes, which are discussed in later chapters.

Why should taxpayers *subsidise* tourism businesses?

While private sector entrepreneurs and the introduction of jet aircraft have largely been responsible for the rapid growth of mass tourism since the 1960s, this would not have been possible without government support in the form of security, stimulation of increased affluence and leisure time, and infrastructure development (Elliott, 1997). Government investment has been necessary to guide the actions of both the private sector and the public sector. In Canada, for example, over 20 government agencies have an active interest in tourism (Vallee, 2005). Mill and Morrison (1985) noted in the USA during the 1980s that there were over 150 government programmes across 50 departments that directly affected tourism. Similarly, in the UK, a 1982 report identified over 70 pieces of legislation that affected tourism (Jeffries, 2001). In effect, it is the government that is the destination *management* organisation by default.

It is not uncommon for those outside the tourism industry to question why taxpayers should *subsidise* the tourism sector. A diverse range of groups can pose this challenge, from retiree associations that have no vested interest in business, to representatives of other industries such as horticultural/ agricultural producer boards that might not receive the same level of *support*. This issue has been a major hurdle for tourism interests in the USA, where a lack of Congress support for an NTO over such a long period had been attributed to strong political views that this would represent *corporate welfare* (Gatty and Blalock, 1997). This is not unreasonable if they are ignorant of the indirect benefits of a thriving tourism industry. The onus is on the tourism industry to educate the host community on the wider benefits of visitor spending.

There have been increasing calls for the public sector to focus on the core tasks required to operate in a market economy. These include the provision of essential services, assurance of macro environment economic stability, protection of the environment and, increasingly, security of citizens from terrorism. Implications of this include a smaller state enterprise sector, the privatisation of infrastructure and a user-pays approach to the operation of museums and parks. Tourism would rarely be regarded as an essential government service such as health, education and security. However, the case for government involvement in tourism may be made through the arguments that:

- tourism is an enabler of *economic development* for society;
- there would be a risk of *market failure* if responsibility for destination marketing was solely the responsibility of the private sector and the free market;
- *provision of infrastructure* stimulates inward private sector investment;
- tourism provides *fiscal revenue* opportunities for government;
- *border control* policies impact on tourism development;
- *regulatory safeguards* are needed to ensure the safety of visitors;
- *disaster response* management is required to avert a tourism crisis;
- *protection of resources* is required to maintain an attractive environment;
- tourism presents *socio-cultural benefits* for communities.

Tourism as an enabler of economic development

Attracting visitors has long been recognised as a means for stimulating economic growth for communities. For example, the emergence of a bathing season for visitors to Margate during the 1730s is credited with rescuing the English port town from ruin, following tough economic times (Walton, 1983). Opportunities exist for the smallest communities to benefit from tourism as a vehicle for economic development. In the USA, for example, Pigeon Forge in Tennessee, Branson in Missouri and Jackson in Wyoming are places with populations of fewer than 5,000 people, but attract over 5 million visitors every year (Ioannides, 2003).

Tourism has generally proved a stable investment vehicle, with overall global growth averaging 6 per cent annually during the 1960s–1990s (Bull, 1995). International tourism receipts grew faster than world trade during the 1980s and, by the 1990s, constituted a higher proportion of the value of world exports than all sectors other than petroleum products and motor vehicles (UNWTO, 1995). Global international arrivals have been forecast to increase by 3.3 per cent a year to reach 1.8 billion by 2030, with growth rates for emerging nations doubling that for advanced economies (UNWTO, 2014).

Recognition that visitor increases lead to new job creation has seen tourism move from the shadows of fiscal policy to a place in centre stage in many economies (Hall, 1998). For example, in the USA, the meetings and conventions sector alone supports 7 million jobs (DMAI, 2013). In California travel spending in the state during 2014 supported 1 million jobs (Travelindustrywire.com, 2015). Globally, tourism supports 1 in every 11 jobs, or 9 per cent of all jobs (UNWTO, 2014). Table 3.1 highlights the ratio of full-time equivalent jobs for a selection of macro regions, countries and communities. In general terms, it is useful to consider tourism as contributing *1 in 10* worldwide, in terms of jobs and also dollars spent by consumers. As at June 2013 there were approximately 267,000 tourism businesses, or 13 per cent of all Australian businesses. However, in the wake of the 2008 global financial crisis, Australia lost an estimated 17,000 tourism businesses between 2010 and 2013, representing 40 per cent of the total businesses lost in the nation for the period (see Backpackertradenews.com, 2015).

Table 3.1 Full-time equivalent tourism jobs

Destination	Ratio of full-time equivalent tourism jobs in the economy	Source
Greece	18%	SETE (2014, in Trihas et al., 2013)
United Kingdom	14%	UNWTO (2011)
Central and Eastern Europe	12%	WTTC/WEFA (1997, in Hall, 2002)
Queensland, Australia	10%	QTIC (2015)
Mexico	10%	WTTC (2004, in Berger, 2006)
The world	9%	UNWTO (2014)
South Africa	9%	www.tourism.gov.za, 2/3/15
Australia	8%	Tourism Research Australia (2013)
Saudi Arabia	7%	UNWTO (2011)
Brazil	6%	UNWTO (2011)
Kansas City, USA	5%	www.visitkc.com/about-visit-kc, 2/3/15

Spatial redistribution

Tourism can be an effective way of redistributing wealth from prosperous cities to rural and industrial areas that have a narrow economic base. With increased diversification into tourism, these regions can counter the risk of decline in traditional industries. The resultant employment opportunities also help to reduce the impact of urban drift among younger members of the population. Rural America has long been in economic decline, and Edgell (1999) cited a number of reports initiated by Congress that promoted tourism as a major opportunity for revival. Edgell asserted most of rural America, which contains 25 per cent of the USA's population and 90 per cent of the natural resources, is conducive to tourism. One proactive approach developed in the USA is Civic Tourism (see www.civictourism.org), which aims 'to provide a forum for communities to decide if and how the individual ingredients of place (cultural, built, and natural) can be integrated to create an appealing, dynamic, and distinctive community identity'. The initiative emerged from those concerned about the urban drift from the old mining towns in the country's south west.

The imbalance of the London-centric nature of British inbound tourism has long been controversial in Britain (Jeffries, 1989). Around two-thirds of all holiday visitors to Britain arrive in London (Bowes, 1990). Likewise, in Australia, 80 per cent of tourism businesses are located in the three states of New South Wales, Queensland and Victoria (backpackertradenews, 2015). Using redistribution policies involving a combination of taxation and spending, it is possible for governments to spread economic benefits throughout the economy (Bull, 1995). For example, the government in Egypt introduced a ten-year tax holiday for developments in remote areas (Wahab, 1995, in Gartner, 1996). Malaysia, Italy, Thailand and the UK have used regionally variable taxation and development grants as incentives for development in outlying areas. The 2015 VisitBritain mission statement explicitly aims to increase visitor spending to all parts of Britain (see Chapter 8). Other notable examples of spatial redistribution policies to improve regional economic opportunities by government include the Languedoc Roussillon development in France (see de Haan *et al.*, 1990; Jeffries, 2001), Cancun in Mexico (Jeffries, 2001) and Korea's Cheju Island (Jeffries, 2001).

Market failure

If funding for destination marketing was left to the private sector, market failure would probably result, since the priority for individual businesses would be to do what is best for their own operation rather than the destination. Thus, the free market in this regard is not efficient due to the effect of stakeholders' self-interests. Would small tourism businesses survive against unfair competition from larger and better resourced operators without government investment in destination marketing? What constitutes membership of the tourism industry? It is extremely difficult for tourism to adopt a cooperative producer board approach, such as is found in the horticulture and agriculture industries, due to the difficulty in delineating those businesses that benefit from tourism spending. Generally, it is for this reason that destination marketers need government support more than other industries. Also, a vast pooling of resources would be required to achieve a reasonable destination marketing budget, since the vast majority of tourism businesses are small family-owned ventures employing fewer than ten people:

- Of Australia's 267,000 tourism businesses 95 per cent are classified as self-employed, micro or small business (backpackertradenews.com, 2015).

- Around 98 per cent of over 1 million US travel businesses are classified as small businesses (Edgell, 1999; Jeffries, 2001).

- An estimated 70 per cent of accommodation houses in England have only 10 or fewer guest rooms (McIntyre, 1995, in Davidson and Maitland, 1997).

- In Europe about 95 per cent of tourism businesses employ fewer than 10 staff (Middleton, 1998), and 96 per cent of the 1.3 million hotels and restaurants have fewer than 9 employees (UNWTO, 1997 in Jeffries, 2001).

Torbay, an English seaside destination, is another useful example of the importance of government investment in tourism (see English, 2000). Torbay had traditionally enjoyed a reputation as the *English Riviera*, but suffered a decline in popularity from the 1970s due to the increased affordability and availability of European holiday packages. Tourism has a significant economic impact on the area with an estimated 16,000 people employed in the local tourism industry. English cited a leading local official to highlight the need for government investment: 'We all know the story of Torbay's decline but it's trying to persuade Government that we suffer measurable deprivation that's the big challenge' (English, 2000: 91). There was a lack of direct involvement by central government, and poor communication between the regional tourism board and local operators. English's synopsis (2000) provides sobering reading for one of Britain's leading resort areas, where tourism was the core industry, where standards were declining and where strong government leadership was lacking:

> *In Torbay the major problem is a lack of professionalism and the belief that they do not need help. Many come to the industry with no prior background or training and very little knowledge . . . Businesses also feel they are only in competition locally . . . and thus do not work together. On the whole few seem to be investing for long-term benefits and standards vary considerably. This research has shown that many supporting the industry would like to see more Government involvement and feel that Government has an important leadership and co-ordination role to play.*
>
> *(English, 2000: 96)*

Therefore, an impartial coordinator is required to stimulate the pooling of destination resources to create a greater impact in the market than would otherwise be achieved by disparate individual efforts. This is similar to the efficient market hypothesis in behavioural finance (see Fama, 1970). If left to the private sector to organise and fund collective destination promotion, the likely result will be failure.

Provision of infrastructure to encourage inward investment

Traditionally, governments have been responsible for the development of infrastructure to enable tourism, such as utilities, sewerage, health, communication and transport facilities (Bull, 1995). The case of the rise and fall and rise of Rotorua in line with government investment in infrastructure, reported in the Preface, is a prime example. In the USA Billington (2008, in Pike, 2008) reported that investors were returning to the Blackstone Valley, America's industrial birthplace, on the back of new government investment. Beginning in 1790 with cotton manufacturing, the Valley became the place to achieve the American Dream. However, by the 1940s, industry was leaving. The Valley went into an economic free-fall, people moved on and mill villages decayed. It took several years of work and support by the Rhode Island and Massachusetts US Congressional delegation, and extensive state, local and organisational support, before President Ronald Regan signed the Blackstone Valley National Heritage Corridor Act into law in November 1986. Since the creation of the Blackstone River Valley National Heritage Corridor, approximately US$21 million in federal funds had been invested in the Valley. As a result, over US$73.5 million in private funds had been attracted to the Rhode Island riverfront portions of the National Heritage Corridor.

Hazbun (2000) reported the difficulty faced by Jordan in attracting visitors prior to the 1990s, due to a lack of infrastructure, access and attractions. Poor quality infrastructure has also been one of the major challenges to overcome for destinations in Eastern Europe. During 2003 the Albanian government began an ambitious development tourism redevelopment programme in a bid to appeal to international visitors. The government organised the demolition of rundown buildings along the best beaches, which would be replaced with 5-star accommodation developments. Albania's Minister of Tourism suggested only Kosovans were willing to put up with the poor roads and other inconveniences of travelling within Albania. Apparently hundreds of illegally erected kiosks, shops and hotels did not have access to water and sewerage facilities. A similar problem exists in Kazakhstan today, where significant government investment in infrastructure is required to enable the fledgling tourism industry to develop. Likewise, it has been suggested Papua New Guinea's tourism potential will remain untapped unless there is the political will by government to develop necessary infrastructure (Wright, 2004).

In recent years India has been investing heavily in infrastructure projects, such as over 18,000 kilometres of highways (D'Silva and Bharadwaj, 2004). In 2003 the first annual Africa tourism investment summit was announced by the Ugandan Minister of Tourism. One of the principal aims of the forum was to promote infrastructure development, in a continent that was attracting only 2 per cent of global tourism spending. Almost half of the population of sub-Saharan Africa live in absolute poverty, each surviving on less than US$1 per day (Kadel et al., 2011). Kadel et al. highlighted two infrastructure projects in the German government's KfW Entwicklungsbank economic development programme that will boost tourism to the region and enhance job opportunities: the Trans Caprivi Highway in Namibia and the Zambezi Bridge linking Namibia with Zambia. The projects are part of long overdue infrastructure that will help the region tap into the average 6 per cent year on year growth in visitor arrivals to Africa, estimated to reach 50 million by 2020. The growth in visitors has been estimated to create 2 million new jobs in sub-Saharan Africa in the decade ending 2020.

Fiscal revenue opportunities for the government

A government has no money of its own and so the more it can collect in taxes from tourism businesses the more it can spend on enhancing a social, environmental and economic climate where entrepreneurs can flourish. The tourism industry can therefore be a source of increased tax revenue to help fund government's essential services. Brand USA explicitly recognises this in the NTO's vision statement, which is tabled in Chapter 8. Reports of fiscal revenue generation have included:

- In 2015 the Arizona Office of Tourism reported the 2013 US$2.7 billion in visitor tax revenue saved every household US$1,100 (https://tourism.az.gov/research-statistics/economic-impact, 21 March 2015).

- In 2015 the Kansas City CVB reported that taxes paid by visitors saved the average local household US$490 in taxes each year (www.visitkc.com/about-visit-kc, 2 March 2015).

- In 2015 Visit California announced the 251 million people who travelled in the state during 2014 spent US$117.5 billion generating US$9.3 billion in state and local tax revenue (Travelindustrywire.com, 2015).

- In 2014 Visit North Carolina's *Beauty Amplified* campaign yielded a 15–1 return on investment to the state. Every advertising dollar generated US$184 in new visitor spending, US$9 in extra state tax revenues and US$6 in extra local tax revenues (Longwoods International, 2015).

- Brand USA claimed 1.1 million additional international visitors generated US$3.4 billion in new spending and US$1 billion in federal, state and local taxes (Travelindustrywire.com, 2014).

- The meetings and conventions sector in the USA generates US$1 billion in tax revenue annually (DMAI, 2013).

- The April 2003 newsletter of the Colorado Tourism Office reported the results of the study that estimated every advertising dollar spent by the STO generated US$12.74 in state taxes.

- In Florida tourism generated US$51 billion in taxable sales during 2002, with the US$3.1 billion in tax representing 20 per cent of the government's total sales tax take.

Taxes also commonly target international travellers at gateways. These include an airport departure fee, such as in Costa Rica and New Zealand, and an arrival tax such as has occurred in Paraguay and Venezuela. In other cases revenue may be raised through visa application fees. A visa fee levied on entry, as is the case in China and Indonesia, for example, might also be considered an arrivals tax. The USA introduced a fee for its visa waiver programme in 2009, to help fund airport infrastructure. Another tax example is permit fees for admission to national and forest parks and marine reserves. Such tourist taxes help to pay for their use of public amenities (Wanhill, 2000), which would otherwise be funded by local taxpayers.

Some taxes can be divisive. Internet news wire service TravelMole.com reported news of a controversial eco-tax, introduced in May 2003 in Spain's Balearic Islands, which was in danger of being scrapped only one year later. The purpose of the tax was to offset environmental damage caused by tourism. At the same time as the levy was imposed, however, visitor numbers declined significantly. The report cited the spokespersons from the Federation of Tour Operators and the *Majorca Daily News* who suggested strongly that the tax had made a significant negative impact on the affordability of the islands. So there is a paradox in the balance between government realisation of tourism's economic development potential versus tourism as an easy target for taxes. While tourists are a valuable part of the tax base, they are not voters (Wanhill, 2000).

In India the government abolished the Inland Air Travel Tax and Foreign Travel Tax (D'Silva and Bharadwaj, 2004). State governments there have also reduced tourism taxes. In 2004 Mexico became the second country, following Chile, to reduce the VAT rate to zero for international conventions (Cerda, 2005). The initiative, which was proposed by the tourism industry, covers venue hire, accommodation, transfers and related services.

Border control policies

Since so much travel crosses national borders, governments have been forced to develop improved policies for entry and exit by residents and visitors. For example, in 2015 the UK government announced major changes to visa rules in an effort to attract more visitors (TravelandTourWorld.com, 2015a). Also in 2015, India extended its *visa on arrival* programme from 43 countries to 150, in a move designed to increase visitors from countries such as the USA, Israel and Japan (TravelandTourWorld.com, 2015b). The UNWTO reported visa facilitation around the world had made strong progress in recent years, with 62 per cent of the world's population requiring a visa prior to departure in 2014, down from 77 per cent in 2008 (TravelandTourWorld.com, 2015c).

While there has been a lack of published research related to the impact of visa policies on tourism, Liu and McKercher's (2014) literature review found a general link between liberalising policies and increased visitors, as in the case of the USA's visa waiver programme introduction for example. They also provided a detailed discussion on the positive and negative economic and social effects of visa liberalisation between Hong Kong and China. Often the tourism industry lobbies for the easing of visa restrictions to improve access from emerging markets. In some cases coordination between tourism policy and immigration policy has resulted in visa regulations designed to enhance international visitor arrivals. For example, a relaxed visa policy introduced by Oman in 2003 was promoted by officials as a measure to boost tourism to the Gulf nation (Rahman, 2003). The European Union is a tourism example of a free trade agreement, where the entry/exit process has been hugely simplified for citizens, much to the envy of tourism interests in most other parts of the world.

Many countries will need to relax their visa policies if they are to take advantage of the potential offered by the China outbound travel market (Liu and McKercher, 2014). Liu and McKercher noted that by 2014 China had signed Approved Destination Status (ADS) with 146 countries. The ADS is used by China to minimise the risk of illegal immigration and enable safe and reliable tourism services for its citizens. In Australia, for example, the government requires all local tour operators and tour guides involved in hosting Chinese ADS visitors to be licensed under the scheme, for which a formal Code of Business Standards and Ethics sets out responsibilities (see www.austrade.gov.au/Tourism/Tourism-and-business/ADS). In 1999 Australia became one of the first countries to be granted ADS and has approval to market directly to Chinese consumers. Liu and McKercher (2014) cited sources suggesting there were 100 million outbound Chinese departures in 2013, with forecasts of up to 350 million by 2020.

International policy decisions

The case of the Karelian Isthmus also highlights the rise and fall and rise of a destination through government intervention, albeit of a different kind (see Kostianen, 2011). This historical border region had a strong tourism base out of St Petersburg in Russia until the Bolshevik Revolution in 1917 saw the area become part of the newly independent Finland. As a result, the border with Russia was closed to travellers and the destination's visitor numbers collapsed. The Isthmus was re-conquered by the Soviet Union during the Second World War and the destination named 'a tourist and "sanitary" region for the Soviet people' (Kostianen, 2011: 144). Indeed the end of the Cold War and the demise of communism from 1989 in Europe removed barriers to travel entry in many countries, which did not exist prior to the Second World War. Likewise, a number of Asian economies are now benefiting from the reduction in travel restrictions for foreigners, such as Myanmar, Cambodia and Vietnam.

Cuba's tourism development has suffered as a result of the US embargo of 1960. Even though the island nation lies less than 100 kilometres from Florida, direct transport links are prohibited. At the time of writing, Cuba and US diplomats had commenced talks about the possibility of closer relations, which could lead to an end to the world's longest running trade embargo. It should be noted, however, that Americans have been visiting the island nation and that immigration officials have been instructed not to stamp US passports to avoid potential problems for these travellers (see L'Etang *et al.*, 2007).

Regulatory safeguards

Key motives for government policies relating to regulatory safeguards are concerned with economic controls, consumer protection and orderly markets (Bull, 1995). Economic controls impact on international travel where a generating country might impose restrictions on the export of the local currency, or regulations concerning tax deductibility for business travel. Consumer protection areas include the licensing and bonding of goods and services providers, accommodation classification systems and the fulfilment of contracts. As temporary residents of a community, travellers also have a right to expect protection from unfair practices and to safe passage. For example, ensuring the safety and security of travellers is a major obstacle to Papua New Guinea's tourism growth. Clearly, however, regulatory safeguards need to avoid unnecessary bureaucracy. In this regard, Bermuda has been labelled 'red tape island' by the government opposition due to the problems being encountered by hotel developers there.

Disaster response management

An emerging area of interest in the tourism literature is the impact of disasters on the tourism industry, both at global and local levels. Quick decisions are required in times of crisis. Such decision making and resultant responses should also be of a cooperative nature and therefore coordinated. Individual businesses are at the mercy of exogenous events, but few have the resources individually to engage in strategic planning for crises, particularly at a destination level. The government therefore has a vested interest in ensuring adequate leadership, to mitigate the chance of a disaster developing into a long-term crisis for the destination and its stakeholders. The topic of tourism disaster response management is discussed in Chapter 7.

Protection of resources to maintain an attractive environment

A completely free market philosophy might not be congruent with a community's wider interests such as the protection of the environment and public goods (Jeffries, 2001). Would an unfettered tourism industry ensure all members of the host and visiting community retained access to natural features such as beaches and rivers? Would unrestricted access to such assets by private sector developers place an undue strain on public sector infrastructure responsibilities? Could we rely on all entrepreneurs to adopt sustainable resource practices without government regulations or inducements? For example, tourism can be used as an economic incentive for protecting native wildlife from poaching (Ritchie and Crouch, 2003).

In general there is increasing conflict between the tourism industry and the conservation movement (Carroll, 1991). This conflict has played a role in stimulating government policies relating to the protection of natural resources for sustainable use. Tourism depends on the protection of environmental and community resources. Is sustainable tourism an oxymoron? There has been increasing criticism about the negative impacts of tourism on societies and environments (Elliott, 1997). Problems include the pressure of mass tourism on communities, natural and built environments and infrastructure; lack of control over tourist developments; and lack of controls over sex tourism. Government investment is required to identify solutions that are in the public interest. Examples of government leadership in environmental protection have included:

- the 1841 establishment of a state-owned natural preservation area in the Karelian Isthmus, Russia (Kostianen, 2011);

- the establishment of the world's first national park in the USA in 1872 (Elliott, 1997);

- the 1887 establishment of the Rocky Mountains Park by the Canadian federal government (Go, 1987);

- the establishment of Tongariro National Park in New Zealand in 1903, which was the first in the world on land gifted by indigenous people;

- Hawaii's Land Use Law of 1961 in the face of rapid tourism developments (National Tourism Resources Review Commission, 1973, in Doering, 1979);

- the Bruges government's Reien Project, to better manage the quality of the destination's canals (see Vanhove, 2002);

- New Zealand's Resource Management Act (1991), which provided a legislative framework for land use planning, water and soil management, pollution, waste control, coastal management and land subdivision;

- by 2009 Namibia had 53 conservation areas, which represented 15 per cent of the country's territory (Kadel *et al.*, 2011).

IN PRACTICE

3.4 The threat to the Great Barrier Reef

Tourism activity around the Great Barrier Reef World Heritage area generated an estimated AUD$5.7 billion in 2013 to the Australian economy (QTIC, 2015). While resource management processes guide commercial tourism in the area, global warming, the invasion of the Indonesian coral eating crown of thorns starfish and significant ongoing coastal industrial development represent very serious threats to the health of the reef. In regard to the latter, a major focus of the *Australian Government Reef Programme* (see www.nrm.gov.au/national/continuing-investment/reef-programme) is to manage the quality of water running into the lagoon, most of which is from non-tourism sources. During 2015 the reef was close to becoming classified as *in danger* by the world heritage body, UNESCO.

Socio-cultural benefits

A key factor in the rise of tourism during the 1950s and 1960s was the introduction of the social policy of leave with pay from work. Cadieu (1999, in Jeffries, 2001) noted French government initiatives in the 1930s to promote social tourism through publicly subsidised holidays for low-income earners as part of a welfare programme. Long's (1994) survey of British local authorities found that, after increased employment opportunities, the social benefits of an increase in the range and quality of facilities, services and events designed for the visitor industry was the next most cited benefit of tourism development in their community. Bramwell and Rawding (1996) cited the head of the Manchester City Council tourism section:

> *Tourism can make the city a better place to live, visit, work and invest in and so the standard of living goes up, and the quality of life improves and the profile of the city is raised, and (this process) goes round in a circle.*

> *(Bramwell and Rawding, 1996: 430)*

Negative impacts of tourism

With so many policy areas impacting on tourism, it would seem it is very much in a government's interests to support a coordinating body, such as a DMO. However, just as lobbying for government support is undertaken by the tourism industry leaders, other stakeholders can be just as passionate in arguing government has no place supporting tourism marketing. Some in industry, such as the director of the British Travel Trade Fair, argue that the benefits of tourism are not fully recognised by governments:

> *In marketing terms, tourism's return on investment is exceptional, reaping nearly £50 in income for every £1 spent. It's another example of why MPs of all parties need to wake up to the fact tourism needs to be moved right up the government agenda.*
>
> *(Barnett, 2006: 1)*

Likewise, Kubiak (2002), a senior policy advisor to the Southern Governors' Association in the USA, suggested the potential of tourism as an economic enabler had been underestimated by state governments, and questioned why more had not been done to promote the benefits offered by tourism. Kubiak (2002: 19) referred to tourism as the 'red-headed step-child' of state government policy makers.

Government recognition of the economic value of tourism to communities, as well as subsequent social benefits, has to a large extent been responsible for the proliferation of DMOs worldwide. The focus of DMO operations has generally been selling a place, with the desired end results being increases in visitor arrivals, length of stay and spending. As is discussed in Chapter 15, however, one of the problems with destination marketing is that it has been difficult to actually quantify the contribution of DMO efforts to the overall success of the destination, both for short-term measures of marketing campaign effectiveness and for long-term destination competitiveness. The lack of performance metrics rightly leaves the industry open to attack from politicians and other industries seeking justification for public funding of place promotion, high costs of infrastructure (sewerage and water) and superstructure (tax breaks for developers), and the impact of export leakage (foreign owned hotels). For example, in the late 1980s a British government review of the British Tourism Authority examined the extent to which the private sector should be responsible for overseas marketing. Jeffries (1989: 75) cited the then minister responsible as stating the government's wish was 'to see such activities carried out in the private sector wherever possible'.

There are essentially two key arguments against public funding involvement in the support of commercial tourism development (Bull, 1995). First, such investments may distort markets. This may occur when a project would not ordinarily succeed in a free market and the net welfare benefits such as employment creation are used to support commercial inefficiencies. Also, larger entities may receive a larger share of resources. Stimulated by the decline in oil prices in the 1980s and a peace accord with Israel in the early 1990s, tourism was promoted in Jordan as the panacea to that country's economic woes (Hazbun, 2000). Tourism would be the oil of the Jordanian economy. However, Hazbun warned of the danger of false expectations created by unrealistic or overly optimistic projections by the Jordanian state. Jordan, which relied on Arab aid and remittances from expatriates abroad, announced ambitious plans to encourage private sector tourism developments. The strategy was to stimulate a rush of investment in mega projects, such as 30,000 new hotel beds in the Dead Sea area by 2010, to overcome the low equilibrium trap of low visitor arrivals generating little revenue for future tourism development. One of the results of this was a 68 per cent increase in hotel beds during the period 1993–1996. However, by 1997 hotel occupancy rates had decreased to only 38 per cent. Khouri (1998, in Hazbun, 2000) cited a Jordanian economist:

Hotels, tourist buses and travel agencies are real and sad examples of how parts of the economy went on an investment binge in 1995, only to come down to earth with a thud a year later and then start to wallow in a depression which continues.

(Khouri, 1998, in Hazbun, 2000: 195)

One of the problems with Jordan's *big push* in stimulating new tourism developments and infrastructure was a failure to balance this with adequate initiatives to stimulate increased demand for the new products (Hazbun, 2000). Part of the problem was a lack of public or private promotional organisations, resulting in a lack of information flow and cooperation between individual tourism businesses.

Bull's (1995) second argument against funding tourism is that subsidies may ultimately benefit visitors rather than suppliers through lower tariffs. This might not be an issue for domestic tourism, but in such cases governments may in effect unintentionally subsidise international visitors. Unfortunately, it is the term *subsidise* that is often used by some to describe government funding of destination marketing.

Even though few countries are self-sufficient and therefore require foreign exchange earnings to purchase necessary imports, not all have embraced the idea of an international tourism trade. Historically, authoritarian regimes have either banned tourism or tightly controlled it (Gartner, 1996). In this regard, readers are referred to Roper (2001) for a comprehensive discussion on the perceived problems with tourism. Roper summarised these points of view as primarily falling into six categories, which are shown in Figure 3.2.

A dislike of strangers and xenophobia

While such views are probably in the minority, there are many closed societies where outsiders are not welcome. The Hawaiian island of Ni'ihau is an example of a place virtually off limits to tourists. Other examples include towns and rural communities that are the base for religious sects such as the Jews of Mea Sharim in Israel and the Amish of Ohio.

Changes to the character of the destination

The character of a destination and its people can be negatively affected by the very people who come to experience it. The number, characteristics, morality and behaviour of visitors can spoil the very nature of what attracted interest in the first place.

Negative social and cultural impacts

New visitors not only bring money into a destination but they can also bring crime, ideas that create disharmony and envy among the host community. To cater to the entertainment tastes of mass tourists, traditional cultures have been replaced with ersatz rituals.

Economic damage

Critics of tourism argue the majority of jobs are low paid and servile in nature, and that most of the profits flow out of the community to outside investors.

Negative environmental impacts

Tourism developments have been the cause of damage to the environment. Also, ironically, increasing numbers of eco-tourists are spoiling the very serenity of the nature they seek to enjoy.

Colonialism or external control

It has been argued that tourism is the new form of colonialism and is even more powerful than any imperial power.

Figure 3.2 Perceived problems with tourism

Source: Adapted from Roper (2001).

While a full discussion on the negative impacts of tourism is beyond the scope of the text, it is important to acknowledge that there are often strong arguments by sections of society against tourism. Some of the claims are fair . . . some are not. Students of destination marketing should be aware of the nature of these points of view to develop a balanced perspective and recognise the need for consistent messages to local residents who might be ignorant of the wider community benefits of a strong and competitive tourism industry.

CHAPTER SUMMARY

Key point 1: The importance of government support for sustained destination competitiveness

Sustained destination competitiveness is unlikely without government support. Coordination is required within and between government departments, within industry and between government and industry. Only governments can provide such coordination through their access to taxation revenue and their ability to legislate. Governments generally support tourism development for the following reasons: increased economic growth and jobs, potential for market failure in a free market, infrastructure is required to attract private sector investment, fiscal revenue opportunities, the need for border controls, the need to protect natural resources and maintain an attractive environment, the need for regulatory safeguards to protect visitors, leadership during times of exogenous events and socio-cultural benefits.

Key point 2: The rational for long-term government funding of destination marketing

The majority of DMOs rely to a large extent on government funding, either by financial grants or by a visitor tax. The overreliance on government support is a concern going into an uncertain future, and more research is needed investigating other revenue sources. Many DMOs, at national, state and local levels, would simply not be able to function in their current form without the resources of government. Private sector contributions are difficult to secure and generally pale in comparison to public sector funding. When public sector funding is reduced for political reasons, such as in times of economic austerity, it is unlikely private sector funding is able to make up the shortfall. Two key problems with sourcing private sector funding are the difficulty in classifying which businesses benefit from tourism, and the potential for self-interest of big business to influence DMO decision making.

Key point 3: The opposing view that governments should not subsidise the tourism industry

Anyone with an interest in tourism management should be able to debate the argument for and against government support of DMOs and be open-minded as to why critics might argue this is a form of subsidy. Some stakeholders from other industries see this as unfair, while others in the community suggest tourism benefits a select few. It must also be acknowledged that there are many potential negative impacts of tourism at a destination.

REVIEW QUESTIONS

1. Why do some outside the industry criticise government for *subsidising* tourism businesses?

2. What is commonly the most compelling reason for government support of tourism development?

3. Why is it so difficult for DMOs to raise direct funding, such as membership subscriptions, from tourism businesses at their destination?

REFERENCES

Akehurst, G., Bland, N. and Nevin, M. (1993). Tourism policies in the European Community member states. *International Journal of Hospitality Management* 12(1): 33–66.

Ateljevic, I. and Doorne, S. (2000). Local government and tourism development: Issues and constraints of public sector entrepreneurship. *New Zealand Geographer* 56(2): 25–31.

Backpackertradenews.com. (2015). Aus tourism sheds 17,000 businesses. Available at: http://backpackertradenews. com.au/aus-tourism-sheds-17000-businesses-28510

Barnett, G. (2006). *Government Apathy Could 'Wipe Millions' off Tourism Earnings.* www.TravelMole.com. 1 March.

Berger, D. (2006). *The Development of Mexico's Tourism Industry: Pyramids by Day, Martinis by Night.* New York: Palgrave Macmillan.

Bolson, F. (2005). Alliances. In Harrill, R. (ed.) *Fundamentals of Destination Management and Marketing.* Washington, DC: IACVB, pp. 219–228.

Bonham, C. and Mak, J. (1996). Private versus public financing of state destination promotion. *Journal of Travel Research* Fall: 3–10.

Bowes, S. (1990). The role of the tourist board. In Goodall, B. and Ashworth, G. (eds) *Marketing in the Tourist Industry: The Promotion of Destination Regions.* London: Routledge.

Bramwell, B. and Rawding, L. (1996). Tourism marketing images of industrial cities. *Annals of Tourism Research* 23(1): 201–221.

Bull, A. (1995). *The Economics of Travel & Tourism.* Melbourne, Australia: Longman.

Carroll, P. (1991). Policy issues and tourism. In Carroll, P., Donohue, K., McGovern, M. and McMillen, J. (eds) *Tourism in Australia.* Sydney, Australia: Harcourt Brace Jovanovich, pp. 20–43.

Carson, D., Beattie, S. and Gove, B. (2003). Tourism management capacity of local government: An analysis of Victorian local government. In Braithwaite, R.W. and Braithwaite, R. L. (eds) *Riding the Wave of Tourism and Hospitality Research: Proceedings of the Council of Australian University Tourism and Hospitality Education Conference.* Coffs Harbour, NSW: Southern Cross University, Lismore. CD-ROM.

Cerda, E. L. (2005). Destination management in Mexico. In Harrill, R. (ed.) *Fundamentals of Destination Management and Marketing.* Washington, DC: IACVB, pp. 259–272.

Coles, T., Dinan, C. and Hutchison, F. C. (2014). Tourism and the public sector in England since 2010: A disorderly transition. *Current Issues in Tourism* 17(3): 247–279.

Coventry, N. (2006). *Inside Tourism.* 621. 1 December. Hard copy newsletter.

Davidson, R. and Maitland, R. (1997). *Tourism Destinations.* London: Hodder & Stoughton.

Davidson, R. and Rogers, T. (2006). *Marketing Destinations & Venues for Conferences, Conventions and Business Events.* Oxford: Elsevier.

De Haan, T., Ashworth, G. and Stabler, M. (1990). The tourist destination as product: The case of Languedoc. In Ashworth, G. and Goodall, B. (eds) *Marketing Tourism Places.* New York: Routledge, pp. 156–169.

DMAI. (2013). *2013 Convention Sales and Marketing Activities Study.* Destination Marketing Association International. Available at: www.destinationmarketing.org/2013-convention-sales-marketing-activities-study-0

Doering, T. R. (1979). Geographical aspects of state travel marketing in the USA. *Annals of Tourism Research* 6(3): 307–317.

Donnelly, M. P. and Vaske, J. J. (1997). Factors affecting membership in a tourism promotion authority. *Journal of Travel Research* Spring: 50–55.

D'Silva, C. and Bharadwaj, M. (2004). The sleeping giant: India wakes up to the tourism challenge. *Executive Report* July: 5–7.

Edgell, D. L. (1999). *Tourism Policy: The Next Millennium.* Champaign, IL: Sagamore.

Elliott, J. (1997). *Tourism: Politics and Public Sector Management.* London: Routledge.

English, G. (2000). Government intervention in tourism: Case study of an English seaside resort. In Robinson, M., Evans, N., Long, P., Sharpley, R. and Swarbrooke, J. (eds) *Management, Marketing and the Political Economy of Travel and Tourism.* Sunderland, UK: The Centre for Travel and Tourism, pp. 86–101.

Fama, E. F. (1970). Efficient capital markets: A review of theory and empirical work. *Journal of Finance* 25(2): 383–417.

Fenich, G. G. (2005). *Meetings, Expositions, Events and Conventions: An Introduction to the Industry.* Upper Saddle River, NJ: Pearson.

Gartner, W. C. (1996). *Tourism Development: Principles, Processes, and Policies.* New York: John Wiley & Sons.

Gatty, B. and Blalock, C. (1997). New organization brings new energy to marketing the U.S. *Hotel & Motel Management* 17 (17 February).

Go, F. M. (1987). Selling Canada. *Travel & Tourism Analyst* Dec: 17–29.

Hall, C. M. (1998). *Introduction to Tourism: Development, Dimensions and Issues* (3rd edition). Sydney, Australia: Pearson Education Australia.

Hall, D. (2002). Brand development, tourism and national identity: The re-imaging of former Yugoslavia. *Journal of Brand Management* 9(4/5): 323–334.

Hashimoto, A. and Telfer, D. J. (2001). Tourism distribution channels in Canada. In Buhalis, D. and Laws, E. (eds) *Communication Issues in NTO Distribution Strategies.* London: Continuum, pp. 243–258.

Hays, S., Page, S. J. and Buhalis, D. (2013) Social media as a destination marketing tool: Its use by national tourism organisations. *Current Issues in Tourism* 16(3): 211–239.

Hazbun, W. (2000). Enclave orientalism: The state, tourism, and the politics of post-national development in the Arab world. In Robinson, M., Evans, N., Long, P., Sharpley, R. and Swarbrooke, J. (eds) *Management, Marketing and the Political Economy of Travel and Tourism.* Sunderland, UK: The Centre for Travel & Tourism, pp. 191–205.

Hopper, P. (2002). Marketing London in a difficult climate. *Journal of Vacation Marketing* 9(1): 81–88.

Horn, C., Fairweather, J. R. and Simmons, D. C. (2000). *Evolving Community Response to Tourism and Change in Rotorua.* Rotorua Case Study Report No. 14. Christchurch, NZ: Lincoln University.

Ioannides, D. (2003). The economics of tourism in host communities. In Singh, S., Timothy, T. J. and Dowling, R. K. (eds) *Tourism in Destination Communities.* Oxford: CABI Publishing, pp. 37–54.

Jeffries, D. (1989). Selling Britain – A case for privatisation? *Travel & Tourism Analyst* 1(1): 69–81.

Jeffries, D. (2001). *Governments and Tourism.* Oxford: Butterworth-Heinemann.

Jenkins, J. (2000). The dynamics of regional tourism organisations in New South Wales, Australia: History, structures and operations. *Current Issues in Tourism* 3(3): 175–203.

Johnson, B. (2011). VisitBritain to cut jobs and refocus. *Marketing Week.* Available at: http://www.marketingweek.co.uk/sectors/travel-andleisure/visitbritain-to-cut-jobs-and-refocus/3023241.article

Kadel, R., Rodl, M. and Wollenzien, T. (2011). Tourism tackles poverty: A case study of Africa. In Conrady, R. and Muck, M. (eds) *Trends and Issues in Global Tourism 2011.* Heidelberg, Germany: Springer-Verlag.

Kerr, W. and Wood, R. C. (2000). Tourism policy and politics in a devolved Scotland. In Robinson, M., Evans, N., Long, P., Sharpley, R. and Swarbrooke, J. (eds) *Management, Marketing and the Political Economy of Travel and Tourism.* Sunderland, UK: The Centre for Travel & Tourism, pp. 284–296.

Kostianen, A. (2011). Tourism and political change in Northern European borderlands: The Karelian Isthmus, c. 1870–1940. *Journal of Tourism History* 3(2): 129–145.

Kubiak, G. D. (2002). Travel & tourism: Export of tomorrow. *Spectrum: The Journal of State Government* Spring: 18–20.

La Page, W. F. (1995). Case studies of partnerships in action. *Journal of Park and Recreation Administration* 13(4): 61–74.

Laden, R. (2015). Colorado Springs should spend more – and hike taxes – to promote tourism, study says. *The Gazette* 11 March. Available at: http://gazette.com/colorado-springs-should-spend-more-and-hike-taxes-to-promote-tourism-study-says/article/1547686

L'Etang, J., Falkheimer, J. and Lugo, J. (2007). Public relations and tourism: Critical reflections and a research agenda. *Public Relations Review* 33(1): 68–76.

Liu, A. and McKercher, B. (2014). The impact of visa liberalization on tourist behaviours: The case of China outbound market visiting Hong Kong. *Journal of Travel Research.* Available at: http://jtr.sagepub.com/content/early/2014/12/29/0047287514564599.abstract

Long, J. (1994). Local authority tourism strategies: A British appraisal. *The Journal of Tourism Studies* 5(2): 17–23.

Longwoods International. (2015). *2014 North Carolina Image & Accountability Research.* January. Available at: http://longwoods-intl.com/travel-tourism-research

Marketing News. (1997). Hard copy magazine article, 29 September.

Marks, J.A. (2004). Convention and visitors bureaus. In Dickenson, B. and Vladimir, A. (eds) *The Complete 21st Century Travel & Hospitality Marketing Handbook*. Upper Saddle River, NJ: Pearson, pp. 139–146.

McGehee, N. G., Meng, F. and Tepanon, Y. (2006). Understanding legislators and their perceptions of the tourism industry: The case of North Carolina, USA, 1990 and 2003. *Tourism Management* 27(2): 684–694.

McKercher, B. and Ritchie, M. (1997). The third tier of public sector tourism: A profile of local government tourism officers in Australia. *Journal of Travel Research* 36(1): 66–72.

Middleton, V. T. C. (1998). New marketing conditions, and the strategic advantages of products similar to destination. In Keller, P. (ed.) *Destination Marketing: Reports of the 48th AIEST Congress, Marrakech*, pp. 153–165.

Mill, R. C. and Morrison, A. M. (1985). *The Tourism System: An Introductory Text*. Englewood Cliffs, NJ: Prentice Hall.

Morrison, A. M., Bruen, S. M. and Anderson, D. J. (1998). Convention and visitor bureaus in the USA: A profile of bureaus, bureau executives, and budgets. *Journal of Travel & Tourism Marketing* 7(1): 1–19.

Nicholas, C. L. (2004). New York City and Company. In Dickenson, B. and Vladimir, A. (eds) *The Complete 21st Century Travel & Hospitality Marketing Handbook*. Upper Saddle River, NJ: Pearson, pp. 147–153.

Oliveira, E. and Panyik, E. (2015). Content, context and co-creation: Digital challenges in destination branding with references to Portugal as a tourist destination. *Journal of Vacation Marketing* 21(1): 53–74.

Pike, S. (2004). *Destination Marketing Organisations*. Oxford: Elsevier Science.

Pike, S. (2007). A cautionary tale of a resort destination's self-inflicted crisis. *Journal of Travel & Tourism Marketing* 23(2/3/4): 73–82.

Pike, S. (2008). *Destination Marketing: An Integrated Marketing Communication Approach*. Burlington, MA: Butterworth-Heinemann.

Pike, S. and Page, S. (2014). Destination marketing organizations and destination marketing: A narrative analysis of the literature. *Tourism Management* 41: 202–227.

Pike, S., May, T. and Bolton, R. (2011). RTO governance: Reflections from a former marketing team. *Journal of Travel & Tourism Research* Fall: 117–133.

Pritchard, G. (1982). Tourism promotion: Big business for the states. *HRA Quarterly* 23(2): 48–57.

QTIC. (2015). *2015 Queensland Election: Priorities for Tourism*. Brisbane, QLD: Queensland Tourism Industry Council. January.

Rahman, F. (2003). *New Visa Rule to Boost Oman's Tourism Sector*. www.eTurboNews.com. 29 July.

Reinhold, S., Läesser, C. and Beritelli, P. (2015). 2014 St. Gallen consensus on destination management. *Journal of Destination Marketing & Management* (in press).

Ritchie, J. R. B. and Crouch, G. I. (2003). *The Competitive Destination: A Sustainable Tourism Perspective*. Oxford: CABI Publishing.

Rogers, T. (2005). Destination management in the UK. In Harrill, R. (ed.) *Fundamentals of Destination Management and Marketing*. Washington, DC: IACVB, pp. 245–258.

Roper, P. (2001). The case against tourism: Doubters and sceptics. In Jeffries, D. (ed.) *Governments and Tourism*. Oxford: Butterworth-Heinemann, pp. 27–50.

Shankman, S. (2015). *How California Doubled Its Tourism Budget to More Than $100 Million*. Available at: http://skift.com/2015/03/02/why-california-doubled-its-tourism-budget-to-more-than-100-million

Sheehan, L. R. and Ritchie, J. R. B. (1997). Financial management in tourism: A destination perspective. *Tourism Economics* 3(2): 93–118.

The News Mail. (2003). Hard copy newsletter article, p. 3.

Tourism Research Australia. (2013). *Tourism Businesses in Australia: June 2010 to June 2012*. Available at: http://www.tra.gov.au/research/Economic_reports.html

TravelandTourWorld.com (2015a) Available at: http://www.travelandtourworld.com/news/article/uks-traveller-friendly-new-visa-rules-boost-economy

TravelandTourWorld.com (2015b) Available at: http://www.travelandtourworld.com/news/article/indian-tourism-rise-voa-extended-150-countries

TravelandTourWorld.com (2015c) Available at: http://www.travelandtourworld.com/news/article/unwto-governments-recognize-benefits-visa-facilitation

Travelindustrywire.com. (2014). *Travel Leaders Applaud Bipartisan Effort to Extend Travel Promotion Program in Omnibus Bill*. Available at: http://www.travelindustrywire.com/article81260.html

Travelindustrywire.com. (2015). *Record-Breaking Year for California's Travel Economy.* Available at: http://www.travelindustrywire.com/article83447.html

Trihas, N., Perakakis, E., Venitourakis, M., Mastorakis, G. and Kopanakis, I. (2013). Social media as a marketing tool for tourism destinations: The case of Greek municipalities. *Journal of Marketing Vistas* 3(2): 38–48.

UNWTO. (1995). *Tourism to the Year 2000 and Beyond: Volume 1 the World.* Geneva, Switzerland: UNWTO.

UNWTO. (2011). *Global Tourism Policy and Practice.* Madrid, Spain: UNWTO.

UNWTO. (2014). *UNWTO Tourism Highlights: 2014 Edition.* Geneva, Switzerland: UNWTO. Available at: http://www.e-unwto.org/doi/pdf/10.18111/9789284416226

Vallee, P. (2005). Destination management in Canada. In Harrill, R. (ed.) *Fundamentals of Destination Management and Marketing.* Washington, DC: IACVB, pp. 229–244.

Vanhove, N. (2002). Tourism policy – Between competitiveness and sustainability: The case of Bruges. *Tourism Review* 57(3): 34–40.

Walton, J. K. (1983). *The English Seaside Resort: A Social History 1750–1914.* Leicester, UK: Leicester University Press.

Wanhill, S. (2000). Issues in public sector involvement. In Faulkner, B., Moscardo, G. and Laws, E. (eds) *Tourism in the 21st Century: Lessons from Experience.* London: Continuum, pp. 222–242.

Wright, J. (2004). PNG tourism completely off track. *The Courier-Mail.* Business. 25 September, p. 79. Hard copy newspaper article.

Chapter **4**

The destination marketing organisation (DMO) and social media

AIMS

To enhance understanding of:

- the rise in influence of social media in travel and tourism;
- how DMOs have been adapting to the Web 2.0 era;
- the benefits and challenges of social media for DMOs.

ABSTRACT

Almost half of the world's population are now internet users. The emergence of Web 2.0 in the early 2000s has revolutionised the way in which all internet users can contribute content. This democratisation of the web has presented the visitor industry with opportunities and challenges on a level not previously experienced. The sheer scale of user-generated content (UGC) that can be published at the *speed of thought* means DMOs have a declining influence in their destination's brand image in comparison to consumers' increasing access to *word of mouse* UGC content. Travellers trust and use social media in travel planning, during travel and after they return home, for a variety of reasons. While DMOs have been experimenting with Web 2.0 technologies in a mostly *ad hoc* way, they have generally been slow to maximise the potential of social media, particularly in terms of enhancing *engagement* with, and between, consumers and stakeholders. Common barriers to DMO engagement have been lack of resources, organisational culture and concerns about loss of control of online content and the potential for negative UGC. It is clear, however, that a new paradigm shift in destination marketing is about to occur as a result of the rise of influence of Web 2.0 technology-based UGC; one that will see destination competitiveness underpinned by DMOs harnessing the opportunities presented by Web 2.0 in a true marketing orientation, using UGC to inform decision making and to engage in relationship marketing. DMOs need a clear strategy for social media engagement, which has at its core a philosophy of *social* (engagement) rather than *media* (placement). Simply applying traditional marketing communications in social media to reach the most technologically sophisticated population the world has seen is a waste of scare resources and a sure path to failure.

An emerging DMO paradigm shift

As at June 2014 just over 3 billion people (42 per cent of the world's population) were internet users (Internet World Stats, 2015a). Table 4.1 summarises the increases in internet use, by continent, between 2000 and 2014. The growth rate figures for the decade were phenomenal: Africa (up 6,499 per cent), Middle East (up 3,304 per cent), Latin America/Caribbean (up 1,673 per cent), Asia (up 1,113 per cent), Europe (up 454 per cent), Oceania/Australia (up 252 per cent) and North America (up 187 per cent). As can be seen, the population penetration levels in Asia (34.7 per cent) and Africa (26.5 per cent), in particular, allude to continued impressive growth into the future. For example, in 2005 there were 2.5 billion connected devices, but by 2020 it has been estimated there will be over 30 billion and these will be mostly mobile (Gartner, 2013, in Trendwatching, 2014). In early 2015 there were 6.8 billion smartphones in use around the world (see SMK, 2015), led by China (1.2 billion), India (924 million) and the USA (327 million). The number of mobile-only internet users is estimated to have grown from 14 million in 2010 to 788 million (Internet World Stats, 2015b).

From a marketing perspective, a major advantage the internet has over traditional media is the ability to integrate five key functions (Gretzel *et al.*, 2000: 147):

1. information representation;
2. collaboration;
3. communication;
4. interactivity;
5. transactions.

Table 4.1 World internet usage as at June 2014

	Internet users December 2000 (millions)	Internet users June 2014 (millions)	Penetration of population	% of table
Asia	114,304	1,386,188	34.7%	45.7
Europe	105,096	582,441	70.5%	19.2
Latin America/Caribbean	18,069	320,312	52.3%	10.5
North America	108,096	310,322	87.7%	10.2
Africa	4,514	297,886	26.5%	9.8
Middle East	3,284	111,809	48.3%	3.7
Oceania/Australia	7,620	26,789	72.9%	0.9
World total	360,985	3,3035,749	42.3%	100.0

Source: Adapted from Internet World Stats (2015a).

However, such potential integration brings with it a minefield of complexity. Keeping up with the speed of *continuous discontinuous change* (perpetual continuous change, but differing types of changes rather than incremental improvements) taking place in the digital world, with increasing adoption rates of mobile devices, increasing internet connectivity and new and disappearing media platforms, presents enormous opportunities and challenges for the visitor industry, the likes of which DMOs have never before been confronted with. For example, by 2009 the internet had become China's most influential medium, with 420 million users (Arlt and Thraenhart, 2011) and, in 2014, *apps* for mobile devices generated more revenue than the Hollywood movie industry (*The Courier-Mail*, 2015). There should be no doubt that a paradigm shift in destination marketing is occurring, as destination marketers are forced to adapt. Exactly how they will achieve this is yet to unfold, but at the core will be a *marketing orientation* (see Chapter 1) with a culture of collaboration and *engagement* between the DMO, stakeholders and consumer-travellers.

The evolution to Web 2.0 will be seen as having the most important impact on written communications since the advent of the printing press (Christou, 2012). Indeed, already in these formative stages, new information is appearing online at the *speed of thought*, with claims:

- by the first half of 2015, 1.44 million people, almost half of all internet users, had active Facebook accounts;
- in 2014 TripAdvisor.com reached 100 million downloads of its app, a six-fold increase since 2011 (www.travelandtourismworld.com, 16 April 2014);
- 100 *things* are uploaded to the internet every second of every day (Cisco, 2013, in Trendwatching, 2014);
- every minute sees 10 hours of content uploaded to YouTube, while over 100 million videos are served daily (Kaplan and Haenlein, 2010);
- every day over 3 million photos are uploaded to Flickr (Bodnar, 2010, in Leung *et al.*, 2013);
- a new blog is created around the world every second of every day (Gretzel, 2006);
- there were 162 million Chinese bloggers by 2009 (Arlt and Thraenhart, 2011);
- 1 billion Tumblr pages are viewed every month (Andrews, 2014);
- Facebook users check their account more than five times a day (Chung and Koo, 2015).

A clear indicator of the impact this new era has had on the tourism world is in the way in which travellers make reservations, which has changed in a relatively short period of time. Table 4.2 highlights the major shift in travel booking methods used by European consumers between 2003 and 2013, as reported by Oliveira and Panyik (2015). As can be seen, the use of the internet for bookings increased from 13 per cent to 76 per cent of travellers. The generation of digital natives who grew up in the internet era might think little of this, but should pause and consider the tourism implications of that one simple statistic . . .

Table 4.2 Changes in European travellers' booking methods

	2003	2013
Travel agent	65%	18%
Phone	22%	5%
Internet	13%	76%

Source: Adapted from Oliveira and Panyik (2015).

before 1995 most people did not have access to the internet and so we can see how far the world has moved from virtually zero per cent bookings online in only 20 years.

Web 2.0

The internet era of corporate websites and e-commerce began in 1995 with the launch of Amazon.com and eBay.com (Kaplan and Haenlein, 2010). The Australian Tourism Commission launched its first consumer website in 1996, with 11,000 pages of information (Buhalis, 2003). For a review on the literature relating to success factors for destinations' websites see Park and Gretzel (2007). During this Web 1.0 period the internet was used to push mostly static information in one direction, in a *read-only* format, which allowed almost no interaction with, or between, other users (Borges, 2009). The technology enabled a new style of presenting marketing communications to a greater audience, but was still generally representative of the *talking at consumers* approach of traditional media marketing. The development of Web 2.0 made it much easier for UGC to be published, through what we now know as social media. While UGC was possible in the Web 1.0 era, it was only in a limited capacity (see Kaplan and Haenlein, 2010). For example, Usenet, a global discussion forum enabling internet users to post messages, was developed in 1979. Also, the TRINET (Tourism Research Information Network) discussion forum was founded in 1988. TRINET is an electronic bulletin board that connects the global tourism research and education community (see http://www.tim.hawaii.edu/timlistserv/about_trinet.aspx). Hosted by the University of Hawaii, TRINET now has over 2,000 members around the world, mostly academics and graduate research students.

The term Web 2.0 was first used in 2004 to describe a platform facilitating content and applications to be continuously modified by all users in a collaborative way (Kaplan and Haenlein, 2010). Web 2.0 was not some mystical upgrade of the internet that occurred at one point in time. Rather it was the availability of a new group of programmes such as Adobe Flash, RSS (really simple syndication) and Java Script. These Web 2.0 technologies, or *tools of mass collaboration* (Sigala, 2012: 7), radically changed the way information could be created, disseminated and viewed by any internet user. For example, the traffic attracted to the world's top two websites, facebook.com and youtube.com, has dwarfed that of sites for traditional mass media such as cnn.com, nytimes.com, espn.go.com and bbc.co.uk (see Pan and Crotts, 2012). The shift in power from organisations to internet users and virtual communities has occurred in a very short period of time, and the tourism industry has been forced to try to adapt quickly to the social media phenomenon.

Social media

To acknowledge the democratising power of social media, *TIME Magazine* named its 2006 person of the year as **You**, the website users (Bodnar, 2010, in Leung *et al.*, 2013). By 2013 engaging with social media had become the most popular activity on the internet (GWI, 2014 in Oliveira and Panyik, 2015), and it has even been suggested consumers devote almost a third of their day to participation on social media (Lang, 2010, in Laroche *et al.*, 2013). Over 90 per cent of China's internet users were engaging in social media by 2010 (Arlt and Thraenhart, 2011). While the communist regime blocked popular Western sites such as Facebook, YouTube and Twitter, the local equivalents Baidu, YouKu and Sina Weibo filled the social media gap. Social media has been defined as:

> [a]ctivities, practices, and behaviours among communities of people who gather online to share information, knowledge, and opinions using conversational media. Conversational media are Web-based applications that make it possible to create and easily transmit content in the form of words, pictures, videos, and audios.
>
> (Brake and Safko, 2009: 6)

The term *virtual community* may have first been coined by Rheingold (1993, in Lange-Faria and Elliot, 2012: 195), who drew on the fields of anthropology and sociology to offer the following definition: 'Social aggregations that emerge from the Net when enough people carry on those public discussions long enough, with sufficient human feeling, to form webs of personal relationships in cyberspace'.

Impact on tourism

Arguably, UGC has the potential to impact on the travel and tourism world in a greater way than on any other industry, for a number of reasons:

- As highlighted in Table 4.2, the internet has emerged as a dominant medium for travel bookings.
- So much of travel requires high levels of information seeking in the planning stages, and UGC is increasingly used as a source.
- Travel and tourism services are predominantly intangible offerings with many types of inherent risk, and UGC is regarded as a credible form of word-of-mouth recommendation.
- There is increasing adoption of mobile social media applications and portable navigation devices.
- There is a move towards providing wider geographic *free wifi* for visitors and residents at destinations.
- There are high levels of *brag value* UGC posts to travellers' virtual social networks.
- Unlike any other brand category, travellers are spoilt for choice with an almost unlimited number of destinations with an online presence.

IN PRACTICE

4.1 Australia's first professional Instagrammer

In 2013 chef and part-time photographer, Lauren Bath, quit her day job to embark on a journey that would lead to her becoming Australia's first professional Instagrammer. At the time Lauren had already built up a huge following of over 200,000 people on Instagram since becoming involved in 2011. Using a top of the range Nikon camera, Lauren now travels the world, working with DMOs, advertising agencies and travel writers, posting pics to her Instagram account, which now has over 400,000 followers. In addition, Lauren has around 200,000 followers across her other social media platforms (Facebook, Google+, Steller and Trover). To date, Lauren has worked on over 100 tourism campaigns, more than any other international Instagrammer. Recently Lauren diversified into public speaking and consulting on social media, as well as project management, as a backup in case the popularity of Instagram starts to fade.

Lauren has a very hands-on approach to working with DMOs and prefers to speak to potential clients at length to make sure they are comfortable with her and her work. She was the first person in Australia to actively present KPIs (Key Performance Indicators) against her campaigns and to broach the difficult topics of media value and return on investment (ROI). Lauren also offers introductory workshops to all clients so that they can better benefit from her social media services.

Figure 4.1 Lauren Bath, Australia's first professional Instagrammer

Follow Lauren Bath

Facebook: https://www.facebook.com/LaurenBathServices
Instagram: www.instagram.com/laurenepbath, @laurenepbath
Twitter: #laurenepbath
Web: www.laurenbath.com

Further reading

News.com.au. (2014).

Tourism academic research

Social media/information communication technologies (ICT) is a relatively new field of research for tourism academics, with the first dedicated journal, the *Journal of Information Technology & Tourism*, launched in 1998. The roots of the journal were created at an earlier meeting of ENTER (http://www.enter2015.org), which is the annual conference of the International Federation for Information Technologies in Travel and Tourism (IFITT). IFITT provides a free digital library of abstracts from all the ENTER conference proceedings from 1998 onwards (see http://www.ifitt.org/resources). The word cloud from the research paper abstracts accepted for ENTER2015 highlights *destination* as a central theme of the conference.

The exponential growth in ICT research has already attracted a number of literature reviews of the field (see O'Connor and Murphy, 2004; Leung and Law, 2007; Hu and Racherla, 2008; Buhalis and Law, 2008; Wang *et al.*, 2010; Gretzel, 2011; Ricci, 2011; Leung *et al.*, 2013). Buhalis and Law (2008) reviewed 149 studies from the first 20 years of ICT research in tourism. Leung and Law (2007) found 410 ICT papers published between 1986 and 2005 in the leading 6 tourism journals. Leung *et al.* (2013) located 44 journal articles specifically on social media in tourism and hospitality that were published between 2007 and 2011.

They reported the number of published journal articles on tourism social media increased from 2 in 2007 to 22 in 2011. The exponential growth in academic interest was highlighted in the 2013 special issue of the *Journal of Travel and Tourism Marketing* (30(1/2)), which attracted 40 submissions (see Law and Xiang, 2013). In 2017 the *Journal of Destination Marketing and Management* will publish a special issue on 'digital destinations'. The first academic conference on tourism blogging was convened in Austria in 2007. The first scholarly book taking a holistic perspective of social media in tourism was by Sigala *et al.* (2012), while the first book specifically interpreting travellers' mobile sociality, using *mobile virtual ethnography*, was by Molz (2012).

Due to the scale of competition in tourism markets and the rise in influence of UGC, it is arguably DMOs that face the greatest level of impacts, opportunities and challenges of social media. It has been suggested that in the future the successful destinations will 'be those that abandon the top-down approach in favour of bottom-up and co-created branding strategies' (Oliveira and Panyik, 2015: 53). To date there has been little empirical research in relation to the effects of social media marketing on destination brands. However, this is not surprising given this is also the case in the wider marketing literature (see Laroche *et al.*, 2013). Nevertheless, the concept of consumers as co-creators of destination brands (by providing UGC), labelled *travellers 2.0* by Sigala *et al.* (2012), requires a radical shift in thinking by destination marketers. DMOs have been criticised for only providing positive views of their destination, with today's sophisticated consumers well aware of the role of destination marketers (see Lange-Faria and Elliot, 2012). However, to date most early practice of generating UGC on tourism websites has been in the form of edited testimonials (Gretzel, 2006).

Types of social media

Kaplan and Haenlein (2010) drew on theories from the fields of media research (social presence, media richness) and social processes (self-presentation, self-disclosure) to classify six categories of social media. *Social presence* (see Short *et al.*, 1976) is influenced by the level of intimacy in communication between two people through different types of media. High social presence leads to greater social influence over each partner's behaviour. *Media richness* (see Daft and Lengel, 1986) recognises the goal of communication is to avoid ambiguity and reduce uncertainty, and that types of media transmissions will differ in the extent they can resolve this. *Self-presentation* (Goffman, 1959) represents the level that people desire to control the impressions others form of them. *Self-disclosure* is the conscious or unconscious revelation of personal information. The classification of social media is shown in Table 4.3.

Collaborative projects, which are designed to allow multiple and simultaneous content contributions by many end users, are the most democratic demonstration of UGC (Kaplan and Haenlein, 2010). There

Table 4.3 Classification of social media

| | | Social presence/media richness | | |
		Low	Medium	High
Self-presentation/ Self-disclosure	**High**	Blogs	Social networking sites	Virtual social worlds
	Low	Collaborative projects	Content communities	Virtual game worlds

Source: Adapted from Kaplan and Haenlein (2010).

are two main types of collaborative projects. One is wikis, which enable users to add, amend or delete content, such as the online encyclopaedia Wikipedia. The other is bookmarking sites, such as Delicious, which allow users to share web bookmarks. Underpinning this social knowledge sharing is the notion that a collective outcome is greater than the sum of the individual parts. Kaplan and Haenlein warned corporates of the danger, particularly during crises, of the high believability of collaborative project content, even though it is not always factual.

Blogs were among the earliest forms of social media to be used, originally known as web-logs, where text writings by one individual were posted in reverse date order, usually anonymously (see wordpress.com). Kaplan and Haenlein (2010) suggested the first social media was Bruce and Susan Abelson's Open Diary, bringing together diary writers, which operated from 1998 to 2014. Indeed blogs have been defined as 'virtual diaries' (Sharda and Ponnada, 2007: 2, in Volo, 2010). More recent developments have included microblogs that limit the number of characters enterable in a single post (e.g. Twitter), multi-author blogs, video blogs (vlogs), audio blogs, photoblogs, sketch blogs and so on. Blogs are regarded as uncensored, and it has been suggested that for a new blog to be taken seriously by search engines at least eight quality blog posts need to be made as early as possible, followed by regular posts (Andrews, 2014). Using Twitter to *favourite* or reply to relevant tweets in a timely manner is an opportunity for the DMO to build trust and rapport (LeadSift, 2013). The style of blogs is quite different to DMO marketing communications, since they are often spontaneous observations that can be positive or negative (Volo, 2010). Molz's (2012: 61) research found readers of travel blogs appear to share an approach of 'living vicariously through you'. So while some might view blogs as a narcissistic outlet, they are also seen as a gift enabling readers to escape their own current environment. The first city tourism destination Twitter account was set up by Portland, Oregon in 2008 (Hey, 2010, in Antoniadis *et al.*, 2014). The first blog dedicated to those working, studying and teaching in tourism was talkingtourism.org. For a critique of the literature relating to blogs in tourism see Volo (2010, 2012).

IN PRACTICE

4.2 The launch of microblogs in China

The first microblog service in China was launched in 2009 by sina.com, one of the country's main web providers. In January 2010 Harbin Tourism Bureau was the first Chinese RTO to register a microblog. By October of that year the account had published 703 messages and attracted 4,475 followers. The first STO microblog account was set up by The Tourism Bureau of Sichuan Province in July 2010 and in the first six months posted 604 messages and attracted 4,908 followers. As well as promoting tourism attractions, the STO microblog encourages input to the strategic plan with prizes for *best advice*.

Source

Shao *et al.* (2012).

Content communities function as media sharing portals, where users do not require a personal profile page. Such sharing between users includes photos (Flikr), videos (YouTube), PowerPoint presentations (Slideshare), text (Bookcrossing) and brochures/books (Scribd, ISSUU). One of the dangers with content community sites is the potential for the sharing of copyright protected material. For example, during 2014 the entire contents of two of my books (Pike, 2004, 2008) had been digitally scanned and uploaded to Scribd by a student in the UK. I was alerted by the student's university plagiarism officer. *Social networking sites*, such as Facebook, enable individuals to create a personal profile page and to provide access to select others, so that information can be shared publicly or privately. Professional networking is enabled by sites such as Linkedin and Academia.Edu. *Virtual game worlds*, such as World of Warcraft, and *virtual social worlds*, such as SecondLife, offer the highest levels of social presence and media richness through multi-user engagement in a three-dimensional space. Lee and Wicks (2010) noted several DMOs had created virtual offices for marketing in SecondLife, including New York, Mexico and Korea.

How consumer-travellers are using social media

People participate in virtual travel communities, as with social media in general, for a diverse range of reasons such as: entertainment, bragging, following, information provision/seeking, social and professional networking and sense of belonging. For a brief review of some of the relevant theories that could be useful for understanding why tourism consumer-travellers use social media, see Pan and Crotts (2012). Pan and Crotts acknowledged opposing opinions that have suggested theories will become obsolete in the information age, but present an argument for how theories from the fields of communications, sociology and computer sciences, for example, can help tourism marketing researchers *make sense* of what the mass of all the social media behavioural data and performance metrics actually represent. They separated the theories into three levels:

1. Micro theories dealing with the contribution of online information and communication of individuals in social settings. These include word-of-mouth, psychological ownership, social exchange and social penetration.

2. Macro theories are concerned with global or abstract perspectives of the structure and forces at play between content and participants. These include social network theories and McLuhan's media theory.

3. Pseudo-theories developed by practitioners, which might intuitively make sense in practice, but have yet to be empirically tested, such as social graphics and purchase funnel.

Figure 4.2 graphically illustrates Pan and Crotts' framework, which links these theories with topical research questions.

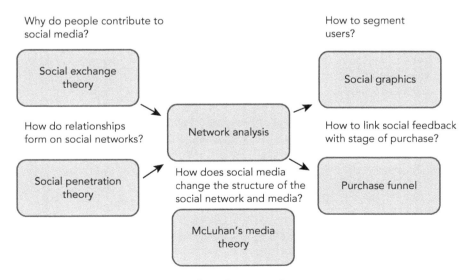

Figure 4.2 Links between theories and social media research questions
Source: Adapted from Pan and Crotts (2012).

Travel planning

Around 85 per cent of leisure travellers use the internet in travel planning (Torres, 2012, in Leung *et al.*, 2013). A study by Allianz Global Assistance that reviewed 32 million exchanges on travel forums in 11 countries found the internet has made consumers much more travel savvy (Travelindustrywire, 2015). The research suggested the emergence of a new breed of traveller, whose use of the internet had equipped them with new skills in buying travel that best met their goals, who they labelled *the skilful tourist*. These skills included the ability to:

- optimise the itinerary to find the best mix of price and quality;
- take advantage of short-term offers;
- anticipate travel constraints such as security, scheduling and comfort;
- adapt travel goals to meet travel realities.

Leung *et al.*'s (2013) literature review concluded that consumers mostly used social media in the trip planning phase and that the key antecedent in decision making was trustworthiness. UGC is regarded as a form of online *word-of-mouth* (WoM), also referred to as *word of mouse* (see Gelb and Sundaram, 2002), WOM² (see Arlt and Thraenhart, 2011) and more commonly eWoM. In this regard, Oliveira and Panyik (2015) cited European Travel Commission reports in 2013 that recommendations from significant others was the most frequently used source of trip planning information (56 per cent), followed by websites (46 per cent), personal experience with a destination (34 per cent), travel agents and tourism offices (21 per cent) and tourism brochures (11 per cent). As such, UGC is a form of organic image development (see Chapter 10), which potentially has a higher credibility than induced images formed through supplier-pushed information (e.g. advertising). MX (2015) cited a report from lastminute.com suggesting one in four Australians have booked a trip after seeing a friend's photos online. The report suggested *social media envy* was a key travel motivator for Gen Y in particular.

From a content analysis of Twitter feeds, LeadSift (2013) found 52 per cent of consumers use social media for summer holiday inspiration, while 92 per cent of consumers expressed that they trust recommendations from *friends* (including online followers) over advertising, with 59 per cent having posted about an upcoming holiday on social media. The ITB World Travel Trends Report (2013, in Oliveira and Panyik, 2015) suggested 40 per cent of travellers were influenced by social media comments in travel planning and 50 per cent of travellers based their travel plans on other people's experiences. A survey of @australia Instagram followers found 91 per cent of international followers were inspired by the account to learn more about Australia as a holiday destination, with 87 per cent suggesting the content increased the likelihood of them visiting the country (Tourism Australia, 2014a). One US respondent said 'I never thought I would want to go to Australia before I joined Instagram. Now I can't imagine not going! So beautiful'. For a review of the literature relating to eWoM in tourism, which is in its infancy, see Luo and Zhong (2015). Their exploratory study found that travel-related eWoM communications via social networking sites relied strongly on existing social relationships.

Search engine optimisation

Search engine optimisation involves adapting online content by the DMO to gain priority positions in popular travel searches on search engines such as google.com and bing.com, and requires an understanding of the key search terms being used by consumers. Another approach is paid search engine marketing, where bidding takes place for advertising space at the top of search engine results (see Pan *et al.*, 2007; Pan and Li, 2011). For a detailed discussion on the mechanics of travel-related search engine optimisation see Xiang and Pan (2011). Their study found there are a relatively small number of key words used in destination information searches.

UGC is search engine friendly and so destinations and their local tourism businesses are at risk of negative or malicious reviews appearing in search results. However, it seems established brand websites have higher perceptions of trust than one unknown individual UGC (Gretzel, 2006). So, while eWoM has the advantage of being a wider network than an individual's real world social circle, credibility of unknown individual users is lower. UGC is regarded as trustworthy, in that it represents the views and experiences of real people, but the information is not always reliable (Burgess *et al.*, 2011). For example, some content can be uploaded by a person with a vested interest. There has been little academic research reported on the role of social media in online travel information searches.

RESEARCH SNAPSHOT

4.1 The role of social media in online travel information searching

Recognising the increasing and dominant use of the internet for travel information searching, Xiang and Gretzel (2010) pointed out the need for research investigating the likelihood that a traveller will be exposed to social media content, compared to other tourism websites, when undertaking an online travel search. Their exploratory study used the Google search engine, which at the time accounted for almost 50 per cent of queries on the internet, to undertake a series of searches using a mix of nine US destination names combined with ten keywords, and limited the results to ten pages. The search generated 10,383 results, of which 1,150 (11 per cent) were identified as social media sites. Of these, the top 20 unique domain names (e.g. TripAdvisor.com) represented half of the 1,150, suggesting a *core* group of 'big player' sites, and then a *long tail* of others in the distribution (Xiang and Gretzel, 2010: 184). The breakdown by category of social media was:

Virtual communities (e.g. igougo.com and lonelyplanet.com)	40 per cent
Consumer review sites (e.g. TripAdvisor.com and zagat.com)	27 per cent
Blogs (e.g. blogspot.com)	15 per cent
Social networking sites (e.g. Facebook)	9 per cent
Media sharing sites (e.g. YouTube)	7 per cent
Others	2 per cent

Xiang and Gretzel concluded that social media plays a major role in online travel searches, given such sites appeared in the first few pages of the search. Virtual community sites were closely related to key tourism businesses such as accommodation and attractions. Consumer review sites were tied to hotels, restaurants and shopping. Social networking sites, blogs and media sharing sites were linked with nightlife, events and parks. However, since social media did not occupy the whole space there was room for tourism websites to compete. Three approaches were recommended:

1. Search engine optimisation and search engine advertising are essential to ensure the tourism website appears in search results. In this regard it was noted certain keywords such as *nightlife* and *restaurants* generated more social media results than others such as *attractions*.

2. Advertising or providing content on social media sites.

3. Integrating components of social media on the tourism website.

Further reading

Xiang, Z. and Gretzel, U. (2010).

During travel

UGC provides travellers with unprecedented levels of diverse and up-to-date information formats (Yoo and Gretzel, 2012; Leung *et al.*, 2013). During travel, social media is used for many varied reasons, including online dating (e.g. PlentyofFish), staying in touch with friends and family (e.g. Facebook), sharing experiences (e.g. Instagram) and onward travel planning (e.g. TripAdvisor). LeadSift (2013) found 85 per cent of Twitter travellers used a smartphone while overseas, 75 per cent used social media and 44 per cent shared videos and photos online. Social media engagement by travellers can influence travel plans while on tour. For example, from a content analysis of Twitter feeds, LeadSift (2013) suggested only 47 per cent of consumers stuck with their original plans. They found travellers were actively looking for recommendations from virtual communities. One study estimated 84 per cent of travellers have made purchase decisions influenced by travel review UGC (comScore, 2007, in Leung *et al.*, 2013). For a review of the literature relating to consumers' use of social media while travelling see Parra-Lopez *et al.* (2012).

After travel

LeadSift (2013) found 76 per cent of Twitter travellers shared information about their holiday on social media after they arrived home. Further, 55 per cent *liked* Facebook pages or Twitter accounts related to a recent holiday, 46 per cent posted hotel reviews and 40 per cent posted restaurant reviews.

Sharing post-trip experiences with friends, such as blogging, is a common reason for UGC, along with providing travel reviews for other travellers. Such altruistic or enjoyment motives are dependent on personality type, which plays a role in the level to which an individual will contribute travel-related UGC. An example of the increasing influence of traveller UGC is TripAdvisor's (2014) annual list of top destinations, based on traveller's reviews. The selection process uses an algorithm that factors in the quantity and quality of reviews and ratings over a year for destinations' hotels, restaurants and attractions. The 2014 top 20 destinations are listed in Table 4.4. For an in-depth study of the determinants of sharing travel experiences on social media see Kang and Schuett (2013).

How DMOs are using social media

In terms of absolute fan base size, Tourism Australia is the global leader. The NTO's Facebook page (https://www.facebook.com/SeeAustralia?ref=br_tf) is the most liked destination with over 6 million followers. In December 2014 Tourism Australia also celebrated the milestone of over 1 million Instagram

Table 4.4 TripAdvisor's top 20 destinations for 2014

Rank	Destination	Change from 2013
1	Istanbul, Turkey	+11
2	Rome, Italy	+2
3	London, England	0
4	Beijing, China	+17
5	Prague, Czech Republic	+4
6	Marrakech, Morocco	+13
7	Paris, France	−6
8	Hanoi, Vietnam	New
9	Siem Reap, Cambodia	+14
10	Shanghai, China	+12
11	Berlin, German	0
12	New York City, USA	−10
13	Florence, Italy	−5
14	Buenos Aires, Argentina	+4
15	Barcelona, Spain	−10
16	St Petersburg, Russia	+4
17	Dubai, UAE	New
18	Chicago, USA	−4
19	Cape Town, South Africa	−3
20	Bangkok, Thailand	−7

Source: TripAdvisor (2014).

followers for @australia and becoming the most popular NTO page in the world (Tourism Australia, 2014a). The number of Instagram followers of @australia was more than that for @explorecanada, @purenewzealand, @lovegreatbritain and @meetsouthafrica combined. Tourism Australia's annual online marketing prospectus (see Tourism Australia, 2014b) provided instructions for individual tourism businesses to participate in the NTO's key social media platforms: Facebook, Twitter, Google+, Instagram, WeChat and Sina Weibo.

However, apart from sheer numbers of followers, there are other factors to consider, such as DMO responsiveness and level of engagement. At the end of the day the number of DMO followers is meaningless to stakeholders unless increased website traffic and ensuing travel bookings are generated.

IN PRACTICE

4.3 HelloBC.com

Tourism British Columbia uses professional social media marketing consultants to assist the DMO to: (1) learn from users' content; and (2) engage with them to help distribute viral marketing. Their social media activities attempt to involve the host community, tourism industry and stakeholders in spreading the message. The DMO's experience with initiatives such as contests on Facebook, Twitter and Flikr has made them adept at *reading, responding and engaging* users. HelloBC.com features a blog enabling consumers and local residents to share experiences and participate in live discussions. The 'Field reporting' section of the blog, hosted on YouTube, saw selected enthusiasts sent to different locations to upload video reports that successfully drove traffic to the website. Other sections included podcasts, tips from travellers and tips from the DMO. The podcast section featured clips from a CBC radio show. Website visitors could become registered blog users and propose travel stories, which the DMO reserves the right to accept and edit. Bloggers were encouraged to: be experiential, be non-commercial, be 'clean' and include fun and videos. Blog content is protected under privacy legislation and users can request removal at any time.

Source

Volo (2012).

Manolo (2015) presented a report by SkiftIQ ranking the top destinations on social media as at December 2014. While the ranking is subjective and based on a complex in-house metric, labelled the Skift Score, out of a possible 1,000 (see https://iq.skift.com/score), the data shown in Table 4.5 provides a guide to the innovative organisations. Of the top ten destinations, four are states, two are countries, two are cities, one is the US National Park Service and one is Disney Resorts. Interestingly seven of the ten destinations are in the USA. The SkiftIQ ranking is updated monthly. At number one in Table 4.5, STO Tourism Queensland's social media prominence rose to fame with their *The Best Job in the World* campaign in 2009.

Table 4.5 Top ten destinations on social media (December 2014)

	Skift score	Facebook likes	Twitter followers	Instagram followers	YouTube views
Tourism and Events Queensland	813	1,172,001	74,363	126,286	3,123,442
Walt Disney World Resorts	811	15,077,512	903,945	890,622	189,972,767
Tourism Australia	805	6,319,867	189,118	1,045,523	30,828,249
Visit Philly	743	437,874	90,408	31,453	720,739
U.S. Dept. of the Interior	733	88,644	260,526	436,773	760,506

Visit Florida	720	632,470	86,966	10,760	11,680,183
Visit Argentina	714	577,611	24,233	2,617	2,881,150
Visit Colorado	714	476,200	99,653	26,832	2,638,863
Explore Georgia	712	270,855	52,581	13,879	66,587
Discover Los Angeles	710	1,145,758	99,322	69,473	1,541,249

Source: Adapted from Manalo (2015).

IN PRACTICE

4.4 The Best Job in the World

Tourism Queensland used Brisbane creative agency SapientNitro to develop the now iconic social media campaign. The agency's impressive list of clients included famous brands such as Coca-Cola, Audi, Hugo Boss, Marks and Spencer and Ladbrokes (see www.sapientnitro.com). SapientNitro's challenging brief was to create international attention for Queensland's Great Barrier Reef, with a relatively minimal budget of AUD$1 million, inclusive of the agency's fees and production costs. While the Great Barrier Reef was already a famous world heritage listed natural wonder, the individual island resort destinations were not well-known relative to Hawaii, the Greek Islands, the Maldives and the Caribbean. To attract global attention, a prize of a job was offered . . . simply, the best job in the world . . . living as a caretaker on the islands of the reef, reporting to the world. Anyone from anywhere in the world could apply. The six-month job carried with it a salary of AUD$150,000, with duties advertised including: feeding the fish, cleaning the pool, collecting the mail, exploring and reporting back. The announcement of the campaign in February 2009 was timed to coincide with the northern hemisphere winter. Classified job ads were strategically placed in target markets, directing interested people to www.islandreefjob.com, supported by media releases from Tourism Queensland. On the first day of the campaign www.islandreefjob.com received an average of 4 million views per hour! In total, 34,684 one-minute video job applications were received from 200 countries. Key results were impressive:

- 8.7 million website hits at an average of 8.25 minutes each, with 55 million page views.
- An estimated 3 billion people were reached through the media.
- Media coverage worth over AUD$400 million in equivalent advertising value.
- From a creative perspective, the campaign won 35 international advertising awards.

Further reading

Belch *et al.* (2009).

Many DMOs have been late adopters of social media as a marketing communication platform. Case study 4.1 discusses how communist country Vietnam's NTO only embraced social media in late 2013, but has since allocated 15 per cent of the marketing budget to the medium.

CASE STUDY

4.1 Vietnam's late adoption of social media

Dam Phuong Lien (June)
Manager, Marketing and Sales Department, Vietnam Airlines

Founded in 1960 as the Vietnam Tourism Corporation, the NTO became the Vietnam National Administration of Tourism (VNAT) in 1992. Today, VNAT is still a government department, as part of the Ministry of Culture, Sport and Tourism. In 2014 Vietnam welcomed a total of 7.9 million international visitors (http://vietnamtourism.gov.vn/index.php/items/16397), which was moderate compared to neighbouring competitors such as Thailand, which attracted 24.8 million visitors (http://www.tourism.go.th/home/details/11/221/23044) and Malaysia, which attracted more than 13.9 million visitors (http://corporate.tourism.gov.my/images/research/pdf/2014/arrival/Tourist_Arrivals_Dec_2014.pdf).

One of the main challenges facing VNAT has been a small marketing budget relative to competing destinations. According to an assessment of Hanoi-based Institute For Tourism Development Research in June 2014, VNAT's average annual expenditure on promoting tourism was less than US$3 million, in contrast to the US$80 million spent by the Tourism Authority of Thailand (TAT), and US$98 million spent by Tourism Malaysia (http://www.itdr.org.vn/thong-tin-tu-lieu/cac-tu-lieu-khac/819-bao-cao-ldu-lich-viet-nam-n-thuc-trang-va-giai-phapr.html). Chief of VNAT, Nguyen Van Tuan, admitted that the tight budget for promoting tourism was spread over so many different activities and as a consequence it was hampering tourism promotion campaigns and reducing the country's ability to grow visitor arrivals (http://www.ttrweekly.com/site/2015/04/shoestring-budget-slows-vietnams-tourism). Therefore VNAT must become more creative in its approach to marketing communications and take advantage of below-the-line opportunities, such as those presented by social media.

Other countries in South East Asia have successfully embraced social media to promote their destinations. For example, TAT has maintained a Facebook page since 2009. With approximately three daily postings related to their destinations, cuisine, events and travel packages, TAT has been able to attract a fan base of 790,000 followers. This is in addition to their Twitter feeds that provide a constant stream of information, pictures and videos about destinations throughout the country. Similarly, information about travel to and in Malaysia is also abundantly and attractively available through their tourism Facebook, Twitter, Flickr and YouTube presence since early 2010.

However, it has only been recently that VNAT has embraced the internet as part of its marketing. The first Facebook page for the destination was established at the end of 2013, with a YouTube presence following in 2014. VNAT focuses on four main themes on social media: destinations and people; traditional cuisines; Vietnamese tourism news; and travel packages and events. To date these themes have been consistently delivered with a frequency of at least two per week for each theme. In VNAT's marketing strategy to 2020, one of the key strategies is maintaining their website and boosting e-marketing in which the above activities on social media platforms such as Facebook and YouTube will be prioritised and developed in both content delivered and graphics designed to increase potential tourists' engagement and, accordingly, promote their destination (http://vietnamtourism.gov.vn/index.php/docs/736). Details of their action plan for e-marketing in the period 2015–2020 are as follows:

In 2015: Step by step apply e-marketing tools through boosting the NTO's Facebook page and building up tourist database.

In 2016: Create and produce tourism e-books and Vietnam Tourist Guide, Vietnam Today, Vietnam destination map or other e-leaflets about Vietnam culture tourism to advertise on their own website, Facebook, YouTube and other recognised tourism websites or travel blogs.

In 2017: Coordinate with other tourism associations in the region, marketing agents, tour companies and travel agents to join in VNAT's e-marketing programmes of co-producing video clips to upload on Facebook and YouTube.

In 2018/2019/2020: Continue to boost and expand e-marketing through increasing the presence on social media networking sites, search engine tools (SEO), email marketing, marketing on other recognised websites by tourists.

VNAT will allocate about 15 per cent of the annual marketing budget to promote products and destinations on digital platforms. As at May 2015 the VNAT tourism Facebook page had only attracted 17,400 followers in the 18 months of its existence and was well below that for Thailand and Malaysia.

Discussion question

In the short term, what initiatives could VNAT undertake to boost the number of Facebook followers?

Generic DMO strategies

From an in-depth investigation of Scandinavian NTOs' social media activity, five generic DMO strategies were identified (Munar, 2012; Gyimothy et al., 2014): mimetic, advertising, analytic, immersion and gamification. DMOs use a *mimetic* strategy to mime the style and e-culture of popular social media sites on their webpage, providing users with opportunities to share experiences. This is representative of an artificial social network, since the main purpose of the site is to officially promote the destination rather than feature inter-user communication. Munar's Scandinavian NTO interviewees' comments about the failure of this approach to develop a strong community included:

> *We would like to encourage people to join the conversations but so far . . . well, we have many members but for some reason they are not active, they are not writing. People are not stupid. They can feel if in the community there is no real involvement.*

> *(Munar, 2012: 110)*

In an *advertising* strategy, DMOs attempt to redirect users of a social media site to increase traffic to destination sites, through the use of banners and URL links, for example, on Facebook, YouTube and Twitter. Neither the *mimetic* nor *advertising* strategy takes advantage of the mass of UGC available for analysis. The weakness of this approach is the broadcast style of message pushed to consumers. The *analytic* strategy uses UGC to monitor trends to enhance forecasting and to prevent escalation of potential negative impacts. There was minimal evidence of using UGC for trend monitoring (Munar, 2012; Gyimothy et al., 2014).

The *immersion* strategy is the creation of a new online community by the DMO, separate from the official destination website, such as that created by Visit Sweden in 2006. Communityofsweden.com was completely based on UGC with minimal control mechanisms, in line with other social networking sites. The site was closed in April 2013, and as at February 2015 visitors to the URL were being directed to different language sites on:

- Facebook (e.g. www.facebook.com/swedentravel);
- Twitter (e.g. twitter.com/VisitSwedenUS);
- Pinterest (e.g. www.pinterest.com/PinsofSweden);
- Flikr (www.flickr.com/photos/outdooracademyofsweden);
- Sina Weibo in China (www.flickr.com/photos/outdooracademyofsweden);
- Kaixin001 in China (www.kaixin001.com/visitsweden);
- Tencent Weibo in China (t.qq.com/visitsweden).

By 2014 around 80 per cent of Visit Denmark's marketing communications were via digital media (Gyimothy *et al.*, 2014). Staff responsible for social media marketing had increased from one junior employee in 2010 to seven positions in 2014. Embratur, Brazil's NTO, created a YouTube channel in June 2009 (Shao *et al.*, 2012). In the first two years the channel attracted 2,000 subscribers and over 500,000 views. Embratur employed the tactic of replying to all postings to stimulate continued conversations.

A key concern with the immersion strategy is the potential for negative UGC and the danger in DMO censoring. In this regard, in relation to communityofsweden.com, one of Munar's (2012) NTO interviewees claimed: 'It does not have the freedom that a social network demands: it is too heavily top-down controlled'. Munar found the NTOs lacked any formal social media strategy and had been making decisions on an *ad hoc* basis, motivated by pressure from stakeholders and a fear of being left behind. As a result, 'the majority of these initiatives are partial and disconnected: there is no common picture of what the organization wants to achieve through social media' (Munar, 2012: 115).

The *gamification* strategy applies gaming technologies to non-game sites, which can be successful in reaching a wide audience, but often fails to generate continued engagement with users. Gyimothy *et al.* (2014) suggested this type of initiative was increasingly being used by DMOs and provided two NTO examples:

- Fans of VisitBritain's Love UK Facebook page were challenged to check in using Facebook places at one of 300 tourism spots to enter a draw for holiday and shopping vouchers.
- Visit Norway developed The Homenkollen Ski Jump game, which has been played more than 600 million times since 2009.

During 2015 the first book on gamification in tourism was announced, but not yet published at the time of print (see http://www.gamification-in-tourism.com).

DMO tactics

One of the greatest challenges facing DMOs has always been reaching so many individual consumers with marketing communications at the time their travel planning is taking place. Eureka! For the first time in the history of destination marketing the opportunity to do so has arrived, in the form of Web 2.0. However, exactly how this will be achieved effectively is not yet known. Due to the current lack of ROI metrics for social media marketing (see Chapter 15), and the sheer pace of its evolution, this chapter does not attempt a detailed *how to* guide on the tactical aspects of online marketing for DMOs. Rather the focus is on the importance of strategic decisions that must be made in terms of goals, resources and organisational commitment, to meet the opportunities and challenges Web 2.0 has created for DMOs. Destination marketers have generally been slow to engage with Web 2.0, but this medium has become such an integral part of most people's lives that no DMO can afford to delay serious investment. To date, a small number of published case studies have described aspects of destination social media marketing tactics in:

- Portugal (Oliveira, 2013, in Oliveira and Panyik, 2015);

- Scandinavia (Munar, 2012; Gyimothy *et al.*, 2014);

- Balkan countries (Bayram and Arici, in Antoniadis *et al.*, 2014);

- European NTOs (Hamill *et al.*, 2012; Antoniadis *et al.*, 2014);

- Ierapetra, Greece (Trihas *et al.*, 2013b);

- China (Wang *et al.*, 2013);

- USA (Sevin, 2013; Milwood *et al.*, 2013);

- Switzerland (Milwood *et al.*, 2013);

- Glasgow, Scotland (Hamill and Stevenson, 2012);

- Chengdu, China (Shao *et al.*, 2012);

- British Columbia (Volo, 2012).

Also, the reader is referred to the work of Mistilis *et al.* (2014), who reported a long list of recommendations from Australian stakeholders' workshops, in relation to how the NTO could better utilise digital technologies during each of the pre-trip planning, during travel and post-trip stages.

IN PRACTICE

4.5 The year of Chengdu

Starting in 2008 'The year of Chengdu' has been an annual marketing initiative designed to attract visitors during the important Chinese New Year national holiday week. Chengdu is the capital city of the Sichuan province in China's southwest. In 2010 the theme of the campaign was *Create and Share Together*, and the DMO cooperated with Microsoft MSN in a social media promotion. MSN China invited users to: (1) insert 'I am enjoying Chinese New Year in Chengdu' on their personal profile, which is similar to a Facebook status update; and (2) vote for the top ten winter tourism attractions in Chengdu. The incentive was a prize draw for ski tickets. In the first week of the initiative over 400,000 users had viewed MSN China's link to the promotion, and at the close of the prize draw there were 500,000 entries. Although not able to be directly attributed to the online promotion, visitor arrivals to Chengdu for Chinese New Year in 2010 were ten per cent higher than in the previous year.

Source

Shao *et al.* (2012).

A major benefit of social media for destination marketers is the opportunity to reach a global audience at a lower cost than traditional media. This is particularly advantageous for three categories of DMOs. The first are small RTOs with few resources, such as Ierapetra in Greece (see Trihas *et al.*, 2013a, 2013b). In an investigation of the use of social media adoption of Greece's 325 municipalities, Trihas *et al.* (2013a) found the majority were unfamiliar with Web 2.0 technology, categorising them as *reluctant adopters*. However, among the top ten municipalities (in terms of online community size) was Ierapetra, which is neither a large city nor a famous tourism destination. Case study 4.2 summarises Ierapetra's early social media marketing activity. The second category involves those DMOs at destinations that are a long distance from major markets. This group is exemplified by the positions held by Queensland and Australia in Table 4.5, and highlighted by scholars (see North, 2013 in Oliveira and Panyik, 2015; Gyimothy *et al.*, 2014). The third category is larger DMOs facing budget cutbacks, particularly since the 2008 global financial crisis, as has been reported for Portugal (see Oliveira and Panyik, 2015) and England (Coles *et al.*, 2012).

CASE STUDY

4.2 Visit Ierapetra

Ierapetra is one of the least known towns on the island of Crete and has a population of less than 20,000 residents. Tourism is second to agriculture in terms of economic contribution.

Visit Ierapetra is the official tourism e-marketing campaign for this small town and began in 2012 as a practitioner/academic collaboration between the municipality's DMO and the Technological Educational Institute of Crete. The aim was to use Web 2.0 technology in a cost-effective way to improve perceptions in key European target markets and increase visitor arrivals at a time of increasing economic uncertainty in Greece. All municipalities faced public sector funding cuts, and the local tourism board made the decision to reduce traditional promotional activity in favour of social media marketing.

Most of the strategy was directed towards Facebook, with one profile page for municipality issues and an English language site for tourism information. The plan was to post a photo or story three times daily and to collaborate with related pages to facilitate sharing. Profiles were also set up for trials on other social media platforms such as Flickr, Pinterest, YouTube, Foursquare, Scribd, ISSUU and Twitter. Since the tourism board's photo library was not of suitable digital quality, a group of local volunteer amateur photographers was used to generate appropriate content at little cost. The decision was also made to have the photos watermarked with the destination name, but available under Creative Commons licence, to enable free sharing.

Preliminary results

- In less than two months the tourism page had attracted over 3,000 followers.
- A summer festival brochure on Scribd was viewed 8,000 times in four months.
- After 500 tweets the Twitter account had only attracted 55 followers.

Further reading

Trihas *et al.* (2013a, 2013b).

Epilogue

As at 18 January 2015 the Visit Ierapetra Facebook page had attracted 4,390 *likes*. The cover page had remained unchanged since 3 June 2014 and had attracted 11 *likes*. Prior to January 2015, the most recent activity had been five months previously when three posts were made in August 2014.

Discussion question

What are the possible reasons for the slowdown in Facebook activity by the DMO in 2014?

The need for a clear DMO online strategy

The increasing influence of social media on consumers' travel planning means DMOs can no longer ignore it. Indeed, the rise of social media has the potential to undermine the authority of DMOs (Gretzel, 2006). However, more important than simply having a social media presence 'to appear to be keeping up with the times' (Hays, 2011: 10, in Hays *et al.*, 2013) is having the right strategy, since clumsy implementation could be damaging. Whereas it is relatively easy to install online marketing communication platforms, managing and monitoring UGC is not. A key issue facing DMOs at all levels is level of resource allocation to the latter. Therefore, it is critical the DMO has a clear vision for what is to be achieved by investing in social media marketing, rather than just seeking to be seen by stakeholders to be involved. Further, there needs to be flexible strategy for which social media is to be used and how it will be employed to facilitate engagement with and between internet users. In this regard, Gunelius (2011, in Shao *et al.*, 2012: 91) proposed ten laws of social marketing to guide strategy development. These are listed in Table 4.6.

As has been shown, the adoption of social media marketing by DMOs has only occurred in recent years. Leung *et al.*'s (2013) review of the 2007–2011 literature concluded there was little evidence of financial ROI in social media, and so travel firms had harboured doubts about how to invest wisely. Lee and Wicks (2010) found the two main barriers to social media marketing by CVBs in the USA were the lack of: (1) funding to implement the technology; and (2) the lack of time to learn how to manage content. Their literature review found scant attention had been paid towards research into training DMOs in the practical use of social media technologies, with studies leaning towards higher education rather than practical training. The use of social media by DMOs has generally been experimental (Gretzel, 2006; Hays *et al.*, 2013: 234): 'many DMOs' understanding of social media is often vague and varied. Very seldom are the rights and wrongs of general marketing rules precisely defined, but rules surrounding social media marketing are even more ambiguous and unclear'.

Table 4.6 Social media marketing laws

1	Listening	Learning how consumers engage in specific social media type and understanding what is important to them
2	Focus	Since it is impossible to be involved in all social media, focus on the most relevant
3	Quality	Connecting to a small group of influential consumers is more important than trying to reach everyone
4	Patience	This is a long-term commitment
5	Compounding	Consumers will share quality content
6	Influence	Identify consumers with the greatest influence
7	Value	Interesting and trustworthy content adds value to a conversation
8	Acknowledgement	Acknowledge everyone who reaches out to establish relationships
9	Accessibility	Be available to the audience on a continual basis
10	Reciprocity	Share content published by others

Source: Adapted from Gunelius (2011, in Shao *et al.*, 2012).

In one of the first studies to investigate how 25 European NTOs were responding to Web 2.0 opportunities, Hamill *et al.* (2009, in Hamill *et al.*, 2012: 99) found only three *progressive adopters* and only seven with a Facebook presence. Likewise, Stankov *et al.* (2010) found fewer than half of NTO members of the European Travel Commission had a Facebook site. At that time the average number of Facebook *friends* for participating NTOs was 4,919, with the highest being 32,402 and the lowest only 45. A content analysis of the world's top ten international tourism destinations in 2011 found Italy and China had no Facebook or Twitter presence at that time (see Hays *et al.*, 2013). Hays *et al.* (2013: 222) found the NTOs for the world's top ten destinations were using Facebook and Twitter 'to simply advertise and market via an additional medium, changing little about the content of the message'. The other destinations in the study had established Facebook and/or Twitter accounts as recently as 2008 (Germany, Spain, Malaysia), 2009 (UK, France, Mexico) and 2011 (Turkey). Hamill *et al.* found the European NTOs were aware of the potential of social media marketing, were enthusiastic to move forward, but were faltering due to major barriers relating to:

- lack of resources;
- organisational culture;
- the lack of a clear vision and strategy;
- concerns about loss of control and potential for negative UGC.

A follow-up study again found most European NTOs were not fully utilising the potential to develop customer networks or engage with virtual communities (Hamill *et al.*, 2012). While 21 of the 25 NTOs had a presence on Facebook or Twitter and 20 had a YouTube channel, only 5 of the DMOs encouraged UGC on their website. They highlighted VisitEngland as the standout performer for the following reasons (Hamill *et al.*, 2012: 107):

- active encouragement of UGC (text, photos, videos);
- visitor ratings and reviews;
- the use of widgets, mashups and podcasts to enhance the online customer experience;
- social bookmarking;
- RSS feeds;
- clear links to external links used;
- iTunes podcasts;
- Enjoy England blog;
- mapping tools;
- over 45,000 Facebook fans and 9,000 Twitter followers.

Hamill *et al.* (2012) concluded the growing experimentation by NTOs was leading to the recognition that a strategy featuring sound planning and professional project management, such as demonstrated by the leading NTO social media marketers, England and Switzerland, was required. They recommended a ten-step social media development cycle, which is briefly summarised below, as a practical framework for not only guiding the strategy process but also for communicating the key goals, objectives, tactics and KPIs to internal and external stakeholders (Hamill *et al.*, 2012: 113–117).

1. Evaluate your social media landscape in terms of understanding how the target market is using social media, what they are saying in relation to destinations and determining the most appropriate applications.

2. Agree the overall general strategy in terms of selecting the channel and then deciding the depth of engagement for each.

3. Develop KPIs, underpinned by the level of available resources and questioning the organisation mindset . . . 'are you willing to engage?'

4. Internal social media audit to evaluate the existing approach relative to the opportunities and the ideal strategy.

5. Be ready to engage.

6. Develop the strategy.

7. Channel action plans.

8. Organisation, resources and people: roles, responsibilities, decision process, control structure, etc.

9. Implementation via professional project management.

10. Performance measurement (see Chapter 15).

If NTOs have struggled, consider how the challenge of social media engagement is magnified for small RTOs. For example, it is ironic, given Hamill *et al.* (2012) highlighted the Swiss NTO for its social media leadership, that a study of RTOs in that country found most to be *laggards* in social media adoption (see Milwood *et al.*, 2013). Their investigation identified some RTOs as either having abandoned a social media strategy or having no intention to adopt.

CHAPTER SUMMARY

Key point 1: The meteoric rise in influence of social media in travel and tourism

In the space of 20 years we have seen internet develop to the point where it is now being used by almost half of the world's population. The emergence of Web 2.0 in the early 2000s has revolutionised the way in which all internet users can contribute UGC. Travellers trust and use UGC in travel planning, during travel and after they return home.

Key point 2: How DMOs have been adapting to the Web 2.0 era

While DMOs have been experimenting with Web 2.0 technologies in a mostly *ad hoc* way, they have generally been slow to maximise the potential of social media, particularly in terms of enhancing *engagement* with, and between, consumers and stakeholders. It is critical that DMOs have a clear vision and a flexible strategy for investing in social media marketing. A new paradigm shift in destination marketing is about to occur as a result of the rise of the influence of Web 2.0 technology-based UGC; one that will see destination competitiveness underpinned by DMOs harnessing the opportunities presented by Web 2.0 in a true marketing orientation, using UGC to inform decision making and to engage in relationship marketing. DMOs need a clear strategy for social media engagement, which has at its core a philosophy of *social* (engagement) rather than *media* (placement). Simply applying traditional marketing communications in social media, to reach the most technologically sophisticated population the world has seen, is a waste of scare resources and a sure path to failure.

Key point 3: The benefits and challenges of social media for DMOs

The democratisation of the online world has presented the visitor industry with opportunities and challenges on a level not previously experienced. The sheer scale of UGC that can be published at the *speed of thought* means DMOs have direct access to a global audience, with greater cost efficiency than traditional media; but face a declining influence in their destination's brand image in comparison to consumers' increasing access to *word of mouse* UGC content.

REVIEW QUESTIONS

1. Why is social media likely to have a far greater impact on travel and tourism than any other industry?

2. Why have DMOs generally been slow to maximise the potential of social media?

3. Summarise why DMOs are losing control over online content about their destination and what the key implications are of this?

REFERENCES

Andrews, A. (2014). *Social Media Marketing*. Available at: http://internetcheatsheets.blogspot.com.

Antoniadis, K., Vrana, V. and Zafiropoulos, K. (2014). Promoting European countries' destination image through Twitter. *European Journal of Tourism, Hospitality and Recreation* 5(1): 85–103.

Arlt, W. G. and Thraenhart, J. (2011). Social media tourism marketing in China. In Conrady, R. and Buck, M. (eds) *Trends and Issues in Global Tourism 2011*. Berlin: Springer-Verlag, pp. 149–154.

Belch, G., Belch, M., Kerr, G. and Powell, I. (2009). *Advertising and IMC*. Sydney, Australia: McGraw-Hill.

Borges, B. (2009). *Marketing 2.0: Bridging the Gap between Seller and Buyer through Social Media Marketing*. Tucson, AZ: Wheatmark.

Brake, N. and Safko, L. (2009). *The Social Media Bible*. Hoboken, NJ: John Wiley & Sons.

Buhalis, D. (2003). *eTourism: Information Technology for Strategic Tourism Management*. Harlow, UK: Pearson Education Limited.

Buhalis, D. and Law, R. (2008). Progress in information technology and tourism management: 20 years on and 10 years after the internet – The state of eTourism research. *Tourism Management* 29: 609–623.

Burgess, S., Sellitto, C., Cox, C. and Buultjens, J. (2011). Trust perceptions of online travel information by different content creators: Some social and legal implications. *Information Systems Frontiers* 13(2): 221–235.

Christou, E. (2012). In Sigala, M., Christou, E. and Gretzel, U. (eds) *Social Media in Travel, Tourism and Hospitality: Theory, Practice and Cases*. Farnham, UK: Ashgate Publishing Limited, pp. 69–71.

Chung, N. and Koo, C. (2015). The use of social media in travel information search. *Telematics and Informatics* 32: 215–229.

Coles, T., Dinan, C. and Hutchison, F. (2012). May we live in less interesting times? Changing public sector support for tourism in England during the sovereign debt crisis. *Journal of Destination Marketing & Management* 1(1–2): 4–7.

Daft, R. L. and Lengel, R. H. (1986). Organizational information requirements, media richness, and structural design. *Management Science* 32(5): 554–571.

Gelb, B. D. and Sundaram, S. (2002). Adapting to 'word of mouse'. *Business Horizons* 45(4): 21–25.

Goffman, E. (1959). *The Presentation of Self in Everyday Life*. New York: Doubleday Anchor Books.

Gretzel, U. (2006). Consumer generated content: Trends and implications for branding. *E-Review of Tourism Research* 4(3): 9–11.

Gretzel, U. (2011). Intelligent systems in tourism: A social science perspective. *Annals of Tourism Research* 38(3): 757–779.

Gretzel, U., Yuan, Y. and Fesenmaier, D. R. (2000). Preparing for the new economy: Advertising strategies and change in destination marketing organizations. *Journal of Travel Research* 39(2): 149–156.

Gyimothy, S., Munar, A. N. and Larson, M. (2014). Consolidating social media strategies. *The 5th International Conference on Destination Branding and Marketing.* IFT Macau. December.

Hamill, J. and Stevenson, A. (2012). 'Creating the buzz': Merchant city (Glasgow) case study. In Sigala, M., Christou, E. and Gretzel, U. (eds) *Social Media in Travel, Tourism and Hospitality: Theory, Practice and Cases.* Farnham, UK: Ashgate Publishing Limited, pp. 39–52.

Hamill, J., Stevenson, A. and Attard, D. (2012). National DMOs and Web 2.0. In Sigala, M., Christou, E. and Gretzel, U. (eds) *Social Media in Travel, Tourism and Hospitality: Theory, Practice and Cases.* Farnham, Surrey: Ashgate Publishing Limited, pp. 99–120.

Hays, S., Page, S. J. and Buhalis, D. (2013). Social media as a destination marketing tool: Its use by national tourism organisations. *Current Issues in Tourism* 16(3): 211–239.

Hu, C. and Racherla, P. (2008). Visual representation of knowledge networks: A social network analysis of hospitality research domain. *International Journal of Hospitality Management* 27(2): 302–312.

Internet World Stats. (2015a). *Internet Usage Statistics: The Big Picture.* Available at: http://www.internetworld-stats.com/stats.htm

Internet World Stats. (2015b). Facebook daily active users. *Internet World Stats Newsletter.* Number 084. 7 May. Available at: http://www.internetworldstats.com/pr/edi084.htm

Kang, M. and Schuett, M. A. (2013). Determinants of sharing travel experiences in social media. *Journal of Travel & Tourism Marketing* 30(1–2): 93–107.

Kaplan, A. M. and Haenlein, M. (2010). Users of the world unite! The challenges and opportunities of social media. *Business Horizons* 53(1): 59–68.

Lange-Faria, W. and Elliot, S. (2012). Understanding the role of social media in destination marketing. *Tourismos: An International Multidisciplinary Journal of Tourism* 7(1): 193–211.

Laroche, M., Habibi, M. R. and Richard, M. (2013). To be or not to be in social media: How brand loyalty is affected by social media? *International Journal of Information Management* 33(1): 76–82.

Law, R. and Xiang, Z. (2013). *Journal of Travel & Tourism Marketing* special issue on social media: Preface. *Journal of Travel & Tourism Marketing* 30(1–2): 1–2.

Leadsift. (2013). *The Future of Social Media & Destination Marketing.* Infographic viewed online at: http://leadsift.com/future-social-media-destination-marketing-infographic

Lee, C. L. and Wicks, B. (2010). Tourism technology training for destination marketing organisations (DMOs): Need-based content development. *Journal of Hospitality, Leisure, Sport & Tourism Education* 9(1): 39–52.

Leung, D., Law, R., van Hoof, H. and Buhalis, D. (2013). Social media in tourism and hospitality: A literature review. *Journal of Travel & Tourism Marketing* 30(1/2): 3–22.

Leung, R. and Law, R. (2007). Analysing research collaborations of information technology publications in leading hospitality and tourism journals: 1986–2005. In Sigala, M., Mich, L. and Murphy, J. (eds) *Information and Communication Technologies in Tourism*, pp. 547–557.

Luo, Q. and Zhong, D. (2015). Using social network analysis to explain communication characteristics of travel-related electronic word-of-mouth on social media networking sites. *Tourism Management* 46: 274–282.

Manolo, J. (2015). Top 10 travel destinations on social media for December 2014. www.skift.com. 26 January. Available at: http://skift.com/2015/01/26/top-10-travel-destinations-on-social-media-for-december-2014

Milwood, P., Marchiori, E. and Zach, F. (2013). A comparison of social media adoption and use in different countries: The case of the United States and Switzerland. *Journal of Travel & Tourism Marketing* 30(1–2): 165–168.

Mistilis, N., Buhalis, D. and Gretzel, U. (2014). Future eDestination marketing: Perspective of an Australian tourism stakeholder network. *Journal of Travel Research* 53(6): 778–790. Available at: http://jtr.sagepub.com/content/early/2014/02/28/0047287514522874

Molz, J. G. (2012). *Travel Connections: Tourism, Technology and Togetherness in a Mobile World World.* New York: Routledge.

Munar, A. M. (2012). Social media strategies and destination management. *Scandinavian Journal of Hospitality and Tourism* 12(2): 101–120.

MX. (2015). Bookings rush: Tripped up by holiday envy. *MX.* 25 February, p. 2. Hard copy newspaper article.

News.com.au. (2014). *Australia's First Professional Instagrammer, Lauren Bath, Shares Her Secrets for Career Success.* 4 April. Available at: http://www.news.com.au/finance/work/australias-first-professional-instagrammer-lauren-bath-shares-her-secrets-for-career-success/story-fnkgbb3b-1226874508436

O'Connor, P. and Murphy, J. (2004). Research on information technology in the hospitality industry. *International Journal of Hospitality Management* 23(5): 473–484.

Oliveira, E. and Panyik, E. (2015). Content, context and co-creation: Digital challenges in destination branding with references to Portugal as a tourist destination. *Journal of Vacation Marketing* 21(1): 53–74.

Pan, B. and Li, X. (2011). The long tail of destination image and online marketing. *Annals of Tourism Research* 38(1): 132–152.

Pan, B. and Crotts, J. C. (2012). Theoretical models of social media, marketing implications, and future research directions. In Sigala, M., Christou, E. and Gretzel, U. (eds) *Social Media in Travel, Tourism and Hospitality: Theory, Practice and Cases*. Farnham, UK: Ashgate Publishing Limited, pp. 73–86.

Pan, B., Litvin, S. W. and O'Donnell, T. E. (2007). Understanding accommodation search query formulation: The first step in putting 'heads in beds'. *Journal of Vacation Marketing* 13(4): 371–381.

Park, Y. A. and Gretzel, U. (2007). Success factors for destination marketing web sites: A qualitative meta-analysis. *Journal of Travel Research* 46(1): 46–63.

Parra-Lopez, E., Gutierrez-Tano, D., Diaz-Armas, R. J. and Bulchand-Gidumal, J. (2012). Travellers 2.0: Motivation, opportunity and ability to use social media. In Sigala, M., Christou, E. and Gretzel, U. (eds) *Social Media in Travel, Tourism and Hospitality: Theory, Practice and Cases*. Farnham, UK: Ashgate Publishing, pp. 171–187.

Pike, S. (2004). *Destination Marketing Organisations*. Oxford: Elsevier Science.

Pike, S. (2008). *Destination Marketing: An Integrated Marketing Communication Approach*. Burlington, MA: Butterworth-Heinemann.

Ricci, F. (2011). Mobile recommender systems. *The Journal of Information Technology & Tourism* 12(3): 205–231.

Sevin, E. (2013). Places going viral: Twitter usage patterns in destination marketing and place branding. *Journal of Place Management and Development* 6(3): 227–239.

Shao, J., Rodriguez, M. A. D. and Gretzel, U. (2012). Riding the social media wave: Strategies of DMOs who successfully engage in social media marketing. In Sigala, M., Christou, E. and Gretzel, U. (eds) *Social Media in Travel, Tourism and Hospitality: Theory, Practice and Cases*. Farnham, UK: Ashgate Publishing Limited.

Short, J., Williams, E. and Christie, B. (1976). *The Social Psychology of Telecommunications*. Hoboken, NJ: John Wiley & Sons.

Sigala, M. (2012). Introduction to Part 1. In Sigala, M., Christou, E. and Gretzel, U. (eds) *Social Media in Travel, Tourism and Hospitality: Theory, Practice and Cases*. Farnham, UK: Ashgate Publishing Limited, pp. 7–10.

Sigala, M., Christou, E. and Gretzel, U. (eds) (2012) *Social Media in Travel, Tourism and Hospitality: Theory, Practise and Cases*. Farnham, UK: Ashgate Publishing Limited.

SMK. (2015). Number crunch: Mobile marketing. *SMK.co*. 19 January. Available at: http://smk.co/article/number-crunch-mobile-marketing

Stankov, U., Lazic, L. and Dragicevic, V. (2010). The extent of use of basic Facebook user-generated content by the national tourism organizations in Europe. *European Journal of Tourism Research* 3(2): 105–113.

The Courier-Mail. (2015). *Bigger Than Hollywood: Apps Earnings a Blockbuster*. 25 January: 33. Hard copy newspaper article.

Tourism Australia. (2014a). *Lots to 'Like' about @australia's Instagram Account*. 15 December. Available at: http://www.tourism.australia.com/news/news-tourism-australia-instagram-1-million.aspx

Tourism Australia. (2014b). *Working with Tourism Australia: Global Marketing Prospectus 2014/2015*. Available at: http://www.tourism.australia.com/documents/Markets/Report_WorkingwithTA_May14.pdf

Travelindustrywire (2015). *Study Shows Web Has Transformed Consumers into More Selective Travel Buyers*. Available at: http://www.travelindustrywire.com/article81708.html

Trendwatching. (2014). *Internet of Caring Things*. April. Available at: online.http://trendwatching.com/trends/internet-of-caring-things

Trihas, N., Perakakis, E., Venitourakis, M., Mastorakis, G. and Kopanakis, I. (2013a). Social media as a marketing tool for tourism destinations: The case of Greek municipalities. *Journal of Marketing Vistas* 3(2): 38–48.

Trihas, N., Perakakis, E., Venitourakis, M., Mastorakis, G. and Kopanakis, I. (2013b). Destination marketing using multiple social media: The case of 'Visit Ierapetra'. *Tourism Today* Fall: 114–126.

TripAdvisor. (2014). *World's Top Destinations Named in TripAdvisor Travelers' Choice Awards*. April 8. Available at: http://www.multivu.com/mnr/70425520-tripadvisor-travelers-choice-awards-top-destinations

Volo, S. (2010). Bloggers' reported tourist experiences: Their utility as a tourism data source and their effect on prospective tourists. *Journal of Vacation Marketing* 16(4): 297–311.

Volo, S. (2012). Blogs: 're-inventing' tourism communication. In Sigala, M., Christou, E. and Gretzel, U. (eds) *Social Media in Travel, Tourism and Hospitality: Theory, Practice and Cases.* Farnham, UK: Ashgate Publishing Limited, pp. 149–163.

Wang, D., Fesenmaier, D. R., Werthner, H. and Webber, K. (2010). *The Journal of Information Technology & Tourism*: A content analysis of the past 10 years. *The Journal of Information Technology & Tourism* 12(1): 3–16.

Wang, D., Li, X. and Li, Y. (2013). China's 'smart tourism destination' initiative: A taste of the service-dominant logic. *Journal of Destination Marketing & Management* 2(1): 59–61.

Xiang, Z. and Gretzel, U. (2010). Role of social media in online travel information search. *Tourism Management* 31(2): 179–188.

Xiang, Z. and Pan, B. (2011). Travel queries on cities in the United States: Implications for search engine marketing for tourist destinations. *Tourism Management* 32(1): 88–97.

Yoo, K. H. and Gretzel, U. (2012). Use and creation of social media by travellers. In Sigala, M., Christou, E. and Gretzel, U. (eds) *Social Media in Travel, Tourism and Hospitality: Theory, Practice and Cases.* Farnham, UK: Ashgate Publishing, pp. 189–205.

Chapter **5**

Governance of destination marketing organisations (DMOs)

AIMS

To enhance understanding of:

- the shift towards public–private partnership (PPP) DMO governance structures;
- the politics of DMO decision making;
- the multiple accountability of DMOs.

ABSTRACT

The necessity of impartiality in holistic destination strategies, the need for opportune market-based tactical decision making and the difficulty in getting industry to contribute direct funding have led to the emergence of PPP DMO structures to coordinate a destination-wide effort. The early DMOs were formed as either government departments or private sector cooperatives. The former were perceived as bureaucracies lacking industry expertise, while the latter lacked the security of long-term funding and were concerned with members' interests. Increasing recognition that a foundation of a destination's competitiveness is the establishment of a partnership approach between stakeholders led to the PPP governance structure of government funding and private sector tourism expertise. However, as discussed in Chapter 4, the destination marketing paradigm is changing due to the rise in the democratising influence of social media. The rise in influence of user-generated content will not only be seen in the market place but also with stakeholders in DMO decision making. The challenge lies in collaboration between the DMO and stakeholders to stimulate a cohesive destination-wide approach in a manner that will satisfy the entrepreneurs and the wider community through the influence of public sector governance transparency. How this more entrepreneurial and open approach will impact on

DMO governance, structure and operations is yet to unfold. What will not change, however, is the multiple accountability of DMOs to a multiplicity of stakeholders with an active interest in destination marketing decision making.

The challenge of positioning multi-attributed destinations in dynamic and heterogeneous markets

The fundamental challenge facing all DMOs is effectively positioning a multi-attributed destination in dynamic and heterogeneous markets. A position means the destination stands for something very focused (as in a single value proposition) and is clearly differentiated from competitors, in consumers' minds, in a meaningful way. However, a destination's diverse range of stakeholders will rarely agree that there is one obvious attribute with which to base such a value proposition, given that no matter the scale of the destination, the geographic space will usually contain a large and often eclectic range of features, such as those highlighted in Table 5.1.

Table 5.1 Diversity of potential destination attributes

Nature-based attractions

Forests, mountains, tundra, glaciers, deserts, flora and fauna wildlife sanctuaries, lakes, rivers, coastlines, islands, harbours, beaches, lagoons, swamps, waterfalls

Built attractions

Theme parks, bridge climbs, casinos, mazes

Water-based activities

Sightseeing cruises, whale watching, white water rafting, jetboating, boat hire, fishing guides, swimming with dolphins, sharks and crocodiles

Adventure activities

Bungee jumping, parachuting, trekking, skiing, off road driving

Entertainment venues

Theatres, cinemas, exhibitions, race tracks

Sports venues

Stadia, golf courses, mountain bike trails, swimming pools, skating rinks

Cultural attractions

Indigenous culture, performing arts, theatres, art galleries, museums, historic sites, castles, palaces, architecture

Retail

Shopping malls, boutiques, megastores, craft markets

Accommodation

Hotels, exclusive lodges, motels, resorts, backpacker hostels, bed and breakfast guest houses

Nightlife

Casinos, nightclubs, bars, pubs, dancehalls

(continued)

Table 5.1 *(continued)*

Gastronomy

Restaurants, cafes, cooking schools, farmers' markets, wineries, orchards

Dark tourism

Battlefields, torture chambers, scenes of natural and man-made disasters

Spiritual sites

Indigenous sites, cathedrals, churches, temples, mosques, pagan sites

Community amenities

Picnic areas, children's playgrounds, golf courses

Host population

Ethnic quarters, customs, language

Climate

Seasonality, climate-based activities

Also, there is not just a single tourism market in which to position the destination. The DMO's tourism operators will have financial interests in a range of geographically dispersed market segments, which are heterogeneous (distinctly different) in terms of needs and dynamic (constantly changing). Since the tourism literature commenced in the 1970s there has been acknowledgement that, on the demand-side of destination marketing, the global market of consumer-travellers is not homogenous in terms of needs (Wahab *et al.*, 1976). Travellers from different geographic areas, socio-demographic groups and lifestyle clusters will respond to different offers at different times, for a complex array of reasons, including the purpose of travel, individual motivation(s), amount of leisure time available, the time of year and availability of other substitute discretionary spending opportunities. Consumers will engage in different types of travel at different times of the year and throughout their lifetime. Thousands of DMOs now compete for the attention of busy consumers through communication channels cluttered with noise from rival and substitute offerings. The greatest challenge facing DMOs is to effectively differentiate their offering at decision time. The concept of destination positioning is discussed in Chapter 11.

A DMO serves as the coordinating body for the many public and private sector organisations and individuals that have an active interest in tourism at a destination. Underpinning the rationale for a DMO to overcome the positioning challenge and enhance destination competitiveness is the need to foster a *cooperate to compete* approach. An impartial coordinator is required to stimulate the pooling of destination resources to create a greater impact in the market than would otherwise be achieved by disparate individual efforts. As discussed in Chapter 3, this is similar to the efficient market hypothesis in behavioural finance (see Fama, 1970). If left to the private sector to organise and fund collective destination promotion, the likely result will be market failure. Simply put, entrepreneurs have a vested interest in the profitability of their own business, and there are few examples of long-term success of destinations where marketing is undertaken either by a private sector cooperative or by individual businesses, in lieu of a DMO. Case study 5.1 highlights tensions that can emerge at destinations undergoing a change in DMO governance.

CASE STUDY

5.1 Black Forest tourism: DMO competition, collaboration and innovation

Professor Florian Hummel
Cologne Business School, Germany

It was in 1906 that the forerunner of today's Black Forest Tourism Association (Schwarzwald Tourismus GmbH (STG)) was established in southern Germany. This is a marketing organisation and governing body for the Schwarzwald (Black Forest) holiday region. The STG performs all the functions of a DMO responsible for the brand name *Black Forest*, which the STG owns. The STG represents a total of 321 municipalities in their tourism interests at home and abroad.

However, in recent years, 15 municipalities have formed their own DMO. These municipalities account for the largest number of tourism visitors and income of the whole Black Forest region. With a similar name to the Black Forest Tourism Association (STG), the newly formed Black Forest Tourism GmbH (Hochschwarzwald Tourismus GmbH (HTG)) manages 23 tourist information offices in towns around this high income region of the Black Forest. With around 3.5 million overnight stays, the HTG now represents the strongest tourism region of the southern Black Forest and has in its geographical portfolio the Schluchsee as the largest lake in the Black Forest. Also, Lake Titisee as the most famous lake, the Feldberg is the highest mountain of the Central German Uplands and the Wutachschlucht as the largest canyon in Germany.

Tourism is the main source of income in this unique but remote area. Politically and economically, this new breakaway DMO entity has created friction within the overall Black Forest region tourism community.

Discussion question 1: Discuss the potential *frictions* that the split up of these two DMOs might generate. In particular, take into account sustaining and developing the brand image of the Black Forest as well as operational issues that tour operators and tourists might face.

In addition, the HTG seems to be a more innovative entity than the older STG. A recent development and initiative are the *Cuckoo Nests – Design Apartments*, which the HTG is marketing to visitors. The apartments feature lovingly designed decor with wood and stone walls, real wood design kitchens, many natural materials, tree stumps as bedside tables and their own furniture line. The staged authenticity of the interior shows off the well-known attributes of the Black Forest region.

Overall 40 such *Cuckoo Nests – Design Apartments* are planned to open and be offered to visitors, scattered around all 15 Black Forest villages that the HTG represents. The *Cuckoo Nests* are located in the mid to upper quality segment, with prices starting at just under €100 per night for two people and are distributed through the HTG website. The apartments are secured initially for 5 years by HTG from the local owner who receives 18 per cent commission on the revenue generated through HTG, but who needs to initially invest €20,000 for furniture and fittings.

A background of the initiative is to help apartment owners with successor problems, difficulties in dealing with modern marketing tools (e.g. online booking facilities) and overcoming an outdated product. The aim is to develop a standardised apartment brand that guarantees the owner a secure income and, overall, to secure the future of this important tourism market in the Black Forest.

> **Discussion question 2: What might be the reception of such standardised hospitality offerings in a very rural and traditional region?**
>
> **Discussion question 3: How will local owners of holiday apartments react when the regional DMO adds these specially designed apartments to the region's portfolio and exclusively makes them available through its website?**

DMO entity

It must be recognised that even though there is an interdependence of multiple stakeholders, a destination typically has an 'almost complete lack of hierarchy and authority' (Lemmetyinen and Go, 2009: 31). Following Gretzel *et al.* (2000), a key problem for all DMOs confronting rapid change in the macro environment is the inability to deal with that change, which is a function of traditional bureaucratic approaches to management. However, to what extent is a fast moving entrepreneurial business model either appropriate or practical for publicly funded DMOs, with a holistic destination responsibility? There has been little research into the relationships between the organisation, strategy and effectiveness of DMOs to guide destination marketers on effective organisation. Indeed, there has been little published at all about the structure of NTOs (Choy, 1993; Morrison *et al.*, 1995; Pike and Page, 2014). What is apparent is that no universally accepted model for DMO structure currently exists. For example, there currently exist myriads of DMO titles:

- agency (Latvian Tourism Development Agency);
- alliance (Warsaw Destination Alliance);
- association (Christmas Island Tourism Association);
- authority (The Gambia Tourism Authority);
- board (British Virgin Islands Tourist Board);
- bureau (Hawaii Visitors Bureau);
- centre (Le Centre Gabonais de Promotion Touristique);
- and co (Goteborg and Co);
- coalition (North Carolina Travel and Tourism Coalition);
- commission (Nevada Commission on Tourism);
- company (New York City and Company);
- corporation (Virginia Tourism Corporation);
- council (Swedish Travel and Tourism Council);
- department (Dubai Department of Tourism and Commerce Marketing);
- directorate (Crete Tourism Directorate);
- Inc. (Northand Inc.).
- institute (Nicaraguan Institute of Tourism);

- ministry (Israel Ministry of Tourism);
- network (North Coast Destination Network);
- office (China National Tourism Office);
- organisation (South Coast Regional Tourism Organisation);
- organization (Cyprus Tourism Organization).

Since the early 1990s, new types of DMO names have emerged to denote organisation focus, such as those incorporating *travel* (Travel Alberta), *tourism* (Falkland Islands Tourism), *destination* (Destination Lake Taupo), *innovation* (Innovation Norway), *explore* (Explore Georgia), *enterprise* (Enterprise Dunedin), *brand* (Brand USA), *venture* (Venture Taranaki Trust) and *visit* (Visit Heart of England), and then others that are difficult to categorise such as Maison de la France, Fáilte Ireland, Latitude Nelson and Positively Wellington Tourism. While there is no one naming theme common to DMOs, there has been a shift in recent years away from the more bureaucratic sounding entities that are representative of government departments. A selection of examples is provided in Table 5.2, which compares the current name to one used in the past. Such name changes generally reflect the general shift to PPP governance.

When VisitBritain (see www.visitbritain.com) was chosen as the name for the UK's new DMO, it had to be purchased from a company that had owned it for 25 years. The chairman of VisitBritain discussed some of the difficulties associated with selecting an appropriate name:

> *You have no idea how much trouble goes into creating a new name. It has to be legal, we have to make sure it means the same thing in different languages, and that it sounds good over the phone, and works in different media.*

Governance

Governance concerns the *process* of decision making, as opposed to the perceived correctness/effectiveness of actual decisions. Good governance can still lead to perceived incorrect and ineffective decisions. Table 5.3 highlights six key characteristics of good governance.

DMOs will always be under constant review and threat from their principal funding sources, and so academic research that proves critical and undermines their arguments for additional funding due to poor or

Table 5.2 DMO name changes

Current name	A previous name
Visit Florida	Florida Department of Commerce
VisitBritain	British Tourist Authority
Tourism Australia	Australian Tourist Commission
Tourism New Zealand	New Zealand Tourist and Publicity Department
Tourism and Events Queensland	Queensland Tourist and Travel Corporation

Table 5.3 Characteristics of good governance

Accountability

There is an obligation to report, explain and be answerable for the consequences of decisions made on behalf of stakeholders

Transparency

Stakeholders should be able to follow and understand the decision making process, clearly seeing how and why a decision was made and what information was considered

Lawful

Decisions follow the rule of law, being consistent with the relevant legislation governing the legal entity of the organisation

Responsive

Balancing competing interests in a timely and appropriate manner for the benefit of the wider community

Equitable and inclusive

All stakeholders should feel their interests have been considered in the decision making process and should have the opportunity to participate in some way

Effective and efficient

Decisions should be made and implemented with the best use of available resources and time to ensure the best results for the community

Source: Adapted from www.goodgovernance.org.au

perceived lacklustre performance means wider academic scrutiny is rarely welcomed in a public setting (Pike and Page, 2014). Most internal reviews remain confidential given the political challenge of maintaining a positive relationship at a distance from funding sources such as government or private sector. And so, while there has been a 2010 special issue in *Tourism Review* (65(4)) and literature reviews on destination governance by Ruhanen *et al.* (2010), Wang (2013) and Zhang and Zhu (2014), research into the governance of DMOs remains limited, and currently there is no accepted model. In particular, there has been little research reported about DMO governance from an emic (inside) perspective. Ruhanen *et al.*'s (2010) review of 53 published governance studies from the wider literature identified six most frequently included dimensions:

1. accountability;

2. transparency;

3. involvement;

4. structure;

5. effectiveness;

6. power.

Also, it has been suggested that governance of globally competitive destinations features four critical success factors (Poetschke, 1995: 62–63):

1. a significant level of private sector control over authority spending;

2. an understanding of the need to incorporate public sector objectives to achieve a balance between marketing and new product development;

3. a dedicated revenue stream that is not subject to annual government control;

4. a broad, integrated, mandate encompassing all functions critical to developing a strong tourism industry, such as marketing, education, research and infrastructure development.

Palmer's (1998) review of the governance literature identified a loose–tight or informal–formal continuum of managing organisational relationships. Loose styles are likely to be more suited to creative tasks, and important considerations are trust and levels of access to resources. Informal relationship controls are self-control, based on financial or psychological incentives, and socio-cultural control, based on group norms. Tight styles are governed by more formal legal controls. The former might signal unclear objectives and strategy, but be more flexible, creative and fast moving. The tight style, on the other hand, is more likely to generate clear and formal goals, contractual rights and obligations, but also be more bureaucratic, particularly in terms of decision making. This approach can be frustrating to entrepreneurial tourism operators.

Palmer (1998) hypothesised that while a loose style might suit a local tourism association because of the dynamic nature of tourism markets, a tight governance style would be more effective in terms of maintaining a strategic focus. In a survey of 172 members of 13 English LTAs, there was evidence to suggest a strong link between a tight governance style and organisation effectiveness. The most effective local tourism associations were ones with formal rules governing relationships between members, an efficient and effective secretariat and opportunities for discussing the management of the association.

The politics of DMO decision making

In the practice of management there is always a danger of politicians, public and private organisations and managers becoming self-serving and consequently failing in their official responsibilities. Public organisations and resources can be misused for private purposes. There can be financial corruption, but more insidious is organisational corruption, where public objectives and principles are displaced by private objectives (Elliott, 1997: 7). In many communities the conservationists and social scientists are not as powerful a lobby as the government sponsor, entrepreneurs and intermediaries.

Politics in decision making is a significant aspect of DMO governance and is unavoidable. From one perspective politics may be viewed as the art of getting things done. From another perspective, politics has been described as 'the striving for power, and power is about who gets what, when and how in the political and administrative system and in the tourism sector' (Elliott, 1997: 10). The political environment in tourism at national and local levels includes: governments and ministers, bureaucratic cultures, competing entrepreneurs, the media, other industry sectors, the host community, special interest groups and external travel intermediaries. The industry is made up of a diverse range of organisations and individuals involved in a complex array of relationships, and it is the challenge of the manager to understand this and work within the system to achieve objectives (Elliott, 1997).

Working through the minefield of tourism politics is a challenging reality. The best laid plans of well-meaning destination marketers can come unstuck due to the differences in opinions of influential stakeholders. While this occurs at national, state and regional levels, the political coalface can be most challenging at a local community level, where there is little escape from daily interactions with stakeholders. For example, Denmark's tourism competitiveness has been hindered since the 1980s by the governance style of RTOs, which have suffered from 'geographic localism and short-term interests' in policy making (Halkier, 2014: 1664). The discussion of politics at destinations has been rare in the academic literature. There have been calls for increased coverage of the study of the politics in tertiary tourism education (see Dredge, 2001; Hollingshead, 2001; Fayos-Solà, 2002). Pike and Page (2014) suggested the seminal study in this regard was Kerr (2004) who undertook an in-depth analysis of the *management of strategic failure* in Scottish tourism, to provide an insightful, theoretical and empirical analysis of the politics of tourism, where the DMO received detailed criticism.

Also, there has been little research attention towards the influence exerted by special interest groups on DMO governance. Greenwood (1993) suggested interest groups are usually more successful the less they use public channels of communication. Media is only used as a last resort. In tourism, groups with an active interest in DMO governance at all levels include sector associations and local/national tourism umbrella associations. In some cases there are organised lobby groups such as the Tour Operators Study Group in the UK. An interest group has been defined as a 'Domain based in economic fields of operation, operating with a degree of permanence, where membership is restricted to organizations such as firms and pressure is exerted through developing permanent relations with government, often in "behind closed doors" environments' (Greenwood, 1993: 336).

PPPs

The necessity of impartiality in holistic destination strategies, the need for market-based tactical decision making and the difficulty in getting industry to contribute funding have led to the emergence of PPP DMO structures. DMOs have historically been established as government departments, particularly at NTO and STO levels. For example, in a 1975 survey of 95 NTOs the UNWTO (1975) found only 6 that were non-governmental. However, there has been a general shift to PPP governance structures since the 1990s. The UNWTO adopted the theme of *Public–private sector partnership: The key to tourism development and promotion* for world tourism day in 1998 (Pike, 2004). In the UK PPPs became a means towards generating larger budgets for local destination marketing during the 1980s and 1990s when tight spending restrictions on local governments were applied by central government (Bramwell and Rawding, 1996). Visit Florida was established in 1996 when the Department of Commerce was disbanded to make way for a PPP to promote tourism in Florida.

In Australia Tourism Tasmania was established as a PPP by legislation in 1996 (Pike, 2008). Smith (2003) described the evolution in 1995 of Canada's NTO into a new PPP, the Canadian Tourism Commission. A major impetus for change was complaints by industry that the previous administration was under funded and not market-driven. By 2000 most provincial and territorial DMOs in Canada had become industry led and publicly funded (National Tourism Strategy, 2003, in Vallee, 2005).

During 2006 there were strong calls by the government opposition in Bermuda to replace the Ministry of Tourism with a PPP that would be 'more in tune . . . forward thinking and fiscally prudent . . . we don't want politicians running tourism'. In 2014 the Bermuda Tourism Authority was established as a PPP with an independent board of directors. However, a scathing editorial in January 2015 highlighted the types of criticism and politics faced by DMOs (*The Royal Gazette*, 2015). The editor did not hold anything back in a commentary on the island nation's bitter politics, with such comments as:

> [i]ts critics, politically motivated, opportunistic and intent on dividing and ruling by any means to hand, routinely paint the BTA as if it is a Trojan horse of darkest design cunningly slipped into our camp . . . Its CEO is routinely depicted as so very odious, cunning and cruel that he has no real-world counterpart . . . The reality is the organisation has been reduced to just another pawn on the chessboard of parochial party politicking . . . We all have a vested interest in the outcomes of initiatives taking place in these areas and the Island's best interests must be placed ahead of political self-interest.

Potential benefits of the PPP structure, compared to a government department of industry and/or a subscription-based collective, include:

- private sector efficiency, and knowledge of the industry;
- increased surety of ongoing government funding;
- increased collaboration between stakeholders;
- less duplication in marketing efforts;
- representative inclusion of all stakeholders;
- more transparency in decision making and auditing;
- reduced conflicts of interest;
- more strategic approach, with a societal marketing orientation;
- improved access to government leadership.

Attempts at RTO rationalisation

England has recently witnessed a major change with the existing structure of tourism promotion being redefined (see Page and Connell, 2009 for a detailed outline of the structure and funding of the DMO structure in the UK) as many regional and locally focused DMOs have been abolished or have had their funding cut as part of public sector austerity cuts. Instead, the development of Local Economic Partnerships (LEP) has replaced the DMOs formerly funded by the Regional Development Agencies (RDAs) that were abolished. Now tourism is subsumed under a wider economic development agenda, as a partnership between local authorities and businesses, and it is their responsibility if they wish to assume any of the former DMO functions. In this respect, tourism as an economic driver of the economy has been downgraded from its former priority status under the RDAs to a position where it is effectively in limbo, and destination marketing is an *ad hoc* activity determined by each LEP (or local authority) if they choose to assume this role (Pike and Page, 2014).

There have been moves in different parts of the world towards rationalisation of RTOs in order to improve the efficiency of resources. In Scotland the 32 area tourist boards (ATBs) established during the 1980s were amalgamated into 14 in 1996, following a 1993 government review of tourism (Davidson and Maitland, 1997; Kerr and Wood, 2000). A similar restructuring strategy was announced in Western Australia during 2004 (www.tourism.wa.gov.au/media/discussion_03.asp, 22 February 2004). As part of the 'New concept for state tourism strategy', the number of official RTOs in the state would be reduced from ten to five. A commitment of AUD$3.25 million annual funding for the five RTOs was announced by the Western Australian state government to 'increase economies of scale, and empower the regions'. Denmark's nationwide system of RTOs was restricted by government in 2007 to be part of six *Regional Growth Fora* (Halkier, 2014). The move was part of attempts to stimulate more innovation and reverse a decline in Denmark's tourism competitiveness.

Implementation of such rationalisation can be problematic. For example, a reduced number of RTOs was called for in the New Zealand Tourism Strategy released in 2001 (see Tourism Strategy Group, 2001). One of the strategy goals was for a smaller number of new RTOs to be established from the existing 25 RTOs. Through sharing common back-office functions, it was suggested the reduced number of RTOs would make significant savings in overhead costs, which could then be more effectively used in promotion. However, the strategy did not discuss how the proposal would be implemented and, in particular, how the political implications would be addressed. Three years later the issue remained problematic despite the efforts of a Regional Tourism Organisations New Zealand (RTONZ) taskforce, as explained to me by the then RTONZ Executive Officer (Pike, 2008): 'Obviously it's a delicate one with lots of political overtones, but it has to be addressed'. Interestingly, by 2015 the number of New Zealand RTOs had actually increased to 30.

Board of directors

The role of the board of directors is to assume overall responsibility for both the strategic planning process and the monitoring of performance in relation to the DMO's goals. The composition of the board will likely reflect the local tourism industry and the dynamics between important stakeholder groups (Wang, 2008).

Some boards can be quite large and cumbersome. Scantlebury (2008, in Pike, 2008) described the failed 1990s initiative of the Barbados Tourism Authority to have all sectors of the tourism industry represented on the board. This resulted in 19 directors on a board that became so cumbersome that board meetings would sometimes take two days to complete, stymying effective decision making. Bramwell and Rawding (1996) reported Birmingham's RTB board comprised 25 directors, with 7 representatives from the local authority and 18 from industry. The first Canadian Travel Commission board contained 26 members, of which 16 were from the private sector and the remainder from the public sector (Smith, 2003). The large size of the board reflected the effort to ensure all regions of Canada were represented. A survey of IACVB members (IACVB, 2001, in Fenich, 2005) found that the average size of CVB boards was 16 voting directors. Lathrop (2005: 198–199) reported the case of Townsville in the USA, where the CVB had a board of 60 directors. Lathrop's (2005) case study of how one group of dissatisfied stakeholders were excluded from decision making concluded with the following governance lessons:

- Bylaws must clearly define the role, responsibility, and code of conduct for the board and staff. The importance of effective bylaws cannot be overstated.

- Do not exclude key community constituents simply because they might not agree, or because it is easier not to deal with them. The old adage – 'keep your friends close and your enemies closer' – holds true in the case of board composition.

- Limit the size of the board. Because of the sheer size of the board in this case study, it was virtually impossible for the chair or executive to manage it effectively.

- Board turnover is a good thing and should be a key aspect of the bylaws. As long as [there is] a nucleus of experienced board members and an effective orientation process, the regular introduction of new members should not be a problem.

- Embrace board governance as an effective management and leadership tool.

In the USA (see Lathrop, 2005) and Canada (see Vallee, 2005), most CVBs are required by federal and state regulations to have an elected non-compensated board and a set of bylaws dictating governance and fiduciary responsibilities. Typically a CVB board is responsible for the following (Lathrop, 2005: 191):

- defining the purpose of the bureau and establishing its governing principles;

- providing advice and consent with respect to overall policy;

- approving the annual operating budget and monitoring the bureau's finances;

- approving the membership structure and fees;

- providing direction and oversight for the bureau's operations;

- monitoring the performance of the CEO;

- representing the bureau's interests among external audiences and serving as an advocate for tourism and destination management issues.

The two main options for selecting directors are by appointment or by election. A danger in any board election system is the appointment of those who are popular, or even *articulate incompetents*, rather than those best qualified. An articulate incompetent is someone who is great at expressing issues and explaining solutions, but fails to act on them (Wintermans, 1994). Bramwell and Rawding (1996: 431) suggested that when appointments are made to publicly funded RTOs by selection, the organisation is 'less democratic and less accountable to the local electorate'. However, local government representatives on the board can serve this purpose. If government representatives are not included on the board, the issue of accountability needs to be carefully addressed in the funding contract and government reporting process. For example, Tourism New Zealand has a board of nine directors appointed by the government's Minister of Tourism for a term of three years. Directors receive an annual fee of NZ$15,000. Qualities sought in directors, and expectations of Tourism New Zealand by the government, are highlighted in Table 5.4. See Pike (2008) for a full position description of the New Zealand Tourism Board.

Table 5.4 Government expectations of Tourism New Zealand directors and operations

Expectations of Tourism New Zealand operations	Skills and experience of directors
<ul><li>integrity;</li><li>frugality and due care in the use of taxpayer money;</li><li>advancing activities beneficial to the tourism sector and wider community rather than to any individual business;</li><li>focusing on medium- to long-term strategies rather than short-term gains;</li><li>showing openness and having good communications with the Minister, the Ministry of Tourism and other government agencies;</li><li>partnering with the private sector to add value rather than displace or duplicate private businesses.</li></ul>	<ul><li>a wide perspective on issues;</li><li>good oral and written communication;</li><li>understanding of public sector governance and accountability;</li><li>previous experience as a company director;</li><li>ability to work in a team and work collaboratively;</li><li>strategic skills;</li><li>experience in developing and maintaining partnerships with other organisations and companies;</li><li>experience with financial statements;</li><li>understanding of and/or experience in the tourism sector at a senior level;</li><li>understanding the importance of value creation, innovation and international best practice comparisons;</li><li>experience of marketing issues.</li></ul>

Source: Pike (2008).

Gee and Makens (1985) provided a candid explanation of the opportunities, challenges and conflicts that face members of tourism boards:

> *Tourism boards can be an effective force for a community's hospitality industry, and the hotel manager is a crucial part of such a board. But to do its job, the board may have to resist the influences of politics, unrealistic community 'cheerleading', and intra-industry competition.*
>
> *(Gee and Makens, 1985: 25)*

While Gee and Makens were writing specifically for hotel managers, their paper is a worthwhile read for any prospective DMO board member. Another account of DMO governance issues likely to be faced was provided in Kelly and Nankervis's (2001) observations of the challenges in Australia faced by one of the state of Victoria's RTOs, the Yarra Valley, Dandenong and the Ranges Tourism Board:

- the diversity of features;
- board representatives not focused on the 'big picture';
- operators' suspicions of others' sectoral interests;
- cumbersome organisational name to reflect all areas covered;
- a regional community not fully informed on the advantages of tourism;
- lack of reliable visitor statistics.

Multiple accountability

Destination marketing staff have many perceived *bosses*, including the board of directors, taxpayers, local tourism businesses, travel trade intermediaries and government funding agencies. In some cases the DMO is accountable to more than one funding agency. The challenge of spending scarce resources and lobbying several local authorities in an RTO's regional catchment area is common. Consider, for example, Outback Queensland (www.outbackqld.com.au) in Australia. The RTO's catchment area represents 50 per cent of the state's land area and includes 21 local government authorities. The structure of local government can make a regional approach to regional problems extremely difficult. Clearly, managing relationships with multiple funding agencies is time consuming. Tourism Auckland CEO, Graeme Osborne, strongly lamented the impact of the resultant multiple accountability and multiple governance, where the RTO reported to the committees of each council as well as to the tourism industry:

> *It prevents truly visionary leadership being exercised at a regional level, which of course is the correct approach for destination marketing. The fundamental flaw then is the structure and (ridiculously excessive) scale of local government, the ensuing lack of regional vision, the 'sovereignty driven', duplicative, parochial leadership offered by generally low-average-quality local government politicians.*
>
> *(Pike, 2008)*

The Tourism Auckland region contains seven local city governments. Manchester's CVB, in the UK, reports to ten local authorities (Bramwell and Rawding, 1996), Bundaberg Region Ltd, an RTO in Australia, reports to ten local authorities (www.bundabergregion.info), and the former West Country Tourist Board in the UK was responsible to six and a half counties (Meethan, 2002).

DMO roles

In the pursuit of destination competitiveness, there is a commonality of roles of DMOs around the world. Analyses of DMO roles have been reported by Pattinson (1990), Choy (1993), Pearce (1996), Getz *et al.* (1998), Morrison *et al.* (1998), Pike (2004, 2008), Harrill (2005a, 2005b), Lennon *et al.* (2006), Ford and Peeper (2008) and Wang (2008). Key themes at all DMO levels, which are discussed in more detail in later chapters, include:

- development and coordination of a cooperative tourism strategy;
- providing advice to government and entrepreneurs;
- lobbying the interests of the tourism industry with government agencies;
- conducting marketing research;
- stimulating new product development;
- undertaking promotional activities;
- information provision;
- promoting quality service standards;
- stimulating new event developments;
- fostering civic pride, along with awareness of, and support for, tourism, among the host community;
- disaster response preparedness.

CHAPTER SUMMARY

Key point 1: PPP DMO governance structures

There is a plethora of DMO structures, with no widely accepted model. Historically, DMOs emerged either as government departments or as industry association collectives. More recently there has been a shift towards the establishment of PPPs as a way of ensuring destination marketing programmes are industry-driven, but also accountable to public funders. PPPs, at both a national and local level, are generally governed by a private sector board that is appointed by, and reports to, a government representative.

Key point 2: The politics in DMO decision making

The politics of decision making is a critical element of DMO effectiveness. Of concern to government funders is the need for industry expertise and accountability from the board of directors. However, stakeholders also demand fair representation in decision making, which can lead to large and cumbersome boards and slower decision making. A critical question is whether directors should be appointed on the basis of expertise, or be democratically elected.

Key point 3: The multiple accountability of DMOs

A key role for the DMO is stimulating the divergent and eclectic mix of stakeholders to work collaboratively for the wider community benefit. The success of individual businesses is reliant to some extent on the competitiveness of the destination and necessitates their self-interests to be tempered by the knowledge that decision making at well-governed DMOs focuses on the wider public good. Nevertheless, political tensions are an unfortunate reality for all destination marketers.

REVIEW QUESTIONS

1. Design an effective board structure for your local DMO. How many directors are appropriate? Who would be most effective, and should directors be appointed on merit or democratically elected? Who should make the appointment decisions? What length of term should directors serve?

2. The chapter discussed the failure in New Zealand's tourism strategy to reduce the number of RTOs. Summarise the potential advantages for doing so, and discuss the potential disadvantages that have stalled the initiative.

3. What are the key advantages of a PPP governance structure?

REFERENCES

Bramwell, B. and Rawding, L. (1996). Tourism marketing images of industrial cities. *Annals of Tourism Research* 23(1): 201–221.

Choy, D. J. L. (1993). Alternative roles of national tourism organizations. *Tourism Management* 14(5): 357–365.

Davidson, R. and Maitland, R. (1997). *Tourism Destinations*. London: Hodder & Stoughton.

Dredge, D. (2001). Local government tourism planning and policy-making in New South Wales: Institutional development and historical legacies. *Current Issues in Tourism* 4(2/4): 355–380.

Elliott, J. (1997). *Tourism: Politics and Public Sector Management*. London: Routledge.

Fama, E. F. (1970). Efficient capital markets: A review of theory and empirical work. *Journal of Finance* 25(2): 383–417.

Fayos-Solà, E. (2002). Globalization, tourism policy and tourism education. *Acta Turistica* 14(1): 5–12.

Fenich, G. G. (2005). *Meetings, Expositions, Events and Conventions: An Introduction to the Industry*. Upper Saddle River, NJ: Pearson.

Ford, R. C. and Peeper, W. C. (2008). *Managing Destination Marketing Organizations*. Orlando, FL: ForPer Publications.

Gee, C. Y. and Makens, J. C. (1985). The tourism board: Doing it right. *The Cornell Quarterly* 26(3): 25–33.

Getz, D., Anderson, D. and Sheehan, L. (1998). Roles, issues, and strategies for convention and visitors' bureaux in destination planning and product development: A survey of Canadian bureaux. *Tourism Management* 19(4): 331–340.

Greenwood, J. (1993). Business interest groups in tourism governance. *Tourism Management* 14(5): 335–348.

Gretzel, U., Yuan, Y. and Fesenmaier, D. R. (2000). Preparing for the new economy: Advertising strategies and change in destination marketing organizations. *Journal of Travel Research* 39(2): 149–156.

Halkier, H. (2014). Innovation and destination governance in Denmark: Tourism, policy networks and spatial development. *European Planning Studies* 22(8): 1659–1670.

Harrill, R. (2005a). *Fundamentals of Destination Management and Marketing*. Washington, DC: IACVB.

Harrill, R. (2005b). *Guide to Best Practises in Tourism and Destination Management: Volume 2*. Lansing, MI: EIAHLA.

Hollingshead, K. (2001). Policy in paradise: The history of incremental politics in the tourism of island-state Fiji. *Tourism* 49(4): 327–348.

Kelly, I. and Nankervis, K. (2001). *Visitor Destinations*. Milton, QLD: John Wiley & Sons.

Kerr, W. (2004). *Tourism Public Policy and the Strategic Management of Failure*. Oxford: Elsevier.

Kerr, W. and Wood, R. C. (2000). Tourism policy and politics in a devolved Scotland. In Robinson, M., Evans, N., Long, P., Sharpley, R. and Swarbrooke, J. (eds) *Management, Marketing and the Political Economy of Travel and Tourism*. Sunderland, UK: The Centre for Travel & Tourism, pp. 284–296.

Lathrop, J. (2005). Board governance. In Harrill, R. (ed.) *Fundamentals of Destination Management and Marketing*. Washington, DC: IACVB, pp. 191–218.

Lemmetyinen, A. and Go, F. (2009). The key capabilities required for managing tourism business networks. *Tourism Management* 30(1): 31–40.

Lennon, J. J., Smith, H., Cockerell, N. and Trew, J. (2006). *Benchmarking National Tourism Organisations and Agencies: Understanding Best Practice*. Oxford: Elsevier.

Meethan, K. (2002). Selling the difference: Tourism marketing in Devon and Cornwall, South-West England. In Voase, R. (ed.) *Tourism in Western Europe: A Collection of Case Histories*. Oxford: CABI Publishing, pp. 23–42.

Morrison, A. M., Braunlich, C. G., Kamaruddin, N. and Cai, L. A. (1995). National tourist offices in North America: An analysis. *Tourism Management* 16(8): 605–617.

Morrison, A. M., Bruen, S. M. and Anderson, D. J. (1998). Convention and visitor bureaus in the USA: A profile of bureaus, bureau executives, and budgets. *Journal of Travel and Tourism Marketing* 7(1): 1–19.

Page, S. J. and Connell, J. (2009). *Tourism: A Modern Synthesis* (3rd edition). Andover, UK: Cengage Learning.

Palmer, A. (1998). Evaluating the governance style of marketing groups. *Annals of Tourism Research* 25(1): 185–201.

Pattinson, G. (1990). Place promotion by tourist boards: The example of 'Beautiful Berkshire'. In Ashworth, G. and Goodall, B. (eds) *Marketing Tourism Places*. New York: Routledge, pp. 209–226.

Pearce, D. G. (1996). Tourist organizations in Sweden. *Tourism Management* 17(6): 413–424.

Pike, S. (2004). *Destination Marketing Organisations*. Oxford: Elsevier Science.

Pike, S. (2008). *Destination Marketing: An Integrated Marketing Communication Approach*. Burlington, MA: Butterworth-Heinemann.

Pike, S. and Page, S. (2014). Destination marketing organizations and destination marketing: A narrative analysis of the literature. *Tourism Management* 41: 202–227.

Poetschke, B. (1995) Key success factors for public/private-sector partnerships in island tourism planning. In Conlin, M. V. and Baum, T. (eds) *Island Tourism*. Chichester, UK: John Wiley & Sons Ltd.

Ruhanen, L., Scott, N., Ritchie, B. and Tkacynski, A. (2010). Governance: A review and synthesis of the literature. *Tourism Review* 65(4): 4–16.

Smith, S. L. J. (2003). A vision for the Canadian tourism industry. *Tourism Management* 24(1): 123–133.

The Royal Gazette. (2015). Available at: http://www.royalgazette.com/article/20150124/COMMENT01/150129828

Tourism Strategy Group. (2001). *New Zealand Tourism Strategy: 2010*. Tourism New Zealand. Available at: www.tourisminfo.co.nz. May.

UNWTO. (1975). *Aims, Activities, and Fields of Competence of National Tourism Organizations*. Madrid, Spain: UNWTO.

Vallee, P. (2005). Destination management in Canada. In Harrill, R. (ed.) *Fundamentals of Destination Management and Marketing*. Washington, DC: IACVB, pp. 229–244.

Wahab, S., Crampon, L. J. and Rothfield, L. M. (1976). *Tourism Marketing*. London, UK: Tourism International Press.

Wang, L. (2013). Review on tourist destination governance in foreign countries. *Tourism Tribune* 28(6): 15–25.

Wang, Y. (2008). Collaborative destination marketing: Roles and strategies of convention and visitors bureaus. *Journal of Vacation Marketing* 14(3): 191–209.

Wintermans, J. (1994). The problem of articulate incompetence. *Canadian Business Review* Spring: 42–43.

Zhang, H. and Zhu, M. (2014). Tourism destination governance: A review and research agenda. *International Journal of e-Education, e-Business, e-Management and e-Learning* 4(2): 125–128.

Chapter **6**

The destination marketing organisation (DMO), meetings and events

AIMS

To enhance understanding of:

- the importance of the meetings and events sectors for destinations;
- the importance of a destination's image in attracting meetings, events and participants;
- key objectives in the DMO's strategy to attract meetings and events.

ABSTRACT

Travel to attend business, sporting, spiritual and cultural events represents a major sector of the visitor industry and therefore presents opportunities for destinations worldwide to stimulate the creation of new events and to bid for existing special events that periodically rotate venues. Importantly, for the majority of DMOs, event tourism represents one of the few opportunities to be directly involved in new product development. Also, meetings and events provide opportunities to enhance occupancy and patronage at a wide range of local businesses and are particularly sought after during off-peak periods or extensions of peak periods. Recognition of the value of the meetings and events sectors has seen an increasing number of DMOs develop convention bureaus and event tourism specialists to enhance destination competitiveness. While there has been relatively little published research into meeting and event destination attractiveness, it is clear that in addition to the functional facilities, a critical factor is the promotional appeal of the destination to participants. DMOs and convention and visitors bureaus (CVBs) use a range of promotional activities to enhance perceptions of the destination in the minds of influential event planners responsible for destination selection, since destination image plays a major role in both the venue selection process and the ensuing attendance by participants and their partners.

Meetings, incentives, conferences and exhibitions (MICE)

Travel to attend meetings is a major sector in the visitor industry, representing one of the fastest growing tourism segments and second main purpose for travel around the world (TravelandTourWorld, 2015a). Destination Marketing Association International (DMAI) (2013) estimated the value of the meetings sector in the USA to be worth over US$1 trillion annually, supporting 7 million jobs and generating over US$1 billion in tax revenue. In Australia over 37 million people attended over 412,000 business events during the 2013–2014 financial year, generating AUD$28 billion and directly employing 180,000 workers (www. travelandtourworld.com, 23 February 2014). In South Korea spending by MICE-related visitors exceeds that for leisure travellers (see http://investseoul.com/industries/mice-industry). In the UK the meetings and events industry is estimated to be worth around £60 billion annually, which is three times that of the agricultural sector (Hall and Ledger, 2015). Over 1.3 million meetings were staged in the UK in 2011, attended by 116 million people, who each spent an average of £40, employing over half a million people and generating over £20 billion in tax revenue.

While the need to meet in person to discuss common interests has been a major part of human activity since ancient times (see Fenich, 2005), views are divided about the impact of electronic meeting mediums, such as teleconferencing. On the one hand, it has been suggested that internet technologies have not made a significant impact on the growth of the meetings sector (Davidson and Rogers, 2006: 3):

> *Man is, above all, a gregarious animal, and there can be no doubt that the need to gather regularly with others who share a common interest is one of the most human of all activities.*

> *Business works best in real time, real touch networks. Meeting face to face remains the ultimate way to plug into a business network.*
>
> *(Queensland Business Acumen, May, 2007, in Pike, 2008: 308)*

Also, in 2007, *Future Watch*, an annual survey of the meetings industry undertaken by Meetings Professionals International, found virtual meetings were not a major component of participants' activities. More recently, however, a survey of 2,000 employees of UK companies found 54 per cent agreed a Skype call would have been preferred to their recent travel to attend a meeting (TravelIndustryWire, 2015). Nevertheless, the sector continues to have significant year-on-year growth, even since the 2008 global financial crisis (ICCA, 2014).

Since the majority of meetings involve fewer than 1,000 delegates, most tourism destinations are able to cater to the market (Abbey and Link, 1994, in Oppermann, 1996). The meetings market is generally more resilient than holiday segments during periods of economic downturn and also offers the destination the opportunity to build additional business during the off-peak periods and to extend peak periods. The most common form of meetings are *corporate* events such as annual general meetings, sales meetings, staff training retreats, product launches and incentive trips. Other buyers of destination meeting services are associations, the public sector and SMERFs, the name given to social, military, religious and fraternal groups. The characteristics of these major segments are summarised in Table 6.1. ICCA's (2014) annual worldwide ranking of the top ten association meetings destinations for 2013, based on the number of international meetings, is summarised in Table 6.2. The top ten cities based on the number of international association meetings held were: Paris (204), Madrid (186), Vienna (182), Barcelona (179), Berlin (178), Singapore (175), London (166), Istanbul (146), Lisbon (125) and Seoul (125).

The term *meeting* is used to describe a multiplicity of business and social events. For example, Fenich (2005) listed 47 synonyms, ranging from *buzz session* to *congress*. For a set of definitions of the key forms of meetings of interest to destination marketers, refer to the Convention Industry Council's Accepted

Table 6.1 Characteristics of major meetings segments

Corporate	The process of deciding to hold events is relatively straight forward.
	However, the actual corporate meeting buyer may be difficult to identify within the initiator's organisation: secretaries, personal assistants, marketing executives, directors of training and many others may book corporate events.
	• Attendance is usually required of company employees.
	• Lead times can be short.
	• A higher budget per delegate.
	• Venues used include hotels, management training centres and unusual venues.
	• Delegates' partners are rarely invited, except in the case of incentive trips.
Association	The process of choosing a destination can be prolonged. A committee is usually involved in the choosing of the destination, and the organisers may be volunteers from the association's membership.
	• Attendance is voluntary.
	• A lower budget per delegate, since for some attendees, price is a sensitive issue and they may be paying their own costs.
	• Venues used include conference centres, civic and academic venues.
	• Delegates' partners frequently attend.
Government	Considerable variety in terms of length of event and budgets available. However, budgets are usually highly scrutinised, since public money is being used. High security measures are indispensable: these meetings are frequently accompanied by demonstrations and disruptions.
SMERF	Price sensitive regarding accommodation rates and venue rates, but more recession proof than corporate meetings. Held by organisations that are run by volunteers – so the task of identifying them can be challenging.
	• Frequently held over weekends and in off-peak periods.
	• Often held in second tier cities, using simple accommodation and facilities.
	• Attended by delegates who bring their spouses/families and are likely to extend their trips for leisure purposes.

Source: Adapted from Davidson and Rogers (2006).

Practices Exchange (APEX – see www.conventionindustry.org/glossary). APEX is an initiative that aims to unite the meetings industry in the development and implementation of voluntary standards of accepted practices.

Retreats involve relatively small business groups, such as a board of directors, a sales team or a faculty's academic team for example, who benefit from a change of scenery for private meetings necessitating creative thinking such as strategic and marketing planning brainstorming. The venue will commonly be an all-inclusive resort to keep the team together and enhance bonding and sharing of ideas. *Conclaves* are political, religious and business gatherings that are held in secret behind closed doors. Probably the most famous conclave is when a meeting of the Roman Catholics' College of Cardinals is

Table 6.2 The world's top ten association meetings destinations

Ranking	Country	Number of international meetings in 2013
1	USA	829
2	Germany	722
3	Spain	562
4	France	527
5	UK	525
6	Italy	447
7	Japan	342
8	People's Republic of China	340
9	Brazil	315
10	Netherlands	302

Source: Adapted from ICCA (2014).

convened in Rome to elect a new Pope. *Seminars* and workshops are usually shorter meetings of up to a day, for the purposes of information sharing and/or staff training. *Conferences* are an event where the primary activity of the attendees is to attend educational sessions, participate in meetings/discussions, socialise or attend other organised events. There is no exhibition component to this type of meeting. *Conventions* are an event where the primary activity of the attendees is to attend educational sessions, participate in meetings/discussions, socialise or attend other organised events. There is a secondary exhibit component. *Congresses* are very large international meetings involving representatives from many countries. For example, the annual Federation Internationale de l'Art Photographique Congress, which will be held in Seoul, South Korea in 2016, brings together over 800 top photographers from 60 countries (see http://webzine.miceseoul.com/seoul-wins-bid-for-2016-international-photography-congress). However, the attendance number pales in comparison to medical congresses in the USA, the largest of which attract over 20,000 delegates (see http://www.medical.theconferencewebsite.com/medical-conferences-2015).

Trade exhibitions/shows are events at which products and services are displayed. The primary activity of attendees is visiting exhibits on the show floor. These events focus primarily on business-to-business (B2B) relationships and are not usually open to the general public. *Public exhibitions/expos* are displays of products and/or services, which are open to the public, and usually have an admission fee. For example, the 2015 Leather Expo in Bangkok, which is organised by the Thai government, was expected to attract over 200 leather manufacturing companies and 25,000 visitors (TravelandTourWorld.com, 2015b). These extend to outdoor events such as the annual agricultural shows that are popular in the UK, New Zealand and Australia. For example, the *Ekka*, which is the Royal Queensland Show held in Brisbane every August, is typical of these city-meets-country events. *Ekka* is Queensland slang for *exhibition*. Over 400,000 people visit the 10-day event that features around 20,000 rural competition entries. A similar type of gathering is horticulture-based. Arguably the best known of these is the Chelsea Flower Show, which has been held annually in London since 1913. The event is so popular that a cap has had to be placed on the maximum number of visitors to the showground.

Incentive travel programmes

Incentive travel programmes were introduced by corporations as a means to motivate staff to achieve targets and improve productivity. Such targets are related to business objectives and commonly involve sales increases or cost reductions. In addition to the achievement of the corporate objectives, other benefits to the organisation of incentive travel include (Witt and Gammon, 1994):

- opportunities for networking and communication between staff and management;
- opportunities for social interaction between those working independently, such as sales reps and dealers;
- conveys a sense of belonging;
- generates enthusiasm;
- fosters loyalty to the company and retains top performers.

There are two characteristics of the incentive travel market that have particular appeal to DMOs. First, this type of travel usually takes place in groups, and often very large groups, such as the 10,000 Japanese door-to-door bra saleswomen hosted by Sydney, Australia (Pike, 2004). Second, the tailored nature of reward packages tends to generate a higher than average yield for service providers.

Incentive travel planning is a specialised craft, and destinations targeting this segment need to carefully consider the resources required to effectively cater for their unique requirements. Itineraries are custom-made to suit the needs of the group, rather than off-the-shelf offerings, and tend to be creative in terms of inventive activities at distinctive venues. Witt and Gammon (1994) suggested only destinations at the mature stage of the lifecycle need apply, since there needs to be a well-developed infrastructure, good accessibility and a sufficient mix of attractions.

For the incentive to appeal to staff, the itinerary needs to be attractive, and the destination needs to be well-known and have a certain *brag value*. Travel time to the destination is also important, given that incentive group travel is commonly in the form of a short break. Promotion is clearly very targeted, usually involving personal selling, coordinated by the DMO, to incentivise travel specialists who are contracted by the corporation.

IN PRACTICE

6.1 The million dollar memo

During 2011, to increase awareness of incentive travel opportunities in Queensland, the STO sent out a *million dollar memo* to businesses inviting them to compete for a prize of AUD$1 million worth of incentive travel experiences, which would be tailored for the winning company. The incentive trip competition was open to any organisation around the world. Entry required the submission of a video outlining why the organisation was a great place to work and why Queensland is the ultimate incentive travel destination.

Within a week of the launch of the AUD$6.9 million campaign, the *million dollar memo* website had attracted 32,000 visitors and the story picked up by 270 media outlets around the world. Eventually, 20 organisations were shortlisted and required to send a staff representative to a 10-day long Incentive Challenge Event to decide the winner.

In 2014 and 2015 the concept was copied by Meet Taiwan, which ran the online incentive business competition *Asia super team: Team up for good*. The competition was limited to businesses in Australia, Japan, Malaysia, South Korea and Thailand, where one team from each was selected to visit Taiwan for an incentive travel trip. The winning team received a prize of US$50,000.

Further reading

http://www.campaignbrief.com/2011/03/tourism-queensland-sends-out-m.html

http://www.news.com.au/travel/travel-updates/queensland-offers-ultimate-million-dollar-holiday/story-e6frfq80-1226025946164

http://www.travelandtourworld.com/news/article/meet-taiwan-asia-super-team-campaign-returns-successful-launch-2014

Convention bureaus

The meetings market brings together a diversity of businesses such as hotels, convention centres, transport operators, attractions, caterers, professional conference organisers (PCO) and entertainers. The complex web of relationships between stakeholders necessitates coordination at the destination level, ranging from a dedicated DMO staff member to a fully fledged CVB. Not all DMOs operate a convention bureau, due to the specialised nature of operations and the level of investment required. For example, in Queensland Australia, only 6 of the state's 14 RTOs have a convention bureau.

As discussed in Chapter 2, the CVB format emanated in the USA, where the first were established in Milwaukee and Des Moines in 1888 (Ford and Peeper, 2008), followed by Detroit in 1896 (Gartrell, 1994), Atlantic City in 1908, Denver in 1909 and Atlanta in 1913 (www.iacvb.org, in Pike, 2008). The USA also developed the first purpose built convention centres during the 1960s. For a wealth of practitioner insights about management and best practice at CVBs in the USA, see Harrill (2005a, 2005b) and Ford and Peeper (2008). In Mexico the first CVB was established in Guadalajara in 1969 (Cerda, 2005). However, it was not until the 1980s that the Mexican government provided funding for the CVBs, and this stimulated the establishment of over 40 CVBs during the late 1990s and early 2000s. The first UK CVBs were formed in the 1980s (see Rogers, 2005). Interestingly, the first national CVBs were not established until 1973 (Germany) and 1974 (Finland).

Associations of CVBs and stakeholders

DMOs understand relatively few conferences will return to the same destination every year. National association conferences commonly circulate around a country in a cyclical manner. Consider the locations of the academic Tourism and Travel Research Association (TTRA) (responsible for the *Journal of Travel Research*) conference from 1970 to 2015 (see http://www.ttra.com/about-us/history-of-ttra). Like the Olympic Games, it is possible to secure a return conference after a period of time. Some DMOs, therefore, see merit in forming alliances with other destinations. The key rationales for this are the sharing of resources and a greater presence in the market. For example, imagine an association conference in the USA that alternates between the West Coast, East Coast and Mid-West. If a member of the alliance on the West Coast has successfully hosted the association's conference this year, a member on the East Coast seeking to bid the following year can obtain insights into the bid process's critical success factors for that particular association. This is mutually beneficial to the association and the DMO alliance.

In 1914 the International Association of Convention Bureaus, later to become the International Association of Convention and Visitor Bureaus in 1974 (IACVB), and now known as DMAI, was formed with 28 members. DMAI now has 600 members, predominantly in North America. From a meetings marketing perspective, membership benefits of DMAI include (see www.iacvb.org):

- The Destination Showcase. In the USA, the only tradeshow purposefully designed for destination exhibitors is the DMAI's annual Destination Showcase. An average of 70 per cent of meeting planners in attendance walk the floor with a Request for Proposals (RFP) in hand. These attendees on average plan 11 meetings a year, including one outside the USA (see www.destinationsshowcaseonline.com).

- The Meeting Industry Network. An online database of over 32,000 past and future meetings by over 16,000 organisations.

- Lead generation. DMAI provides online RFP distribution by meeting planners.

- Meeting Industry Almanac. Convention bureaus can host over 30,000 meetings professionals in the annual *Meeting Industry Forecast*.

- Professional in Destination Management Certificate programme.

The BestCities Global Alliance (www.bestcities.net) was the first truly international alliance of convention bureaus, with eight partners in five continents: Cape Town, Copenhagen, Dubai, Edinburgh, Melbourne, San Juan, Singapore and Vancouver. The alliance promotes the following advantages to conference organisers:

- Global access – one email or phone call provides access to the most professional convention bureaus and attractive destinations in the world.

- Innovative bid proposals – members work with local industry suppliers, public sectors and DMOs to ensure the client's requirements are met.

- Expert advice – on all aspects of planning a meeting at the chosen destination.

- Quality assurance – all member bureaus undergo a rigorous inspection and approval process and are continuously monitored by client evaluations.

- Client forums – a platform for peer-to-peer networking and discussion of topics related to managing international organisations and planning their meetings.

Seventeen countries banded together in 2014 to form the European National Convention Bureaux (Oates, 2014). The purpose of the collaboration was to better compete with emerging meeting destinations who had become more aggressive in the US market, such as Brazil and New Zealand. By 2015 membership had increased to 22 member nations, although no website had been developed. Leading professional bodies for the meetings sector are listed in Table 6.3.

Bidding process

The CVB or DMO is seen as an impartial information source for meeting professionals. When a PCO, organisation or association contacts the CVB, the office acts as a facilitator of tailored information on suitable facilities. The CVB in turn manages a leads process for members to bid for the business. This can extend to social and entertainment services, in addition to meeting space and accommodation requirements. For example, the Las Vegas CVB sent out 3,000 leads to local businesses during 2003

Table 6.3 Professional meetings organisations

Organisation	URL
Destination Marketing Association International	www.iacvb.org
Meeting Professionals International	http://www.mpiweb.org
Union of International Associations	www.uia.org
International Congress and Convention Association	www.iccaworld.com
Meetings Industry Association of Australia	www.meetingsevents.com.au
Meetings Industry Association of the UK	www.mia-uk.org
Trade Show Exhibitors Association	www.tsea.org
Joint Meetings Industry Council	www.themeetingsindustry.org
International Association of Exposition Managers	www.iaem.org
International Association of Fairs and Expositions	www.fairsandexpos.com
Convention Liaison Council	www.conventionindustry.org
Professional Convention Management Association	www.pcma.org
Society of Incentive Travel Executives	www.site-intl.org
International Association of Professional Congress Organisers	www.iapco.org
Convention Industry Council	www.conventionindustry.org
Association of British Professional Conference Organisers	www.abpco.org
Association of Australian Convention Bureaux	www.aacb.org.au

(Cortez, 2004). In June 2015 the European Travel Commission and the UNWTO organised a two-day seminar in Antwerp to present 'the key criteria that influence the choice of a destination by meeting planners' (TravelandTourWorld, 2015c). The general steps in the meeting bidding process involve (Harris *et al.*, 2005: 33):

- identifying meetings with the potential to be hosted by the destination and encouraging local associations and firms to bid for their organisation's conference;

- obtaining the bid criteria from the association;

- seeking clarification on the bidding process and working with the local association to develop a bid document;

- involving a professional meeting planner in budget development;

- conducting a site inspection;

- lodging the bid and undertaking destination promotional activities;

- for successful bids, engaging in promotional activity aimed at potential delegates.

Digital destination planning guides

Tourism Toronto claimed the launch of its new digital destination planner in 2005 was the first of its kind in North America. Designed for meeting professionals and tour operators, *Digital Toronto* provides a link to a product and services directory that is updated monthly (see www.tourismtoronto.com). Online planner's guides are now expected at destinations. For example, while the Melbourne Convention Bureau's 2015 Melbourne Planners' Guide was freely available in print form, an updated version was available online (see http://www.melbournecb.com.au/meetings-events/planners-guide).

Local support

Encouraging local business associations and clubs to bid for meetings is a major part of conference marketing. The stimulus for destinations hosting associations' meetings, for example, is usually the local members of the association. The DMO should alert such groups to the value for the destination of attracting meetings of their national and international associations, as well as the availability of DMO staff to help coordinate the bid process.

Destination attractiveness

The promotional activities of convention bureaus are still based on the marketing orientation of matching available resources with environment opportunities. The convention bureau is engaged in targeting appropriate buyers with a meaningful value proposition. It is just as important to monitor how the destination is perceived by meeting planners as it is by consumers. Image is important in the meetings market, since conventions are usually held in places that are attractive to potential delegates. However, Oppermann (1996), Chacko and Fenich (2000) and Pike (2002, 2007) have highlighted the lack of research into what makes an attractive convention destination. Of the 263 destination image studies tabled by Pike (2002, 2007), only 6 were in the context of conventions. Chacko and Fenich's (2000) content analysis of previous studies enabled a synthesis of important convention destination attributes. They identified 12 such attributes for use in their survey of convention planners' perceptions of 7 destinations. Regression analysis identified *promotional appeal* as a significant predictor for overall convention destination attractiveness for most of the cities in the study. The most critical factor, they concluded, was the convention planner's ability to sell the destination to potential delegates.

RESEARCH SNAPSHOT

6.1 Convention destination image

Oppermann (1996) identified a paucity of published research into convention destination images with which to guide destination marketers. He chose to gain insights into how 30 North American cities were perceived as convention destinations from the perspective of association meeting planners. Association conferences are reasonably flexible in terms of destination selection, and association planners are akin to tour operators who are involved in selecting a destination and on-selling to members. Planners are only too aware that potential delegates usually have a selection of conferences on offer each year, and the choice of destination plays a role in decision making. The study targeted members of the Professional Convention Management Association. In the sample, 79 per cent of participants indicated their responsibilities included selection of the conference destination. The results provided rankings of the importance of 15 convention destination attributes, along with how each of the 30 destinations was perceived on each attribute. This approach enabled an understanding of how each destination is positioned relative to competing places. Two further implications were noted. First, the association convention planners differed in their destination selection criteria, in terms of attribute importance. Second, previous experience with a destination emerged as a crucial factor in destination image.

Further reading

Oppermann, M. (1996).

Activities for delegates' partners

It is common practice at major meetings to offer social activities and sightseeing tours for delegates' partners, while meetings are in session, in order to increase visitor numbers. Pre and post meeting tours are also used to increase length of stay. Hence the importance of a destination's promotional appeal in luring delegates' partners.

Cruise lines as new competition to conference destinations

Cruise companies see the same benefits in conference events as DMOs and are increasingly competing with destinations for a share of the market. In this regard, it is worth noting Plog's (2000) prediction that *managed* destinations, such as resorts and cruise ships, would become increasingly popular in the future due to their ability to manage capacity and maintain consistency of quality. Many ships now feature conference facilities and are price competitive due to the all-inclusive nature of their product. For example, recent academic conference cruises have included:

- The 5th International Interdisciplinary Business and Economics' (IIBA) conference in November 2015 was held on the Royal Caribbean cruise line out of Fort Lauderdale, USA.

- The 3rd International Interdisciplinary Business and Economics' (IIBA) conference in March/April 2015 was held on the Royal Caribbean cruise line out of Fort Lauderdale, USA.

- The International Society of Travel and Tourism Educators' (ISTTE) 2010 conference was held on the Carnival cruise line out of Los Angeles, USA.

Event tourism

In the modern era, the first *special event* was probably London's Great Exhibition of 1851, which attracted the curiosity of visitors in their millions. The success of the event led to Vienna copying the concept in 1863, followed by Paris in 1878 (see Elliott, 1997). Then in 1885 the International Association of Fairs and Expositions launched half a dozen fairs (Getz, 2008). The scale of the special events sector is now so great that the International Festival and Event Association, established in 1956, estimates that over 1 million events each year are now of a size necessitating government support (http://www.ifea.com). The scale of the sector has motivated many destinations to establish specialist event tourism units or coordinators. For example, the 2004 Tourism Australia Act of Parliament required the NTO to establish a unit focusing on the business and event tourism sectors (Stokes, 2008).

Getz (2008) reported the first academic conferences on special events were convened by TTRA Canada in 1985 and the International Association of Scientific Experts in Tourism in 1987. The topic's increasing importance in tourism literature has been recognised with a number of specialist journals commencing since the 1990s, such as *Event Management*, *Convention and Event Tourism*, *Journal of Event Management Research* and the *World Journal of Managing Events*. A special issue on 'Contemporary issues in events, festivals and destination management' was announced for 2016 in the *International Journal of Contemporary Hospitality Management*. The first book was by Getz (1997). For an in-depth review of the literature related to event tourism, which commenced in 1974, see Getz (2008). At the time of writing in 2015 this was the most downloaded article from leading journal *Tourism Management*, which reflects the popularity of the topic among academic researchers. The introduction by Getz (1997: 403) stated:

> *Events are an important motivator of tourism, and figure prominently in the development and marketing plans of most destinations. The roles and impacts of planned events within tourism have been well documented, and are of increasing importance for destination competitiveness. Yet it was only a few decades ago that 'event tourism' became established in the research community, so that the subsequent growth of this sector can only be described as spectacular.*

Destinations host a range of events that are gained from competitive bids, created locally for tourism, or were developed as grassroots community occasions (Stokes, 2008). As well as attracting visitors, such events also provide opportunities for the local community to be involved as either participants or spectators. A typology of such planned events is shown in Table 6.4.

It has been suggested by Getz (2008) that the term *event tourism* was possibly first used in 1987 by the New Zealand Tourist and Publicity Department. The term has been defined as (Getz, 1997: 16): 'The planning, development and marketing of events as tourist attractions to maximise the number of tourists participating in events as either primary or secondary attractions'.

Explicit in this definition is the notion that events can be a form of product development. Events therefore are one of the few, if not only, forms of direct involvement in new product development for the majority of DMOs. The different types of initiatives in this regard have included:

Table 6.4 Typology of planned events

Cultural celebrations
Festivals, carnivals, commemorations and religious events

Political and state
Summits, royal occasions, government events and VIP visits

Arts and entertainment
Concerts and award ceremonies

Sporting competitions
Amateur and professional

Private
Weddings, parties and socials

Source: Adapted from Getz (2008).

- During 2015 NTO EventScotland launched a new £200,000 grant fund to help develop new events for the planned 2016 Year of Innovation, Architecture and Design.

- To increase awareness of new events, STO Events Victoria provides an online database. The event listings are self-authored so that anyone can create a listing for their event (see http://www.eventsvictoria.com/about/what-is-events-victoria).

- At the larger RTO level, the city of Melbourne provides an online event management guide to planning events in the state of Victoria (http://www.melbourne.vic.gov.au/enterprisemelbourne/promote/documents/eventsguide181207.pdf).

- At a smaller RTO level, the Dubbo events strategy promotes a *whole of council* approach to the way different departments of the local government can support new event development (DCC, 2012).

Sports events

Sports events are, of course, not a modern phenomenon. As early as the eighth century BC in ancient Greece, travellers visited places such as Olympia and Delphi for the games. Romero (2013), for example, cited reports from the 143rd Olympic Games that were staged in the year 208 BC, the games at Delphi occurring before in 425 BC and another which estimated that up to 50,000 people had travelled to these ancient games at Olympia. The three types of people present at these games, as summarised in this quote about a view of philosophy from Pythagoras, are the same as in event tourism today – the competitors, the vendors and the spectators:

> *Pythagoras replied that the life of man seemed to him to represent the festival which was celebrated with [the] most magnificent games before a concourse collected from the whole of Greece; for at this festival [were] some men whose bodies had been trained so as to win the glorious distinction of a crown, others were attracted by the prospect of making gain by buying or selling, whilst there was on the other hand a certain class, and that quite the best type of free-born man, who looked neither for applause nor gain, but came for the sake of the spectacle and closely watched what was done and how it was done.*
>
> *(Romero, 2013: 149)*

The city of Indianapolis in the USA has been described as a classic case study of how sporting events can be used to generate a civic turnaround (Rozin, 2000, in Getz, 2008). As an aside, 2016 will mark the 100th running of the Indianapolis 500 motor race. Similarly, during 2003, the Dublin Chamber of Commerce reported an otherwise flat tourism season was 'kept alive' by a series of major events, including the Special Olympics. Today the highest profile events in the world are sports-related. At the pinnacle of these are, of course, the FIFA World Cup and the Olympic Games. In a remarkable coup for Brazil, the country secured the rights to host both events in quick succession, in 2014 and 2016. The 2008 Olympics in China attracted over 11,000 athletes and set a record for the most viewed games ever, watched by an estimated 70 per cent of the global population (Neilson, 2008, in Li and Kaplanidou, 2013). Li and Kaplanidou cited evidence suggesting increases in visitors for the host nation of just over two per cent in the four years leading up to the games and in the four years afterwards. Bidding for mega-events such as the Olympic Games and FIFA World Cup are beyond the reach of the majority of DMOs. However, there are a plethora of smaller events that are within the reach of most DMOs, and so the sector is an important target in any destination marketing plan. After all, it has been suggested that sports and related recreation make up at least 25 per cent of tourism activity (Research Unit, 1994, in Pitts and Ayers, 2000). At the time of writing, the *Journal of Sport and Tourism* had planned a 2016 special issue on 'Sport tourism destinations'. An example of one little known sports event attracting around 4,000 visitors, which DMOs can help bidding for, is discussed in case study 6.1.

CASE STUDY

6.1 Interhash: The drinking club with a running problem

The little known Interhash (see www.interhash.com) is the gathering of hash house harriers from around the world and has since the early 1990s regularly attracted over 4,000 participants. Importantly the participants are not competitors, as this is mostly a series of social events for the organisation that describes itself as a *drinking club with a running problem*. Until recently, the number of participants at this Interhash event has been greater than the number of competitors at the Commonwealth Games, which is an Olympic Games style event for countries belonging to the British Commonwealth. Interhash is held in a different region every two years and, like most global events, operates a bid process for interested destinations. DMOs usually support a bid by the local hash house harriers clubs, who are required to lodge a bid document with the following information, as listed on www.interhash.com in May 2015:

Interhash bidders should prepare a 1 page outline of their business plan and provide it to the next Interhash magazine editor for inclusion in the magazine given to every attending Interhasher. It is also recommended that every bidder presents this plan on their Interhash bid website.

Details of location, date, venue, running areas, planned program, goodie bag, accommodation availability, transportation arrangements, etc.

Information about the Hashers and Hash Chapters who are committing to hosting the Interhash.

Information on registration costs for the basic Interhash comprising welcoming party with hash runs on the following 2 days including registration fee structure.

Information on additional activities including Charity Run, pre and post ambles.

Commitment to audited financial report within six months of the Interhash conclusion with details of plans for distribution of surplus funds.

Global members on the Interhash delegates mailing list then democratically vote for their preferred destination. What heightens the intrigue in the destination selection process is the requirement for all bids to be posted on the Interhash website for all members to consider, a practice that is quite unusual since event bidding is usually a confidential process.

Discussion question

For a destination to host Interhash, what key attributes would impress members in the competitive bid process?

Festivals

A festival has been defined as a 'public, themed celebration' (Getz, 1997: 8). Such events have the potential to increase a community's sense of place and local pride, as well as increase visitor arrivals as part of the experience economy. For a review of the academic literature related to festivals, see Getz (2008). For an overview of event management and a series of destination case studies see Allen *et al.* (2005).

Despite the high profile of national and international sports events, as many if not more people attend events related to culture and the arts, which are not the sole domain of the major cities. There are various forms of sports-related festivals. One is in the style of the Golden Oldies amateur sports movement, which offers opportunities for people over 35 years of age to participate in a week of social events and games related to their favourite sport (see http://www.goldenoldiessports.com). The organisation, which has over 20,000 members, offers annual festivals of rugby, golf, cricket, hockey and netball, each at a different destination each year, underpinned by the motto *fun, friendship and fraternity*. Recent destinations hosting one of the festivals have included: Cardiff, Wales (rugby); Barbados, West Indies (cricket); Rotorua, New Zealand (golf); Hawaii (hockey); and Hobart, Australia (netball). Another type of sports festival is one wrapped around a major event. These can be one-off, due to the rotation of the venue, such as the Festival of Rugby 2015 in the UK for the Rugby World Cup. Over 250,000 people are expected to attend the festival events at a range of locations around England and Wales. The rugby tournament, which is held in a different country every four years, is expected to generate £2.2 billion in the UK economy. To raise awareness of the festival, Visit England coordinated a year-long domestic *Home of Sport* marketing campaign on social media and television, which was based on England's historic sporting heritage (Travelandtourworld.com, 2015d). In other cases a festival might be developed to wrap around a regular major sporting event. For example, the Grand Prix weekend festival in Montreal attracts around 300,000 visitors. A further sports-related festival is where a group of small events are combined under a theme, such as in the case of the Hunter Festival of Sport in New South Wales, Australia. The festival, which is held during the mid-year school break each year, combines a series of come-and-try events and coaching clinics.

Other common themes tend to be festivals which are a celebration of:

- **Writers**

The coastal New South Wales town of Byron Bay is a useful example of how a small community can develop an attractive festival based around writing. The largest regional event of its type in Australia, the 2015 Byron Bay Writers Festival brought around 140 influential writers, TV presenters and even a former Prime Minister and former state Premier for three days of talks and workshops. Byron Bay is well-known as a summer beach holiday destination and the festival, which takes place during the off-peak winter period, coincides with the annual migration of whales along the coast.

- **Music**

All day music festivals are now common in many parts of the world, staged either annually or as one-off events. Genres are varied and include bluegrass (e.g. North Wales Bluegrass Festival), blues and roots (Bluesfest, Byron Bay), classical and opera (e.g. Edinburgh International Festival), heavy metal and rock (e.g. Whitby Goth Festival), tribute bands (e.g. Glastonbury), jazz (Monterey Jazz Festival), punk (e.g. Manchester Punk Festival), folk (e.g. Woodford Folk Festival), ethnic (e.g. Leeds Asian Festival) and electronic (e.g. Chemical Music, Rio de Janeiro). In recent years there has been a trend towards a franchise of touring festivals such as Big Day Out in Australia and Radio 1's Big Weekend in the UK. The Isle of Wight in the UK is well-known for hosting music festivals of a longer duration, such as Bestival and Isle of Wight Festival, which are three-day events.

- **Gastronomy**

Ho Chi Minh City holds an annual Southern Cuisine Festival to celebrate the culinary delights of Southern Vietnam. In New Zealand many towns and cities hold traditional Maori kai (food) festivals. Among the best known are: Hokitika Wild Foods Festival on the South Island's West Coast; Maketu Kaimoana (seafood) Festival in the Bay of Plenty; Kawhia Kai Festival in the Waikato; and Te Ra o Waitangi in Wellington.

- **Fashion**

One of the most creative fashion festivals in the world is the annual World of Wearable Art in New Zealand. The festival originated as the Wearable Art Awards in the city of Nelson, but became so popular it had to be moved to the capital, Wellington. For a brief glimpse into the way in which fashion, art and theatre collide see http://worldofwearableart.com/about.

- **Culture**

It has been claimed the Gangneung Dano-je Festival has been held annually in the South Korean city for over 1,000 years (TPO, 2015). New Zealand's preeminent celebration of Maori culture is the annual Te Matatini National Kapa Haka Festival. At the core of the festival is a prestigious performing arts competition. The festival is held in a different town each year.

- **Spiritual**

The four-day MindBodySpirit Festival in Sydney is Australia's largest health and wellbeing event, featuring performances, displays and products related to spirituality, food, meditation and yoga, psychics, crystals and so on. The small Balinese town of Ubud, made famous in Elizabeth Gilbert's 2006 bestselling book *Eat, Pray, Love*, holds a six-day Bali Spirit Festival of yoga, dance and music.

- **Film**

Many communities now host some type of film festival. For example, Miami Film Month is a festival of film-related events organised by the Greater Miami Convention and Visitors Bureau in June each year. The small country town of Maryborough in Australia hosts their annual Mary Poppins Festival, which while not being a festival of films, celebrates the town's connection with Mary Poppins. Maryborough is the birthplace of Mary Poppins' writer P. L. Travers, whose novels inspired two Disney movies.

- **Art**

In the USA The Age of Rubens exhibition attracted 234,000 visitors to Toledo, mostly from interstate (Holcolmb, 1999). Gartrell (1994) reported the Street Art Fairs in Ann Arbor, Michigan, attracted over 500,000 attendees.

Wacky events

Another event category could be labelled odd, wacky or off-beat. For example, in August each year the tomato fight in the Spanish town of Bunol attracts around 30,000 participants (http://www.huffingtonpost.com/entry/la-tomatina-spain-tomato-fight-photos_55ddfbbee4b0a40aa3ad20ec).

Examples of wacky events that have been developed in the UK include (Ross, 2003):

- the world bog snorkelling championships at Llanwrtyd;
- Shrovetide football, with goalposts 4.8 kilometres apart, at Ashbourne;
- Up-Helly-Aa Viking Festival, which originated in the nineteenth century, in Lerwick;
- the Shrove Tuesday pancake race at Olney;

- the world coal carrying championships at Onsett;
- cheese rolling races, which date back 400 years, at Brockworth;
- the world toe wrestling championships at Wetton;
- the world stinging nettle challenge at Marchwood;
- gurning competition (pulling grotesque faces) at the Egremont Crab Fair;
- Stonehaven Fire Balling Festival.

Examples in other parts of the world include:

- the annual camel beauty pageant in Abu Dhabi, United Arab Emirates;
- Groundhog Day on 2 February in Punxsutawney, Pennsylvania, which attracts over 30,000 visitors to see groundhog *Punxsutawney Phil* emerge from hibernation;
- the world cow chip throwing championship in Beaver, Oklahoma;
- the Whitestone cheese rolling competition in Wendon Valley, New Zealand;
- the wife-carrying world championships in Sonkajarvi, Finland;
- the Palio of Siena horseraces around the central square in the medieval town of Siena, Italy;
- the Henley-on-Todd regatta in Alice Springs, Australia, where curious looking boats are raced by foot along the dry riverbed. The regatta is only cancelled when rain creates water in the Todd River!

IN PRACTICE

6.2 Zombie-infested obstacle courses

One creative event that has captured the interest of many destinations and people around the world is a zombie run, where runners try to complete a five kilometre course while being forced to evade zombies. Runners wear one or more tags or flags, which the zombies attempt to take from them to eliminate them. The races are often held near famous landmarks or in stadiums. Some events are held in the dark, such as the annual Dusk 'til Dawn race near London (http://zombieevacuation.com/one-event/dusk-till-dawn). Believed to have started in the USA, one of the major events is Run for Your Lives, organised by Singapore-based entertainment company Action X. In 2015 it was announced that the event would be staged in Australia for the first time (see https://www.facebook.com/rfylau?fref=ts). Promoted as 'part obstacle course, part music festival, and a full on encounter with the running dead', the event offers entrants to register as either runners or zombies. Both the one-off Sydney and Melbourne events, which would culminate in an Apocalypse party, were expected to attract visitors from around the country.

DMO event strategy

The strategy process for DMOs is presented as the subject of Chapter 8. For the event tourism component of the DMO strategy, Stokes (2008) identified three frameworks for decision making:

1. corporate, market-led;

2. community, destination-led;

3. synergistic.

Within the *corporate, market-led framework*, the strategy focus is on major events that represent significant tourism generators. Decision making is likely to be made by one or two agencies in this corporate-driven environment, rather than a collaborative process involving stakeholders. Also, decision criteria would focus on visitor numbers, spending and media exposure, rather than non-monetary criteria. In the *community, destination-led framework*, the focus is on a mix of events and where decision making involves consensus making among a wider group of stakeholders. Decision criteria involve more consideration of environmental, social and cultural impacts, rather than just economic benefits. For reviews of the range of possible positive and negative impacts of events see Allen *et al.* (2005) and Page and Connell (2009). This framework is particularly suited to smaller towns that are not usually involved in bidding for events, but which have a greater incidence of festivals. The *synergistic* framework straddles the other two approaches and is structured in a manner that seeks equitable input from government, business and the community. The strategy focus might seek to strive for a balanced portfolio of events.

Goals

The key goals in a DMO's event tourism strategy will generally be to:

- develop a reputation as a well-known event destination;
- retain and grow existing events;
- lobby government for development of event facilities and expeditious planning permits;
- strengthen relations between government and events stakeholders;
- maximise existing destination strengths;
- develop new destination strengths;
- attract high profile events;
- develop a cooperative stakeholder approach to event bidding;
- raise community awareness of the value of events;
- encourage the development of local community events;
- maximise the economic benefits of event tourism for the wider community;
- maximise longer-term growth opportunities;
- mentor and support event organisers.

DMO objectives relating to the meetings and events sectors

Depending on the strategy framework at a destination and the ensuing event tourism strategy goals, the tactical objectives should consider the extent to which events have the potential to:

- maximise opportunities for stakeholders' involvement in planning, organising and participating;
- be supported in their development by stakeholders;

- justify public sector spending on supporting infrastructure;
- link with other local events;
- enhance local pride;
- generate economic benefits, particularly for communities in need;
- enhance usage of tourism facilities;
- celebrate the local culture;
- support the destination brand identity;
- help to differentiate the destination's uniqueness;
- enhance destination image;
- be promoted to attract a wider tourism mix;
- provide a boost in visitor arrivals during off-peak periods or extend peak periods;
- increase average length of stay;
- enhance the visitor experience at the destination;
- stimulate repeat visitation to the destination;
- attract major sponsorship;
- attract media attention.

CHAPTER SUMMARY

Key point 1: The importance of the meetings and events sectors for destinations

Travel for the purpose of MICE has emerged as one of the largest, fastest growing and most resilient tourism segments of the visitor industry for destinations worldwide. Since the majority of annual meetings are small to moderate size events, the market provides most DMOs with opportunities to enhance occupancy and attendance at a wide range of local businesses, often during off-peak periods.

Key point 2: The importance of a destination's promotional appeal

While there has been relatively little published research into meetings and events destination attractiveness, it is clear that in addition to meeting facilities, a critical factor is the promotional appeal of the destination to delegates, participants, spectators and partners. DMOs and CVBs use a range of promotional activities to enhance perceptions of the destination in the minds of influential meetings and events planners responsible for destination selection.

Key point 3: The key objectives in the DMO's strategy to attract meetings and events

For the majority of DMOs, event tourism represents the main opportunity to be directly involved in new product development. Recognition of the value of the MICE and events sectors has seen an increasing number of DMOs develop convention bureaus, along with specialists in event tourism, to enhance competitiveness. Other DMOs without convention bureaus still compete as information brokers and by assisting local groups in the coordination of bids.

REVIEW QUESTIONS

1. Explain why promotional appeal is such an important aspect of a MICE destination.

2. Discuss the potential for your destination to successfully bid for, and host, the Interhash event discussed in case study 6.1.

3. Discuss the range of tailor-made service options your destination could offer incentive travel planners.

REFERENCES

Allen, J., O'Toole, W., McDonnell, I. and Harris, R. (2005). *Festival and Special Event Management* (3rd edition). Milton, QLD: John Wiley & Sons.

Cerda, E. L. (2005). Destination management in Mexico. In Harrill, R. (ed.) *Fundamentals of Destination Management and Marketing*. Washington, DC: IACVB, pp. 259–272.

Chacko, H. E. and Fenich, G. G. (2000). Determining the importance of US convention destination attributes. *Journal of Vacation Marketing* 6(3): 211–220.

Cortez, M. J. (2004). Las Vegas: To brand the new destination. In Dickenson, B. and Vladimir, A. (eds) *The Complete 21st Century Travel & Hospitality Marketing Handbook*. Upper Saddle River, NJ: Pearson, pp. 159–167.

Davidson, R. and Rogers, T. (2006). *Marketing Destinations & Venues for Conferences, Conventions and Business Events*. Oxford: Elsevier.

DCC. (2012). *Dubbo City Events Strategy*. Dubbo, NSW: Dubbo City Council.

DMAI. (2013). *2013 Convention Sales and Marketing Activities Study*. Destination Marketing Association International. Available at: http://www.destinationmarketing.org/2013-convention-sales-marketing-activities-study-0

Elliott, J. (1997). *Tourism: Politics and Public Sector Management*. London: Routledge.

Fenich, G. G. (2005). *Meetings, Expositions, Events and Conventions: An Introduction to the Industry*. Upper Saddle River, NJ: Pearson.

Ford, R. C. and Peeper, W. C. (2008). *Managing Destination Marketing Organizations*. Orlando, FL: ForPer Publications.

Gartrell, R. B. (1994). *Destination Marketing for Convention and Visitor Bureaus*. Dubuque, IA: Kendall/Hunt.

Getz, D. (1997). *Event Management and Event Tourism*. New York: Cognizant Communications Corp.

Getz, D. (2008). Event tourism: Definition, evolution and research. *Tourism Management* 29(3): 403–428.

Hall, T. and Ledger, A. (2015). UK events industry worth £60 billion, reveals MPI study. *Citmagazine.com*. 10 July. Available at: http://www.citmagazine.com/article/1190234/uk-events-industry-worth-60bn-reveals-mpi-study

Harrill, R. (2005a). *Fundamentals of Destination Management and Marketing*. Washington, DC: IACVB.

Harrill, R. (2005b). *Guide to Best Practices in Tourism and Destination Management: Volume 2*. Lansing, MI: EIAHLA.

Harris, R., Jago, L. and King, B. (2005). *Case Studies in Tourism & Hospitality Marketing*. Frenchs Forest, NSW: Pearson.

Holcolmb, B. (1999). Marketing cities for tourism. In Judd, D. R. and Fainstein, S. S. (eds) *The Tourist City*. Newhaven, CT: Yale University Press, pp. 54–70.

ICCA. (2014). *2013 ICCA Statistics Report – Country & City Rankings: International Association Meetings Market*. Amsterdam, The Netherlands: International Congress and Convention Association. June. Available at: www.iccaworld.com/newsarchives/archivesearch.cfm

Li, X. and Kaplanidou, K. (2013). The impact of the 2008 Beijing Olympic Games on China's destination brand: A US-based examination. *Journal of Hospitality & Tourism Research* 37(2): 237–261.

Oates, G. (2014). 17 European countries band together to create meetings-themed organization. Available at: http://www.skift.com/2014/12/29/17-european-countries-band-together-to-create-super-destination-marketing-organization

Oppermann, M. (1996). Convention destination images: Analysis of association meeting planners' perceptions. *Tourism Management* 17(3): 175–182.

Page, S. and Connell, J. (2009). *Tourism: A Modern Synthesis* (3rd edition). Andover, UK: Cengage Learning.

Pike, S. (2002). Destination image analysis: A review of 142 papers from 1973–2000. *Tourism Management* 23(5): 541–549.

Pike, S. (2004). *Destination Marketing Organisations*. Oxford: Elsevier Science.

Pike, S. (2007). Destination image literature: 2001–2007. *Acta Turistica* 19(2): 107–125.

Pike, S. (2008). *Destination Marketing: An Integrated Marketing Communication Approach*. Burlington, MA: Butterworth-Heinemann.

Pitts, B. G. and Ayers, K. (2000). Sports tourism and the gay games: The emerging use of destination marketing with the gay games. In Robinson, M., Evans, N., Long, P., Sharpley, R. and Swarbrooke, J. (eds) *Management, Marketing and the Political Economy of Travel and Tourism*. Sunderland, UK: Business Education Publishers, pp. 389–401.

Plog, S. T. (2000). Thirty years that changed travel: Changes to expect over the next ten. *Keynote Address at the 31st Travel and Tourism Research Association Conference*. Burbank, CA. June. Available at: www.ttra.com

Rogers, T. (2005). Destination management in the UK. In Harrill, R. (ed.) *Fundamentals of Destination Management and Marketing*. Washington, DC: IACVB, pp. 245–258.

Romero, F. G. (2013). Sports tourism in ancient Greece. *Journal of Tourism History* 5(2): 146–160.

Ross, P. (2003). It's a wacky world out there. *The Sunday Mail*. Brisbane. 27 July: 4–5. Hard copy newspaper article.

Stokes, R. (2008). Tourism strategy making: Insights to the events tourism domain. *Tourism Management* 29(2): 252–262.

TPO. (2015). Gangneung Dano-je Festival 2015. *TPO Newsletter No.124 Issue*. Distributed in a broadcast email from admin@top.org. 12 June.

TravelandTourWorld.com. (2015a). *Macroeconomic Forecasts for Travel Industry 2020*. January, pp. 18–21. Available at: http://www.travelandtourworld.com/flipbook/jan2015/flipviewerxpress.html

TravelandTourWorld.com. (2015b). *Leather Expo in Thailand to Attract over 25,000 Foreign Visitors*. Available at: http://www.travelandtourworld.com/news/article/leather-expo-thailand-attract-25000-foreign-visitors

TravelandTourWorld.com (2015c). *ETC and UNWTO to Unveil the Secrets to Success in the Meetings Industry*. Available at: http://www.travelandtourworld.com/news/article/etc-unwto-unveil-secrets-success-meetings-industry

TravelandTourWorld.com. (2015d). *100 Days Until Rugby World Cup 2015 Consumer Competition Launch*. Available at: http://www.travelandtourworld.com/news/article/100-days-rugby-world-cup-2015-consumer-competition-launch

Travelindustrywire. (2015). *U.K. Companies Losing Millions Per Year on Travel Costs Due to 'Wasted' Meetings*. Available at: http://www.travelindustrywire.com/article83884.html

Witt, S. F. and Gammon, S. (1994). Incentive travel. In Witt, S. F. and Moutinho, L. (eds) *Tourism Marketing and Management Handbook* (2nd edition). Hertfordshire, UK: Prentice Hall.

Chapter **7**

The destination marketing organisation (DMO), disasters, crises and dark tourism

AIMS

To enhance understanding of:

- destination disaster contingency marketing planning to avert a crisis;
- DMO responses to disasters;
- the dark side of tourism marketing.

ABSTRACT

An emerging role of DMOs is leading the tourism community in the development of contingency marketing planning for possible future catastrophic events that have the potential to render the destination uncompetitive overnight. Since no destination is immune to disaster, every DMO should consider the possibility of such an occurrence at some stage in the future. Disasters can be man-made or *acts of God*, and the effects can be short term or long term. Almost all will be unpredictable and beyond the control of the DMO. The level of preparedness for a disaster at a destination will determine the extent to which a management crisis manifests. Since a state of crisis can affect the viability of the destination and the survival of local businesses, DMOs have a responsibility to prepare marketing contingency plans. The level of such planning by DMOs has until recently been very low, particularly in terms of garnering stakeholder involvement, and the topic of destination crisis management has only recently emerged as a research field within the tourism academic literature. A number of case studies of disasters at destinations have been reported in recent years and provide a valuable resource for DMOs considering contingency planning. Key activities that DMOs should consider include: the formation of a permanent disaster task-force, future scenario thinking and risk analysis, coordinated marketing responses, market concentration, outsourcing of media relations and initiatives to support local businesses. Also, there is a dark side to tourism marketing related to facilitating travellers' curiosity in experiencing scenes of disasters, death and morbid and macabre events. Human curiosity has driven visits to sites of death and destruction for centuries. While DMOs lack any control over commercial and visitor activities at such sites, destination marketers do engage in ethical promotion of positive aspects of visits for the purposes of pilgrimage, remembrance and respect.

Disaster contingency marketing planning to avert a crisis

The Indonesian island of Bali was the most visited overseas destination for Australian travellers when *disaster* struck in October 2002 in the form of terrorist bombings, including one at a crowded tourist bar. The attacks killed 202 people and injured over 200 others from Australia, the UK, USA, Scandinavia and Indonesia. The event left the destination in a state of *crisis* from which it has still not fully recovered, due in part to a further terrorist bombing in 2005 and regular Australian government terrorism-related travel advisories, including a warning to avoid travel to the destination in January 2015. Also, throughout 2015 there were public calls from many Australians to boycott Bali tourism due to the executions of two convicted Australian drug smugglers on 29 April 2015. eGlobaltravelmedia.com (2015a) cited a study finding 34 per cent of Australians saying they were less likely to visit the island because of the executions.

The emerging literature on destinations in crisis contains an increasing number of case studies that will be of practical value in enhancing DMOs' ability to rally following disastrous events such as that faced by Bali. The first journal special issue was 'Tourism crises caused by war, terrorism and crime', which was published in 1999 by the *Journal of Travel Research* (38(1)). The guest editors advised the 11 published articles represented a cross-section of those presented at the 1997 'War, Terrorism: Times of Crisis and Recovery' conference held in Dubrovnik, Croatia. The conference was the second, following a meeting in Sweden in 1995, to focus on the relationship between tourism, security and safety. A 2005 special issue on the topic by the *Journal of Travel and Tourism Marketing* (19(2/3)) generated a further 12 papers. See Pike (2008) for a list of these 34 papers describing disastrous events in the USA, Egypt, Israel, Sri Lanka, Italy, Northern Ireland, Philippines, Pakistan, Cyprus, the UK, Canada, Fiji, Turkey, South Africa, Yugoslavia and Australia. At the time of writing, a 2016 *Journal of Destination Marketing and Management* special issue on 'Marketing and branding of conflict-ridden destinations' has been announced. The first tourism crisis text, by Beirman (2003a), examined the crises and responses of 11 case studies. This has since been followed by Avraham and Ketter (2008).

Disaster or crisis?

The seemingly increasing and intensifying effects of climate change will probably see more frequent and more severe weather events, which will place many destinations, particularly in coastal regions, at greater risk of potential disasters. It is important to note the distinction between the terms *disaster* and *crisis*. Faulkner (1999) suggested a crisis was representative of a self-inflicted situation caused by inept management practices or inability to adapt to a rapidly changing environment. A disaster on the other hand is a sudden catastrophic change over which the organisation has little or no control. From the DMO perspective a crisis could be considered as occurring during the period between when a disaster strikes a destination and when recovery has been achieved. The degree of internal crisis caused by the external disaster (see Figure 7.1) will vary between DMOs, depending on the nature of the event, as

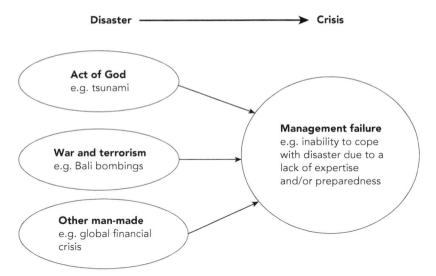

Figure 7.1 Disaster or crisis?

well as management's expertise and preparedness to deal with such events, access to resources and ability to react quickly.

All destinations are at risk of a future disaster, with some more likely than others. For example, Tsai and Chen (2011) cited the World Bank's (2005) *Natural Disaster Hotspots: A Global Risk Analysis* report (Dilley *et al.*, 2005), which found that 73 per cent of the land area and population of Taiwan are at risk of three types of disaster. Taiwan has in the past had an average of over 200 earthquakes and 5 typhoons each year (Chiang, 2003 in Tsai and Chen, 2011). Since a destination in crisis is not a modern phenomenon, it would be expected that preparing contingency plans to avert a crisis has been an important element of any DMO planning. Historically, however, it has been rare for such a topic to dominate much meeting time among stakeholders until disaster strikes. Observations of publicly available strategic plans for NTOs and STOs also indicate contingency planning for many has not been a priority until recently. For example, Pacific Area Travel Association (PATA) (1991, in Litvin and Alderson, 2003) noted the majority of its members, including NTOs, did not include crisis management in strategic planning at that time. A decade later, Faulkner and Vikulov (2001) noted that the tourism industry was still not planning sufficiently for disasters. The key challenge has been for the DMO to balance the need to prepare for any future disaster with the reality of stakeholders' expectations that limited resources should be used in the market place today in order to generate tomorrow's cash flow, as opposed to spending time planning for some unknown event that might or might not eventuate at some point in the future.

In the quest for increased visitors and spending, which is how a DMO is ultimately critically judged, crisis planning may be viewed as a luxury of time if a disaster has not actually occurred nearby in living memory. I am aware of one RTO board of directors that had regularly ignored pleas from the local civil defence coordinator to consider contingency plans in what is a recognised earthquake zone. The coordinator's concern was that all entrances to the destination were via bridges, which were at risk of collapse in a significant quake. This would severely impact the ability to evacuate visitors. The rationale for contingency planning was that a major unpredictable earthquake is highly likely to strike the destination at some unknown time in the future – maybe not for 10,000 years, but maybe next week. The approaches literally fell on deaf ears at the RTO. However, as warned by Litvin and Alderson (2003: 189): 'The intensity of the moment during a crisis is clearly not the time to commence such planning'.

IN PRACTICE

7.1 Sitting in the hot seat

Hanbury (2005) provided a first-hand account of what it is like to be in the hot seat during a disaster at a DMO without a contingency marketing plan. Hanbury had been in the position of CEO at the Washington, DC Convention and Tourism Corporation (WCTC) for only five months during the 9/11 attacks. The WCTC was not organised to deal with even a minor disaster at the time, let alone the largest economic crisis to face the US capital. Having been formed only five months previously, following the underperformance of the previous DMO, the WCTC was in the midst of major restructuring. The new DMO had no disaster response plan. Hanbury described how the team responded to ultimately manage the situation and outlined a summary of lessons learned from the experience.

Further reading

Hanbury, W. A. (2005).

Some disasters may be of a short-term nature, such as a severe weather event or act of violence. Others might be long term, such as the political ban on US citizens visiting Cuba. The ban was imposed by President Kennedy in 1963, was later lapsed by President Carter, and then re-imposed by President Reagan in 1982. The Middle East is a region that has suffered from ongoing acts of war and terrorism. Mansfield (1999) outlined six major cycles of tourism decline and recovery in Israel due to ongoing security situations since 1967. As a result, Israel has suffered a prevailing image of a high-risk destination. The cycles were caused by:

- the Six Day War in 1967;
- the 1973 Yom Kippur war between Israel, Egypt and Syria;
- the 1981 intensity of Palestine Liberation Organization attacks;
- the late 1980s double cycle of international and domestic terror;
- the 1990–1991 Gulf War;
- the terrorised peace cycle of the 1990s.

Unfortunately, however, from the analysis of these events, Mansfield (1999) concluded that once each crisis had ended and recovery in visitor arrivals was evident, neither the government nor tourism industry planned for a future disaster. This was evident in Bierman's (2008, in Pike 2008) examination of Israel's marketing recovery efforts between 2001 and 2006. Bierman was the director of the Israel NTO's Australasia office between 1994 and 2006 and was directly involved in the recovery strategy. International tourism arrivals to Israel reached a peak during 2000, which was the year of Christianity's bimillennium. During that year 2.7 million visitors arrived in Israel. At the end of September 2000 the Palestinian intifada broke out, which resulted in an immediate decline of tourism arrivals to Israel. The massive decline reached its lowest point in 2002 when only 864,000 visitors arrived.

The Israel Ministry of Tourism and its representative offices around the world undertook a major recovery campaign, which resulted in tourism numbers beginning to increase in 2003 to 1.03 million, growing to 1.5 million in 2004 and reaching 1.9 million in 2005. Until the outbreak of border conflict on the Lebanese frontier in July 2006, Israel tourism growth for the first half of 2006 was a further 25 per cent. During the recovery phase, Israel hosted many travel agents, travel writers, religious leaders and high profile celebrities who readily provided positive testimonials that were publicised by Israel government tourism offices in targeted consumer and trade media campaigns in their respective markets. By the beginning of 2006 the Israel Ministry of Tourism undertook a more aggressive marketing campaign to attract a growing range of tourists in all key source markets. The recovery came to an abrupt end with the outbreak of military conflict on the Israel–Lebanon border in July 2006, but since the end of this conflict in August 2006 the Israel Ministry of Tourism immediately utilised a similar approach to recommence recovery.

Events such as these have increased the global profile of the link between terrorism and tourism. Terrorists have recognised the symbolism of tourism and the vulnerability of tourists. Unfortunately, the issue is one that is likely to confront the tourism industry for generations. It therefore behoves DMOs to consider contingencies for the effects of such events in their own region and in other parts of the world.

Violence and crime

In 1996, at a popular tourism attraction in Tasmania, Australia, a lone gunman killed 35 domestic and overseas visitors. During October 2003 there was violent rioting in the streets in leading Jamaican destination, Montego Bay. A month earlier, the tranquil Maldives was hit by rioting that led to late-night curfews. L'Etang *et al*. (2007) discussed the examples of rape and murder of young female travellers in Thailand's Koh Samui island and the Caribbean island of Aruba and the resultant global media attention and decline in hotel occupancy. These are but a few of the many acts of violent crimes that have affected destinations in the modern era.

Excessive crime and unruly behaviour can affect the image of a destination, and crime against visitors has led to negative reputations for many urban destinations around the world. For example, violent crimes in Miami and Orlando reached such a level in 1993 that they caused a decrease in visitor arrivals to the entire state (Pizam, 1999). Dimanche and Lepetic (1999) provided a case study of the impact of crime levels on tourism in New Orleans, where the murder rate was eight times the national average and five times that of New York. In 1997 the New Orleans CVB hired an outside consultant to develop a marketing plan to address the negative crime image of the city. However, Dimanche and Lepetic (1999) found that while the tourism industry in the city was under siege from a high crime rate, there was a lack of concern among stakeholders, due to no noticeable drop in revenues. They strongly urged operators to heed the warning signals before the situation became a crisis.

Other types of 'man-made' disasters

Other examples of man-made disasters impacting on the tourism industry have included:

- the 2015 terrorism bombings in Egypt's Sinai Peninsula;
- the 2014 violent mass protest in Istanbul's Taksim Square;
- the twin 2014 Malaysian Airlines crashes;
- the 2013 Westgate Mall shooting massacre in Nairobi, Kenya;
- the 2008 global financial crisis;

- the 2002 collapse of Australia's major domestic air carrier, Ansett Airlines;

- the gunning down in 1997 of 58 overseas visitors and 4 Egyptians outside one of Egypt's most famous temples in Luxor. The attack cost Egypt's tourism industry US$2 billion in lost earnings (Edgell, 1999);

- Pacific nuclear testing in the South Pacific in 1995 (see Elliott, 1997);

- labour strikes such as those by Australian airline pilots in 1989–1990 (see Lavery, 1992) and US air traffic controllers in 1981;

- the 1989 Exxon Valdez oil spill at Prince William Sound, Alaska;

- the 1989 political uprising in Tiananmen Square, China (see Gartner and Shen, 1992; Roehl, 1990);

- the 1970s global oil crisis. The impact in New Zealand was so significant that the government ordered the closure of petrol stations on Sundays. Another initiative that impacted on tourism was the introduction car-less day stickers, where every car was forced to carry a sticker indicating one day of the week when it could not be used;

- the nationalisation of Mexico's oil industry in the 1930s causing an immediate decline in self-drive tourists from the USA (Berger, 2006).

Uncertainty

Tourism destinations have always been, and will continue to be, at risk of exogenous events. Such *wildcard* events have been described by Hall (2005) as being low probability, but high impact. Arguably the greatest impact of these on the tourism industry is uncertainty.

- Uncertainty of travellers to risk personal safety on what is after all a discretionary activity. During periods of insecurity, consumers can choose either to travel somewhere perceived to be safe or delay travel plans. For example, Hopper (2002) reported that within hours of the 9/11 strikes in the USA, hotels in London were receiving cancellations from all over the world. In France visitors from the USA declined by an estimated 90 per cent in the month immediately following 11 September 2001.

- Uncertainty of investors and small business owners to invest or reinvest in repairs, maintenance, upgrades or new developments.

- Uncertainty of tourism staff on the future of their career. This even extends to tourism degree and diploma courses, which can suffer from concerns held by prospective students and parents.

Resilience

On a global basis the tourism industry has historically proven resilient, with remarkably quick recoveries following major crises. For example, International Air Transport Association (IATA) CEO Giovanni Bisignani suggested that following the 1991 Gulf War, a year when tourism arrivals only increased by 1 per cent, growth in 1992 was 8 per cent. Even with the events of 9/11, international arrivals exceeded 700 million for the first time in 2002, representing an increase of 3 per cent over 2001 and 19 million more than *millennium year*. However, recovery for individual destinations might take place over a longer term. For example, one year after the 2002 Bali bombings, a United Nations report estimated the unemployment rate to be up by almost one third and that street vendors' sales were down by 50 per cent.

Costs

Aside from the effects of human suffering caused by disasters, of concern to destination stakeholders are negative economic impacts:

- A KPMG report estimated Toronto's tourism industry lost CAD$190 million in the first two months of severe acute respiratory syndrome (SARS) (McClelland, 2003).

- The ILO (2003) estimated the total loss of jobs in world tourism at over 11 million following the terrorist attacks of 9/11, representing a loss of 1 in every 7 jobs in tourism and travel.

- The CEO of IATA, Giovanni Bisignani, predicted the 2003 war in Iraq would cost the global airline industry US$10 billion in losses, on top of the US$30 billion in losses following 11 September 2001. At the time, a survey by the Tourism Association of America estimated over 70 per cent of Americans were not interested in travelling overseas.

Negative media impacts

Often the perception of risk when a disaster strikes will impact on travellers' decision making. For example, the mass political protests in 2014 in Istanbul's Taksim Square, involving over 1 million residents, military tanks and water cannon, caused mass cancellations of travel bookings, even though the famous attractions in the old city precinct, such as the Blue Mosque and Grand Bazaar, were well away from the troubles and quite safe for visitors. Other examples of perceptions problems have included:

- eGlobaltravelmedia.com (2015b) cited research by Roy Morgan, which showed a decline in interest by Australians to visit Christchurch three years after the 2010 earthquakes that devastated the city. Since Christchurch is the airport gateway to New Zealand's South Island, the earthquake effect was causing a knock-on effect in terms of a downturn in popularity of other nearby destinations, which were not hit by the quake.

- Like Israel, Northern Ireland tourism has suffered a negative image from terrorism over three decades, during the ethno-nationalist *troubles* between the 1960s and 1990s. However, Leslie (1999) found that even though the associated negative publicity of the 1970s had decreased considerably, Northern Ireland had become increasingly substitutable as a destination for UK travellers. O'Neill and McKenna (1994) found by comparison that in the 1990s, visitor numbers to Northern Ireland had merely re-established the 1960s pre-troubles levels, whereas volumes in Great Britain and the Republic of Ireland had increased by over 50 per cent.

- Visitor arrivals in Egypt during 2014 had declined by 30 per cent compared to the previous year, due to the political chaos (see TravelandTourWorld, 2014). Revenues from tourism during the same period were estimated to have declined by 50 per cent.

- The political unrest in Thailand during late 2013/early 2014, spearheaded in Bangkok with mass demonstrations, had an immediate effect on the MICE sector with the cancellation and postponement of numerous conferences (see eGlobaltravelmedia, 2015c).

Arguably, the management of negative perceptions in the market place related to a disaster is one of the greatest challenges confronting DMOs, since as noted (see Cavlek, 2002; Pike 2007; Pike *et al.*, 2011), incorrect beliefs can inhibit visitation. Misinformation in the USA about the 2001 outbreak of foot-and-mouth disease in the UK led to perceptions that the disease was a human condition and that all of England was *closed*. One of the greatest communication challenges was maintaining a positive outlook in destination promotion, while simultaneously promoting the negative impacts to government (Hopper,

2002: 83). Frisby (2002) provided a detailed first-hand account of the PR activities undertaken by the BTA during the foot-and-mouth outbreak. Initiatives undertaken during the crisis included: media releases, fortnightly newsletters, sponsored overseas media visits, video news releases and background tapes and development of a media extranet. At the peak of the outbreak, the BTA's call centre in New York received an average of 700 calls each day about the crisis. Frisby (2002: 90) claimed media misinformation was such that enquiries included, for example: 'Should we bring our own food?' and 'Can we travel around safely?' At the time of the outbreak, the London Tourism Board was conducting around six broadcast interviews a week with media, which were focused heavily on the negative perceptions.

During the first half of 2003, SARS caused panic in the travel industry worldwide. SARS was estimated to have affected over 8,000 people and was responsible for over 800 deaths (Manning, 2003). China was the worst affected, with the emerging destination giant experiencing its first decline in international visitor arrivals in 2003. Other than the loss of life, the most significant aspect of the SARS outbreak to impact on the tourism industry was the mass media coverage. A March 2003 press release by PATA called for 'accurate, restrained and sensible travel advice and media reporting' of SARS. PATA urged all those reporting to be geographically specific and avoid alarmist statements. The following day in an email to the TRINET online tourism research community, Professor Bob McKercher of The Hong Kong Polytechnic University lamented how the global media frenzy was feeding perceptions of a disaster:

> *While the health scare is no doubt of concern, we must keep a proper perspective on it. The local and global media is in something of a feeding frenzy. As a resident of HK, it is worrying, but remember that, out of a population of 7 million, only 100 people have fallen ill, so far.*

Government travel advisories

All national governments have a responsibility to provide a travel security advisory service for their citizens, identifying potentially risky travel destinations. Most countries provide regularly updated travel advisories on government websites, and the implications for the DMOs of those countries listed are significant in terms of the damage to the image of their destination and the necessary recovery marketing efforts, given the difficulty in correcting a negative image. The extent to which promotional efforts are negated by government travel advisories is a very real issue warranting more research. It is important to consider that, unfortunately, the negative images created by publicity surrounding a disaster can last far longer than any physical destruction to infrastructure or tourism facilities, and so the NTO must lobby their own government to use public diplomacy to ensure travel advisories of other governments are fair, accurate and current. Recognising the potentially negative impacts of travel advisories, the UNWTO promotes a set of guidelines to governments in this regard.

Government travel advisories have been regarded as extremely controversial in many quarters for their role in exacerbating negative economic impacts, particularly on poorer nations. Rarely if ever has a travel advisory been posted about Western industrial countries. This was particularly noticeable for the USA after 9/11 and the United Kingdom during the 2002 foot-and-mouth outbreak. Unfortunately, most advisories are issued against less developed countries that can ill afford the resultant tourism downturn. Philippines tourism secretary and PATA associate chairman Richard Gordon suggested travel advisories reward the terrorists (Alcantara, 2003): 'It is really a cover-your-behind memo issued by a foreign bureaucrat. Jobs have been lost and it's time issuing countries take responsibility for their actions'.

Opanga (2003) even suggested travel advisories from UK and US governments were responsible for the collapse of tourism in Kenya. Beirman (2003b) reported on a recovery seminar in Kenya during 2003, which was convened by the Kenyan Association of Tour Operators to 'establish what was required to alter the negative travel advisories which had crippled Kenyan tourism during the first half of 2003'. Beirman questioned the motives for the continuation of travel advisories by the US and Australian governments that warned of an 'imminent terrorism attack', even though this had not materialised after six months. Kenya's Minister of Tourism visited the UK in mid-2003 in a failed attempt to urge the government to change the travel advisory. The country's tourism industry was struggling again in 2015 when, following a series of terrorist attacks killing over 400 people, visitor arrivals decreased by 25 per cent in the first 5 months of the year (Travelandtourworld.com, 2015). Kenya had been hit by a series of attacks by Somalia's Shabaab Islamists including the Nairobi shopping mall massacre in 2013, attacks in coastal towns in 2014 and at a university in 2015. In June 2015 many countries were advising citizens *not to travel* to Kenya's border regions and to *reconsider your need to travel* to the capital Nairobi.

Stop press: Middle East respiratory syndrome (MERS)

At the time of writing (June 2015) the World Health Organization (WHO) recommended against imposing travel bans or airport screenings in the Middle East and South Korea, where there had been 145 cases of MERS reported between 20 May and 15 June, including 14 deaths among the elderly. At the time, WHO advised most cases were occurring in hospitals, and the virus was being contained. Authorities in the Middle East were working to bring MERS under control before the next Hajj pilgrimage of millions of Muslims to Mecca in September 2015.

Helpful resources

Any destination hit by a disaster will be forced to implement recovery strategies to avoid or minimise a crisis situation. Since no destination is immune to disasters, it surely behoves the DMO to develop some form of marketing response strategy, in conjunction with civic authorities, in advance of an admittedly unknown exogenous event. However, until recently there have been few resources available to advise DMOs. The UNWTO now plays a major role in assisting DMOs to work with governments to integrate tourism into disaster emergency procedures, since in many parts of the world tourism is regarded as a non-essential activity and therefore low priority. In addition, the UNWTO is part of the Tourism Emergency Response Network (TERN), which was activated during the 2009 H1N1 pandemic and 2010 volcanic eruption in Iceland. Regular simulation exercises are also held. Guidelines for contingency marketing communications are available from the UNWTO (http://www.e-unwto.org/action/showPublications?category=40000095) and PATA (www.pata.org). Following a recommendation of the PATA Bali Tourism Recovery Taskforce, PATA created a crisis manual for member governments (see PATA, 2003). The manual provides a checklist of critical tasks to be undertaken during a crisis, as well as a directory of crisis specialists. The Federal Emergency Management Agency (FEMA) website (see www.fema.org) provides a valuable resource on disaster management, including education and training information.

While ensuring the safety of visitors and rebuilding infrastructure and tourism facilities will be paramount, these activities are beyond the scope of DMOs. This section is therefore limited to discussing the marketing aspects of recovery from disasters. One RTO that did have a disaster plan on 11 September 2001 was Charleston in South Carolina (Litvin and Alderson, 2003). The first meeting of the Charleston Area Convention and Visitors Bureau (CACVB) crisis team took place on the afternoon of 11 September. However, the CACVB plan immediately proved to be of limited value as all scenarios were based on local events such as localised hurricanes and floods. There was no scenario for an incident 500 miles away.

Clearly a DMO's ability to respond effectively to a disaster will depend on the level of resources available. Depending on the scale of the disaster, this will likely require strong lobbying by DMOs for government intervention. Examples include:

- In 2003 the Hong Kong Tourism Board announced funding of HK$400 million for a series of special events to repair the post-SARS image of Hong Kong.

- In China post-SARS initiatives included visa exemptions for some nationalities.

- The Indonesian government allocated US$44.6 million for a global campaign to lure visitors back to Bali following the October 2002 bombings (Osborne, 2003 in Pike, 2008: 338).

- At the height of the SARS publicity the Canadian federal government pledged an additional CAD$15.5 million to promote Toronto and Canada as safe destinations.

- The Thailand government took the unusual step of promising US$100,000 to any tourist catching SARS while visiting the country. Authorities made the offer due to concern over the April arrival figures, which were down by almost half even though Thailand had been declared a SARS-free zone. The initiative followed a US$100,000 SARS-free guarantee by Thai Airways.

- Following the events of 9/11 the Southern Governors' Association adopted a resolution involving federally funded advertising and tax credits (Kubiak, 2002). The Florida state government provided US$20 million for tourism advertising following 9/11 (Word, 2003 in Pike, 2008: 338). This stimulated a further US$25 million in private sector funding (Bush, 2004).

- In 2002 the British government announced a £40 million marketing package to reverse the estimated £2 billion drop in tourism revenue from the foot-and-mouth outbreak (Kleinman and Bashford, 2002).

- In response to the 1989–1990 pilots' strike in Australia, which resulted in a decrease of over 100,000 international visitor arrivals, the Australian federal government provided an additional recovery plan fund of AUD$18.5 million to the NTO (Lavery, 1992).

Not all DMOs are fortunate to receive extra government funding following a disaster. For example, as discussed in Chapter 3, destinations reliant on a bed tax for revenue generation, such as North American CVBs like Las Vegas, face a decline in budget when bed nights are down. Also, during the 1997 Asian economic crisis, the Indonesian Tourist Promotion Board was forced to close important overseas offices in Frankfurt, London, Los Angeles, Singapore, Taipei and Tokyo as a result of a lack of funding and huge debts (Henderson, 2002).

Tactical responses

Faulkner (1999, 2001) developed a tourism disaster management framework for communities, based on six phases of the disaster process:

1. **pre-event**, when action can be taken to mitigate effects of potential disasters;

2. **prodromal**, when it is apparent a disaster is imminent;

3. **emergency**, when the effect of a disaster is felt and action is necessary to protect people and property;

4. **intermediate**, when the immediate needs of people have been addressed and the focus shifts to restoring services and the community to normal;

5. **long-term (recovery)**, which is a continuation of the intermediate stage, but now includes items that could not be addressed quickly, along with a post-mortem;

6. **resolution**, when routine has been restored or a new improved state has been established.

As a marketing organisation, the DMO can only be responsible for some of the actions required in such a framework for a community. The Department of Resources, Energy and Tourism (2012: 8) proposed a *being prepared* checklist, asking DMOs if they had the following:

- a tourism crisis management group who are aware of their roles and responsibilities;
- a tourism risk management plan that identifies your region's most likely areas of risk exposure;
- an action plan to minimise risks to the region;
- a programme to prepare the tourism industry to face a crisis;
- an understanding of the role the DMO can play at the time of a crisis;
- a media spokesperson;
- a programme to practise responding to a crisis;
- a plan for managing the tourism crisis management group's communications response to the media and tourism industry;
- a contacts database that is easily accessible and can be activated at the time of a crisis;
- awareness of the tourism industry protocol for responding to the media during a crisis.

IN PRACTICE

7.2 A practical guide for RTOs to prepare, respond and recover

As part of implementing *Tourism 2020* strategy, the Australian government's Standing Committee on Tourism's Industry Resilience Working Group developed a guide to assist RTOs to better prepare, respond and recover from a crisis (see Department of Resources, Energy and Tourism, 2012). The guide comprised the following sections, which provide a useful format for DMOs in the formative stages of preparing a disaster resilience plan:

1. **Prepare**
   - being prepared checklist;
   - share the load;
   - plan to manage your risk;
   - prepare the tourism industry;
   - plan your emergency response;
   - communication is essential.

2. **Respond**
   - immediate actions checklist;
   - the first 24 hours;

- short- to medium-term activities (days 2–12);
- long-term actions (day 15 and beyond).

3. **Recover**

- incident recovery checklist;
- back to business;
- step to recovery;
- recovery marketing and communications;
- planning the restoration;
- evaluate and re-assess.

4. **Templates**

- tourism crisis management group roles and responsibilities;
- tourism crisis management group training scenarios;
- tourism crisis management group risk management plan;
- SWOT analysis;
- tourism crisis communications plan;
- crisis impact questionnaire;
- tourism crisis assessment checklist.

Further reading

Department of Resources, Energy and Tourism (2012).

Successful tactics implemented by DMOs at various stages of the disaster process have included:

- a disaster management taskforce;
- scenario thinking;
- public relations;
- outsourcing expertise;
- coordinating cooperative campaigns;
- travel trade familiarisation visits;
- supporting local businesses;
- stimulating discounts and adding value;
- market concentration.

Disaster management taskforce

The purpose of a management taskforce is to minimise the level of guesswork during a disaster. The DMO is in an ideal situation to coordinate immediate and ongoing marketing responses, working closely with any damage response agencies to ensure consistency of messages. DMOs at all levels may form a taskforce that fits within the existing governance structure. Meetings need not have the same frequency as other panels, but should draw on expertise from relevant fields, such as civil defence, public health and infrastructure. Sönmez *et al.* (1999) suggested organising teams within the taskforce with different responsibilities, such as: public relations, promotion, information coordination and fundraising.

In most cases a taskforce has historically been instigated reactively following a disaster. For example, the PATA Bali Recovery Taskforce was established immediately following the October 2002 bombings to assist Indonesia. Within a week of the 2001 outbreak of foot-and-mouth disease in the UK, the BTA had set up its Immediate Action Group (Frisby, 2002). Two weeks after 9/11, the London Tourist Board (LTB) established the London Tourism Recovery Group (London Tourist Board, 2001, in Hopper, 2002).

From a marketing perspective, the first role of the taskforce is to assess the situation for impact in the market on visitor arrivals. Primary impact concerns will be the level of visitation decrease (visitor numbers, nights, spend) and forecasting the period of time. The second role is to respond as quickly as possible, initially focusing on information dispersal in a manner that fosters a sense of trust in the DMO by the media and travelling public. This may be necessary to clearly demarcate where the problem is, particularly if a number of areas have been unaffected. For example, Florida has a coastline of over 1,000 miles, and Hurricane Andrew in 1992 affected a relatively small 10 miles of beaches (Portorff and Neal, 1994). Portorff and Neal cited a UK newspaper headline that read 'Hurricane bearing down on Disney beaches', and yet the distance between Orlando and the affected beaches was over 200 miles.

Scenario thinking

Disasters, whether natural or man-made, are rarely predictable. If destinations are to prepare marketing contingency plans for possible disasters, it is important to look forwards as well as backwards, with the caveat that history is no predictor of the future. While it would be futile to attempt to predict the future, what can be valuable is the use of scenario thinking. As discussed in Chapter 8, scenario building attempts to construct views of possible futures, in an effort to better plan for uncertainty (see Schwartz, 1992; Johnson and Scholes, 2002). Strategic choices can be made based on how the different scenarios might unfold. In theory, this then offers the relative security of being prepared for, to varying degrees, whatever type of scenario happens. Scenarios should be seen as carefully constructed plots, rather than predictions. When attempting to envision the future, assumptions must be made for each scenario. Since the assumptions are the key elements in determining the basis for each plot, the number should be kept to a minimum to reduce complexity. For each scenario, a number of questions can be developed, including:

- What might lead to success or a speedy recovery where others may fail?
- What might happen to current customers?
- What might happen to future suppliers?
- What type of businesses will fare best/worst?
- What are the most important activities that need to be addressed first?
- Where should marketing resources be directed?

During 2005 a media *frenzy* developed over the threat of avian flu spreading from Asia to Europe in the form of a pandemic. Visit Scotland undertook scenario planning for such an eventuality. Page *et al.* (2006) provided a rare insight into the scenario building exercise from the perspective of a DMO. The case is an example of best practice in the tourism industry, both in terms of the planning process and the sharing of information with other NTOs.

Public relations

As discussed, the media plays an important role in communicating the impacts of disasters to the public. Therefore, public relations initiatives are a critical component in any disaster response strategy. This topic is addressed in Chapter 13. For a review of media strategies used by places in crisis, see Avraham and Ketter (2008). Recovery from a disaster or negative issue requires planning. During a serious crisis all international marketing should cease, given these will be worthless if consumers are bombarded with negative news images on their televisions (Mansfield, 1999). The focus of communications at this stage should be on providing accurate information dissemination. Strengthening of relations with the media will be necessary to generate greater positive publicity, since misinformation is one of the greatest challenges to overcome.

Effective media relations is one of the most important aspects of a destination recovery response, since as discussed the negative reporting in the mass media can affect the viability of a destination. The media has a propensity for relaying *bad news* rather than positive coverage of the destination's recovery. Beirman (2003a: 25–26) advised that DMO media managers should be prepared for the following questions:

- What is being done to assist victims?
- What is the extent of the damage/casualties?
- What is being done to reduce, minimise or eliminate future risks?
- What can the government/destination authorities do to guarantee safety?
- Why did this event occur in the first place?
- Who is to blame?
- How long will the crisis last?

Quarantelli (1996, in Faulkner, 1999) observed four key characteristics in the role of the media in US disasters. Interestingly, the first had been a lack of disaster preparedness planning by the mass media. Second, tensions emerged between local media and national media over disaster ownership. Third, the media tended to selectively report activities of organisations with which they have an established relationship. Fourth, television had been prone to perpetuate disaster myths.

Outsourcing expertise

Few DMOs are likely to have the resources to employ a permanent disaster media specialist, and few DMO staff are likely to have been trained in crisis management. Depending on the level of disaster/crisis, such a specialist might need to be outsourced to work with the taskforce. In 2003 the LTB took the step of offering a three-month contract for a marketer to focus on encouraging Londoners to spend more in their own city during the war in Iraq. The temporary position reported to a committee formed by the RTO, the Greater London Authority and the London Development Agency. Outsourcing of PR specialists may be needed to temporarily coordinate public information dissemination. For example, at the RTO level, the Katherine Regional Tourism Association employed a journalist to work with the media following the 1998 Australia Day flood (Faulkner and Vikulov, 2001). At the NTO level, during the 2001 UK outbreak of foot-and-mouth disease the BTA contracted a global PR agency to minimise the negative perceptions of Britain overseas (Frisby, 2002). However, BTA PR director, Frisby, candidly acknowledged a post-crisis recommendation to not outsource to a global agency in the future:

Although the appointed agency performed well in the initial rebuttal phase, after six weeks it became clear that a lack of product knowledge meant that enormous inputs of time and expertise were required in order to continue to produce results.

(Frisby, 2002: 99)

Coordinating cooperative campaigns

Key advantages of a coordinated marketing response include (Mansfield, 1999): economies of scale, consistency of image-related messages, more effective assessment of performance, reduced infighting between different tourism sector groups and positive signals for the travel industry and target markets. Regarding the last point, during the 2001 UK foot-and-mouth disease outbreak a feature of the BTA's response was working closely with national and regional tourist boards and key government departments, in an effort to minimise negative media coverage and to provide reassurance to the public (Frisby, 2002).

The events of 9/11 enabled the CACVB to successfully implement cooperative packages, which it had previously been unable to stimulate in more settled times (Litvin and Alderson, 2003). Similarly, Hopper (2002) reported one of the key lessons learned by the London Tourism Board in the wake of 9/11 was the need for effective dialogue with tourism operators. Hopper suggested a legacy of the improved public–private sector relationship established during the crisis became a model for future marketing of the destination.

Case study 7.1 summarises a cooperative marketing campaign by an STO and 3 RTOs to mitigate the effects of a major oil spill along a 60 kilometre stretch of coastline in Queensland, Australia. As well as combatting the environmental impacts of spill, recognised as the worst disaster ever experienced by the state, there was an urgent need to reassure the market that many beach areas were not affected and were still open for business.

CASE STUDY

7.1 Beaches *open for business*

In March 2009, during Cyclone Hamish, the *MV Pacific Adventurer* spilled 260 tonnes of fuel, along with 31 shipping containers housing 620 tonnes of ammonium nitrate, into the Coral Sea, just north of Brisbane, Australia. The following week the spillage washed ashore along 60 kilometres of coastline that included 4 popular beach destinations: Sunshine Coast, Moreton Bay, Bribie Island and Moreton Island. Affected areas included surf beaches, reefs and wetlands. Many of these areas had also already been battered by the cyclone. The ship continued through into the Port of Brisbane, leaving a 500 metre oil slick at the mouth of the Brisbane River. A state of emergency was declared by the Queensland state government, with Premier, Anna Bligh, describing the event as 'the worst environmental disaster Queensland has ever seen'. The spillage took 16 months of work by over 1,400 people to clean, at a direct cost of millions of dollars, along with the ensuing loss of revenue by affected businesses.

Nine days after the spill, Tourism Queensland announced details of a coordinated, cooperative campaign involving the STO and three RTOs: Brisbane Marketing, Tourism Sunshine Coast and Fraser Coast South Burnett Tourism. The aim was to reassure the domestic market and local residents that most beaches in south-east Queensland were *open for business*. The initiative was anchored by a AUD$750,000 television advertising campaign in Sydney, Melbourne, Brisbane and northern New South Wales. Other tactics included:

- a three-week newspaper advertising campaign linked to the television advertising;
- a campaign featuring local cricketing legend, Matthew Hayden, encouraging Queenslanders to *Donate a day to the bay* to assist the clean-up operation;
- a local radio blitz promoting the Sunshine Coast to Brisbane residents;
- weather segments and live weather crosses on a national television network;
- television and print publicity in high profile television travel shows and newspaper travel sections;
- a special travel promotion via the STO's email newsletter to a database of over 400,000 consumers;
- updates to the local tourism industry encouraging them to make sure frontline staff were aware of unaffected beach areas and operations;
- a dedicated STO email account and Maritime Services Queensland phone hotline for tourism operators to direct tourism-related questions and concerns.

Further reading

Ironside *et al.* (2009).
https://www.youtube.com/watch?v=cFJALMXLf9k
http://en.wikipedia.org/wiki/2009_southeast_Queensland_oil_spill

Discussion question

Why did the DMOs target communications towards the local host community as well as the major domestic markets of Sydney and Melbourne?

Travel trade familiarisation visits

Following the 2003 terrorist attacks in Turkey, the Balkan Federation of Travel and Tourist Agencies Associations planned travel trade familiarisations to develop solidarity with intermediaries in the region. On the assumption that negative images of Turkey would affect tourism to nearby member countries, the federation planned familiarisation visits to Istanbul for leading world tourism authorities during 2004. Hosting large groups of travel industry personnel on familiarisations by the Turkish Ministry of Tourism was a major reason for that country's rapid recovery following the 1999 Izmit earthquake (Beirman, 2003a). The topic of travel trade familiarisations is discussed in Chapter 14.

Supporting local tourism businesses

Mansfield (1999) suggested governments in high-risk areas should provide financial incentives for tourism investors, given the probability of future losses. A number of cases in the literature have reported initiatives to support local tourism operators during a crisis:

- VAT was reduced from 13 per cent to 3 per cent on hotels in Jordan during the 2003 war in Iraq.
- The Israel Ministry of Tourism has provided subsidies for tourism operators marketing the destination (Beirman, 2002).
- Following 9/11, the CACVB enlisted an online booking company to conduct workshops for local tourism businesses (Litvin and Alderson, 2003).
- Following 9/11, one of the recovery initiatives of the London Mayor was a £500,000 contribution towards free and discounted tickets to the city's theatres (Frisby, 2002).

Stimulating discounts and adding value

The introduction of special deals has been a regular component of Israel's post-crisis recovery programmes (Beirman, 2002). Beirman (2003a) cited the examples of Delta Airlines, which provided 10,000 free seats to New York following 9/11, and Insight Vacations, which provided a one-week package in Egypt for US$1 as a value add-on to its European tour product following the 1997 Luxor massacre. During the 2001 UK outbreak of foot-and-mouth disease, the BTA used the organisation's trade website to ask operators to provide details of special deals, details of which were used in media releases and publicised on the organisation's consumer website (Frisby, 2002).

Market concentration

As highlighted in the case of Israel (Bierman, 2008, in Pike, 2008), one of the most important crisis decisions concerns trade-offs about which markets to focus recovery efforts on (Bierman, 2008, in Pike, 2008). The key strategic foundation for rebuilding tourism to Israel, which was developed in January 2001, centred on stratifying the market into three key segments:

1. stalwarts – travellers with high commitment and high affiliation;

2. waverers – travellers with modest commitment and high affiliation;

3. discretionaries – travellers with low commitment and low affiliation.

During the first phase of recovery, 2001–2004, most marketing activity was focused on the stalwart market, which comprised Jews, Christian Zionists and business travellers with many solidarity groups being encouraged and formed. During 2004–2005 there was a focus on the waverer market, which comprised Christian pilgrims and other groups in Europe, North America, East Asia and Australasia with a high level of affiliation. By 2005 there was a switch in emphasis to attract the discretionary (vacation) market through partnerships with tour wholesalers and airlines, which resumed flights and tour programmes in Israel.

During the Asian economic crisis the Singapore Tourism Board concentrated on markets unaffected by the economic downturn (Henderson, 2002). During the UK foot-and-mouth disease outbreak in 2001 the BTA focused attention on 11 key markets (Frisby, 2002). On the correct assumption that Americans would be reluctant to fly in the short term following 11 September, the CACVB focused attention on cities within a 10-hour drive (Litvin and Alderson, 2003). All scheduled advertising was pulled immediately and replaced with a new campaign featuring the tagline: *A short drive down the road, a million miles away*. During the foot-and-mouth disease outbreak in the UK, the LTB directed attention towards the domestic market (Hopper, 2002). The LTB particularly focused on promoting domestic short breaks to the capital. However, by February 2002 PATA had stated concern at the trend towards stronger domestic promotion in many PATA countries (PATA, 2002). The concern was due to the potential for discouraging outbound travel, resulting in lower inbound arrivals within the region, which would further impact on airline profitability.

Social media

The future will see increasing DMO use of social media, such as Twitter, for example, for broadcasting updates during and post disaster. However, little has been reported about the use of social media related to disasters in the tourism literature to date. Cakmak and Issac (2012) discussed analysing visitors' blogs as a means of interpreting the image of a destination experiencing troubles, such as in the case of Bethlehem. Hays *et al.* (2013) noted during the 2010 Queensland floods that the STO's domestic Facebook fans were encouraged to upload pictures to show the world that most tourist areas were unaffected. They found this was a useful way to get a community talking positively about the destination at a time when the news media were using headlines such as 'half of Queensland underwater', 'it's a nightmare' and 'it's a disaster' (Hays *et al.*, 2013: 233). Due to a history of severe weather events in the state, Tourism and Event Queensland and other stakeholders have been particularly proactive in the use of social media initiatives. In addition to the Facebook tactics, the STO has also developed a series of YouTube video resources for communities (https://www.youtube.com/user/tourismqld). Also, the *Ready, set, go!* mobile app was developed by the Queensland Tourism Industry Council, in conjunction with EC3 Global and the National Centre for Studies in Travel and Tourism, to enable tourism businesses to enhance their disaster readiness (https://www.qtic.com.au/project-service/ready-set-go-mobile-app). For insights into the driver of travellers' social media usage during a crisis see Schroeder *et al.* (2013).

Dark tourism

There is a dark side to tourism marketing, where some travellers are attracted to the negative images of places that have suffered disasters (Ahmed, 1991). It has been suggested that the First World War of 1914–1918 represented the start of the modern dark tourism era, due to the global introduction of battle scene footage at the new invention of movie cinemas at that same time (Seaton, 1996). The phenomenon is most commonly labelled *dark tourism* (see, for example, Lennon and Foley, 2000) where tourists visit scenes of death, disaster, violence and crime, for reasons of remembrance, education, entertainment and morbidity. Another term used in the academic literature to describe aspects related to this phenomenon has included *thano tourism* (see Seaton, 1996), which comes from the ancient Greek word *thanatos* for the personification of death. In 2005 the level of academic interest in the topic led to the launch of dark tourism website www.dark-tourism.org.uk, by the Institute for Dark Tourism, with the goal to become the one-stop shop for researchers and students interested in accessing information on the topic. In 2014 the Institute launched the world's first master's degree in dark tourism at the University of Central Lancashire, UK.

While the label *dark tourism* is relatively new, the activities the term represents are not. That so many travellers are attracted to scenes of disaster is perhaps representative of human curiosity, which in part manifests itself in our innate desire for travel to explore our world. In some cases, travellers' morbid curiosity is temporary, immediately following an event, such as:

- 'Ghoulish Aussie tourists flocking to the jail housing convicted drug smugglers Schapelle Corby and the Bali Nine' (Wockner and Weston, 2006: 9). The Indonesian jail was becoming a must-see for some *jail tourists*, wanting a glimpse of the ten infamous young Australians, including two on death row, who were eventually executed in 2015.

- Shortly after the war in Iraq in 2003, UK travellers were signing up for tours of the country. A report in the Daily Express cited bookings by travellers to a tour organised by Hinterland Travel to 'see what has happened to the country', rather than for cultural or natural attractions.

CASE STUDY

7.2 Tours to Christchurch's earthquake Red Zone

Dr Anne Lane
Queensland University of Technology, Australia

Christchurch is New Zealand's second-largest city with a population of about 360,000 people. It is the capital of the Canterbury region, situated on the eastern coast of New Zealand's South

Island in an area renowned for earthquake activity – which is why NZ is sometimes referred to as the Shaky Isles. Although Christchurch's economy is based largely on agriculture, it has also has a thriving tourism industry. Tourists visit Christchurch because of its proximity to the snow fields of the Southern Alps, its growing reputation as a base camp for action and adventure activities and the charm of its architecture and culture. These and other attractions also make Christchurch a favoured destination for cruise ship passengers.

On 4 September 2010 a severe earthquake with a magnitude of 7.1 on the Richter scale rocked Christchurch. The area was still recovering from this when, on 22 February 2011, another major quake occurred. This second shock caused widespread damage and destruction in the Christchurch area and resulted in the deaths of 185 people.

Once the immediate after effects of the disaster had been addressed, and parts of the city had been made safe, the council set up the Canterbury Earthquake Recovery Authority (CERA) to look for ways to help local residents and businesses recover. As part of these efforts, CERA began to run bus tours to the Red Zone, the area of Christchurch hardest hit by the earthquakes. Over 37,000 tourists and locals paid a gold coin donation to take a trip to view the devastation.

The initial purpose of these bus tours was to allow those interested to see the reality of the disaster site for themselves, rather than relying on the often sanitised images portrayed in the media. Other visitors, particularly locals, wanted to go to pay their respects and to grieve for those who had lost their lives. Tour operators provided warnings about the danger of visiting the city centre, which was still experiencing aftershocks, and gave participants two chances to get off the bus before the tour began. Support facilities were provided for those who became distressed. Visitors were asked to listen to a provided audio track using headphones to respect the wishes of those who wanted to view the situation in silence. Red Zone tours were also provided for celebrities and politicians. Despite these efforts, local tourism operators experienced an 80 per cent drop in visitor numbers.

By March 2012, it became apparent that CERA could no longer afford to keep running the loss-making Red Zone bus tours. They put out a tender for a private company to offer the tours instead. Interested parties initially indicated they would need to charge visitors a minimum of NZ$10 per ticket to make the trips financially viable. The company whose tender bid was successful now brands the trips as The Rebuild Tour (see http://www.redbus.co.nz/christchurch/rebuild-tour), and focuses on showing visitors the rebuilding and regeneration of Christchurch in their NZ$29 tours. The tour is rated eighth out of 69 tours and activities in Christchurch by TripAdvisor with a user score of 4.5 out of 5.

Discussion question

What is the tourism benefit of offering tours of a disaster zone?

In many cases a sustained curiosity is developed. For example, the site of the 1985 air crash in which 256 members of the US 101st Airborne Division were killed remains one of the most popular visitor attractions in Gander, Canada (see Butler and Baum, 1999). In Rotorua, New Zealand, disaster struck in June 1886 when Mount Tarawera erupted, destroying 3 Maori villages with the loss of 150 lives and obliterating the fledgling destination's most notable tourism attraction at the time, the Pink and White Terraces. This was a devastating blow for tourism (Stafford, 1986), only 40 years after the first tourist arrivals. However, within two years Rotorua's annual visitor arrivals were higher than pre-eruption levels (Reggett, 1972). Part of the continued interest in Rotorua was the eruption aftermath and new volcanic craters, which remain attractions today. The city of San Francisco marked the 100th anniversary of the 1906 earthquake with a series of events and promotions. Similarly the city of Napier in New Zealand strongly promotes its art deco architecture, which was a result of rebuilding after a devastating earthquake in 1931.

RESEARCH SNAPSHOT

7.1 The nineteenth-century rise of Pompeii as a site of secular tourism pilgrimage

The site of the ancient city of Pompeii, Italy, remained inaccessible to the public for 1,700 years, from the time the town was buried in ash from the AD 79 eruption of Mount Vesuvius until Charles de Bourbon's extensive excavations of the eighteenth century. Kovacs (2013) traced the history of the evolution of the site as a tourism destination in the latter half of the nineteenth century, through analyses of artworks, guidebooks, souvenir production and the 1834 novel *The Last Days of Pompeii* by Edward Bulwer-Lytton. The analysis examined why Pompeii has become a Mecca of secular travel, where visitors are able to pay homage to the lives lost and experience an authentic slice of ancient Roman life, ever since the excavated site was founded as a museum in the late 1800s.

Further reading

Kovacs, C. L. (2013).

Scenes of death, human suffering and remembrance

In what could be described as a macabre tourism activity, walk down the restaurant strip along Miami South Beach's Ocean Drive on any day or night and you will see the curious sight of visitors posing for photos and selfies on the steps of the mansion where famous fashion guru, Gianni Versace, was gunned down in 1997. Other popular sites of human suffering include:

- The grounds of the Tower of London, where visitors can stand on the spot where Queen Anne Boleyn was beheaded in 1536 on the orders of her husband King Henry VIII.

- Cambodia's Killing Fields, where over 1 million people died during the 1970s civil war.

- The Alma tunnel in Paris where Princess Diana was killed in 1997.

- Dealey Plaza in Dallas, where US President John F. Kennedy was assassinated in 1963. Two large X marks on the roadway indicate where the sniper's bullets hit their target.

- The treacherous Kakoda trail in Papua New Guinea, scene of Second World War battles between Japanese and Australian forces.

- Robben Island, near Cape Town in South Africa, where the late Nelson Mandela was jailed from 1964 to 1982 before becoming the country's first black president a decade later.

- Second World War prisoner of war camps, such as Colditz Castle, Germany.

The year 2015 marked the 100th anniversary of the Australia and New Zealand Army Corps (ANZAC) landing on the Gallipoli peninsula in Turkey during one of the bloodiest campaigns of the First World War with 36,000 British Commonwealth troops killed. The site, now known as ANZAC Cove, is protected by the Turkish government as a memorial, and there are no built commercial facilities. There is a memorial walking track and 31 battlefield cemeteries. ANZAC Day is commemorated by Australians and New Zealanders on 25 April each year, and many have travelled to Gallipoli over the years to attend the annual dawn service. The memorial site has a capacity for 8,000 visitors, who stay overnight in sleeping bags on the clifftop grass, and is full every year. Interest in the 2015 centenary was so great that the governments of Australia and New Zealand held a coordinated ballot 12 months in advance, and in both countries the number of registrants on the waiting list was over double the number of tickets allocated for the service. In fact, 42,000 Australians applied in the ballot (Miranda, 2015).

Also commemorated in 2015 was the 200th anniversary of the Battle of Waterloo in Belgium (Backpackertradenews.com, 2015). Around 200,000 visitors were expected to visit the town during the three-day commemoration. The short battle in 1815 between the Duke of Wellington's Anglo-allied forces and Napoleon Bonaparte's French army ended 20 years of war and marked the beginning of 50 years of peace.

Other well-visited memorial sites include:

- the Bali bomb memorial at Kuta, Indonesia;
- Hawaii's USS Arizona Second World War Pearl Harbour memorial;
- the Holocaust Memorial Museum, USA;
- Auschwitz-Birkenau Memorial and Museum, Poland;
- Peace Memorial Park in Hiroshima, Japan;
- New York's Ground Zero, USA;
- Nanjing Massacre Memorial, China;
- the US civil war Petersburg National Battlefield.

The DMO's role in ethical promotion of dark tourism

The popularity of sites of death and disaster has demonstrated that there can also be a positive effect of such events. However, there is a fine moral line between preserving sites for memorial purposes and their commercial exploitation. In 2005 the government of Phnom Phen in Cambodia signed a deal with Japanese entrepreneurs to manage the Choeung Ek Memorial, which proved contentious with some local residents (Cripps, 2005). The Killing Fields genocide memorial houses a tower of an estimated 8,000 human skulls, some of the estimated 3 million victims who died at the hands of former dictator Pol Pot's Khmer Rouge. Cripps cited relatives who suggested victims were being 'sold for profit'. However, the local mayor argued the decision was justified since most package tours featured the memorial as a regular stop: 'This project will benefit our country's tourism as some tourists do not just want to visit our historic temples. They also what to see with their own eyes the past violence of the "Killing Fields"'.

Since DMOs are rarely destination *management* organisations, they have no control over commercial activities or visitor behaviours at dark tourism sites. Instead, their role is one of encouraging ethical and sensitive visitation and respect.

CHAPTER SUMMARY

Key point 1: Disaster contingency marketing planning to avert a crisis

No destination is immune to a disaster, and so every DMO should consider the possibility of such an event occurring at some stage in the future. Disasters can be man-made or *acts of God* and can be short term or long term. Almost all will be unpredictable and beyond the control of the DMO. The level of preparedness for a disaster at a destination is likely to determine the extent to which a management crisis manifests.

Key point 2: DMO responses to disasters

Since a state of crisis can affect the viability of the destination, DMOs have a responsibility to prepare disaster marketing plans. The level of such planning has historically been very low. However, the recent increase in acts of war and terrorism has forced more destinations to act. The topic of destination disaster response management is an emerging research field within the tourism literature. A number of case studies have been reported in recent years and provide a valuable resource for DMOs considering contingency planning. Key activities that DMOs should consider include: the formation of a permanent disaster taskforce, scenario building and risk analysis, coordinated marketing responses, market concentration, outsourcing of media relations and initiatives to support local businesses.

Key point 3: The dark side of tourism marketing

There is a dark side to tourism marketing related to facilitating travellers' interests in experiencing scenes of death, disasters and other morbid and macabre events. Since the DMO has no control over the commercial activities and behaviour of visitors at such sites, the main role is one of using ethical and sensitive marketing communications to promote the positive aspects of visitation for remembrance and respect.

REVIEW QUESTIONS

1. Discuss the importance of a disaster marketing strategy for your destination. Does your DMO have a disaster response strategy published in the public domain?

2. What are the potential risks to your destination that could lead to a disaster and crisis in the future?

3. Why have DMOs in general been slow to develop a disaster response strategy?

REFERENCES

Ahmed, Z. U. (1991). The dark side of image marketing. *The Tourist Review* 4(2): 36–37.

Alcantara, N. (2003). *Travel Advisories Reward Terrorists, Says Gordon*. Available at: www.eturbonews.com. 24 October 2003.

Avraham, E. and Ketter, E. (2008). *Media Strategies of Marketing Places in Crisis: Improving the Image of Cities, Countries and Tourist Destinations*. Burlington, MA and Oxford, UK: Butterworth-Heinemann.

Backpackertradenews.com. (2015). *2000 Aussies to Meet Their Waterloo*. 10 June. Available at: http://www. backpackertradenews.com.au/2000-aussies-meet-their-waterloo

Beirman, D. (2002). Marketing of tourism destinations during a prolonged crisis: Israel and the Middle East. *Journal of Vacation Marketing* 8(2): 167–176.

Beirman, D. (2003a). *Restoring Destinations in Crisis*. Crows Nest, NSW: Allen & Unwin.

Beirman, D. (2003b). *Kenyan Tourism's Recovery*. Available at: www.eturbonews. 1 October.

Berger, D. (2006). *The Development of Mexico's Tourism Industry: Pyramids by Day, Martinis by Night*. New York: Palgrave Macmillan.

Bush, J. E. (2004). The story of a public/private tourism marketing partnership. In Dickenson, B. and Vladimir, A. (eds) *The Complete 21st Century Travel & Hospitality Marketing Handbook*. Upper Saddle River, NJ: Pearson, pp. 121–127.

Butler, R. W. and Baum, T. (1999). The tourism potential of the peace dividend. *Journal of Travel Research* 38(1): 24–29.

Cakmak, E. and Issac, R. (2012). What destination marketers can learn from their visitors' blogs: An image analysis of Bethlehem, Palestine. *Journal of Destination Marketing and Management* 1(1/2): 124–133.

Cavlek, N. (2002). Tour operators and destination safety. *Annals of Tourism Research* 29(2): 478–496.

Cripps, K. (2005). Cambodia's mass grave site privatized. Available at: www.travelwirenews.com. 12 April.

Department of Resources, Energy and Tourism. (2012). *Don't Risk it! A Guide to Assist Regional Tourism Organisations to Prepare, Respond and Recover from a Crisis*. Canberra, Australia: Australian Government.

Dilley, M., Chen, R. S., Deichmann, U., Lerner-Lam, A. L. and Arnold, M. (2005). *Natural Disaster Hotspots: A Global Risk Analysis*. Washington, DC: World Bank. © World Bank. Available at: https://openknowledge.worldbank.org/handle/10986/7376

Dimanche, F. and Lepetic, A. (1999). New Orleans tourism and crime: A case study. *Journal of Travel Research* 38(1): 19–23.

Edgell, D. L. (1999). *Tourism Policy: The Next Millennium*. Champaign, IL: Sagamore.

eGlobaltravelmedia.com. (2015a). *Poll Indicates Drug Duo Executions May Affect Bali Travel*. 11 May. Available at: http://www.eglobaltravelmedia.com.au/poll-indicates-drug-duo-executions-may-affect-bali-travel

eGlobaltravelmedia.com. (2015b). *Aussies Still Love NZ But 'Quake Effect' Shakes Things up*. 7 January. Available at: http://www.eglobaltravelmedia.com.au/aussies-still-love-nz-but-quake-effect-shakes-things-up

eGlobaltravelmedia.com. (2015c). *Bangkok Unrest: Cancellations Start to Hit Mice Industry*. 16 January. Available at: http://www.eglobaltravelmedia.com.au/bangkok-unrest-cancellations-start-to-hit-mice-industry

Elliott, J. (1997). *Tourism: Politics and Public Sector Management*. London: Routledge.

Faulkner, B. (1999). *Tourism Disasters: Towards a Generic Model*. CRC Tourism Work-in-Progress Report Series: Report 6. Hard copy publication.

Faulkner, B. (2001). Towards a framework for tourism disaster management. *Tourism Management* 22(2): 135–147.

Faulkner, B. and Vikulov, S. (2001). Katherine, washed out one day, back on track the next: A post-mortem of a tourism disaster. *Tourism Management* 22(4): 331–344.

Frisby, E. (2002). Communicating in a crisis: The British Tourist Authority's responses to the foot-and-mouth outbreak and 11th September, 2001. *Journal of Vacation Marketing* 9(1): 89–100.

Gartner, W. C. and Shen, J. (1992). The impact of Tiananmen Square on China's tourism image. *Journal of Travel Research* Spring: 47–52.

Hall, C. M. (2005). The future of tourism research. In Ritchie, B. W., Burns, P. and Palmer, C. (eds) *Tourism Research Methods: Integrating Theory with Practice*. Wallingford, UK: CABI Publishing.

Hanbury, W. A. (2005). Case study in crisis management: Management lessons learned from 9/11 and its aftermath. In Harrill, R. (ed.) *Fundamentals of Destination Management and Marketing*. Washington, DC: IACVB, pp. 99–108.

Hays, S., Page, S. J. and Buhalis, D. (2013). Social media as a destination marketing tool: Its use by national tourism organisations. *Current Issues in Tourism* 16(3): 211–239.

Henderson, J. (2002). Managing a tourism crisis in Southeast Asia: The role of national tourism organizations. *International Journal of Hospitality & Tourism Administration* 3(1): 85–105.

Hopper, P. (2002). Marketing London in a difficult climate. *Journal of Vacation Marketing* 9(1): 81–88.

ILO. (2003). *ILO Sees Further Tourism Job Losses Due to Travel Woes: SARS, Economic Doldrums Cited as Causes*. Media Release. International Labour Organization. 14 May.

Ironside, R., Caldwell, A. and Williams, B. (2009). Pacific Adventurer oil spill a disaster says Anna Bligh. *The Courier Mail*. 13 March. Hard copy newspaper article.

Johnson, G. and Scholes, K. (2002). *Exploring Corporate Strategy* (6th edition). Harlow, UK: Pearson Education.

Kleinman, M. and Bashford, S. (2002). BTA set for 40m blitz to tempt back tourists. *Marketing* February 28(6). Hard copy article.

Kovacs, C. L. (2013). Pompeii and its material reproductions: The rise of a tourist site in the nineteenth century. *Journal of Tourism History* 5(1): 25–49.

Kubiak, G. D. (2002). Travel & tourism: Export of tomorrow. *Spectrum: The Journal of State Government* Spring: 18–20.

Lavery, P. (1992). The financing and organisation of national tourist offices. *EIU Travel & Tourism Analyst* 4: 84–101.

Lennon, J. and Foley, M. (2000). *Dark Tourism: The Attraction of Death and Disaster.* London: Continuum.

Leslie, D. (1999). Terrorism and tourism: The Northern Ireland situation – A look behind the veil of certainty. *Journal of Travel Research* 38(1): 37–40.

L'Etang, J., Falkheimer, J. and Lugo, J. (2007). Public relations and tourism: Critical reflections and a research agenda. *Public Relations Review* 33(1): 68–76.

Litvin, S. W. and Alderson, L. L. (2003). How Charleston got her groove back: A convention and visitors bureau's response to 9/11. *Journal of Vacation Marketing* 9(2): 188–197.

Manning, A. (2003). *WHO Lifts Last SARS Travel Warning.* Available at: www.eTurboNews.com. 25 July.

Mansfield, Y. (1999) Cycles of war, terror, and peace: Determinants and management of crisis and recovery of the Israeli tourism industry. *Journal of Travel Research* 38(1): 30–36.

McClelland, C. (2003). *Toronto Tourism Loses $190 Million, Says Report.* Available at: www.eTurboNews.com. 18 June.

Miranda. C. (2015). United they pay respect. *The Courier Mail.* 25 April, pp. 6–7. Hard copy newspaper article.

O'Neill, M. A. and McKenna, M. A. (1994). Northern Ireland tourism: A quality perspective. *Managing Service Quality* 4(2): 31–35.

Opanga, K. (2003). *Kenya Suffers for the US and Because of America.* 24 June. Available at: www.eTurboNews.com

Page, S., Yeoman, I., Munro, C., Connell, J. and Walker, L. (2006). A case study of best practice: Visit Scotland's prepared response to an influenza pandemic. *Tourism Management* 27(3): 361–393.

PATA. (2002). *Issues & Trends: Pacific Asia Travel* 7(2). Hard copy only.

PATA (2003). *Crisis: It Won't Happen to Us!* Bangkok: Pacific Asia Travel Association.

Pike, S. (2007). A cautionary tale of a resort destination's self-inflicted crisis. *Journal of Travel & Tourism Marketing* 23(2/3/4): 73–82.

Pike, S. (2008). *Destination Marketing: An Integrated Marketing Communication Approach.* Burlington, MA: Butterworth-Heinemann.

Pike, S., May, T. and Bolton, R. (2011). RTO governance: Reflections from a former marketing team. *Journal of Travel & Tourism Research* Fall: 117–133.

Pizam, A. (1999). A comprehensive approach to classifying acts of crime and violence at tourism destinations. *Journal of Travel Research* 38(1): 5–12.

Portorff, S. M. and Neal, D. M. (1994). Marketing implications for post-disaster tourism destinations. *Journal of Travel & Tourism Marketing* 3(1): 115–122.

Reggett, R. S. (1972). *The Tarawera Eruption: Its Effects on the Tourist Industry.* Unpublished MA Thesis. Dunedin, NZ: University of Otago. Hardbound copy thesis.

Roehl, W. S. (1990). Travel agent attitudes toward China after Tiananmen Square. *Journal of Travel Research* Fall: 16–22.

Schroeder, A., Pennington-Gray, L., Donohoe, H. and Kiousis, S. (2013). Using social media in times of crisis. *Journal of Travel & Tourism Marketing* 30(1/2): 126–143.

Schwartz, P. (1992). *The Art of the Long View.* London: Century Business.

Seaton, A. V. (1996). Guided by the dark: From thanatopsis to thanatourism. *International Journal of Heritage Studies* 2(4): 234–244.

Sönmez, S. F., Apostolopoulous, Y. and Tarlow, P. (1999). Tourism in crisis: Managing the effects of terrorism. *Journal of Travel Research* 38(1): 13–18.

Stafford, D. (1986). *The Founding Years in Rotorua: A History of Events to 1900.* Auckland, NZ: Ray Richards.

TravelandTourWorld.com. (2014). *Egypt's Tour Guides' New Business: Producing Opium.* Available at: http://www.travelandtourworld.com/news/article/egypts-tour-guides-new-business-producing-opium

TravelandTourWorld.com. (2015). *Kenya Tourist Arrivals Fell by 25% in the First Five Months This Year.* Available at: http://www.travelandtourworld.com/news/article/kenya-tourist-arrivals-fell-25-first-five-months-year

Tsai, C. H. and Chen, C. W. (2011). The establishment of a rapid natural disaster risk assessment model for the tourism industry. *Tourism Management* 32(1): 158–171.

Wockner, C. and Weston, P. (2006). Anger over 'sick' Bali prison tours. *The Sunday Mail.* 12 March, p. 9. Hard copy newspaper article.

Chapter 8

Destination marketing strategy development

> **AIMS**
>
> To enhance understanding of:
>
> - the DMO vision, values, mission, goals and objectives;
> - a destination marketing strategy design framework;
> - sources of comparative and competitive advantage for destinations.

> **ABSTRACT**
>
> The DMO's mission is to enhance destination competitiveness. The increasing competition in tourism markets, cluttered with the noise of substitute products and countless destinations promoting similar benefits, forces DMOs at all levels to develop effective marketing communication strategies. Strategic marketing planning is a proactive attempt by the DMO to enhance destination competitiveness by establishing a differentiated and meaningful position in the minds of target consumers. In Chapter 1 it was proposed that destination marketing is a forward-thinking communication discipline, which involves matching destination resources with environment opportunities. These two concepts underpin strategy design. Also, the ability to implement strategy is as critical as the quality of the plan. One of the main shortcomings in strategy implementation is the failure to translate strategic goals into a practical guide for all stakeholders on those factors that are critical to the achievement of the targets. While later sections of the text focus on collaboration, implementation and performance measurement, this chapter provides a framework for developing strategic goals and articulating the strategy rationale to stakeholders. Central to the framework are three tools: the STEEPL analysis is used to scan the macro environment to identify potential opportunities and threats; the VRIO resource model categorises the destination's resources to identify sources of competitive advantage; and the SWOT matrix is a visual tool for:

(1) developing goals and objectives that match destination resources with environment opportunities; and (2) demonstrating the rationale for the marketing communication tactics to stakeholders.

Destination marketing strategy framework

In the pursuit of destination competitiveness it has only been relatively recently that DMOs have begun to develop coordinated tourism strategies. Published research relating to DMO strategy development is scant (see Gilbert, 1990; Long, 1994; Kim *et al.*, 2000; Smith, 2003; Stokes, 2008). The contributions to date indicate an *ad hoc* approach that appears to be typical of the wider destination marketing literature (Pike and Page, 2014). The need for an industry-wide tourism strategy has been called for in most parts of the world in recent years, including, for example, Canada (Go, 1987), New Zealand (NZTPD, 1989; OTSP, 2001), USA (Ahmed and Krohn, 1990), Central and Eastern Europe (Hall, 1999), Scandinavia (Flagestad and Hope, 2001) and Australia in the federal government's 2004 AUD$235 million white paper. Leslie (1999) was particularly critical of the then Northern Ireland Tourist Board for a lack of long-term strategic planning, which had resulted in the destination losing touch with changing patterns of demand:

> *For those involved, to consider publicly that the troubles have masked attention to significant underlying trends counteracting demand for the province would not only bring into question their personal role and job but also that of the value of the organization.*

> *(Leslie, 1999: 40)*

Figure 8.1 presents a framework for the challenging task of formulating strategy to achieve the goals, remembering the fundamental purpose of the DMO is to enhance destination competitiveness. The approach is based on the view of destination marketing as a forward-thinking communication discipline that is based on *matching destination resources with environmental opportunities*. Destination resources are assets that represent potential strengths and weaknesses, relative to competing places. Environment opportunities represent forces in the macro environment that might or might not be directly related to the travel industry, over which the DMO has no control, but which represent potential opportunities and threats for the destination. The framework involves undertaking an analysis of macro and internal environments to identify sources of strengths, weaknesses, opportunities and threats (SWOT), in a manner

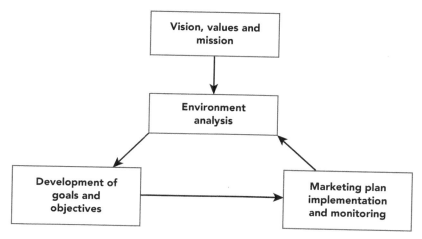

Figure 8.1 DMO strategy framework

that leads to the development of offensive and defensive goals and objectives, which will in turn guide the development of the promotional tactics. The framework is useful for explaining the rationale for the DMO's promotional tactics to stakeholders; a critical step in navigating destination politics and gaining buy-in for a collaborative effort from stakeholders.

DMO vision, values and mission

Much of marketing planning is about finding ways to meet unmet consumer wants. Marketing is therefore a forward-thinking exercise, and it is often useful for DMOs to articulate an envisioned future as a way of rallying and motivating stakeholders. A destination vision has been described as an 'inspirational portrait of an ideal future that the destination hopes to bring about at some defined future' (Goeldner *et al.*, 2000: 445). Table 8.1 highlights a number of DMO vision statements from around the world in 2015, which tend to articulate aspects of future destination competitiveness.

Table 8.1 DMO vision statements

DMO	Vision
VisitBritain http://www.visitbritain.org/aboutus/overview.aspx	To inspire the world to explore Britain
Visit Orlando, USA http://www.visitorlando.com/about-us	To be the most visited destination in the world
Tourism New Zealand http://traveltrade.newzealand.com/en/about	To motivate our target market to come now, do more and come back
Brand USA www.thebrandusa.com	Brand USA will be responsible for positioning and promoting the United States as a compelling destination for international travellers, inspiring visitors with a refreshed understanding that there is no place in the world like the United States of America with its limitless destinations and attractions. We will build a world-class team and organization that will execute an integrated marketing and communication strategy designed to deliver the highest possible return for the United States – in the form of job creation, GDP and export growth, and increased federal tax revenues
Destination New South Wales, Australia www.destinationnsw.com.au/about-us	To make Sydney and NSW one of the world's most successful tourism and event destinations
Vancouver Convention and Visitors Bureau, Canada www.tourismvancouver.com/about-us	To be the global leader in destination sales, marketing and visitor experiences

It is important to recognise vision statements should essentially be verbalising what the organisation already stands for, rather than an attempt to calculate what would be the most pragmatic or popular (Collins and Porras, 1997: 87). An important element in the vision design is therefore an understanding of the organisation's values, which are a small set of deeply held and enduring beliefs. Collins and Porras found visionary organisations tended to have between three and six simply stated core values, but that there was no single common ideology. Some firms feature customers at the core, others feature staff, some feature services, some feature risk taking, while others feature innovation. The core values of three tourism service-related firms from an extensive list compiled by Collins and Porras (1997: 68–71) are highlighted in Table 8.2.

There is a dearth of published research investigating the role of DMO values. Table 8.3 lists a variety of DMO value statements in use in 2015.

While a vision statement serves as a motivational aspiration, a mission is a statement about what is expected to be achieved and measured. Senior management and directors are held accountable to the mission. Even though mission statements are often criticised as being bland, it is important to clearly articulate to stakeholders the overall purpose of the organisation (Johnson and Scholes, 2002). Given the political dynamics of tourism destination marketing and the often divergent interests of stakeholders, a succinct and clear mission is important for DMOs. There should be no confusion as to the DMO's reason for being. However, in practice it is often difficult to distinguish vision statements from mission statements. Examples of DMO mission statements in 2015 are listed in Table 8.4.

Table 8.2 Examples of core values

Firm	Values
Disney	• No cynicism allowed • Fanatical attention to consistency and detail • Continuous progress via creativity, dreams, and imagination • Fanatical control and preservation of Disney's *magic* image • To bring happiness to millions, and to celebrate, nurture, and promulgate wholesome American values
Marriott	• Friendly service and excellent value (customers are guests) to make people away from home feel that they're among friends and really wanted • People are number 1 – treat them well, expect a lot, and the rest will follow • Work hard, yet keep it fun • Continual self-improvement • Overcoming adversity to build character
American Express	• Heroic customer service • Worldwide reliability of services • Encouragement of individual initiative

Source: Adapted from Collins and Porras (1997).

Table 8.3 DMO values

DMO	Values
Republic of South Africa Ministry of Tourism www.tourism.gov.za	• **Innovative**: Leveraging the resources and partnerships to optimise delivery to our stakeholders, and responsive to change • **Ethical** (Good corporate governance): Encapsulates principles of integrity, transparency and accountability • **Customer focus**: Provide services and solutions in a manner that is efficient, effective and responsive
Destination Wollongong, Australia www.visitwollongong.com.au	• **Resourceful**: Our highly adaptable 'can do' attitude taps into current trends • **Enthusiastic**: We love what we do! • **Innovative**: We challenge traditional thinking and look beyond the obvious • **Collaborative**: We achieve through teamwork and engage stakeholders to strengthen the region's brand appeal • **Integrity**: We represent the appeal and authentic experiences of our destination with honesty and originality
Destination Bristol, England www.visitbristol.co.uk/destinationbristol/about-us	• Being effective partners • Working with integrity • Delivering excellence • Valuing people • Providing leadership • Delivering customer satisfaction • Being successful
Scandinavian Tourist Board www.visitiscandinavia.org/en/corporate2/about-stb/english	• Facilitator • Innovator • Strategist • Knowledgeable

Macro environment analysis

A DMO does not operate within a vacuum. The best-laid plans will come unstuck because of events in the external environment over which the DMO has little or no control. Determinants of tourism and travel comprise exogenous forces, which are events or trends that may or may not be directly related to tourism, but which have the potential to influence the extent and nature of demand for tourism activity. A useful starting point therefore is to consider the range of macro environment influences that have the potential to impact on the tourism industry either positively or negatively.

Table 8.4 DMO mission statements

DMO	Mission statement
Goteborg & Co. (Gothenburg, Sweden) www.gotenborg.com	To market and take part in developing Gothenburg as a tourist, meeting and event destination
Zanzibar Commission for Tourism www.zanzibartourism.net	To be the most exotic, diverse island destination in the Indian ocean region
Las Vegas Convention and Visitors Authority, USA www.lvcva.com	To attract visitors by promoting Las Vegas as the World's most desirable destination for leisure and business travel
South Australian Tourism Commission, Australia www.tourism.sa.gov.au/about-satc.aspx	The SATC is committed to achieving $8 billion in tourism expenditure potential by 2020
Visit Kansas City, USA www.visitkc.com/about-visit-kc	To ignite global passion for visiting Kansas City
VisitBritain www.visitbritain.org	To grow the value of inbound tourism to Britain, working with a wide range of partners in both the UK and overseas. Through our global reach, we aim to increase visitor spending to all parts of Britain and improve Britain's ranking in the eyes of international visitors
Travel Portland www.travelportland.com	To strengthen the region's economy by marketing the metropolitan Portland region as a preferred destination for meetings, conventions, and leisure travel

As shown in Figure 8.2, it is useful to visualise the environment in the shape of a doughnut. The outer layer is representative of the external macro environment, the source of *opportunities* and *threats* over which the DMO has no control.

This is an important consideration for the SWOT. For example, weather-induced seasonality is a key macro environment issue affecting Canada's competitiveness (Smith, 2003: 125) and is therefore regarded as a *threat*. However, *to develop and promote new summer events* is not representative of an *opportunity*, as it is a goal the DMO has control over. The macro environment, which surrounds the organisation's internal environment, consists of **S**ocio-cultural, **T**echnology, **E**conomic, **E**cological, **P**olitical and **L**egal (STEEPL) forces. The internal operating environment consists of sources of *strengths* and *weaknesses* over which the organisation has varying degrees of control, such as stakeholders, competitors and customers. While it can be argued that a DMO does not have control over the actions of customers or competitors, destination marketers do have some control over which segments to target and, in doing so, which competitors. Case study 8.1 summarises a DMO/operator collaboration to adapt a destination resource to take advantage of an opportunity.

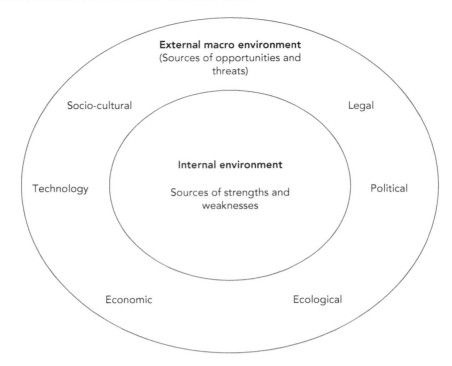

Figure 8.2 Macro environment and internal environment

8.1 Collaborative marketing research for product development

Sarah Gardiner and Noel Scott
Griffith University, Gold Coast, Australia

To remain competitive in a changing tourism market DMOs need to support and encourage tourism operators to continue to evolve their experiences to meet their changing visitors' mix and market-specific needs. The Gold Coast is Australia's major leisure tourism destination, providing a fun holiday environment built around its core resources of surf beaches, waterways and rainforest environments combined with its relaxed lifestyle and built attractions, centred on theme parks, shopping and dining activities. Not unlike many other tourism destinations around the world over the past century, Gold Coast tourism experiences have historically catered for mostly Western travellers, chiefly Australian (domestic) visitors from Brisbane, Sydney and Melbourne and visitors from New Zealand, Europe and the United States. However, the recent dramatic growth in first Japanese (1980s onwards) and later in Chinese (2000s onwards) visitors presents a challenge for operators who need to evolve their experiences to accommodate the important cultural differences of these new markets.

China is the fastest growing international travel source market in the world, and many Australian destinations, like the Gold Coast, have benefited from this boom in Chinese travellers. Australia was one of the first Western countries to be given Approved Destination Status (in 1999) for

Chinese travellers and, since then, this market has grown around 13 per cent per annum (2002 to 2012) to become Australia's second largest inbound market (after New Zealand and exceeding visitors from the United Kingdom). This growth is expected to continue with the Australian Government estimating total expenditure by Chinese travellers to reach between AUD$7.4 billion and AUD$9 billion by 2020.

Cognisant of this market trend, Gold Coast operators saw a significant opportunity to grow their businesses to attract Chinese visitors, but required insightful and actionable research on the preferences of Chinese visitors to make their experience 'China ready'. Accordingly, the region's DMO, Gold Coast Tourism, and local government agency, City of Gold Coast, partnered with Griffith University to investigate ways in which Gold Coast tourism businesses could make changes to their guest experience to better accommodate Chinese visitors, in particular Chinese youth and student travellers. To make sure the research results were practical and actionable, the researchers worked with a surf school that was interested in getting into the China market. Chinese university students living in Brisbane and the Gold Coast were invited to participate in a focus group where they were asked qualitative questions about their perceptions and attitude towards participating in a surf lesson as part of a Gold Coast holiday. Further insights were gathered when some participants later participated in a surf lesson and were interviewed about their perceptions, emotions and attitudes to the activity following the lesson.

Results suggest they really liked the beach and it was one of their main reasons for visiting and studying on the Gold Coast. Yet, most of the time, they just tended to look and visit the beach, they did not actually enter the water, because they were unfamiliar with the surf and had a fear of the water. Many of them could not swim and had never experienced the surf before. They are interested in surfing, but perceived it as too difficult. Yet, the idea of standing up and surfing a wave was viewed as a significant goal achievement. Sending an image of surfing a wave back home would provide social kudos. Sun exposure was also a concern. Darker skin was associated with farmers and agricultural workers who were perceived as lower class than Asian international students from cities and middle to upper class families who preferred fairer skin to represent their social status.

For those who went on the surf lesson there was a lot of excitement and students were proud and satisfied, because they confronted their fears of the activity. They really did not expect to stand up on a surfboard, so when they did stand, it was a moment of great joy. The professionalism and enthusiasm of the instructor also rated highly. They were keen to share their experiences on social media and used a Weibo account because Facebook is not accessible in China.

The surf school modified their products to suit the new Chinese market. Based on these findings, the surf school changed its emphasis from thrill and adventure to focus on learning about the beach, surfing safety and water skills as well as ensuring their instructors were more sensitive to various guest cultural needs and backgrounds. Sun sensitivity was addressed with long sleeve rash vests available to avoid sun exposure. International students also tended to partake in activities in friendship groups, and so the surf school offers group discounts and social activities, like a 'Surf and Sizzle' beach barbeque to extend the experience beyond just riding a wave.

Further reading

Scott, N., Gardiner, S. and Carlini, J. (2014).
http://www.griffith.edu.au/__data/assets/pdf_file/0004/678307/Experience-Gold-Coast-Innovative-Products-for-Asian-Visitors-2.pdf

Discussion question

Identify an ecotourism experience at your destination that might need adapting to suit Chinese visitors. What type of market research could you undertake to test the proposed changes to the experience?

Forward thinking

Marketing is as much a forward-thinking exercise about unmet consumer wants as it is about catering to current wants. Hamel and Prahalad (1989) argued the importance of devoting time to thinking about the future. They urged organisations to develop a view about the future as an ongoing project sustained by continuous debate, rather than a massive one-time effort. While it would be futile to attempt to predict the future (Drucker, 1995), it is critical that emerging megatrends, which have the potential to shape the future of the tourism industry, either positively or negatively, are explored. In examining the historical time lag from technological invention to market use and acceptance, Drucker suggested the future is already here, and that we should look to the fringes of society to observe future applications that are currently in the exploratory design stages. Everything that will be in common use in 30 years' time already exists in some form today, being developed somewhere on the *fringes of society*.

There exists a rich resource of views offered by futurists, whose research explores trends in mainstream society as well as developments occurring on the fringes. A sample of futurists' thoughts in 2015, which might have tourism implications, is provided in Table 8.5. Other well-known futurists include: John Naisbitt (www.naisbitt.com), Faith Popcorn (www.faithpopcorn.com), Alvin Toffler (www.alvintoffler.net), Ray Kurzweil (www.kurzweilai.net) and Nick Bostrom (www.nickbostrom.com). Unfortunately, tourism as a topic has received little attention from futurists (Cole and Razak, 2009). Most notable to date have been the books of tourism *futurologist* Ian Yeoman (2008, 2012). Yeoman was formerly a scenario planner for Visit Scotland. Tourism academics are canvassed on the most important issues facing the global tourism each year by Professor David Edgell Sr., of East Carolina University. Using the TRInet list-serve of over 2,000 tourism academics, Edgell posts a summary of the top 10 trends that year. Table 8.6 summarises the most important issues, which represent potential opportunities and threats, for 2014 and 2015.

Scenario thinking

Scenario planning was developed by Wack (1985) and promoted by Schwartz (1991) as a structured way of thinking about the future. In the form of carefully constructed plots, scenario thinking is underpinned by: (1) adopting the long view; (2) outside-inside thinking; and (3) drawing from multiple perspectives. In a world of continuous-discontinuous change (continuous but differing types of change rather than incremental adjustments) the approach is ideal for DMOs to tap the wider community of stakeholders' creativity and entrepreneurship thinking to help make sense of the future. Little has been reported about scenario thinking for DMOs in the tourism literature to date. Formica and Kothari (2008) outlined their use of scenario thinking with stakeholders of the tourism industry in the US tri-state area of Pennsylvania, New Jersey and Delaware, to identify forces likely to drive change in the industry over the next five years. Adopting a longer-term view, Yeoman (2012) described a range of scenarios for global tourism in the year 2050. As suggested in Chapter 7, scenario thinking is particularly useful in developing disaster response strategies. During 2005 a media *frenzy* developed over the threat of avian flu spreading from Asia to Europe in the form of a pandemic. Visit Scotland undertook scenario planning for such

Table 8.5 Views of the future

Futurist	Trends
World Futurist Society 2014–2030 www.wfs.org/forecasts	• Electric cars powered by fuel cells, sell excess electricity back to the grid • Open-source robot blueprints cut the cost of robots by 90% • Smart phones help spur reform in Africa • The world's oceans face mass extinction event • The *cloud* will become more intelligent, not just a place to store data
Skift.com (2015)	• Hospitality sector driving innovation in travel • The conferences and events industry is going through a renaissance • The rise of the boutique destination • Mobile pay and wearable tech move from concept to real-world disruptor • Travel brands reimaging themselves as lifestyle connoisseurs • The real and literal disruption of travel is a real threat • The online travel duopoly will not last forever • Alternative travel is a reality • Downsizing on design and moving towards simplicity • Mobile is moving in-market • Travel brands look to Instagram for the influencer bump
Trendwatching.com	• Instant skills – reducing barriers to creation of high quality output • Fast laning – reducing online waiting times for consumers • Fair splitting – mPayments facilitate cost splitting • Internet of shared things – as more devices become connected • Branded government – corporate brands helping create meaningful change in the civic arena

an eventuality. Page *et al.* (2006) provided a rare insight into the scenario building exercise from the perspective of a DMO. The case is an example of best practice in the tourism industry, both in terms of the planning process and the sharing of information with other NTOs.

STEEPL analysis

The STEEPL analysis provides a structured approach to scanning the macro environment. While a full analysis of key issues, trends and drivers that confront global tourism is beyond the scope of this chapter, an example of a STEEPL summary is shown in Table 8.7. The STEEPL provides a systematic approach to the identification of forces that have the potential to impact on tourism in the future,

Table 8.6 Top ten issues facing global tourism

	2014	2015
1	Global economic slowdown	Global economic slowdown
2	Safety and security	Safety and security
3	Lack of leadership in tourism policy and planning	Sustainability destinations' resources
4	Sustainability destinations' resources	Lack of leadership in tourism policy and planning
5	New technologies and online applications	Barriers to travel such as visas, fuel prices, airline fees and airline delays
6	Transformation effect tourism is having on global socio-economic progress	New technologies and online applications
7	Climate change	Transformation effect tourism is having on global socio-economic progress
8	Increased fuel prices and airline fees	Disasters and political disruptions
9	Disasters and political disruptions	Climate change
10	Changes in tourism demand from increasing travel by emerging nations	Changes in tourism demand from increasing travel by emerging nations

either positively or negatively. These therefore represent environment opportunities and threats for inclusion in the SWOT matrix. (**Note: An opportunity is not a tactic, as is so often seen incorrectly in SWOT analysis, such as *To do something*, but rather a positive external force over which the DMO has no control.**)

Competitive advantage versus comparative advantage

An important question raised by Ritchie and Crouch (2000) was whether destination *stars* are made or born. They offered the example of Russia at that time, well-endowed with natural resources but lacking in deployment, in comparison to destinations such as Singapore, Las Vegas, Branson and San Antonio, all of which had developed successful tourism strategies with limited endowed resources. Ritchie and Crouch suggested an understanding of success drivers was of fundamental importance and categorised these into resources that would represent sources of either comparative or competitive advantage. Endowed resources inherited by a destination, such as climate and scenery, are categorised as sources of *comparative* advantage. However, resources created by the destination, which include the way in which endowed resources are organised and deployed in the market, represent sources of *competitive* advantage. A practical example of this was provided by Dascalu (1997), who cited comments from a former Romanian Minister of Tourism concerned that his country had enormous tourism resources, but that the tourism industry was under performing. These resources might have represented sources of comparative advantage, but were not being used to achieve a competitive advantage. Other examples of sources of comparative advantage that do not yet represent competitive advantage include:

Table 8.7 STEEPL analysis

Socio-cultural	
	• Social media uptake
	• Population growth and ageing population
	• The rise of China outbound travel
	• Mega rich
	• Nostalgia
	• Busier lives
	• Increasing growth in travel
	• Exercise movement
	• Changing work and workforce patterns
	• Increasing consumer sophistication
	• Virtual shopping and demassification
Technology	• Web 2.0 technologies and consumers' expectations
	• Rise in influence in social media user generated content
	• Disintermediation
	• Self-driving cars
	• Rates of obsolescence
	• Virtual reality
	• Artificial intelligence
	• Real-time global media
	• Robotics
	• Nanotechnology
	• Sub-orbital travel
	• Medical tourism
Economic	• Global financial crisis
	• Business alliances, mergers and acquisitions
	• Lessening political control of interest rates and currency exchange rates
	• Value of information
	• Virtual networks
	• Increased competition
	• Foreign direct investment
	• Disposable income
	• Retirement income
	• Low-cost airlines

(continued)

Table 8.7 *(continued)*

Ecological	• Climate change
	• Rising ocean levels
	• Carbon trading
	• Environmental protection
	• Renewable energies
	• Biosecurity
	• Responsibility of citizenship
	• Eco-friendly and organic movement
	• Recycling
	• Overcrowding and pollution
Political	• Terrorism
	• Consumer uncertainty during national elections
	• Regional trading blocs
	• Community-based tourism planning
	• Increasing government stability in South America and decline in Arabian Gulf states
	• Pirates
	• Indigenous peoples' land rights
	• User-pays taxes
	• Increasing bureaucracy
Legal	• Visa facilitation
	• Illegal migration
	• Deregulation
	• Safety standards
	• Information privacy
	• Intellectual property
	• Insurance liability

- Ethiopia's Simien Mountains, home of the biblical Queen of Sheba, with spectacular gorges up to 1,000 metres deep;

- the world's oldest paintings at Cantabria's Altamira Caves in northern Spain, which date back 14,000 years;

- Kazakhstan has the world's largest number of wild wolves;

- some of the world's most complete dinosaur remains can be found in the Fossil Triangle, which links to isolated outback towns of Winton, Hughenden and Cloncurry in Queensland, Australia.

Competitive advantage is expressed in terms of competitors and customers. Porter (1980, 1985) suggested a competitive strategy was one that positioned a business to make the most of strengths that differentiated the organisation from competitors. A firm's success is ultimately achieved through 'attaining a competitive position or a series of competitive positions that lead to superior and sustainable financial performance' (Porter, 1991: 96). A sustainable competitive advantage is gained when consumers perceive a performance capability gap that endures over time (Coyne, 1986). Subjective examples of potential sources of comparative and competitive advantage for DMOs are summarised in Table 8.8.

VRIO resource model

A tourism resource may be viewed as anything that plays a major role in attracting visitors to a destination (Spotts, 1997). Sources of competitive advantage are essentially assets and skills (Aaker, 1991). An asset is a resource that is superior to those possessed by the competition, and a skill is an activity undertaken more effectively than competitors. A resource audit is therefore a key component of marketing planning. However, Ferrario (1979) suggested up to that time the availability of tourism resources was often taken for granted by both practitioners and academics. Since then the process of auditing a destination's resources has received increased attention in the literature (see, for example, Pearce, 1997; Spotts, 1997; Faulkner et al., 1999; Ritchie and Crouch, 2000; Pike, 2002; Beerli and Martin, 2004).

Barney (1991, 1996) developed the VRIO model as a tool for determining the competitive status of resources controlled by a firm. While this resource-based view of the firm is widely accepted in the

Table 8.8 DMO sources of *comparative* advantage representing potential for *competitive* advantage

Natural resources	**Political goodwill**
Location, landscape features and climate	Influence on government fiscal policy such as taxation; investment incentives; and capital expenditure on infrastructure developments
Cultural resources	
People, history, language, cuisine, music, arts and crafts, traditions and customs	**Organisation knowledge**
Human resources	Governance structure and policies; staffing levels, training, experience, skills and retention; organisational culture; innovation; technology adoption; flexibility; customer service orientation; creative response capability; market orientation, marketing information system, specialised knowledge of segment needs
Skills and availability of the region's labour force; industrial relations; industry service standards; and attitudes of locals	
Developed resources	
Accessibility, infrastructure and the scale, range and capacity of man-made attractions and other superstructures	**Implementation**
Financial resources	Marketing orientation, sustainable tourism development planning; brand development, positioning and promotion; ease of making reservations; consistency of stakeholders' delivery
Size and certainty of the DMO budget; private sector marketing resources; size of the local economy; access to capital for product developments and ability to attract new investment	
Legal resources	**Goodwill**
Brand trademarks, licences and visa policies	Destination history; travellers' ancestral links to the destination; friends and/or relatives; novelty or fashionability of the destination; brand salience and ToMA levels; levels of previous visitation and satisfaction; and perceived value
Relationships	
Internal/external industry integration and alliances; distribution; stakeholder cooperation	

Table 8.9 VRIO resource model

Strength	Valuable?	Rare?	(Un)Imitable?	Organised?	Status
Resource A	yes	yes	yes	yes	SCA
Resource B	yes	yes	yes	no	TCA
Resource C	yes	no			CP
Resource D	no				CD

Notes: CP = competitive parity; TCA = temporary competitive advantage; SCA = sustainable competitive advantage; CD = competitive disadvantage.

strategic management literature, the VRIO framework has attracted little attention from destination marketing researchers (Pike, 2004, 2008; Line and Runyan, 2014). The model is based on the assumption that resources are heterogeneous and immobile across firms. Heterogeneity means organisations are not created equal and will vary in terms of the resources they control. Immobility refers to the difficulty of transferring resources from one organisation to another. To achieve a sustainable competitive advantage the VRIO model first requires a resource to be valuable (V) to the firm, for either increasing revenue or decreasing costs. Second, the resource should be rare (R) among competitors. Therefore, resources must be analysed in comparison to the competitive set of destinations. Differentiation alone does not lead to meaningful advantage over others. Exploitation of such organisational strengths must first be converted into (Day and Wensley, 1988): (1) benefits; (2) perceived by a sizeable customer group; (3) who value and are willing to pay for them; and (4) which cannot readily be obtained elsewhere. Third, it should be costly for competitors to imitate (I) the resource. Finally, the firm must be organised (O) in such a way that it is able to exploit the resource in the market. An example of the VRIO resource model is provided in Table 8.9. The table shows how answering yes to each denotes that a resource is a source of sustainable competitive advantage. Answering yes to the first two or three qualities indicates a source of temporary competitive advantage. A resource that is valuable, but not meeting the other criteria, represents a source of competitive parity. Finally, a resource that is not valuable represents a source of competitive disadvantage. The VRIO model determines which strengths should be included in the SWOT matrix.

As with any firm in a fiercely competitive environment, a DMO will realistically only be able to draw on one or a few *strengths* that represent a competitive advantage. A long bullet point list of strengths in the SWOT analysis, as is often seen in marketing plans, is misleading and misrepresentative of the destination's competitive position.

Developing goals and objectives

The ideal is to implement strategies that are not used by existing rivals, which will exploit strengths, neutralise threats and avoid weaknesses. The desired result is to build a source of sustainable competitive advantage, or a defendable position.

Ultimately, organisations are established to achieve goals and objectives. Goals are general statements of intent, related to delivering the mission, and are usually qualitative (Johnson and Scholes, 2002). That is, they provide broad indicators of how the mission will be achieved, but are not necessarily quantifiable. Collins and Porras (1997: 94) promoted the concept of a big hairy audacious goal (BHAG) as a way of capturing the attention of stakeholders. For example, Henry Ford's BHAG was to democratise the automobile, while Bill Gates held a similar dream for computers. A BHAG might seem impossible, but it can be a catalyst for stimulating increased creativity: 'A BHAG engages people – it reaches out and grabs them in the gut. It is tangible, energizing, highly focused. People "get it" right away; it takes little or no explanation' (Collins and Porras, 1997: 94).

Since the key argument for government funding of destination marketing is the potential direct and indirect economic benefits, it would be expected that DMO goals will be related to achieving this. Investigations during the 1990s certainly support this proposition at the level of NTO (see Akehurst *et al.*, 1993; Baum, 1994), STO (see Hawes *et al.*, 1991) and RTO (see Sheehan and Ritchie, 1997). In the time since there has been relatively little published about the role and monitoring of DMO goals. Examples of DMO goals in 2015 are listed in Table 8.10.

Whereas goals are broad statements about how to achieve the mission, objectives are the quantifiable targets of the goals and should clearly describe specific outcomes. Ideally objectives should be SMART (Tribe, 1997: 32):

- **S**pecific;
- **M**easurable;
- **A**greed with those who must attain them;
- **R**ealistic;
- **T**ime-constrained.

Examples of DMO objectives in 2015 that meet these criteria are listed in Table 8.11.

Table 8.10 DMO goals

DMO	Goal
Warsaw Destination Alliance, Poland www.destinationwarsaw.com	Improve the image of Warsaw throughout the world
Destination New South Wales, Australia www.destinationnsw.com.au/about-us	Increase industry stakeholder and customer engagement
Hawaii Tourism Authority, USA www.hawaiitourismauthority.org	Maintain and improve transportation access, infrastructure and services to facilitate travel to, from and within Hawaii
The Cotswolds, England www.cotswolds.com	Counter perceptions of the destination as expensive
Prague City Tourism www.praguecitytourism.cz	Increase average spend per visitor
Tourism Australia www.tourism.australia.com	Increase tourism labour and skills

Table 8.11 DMO objectives

DMO	Objective
Maryland Office of Tourism, USA	Secure 'destination Maryland' media placements that have a value of at least US$15 million in the 2014 fiscal year
Destination New South Wales, Australia	Maintain a full-time position within Destination NSW as a resource dedicated to support Aboriginal tourism businesses
Visit Scotland	Identify knowledge gaps, conduct research and collate evidence required to build a strong case for action to promote sustainable tourism
Tourism Rotorua Destination Marketing, New Zealand	Increase Rotorua's share of the Australian visitor arrivals to New Zealand
Tourism Tasmania, Australia	Implement two domestic PR campaigns
Johnson County, USA	Create Amtrak packages, including train ticket, rental car, hotel, attraction tickets and meal for weekend trip to Johnson County

The SWOT matrix

An effective visual tool for designing and communicating the rationale for tactics to DMO stakeholders, by matching organisation resources with environment opportunities, is the SWOT matrix as shown in Figure 8.3. The SWOT matrix extends the practical value of the traditional SWOT analysis, which is often not used

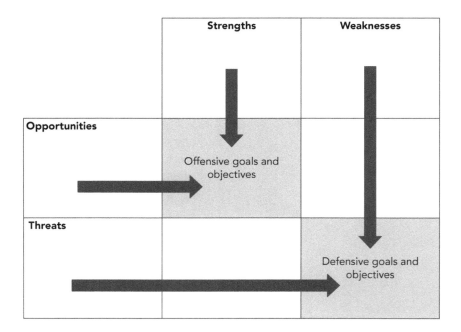

Figure 8.3 SWOT matrix

	Strength Range and diversity of accommodation	Weakness Small regional airport not serviced by major carriers
Opportunity Increasing level of short breaks by consumers	Offensive (matching strength with opportunity). Assist accommodation businesses to develop initiatives to keep in touch with previous visitors from the city to stimulate repeat visitation	
Threat Proliferation of low-cost airlines offering city consumers affordable short break air packages to new destinations		Defensive (matching weakness with threat). Proactively commission feasibility study to identify benefits for low-cost carriers to service the destination

Figure 8.4 SWOT matrix example

effectively in marketing planning. Some marketers carefully prepare a SWOT bullet point list and file it away in the marketing plan's appendices. The point of the SWOT should be to shape strategy and tactics by visually showing stakeholders the matching of internal resources with environment opportunities. The SWOT matrix encourages thinking about offensive strategies, which will maximise strengths to take advantage of opportunities, and defensive strategies, which will minimise weaknesses in relation to threats.

A DMO must then showcase the destination in a way that offers benefits sought by travellers, represents the interests of tourism suppliers and does not commodify residents' sense of place. Communicating matches between destination resources and travellers' wants is the focus of DMO promotional activities. Figure 8.4 illustrates how the SWOT matrix might be used to develop offensive and defensive strategies for the marketing plan. In this case the examples are drawn from a beach resort area located a 4–5 hour drive from a capital city. This matrix provides a simple example of the potential value for guiding stakeholders on the rationale for the DMO's marketing strategies.

CHAPTER SUMMARY

Key point 1: DMO vision, values, mission, goals and objectives

The core purpose of DMOs is enhancing destination competitiveness. Since marketing requires a forward-thinking orientation, a vision statement is used to articulate a motivational aspiration. The mission is a summary statement that makes clear to stakeholders the purpose of the organisation. The role of goals and objectives is to articulate how the mission will be achieved and, in doing so, provide motivational targets by which the success of the organisation can be monitored.

Key point 2: Destination marketing strategy design framework

Destination marketing is a forward-thinking discipline involving matching destination resources with external opportunities. The chapter outlined a framework for developing strategic goals and articulating the strategy rationale to stakeholders. Central to the framework are three tools: the STEEPL analysis is used to scan the macro environment to identify potential opportunities and threats; the VRIO resource model categorises the destination's resources to identify sources of competitive advantage; and the

SWOT matrix is a visual tool for developing goals and objectives that match destination resources with environment opportunities.

Key point 3: Sources of comparative and competitive advantage

A successful strategy achieves a point of difference against competitors on an attribute deemed important by the market. A DMO's resources consist of sources of comparative and competitive advantage. The VRIO resource model helps to identify the one or few destination resources that represent potential sources of competitive advantage for a DMO.

REVIEW QUESTIONS

1. Explain why a destination will realistically have only one or a few *strengths*?

2. Explain why the following is not representative of an *opportunity* in a DMO SWOT analysis/matrix: *To create a Chinese language destination website*.

3. Explain the relationship between a DMO's mission, goals and objectives.

REFERENCES

Aaker, D. A. (1991). *Managing Brand Equity*. New York: Free Press.

Ahmed, Z. and Krohn, F. B. (1990). Reversing the United States' declining competitiveness in the marketing of international tourism: A perspective on future policy. *Journal of Travel Research* 29(2): 23–29.

Akehurst, G., Bland, N. and Nevin, M. (1993). Tourism policies in the European Community member states. *International Journal of Hospitality Management* 12(1): 33–66.

Barney, J. (1991). Firm resources and sustained competitive advantage. *Journal of Management* 17(1): 99–120.

Barney, J. (1996). *Gaining and Sustaining Competitive Advantage*. Reading, MA: Addison-Wesley.

Baum, T. (1994). The development and implementation of national tourism policies. *Tourism Management* 15(3): 185–192.

Beerli, A. and Martin, J. (2004). Factors influencing destination image. *Annals of Tourism Research* 31(3): 657–681.

Cole, S. and Razak, V. (2009). Tourism as future. *Futures* 41(6): 335–345.

Collins, J. C. and Porras, J. I. (1997). *Built to Last*. New York: HarperCollins.

Coyne, K. P. (1986). Sustainable competitive advantage: What it is, what it isn't. *Business Horizons* January/February: 54–61.

Dascalu, R. (1997). Romania plans reparations for nationalised hotels. *Reuters*. August 11.

Day, G. S. and Wensley, R. (1988). Assessing advantage: A framework for diagnosing competitive superiority. *Journal of Marketing* 52(April): 1–20.

Drucker, P. (1995). *Managing in a Time of Great Change*. Oxford: Butterworth-Heinemann.

Faulkner, B., Oppermann, M. and Fredline, E. (1999). Destination competitiveness: An exploratory examination of South Australia's core attractions. *Journal of Vacation Marketing* 5(2): 125–139.

Ferrario, F. F. (1979). The evaluation of tourist resources: An applied methodology. Part 1. *Journal of Travel Research* 17(3): 18–22.

Flagestad, A. and Hope, C. A. (2001). 'Scandinavian winter': Antecedents, concepts and empirical observations underlying a destination umbrella branding model. *Tourism Review* 56(1/2): 5–12.

Formica, S. and Kothari, T. H. (2008). Strategic destination planning: Analyzing the future of tourism. *Journal of Travel Research* 46(May): 355–367.

Gilbert, D. (1990). Strategic marketing planning for national tourism. *The Tourist Review* 1: 18–27.

Go, F. M. (1987). Selling Canada. *Travel & Tourism Analyst*. December: 17–29.

Goeldner, R. C., Ritchie, J. R. B. and McIntosh, R. W. (2000). *Tourism: Principles, Practises, Philosophies* (8th edition). New York: John Wiley & Sons.

Hall, D. (1999). Destination branding, niche marketing and national image projection in Central and Eastern Europe. *Journal of Vacation Marketing* 5(3): 227–237.

Hamel, G. and Prahalad, C. K. (1989). Strategic intent. *Harvard Business Review* May/June: 63–76.

Hawes, D. K., Taylor, D. T. and Hampe, G. D. (1991). Destination marketing by states. *Journal of Travel Research* Summer: 11–17.

Johnson, G. and Scholes, K. (2002). *Exploring Corporate Strategy* (6th edition). Harlow, UK: Pearson Education.

Kim, S., Crompton, J. L. and Botha, C. (2000). Responding to competition: A strategy for Sun/Lost City, South Africa. *Tourism Management* 21(1): 33–41.

Leslie, D. (1999). Terrorism and tourism: The Northern Ireland situation – A look behind the veil of certainty. *Journal of Travel Research* 38(1): 37–40.

Line, N. D. and Runyan, R. C. (2014). Destination marketing and the service-dominant logic: A resource-based operationalization of strategic marketing assets. *Tourism Management* 43: 91–102.

Long, J. (1994). Local authority tourism strategies: A British appraisal. *The Journal of Tourism Studies* 5(2): 17–23.

NZTPD. (1989). *New Zealand Regional Tourism Summary*. Wellington, NZ: New Zealand Tourist & Publicity Department.

OTSP. (2001). *New Zealand Tourism Strategy 2010: Summary of Recommendations*. Wellington, NZ: Office of Tourism and Sport.

Page, S., Yeoman, I., Munro, C., Connell, J. and Walker, L. (2006). A case study of best practice: Visit Scotland's prepared response to an influenza pandemic. *Tourism Management* 27(3): 361–393.

Pearce, D. G. (1997). Competitive destination analysis in Southeast Asia. *Journal of Travel Research* 35(4): 16–24.

Pike, S. (2002). *Positioning as a Source of Competitive Advantage: Benchmarking Rotorua's Position as a Domestic Short Break Holiday Destination*. PhD Thesis. University of Waikato. November. Hard copy only.

Pike, S. (2004). *Destination Marketing Organisations*. Oxford: Elsevier Science.

Pike, S. (2008). *Destination Marketing: An Integrated Marketing Communication Approach*. Burlington, MA: Butterworth-Heinemann.

Pike, S. and Page, S. (2014). Destination marketing organizations and destination marketing: A narrative analysis of the literature. *Tourism Management* 41: 202–227.

Porter, M. E. (1980). *Competitive Strategy*. New York: The Free Press.

Porter, M. E. (1985). *Competitive Advantage*. New York: The Free Press.

Porter, M. E. (1991). Towards a dynamic theory of strategy. *Strategic Management Journal* 12(2): 95–117.

Ritchie, J. R. B. and Crouch, G. I. (2000). Are destination stars born or made: Must a competitive destination have star genes? *Lights, Camera, Action: 31st Annual Conference Proceedings*. San Fernando Valley, CA: Travel and Tourism Research Association.

Schwartz, P. (1991). *The Art of the Long View*. London: Century Business.

Scott, N., Gardiner, S. and Carlini, J. (2014). *Experience Gold Coast: Innovative Products for Asian Visitors Griffith Institute for Tourism Research Report Series Report No 3*. Gold Coast, QLD: Griffith Institute for Tourism.

Sheehan, L. R. and Ritchie, J. R. B. (1997). Financial management in tourism: A destination perspective. *Tourism Economics* 3(2): 93–118.

Smith, S. L. J. (2003). A vision for the Canadian tourism industry. *Tourism Management* 24(2): 123–133.

Spotts, D. M. (1997). Regional analysis of tourism resources for marketing purposes. *Journal of Travel Research* Winter: 3–15.

Stokes, R. (2008). Tourism strategy making: Insights to the events tourism domain. *Tourism Management* 29(2): 252–262.

Tribe, J. (1997). *Corporate Strategy for Tourism*. London: ITP.

Wack, P. (1985). Scenarios: Shooting the rapids. *Harvard Business Review* 63(3): 139–150.

Yeoman, I. (2008). *Tomorrow's Tourist: Scenarios & Trends*. Oxford: Elsevier.

Yeoman, I. (2012). *2050: Tomorrow's Tourism*. Bristol, UK: Channelview Publications.

Chapter **9**

Destination branding

AIMS

To enhance understanding of:

- the role and importance of branding for destinations;

- the concepts of brand identity, brand image and brand positioning;

- the complexity of branding destinations.

ABSTRACT

Today's consumers have more product choice, but less decision time than ever before. Consequently, a brand that can help simplify decisions, reduce perceived purchase risk and create and deliver expectations is invaluable. While the topic of product branding first appeared in the psychology literature in the 1940s, research related to the branding of tourism destinations did not appear until the late 1990s. Many destinations are becoming increasingly substitutable in markets crowded with rival places offering similar features and benefits, and so DMOs have increasingly turned to branding in the past 20 years in an attempt to differentiate. This chapter is underpinned by four themes. The first is the understanding that promoting product features is not sufficient to differentiate against competitors. Second, the already complex process of brand development and management is intensified for destination marketers. Third, and following the previous point, there has been little published research to date to guide DMOs on the long-term effectiveness of destination branding. Fourth, branding is at the very heart of marketing strategy, and so the purpose of all destination marketing activity must be to enhance the brand identity.

Differentiation and the balance of power

Ever since the topic of branding was introduced in the psychology literature during the 1940s (see for example Guest, 1942), there has been consistent recognition that it offers organisations a means of differentiation in markets crowded with similar offerings (see Banks, 1950; Gardner and Levy, 1955; Aaker, 1991;

Keller, 2003; Kotler *et al.*, 2007; Pike and Page, 2014). Gardner and Levy (1955) discussed stereotypes that had emerged in advertising, which failed to differentiate competitive products. They espoused the importance of considering a brand as representing a personality, the sum of which might be more influential than the product's individual attributes:

> *[a] brand name is more than the label employed to differentiate among the manufacturers of a product. It is a complex symbol that represents a variety of ideas and attributes. It tells the consumers many things, not only by the way it sounds (and its literal meaning if it has one) but, more important, via the body of associations it has built up and acquired as a public object over a period of time . . . the net result is a public image, a character or personality that may be more important for the over-all status (and sales) of the brand than many technical facts about the product.*
>
> *(Gardner and Levy, 1955: 35)*

Branding was in practice for thousands of years before becoming an academic field. For example, Keller (2003) cited reports about identification marks of craftsmen being found on pottery in China, Europe and India dating as far back as 1300 BC. In the modern era, the evolution of brand development since the 1870s was examined by King (1970), who suggested the driving force was the cyclical balance of power in the manufacturer–distributor relationship. Branding of manufactured goods emerged during the late nineteenth century to counter the dominating force of wholesalers who controlled what were essentially commodity markets. Retailers purchased what was available in stock from wholesalers, who in turn dictated what manufacturers should produce. From the 1900s to the 1960s the role of the wholesaler was reduced to that of distributor, as manufacturer numbers declined to the level of oligopolies. Brands were then used to build demand for a smaller line of goods, with economies of scale leading to increased profits for manufacturers. By 1970 the balance of power had shifted towards large scale retailers, where economies of scale and their own brand labels enhanced profit levels (King, 1970: 7–8): 'After all, many retail chains are bigger businesses than most consumer goods manufacturers; and on the whole there are more manufacturers still in most fields than the retailer really needs'.

The new role for product marketers was to enhance the value of their brands to the consumer, in the hope they would then exert demand on the mega-retailer. King also used the term brand personality to suggest brands held values beyond their physical and functional attributes:

> *People choose their brands as they choose their friends. You choose your friends not usually because of specific skills or physical attributes (though of course these come into it) but simply because you like them as people. It is the total person you choose, not a compendium of virtues and vices.*
>
> *(King, 1970: 11)*

While there is a lack of published research into the balance of power in the history of tourism distribution, the same dynamics between service provider and travel intermediaries apply. Recent years have witnessed a bifurcation of key travel products (e.g. airlines, hotels) as either large global corporate brands or small niche operators, negotiating with a small number of powerful travel intermediaries. This power balance is currently being challenged by the rise in influence of user-generated content on social media.

Following Aaker (1991), de Chernatony (1993: 173) and Keller (2003: 39–41), there are a number of compelling reasons why branding practice has increased exponentially since the 1990s, in which differentiation is a recurring theme: brand equity, increasing global competition, commodification, the power of intermediaries, sophisticated consumers, media cost effectiveness and a short-term performance orientation.

Brand equity

One of the most important impacts of branding for commercial organisations has been the increasing awareness of the balance sheet value of brands, referred to as *goodwill* or *brand equity*. That is, a brand can be an asset or a liability to the firm over and above its tangible assets and, as such, can affect the valuation of the firm. Given the difficulty and cost of developing new brands, there is a willingness by firms to pay a premium for the purchase of well-known brands. The top ten intangible brand values in 2014 are shown in Table 9.1, where it can be seen that the Apple brand was valued at US$118.9 billion. DMOs compete with these brands for consumers' discretionary spending. No travel-related brands were ranked in the top ten.

The marketing budget should be regarded as an investment in consumers' associations of the brand (Keller, 2000). There is a growing view that branding lies at the core of marketing strategy and that the purpose of the marketing programme should be to focus on developing favourable brand associations, linking the brand's attributes to consumer wants. Therefore, the other motive for measuring brand equity, other than financial asset valuation, is tracking market perceptions. In this regard, consumer-based brand equity (CBBE) might be the most critical for organisations, since financial valuation is irrelevant if no underlying consumer-based value of the brand has been established (Keller, 1993). For destinations the concept of CBBE is clearly more relevant than balance sheet values (see Konecnik and Gartner, 2007; Pike, 2007, 2010; Boo *et al.*, 2009). CBBE is discussed in more detail in Chapter 15 as a means of both monitoring effectiveness of past marketing and providing indicators of future performance.

Increasing global competition

Since the 1990s, competition has intensified through the breaking down of trading barriers between nations and the opening up of former communist states. The new competition phenomenon does not discriminate against famous destinations. For example, Dahles (1998: 56) claimed that, while once competing with London and Paris to be Europe's most popular destination, Amsterdam was 'fighting for survival'. This and other impacts of globalisation, such as Web 2.0, have led to a greater awareness of

Table 9.1 The world's top ten valued brands in 2014

Rank	Brand value US$ billions
1. Apple	118.9
2. Google	107.4
3. Coca-Cola	81.6
4. IBM	77.2
5. Microsoft	61.2
6. GE	45.5
7. Samsung	45.5
8. Toyota	42.4
9. McDonald's	42.3
10. Mercedes Benz	34.3

Source: Adapted from http://www.bestglobalbrands.com/2014/ranking

global competitors by both producers and consumers. Increasing competition between traditional and emerging destinations has significant consequences for most places:

> *The great majority will need to review and adapt their traditional organisational and marketing methods to survive and prosper in the next millennium. One can only speculate that some will be unable to make the change and will not survive as holiday destinations beyond the next decade or so.*
>
> *(Middleton, 1998: 153)*

The split up of the former Yugoslavia in the 1990s is an example of this new competition. Containing most of the former Yugoslavia's coastline, Croatia was a major benefactor of tourism in the region. Following the war years it was important, therefore, for Croatia to establish a national tourism brand strategy that would 'convey a distinct image to clearly differentiate the country from its neighbours and reassure former markets that quality and value had been restored' (Hall, 1999: 234). The challenging development of national brands in the *rebranding* of nations from the former Yugoslavia has also since been discussed by Dosen *et al.* (1998), Hall (2002), Martinovic (2002), Konecnik (2004, 2006) and Konecnik and Gartner (2007). As tabled in Chapter 2 (see Table 2.5) there have been a number of reports in the tourism literature about emerging and established destinations struggling to compete in the new era.

Commodification

There is a *sameness* creeping into destinations around the world, and those places that are perceived to offer the same attributes as others are likely to be substitutable in consumers' minds and, therefore, in their decision making. Commodification of products is increasing, due to the difficulty of differentiating like products in crowded markets. As the craftsmen of a thousand years ago would have been only too aware, product features can be quickly imitated and so do not provide a lasting source of advantage. The effect of continued commodification in markets is ultimately competition based on price (Aaker and Joachimsthaler, 2000: 40): 'Too many brands drift aimlessly and appear to stand for nothing in particular. They always seem to be shouting price, on sale, attached to some deal, or engaging in promiscuous channel expansion – symptoms of a lack of integrity'.

An effective brand strategy can provide a means for successful differentiation. After all, in commodity categories *something* must make a greater difference to a consumer's thinking about the competing products that offer features of a similar quality, and that something is the symbol a brand represents to the consumer (Gardner and Levy, 1955). Pride (2002: 109) succinctly pointed out the difficulty facing Wales: 'For many years that venerable and respected British oracle of information and explanation, the Encyclopaedia Britannica, essentially denied Wales' existence. Under the entry for Wales it simply stated "for Wales please see England"'.

However, Keller (2003) pointed to successful branding within a number of commodity categories, where product differentiation is difficult to achieve, such as water (Perrier), beer (Budweiser), cigarettes (Marlboro), soap (Ivory), pineapples (Dole), oatmeal (Quaker) and bananas (Chiquita).

The power of travel intermediaries

The power of mega travel intermediaries is increasing. Development and distribution of their own brands and access to customers, combined with their control of high profile retail shelf space and online shopping, can be a significant barrier for small product suppliers. This power of wholesalers and retailers not only applies to fast-moving consumer goods in supermarkets but equally to the distribution of tourism services, both traditional and online. In most countries now, outbound travel is controlled by a relatively small number of traditional and online travel intermediaries.

Sophisticated consumers

Today's consumers are the most sophisticated ever to be faced by marketers. We are experienced, having been exposed to unprecedented levels of media communications, and have access to increasing sources of product information and consumer advice. In so many cases we are spoilt for choice, and we know it. The rise in influence of user-generated content in social media has increased awareness of the role marketers are attempting to play, and we are not so easily tricked by false advertising (at least not a second time!).

Media cost effectiveness

Marketers are now faced with escalating media costs, often in tandem with declining advertising budgets. The proliferation of new and niche media is resulting in a diffusion of, and relative decline in, the effectiveness of traditional advertising. This has led to increased interest in below-the-line promotional opportunities, such as social media, relationship marketing and public relations.

Short-term performance orientation

Marketing planning has long been driven by short-term measures of accountability. Such pressures, which may be exerted by shareholders, economic analysts or changes in management, place emphasis on tactical promotional initiatives for short-term gain rather than longer-term strategic marketing.

Destination branding

Destinations can be branded, but do consumers regard places as brands? What exactly is a destination brand? These are questions that have to date been overlooked by researchers (Pike and Page, 2014). Are they *collective hallucinations* as suggested by Professor John Urry in the keynote address to the 2003 *Taking tourism to the limits* conference at the University of Waikato? When considering definitions of the brand construct, it is important to consider the perspectives of both the organisation and the market. From the market perspective, the commonly cited definition provided by Aaker (1991) is pertinent to the ensuing discussion on the branding of destinations, which effectively represent *groups of sellers*:

> *A brand is a distinguishing name and/or symbol (such as a logo, trademark, or package design) intended to identify the goods or services of either one seller or a group of sellers, and to differentiate those goods from those of competitors.*
>
> *(Aaker, 1991: 7)*

However, in the foreword to the first issue of *Place Branding and Public Policy*, editor Simon Anholt (2004: 4) suggested 'almost nobody agrees on what, exactly, branding means' in describing place branding practice as akin to the Wild West. There has been a lack of consistency in defining what constitutes destination branding, both within the industry and within academia (see Blain *et al.*, 2005; Park and Petrick, 2006; Tasci and Kozak, 2006). The most comprehensive definition to date has been that proposed by Blain *et al.* (2005), which followed Berthon *et al.*'s (1999) model of the functions of a brand from both the buyer and seller perspectives:

> *Destination branding is the set of marketing activities (1) that support the creation of a name, symbol, logo, word mark or other graphic that readily identifies and differentiates a destination; that (2) consistently convey the expectation of a memorable travel experience; that (3) serve to*

consolidate and reinforce the emotional connection between the visitor and the destination; and that (4) reduce consumer search costs and perceived risk. Collectively, these activities serve to create a destination image that positively influences consumer destination choice.

(Blain et al., 2005: 337)

A brand must stand for something, a promise to the consumer, and so is much more than merely symbols presented to the public. It is useful to consider a brand as representing an identity for the producer and an image for the consumer. Aaker (1996) distinguished these separate components of a brand as the brand identity (internal organisation orientation), representing self-image and aspired market image, and the brand image (external market orientation), which is the actual image held by consumers and may or may not bear any resemblance to that intended by the DMO. The model in Figure 9.1 highlights these two distinctive components, along with a third overlapping element, which is brand positioning. Brand positioning is the attempt to achieve congruence between brand identity and brand image, over which the DMO has some control. Figure 9.1 attempts to depict brand image as being nebulous relative to the clearly defined and espoused brand identity. Brand positioning is shown as an arrow attempting to pierce the attention of consumers with a succinct message.

This chapter focuses on the development of a destination brand identity. The components and formation of destination brand image are outlined in Chapter 10, and destination positioning is the focus of Chapter 11.

Destination branding literature

The topic of destination branding did not appear in the tourism literature until the late 1990s. Gnoth (1998) suggested the special track on *Branding tourism destinations* he convened at the 1997 American Marketing Science conference was the first meeting of practitioners and academics on the topic. The following year, the Tourism and Travel Research Association (TTRA) conference, which was themed *Branding the travel market*, featured eight destination branding papers. The first destination branding conference was staged in 2005. The initiative of Macau's Instituto De Formação Turistica (IFT), in conjunction with Perdue University, was a test of academic interest in the topic. Ultimately, the decision was justified with around 100 delegates attending from 22 countries. Chapter 1 listed the academic destination branding conferences that have been convened since then.

The first journal special issue on destination branding was published by the *Journal of Vacation Marketing* in 1999 (5(3)). Since then there have been other special issues in 2007 in *Tourism Analysis* (12(5–6)), 2013

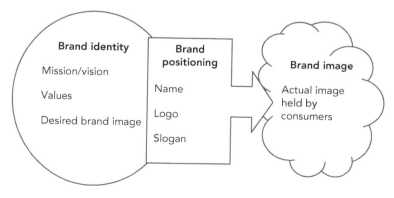

Figure 9.1 Three components of branding

Table 9.2 Destination branding research gaps in the literature

---

- In depth case studies of the politics of destination brand decision making

- Development and management of destination brand umbrella strategies, which reflect linkages and synergies by the NTO and STOs/RTOs, and also between the DMO and stakeholders

- Involvement and 'buy in' of the host community who are an important part of local tourism, both as hosts of visiting friends or relatives and as occasional local tourists. To what extent does the tourism brand identity represent local residents' 'sense of place'?

- The extent to which destinations are able to generate different brand positioning strategies to suit the needs of different markets, given those attributes determining destination preferences might differ between different travel situations

- Involvement and 'buy-in' of the tourism industry. To what extent do destination brand campaigns enhance the competitiveness of business-related stakeholders including local tourism businesses as well as key travel trade intermediaries

- The extent to which customer relationship marketing is possible for DMOs to stimulate increased loyalty and repeat visitation

- The effectiveness of brand slogans and logos

- The potential of brand licencing revenue as an alternative funding source

- Measurement of destination brand performance effectiveness over time

---

Source: Adapted from Pike (2009).

in *Tourism Tribune* (28(1)) and 2014 in the *Journal of Destination Marketing & Management* (3(1)). Destination branding books have been published by Morgan *et al.* (2002b, 2004, 2011), Baker (2007, 2012), Donald and Gammack (2007), Cai *et al.* (2009) and Moilanen and Rainisto (2009). The first destination branding journal articles to be published were Pritchard and Morgan's (1998) report on the brand strategy for Wales and Dosen *et al.*'s (1998) analysis of the appropriateness of Croatia's brand. Since then the topic has become one of the fastest growing in the destination marketing literature (Pike and Page, 2014). For example, a review of the first 10 years of destination branding research (see Pike, 2009) tabled 74 academic publications by 102 authors. The review identified nine research gaps in the literature, which are summarised in Table 9.2.

Critical success factors

In moving towards a structure for destination brand strategy it is useful to consider potential critical success factors. In this regard Keller (2000) identified ten characteristics of the world's strongest brands, which could be used by marketers to identify strengths and weaknesses of a brand and its competitors. While no destination brands were included in the analysis, Keller's brand report card does warrant consideration by destination marketers, albeit with a caveat that the level of control or influence able to be exerted by DMOs makes implementation problematic:

1. The brand excels at delivering the benefits customers truly desire.

2. The brand stays relevant to customers.

3. The pricing strategy is based on consumers' perceptions of value.

4. The brand is properly positioned in the market by offering a distinctive value proposition.

5. The brand is consistent.

6. The brand portfolio and hierarchy make sense.

7. The brand makes use of, and coordinates, a full repertoire of marketing activities.

8. The brand's managers understand what the brand means to consumers.

9. The brand is given proper support and that support is sustained over the long run.

10. The organisation monitors the sources of brand equity.

Case studies similar to Keller's (2000) that analyse leading destination brands to identify critical success factors for DMOs will be invaluable. However, as has been stated, the number of published destination brand case studies has only emerged recently, and there is a need for more case study-based research into the long-term effectiveness of destination brand management over time. Relative to the number of papers published on destination image, there have been few reporting destination branding case studies. Given the recent emergence of the destination branding literature, it is not surprising that the focus of cases published to date has been on brand development. The case studies published to date do, however, provide valuable insights into the practical challenges of applying brand theory to destination brand development, particularly since most have been written by practitioners involved in the brand campaigns. Pike (2008) summarised the contribution of six of the earliest cases: Brand Oregon (Curtis, 2001), Ohio's identity crisis (May, 2001), Wales' natural revival (Pride, 2002), Brand Western Australia (Crockett and Wood, 1999), war-torn Central and Eastern Europe (Hall, 1999) and New Zealand's global niche (Morgan et al., 2002a). For a list of 33 destination branding case studies published between 1998 and 2007, see Pike (2009).

Destination brand identity development

There has been a lack of research into the extent to which the marketing communications of the DMO and key stakeholders align with, and therefore support, the brand identity (Pike and Page, 2014: 218): 'Given the level of investment in brand development globally, insights are required into the links between branding theory and practise'. Cai (2002) was the first to separate destination brand identity development from destination image building. Brand identity has an internal focus on issues such as self-image and a vision for motivating stakeholders, while brand image represents the actual image held in the market. A brand identity will include values, key competitors, a positioning statement, key attributes and benefits and target audience. Pike and Page (2014) pointed to growing interest in testing whether the concept of a brand *personality* can apply to destination brands and brand identities (see Ekinci and Hosany, 2006; Hosany et al., 2006; Ekinci et al., 2007; Murphy et al., 2007a, 2007b; Pitt et al., 2007; Usaki and Baloglu, 2011; Pereira et al., 2012). Destination brand identity development essentially involves five stages:

1. the appointment of a brand champion;

2. the identification of the brand community;

3. a destination audit to identify sources of competitive advantage (see Chapter 8);

4. an analysis of brand image (see Chapter 10);

5. the production of a brand charter for stakeholders.

The appointment of a brand manager is an important precursor to the destination brand development. As evidenced in the case of Wales (see Pride, 2002), a lack of leadership can inhibit the brand's development, particularly in the initial phase. Such a role will vary depending on the size of the DMO, but will nevertheless be driven by the same principles. Branding is a complex and challenging process, and leadership, responsibility and accountability are required. At the NTO level there has been a growing number of brand manager appointments made since the mid-1990s. The Western Australian Tourism Commission's (WATC) approach to branding the state was reported by the STO's CEO and brand manager (see Crockett and Wood, 1999). The authors advised the development of a new brand strategy in the 1990s, which not only resulted in a successful global repositioning but also an 'entire organisational shift' (Crockett and Wood, 1999: 276): 'Brand WA provided the catalyst for an entire organisational restructure within the WATC. This reflects a new corporate culture, new direction, increased accountability, performance measurement, partnerships with industry and a clear customer focus' (Crockett and Wood, 1999: 278).

The effective development and nurturing of the destination brand will depend on the identification of a brand community. Ultimately, the destination brand community will be as important a brand communications' medium as any advertising campaign, since it is they who must deliver the brand promise. Therefore, it is critical the brand identity encapsulates the values of the community and the essence of the visitor experience, as well as provide a vision to guide and motivate active stakeholders. Modelling by Cai (2002, 2009), along with Konecnik *et al.* (2013), provide rare insights into community collaboration in destination branding.

Implications of social media

To date there has been little research in the wider marketing literature into the effects of social media marketing on brands. Laroche *et al.* (2013) discussed the concept of *brand community* taking on a new meaning, given the advent of social media, and the enabling of consumers to take part. In this context Muniz and O'Guinn (2001: 412) defined a brand community as 'a specialized, non-geographically bound community, based on a structured set of social relations among admirers of a brand'. It is essential that 'creation and negotiation of meaning' are the priorities (McAlexander *et al.*, 2002). Oliveira and Panyik (2015) suggested encouraging contributions of actual visitor experiences and engaging with that content by way of identifying patterns in the narratives as a way of guiding the DMO's consistency in brand positioning.

Travel intermediaries

Vial (1997, in Morgan and Pritchard, 1998) cited the example of the *Feast for the senses* brand developed by Publicis for the Morocco Tourist Board. This was an attempt to develop an umbrella brand for use in all markets. Previously, different campaigns had been used in different markets, which had resulted in a confused image. The proposed campaign did gain the support of the tourism industry in Morocco. However, it was derailed by resistance from travel agents and tour wholesalers who viewed the campaign as promoting cultural tourism when they were in the business of catering to the need for sun and sea packages.

Local residents

Any destination brand must represent local residents' sense of place, so that they can help spread an authentic message. Research into the perceptions of *New Asia – Singapore* by Henderson (2000) highlighted the real-world challenges involved in gaining acceptance of the brand from local residents. A small exploratory survey of local residents and English-speaking visitors revealed gaps between actual perceptions (brand image) and the intended brand values (brand identity). Concerns about place commodification were also evident. Sample limitations aside, Henderson's (2000) study insightfully highlighted the importance of consultation with the host community to ensure what is being communicated in brand strategies is both realistic and appropriate:

> *When residents are called on to live the values of the brand in pursuit of tourism goals, it would seem that marketers are in danger of assuming too much influence and a sense of balance needs to be restored. Societies cannot be engineered or places manufactured for tourist consumption without a loss of authenticity which is ultimately recognised by the visitor who will move on to seek it elsewhere.*
>
> *(Henderson, 2000: 215)*

Also important are members of non-tourism businesses, who might not view tourism as being their core business, but who may nevertheless be indirectly involved in providing goods or services to visitors. For example, these include such diverse groups as local produce suppliers, architects, real estate agents, hairdressers and employment agencies. A destination brand community consists, therefore, not only of local tourism providers but also visitors and the host population, the local business community and key travel distribution intermediaries.

The Oregon case (see Curtis, 2001) demonstrated the importance of avoiding a top-down approach by involving the local tourism industry. Indeed, Curtis observed a strong brand became a unifying force for increased cooperation by all stakeholders in Oregon. Likewise, Hawes *et al.* (1991) found a number of US STOs that employed a state-wide slogan as a unification mechanism. The formation of a project group that is representative of the brand community can act as a conduit between the DMO and the community, help identify stakeholder groups warranting involvement in qualitative discussions on place meaning, assist the brand manager with the development of recommendations for the DMO board and help develop a means of briefing the community on the purpose and role of the brand. Admittedly, the selection of such a representative group will always be problematic, in terms of achieving a political balance and a manageable size.

Brand charter

A brand charter can serve to motivate, remind and guide stakeholders. Like any formal planning document, the key to readability and application is succinctness. Essential elements include, but are not limited to: a brand mission, vision, brand identity/essence statement, brand values and guidelines for implementation and auditing. Urde (1999: 126) suggested a brand vision is required to answer the following questions: What do we want to achieve with our brand? How will the organisation realise this vision? The brand essence statement is the articulation of the brand identity. This has also been described as a *brand mantra* by Keller (2003), who suggested a three- to five-word statement that clearly defines the focus and boundary of the brand category, such as authentic athletic performance (Nike) and fun family entertainment (Disney). Aaker and Joachimsthaler (2000) suggested a brand identity will usually have two to four dimensions, as well as a focused brand essence statement. They offered the example of Virgin's core identity dimensions being service quality, innovation, fun and entertainment and value for money, while the brand essence statement is iconoclasm. The purpose of the brand essence statement and core values is to guide and motivate those within the organisation and will not necessarily be explicit in all promotional communications.

A brand charter provides guidelines for the use of symbols by the local tourism industry and intermediaries. The purpose is to ensure a consistency in application. Morgan *et al.* (2012) cited research by the UNWTO and the European Tourism Commission revealing 82 per cent of NTOs provided a toolkit explaining how to use the official destination brand. While earlier guidelines were distributed in brochure form, most DMOs now provide these online. For example, in 2015 Tourism and Events Queensland outlined online the following for the state's 13 destinations (http://teq.queensland.com): brand positioning, core promise, brand values, logo use, upcoming campaigns and advertising opportunities, image library and brand contact person. In the case of Brisbane, the state capital, the brand identity was summarised as:

- **Core promise** – *what we promise our destination brands will deliver to visitors*

  Feel the vitality of city life with a Queensland twist.

- **Brand personality** – *how our destination brands are portrayed, based on human characteristics*

  Friendly, welcoming, relaxed, unpretentious, well-rounded.

- **Brand values**

  Pride in Brisbane, hospitality, authenticity.

IN PRACTICE

9.1 Wales's marketing narrative

By March 2015 Wales had invested 18 months' work in developing a new branding strategy and *marketing narrative* for the country, embracing both tourism and foreign investment. Led by a brand champion, the process involved extensive dialogue with industry. From the tourism perspective, the key recommendations for the new brand were:

- To place our high-quality products and destinations front and centre, helping to make our marketing credible and distinctive. This is a departure from the more generic approach of the past and the approach of some of our competitors.

- To develop a brand that is consistently visible through sustained, targeted promotion and highly credible by showcasing our achievements and delivery in areas of core strength.

- To consistently challenge pre-conceived images of Wales and concerns that deter potential visitors from selecting Wales as a holiday destination: weather, warmth of welcome, ease of travel and product experience. The aim is to invite re-evaluation, investigation and trial.

- To show that Wales is different from its competitors in ways that are relevant to diverse target markets with distinctive brand campaigns.

The core proposition centres on promoting Wales as an exciting place to visit, where there is always something fresh to discover, see and do. The aim was to encourage potential visitors to think again about Wales by showcasing the variety and richness of the experiences available.

Source

http://gov.wales/topics/tourism/marketingl1/wales-brand-update/?lang=en (login and free registration required)

Destination branding complexity

The application of branding is a complex and challenging process, magnified for destinations by the constraints faced by most DMOs. Following Pike (2005) there are at least ten issues that make the application of branding theory to a destination a complex undertaking:

- The DMO promises a destination brand proposition, but lacks control over the actual delivery of the promise by local businesses and the host community.

- Destinations are far more multidimensional than consumer goods and other types of services. As is discussed in Chapter 11, effective positioning requires reaching the minds of busy consumers with a succinct and meaningful proposition focusing on one or a few brand associations; usually in the form of a *seven-word single-minded proposition*. Nowhere is this challenge better highlighted than in the development of a seven-word slogan that encapsulates a destination's diverse and often eclectic range of natural resources, built attractions, culture, activities, amenities, accommodation and the host community's sense of place. As suggested in Chapter 8, a destination will have only one or a few resources that represent a source of competitive advantage, and using the narrow focus necessitates making trade-offs that run the gauntlet of local politics.

- The market interests of the diverse group of active stakeholders are heterogeneous. Counter to a market orientation, where products are designed to suit market needs, DMOs are forced into targeting a multiplicity of geographic markets to attract a wide range of segments for their existing range of products, most of which are rigid in what they can be used for. Is one slogan, such as *Idaho – great potatoes, tasty destinations* or *Slovenia – the grown place of Europe*, likely to be meaningful to all market segments? Designing separate propositions for different segments will be beyond the resources of most DMOs. For example, *100% Pure New Zealand*, launched in 1999, was the country's first global tourism brand (see Morgan *et al.*, 2002a). Prior to this, different campaigns had been used in different markets. New Zealand is a small, geographically disadvantaged player in the international travel market, with a relatively small NTO budget. Tourism New Zealand recognised that to be more competitive on the international stage, particularly against larger neighbour, Australia, required the development of a single niche brand across all markets. Conversely, in 2015 the Singapore Tourism Board unveiled a series of different brand positioning campaigns to appeal to different segments in several different markets (TravelandTourWorld.com, 2015).

- The politics of decision making can render the best of marketing theory redundant. The issues of who decides the brand identity and positioning proposition, and how they are held accountable, are critical. At the level of DMO governance and decision making, politics arises through inequality between tourism organisations. For example, Ritchie and Ritchie (1998) referred to the heavy influence of the Disney Corporation on the *Orlando Magic* destination brand. In the USA there have been concerns at many destinations funded by a bed tax that large hotel chains have undue influence in DMO decision making. In New Zealand Rotorua's *Feel the spirit manaakitanga* was considerably influenced by the local indigenous Maori population. One-third of the local population is Maori, and the district has a proud history of providing cultural experiences and hospitality to travellers. That the theme was designed for use in all markets assumes all markets will have an interest in Maori culture. Research by Pike and Ryan (2004) into how Rotorua was positioned in the important domestic short break market suggested strongly that Maori culture was not regarded as either a salient or determinant attribute. Rotorua has a strong position in the domestic market, but one that is based on other attributes. The research indicated that Rotorua should therefore consider using a different positioning theme in the domestic short break market, to reinforce positively held perceptions. The RTO has since changed the brand slogan to *Famously Rotorua*.

- There is a fine balance to be struck between community consensus and brand theory, since a top-down approach to destination brand implementation is likely to fail. As mentioned, DMOs lack any direct control over the actual delivery of the brand promise by the local tourism community. Therefore without buy-in from these stakeholders the strategy will likely struggle to gain momentum. In the case of Brand Oregon (see Curtis, 2001), to achieve brand consistency, the tourism component of the strategy required all RTOs that received state funding to use the Oregon Tourism Commission's advertising agency. While the rationale for this approach was to achieve a consistency of promotional material, ultimately the top-down approach met with resistance from the regions.

- Brand loyalty, the quintessential goal of marketing, recognises the increased efficiencies and yield to be gained from repeat visitation. Staying in touch with previous visitors is a powerful and efficient means of enhancing the destination brand, but DMOs rarely come into contact with visitors to their destination and have no access to visitors' contact details left at accommodation registration desks.

- Funding is often a continuous problem for DMOs, in both scale and consistency. Even the largest DMO budgets pale in comparison to those of the major corporate brands with which they compete for discretionary consumer spending. Since DMOs have no direct financial stake in visitor expenditure, they must continually lobby for public and private funding. A successful brand campaign leading to increased yields for local businesses does not necessarily translate into increased revenue for the DMO, unless through a visitor levy or bed tax.

- A destination may be viewed as the umbrella brand, with individual products as sub-brands. Hopper (2002) reported how the plethora of brands used by tourism businesses to promote London had led to a dilution of the brand designed by the London Tourist Board. In tourism there might be up to six or more levels in the destination brand family hierarchy, ranging from macro region brand, country brand, state/province brand and regional/city brand, to precinct brands and individual tourism business brands. The issue becomes complex when considering that major attractions, such as Stonehenge in south England, Legoland in California, Sea World on Australia's Gold Coast and Disneyland Resort Paris, for example, might have different destination umbrella brands at the RTO, STO and NTO levels with which they work. Flagestad and Hope (2001) suggested an umbrella brand for Scandinavian tourism suppliers could prove an efficient means of addressing image problems in non-Nordic markets. Such an umbrella brand has since come to fruition. A proactive role is played by Tourism and Events Queensland in developing regional brands within the state. The incentive for the RTOs is funding by the STO, at a level that can exceed the contributions of local shire councils. The concept of destination umbrella branding is related to the consumer goods strategy of applying the name of a brand to a broad range of products, the purpose of which is to spread positive elements of a brand's value over multiple products, through transfer phenomena such as semantic generalisation (see, for example, Mazanec and Schweiger, 1981). Potentially, the marketing efforts of each product within the brand hierarchy can flow across to other partners.

- As will be discussed in Chapter 10, destination image change occurs only slowly over time (see Crompton, 1979; Gartner and Hunt, 1987; Gartner, 1993; Pike, 2010). However, as is discussed in Chapter 11, it appears to be difficult for DMOs to adopt a long-term approach to branding, with so many regularly changing the brand proposition/slogan. Of the 47 USA state slogans used in 1982, only 6 were still in use in 1993, and of the 46 slogans used in 1993, only 13 were still being used in 2003 (see Pike, 2004, 2008). Over a 21-year period, only 6 of the 1982 slogans remained in use in 2003. Often the changes are political. For example, in the case of Valencia in Spain the publicly funded DMO was required to issue new advertising contracts every year (Morgan and Pritchard, 1998). In the state of Louisiana, the Department of Culture, Recreation and Tourism was legislated to review its advertising agency account every three years (Slater, 2002). Prior to establishing a public–private partnership-based Florida STO in 1996, any change in the politician responsible for the tourism portfolio resulted in a change of marketing strategy and slogan (see Bush, 2004). In Australia, for example, the NTO recently changed the branding strategy five times in ten years, often for political reasons, and most recently at a cost of AUD$300 million for design and implementation.

- Arguably the most significant issue to add complexity to destination branding has been the rise in influence in social media user-generated content in the past decade. User-generated content is now having a greater impact in the market place than DMO marketing communications. One study found that two-thirds of consumers feel their relationships with brands are one-sided, with brands benefiting more than consumers (Edelman, 2014, in Trendwatching.com, 2015). The democratisation of the internet is lessening the power of destination marketers who, as discussed in Chapter 4, have to date generally resisted providing consumers with opportunities to upload uncensored content. The result is that the DMO's influence on the destination brand image in the market is declining.

CHAPTER SUMMARY

Key point 1: The role and importance of branding destinations

It has been suggested that the future of marketing will be a battle of the brands and that in tourism, destinations have emerged as the biggest brands. Destinations compete in crowded markets against the clutter of noise from substitute products as well as an almost unlimited number of competing places offering similar attributes and benefits. Effective branding enhances destination salience through differentiation that is meaningful to consumers. The uptake of destination branding research and practice has increased exponentially since the 1990s.

Key point 2: The concepts of brand identity, brand image and brand positioning

The purpose of a brand is to establish a distinctive and memorable identity in the market place that represents a source of value for the consumer. For DMOs, the value of strong CBBE lies in the opportunity to minimise destination switching through a differentiated value proposition and increased loyalty. There are three core components of branding: (1) the fundamental challenge for DMOs is to somehow develop a brand identity that encapsulates the essence or spirit of a multi-attributed destination representative of a group of sellers as well as a host community. Such a brand identity should serve as a guiding focus for the marketing activities of the DMO and stakeholders; (2) brand image (Chapter 10) is the actual image held by consumers and may or may not be reflective of the brand identity; and (3) brand positioning (Chapter 11) is the attempt to enhance congruence between the brand image and the brand identity with a succinct value proposition.

Key point 3: The complexity of branding destinations

The process of branding destinations is a more complex undertaking than that for most consumer goods and services. Some of the many branding challenges facing most DMOs include: the development of an enthusiastic brand community, without an overtly top-down approach; lack of control over the brand promise delivery; the diversity of stakeholders and destination attributes; the multiplicity of markets of interest to stakeholders; the potential influence of powerful travel intermediaries; the rise in influence of user-generated content on social media; the politics of DMO decision making; conflicting brand hierarchies; lack of funding; and inability to keep in touch with previous visitors to stimulate destination loyalty.

REVIEW QUESTIONS

1. Describe the key rationale for DMOs to develop a destination brand.

2. Why can it be difficult for a DMO to develop a brand identity?

3. Briefly describe the purpose of brand positioning.

REFERENCES

Aaker, D. A. (1991). *Managing Brand Equity*. New York: Free Press.

Aaker, D. A. (1996). *Building Strong Brands*. New York: Free Press.

Aaker, D. A. and Joachimsthaler, E. (2000). *Brand Leadership*. New York: Free Press.

Anholt, S. (2004). Editorial. *Place Branding and Public Policy* 1: 4–11.

Baker, B. (2007). *Destination Branding for Small Cities: The Essentials for Successful Place Branding*. Portland, OR: Creative Leap Books.

Baker, B. (2012). *Destination Branding for Small Cities: The Essentials for Successful Place Branding* (2nd edition). Portland, OR: Creative Leap Books.

Banks, S. (1950). The relationship between preference and purchase of brands. *The Journal of Marketing* 15(October): 145–157.

Berthon, P., Hulbert, J. M. and Pitt, L. F. (1999). Brand management prognostications. *Sloan Management Review* 40(2): 53–65.

Blain, C., Levy, S. E. and Ritchie, J. R. B. (2005). Destination branding: Insights and practices from destination management organizations. *Journal of Travel Research* 43(May): 328–338.

Boo, S., Busser, J. and Baloglu, S. (2009). A model of customer-based brand equity and its application to multiple destinations. *Tourism Management* 30(2): 219–231.

Bush, J. E. (2004). The story of a public/private tourism marketing partnership. In Dickenson, B. and Vladimir, A. (eds) *The Complete 21st Century Travel & Hospitality Marketing Handbook*. Upper Saddle River, NJ: Pearson, pp. 121–127.

Cai, L. A. (2002). Cooperative branding for rural destinations. *Annals of Tourism Research* 29(3): 720–742.

Cai, L. A. (2009). Tourism branding in a social exchange system. In Cai, L. A., Gartner, W. C. and Munar, A. M. (eds) *Tourism Branding: Communities in Action*. Bingley, UK: Emerald, pp. 90–104.

Cai, L. A., Gartner, W. C. and Munar, A. M. (eds) (2009). *Tourism Branding: Communities in Action*. Bingley, UK: Emerald.

Crockett, S. R. and Wood, L. J. (1999). Brand Western Australia: A totally integrated approach to destination branding. *Journal of Vacation Marketing* 5(3): 276–289.

Crompton, J. L. (1979). An assessment of the image of Mexico as a vacation destination and the influence of geographical location upon that image. *Journal of Travel Research* Spring: 18–23.

Curtis, J. (2001). Branding a state: The evolution of brand Oregon. *Journal of Vacation Marketing* 7(1): 75–81.

Dahles, H. (1998). Redefining Amsterdam as a tourist destination. *Annals of Tourism Research* 25(1): 55–69.

De Chernatony, L. (1993). Categorizing brands: Evolutionary processes underpinned by two key dimensions. *Journal of Marketing Management* 9(2): 173–188.

Donald, S. H. and Gammack, J. G. (2007). *Tourism and the Branded City: Film and Identity on the Pacific Rim*. Aldershot, UK: Ashgate.

Dosen, D. O., Vranesevic, T. and Prebezac, D. (1998). The importance of branding in the development of marketing strategy of Croatia as tourist destination. *Acta Turistica* 10(2): 93–182.

Ekinci, Y. and Hosany, S. (2006). Destination personality: An application of brand personality to tourism destinations. *Journal of Travel Research* 45(2): 127–139.

Ekinci, Y., Sirakaya-Turk, E. and Baloglu, S. (2007). Host image and destination personality. *Tourism Analysis* 12(5/6): 433–446.

Flagestad, A. and Hope, C. A. (2001). 'Scandinavian winter': Antecedents, concepts and empirical observations underlying a destination umbrella branding model. *Tourism Review* 56(1/2): 5–12.

Gardner, B. B. and Levy, S. J. (1955). The product and the brand. *Harvard Business Review* March/April: 33–39.

Gartner, W. C. (1993). Image information process. *Journal of Travel & Tourism Marketing* 2(2/3): 191–215.

Gartner, W. C. and Hunt, J. D. (1987). An analysis of state image change over a twelve-year period (1971–1983). *Journal of Travel Research* Fall: 15–19.

Gnoth, G. (1998). Branding tourism destinations. Conference report. *Annals of Tourism Research* 25(3): 758–760.

Guest, L. P. (1942). The genesis of brand awareness. *Journal of Applied Psychology* 26: 800–808.

Hall, D. (1999). Destination branding, niche marketing and national image projection in Central and Eastern Europe. *Journal of Vacation Marketing* 5(3): 227–237.

Hall, D. (2002). Brand development, tourism and national identity: The re-imaging of former Yugoslavia. *Journal of Brand Management* 9(4/5): 323–334.

Hawes, D. K., Taylor, D. T. and Hampe, G. D. (1991). Destination marketing by states. *Journal of Travel Research* Summer: 11–17.

Henderson, J. C. (2000). Selling places: The new Asia-Singapore brand. In Robinson, M., Evans, N., Long, P., Sharpley, R. and Swarbrooke, J. (eds) *Management, Marketing and the Political Economy of Travel and Tourism*. Sunderland, UK: The Centre for Travel & Tourism, pp. 207–218.

Hopper, P. (2002). Marketing London in a difficult climate. *Journal of Vacation Marketing* 9(1): 81–88.

Hosany, S., Ekinci, Y. and Uysal, M. (2006). Destination image and destination personality: An application of branding theories to tourism places. *Journal of Business Research* 59(5): 638–642.

Keller, K. L. (1993). Conceptualizing, measuring, and managing customer-based brand equity. *Journal of Marketing* 57(January): 1–22.

Keller, K. L. (2003). *Strategic Brand Management*. Upper Saddle River, NJ: Prentice Hall.

Keller, P. (2000). Destination marketing: Strategic areas of inquiry. In Manente, M. and Cerato, M. (eds) *From Destination to Destination Marketing and Management*. Venice, Italy: CISET, pp. 29–44.

King, S. (1970). Development of the brand. *Advertising Quarterly* Summer: 6–14.

Konecnik, M. (2004). Evaluating Slovenia's image as a tourism destination: A self-analysis process towards building a destination brand. *Journal of Brand Management* 11(4): 307–316.

Konecnik, M. (2006). Croatian-based brand equity for Slovenia as a tourism destination. *Economic and Business Review* 8(1): 83–108.

Konecnik, M. and Gartner, W. C. (2007). Customer-based brand equity for a destination. *Annals of Tourism Research* 34(2): 400–421.

Konecnik, M., Ruzzier, M. and De Chernatony, L. (2013). Developing and applying a place brand identity model: The case of Slovenia. *Journal of Business Research* 66(1): 45–52.

Kotler, P., Brown, L., Adam, S., Burton, S. and Armstrong, G. (2007). *Marketing* (7th edition). Frenchs Forest, NSW: Pearson Education.

Laroche, M., Habibi, M. R. and Richard, M. (2013). To be or not to be in social media: How brand loyalty is affected by social media? *International Journal of Information Management* 33(1): 76–82.

Martinovic, S. (2002). Branding Hrvatska – A mixed blessing that might succeed: The advantage of being unrecognisable. *Journal of Brand Management* 9(4/5): 315–322.

May, C. (2001). From direct response to image with qualitative and quantitative research. *Presentation at the 32nd Annual Conference of the Travel & Tourism Research Association*. Fort Myers.

Mazanec, J. A. and Schweiger, G. C. (1981). Improved marketing efficiency through multi-product brand names. *European Research* January: 32–44.

McAlexander, J. H., Schouten, W. J. and Koening, F. H. (2002). Building brand community. *Journal of Marketing* 66(1): 38–54.

Middleton, V. T. C. (1998). New marketing conditions, and the strategic advantages of products similar to destination. In Keller, P. (ed.) *Destination Marketing: Reports of the 48th AIEST Congress, Marrakech*, pp. 153–165.

Moilanen, T. and Rainisto, S. (2009). *How to Brand Nations, Cities and Destinations: A Planning Book for Place Branding*. Basingstoke, UK: Palgrave Macmillan.

Morgan, N. and Pritchard, A. (1998). *Tourism Promotion and Power: Creating Images, Creating Identities*. Chichester, UK: John Wiley & Sons Ltd.

Morgan, N., Pritchard, A. and Piggott, R. (2002a). New Zealand, 100% pure: The creation of a powerful niche destination brand. *Brand Management* 9(4/5): 335–354.

Morgan, N., Pritchard, A. and Pride, R. (2002b). *Destination Branding: Creating the Unique Destination Proposition*. Oxford, UK: Butterworth-Heinemann.

Morgan, N., Pritchard, A. and Pride, R. (2004). *Destination Branding: Creating the Unique Destination Proposition* (2nd edition). Oxford: Butterworth-Heinemann.

Morgan, N., Pritchard, A. and Pride, R. (2011). *Destination Brands: Managing Place Reputation* (3rd edition). Oxford: Butterworth-Heinemann.

Morgan, N., Hastings, E. and Pritchard, A. (2012). Developing a new DMO evaluation framework: The case of Visit Wales. *Journal of Vacation Marketing* 18(1): 73–89.

Muniz, M. A. and O'Guinn, C. T. (2001). Brand community. *Journal of Consumer Research* 27(4): 412–432.

Murphy, L., Benckdorff, P. and Moscardo, G. (2007a). Destination brand personality: Visitor perceptions of a regional tourism destination. *Tourism Analysis* 12(5/6): 419–432.

Murphy, L., Moscardo, G. and Benckdorff, P. (2007b). Using brand personality to differentiate regional tourism destinations. *Journal of Travel Research* 46(1): 5–14.

Oliveira, E. and Panyik, E. (2015). Content, context and co-creation: Digital challenges in destination branding with references to Portugal as a tourist destination. *Journal of Vacation Marketing* 21(1): 53–74.

Park, S. Y. and Petrick, J. F. (2006). Destinations' perspectives of branding. *Annals of Tourism Research* 33(1): 262–265.

Pereira, R. L. G., Correia, A. L. and Schutz, R. L. A. (2012). Destination branding: A critical overview. *Journal of Quality Assurance in Hospitality & Tourism* 13(2): 81–102.

Pike, S. (2004). Destination brand positioning slogans: Towards the development of a set of accountability criteria. *Acta Turistica* 16(2): 102–124.

Pike, S. (2005). Tourism destination branding complexity. *Journal of Product & Brand Management* 14(4): 258–259.

Pike, S. (2007). Consumer-based brand equity for destinations: Practical DMO performance measures. *Journal of Travel & Tourism Marketing* 22(1): 51–61.

Pike, S. (2008). *Destination Marketing: An Integrated Marketing Communication Approach*. Burlington, MA: Butterworth-Heinemann.

Pike, S. (2009). Destination brand positions of a competitive set of near-home destinations. *Tourism Management* 30(6): 857–866.

Pike, S. (2010). Destination branding: Tracking brand equity for an emerging destination between 2003 and 2007. *Journal of Hospitality & Tourism Research* 34(1): 124–139.

Pike, S. and Ryan, C. (2004). Destination positioning analysis through a comparison of cognitive, affective and conative perceptions. *Journal of Travel Research* 42(4): 333–342.

Pike, S. and Page, S. (2014). Destination marketing organizations and destination marketing: A narrative analysis of the literature. *Tourism Management* 41: 202–227.

Pitt, L. F., Opoku, R., Hultman, M., Abratt, R. and Spyropoulou, S. (2007). What I say about myself: Communication of brand personality by African countries. *Tourism Management* 28(3): 835–844.

Pride, R. (2002). Brand Wales: 'Natural revival'. In Morgan, N., Prichard, A. and Pride, R. (eds) *Destination Branding*. Oxford: Butterworth-Heinemann, pp. 109–123.

Pritchard, A. and Morgan, N. (1998). Mood marketing – The new destination branding strategy: A case of Wales the brand. *Journal of Vacation Marketing* 4(3): 215–229.

Ritchie, J. R. B. and Ritchie, R. J. B. (1998).The branding of tourism destinations: Past achievements and future challenges. In Keller, P. (ed.) *Destination Marketing: Reports of the 48th AIEST Congress, Marrakech*, pp. 89–116.

Slater, J. (2002). Brand Louisiana: 'Come as you are. Leave different.' In Morgan, N., Pritchard, A. and Pride, R. (eds) *Destination Branding*. Oxford: Butterworth-Heinemann, pp. 148–162.

Tasci, A. D. A. and Kozak, M. (2006). Destination brands vs destination images: Do we know what we mean? *Journal of Vacation Marketing* 12(4): 299–317.

TravelandTourWorld.com. (2015). *Singapore Tourism Board Unveils Differentiated Marketing Campaigns*. Available at: http://www.travelandtourworld.com/ttw-archive-2015

Trendwatching.com. (2015). Currencies of change: Why customers will expect good behavior to be more than just its own reward. *March 2015 Trend Briefing*. Available at: http://trendwatching.com/trends/currencies-of-change

Urde, M. (1999). Brand orientation: A mindset for building brands into strategic resources. *Journal of Marketing Management* 15(2): 117–133.

Usaki, A. and Baloglu, S. (2011). Brand personality of tourist destinations: An application of self-congruity theory. *Tourism Management* 32(1): 114–127.

Chapter 10

Destination image

AIMS

To enhance understanding of:

- the role of image in destination marketing;
- consumer decision sets;
- key destination image measurement issues.

ABSTRACT

Images held by consumers play a major role in travel purchase decisions, and so an understanding of the perceptions held of the destination is essential. Chapter 9 introduced the concepts of brand identity, brand positioning and brand image as the key components of branding. Brand identity represents the values and essence of the destination community, is the self-image aspired in the market place and has an internal focus on motivating and guiding stakeholders. This chapter discusses the image component of destination branding. This represents the actual image held of the destination by consumers, which may or may not be similar to that intended in the brand identity. Major objectives of any marketing strategy will usually be to create a new image, to correct negative perceptions or to reinforce positive images already established in the minds of the target audience. The purpose is to achieve brand salience in terms of membership of the small competitive set of destinations considered by the consumer during decision making, which represents a source of competitive advantage. The topic of destination image has arguably been the most prevalent in the tourism literature, and so there exists a rich resource to guide DMOs. However, despite over 40 years of published destination image research, there is no widely accepted method for measuring this construct. The chapter concludes with a summary of the key common limitations in destination image measurement.

Perception is reality

In Chapter 9 destination branding was introduced as comprising the three key components shown in Figure 10.1: *brand identity*, which is the image aspired to in the market place by the DMO; *brand image*,

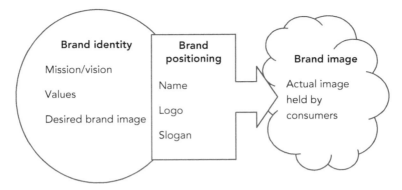

Figure 10.1 Three components of branding

which is the actual image held by consumers and may bear little resemblance to that desired by the DMO; and *brand positioning*, which is the attempt by the DMO to enhance congruence between the brand identity and the brand image.

Unfortunately for the marketer, images held by consumers might only have a tenuous and indirect relationship to fact:

> *Sometimes the notions people have about a brand do not even seem very sensible or relevant to those who know what the product is 'really' like. But they all contribute to the customer's deciding whether or not the brand is the one for me.*
>
> *(Gardner and Levy, 1955: 35; Reynolds, 1965)*

However, whether an individual's perceived images are correct is not as important as what the consumer actually believes to be true. This proposition continues to underpin consumer behaviour research today and is commonly referred to as *perception is reality*, the origin of which was Thomas's theorem: 'What is defined or perceived by people is real in its consequences' (Thomas and Thomas, 1928: 572, in Patton, 2002). That is, while an individual's perceptions about a brand might be incorrect, they still influence their purchase behaviour.

The role of destination image

At the 2000 Tourism and Travel Research Association conference in Hollywood, John Hunt used the metaphor of *three peasants breaking in a new field* to describe the 1970s destination image research undertaken by himself, Edward Mayo and Clare Gunn. In the 40 years since their pioneering work, destination image has been one of the most prevalent topics in the tourism literature (Pike and Page, 2014). For reviews of this literature, see Chon (1990), Gallarza *et al.* (2002), Tasci *et al.* (2007), Stepchenkova and Mills (2010), Zhang *et al.* (2014) and Josiassen *et al.* (2015). For a categorisation of 262 destination image studies published between 1973 and 2007, see Pike (2002a, 2007a).

Chon's (1990) review of 23 of the most frequently cited destination image studies at that time found that the most popular themes were the role and influence of destination image in buyer behaviour and satisfaction. More recently, Zhang *et al.*'s (2014) meta-analysis of the literature found a strong relationship between destination image and destination loyalty. Indeed Hunt's (1975) view, that images held by potential travellers are so important in the destination selection process that they can affect the viability of the destination, has become axiomatic. After all, most tourism products are services rather than physical goods and can often only compete via images. Key implications of this for destination marketers are the issues of intangibility and risk, inseparability and variability, perishability, and substitutability.

Intangibility and risk

Prior to purchase, a guitar may be played in the store, shoes can be fitted and a car taken for a test drive. Products are tangible goods that can generally be inspected, trialled and exchanged. All of our senses are available to us as we shop for products at the mall. Even if planning an online purchase we can usually check out the product in a store first. However, the only physical evidence of a holiday destination we have never previously visited may be in the images and words of travel brochures, web pages, friends' posts on social media or in the broadcast media. Thus, expectations of the holiday are realisable only after purchase and actual travel (Goodall *et al.*, 1988). It follows then that a consequence of intangibility is risk in the travel purchase decision. Several types of risk may be of concern to travellers and suppliers in different travel situations:

- **Performance risk**. Will the service perform as expected? Tourism destination performance risks include a diverse range of factors, such as poor weather, labour strikes, substandard service encounters, civil unrest, grumpy travellers, theft and other crimes, natural disasters, fluctuating exchange rates, traffic delays, airport congestion and terrorism. Since satisfaction with a destination will result from a series of separate service interactions, over which the DMO has no control, the potential for dissatisfaction at a new destination is considerable. Will the destination live up to the consumer's expectations, regardless of whether their *perceptions* are reasonable or not?

- **Social risk**. To what extent will the travel experience be *perceived* to enhance wellbeing or the self-concept? Is there potential for embarrassment? There might be stress involved when travelling in unfamiliar environments. Mansfield (1992) referred to the social stress of tourism, when motivated to travel by membership of a social reference group. For example, social risk may occur when joining a coach tour of strangers, since holidays represent interplay between merging into a group and affirming individuality (Mollo-Bouvier, 1990). Differences between individuals' personalities are as much in evidence during travel as they are in everyday life.

- **Physical risk**. Is there potential for harm? Travellers not only *perceive* the risk of harm at the destination but will also consider the transport facilities and transit environments en route (see, for example, Page *et al.*, 1994; Page and Wilks, 2004). This has been particularly evident immediately following major acts of war and terrorism and outbreaks of disease, which, while restricted to a relatively small geographic area, have led to a decline in travel in other parts of the world. For example, in the cases of the 1990–1991 Gulf War, 9/11 in New York and the outbreak of severe acute respiratory syndrome (SARS) in Asia during 2002–2003, overall worldwide international travel declined for a period.

- **Financial risk**. Does the financial investment represent *perceived* value? The higher the level of involvement in the decision, the higher the perceived risk might be. While pleasure travel might be a psychological necessity, it is usually discretionary spending and therefore competes with other household financial issues such as replacement of a car or major appliances, medical events and home renovations, all of which are tangible. This will have greater implications for destinations not previously visited and those that are long haul.

Inseparability and variability

Customers are actively involved in the delivery of a service, since production and consumption occur simultaneously. Increasingly, travellers have been seeking greater involvement in tourism services, as participants rather than passive observers (Crouch, 2000; Pike and Page, 2014). For example, research investigating service dominant logic and its application to marketing in tourism has shown the shift in thinking towards co-creation and co-production in destination–traveller engagement (Shaw *et al.*, 2011). Also, *perceptions* of the same destination experience may be quite different among different travellers at different times, leading to different levels of satisfaction.

Perishability

Destination services are perishable, since they cannot be stored for sale later during high demand periods. Individual businesses attempt to match capacity with projected levels of demand through measures such as dynamic pricing, yield management and sales promotions. For DMOs, this presents challenges in forecasting the impacts of annual seasonality, periodicity of peaks and troughs during the week, special events and exogenous forces.

Substitutability

Destinations are close substitutes for rival places in crowded markets, since travellers have available to them a myriad of destinations they *perceive* will satisfy their wants. Even taking into account price incentives, what influences a traveller to select a destination they have not previously visited? In such cases images can provide a pre-taste. Influencing these images by DMOs requires insights into the complexity of the image formation process. There has been a lack of attention to date in the tourism literature to the issue of *destination switching*. For example, it is not known the extent to which a consumer will switch between destinations in the decision set due to issues that might occur at the time of decision making, such as awareness of better value packages, a word-of-mouth recommendation from a significant other or events such as natural disasters or terrorism. For example, an exploratory study in the UK (Wilson, 2002) found evidence that short break holiday travellers would change their intended destination if a *bargain* package to another destination became available.

Image formation and the mind's defence system

While it is agreed consumers' perceptions play an important role in travel decisions, defining *destination image* and understanding image formation are not so clear. A number of authors have been critical of attempts to conceptualise the destination image construct. It was even proposed that most of the early destination image studies lacked any conceptual framework (Echtner and Ritchie, 1991; Fakeye and Crompton, 1991). Echtner and Ritchie suggested most definitions were vague, such as *perceptions of an area*. Jenkins (1999) found the term destination image had been used in a number of different contexts including, for example, perceptions held by individuals, stereotypes held by groups and images projected by DMOs. Questions have been raised as to whether researchers were actually certain of the unique properties of destination image and whether it could be accurately measured. However, this is not a problem faced by destination image researchers in isolation, since in the wider marketing literature, there is not yet a consensus on either the definition of the *brand image* construct or on how it should be operationalised.

Our minds often struggle to cope with the daily flood of advertising and other media (Ries and Trout, 1981). In this regard the explosion in destination choice and destination publicity material has only served to increase confusion among potential travellers, particularly since the advent of the internet, Web 2.0 and social media. A central theme within the marketing literature has been the difficulty which the mind has in dealing with this increasingly busy world. However, Jacoby (1984) argued that, while consumers could become overloaded with information, they would not generally allow this to occur. Instead, coping mechanisms are developed. The need for simplified processing by the mind was implicit in the definition of image proposed by Reynolds (1965: 69): 'The mental construct developed by the consumer on the basis of a few selected impressions among the flood of total impressions'.

This viewpoint holds that we develop simplified images through some sort of creative filtering process. We are selective about which messages attract our attention; we are selective about how we interpret and even distort information; and we are selective about which information we retain in memory. This selective filtering is a form of perceptual defence (Moutinho, 1987). Exactly how the mind's *black box* of the filtering of cognitive information occurs in the brain to produce a composite image is not yet fully understood. For example, another important concept for multi-attributed entities, such as destinations, is that of an overall composite image versus consideration of a set of individual attributes (see Mayo, 1973; Dichter, 1985; Gartner, 1986; MacInnes and Price, 1987; Stern and Krakover, 1993; Baloglu and McCleary, 1999). MacInnes and Price described imagery as a process of the representation of multi-sensory information in a *gestalt*. Discursive processing on the other hand is the cognitive elaboration of individual attributes. A key issue for destination image research is whether imagery or discursive processing is used to evaluate destinations. Pike's (2002a, 2007a) review of 262 destination image studies found 187 (71 per cent) used lists of attributes. Studies interested in measuring holistic impressions have included Pearce (1988), Reilly (1990) and Um and Crompton (1990).

A further dimension of destination image is how individuals evaluate common functional attributes versus unique and psychological features (Echtner and Ritchie, 1991). Since most studies require participants to compare destinations across a range of common attributes, there is little opportunity to identify attributes that might be unique to a destination. However, it should also be recognised that unique features may not necessarily explain a destination's competitive position if they do not offer benefits in a specified travel context (Pike, 2004).

Plot value and the halo effect

Given a single fact, a consumer can create a detailed image of a product through simple inferences (Reynolds, 1965). One way this occurs is through *plot value* where certain attributes are seen by an individual to go together. In this way, we construct a plot from a small amount of knowledge. Knowledge of a destination's location may enable the construction of an image including likely climate and geography. For example, New Zealand's location in the South Pacific might incorrectly stimulate an image of a tropical climate, rather than the country's actual temperate weather. A similar phenomenon may occur through the *halo effect* where a product that is rated highly on one attribute is then also assumed to rate highly on others. The reverse may also apply.

Geographers have commonly referred to images held of environments being either designative or appraisive (Stern and Krakover, 1993). The former use a cognitive categorisation of the landscape, while the latter are concerned with attitudes towards the place. These ideas are consistent with Fishbein's (1967) concepts of cognition, affect and conation, which, along with Gunn's (1988) organic/induced images, have been the most cited destination image formation concepts.

Cognition, affect and conation

Fishbein (1967) and Fishbein and Ajzen (1975) argued the importance of distinguishing between an individual's beliefs and their attitudes. While beliefs represent information (knowledge) held about an object, attitude is an overall evaluation (degree of liking). Beliefs and attitude comprise cognitive, affective and conative components.

Cognition is the sum of what is known or believed about a destination and might be organic or induced. Cognition denotes awareness, but not necessarily salience. *Affect* represents an individual's feelings towards an object, which will be favourable, unfavourable or neutral. The number of terms used in the English language to describe affect towards a destination is in the hundreds (Russel *et al.*, 1981). Following Russel (1980), Russel *et al.* factor analysed 105 common adjectives used to describe environments and generated the affective response grid shown in Figure 10.2. Eight adjective dimensions of affect were included in the model. The assumption was that these dimensions were not independent of each other, but represented a circumplex model of affect. The horizontal axis was arbitrarily set to represent *pleasantness*, while the vertical axis represents level of *arousal*. In this way, *exciting*, which is a dimension in its own right, is a combination of arousing and pleasant, while *distressing* is a function of arousing and unpleasant. Walmsley and Jenkins' (1993) principal components analysis of repertory grid data produced the same two factor labels. Using four semantic differential scales, *pleasant/unpleasant*, *relaxing/distressing*, *arousing/sleepy* and *exciting/gloomy*, Baloglu and Brinberg (1997) demonstrated how the affective response model could be applied to destinations. They used multidimensional scaling to plot the affective positions of 11 Mediterranean destinations.

The majority of destination image studies have focused on cognitive attributes. Pike's (2002a, 2007a) review of 262 destination image studies found only 17 showed an explicit interest in measuring affective images. Only recently have destination studies studied both cognition and affect towards destinations together (see Dann, 1996; MacKay and Fesenmaier, 1997; Baloglu, 1998; Baloglu and McCleary, 1999; Baloglu and Mangaloglu, 2001; Sönmez and Sirakaya, 2002; Kim and Richardson, 2003; Kim and Yoon, 2003; Kastenholz, 2004; Pike and Ryan, 2004; Baloglu and Love, 2005; Konecnik, 2005; Hosany *et al.*, 2006; Pike, 2006; San Martin and del Bosque, 2008; Pike and Mason, 2011; Agapito *et al.*, 2013).

The *conative* image is analogous to behaviour since it is the action component, representing intent to purchase (Howard and Sheth, 1969). Therefore, conation may be considered as the likelihood of visiting a destination within a given time period. Figure 10.3 highlights how cognition/affect/conation might apply in decision making. The process is similar to the hierarchy of effects (see Lavidge and Steiner, 1961) or the AIDA model used by advertisers, where the aim is to guide a consumer through the stages of **A**wareness,

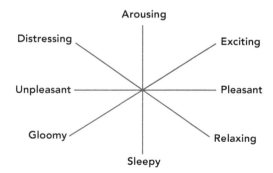

Figure 10.2 Affective response grid
Source: Adapted from Russel *et al.* (1981).

Figure 10.3 Cognition/affect/conation

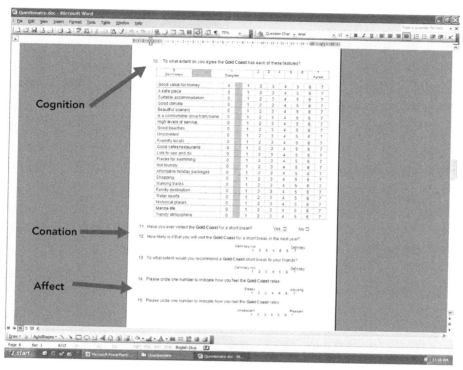

Figure 10.4 Operationalising cognition/affect/conation

Interest, Desire and Action. Figure 10.4 is an excerpt from the questionnaire used by Pike (2009) to operationalise the three concepts.

Organic and induced images

Gunn (1988) suggested destination images were formed in two ways: organically and induced. *Organic* images are developed through an individual's everyday assimilation of information, which includes a wide range of mediums such as school history lessons, word of mouth, social media posts, mass media (editorial) and actual visitation. The *induced* image on the other hand is formed through the influence of tourism promotions directed by marketers, such as advertising. This is more common when an individual begins sourcing information for a holiday. The distinction between organic and induced images is the level of influence held by marketers. This is particularly relevant in the Web 2.0 era, where destination advertising is swamped by the mass of user-generated content (UGC) on social media.

There are two important implications of this. First, it is possible for individuals to have images of destinations that they have not previously visited. Second, destination images can change after visitation (Hunt, 1975; Pearce 1982; Wee *et al.*, 1985; Chon, 1991; Hu and Ritchie, 1993). Milman and Pizam (1995) demonstrated how familiarity with a domestic US destination, measured by previous visitation, led to a more positive image and increased likelihood of repeat visits. Therefore, it is important to separate the images held by visitors from those of non-visitors. Non-visitors will include those who would like to visit, but have not yet been able to for various reasons, as well as those who have chosen not to visit. However, many studies of destination image have excluded non-visitors (Ahmed, 1991; Baloglu and McCleary, 1999; Pike, 2008; Cherifi *et al.*, 2014).

Personal construct theory and learning from experience

Apart from an innate need to explore, all other travel motivations are learned by individuals (Mayo and Jarvis, 1981). For example, no one is born with the need for status. Therefore, an individual's travel preferences and behaviour can change during a lifetime as wants and motives are learned from experience. A useful theory for understanding this phenomena is through the lens of Kelly's (1955) personal construct theory (PCT), which views individuals as scientists whose aim is to predict and control their world. Underpinning PCT is constructive alternativism, which proposed individuals have the creative capacity to interpret their world, rather than respond to it in a stimulus–response manner. People construe the environment in different ways, and it is open to reconstruction. The individual (personal) construct system is the only model used to guide behaviour (Jankowicz, 1987).

Anticipation is at the very core of construing (Landfield and Leitner, 1980: 5): 'If we were not anticipating regularities in behaviour, why should we become upset about sudden change?' Why would you be disappointed with someone's behaviour if you did not have different expectations of them? Therefore everyone has a repertoire of constructs that are continually being tested and amended through life experiences, in an attempt to enhance predictions about the consequences of choices. The basic proposition in the PCT's fundamental postulate was that 'a person's processes are psychologically channelized by the ways in which he anticipates events' (Kelly, 1955: 46).

Kelly designed the repertory test to operationalise PCT, to elicit an individual's range of constructs used to guide their behaviour. Originally developed for use in clinical psychology, the repertory test has been adapted for use in a diverse range of other fields, such as marketing research. While PCT and the repertory test have not been widely reported in the tourism literature, destination image applications have included investigations of the perceptions of: seaside resorts (Riley and Palmer, 1975), countryside places (Palmer, 1978), pre and post travel (Pearce, 1982), holiday photos (Botterill and Crompton, 1987), Austria (Embacher and Buttle, 1989), Japan (Botterill, 1989) and domestic destinations (Walmsley and Jenkins, 1993; Young, 1995; Pike, 2003, 2007b, 2012). In the destination marketing context the repertory test is a structured qualitative technique for identifying the *cognitive* destination attributes consumers use to differentiate a competitive set of places, or laddering analysis can be used to identify *affective* benefits.

Laddering analysis was developed by Hinkle (1965), one of George Kelly's (1955) PhD students, as an extension of the repertory test. Laddering is commonly referred to by marketing researchers as means–end chain (see Gutman, 1982; Reynolds and Gutman, 1984). Laddering facilitates understanding of how cognitive attributes are perceived to provide benefits, which in turn satisfy personal values. In the example shown in Figure 10.5, an individual might differentiate destinations on the basis of the variety of beaches (salient cognitive attribute), which offer the potential benefit of relaxation (affective), to enhance self-esteem (personal value). For an application of the repertory test with laddering to identify how consumers differentiate destinations on the basis of attributes, benefits and personal values, see Pike (2012).

Associative network theory

A number of extensive literature reviews on the topic of memory structure (see, for example, Keller, 1993; Cai, 2002) have found the most commonly accepted conceptualisation has been by a spreading

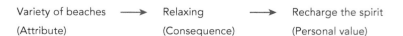

Variety of beaches ⟶ Relaxing ⟶ Recharge the spirit

(Attribute)   (Consequence)   (Personal value)

Figure 10.5 Means–end chain ladder

action. This is consistent with associative network theory, which sees memory as consisting as nodes (neurons) with links to other nodes (see Anderson and Bower, 1979; Anderson, 1983). A node represents stored information about a particular concept and is part of a network of links to other nodes. Activation between nodes occurs either through the action of processing external information or when information is retrieved from memory. When a node concept is recalled, the strength of association will dictate the range of other nodes that will be activated from memory. A destination brand is conceptualised as representing a node with which a number of associations with other node concepts (wants, attributes and benefits) are linked. Key implications of this are destination salience, when a travel situation is considered, and the strength and favourability of associations with important attributes (e.g. variety of beaches) and benefits (e.g. relaxing).

Promote the destination first and your business second

As discussed in Chapter 9, in an attempt to reach the minds of busy consumers it is critical that all marketing communications reinforce the brand identity. With UGC on social media swamping communications by destination marketers, it is advantageous for as many stakeholders as possible to also support the destination brand identity in their own marketing efforts. There is an old adage in destination marketing that it is in the interests of tourism businesses to promote the destination first and their business second. This philosophy, which recognises individual businesses are reliant to some extent on the competitiveness of the destination, is not always obvious to new entrants to the industry. Case study 10.1 highlights how one accommodation business has adopted this approach in their social media programme, recognising that their followers will likely be more interested in being engaged by destination stories rather than updates about individual hotels.

CASE STUDY

10.1 The Wyndham Group: Promoting the destination first and their business second

Jane Gentle
Strategic Business Advisor, Iconic Solutions, Australia

Wyndham Worldwide is one of the world's largest hospitality companies with 80 properties in 6 continents across South East Asia and the Pacific Rim. The group's portfolio of world-renowned hotel and resort brands offer leisure and business travellers a broad array of products and services across a variety of budgets. Wyndham Worldwide recently initiated a new approach to managing their online social media programme, based on the recognition of the need to promote the destination first and the company second, in order to drive traffic to individual properties. The group has achieved this by aligning their initiatives with those of the local DMO at each of their destinations.

Wyndham keeps a tight rein on their corporate Facebook and Instagram pages, with the marketing department, located in their head office on Australia's Gold Coast, being responsible for all content for each property. Wyndham management views Facebook as a way of connecting with followers and providing information that will capture the attention of potential and current visitors, while enabling followers to share, like or comment on their posts. The group has nearly 30 properties located throughout Australia, and Facebook pages for each individual property are not permitted (see https://www.facebook.com/Wyndhamap?fref=ts). Rather, an ambassador is appointed at each property, with the responsibility for creating newsworthy content on the region, which is then sent to head office. These story ideas are then reviewed for potential posting to the 23,000 Facebook followers of the Wyndham corporate page. The idea of the ambassadors in each location is to enable each individual property to have their opportunity to be showcased to the group's wider audience, while providing locale-centric stories to promote the destination over the corporate entity. Adopting a *jab, jab, jab, hook* approach, the strategic plan uses Facebook to post informative articles that link back to the corporate website, which has a dedicated blog page (http://www.wyndhamap.com/wps/wcm/connect/wyndham/home/sitetools/exturl-wandrful).

Recognising the bigger picture of destination competitiveness, the articles are carefully crafted to promote the destination first and the Wyndham property second. For example, one recent article focused on 'how to wine and dine in Torquay', providing readers with a unique guide on how best to tour the region's cuisine offerings. The story was part of an attempt to re-position the region from being known as a surfing community, to one that offers fine dining and vineyards specialising in classic varietals such as Shiraz and Merlot, as well as more exquisite Grenache and Gewürztraminer, all of which 'can be enjoyed while watching a stunning moonlight summer concert in a 200 seat amphitheatre in one of the local vineyards'.

Another recent Facebook posting offered suggestions on 'the best things to do in Melbourne on a rainy day', which recognised the city's renown for sometimes providing all four seasons in one day. The Wyndham Melbourne ambassador asked locals to share their favourite things to do on rainy days, to provide insiders' knowledge. Another article titled 'A photographic vision: Melbourne' detailed an urban walk of the city, complete with a downloadable guided map, navigating photographers through the city's unique laneways, urban graffiti hot spots and historic arcades, providing newcomers with an *off-the-beaten track* and stunning photographic trail of the city.

Discussion question

What initiatives could a DMO use to stimulate stakeholders to promote the destination image in their own marketing communications?

Motivation

Motivation begins the holiday travel decision process, when a want arises that cannot be met at home (Gartner, 1993). The term vacation infers the vacating of one space for another. This applies mentally as well as physically since pleasure travel is considered a psychological necessity. In this regard, motives can therefore be viewed as the psychological determinants of demand (Kotler *et al.*, 1999). Motivation in tourism is a relatively new field of study, and researchers have consistently reported a lack of understanding (see Dann, 1981; Mansfield, 1992; Ritchie, 1996; Baloglu and McCleary, 1999; Pike, 2008). However, the lack of theory is not unique to the tourism industry, since the issue of consumer motivation in the wider marketing literature is not fully understood.

Sunlust and wanderlust

One of the first attempts to explain pleasure travel motivation was Gray's (1970) concepts of wanderlust and sunlust, which subsume many of the motivation categories outlined in more recent studies.

Wanderlust characterised the human need to temporarily leave familiar surroundings to experience different cultures and places. *Sunlust* represents travel for a specific purpose for benefits not available at home, such as winter sun holidays or visits to a larger city.

Push versus pull

Dann (1977) introduced the concept of *push* factors to explain the link between motivation and destination choice. Motivational push factors were proposed to be a logical antecedent to the analysis of *pull* factors such as destination attributes. Within the push category, Dann introduced the concepts of anomie and ego-enhancement from social psychology to explain the core travel motivations. The anomic traveller seeks escape from the mundane and isolation at home to obtain opportunities for social interaction. Ego-enhancement on the other hand seeks increased self-recognition, such as opportunities to recreate oneself at a place where identity is not known, or trip-dropping at home about destinations with *brag value* to reinforce status.

Psychocentric-allocentric continuum of traveller types

Related to travel motivation is the work of Cohen (1972) and Plog (1974) in categorising traveller types. Cohen suggested four types of tourist roles: the organised mass tourist, the individual mass tourist, the explorer and the drifter. While the core motives for most were variety and novelty, each group clearly differed in the level of control and predictability sought from the experience. The key variable in the typology was strangeness versus familiarity. Plog introduced psychocentricity and allocentricity to travel. Psychocentrics were posited to be nervous and non-adventurous, travel to familiar places, preferring to drive rather than fly. Allocentrics on the other hand were more confident and willing to experiment with life. These individuals would prefer new experiences such as non-touristy or remote destinations. Both Cohen and Plog linked their concepts to the evolution of a destination's lifecycle. For example, Cohen suggested strangeness and novelty were important for travellers. Plog proposed allocentrics would be the first to visit or explore a new destination, while psychocentrics would be attracted at the maturity or even the decline stage. However, Cohen suggested mass tourism had created a paradox, where novelty was increasingly difficult to cater to as tourism had become institutionalised (and that was 40 years ago!).

Satisfying consumers' 'wants'

One of the problems for tourism researchers is that motives for travel may not actually be entirely understood by travellers themselves (Crompton, 1979: 421): 'The in-depth interviews caused many respondents to confront for the first time their real motives for going on a pleasure vacation'. Therefore the reasons people give for taking holidays are not necessarily sufficient to explain motivation (Mill and Morrison, 1992). Motivations can be very difficult to recall and to articulate. Instead, following Maslow's (1943) theory of motivation as a hierarchy of needs, Mill and Morrison argued that the key to understanding travel motivation was through the recognition of travel as a needs and wants satisfier: 'Motivation occurs when an individual wants to satisfy a need' (Mill and Morrison, 1992: 17). They suggested this view of motivation is the difference between seeing the destination as a collection of attractions and seeing it as a place for satisfying needs and wants.

Gilmore (2002) succinctly summarised the complex field of tourism motivation into three categories: hedonism, self-improvement and spiritual. Recognising the needs of an individual traveller will be physical, psychological or intellectual, Mill and Morrison (1992) linked the relationships between needs and motives referenced in the tourism literature, as shown in Table 10.1. It could be argued the physiological and safety needs are physical, while the belonging, esteem and self-actualisation needs are psychological. The last two categories are intellectual needs.

Table 10.1 Needs and tourism motives

Need	Want/motive	Tourism literature
Physiological	Relaxation	Escape, relaxation, relief of tension, sunlust, physical, mental relaxation of tension
Safety	Security	Health, recreation, keep oneself active and healthy
Belonging	Love	Family togetherness, enhancement of kinship relationships, companionship, facilitation of social interaction, maintenance of personal ties, interpersonal relations, roots, ethnic, show one's affection for family, maintain social contacts
Esteem	Achievement, status	Convince oneself of one's achievements, show one's importance to others, prestige, social recognition, ego-enhancement, professional business, personal development, status, prestige
Self-actualisation	Be true to one's own nature	Exploration and evaluation of self, self-discovery, satisfaction of inner desires
To know and understand	Knowledge	Cultural, education, wanderlust, interest in foreign areas
Aesthetics	Appreciation of beauty	Environmental, scenery

Source: Adapted from Mill and Morrison (1992: 20).

When motivated to act, the individual consumer-traveller becomes a decision maker (Mayo and Jarvis, 1981). Decisions must be made about where to go, when to go, how to get there and what to do there. Brand decisions then essentially involve alternative brands and the buyer's own choice criteria (Howard and Sheth, 1969). Choice criteria will be associated with motives. Therefore, while a favourable image of a destination is important, it must also be aligned to the traveller's wants, to increase the likelihood of visitation (Mansfield, 1992). Mill and Morrison (1992) suggested one implication of Maslow's hierarchy of needs was that holidays targeting the satisfaction of lower level physical and physiological needs would be treated as a necessity rather than as a luxury. Of particular interest is how travellers select a holiday destination from so many places that could satisfy their wants.

Importantly, therefore, many holiday decisions are made on the basis of activity first, destination second (Gilmore, 2002). Phelps (1986), for example, found visitors to Menorca had a low awareness of the destination they were travelling to on a package tour, since the package product was more important that the destination. This is why so many destinations are substitutable for any given travel situation and why destination salience and decision set inclusion, rather than awareness per se, represent competitive advantage (Pike and Ryan, 2004).

Decision sets

Consumer decision set theory offers some explanation of this most complicated aspect of consumer behaviour. Howard (1963) and Howard and Sheth (1969) introduced the concept of the evoked decision set to propose that the number of brands considered in any purchase decision was considerably lower than those available. The evoked set comprises only those brands the consumer will actually consider in the next purchase decision. In this text, the term *competitive set* is used interchangeably with decision set, because it identifies the small set destinations a DMO is competing against in the consumer's mind, in a given travel decision. Howard proposed the number of brands in an individual's evoked set would remain constant at about three or four. Woodside and Sherrell (1977) were the first to investigate evoked sets of destinations in the holiday decision process. They were motivated by the proposition that the mental processes required to evaluate the features of say 15 or more destinations would represent too great a task for most travellers.

The reduced set of likely alternatives forming the evoked decision set is part of the total set. The evoked set comprises those destinations the consumer has some likelihood of visiting within a given time period (Woodside and Sherrell, 1977). For travellers, this total set would consist of all those destinations that may or may not be available and of which they may or may not be aware. In other words, all destinations. Within this total set of destinations, Woodside and Sherrell (1977) proposed the following possible overlapping subsets:

- unavailable and unaware set;
- awareness set;
- available set;
- evoked set;
- aware and unavailable set;
- available and unaware set;
- inert set;
- inept set;
- chosen destination.

Since consumers will either be aware or unaware of the existence of a product, it is from the awareness set that a purchase choice will ultimately be made (Narayana and Markin, 1975). Clearly, a destination must first make it into the consumer's awareness set for consideration. From a practical perspective this represents a challenge for some destinations. Lilly (1984), for example, discussed the difficulty in promoting North Staffordshire, a region with little tourism image outside its own boundaries. Likewise, strategists appointed by Papua New Guinea's NTO in 2004 found that a major barrier to the development of tourism in that country was a lack of consumer awareness about the destination (Wright, 2004).

It is important to recognise the distinction between an awareness problem and that of a negative image, since the existence of the latter at least denotes awareness. However, more than simply awareness of a destination is required. For example, Milman and Pizam (1995) found awareness of a popular US domestic destination was not necessarily a strong indicator of intent to visit. In short, other determinants of choice exist. The destinations in a consumer's competitive set/decision set are those that are salient during decision making. Destination salience therefore represents a source of competitive advantage.

Competitive set of destinations (evoked decision set)

The competitive set of destinations represents the small number of places a consumer actively considers for a particular travel context during travel planning decision making. The competitive set is defined only by the consumer. Miller (1956) cited a number of studies from the consumer psychology literature to suggest the limit to the number of stimuli people would generally be capable of processing would be around seven. Miller even linked this proposition to the use of questionnaire rating scales, where seven points had generally been considered the limit of usefulness. Woodside and Sherrell's (1977) literature review found this limit had generally been consistent in brand recall tests across product categories as diverse as cars and toothpaste.

Woodside and Sherrell (1977) found the evoked set size averaged 3.4 destinations for selection during the following 12 months. Their proposition of four plus or minus two destinations in the evoked set has been supported in other destination studies (see Thompson and Cooper, 1979; Woodside and Lysonski, 1989; Goodall and Ashworth, 1990; Crompton, 1992; Pike and Ryan, 2004; Pike, 2006, 2010).

For consumer goods, it has been suggested brands excluded from the evoked decision set may have a purchase probability of less than 1 per cent (Wilson, 1981). The concept of the evoked set, therefore, has important implications for DMOs if it is from this set that final destination selection is made. It must be accepted that a hierarchy of destination brand saliency is formed within the evoked set of destinations if a final selection is to be made.

Top of mind awareness (ToMA)

The higher a brand's position in a consumer's mind, the higher the intent to purchase (Burke and Schoeffler, 1980; Wilson, 1981). It has been shown that ToMA, measured by unaided recall, is related to purchase preference among competing brands (Axelrod, 1968; Wilson, 1981; Woodside and Wilson, 1985). Consequently, for the destination that first comes to mind when a consumer is considering travel, ToMA must surely represent a source of advantage (Pike, 2002b). The other destinations in the evoked decision set are considered salient. As discussed in Chapter 11, salience is more than awareness per se, because it is only those places that come to mind when decision making is taking place. So we understand for a given travel situation, the consumer will likely have a preferred ToMA destination and one or a few other salient destinations making up a competitive set, but that there is potential for substitution between the ToMA destination and the other destinations in this competitive set.

RESEARCH SNAPSHOT

10.1 Combining attitudinal and behavioural data

Integrated marketing communications pioneer, Professor Don Schultz, has been critical of the lack of research in the wider marketing literature that combines consumer attitudes with behavioural data. In other words, comparing what people say they intend to do with what they actually do. There has only been a small number of applications of consumer decision set theory to holiday destination choice, and these studies have tended to rely on a single cross-sectional snapshot of research participants' stated preferences. Very little has been reported on the relationship between stated destination preferences and actual travel. To what degree then can marketers rely on consumers' stated attitudes if there is no comparative measure of actual behaviour? This study presented a rare longitudinal examination of destination decision sets and the first in the context of short break holidays by car in Queensland, Australia. Two questionnaires were administered, three months apart, to the same sample of people. The first identified destination preferences, while the second examined actual travel. The findings indicated a general consistency between attitude and behaviour in the short term and supported the proposition that the positioning of a destination into a consumer's decision set represents a source of competitive advantage:

- In terms of unaided ToMA, participants elicited over 100 short break destinations within comfortable driving distance of Brisbane. Brisbane residents are literally spoilt for choice by contiguous destinations.

- Participants indicated a mean of only four destinations in their short break decision set. This has implications for those destinations not included, particularly in light of the competition mentioned in the previous point.

- There was a strong link between stated destination preferences and actual travel. Almost 75 per cent of participants who took a short break during the study visited at least one destination from their stated decision set.

- Familiarity with preferred destinations was apparent, with 92 per cent of participants indicating having previously visited their ToMA destination.

- Intent to visit the destination of interest was significantly higher from previous visitors than non-visitors.

A key implication for destination marketers is the recommendation to monitor competitive decision set composition, which represents an important and practical indicator of future performance, for future marketing planning. A destination not included in a consumer's decision set is at a competitive disadvantage and so remedial action will need to be planned.

Further reading

Pike, S. (2006).

Monitoring destination image

Destination image measurement has been one of the most popular topics in the tourism literature since the 1970s (Pike and Page, 2014). However, in spite of the breadth of research reported, there is still no universally accepted method or instrument for measuring the construct. Destination images reside in the minds of unique individual human beings, and no technology currently exists to beam these images into the light of day. The brain is complex, and it is said that *if the mind was simple enough to understand, we would be too simple to understand it*. So researchers generally rely on three simple, and yet paradoxically complex, methods. For more in-depth discussion on qualitative and quantitative research methods in tourism, there have been a number of specialist texts (see Ryan, 1995; Brunt, 1997; Jennings, 2001; Ritchie *et al.*, 2005; Veal, 2011). The first method used to gain insights into a destination's image is talking to people in small qualitative studies to elicit, in their own words, how they perceive the destination. This of course requires participants to actually understand their own thought processes and to be able to articulate the type of meaning sought by the researcher. Of the 262 destination image studies tabled by Pike (2002a, 2007a), only 97 (37 per cent) employed qualitative methods to either interpret destination image or to elicit attributes for structured questionnaires.

The second approach is interpreting the content of what people write or photograph about either their intent to travel or their actual travel experiences. There has been a lack of published research to date on how to efficiently and effectively monitor UGC in Web 2.0. Stevenson and Hamill (2012) provided an overview of the benefits of social media monitoring and critiqued the range of web crawler tools available at the time. In relation to their research monitoring, which comprised almost a year of social media content related to the world's top ten destinations, they were able to generate information such as: the number of mentions, the channel sources, key influencers and brand sentiment. They acknowledged that the major limitation of such research was the inability to secure access to Facebook content. Crotts *et al.* (2012) provided rare and candid insights into their experiences attempting to analyse travel blog contents to address real world marketing research briefs. They found most major travel blog sites have entered into relationships with commercial marketing research firms that provide dashboard summaries of what consumers are saying about their clients. In the hospitality sector these include chatterguard.com, revinate.com and tnooz.com. As a consequence of these commercial arrangements, academic researchers will be limited in terms of the data they will be granted access to on leading travel blogs and will almost certainly be forbidden from using web crawler tools. Academics will generally be limited to the unregulated blogosphere (see Google's blog index). Crotts *et al.* also discussed the challenges presented by deceptive UGC and some of the quantitative methods available for analysing qualitative travel blog data.

The third approach is asking large samples of people to rate a destination or destinations across a battery of attribute scale items. As has been discussed, this was the most common method, being used by 71 per cent of 262 studies published between 1973 and 2007 (Pike, 2002a, 2007a). Following Pike (2008), there are a number of limitations that should be considered when using structured questionnaires to measure destination image:

- lack of a qualitative stage in questionnaire design;
- risk of uninformed response bias;
- neglect of attribute importance ratings;
- measuring one destination's image in isolation to the competition;
- travel context;
- structural equation modelling.

Lack of a qualitative stage in questionnaire design

Since a questionnaire should be tailored to suit the target sample (Malhotra *et al.*, 2007), it is important to bring the consumer into the research at the questionnaire design stage to enhance the wording and validity of the attribute list. However, many studies have not used a qualitative stage to elicit salient attributes from consumers. Of the 1973–2007 destination image studies tabled by Pike (2002a, 2007a), fewer than half of the 197 structured questionnaires used a qualitative stage involving consumers. Most of the remainder used attributes selected from the literature in other parts of the world, or from expert opinion such as academics and practitioners. The latter approach runs the real risk of selecting attributes that are not relevant or meaningful to the sample. Just because a questionnaire is *valid* in one part of the world does not mean it will be *reliable* in other settings. Pike (2008) suggested screening attributes selected from the literature through focus groups to access local suitability.

Risk of uninformed response bias

Following the previous point, the use of attributes that are irrelevant to members of the sample runs the risk of attracting uninformed responses, which is a form of bias. The purpose of questionnaire scales is for participants to place their perceptions along a continuum, which permits people with differing opinions to respond differently (Likert, 1932). Participants are asked to rate the extent to which they believe a destination provides an attribute, such as *good shopping* using a Likert-type scale anchored at 1 (strongly disagree) and either 5 or 7 (strongly agree). Following Pike (2007c), this begs the question: How should a participant respond if they don't understand what the attribute is, they don't know if a destination features this attribute, or they don't care? Without an explicit *don't know* option, many participants will express an opinion about things on which they have no knowledge or experience (Hawkins *et al.*, 1988). This is then biased data, representative of an uninformed response. Only 4 (2 per cent) of the 187 destination studies that employed structured questionnaires, tabled by Pike (2002a, 2007a) offered a *don't know* option for participants.

Destination image studies by Pike (2007d, 2010) and Bianchi *et al.* (2014) found high percentages of participants using the *don't know* option. While removing the potential problem of uniformed response bias, the *don't know* data also provides useful practical information for destination marketers, which they would not otherwise be aware of. For example, Bianchi *et al.* found up to 80 per cent of their Australian sample used the *don't know* option when asked to rate their perceptions of destination attributes in Brazil, Argentina and Chile. Future marketing communications can then be used to address the lack of awareness of *important* attributes and monitored in future surveys.

Neglect of attribute importance ratings

Many questionnaires measure the perceived performance of a destination across a list of attributes, without any measure of attribute importance. This implies all attributes will be important to the participant. However, as discussed, many destination image studies have used attribute lists developed from previous studies in the literature, often in other parts of the world and without consumer input.

False marketing communication decisions could be made on the basis of attributes where the destination is rated favourably, but where the attribute might not actually be important in the market. Therefore, a measure of attribute importance provides enhanced understanding of which attributes should be used in marketing communications. A graphical tool for enabling this is importance–performance analysis (IPA) (see Martilla and James, 1977). Of the 187 structured destination image studies tabled by Pike (2002a, 2007a), 13 (7 per cent) used IPA to measure attribute importance and destination performance. IPA is useful as a graphical tool for explaining to stakeholders the rationale for which attributes need to be the focus of marketing communications.

Measuring one destination's image in isolation to the competition

Given the role of the DMO is to enhance destination competitiveness, and the purpose of branding is to differentiate against rivals, measurement of a destination's image in isolation does not provide insights into the competitive position, in terms of identifying strengths and weaknesses. While such measurement provides an understanding of the extent to which brand image is congruent with the brand identity, a frame of reference with rival destinations is necessary to identify relative strengths and weaknesses. In Pike's (2002a, 2007a) analyses of destination image studies published between 1972 and 2007, approximately half (129) examined the image of one destination in isolation, without reference to competing places. Such competing places would ideally be those identified by consumers in their competitive (evoked) set for a given *travel context*.

Travel context

There has been a lack of research interest in *distance decay* (see Cooper and Hall, 2008) and *travel context* (see Snepenger and Milner, 1990) on destination image and decision making. Distance decay holds that demand declines exponentially as distance increases (see Cooper and Hall, 2008), and a number of studies have found that the profile and preferences of long haul travellers differs to that for short haul travel (see King, 1994; McKercher and Lew, 2003; McKercher, 2008; McKercher *et al.*, 2008; Pike *et al.*, 2010; Bianchi and Pike, 2011; Yan, 2011; Ho and McKercher, 2012). Related to this is the proposition attribute that importance can vary between travel situations (Barich and Kotler, 1991; Crompton, 1992), as will ToMA destination preference. Travel context refers to the situation or usage of the product, such as the time of year, type of trip or geographic travel range. For example, destination salience will likely differ between the context of a honeymoon and an end of season football team trip. However, there has been limited attention to the importance of context in consumer research. In an assessment of the tourism marketing research state of the art, Ritchie (1996) proposed ten key shortcomings. Among the gaps, which Ritchie labelled the *dark side of the universe*, was travel context.

Thompson and Cooper (1979) noted that no tourism study had examined the effect of travel context on evoked decision set size. However, investigations of decision sets in the context of short break holidays in New Zealand (Pike, 2002b) and Australia (Pike 2006, 2007d) found a consistency in the size of the evoked decision sets with means of three to four destinations. Destination image studies have generally been undertaken without explicitly defining the context in which the traveller decision is being made (Hu and Ritchie, 1993). Even though it was proposed in the 1980s that any list of determinant destination attributes will vary depending on situational context (see Gearing *et al.*, 1974), only 37 (14 per cent) of the 262 published destination image papers tabled by Pike (2002a, 2007a) were explicit about a travel context of interest.

Structural equation modelling (SEM)

SEM is increasingly being used to test relationships between destination branding constructs, such as brand awareness, brand image, brand quality, brand value and brand loyalty (see, for example, Konecnik, 2006; Konecnik and Gartner, 2007; Boo *et al.*, 2009; Kim *et al.*, 2009; Pike and Bianchi, 2014; Zhang *et al.*, 2014; Bianchi *et al.*, 2014). There are two major limitations of SEM in relation to destination image measurement. First, while SEM studies have included destination brand awareness, they do not capture brand salience. This is because brand salience requires an unaided open-ended question, whereas the use of SEM requires the participant be given the name of a destination and asked to rate their awareness using a Likert-type scale. For example, there is a big difference between asking someone if they are aware of France, for example, and using an open-ended question asking them to list their preferred destination. Second, while SEM studies to date have shown relationships exist between destination brand image and other constructs in the model, they have not actually measured the destination's image. This is because in the SEM models destination image has been operationalised with only a few scale items, which is far from sufficient. Therefore, care should be taken when reporting SEM results relating to destination brand awareness and destination brand image.

Fourth, SEM studies to date have tended to measure consumer-based brand equity (CBBE) for one destination in isolation, which does not capture how the destination is positioned in consumers' minds relative to rivals in the competitive set. There is also the question of what the dependent variable should be in SEM modelling of destination CBBE (Pike and Page, 2014). For a critique of the use of SEM in 209 papers published in the wider tourism literature between 2000 and 2011, see Nunkoo *et al.* (2013).

Importantly, SEM studies have also been criticised for producing model outputs that have been statistically manipulated rather than theoretically driven (see, for example, Mazanec, 2009):

> *It is not too big a surprise that a model class named Structural Equation Models (SEMs, or latent-variable multiple-indicator models, where I include Partial Least Squares Path Models) plays a prominent role in generating myths. If a magician, whether experienced as, say, David Copperfield or an apprentice like Harry Potter, were to choose a methodology they most certainly would opt for SEMs. There is no other method where one may wave the magic wand to pull white rabbits out of the black top-hat with little effort and where theoretical progress and nonsense applications are in close vicinity.*
>
> *(Mazanec, 2009: 319)*

Destination image change occurs only slowly over time

While individual components of a destination image may fluctuate greatly over time, their effect on over-all image might not be influential (Crompton, 1979; Gartner, 1986). Gartner and Hunt (1987) found evidence of positive destination image change over a 13-year period, but concluded any change only occurs slowly. Likewise a study by the English Tourist Board (1983, in Jeffries, 2001), which analysed the impact of an advertising campaign to modify Londoners' perceptions of England's North Country over a three-year period, found only minor changes in destination image. Likewise, Anholt's national brand index (see Anholt, 2010: 6) has shown that nation image is a 'remarkably stable phenomenon'. An ongoing study of the perceptions of a competitive set of five short break holiday destinations in Queensland, which found almost no changes in the perceptions of any of the destinations between 2003 and 2012 (see Pike, 2006, 2007d, 2009, 2010), is summarised in Chapter 15. Other than these studies, research investigating the temporal nature of destination image change has been neglected in the tourism literature and therefore represents an important research gap. Gartner (1993) proposed that the larger the entity the slower the image change. This supports the proposition that it is difficult to change people's minds, with the easier marketing communication route being to reinforce positively held images (Ries and Trout, 1981), which underpins the discussion on destination positioning in Chapter 11.

CHAPTER SUMMARY

Key point 1: The role of image in destination marketing

Tourism marketing is generally concerned with the selling of intangible dreams, since expectations of a tourism service can only be realised during travel. The images held of destinations by consumers there-fore play a critical role in their decision making. Since tourism services can only compete via images, it is imperative marketers understand *perception is reality*, and the brand image of the destination may or may not be quite different to the brand identity intended by the DMO. Since the first destination image studies appeared in the 1970s, the topic has become one of the most prevalent in the tourism literature. A destination's image is a repertoire of brand associations held in the mind of the consumer. They may have been developed through organic sources such as previous visitations, or induced sources such as advertising. For today's sophisticated consumers, organic images have a higher credibility than induced images, and UGC in social media is diluting DMOs' marketing communications' impact.

Key point 2: Consumer decision sets

Consumers are spoilt for choice in available destinations, but will only actively consider a limited num-ber in the decision making process. Research has shown the size of the consumer's competitive set of destinations will be limited to around four. The implication for DMOs examining the image of their des-tination is that destinations not included in a consumer's decision set will be less likely to be selected. Competitive set inclusion, particularly ToMA, denotes brand salience and therefore a source of competi-tive advantage over the majority of places not included.

Key point 3: Key destination image measurement issues

Since the 1970s, the destination image has provided a rich resource for practitioners and academics, but there is no widely accepted method for measuring the construct. The vast majority of studies have employed structured questionnaires requiring participants to rate a destination or destinations across a battery of scale items. The chapter raised the issue of six potential limitations to consider when using this approach.

REVIEW QUESTIONS

1. Why is it asserted that brand salience in the form of ToMA and competitive set membership represents a source of competitive advantage?

2. What is meant by the marketing adage, *perception is reality*, and why is this relevant to DMOs?

3. Why is it recommended that DMOs focus on promoting attributes already favourably perceived by consumers, rather than attempt to change negative images?

REFERENCES

Agapito, D., do Valle, P. O. and da Costa Mendes, J. (2013). The cognitive-affective-conative model of destination image: A confirmatory analysis. *Journal of Travel & Tourism Marketing* 30(5): 471–481.

Ahmed, Z. U. (1991). The influence of the components of a state's tourist image on product positioning strategy. *Tourism Management* December: 331–340.

Anderson, J. R. (1983). *The Architecture of Cognition*. Cambridge, MA: Harvard University Press.

Anderson, J. R. and Bower, G. H. (1979). *Human Associative Memory*. Hillsdale, NJ: Lawrence Erlbaum.

Anholt, S. (2010). *Places: Identity, Image and Reputation*. Basingstoke, UK: Macmillan.

Axelrod, J. N. (1968). Attitude measures that predict purchase. *Journal of Advertising Research* 8(1): 3–17.

Baloglu, S. (1998). An empirical investigation of attitude theory for tourist destinations: A comparison of visitors and nonvisitors. *Journal of Hospitality & Tourism Research* 22(3): 211–224.

Baloglu, S. and Brinberg, D. (1997). Affective images of tourism destinations. *Journal of Travel Research* Spring: 11–15.

Baloglu, S. and Love, C. (2005). A cognitive-affective positioning analysis of convention cities: An extension of the circumplex model of affect. *Tourism Analysis* 9(4): 299–308.

Baloglu, S. and Mangaloglu, M. (2001). Tourism destination images of Turkey, Egypt, Greece, and Italy as perceived by US-based tour operators and travel agents. *Tourism Management* 22(1): 1–9.

Baloglu, S. and McCleary, K. W. (1999). A model of destination image. *Annals of Tourism Research* 26(4): 868–897.

Barich, H. and Kotler, P. (1991). A framework for marketing image management. *Sloan Management Review* 32(2): 94–104.

Bianchi, C. and Pike, S. (2011). Antecedents of attitudinal destination loyalty in a long-haul market: Australia's brand equity among Chilean consumers. *Journal of Travel & Tourism Marketing* 28(7): 736–750.

Bianchi, C., Pike, S. and Lings, I. (2014). Investigating attitudes towards three South American destinations in an emerging long haul market using a model of consumer-based brand equity (CBBE). *Tourism Management* 42(1): 215–223.

Boo, S., Busser, J. and Baloglu, S. (2009). A model of customer-based brand equity and its application to multiple destinations. *Tourism Management* 30(2): 219–213.

Botterill, T. D. (1989) Humanistic tourism? Personal constructions of a tourist: Sam visits Japan. *Leisure Studies* 8(3): 281–293.

Botterill, T. D. and Crompton, J. L. (1987). Personal constructions of holiday snapshots. *Annals of Tourism Research* 14(1): 152–156.

Brunt, P. (1997). *Market Research in Travel and Tourism*. Oxford: Butterworth-Heinemann.

Burke, W. L. and Schoeffler, S. (1980). Brand awareness as a tool for profitability. *The Strategic Planning Institute*. Boston, MA: Cahners.

Cai, L. A. (2002). Cooperative branding for rural destinations. *Annals of Tourism Research* 29(3): 720–742.

Cherifi, B., Smith, A., Maitland, R. and Stevenson, N. (2014). Destination images of non-visitors. *Annals of Tourism Research* 49: 190–202.

Chon, K. (1990). The role of destination image in tourism: A review and discussion. *The Tourist Review* 45(2): 2–9.

Chon, K. (1991). Tourism destination image: Marketing implications. *Tourism Management* March: 68–72.

Cohen, E. (1972). Toward a sociology of international tourism. *Social Research* 39: 164–182.

Cooper, C. and Hall, C. M. (2008). *Contemporary Tourism: An International Approach*. Oxford: Butterworth-Heinemann.

Crompton, J. L. (1979). An assessment of the image of Mexico as a vacation destination and the influence of geographical location upon that image. *Journal of Travel Research* Spring: 18–23.

Crompton, J. L. (1992). Structure of vacation destination choice sets. *Annals of Tourism Research* 19(3): 420–434.

Crotts, J. C., Davis, B. H. and Mason, P. R. (2012). Analysing blog content for competitive advantage: Lessons learned in the application of software aided linguistics analysis. In Sigala, M., Christou, E. and Gretzel, U. (eds) *Social Media in Travel, Tourism and Hospitality: Theory, Practice and Cases*. Farnham, UK: Ashgate Publishing Ltd, pp. 281–292.

Crouch, G. I. (2000). Services research in destination marketing: A retrospective appraisal. *International Journal of Hospitality & Tourism Administration* 1(2): 65–85.

Dann, G. M. S. (1977). Anomie, ego-enhancement and tourism. *Annals of Tourism Research* March/April: 184–194.

Dann, G. M. S. (1981). Tourist motivation: An appraisal. *Annals of Tourism Research* 8(2): 187–219.

Dann, G. M. S. (1996). Tourists' images of a destination: An alternative analysis. *Journal of Travel & Tourism Marketing* 5(1/2): 41–55.

Dichter, E. (1985). What's in an image. *The Journal of Consumer Marketing* 2(1): 75–81.

Echtner, C. M. and Ritchie, J. R. B. (1991). The meaning and measurement of destination image. *The Journal of Tourism Studies* 2(2): 2–12.

Embacher, J. and Buttle, F. (1989) A repertory grid analysis of Austria's image as a summer vacation destination. *Journal of Travel Research* Winter: 3–7.

Fakeye, P. C. and Crompton, J. L. (1991). Image differences between prospective, first time, and repeat visitors to the Lower Rio Grande Valley. *Journal of Travel Research* 30(1): 10–16.

Fishbein, M. (1967). *Readings in Attitude Theory and Measurement*. New York: John Wiley & Sons.

Fishbein, M. and Ajzen, I. (1975). *Belief, Attitude, Intention and Behavior: An Introduction to Theory and Research*. Philippines: Addison-Wesley.

Gallarza, M. G., Saura, I. G. and Garcia, H. C. (2002). Destination image: Towards a conceptual framework. *Annals of Tourism Research* 29(1): 56–78.

Gardner, B. B. and Levy, S. J. (1955). The product and the brand. *Harvard Business Review* March-April: 33–39.

Gartner, W. C. (1986). Temporal influences on image change. *Annals of Tourism Research* 13(4): 635–644.

Gartner, W. C. (1993). Image information process. *Journal of Travel & Tourism Marketing* 2(2/3): 191–215.

Gartner, W. C. and Hunt, J. D. (1987). An analysis of state image change over a twelve-year period (1971–1983). *Journal of Travel Research* Fall: 15–19.

Gearing, C. E., Swart, W. W. and Var, T. (1974). Establishing a measure of touristic attractiveness. *Journal of Travel Research* 12(4): 1–8.

Gilmore, F. (2002). Branding for success. In Morgan, N., Pritchard, A. and Pride, R. (eds) *Destination Branding: Creating the Unique Destination Proposition*. Oxford: Butterworth-Heinemann, pp. 57–65.

Goodall, B. and Ashworth, G. (eds) (1990). *Marketing in the Tourism Industry: The Promotion of Destination Regions*. London: Routledge.

Goodall, B., Radburn, M. and Stabler, M. (1988). *Market Opportunity Sets for Tourism*. Reading, UK: University of Reading.

Gray, H. P. (1970). *International Travel: International Trade*. Lexington, MA: Heath Lexington Books.

Gunn, C. (1988). *Vacationscape: Designing Tourist Regions* (2nd edition). Austin, TX: Bureau of Business Research, University of Texas.

Gutman, J. (1982). A means end chain model based on consumer categorization processes. *Journal of Marketing* 46(2): 60–72.

Hawkins, D. I., Coney, K. A. and Jackson, D. W. (1988). The impact of monetary inducement on uninformed response error. *Academy of Marketing Science* 16(2): 30–35.

Hinkle, D. N. (1965). *The Change of Personal Constructs from the Viewpoint of a Theory of Construct Implications*. Unpublished PhD thesis. Ohio State University.

Ho, G. and McKercher, B. (2012). A comparison of long-haul and short-haul business tourists of Hong Kong. *Asia Pacific Journal of Tourism Research* iFirst article 19(3): 1–14.

Hosany, S., Ekinci, Y. and Uysal, M. (2006). Destination image and destination personality: An application of branding theories to tourism places. *Journal of Business Research* 59(5): 638–642.

Howard, J. A. (1963). *Marketing Management: Analysis and Planning*. Homewood, IL: Irwin.

Howard, J. A. and Sheth, J. N. (1969). *The Theory of Buyer Behavior*. New York: John Wiley & Sons.

Hu, Y. and Ritchie, J. R. B. (1993). Measuring destination attractiveness: A contextual approach. *Journal of Travel Research* 32(2): 25–34.

Hunt, J. D. (1975). Image as a factor in tourism development. *Journal of Travel Research* 13(3): 1–7.

Jacoby, J. (1984). Perspectives on information overload. *Journal of Consumer Research* 10(4): 432–435.

Jankowicz, A. D. (1987). Whatever became of George Kelly? Applications and implications. *American Psychologist* 42(5): 481–487.

Jeffries, D. (2001). *Governments and Tourism*. Oxford: Butterworth-Heinemann.

Jenkins, O. H. (1999). Understanding and measuring tourist destination images. *International Journal of Tourism Research* 1(1): 1–15.

Jennings, G. (2001). *Tourism Research*. Milton, QLD: John Wiley & Sons.

Josiassen, A., Assaf, A., Woo, L. and Kock, F. (2015). The imagery-image model: Revisiting destination image. *Journal of Travel Research* (in press). Available before print at: http://jtr.sagepub.com/content/early/2015/05/04/0047287515583358.abstract

Kastenholz, E. (2004). Assessment and role of destination-self-congruity. *Annals of Tourism Research* 31(3): 719–723.

Keller, K. L. (1993). Conceptualizing, measuring, and managing customer-based brand equity. *Journal of Marketing* 57(January): 1–22.

Kelly, G. A. (1955). *The Psychology of Personal Constructs*. New York: Norton.

Kim, H. and Richardson, S. L. (2003). Motion picture impacts on destination images. *Annals of Tourism Research* 30(1): 216–237.

Kim, S. and Yoon, Y. (2003). The hierarchical effects of affective and cognitive components on tourism image. *Journal of Travel & Tourism Marketing* 14(2): 1–22.

Kim, S. H., Han, H. S., Holland, S. and Byon, K. K. 2009. Structural relationships among involvement, destination brand equity, satisfaction and destination visit intentions: The case of Japanese outbound travellers. *Journal of Vacation Marketing* 15(4): 349–365.

King, B. (1994). Australian attitudes to domestic and international resort holidays: A comparison of Fiji and Queensland. In Seaton, A. V., Jenkins, C. L., Wood, R. C., Dieke, P. U. C., Bennett, M. M., MacLellan, L. R. and Smith, R. (eds) *Tourism: The State of the Art*. Chichester, UK: John Wiley & Sons Ltd.

Konecnik, M. (2005). Slovenia as a tourism destination: Differences in image evaluations perceived by tourism representatives from closer and more distant markets. *Economic and Business Review* 7(3): 261–282.

Konecnik, M. (2006). Croatian-based brand equity for Slovenia as a tourism destination. *Economic and Business Review* 8(1): 83–108.

Konecnik, M. and Gartner, W. C. (2007). Customer-based brand equity for a destination. *Annals of Tourism Research* 34(2): 400–421.

Kotler, P., Bowen, J. and Makens, J. (1999). *Marketing for Hospitality and Tourism* (2nd edition). Upper Saddle River, NJ: Prentice Hall.

Landfield, A. W. and Leitner, L. M. (1980). (Eds). *Personal construct psychology: Psychotherapy and Personality*. New York: John Wiley & Sons.

Lavidge, R. E. and Steiner, G. A. (1961). A model for predictive measurements of advertising effectiveness. *Journal of Marketing* 25(1): 59–62.

Likert, R. (1932). *A Technique for the Measurement of Attitudes*. New York: Archives of Psychology.

Lilly, T. (1984). From industry to leisure in The Potteries. *Tourism Management* 5(2): 136–138.

MacInnes, D. J. and Price, L. L. (1987). The role of imagery in information processing: Review and extensions. *Journal of Consumer Research* 13(3): 473–491.

MacKay, K. J. and Fesenmaier, D. R. (1997). Pictorial element of destination in image formation. *Annals of Tourism Research* 24(3): 537–565.

Malhotra, N., Hall, J., Shaw, M. and Oppenheim, P. (2007). *Marketing Research* (3rd edition). Frenchs Forest, NSW: Pearson Education.

Mansfield, Y. (1992). From motivation to actual travel. *Annals of Tourism Research* 19(3): 399–419.

Martilla, J. A. and James, J. C. (1977). Importance–performance analysis. *Journal of Marketing* 41(1): 77–79.

Maslow, A. H. (1943). A theory of human motivation. *Psychological Review* 50: 370–396.

Mayo, E. J. (1973). Regional images and regional travel behaviour. *The Travel Research Association 4th Annual Proceedings*. Idaho.

Mayo, E. J. and Jarvis, L. P. (1981). *The Psychology of Leisure Travel*. Boston, MA: CBI Publishing Company.

Mazanec, J. (2009). Unravelling myths in tourism research. *Tourism Recreation Research* 34(3): 319–323.

McKercher, B. (2008). The implicit effect of distance on tourist behavior: A comparison of short and long-haul pleasure tourists to Hong Kong. *Journal of Travel & Tourism Marketing* 25(3/4): 367–381.

McKercher, B. and Lew, A. A. (2003). Distance decay and the impact of effective tourism exclusion zones on international travel flows. *Journal of Travel Research* 42(2): 159–165.

McKercher, B., Chan, A. and Lam, C. (2008). The impact of distance on international tourist movements. *Journal of Travel Research* 47(2): 208–224.

Mill, R. C. and Morrison, A. M. (1992). *The Tourism System: An Introductory Text* (2nd edition). Englewood Cliffs, NJ: Prentice Hall.

Miller, G. A. (1956). The magical number seven, plus or minus two: Some limits on our capacity for processing information. *The Psychological Review* 63(2): 81–97.

Milman, A. and Pizam, A. (1995). The role of awareness and familiarity with a destination: The central Florida case. *Journal of Travel Research* 33(3): 21–27.

Mollo-Bouvier, S. (1990). Short-break holidays: Where are the children? In Fache, W. (ed.) *Shortbreak Holidays*. Rotterdam: Center Parcs.

Moutinho, L. (1987). Consumer behaviour in tourism. *European Journal of Marketing* 21(10): 1–44.

Narayana, C. L. and Markin, R. J. (1975). Consumer behavior and product performance: An alternative conceptualisation. *Journal of Marketing* 39(October): 1–6.

Nunkoo, R., Ramkissoon, H. and Gursoy, D. (2013). Use of structural equation modelling in tourism research: Past, present, and future. *Journal of Travel Research* 52(6): 759–711.

Page, S. and Wilks, J. (2004). *Managing Tourist Health and Safety*. Oxford: Elsevier Science Ltd.

Page, S., Clift, S. and Clark, N. (1994). Tourist health: The precautions, behaviour and health problems of British tourists in Malta. In Seaton, A. V., Jenkins, C. L., Wood, R. C., Dieke, P. U. C., Bennett, M. M., MacLellan, L. R. and Smith, R. (eds) *Tourism: The State of the Art*. Chichester, UK: John Wiley & Sons Ltd, pp. 799–817.

Palmer, C. J. (1978). Understanding unbiased dimensions: The use of repertory-grid methodology. *Environment and Planning* 10: 1137–1150.

Patton, M. Q. (2002). *Qualitative Research & Evaluation Methods* (3rd edition). Thousand Oaks, CA: Sage.

Pearce, P. L. (1982). Perceived changes in holiday destinations. *Annals of Tourism Research* 9(2): 145–164.

Pearce, P. L. (1988). *The Ulysses Factor*. New York: Springer-Verlag.

Phelps, A. (1986). Holiday destination image: The problem of assessment. *Tourism Management* September: 168–180.

Pike, S. (2002a). Destination image analysis: A review of 142 papers from 1973–2000. *Tourism Management* 23(5): 541–549.

Pike, S. (2002b). ToMA as a measure of competitive advantage for short break holiday destinations. *Journal of Tourism Studies* 13(1): 9–19.

Pike, S. (2003). The use of repertory grid analysis to elicit salient short break holiday attributes. *Journal of Travel Research* 41(3): 326–330.

Pike, S. (2004). *Destination Marketing Organisations*. Oxford: Elsevier Science.

Pike, S. (2006). Destination decision sets: A longitudinal comparison of stated destination preferences and actual travel. *Journal of Vacation Marketing* 12(4): 319–328.

Pike, S. (2007a). Destination image literature: 2001–2007. *Acta Turistica* 19(2): 107–125.

Pike, S. (2007b). Repertory grid analysis in group settings to elicit salient destination brand attributes. *Current Issues in Tourism* 10(4): 378–392.

Pike, S. (2007c). Destination image questionnaires: Avoiding uninformed responses. *Journal of Travel & Tourism Research* 2(Fall): 151–160.

Pike, S. (2007d). Consumer-based brand equity for destinations: Practical DMO performance measures. *Journal of Travel & Tourism Marketing* 22(1): 51–61.

Pike, S. (2008). Five limitations of destination brand image measurement. *Tourism Recreation Research* 33(3): 361–363.

Pike, S. (2009). Destination brand positions of a competitive set of near-home destinations. *Tourism Management* 30(6): 857–866.

Pike, S. (2010). Destination branding: Tracking brand equity for an emerging destination between 2003 and 2007. *Journal of Hospitality & Tourism Research* 34(1): 124–139.

Pike, S. (2012). Destination positioning opportunities using personal values elicited through the repertory test and laddering analysis. *Tourism Management* 33(1): 100–107.

Pike, S. and Bianchi, C. (2014). Destination brand equity for Australia: Testing a model of CBBE in short haul and long haul markets. *Journal of Hospitality & Tourism Research*. Available at: http://jht.sagepub.com/content/early/2013/06/19/1096348013491604.full.pdf+html

Pike, S. and Mason, R. (2011). Destination competitiveness through the lens of brand positioning. *Current Issues in Tourism* 14(2): 169–182.

Pike, S. and Page, S. (2014). Destination marketing organizations and destination marketing: A narrative analysis of the literature. *Tourism Management* 41: 202–227.

Pike, S. and Ryan, C. (2004). Dimensions of short break destination attractiveness: A comparison of cognitive, affective and conative perceptions. *Journal of Travel Research* 42(4): 333–342.

Pike, S., Bianchi, C., Kerr, G. and Patti, C. (2010). Consumer-based brand equity for Australia as a long haul tourism destination in an emerging market. *International Marketing Review* 27(4): 434–449.

Plog, S. T. (1974). Why destination areas rise and fall in popularity. *The Cornell HRA Quarterly* 14(4): 55–58.

Reilly, M. D. (1990). Free elicitation of descriptive adjectives for tourism image assessment. *Journal of Travel Research* Spring: 21–26.

Reynolds, T. J. and Gutman, J. (1984). Advertising is image management. *Journal of Advertising Research* 24(1): 27–36.

Reynolds, W. H. (1965). The role of the consumer in image building. *California Management Review* Spring: 69–76.

Ries, A. and Trout, J. (1981). *Positioning: The Battle for Your Mind*. New York: McGraw-Hill.

Riley, S. and Palmer, J. (1975). Of attitudes and latitudes: A repertory grid study of perceptions of seaside resorts. *Journal of the Market Research Society* 17(2): 74–89.

Ritchie, B. W., Burns, P. and Palmer, C. (2005). (Eds). *Tourism Research Methods: Integrating Theory with Practice*. Wallingford, UK: CABI.

Ritchie, J. R. B. (1996). Beacons of light in an expanding universe: An assessment of the state-of-the-art in tourism marketing/marketing research. *Journal of Travel & Tourism Marketing* 5(4): 49–84.

Russel, J. A. (1980). A circumplex model of affect. *Journal of Personality and Social Psychology* 39(6): 1161–1178.

Russel, J. A., Ward, L. M. and Pratt, G. (1981). Affective quality attributed to environments: a factor analytic study. *Environment and Behavior* 13(3): 259–288.

Ryan, C. (1995). *Researching Tourist Satisfaction: Issues, Concepts, Problems*. London: Routledge.

San Martin, H. and del Bosque, I. A. R. (2008). Exploring the cognitive-affective nature of destination image and the role of psychological factors in its formation. *Tourism Management* 29(2): 263–277.

Shaw, G., Williams, A. and Bailey, A. (2011). Aspects of service-dominant logic and its implications for tourism management: Examples from the hotel industry. *Tourism Management* 32(2): 207–214.

Snepenger, D. and Milner, L. (1990). Demographic and situational correlates of business travel. *Journal of Travel Research* 28(4): 27–32.

Sönmez, S. and Sirakaya, E. (2002). A distorted destination image? The case of Turkey. *Journal of Travel Research* 41(2): 185–196.

Stepchenkova, S. and Mills, J. (2010). Destination image: A meta-analysis of 2000–2007 research. *Journal of Hospitality Marketing & Management* 19(6): 575–609.

Stern, E. and Krakover, S. (1993). The formation of a composite urban image. *Geographical Analysis* 25(2): 130–146.

Stevenson, A. and Hamill, J. (2012). Social media monitoring: A practical case example of city destinations. In Sigala, M., Christou, E. and Gretzel, U. (eds) *Social Media in Travel, Tourism and Hospitality: Theory, Practice and Cases*. Farnham, UK: Ashgate Publishing Ltd.

Tasci, A. D. A., Gartner, W. C. and Cavusgil, S. T. (2007). Conceptualization and operationalization of destination image. *Journal of Hospitality & Tourism Research* 31(2): 194–223.

Thompson, J. R. and Cooper, P. D. (1979). Additional evidence on the limited size of evoked and inept sets of travel destination. *Journal of Travel Research* 17(3): 23–25.

Um, S. and Crompton, J. L. (1990). Attitude determinants in tourism destination choice. *Annals of Tourism Research* 17(3): 432–448.

Veal, A. J. (2011). *Research Methods for Leisure and Tourism* (4th edition). Harlow, UK: Pearson.

Walmsley, D. J. and Jenkins, J. M. (1993) Appraisive images of tourist areas: Application of personal constructs. *Australian Geographer* 24(2): 1–13.

Wee, C. H., Hakam, A. N. and Ong, E. (1985). Temporal and regional differences in image of a tourist destination: Implications for promoters of tourism. *Service Industries Journal* 5(1): 104–114.

Wilson, A. (2002). Satisfaction criteria of short break leisure travellers. *The Hospitality Review* October: 32–36.

Wilson, C. E. (1981). A procedure for the analysis of consumer decision making. *Journal of Advertising Research* 21(2): 31–36.

Woodside, A. G. and Sherrell, D. (1977). Traveler evoked, inept, and inert sets of vacation destinations. *Journal of Travel Research* 16(1): 14–18.

Woodside, A. G. and Wilson, E. J. (1985). Effects of consumer awareness of brand advertising on preference. *Journal of Advertising Research* 25(4): 41–48.

Woodside, A. G. and Lysonski, S. (1989). A general model of traveler destination choice. *Journal of Travel Research* Spring: 8–14.

Wright, J. (2004). PNG tourism completely off track. *The Courier-Mail*. Business. September 25, p. 79. Hard copy newspaper article.

Yan, L. (2011). Uneven distance decay: A study of the tourist market segments of Hong Kong. *International Journal of Tourism Sciences* 11(1): 95–112.

Young, M. (1995). Evaluative constructions of domestic tourism places. *Australian Geographical Studies* 33(2): 272–286.

Zhang, H., Fu, X., Cai, L. A. and Lu, L. (2014). Destination image and tourist loyalty: A meta-analysis. *Tourism Management* 40: 213–223.

Chapter **11**

Destination brand positioning

AIMS

To enhance understanding of:

- positioning as a source of competitive advantage for destinations;

- positioning as the attempt to achieve congruence between brand identity and brand image;

- the challenges involved in developing a narrow positioning focus for multi-attributed destinations in multiple markets.

ABSTRACT

Destination brand positioning is mutually beneficial for the DMO and the consumer, since the process is underpinned by the philosophy of understanding and meeting unique consumer *wants*. On the supply side, positioning can aid the DMO gain *cut-through* to reach the minds of consumers in markets that are crowded with the clutter of promotional messages of competing destinations and substitute products and services. From the demand perspective, effective positioning can enable easier decision making for the consumer. Consumers do not have time to consider the merits of all available brands in a purchase decision and will therefore appreciate a memorable and focused value proposition that appeals to their wants at that particular time. However, positioning requires a narrow message focus, and therefore trade-offs must be made about what to leave out of the proposition. Developing a single-minded proposition that will be meaningful in multiple markets is challenging for multi-attributed destinations. For a variety of external pressures it can be tempting for a DMO to regularly change the positioning theme, and history has shown this has happened all too frequently. However, consumer attention is in short supply out there, which necessitates consistency of message over time, and so brand positioning requires a long-term commitment.

Brand positioning as a source of competitive advantage

Previously, destination branding was introduced as comprising the three key components shown in Figure 11.1. Chapter 9 discussed the development of a *brand identity*, which represents the self-image desired in the market, while Chapter 10 presented *brand image* as representing the actual image held by consumers, which may or may not be quite different to that intended in the brand identity. The focus of this chapter is on positioning as a potential means of enhancing congruence between brand identity and brand image through a succinct value proposition. Aaker (1996: 71) defined a *brand position* as 'the part of the brand identity and value proposition that is to be actively communicated to the target audience and that demonstrates an advantage over competing brands'.

Effective positioning can be a source of competitive advantage for organisations in any industry consisting of close substitutes (Porter, 1980). In most tourism markets, competing destinations are indeed close substitutes for other places offering similar attributes and benefits for a given travel context. There are over 10,000 beaches in Australia, and so for a weekend beach break a beach is a beach is a beach, is it not? For example, the beach scene in Figure 11.2 (Mount Maunganui, New Zealand) could be almost anywhere in the world. In this regard Morley and Stolz (2003: 3) reported the embarrassment in Australia of Gold Coast Tourism Bureau officials after discovering the destination had been inadvertently using a rival Sunshine Coast beach scene in 100,000 copies of the Gold Coast's 2003 *Holiday Guide*. In reference to the ensuing national television coverage of the faux pas, the Sunshine Coast's RTO chairman responded: 'We appreciate all the publicity we can get'. Similarly, in 2007, Australian advertising industry trade magazine *BandT.com.au* mistakenly ran a photo of Chicago's Gold Coast instead of Australia's Gold Coast in a feature on the state of Queensland.

The successful positioning of a destination into a consumer's competitive set of around four places during decision making represents a source of competitive advantage over the majority of competing places that are not salient (Pike and Ryan, 2004). The chapter is underpinned by Figure 11.3, which presents a conceptual model of brand positioning as a potential source of competitive advantage for destinations. The model views positioning as a vehicle for influencing destination image and, therefore, destination attractiveness. An attractive destination is one that achieves:

[a] distinctive top of mind awareness (ToMA) position, based on leadership in determinant attributes, relative to destinations in the competitive set, in the minds of a target group of consumers, who have an intent to visit within a given time period.

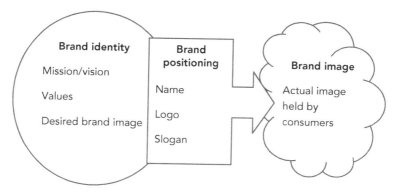

Figure 11.1 Three components of branding

Figure 11.2 A beach is a beach is a beach . . .
Source: Alexandra Pike, the author's daughter.

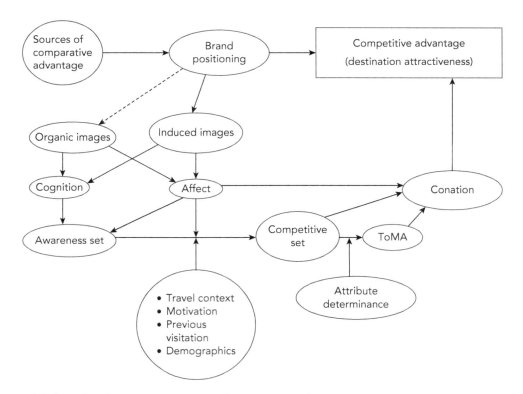

Figure 11.3 Brand positioning as a source of competitive advantage
Source: Adapted from Pike (2002, 2004a, 2008).

The positioning concept

Positioning can enable a brand to effectively compete against a specified set of competitors in a particular market (Keller, 2003: 150). The concept was first introduced to the advertising community as a marketing strategy in 1969 (Trout and Ries, 1979) and has been defined as a process of 'establishing and maintaining a distinctive place in the market for an organisation and/or its individual product offerings' (Lovelock, 1991: 110). At the core of this quest for a distinctive place is recognition that marketing is a battle fought inside the consumer's mind:

> *Marketing battles are not fought in the customer's office or in the supermarkets or the drugstores of America. Those are only distribution points for the merchandise whose brand selection is decided elsewhere. Marketing battles are fought in a mean and ugly place. A place that's dark and damp with much unexplored territory and deep pitfalls to trap the unwary. Marketing battles are fought inside the mind.*
>
> *(Ries and Trout, 1986: 169)*

Brand positioning rationale is based on three propositions. First, we live in an over-communicated society, bombarded with information on a daily basis, at levels that are unprecedented in history. Second, our minds develop a defence system against this media clutter. Third, the only way to cut through the clutter and the mind's defence system is through consistent, simplified and focused messages. Consequently, not selecting a positioning strategy could lead to head-on competition with stronger brands, an unwanted position with little demand, a fuzzy position where distinctive competence is unclear, or no position where the product is unheard of (Lovelock, 1991). Porter (1980) warned that being *stuck in the middle*, with no distinctive position, was the most dangerous place to be: 'A company can outperform rivals only if it can establish a difference that it can preserve'.

Effective positioning offers the customer benefits tailored to solve a problem, in a way that is different to competitors (DiMingo, 1988; Chacko, 1997). The key construct in positioning is brand image. However, positioning requires more than an understanding of what a brand's image is in the mind of the consumer. While such studies enable an indication of perceptions of a destination relative to the brand identity, a weakness of this approach is the inability to determine relative positioning against competing places. Positioning requires a frame of reference with the competition, particularly in relation to those in the competitive set. A position is a product's perceived performance, relative to competitors, on specific attributes (Wind and Robinson, 1972; Lovelock, 1991). Although positioning had featured in the economics literature as early as the 1920s (Myers, 1992), there was little mention of the construct in the destination marketing literature until the 1980s:

> *Few communities have developed a positioning strategy. Instead they yield to the pressure to be all things to all people, and use look-alike promotions and print brochures showing attractions ranging from historic barns to zoos – without any regard to whether these features have any drawing power.*
>
> *(Gee and Makens, 1985: 29)*

The first destination positioning study published in the tourism literature was in 1978 (see Goodrich, 1978). Pike's (2002, 2007a) analyses of 262 published destination image studies between 1973 and 2007 found approximately half (129) examined the image of one destination in isolation, without reference to competing places. While this approach does enable comparison of consumer perceptions with the desired brand identity, ascertaining strengths and weaknesses relative to competitors is not possible. In Pike's (2009) review of 28 research-based destination branding studies, only 3 focused on brand positioning analysis (see Nickerson and Moisey, 1999; Shanka, 2001; Kendall and Gursoy, 2007).

Differentness

Marketers need to think in terms of *differentness* rather than simply *betterness* (Ries and Trout, 1986). This has important tourism implications, given few tourism offerings are unique, and almost every new and innovative tourism service can be imitated. Differentiation is critical for destinations, because they usually offer similar attributes and benefits to competitors for a given travel context. Therefore, they will either become places of status, or commodities, with the latter leading to increased substitutability. Plog (2000) lamented the increasing sameness of most destinations around the world, due to the effects of globalisation. Modernity has all but destroyed the opportunity for travellers to experience different attractions (Dann, 2000). This standardisation of facilities enabled mass tourism by providing travellers with necessary familiarity (Cohen, 1972: 172): 'As a result, countries become interchangeable in the tourist's mind. Whether he is looking for good beaches, restful forests, or old cities, it becomes relatively unimportant to him where these happen to be found'.

While a differentiated positioning to stand out from the crowd is possible for any destination, the task is not easy. The fundamental marketing challenge faced by DMOs is to somehow match a large and diverse product range with the wants of a number of dynamic and heterogeneous markets. The desired market position, assuming one has been designed, articulated and agreed to, must be presented to the market in a way that stands out from other attention-seeking messages of rival destinations and substitute products. If successful, such a position will establish the destination as top of mind in the target audience. If top of mind awareness (ToMA) is an indicator of purchase preference (Axelrod, 1968; Wilson, 1981; Woodside and Wilson, 1985), it follows that such a position in the mind offers destinations a potential source of competitive advantage against rival places that are not salient in the decision process (Pike and Ryan, 2004).

As discussed in Chapter 8, strategy should seek to maximise strengths, correct weaknesses, minimise threats and maximise opportunities. Porter (1980) suggested a competitive strategy was one that positioned a business to make the most of strengths that differentiated the firm from competitors. A sustainable competitive advantage is gained when consumers perceive a performance capability gap that endures over time (Coyne, 1986). To gain an advantage the gap must be through an attribute that represents an important buying criterion. Not all attributes that differentiate a product from competitors are actually important to the consumer, and not all important attributes are used in decision making.

Determinant attributes

The ideal for any brand is to be perceived favourably on attributes that are important to the target segment. Different terms have been used in the tourism literature to describe important attributes. *Salient* attributes come to mind first during decision making, while *determinant* attributes are the one or few salient attributes that determine purchase choice. Not all important attributes will be salient. It is essential then to identify those attributes that determine product choice, to form the basis for any positioning campaign (Ritchie and Zins, 1978; Lovelock, 1991). Myers and Alpert (1968: 13) offered the first definition of determinance in the marketing literature: 'Attitudes toward features which are most closely related to preference or to actual purchase decisions are said to be determinant; the remaining features or attitudes – no matter how favourable – are not determinant'.

For example, Figure 11.4 shows possible important, salient and determinant attributes for a four star city hotel purchase decision. Of course, hotel cleanliness will be an important attribute, but it is not likely to be salient in the context of four star hotels. Rather, it would be assumed all available four star hotels would be clean.

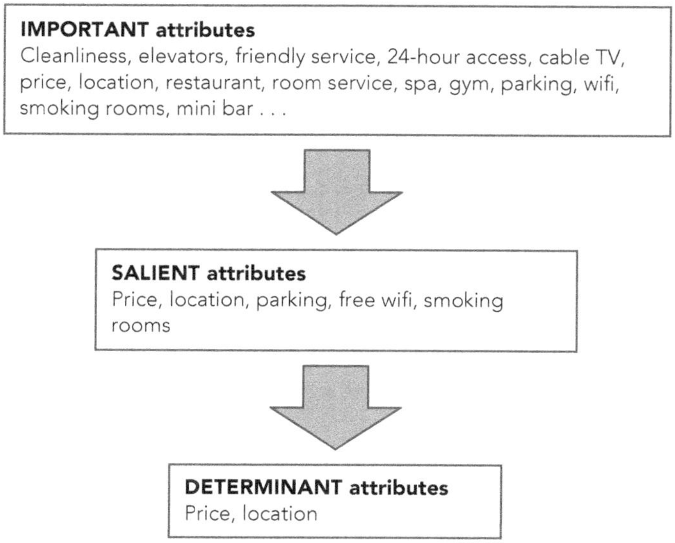

```
┌─────────────────────────────────────────────────────────┐
│ IMPORTANT attributes                                      │
│ Cleanliness, elevators, friendly service, 24-hour access, │
│ cable TV, price, location, restaurant, room service, spa, │
│ gym, parking, wifi, smoking rooms, mini bar . . .         │
└─────────────────────────────────────────────────────────┘
                            ↓
┌─────────────────────────────────────────────────────────┐
│ SALIENT attributes                                        │
│ Price, location, parking, free wifi, smoking rooms        │
└─────────────────────────────────────────────────────────┘
                            ↓
┌─────────────────────────────────────────────────────────┐
│ DETERMINANT attributes                                    │
│ Price, location                                           │
└─────────────────────────────────────────────────────────┘
```

Figure 11.4 Determinant attributes

In an analysis of over 80 published destination image studies that had used lists of attributes in structured questionnaires, Pike (2003) summarised 18 general attribute themes. Of the 80 studies, 37 concluded with resultant *determinant* attributes or factors, which were summarised into the following 15 themes:

- nature/scenery;
- local culture;
- price/value;
- good weather;
- infrastructure;
- friendly locals;
- safe/relaxing environment;
- lots to do;
- accommodation;
- sports activities;
- cafes/restaurants;
- historical sites;
- nightlife;
- accessibility;
- shopping.

Destination–market researchers could screen these themes through focus groups and/or personal interviews to develop a context-specific list of attributes for use in locally tailored destination image surveys.

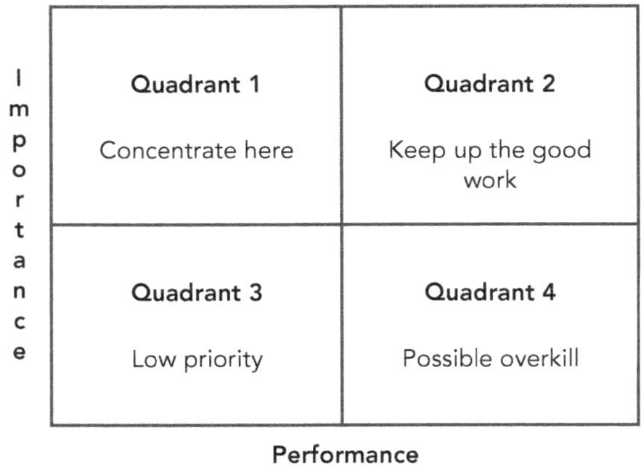

Figure 11.5 Importance–performance matrix

To summarise, a large number of attributes may be important for a given travel context. Since many competing products are likely to offer the same features, it will be a reduced set of salient attributes used to differentiate brands. From these, only one or a few determinant attributes will be used in the final destination selection.

Importance–performance analysis (IPA)

A graphical tool for helping to identify determinant attributes is IPA, introduced by Martilla and James (1977). The graphical output is easily understood by practitioners with little or no research training. The technique enables identification of those attributes that are most important to the market and where the destination is perceived most favourably (Figure 11.5, quadrant 2). It is these attributes that should then be used in marketing communications, since the easiest route to the consumer's mind is to reinforce positively held images rather than attempt to try to change their mind. Pike's (2002, 2007a) categorisation of 262 destination image studies identified 13 that had employed the IPA technique, which ask survey participants to rate the importance of each attribute before rating their perceptions of the performance of the destination(s) for the same attributes.

The positioning process

The destination positioning process involves seven stages:

1. identify the target market and travel context;

2. identify the competitive set of destinations;

3. identify the attributes/benefits sought;

4. identify perceptions of the strengths and weaknesses of each of the competitive set of destinations;

5. identify opportunities for a differentiated positioning proposition based on attribute determinance;

6. select and implement the position proposition;

7. monitor the performance of the positioning strategy over time in terms of destination differentiation and congruence between brand identity and brand image.

The target market

Brand positioning has its roots in segmentation theory. The first task in developing profitable customer relationships is the identification of target markets. The DMO marketing approach differs to the generally accepted definition of the marketing orientation, as presented in general marketing theory in at least one significant way. A marketing orientation was defined in Chapter 1 as a philosophy that recognises the achievement of organisational goals, requires an understanding of the wants of the target market and then delivers satisfaction more effectively than rivals. In other words, making all decisions with the target consumer in mind. Most DMOs have no control over the tourism services they represent, and with the exception of special events (see Chapter 6), devote relatively few resources to encouraging new product development tailored to meet identified consumer needs. Therefore, the marketing process is not one of designing products to meet market needs, but of attempting to find markets that are likely to be interested in the destination's current products and then communicating an attractive and differentiated value proposition.

Identifying market segments that might have an interest in the destination's product range is a critical task for destinations. DMOs have a broad mandate and therefore operate in multiple mass markets with millions of consumers. Tourism demand does not represent a homogenous group of people with identical motivations (Wahab *et al.*, 1976) and, as already discussed, the market interests of a destination's tourism businesses are often divergent. However, the need to focus resources then leads to the need to prioritise target markets. Positioning and segmentation have become inseparable in the marketing process.

Market aggregation represents an undifferentiated approach, where all consumers are treated as one, and is criticised as being a *shotgun* approach. At the opposite end of the continuum is total market disaggregation where every consumer is treated individually as a separate segment. There are obvious limits as to how far this can be taken by DMOs. However, important trade customers such as inbound tour operators (see Chapter 14) are an example of marketing to the needs of an identifiable individual client.

As discussed in Chapter 10, a destination's image might differ between regional markets (Hunt, 1975), between different segments (Phelps, 1986; Fakeye and Crompton, 1991) and in different travel contexts (Pike and Ryan, 2004). Critics have suggested that many NTOs in Europe have paid insufficient attention to the differences between markets, suggesting they were limited to using undifferentiated, but cost effective, marketing, which targeted common interests and needs of all travellers. However, undertaking needs analyses on a segment-by-segment basis provides marketers with opportunities to understand the needs of target segments better than competitors (Lovelock, 1991).

Positioning is based on communicating one or a few key benefits desired by the target segment that will determine choice. Since destinations operate in mass markets containing individuals with differing wants, can one positioning theme be adapted for use in all markets, or do the different characteristics of each market dictate a mix of distinct tailored themes as in the *think global, act local* mantra? In theory, the latter would enable separate advertising briefs to be developed that cater to the needs of different segments, as was the case for the Singapore Tourism Board's new global marketing campaign in 2015. However, from a practical perspective, when considering the range of segments that will be of interest to a DMO's stakeholders, both a multi-market assessment and a differentiated promotion approach appear daunting. As observed by Hooley and Saunders (1993: 154), an organisation taking the multiple segment approach 'may face a diseconomy in managing, supplying and promoting in a different way to each of these segments it has chosen'. Woodside (1982) also presented a warning in this regard, suggesting it is more effective to offer one set of benefits to one significant segment.

Segmentation can be undertaken either by a priori means, where the criterion variable for dividing the market is already known, or by a posteriori means, where no such prior knowledge exists (Calantone and Mazanec, 1991). For practical reasons many smaller DMOs will use an a priori approach to segment the global market. This is undertaken using criteria relating to easily obtainable information on geographic and demographic characteristics.

Market portfolio models

A number of methods for measuring international markets in relative terms has been reported in the literature, such as the market potential index developed by the United States Travel Service (see Lundberg, 1990), Western Australia's market potential assessment formula (see Crockett and Wood, 1999) and the country potential generation index (Hudman, 1979 in Formica and Littlefield, 2000). A more comprehensive method is multifactor portfolio modelling, which has been based on a two-dimensional matrix combining measures of market attractiveness and competitive position (see Mazanec, 1997). The matrix presents a visual tool similar to the growth-share matrix used by businesses to plot their product portfolio by market share and market growth (see, for example, Johnson and Scholes, 2002: 284). For destinations, market attractiveness variables considered for inclusion include market size, growth rate, seasonality effects and price levels, while a competitive position might include variables related to market share, image and advertising budgets. Destinations and markets are rated on each variable, which are subjectively assigned a weighting since not all will be of equal importance. For processing such data Mazanec promoted the use of the IAAWIN software, which was freely available from the Vienna University of Economics and Business Administration (see www.wu-wien.ac.at). A variation of this method, using a 3 × 3 matrix, was reported by Henshall et al. (1985) in a comparative assessment of New Zealand's major markets.

Another portfolio approach, the destination–market matrix (DMM), which provides more balance between quantitative and qualitative analysis, was promoted by McKercher (1995). The DMM incorporates the destination lifecycle as well as the growth-share matrix and displays six relationships between the destination and its markets:

1. the relative importance of each market;

2. each market's lifecycle stage;

3. the age of each market in each lifecycle stage, which forms the basis of the horizontal axis;

4. a prediction of future performance, which forms the basis of the vertical axis;

5. the total number of markets attracted to the destination;

6. the interrelationship existing between all these markets.

The four cells of the DMM, shown in Figure 11.6, represent the lifecycle stages each market would be expected to follow: *new*, *expanding*, *stable* and *tired*. Each circle represents a market of interest, in terms of relative size and future performance. A critical assumption of the model is that markets progress through the matrix in a clockwise direction, starting as a new market in the top left-hand corner. McKercher suggested the benefits of the DMM were its flexibility, in that markets could be segmented by whatever means was most suitable to the DMO, and the ability to track the performance over time. Three Australian case studies were provided to demonstrate its effectiveness as a visual planning tool. The DMM was used by McKercher to graphically highlight unbalanced growth at the Gold Coast, the state of Victoria in decline and balanced growth for Australia as a whole.

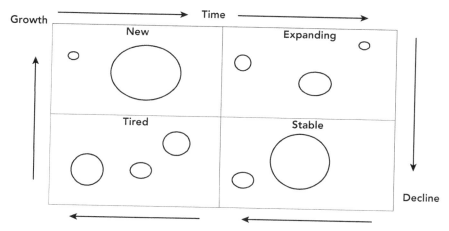

Figure 11.6 Destination–market matrix

Source: Adapted from McKercher (1995).

General utilities of market portfolio modelling techniques include aiding DMO decisions relating to promotional budget allocation for each market and enhancing understanding of the destination's relative reliance on key markets. These can then be graphically presented to stakeholders to promote or justify strategies. Often it is only with hindsight that the full implications of an overreliance on particular markets is realised. This was particularly evident in Australia and New Zealand during the 1990s Asian economic crisis when an overreliance on markets in the region proved a weakness of many tourism businesses. Similarly, one of the major problems in the downturn in visitors to Majorca during the 1980s was an overreliance on the UK and German markets, which accounted for 70 per cent of the island's visitors (Morgan, 1991). As discussed in Chapter 2, Turkey has faced a similar problem since the 2000s (see Okumus and Karamustafa, 2005; Kozak and Martin, 2012; Ozturk and Van Niekerk, 2014). The portfolio approach can also be used by a DMO on a market-by-market basis to plot current and future attractiveness of the destination's individual products. This is useful for destinations with a diverse range of products that have differing levels of appeal for different markets.

The a posteriori segmentation approach usually utilises more sophisticated multivariate techniques, such as cluster analysis, to identify groups within a population that exhibit or state similar psychographic characteristics. These will involve more subjectively defined criteria such as attitudes, desired benefits and behavioural intent. Another means is by travel purpose, including special interest groups. An almost limitless list of these include such diverse examples as: medical tourists, business meetings, incentive groups, school reunions, education field trips, bird watchers, calligraphers, collectors, country music fans, bikers and surfers.

Segmentation by social graphics

An emerging area of segmentation research in the Web 2.0 era is by *social graphics*.

Owyang (2010, in Pan and Crotts, 2012: 81) argued the merits of segmenting customers by asking questions such as:

- Which websites are my customers on?
- What are my customers' social behaviours online?

- What social information or people do my customers rely on?

- What are my customers' social influence?

From these it could be possible to separate individuals into different layers of social media engagement: curators, producers, commenters, sharers and watchers. A study by Allianz Global Assistance that reviewed 32 million exchanges on travel forums in 11 countries shows that the internet has made consumers much more travel savvy, which they labelled *the skilful tourist* (Travelindustrywire, 2015). The study identified four segments of skilful tourist:

1. *Comfort travellers* are focused on the quality of the experience and seek validation of travel plans by like-minded others.

2. *Active travellers* seek a physically challenging trip, experiencing as much as possible, and then sharing.

3. *Money smart travellers* seek a good deal and only spend money on packages that meet their vision.

4. *Stress travellers* are concerned about what might go wrong and seek advice from peers and travel professionals to mitigate potential problems.

The value proposition (attention is in short supply out there)

The development of a value proposition is arguably the greatest challenge in branding (Gilmore, 2002). Once the potential determinant attributes are known, a key decision must be made about which should be used as the focus of the brand positioning. While *focus* may be appropriate for single product marketers, the selection of one determinant attribute by a DMO is problematic. A useful way to understand this challenge is to consider what seven-word proposition and image would be effective for your destination on a roadside billboard or on a postcard. Both mediums are a metaphor for positioning succinctness. There is no time or space to tell the whole story, so the focus must be a simple message that will be noticed as well as be immediately meaningful in the target market. I experienced an interesting example of how the multi-attributed nature of destinations represents a major challenge in the positioning process when managing Tourism Rotorua. I was presented with a request by a national television network for a graphic image of one local icon for use in the nightly weather segment. Only one image was permitted, which would be used consistently each night alongside images from other major centres. However, this high profile opportunity proved a difficult selection due to the vested business interests in different icons by individual representatives of the RTO's board. Industry politics did not dictate the final choice, but it certainly frustrated the decision making.

Making trade-offs

To stand out and be noticed and remembered, DMOs must design a positioning strategy focused on one or few determinant attributes. Success is most likely when the range of differentiated features emphasised is small (Aaker and Shansby, 1982; Crompton *et al.*, 1992) and yet a destination usually comprises a diversity of features. For DMOs, this necessitates making trade-offs. After all, 'you can't stand for something if you chase after everything' (Ries, 1992: 7). The power of focus is due to our mind's dislike of confusion (Trout and Rivkin, 1995). In an age when the information flood is increasing exponentially, the message should not try to tell the product's entire story, but rather focus on one powerful attribute, since more brand variations cause confusion. Ries (1992: 5) suggested that owning a word in the target's mind had become the most powerful concept in marketing. Therefore, the following question should be asked: What single idea or concept does my company (or brand) stand for in the mind of the prospect? For example, Las Vegas (adult playground) and Orlando (family fun) make trade-offs with their differentiated positioning themes.

In the brand literature it has been suggested a value proposition is the promise of functional, emotional and self-expressive benefits to influence purchase decisions (Aaker, 1996). These are relevant to the concepts of cognitive, affect and conative images, which were discussed in Chapter 10. Functional product attributes by themselves do not differentiate and are easy to copy. This relates to the cognitive image or knowledge of a destination's features. Emotional benefits are the stimulation of a positive feeling. This relates to the affective image component. Self-expressive benefits strengthen the link between brand and consumer by representing symbols of our self-concept: 'A brand can thus provide a self-expressive benefit by providing a way for a person to communicate his or her self image' (Aaker, 1996: 99). These may include, for example, *adventurous*, *hip*, *sophisticated* and *successful*, among others. The differences between emotional and self-expressive benefits are that self-expressive benefits emphasise the self rather than feelings, a public setting rather than private, future aspirations rather than memory, and the act of using the product rather than the consequences of using it. For example, the benefit of the pre and post brag value from visiting an exotic destination may be different to the benefit of feelings attained from being there.

RESEARCH SNAPSHOT

11.1 How destination positioning might be undertaken on the basis of attributes, benefits or personal values

Pike (2012) reported the application of two qualitative techniques used to explore the range of cognitive attributes, consequences (benefits) and personal values that represent potential positioning opportunities for destinations in the context of short break holidays. The repertory test is an effective technique for understanding the salient attributes used by a traveller to differentiate destinations, and laddering analysis enables the researcher to explore the smaller set of consequences and personal values guiding such decision making. A key finding of the research was that, while individuals might vary in their repertoire of salient attributes, there was a commonality of shared consequences and values. This has important implications for DMOs, since a brand positioning theme that is based on a value will subsume multiple and diverse attributes. It was suggested that such a theme will appeal to a broader range of travellers, as well as appease a greater number of destination stakeholders than would a functional attribute-based theme.

Further reading

Pike, S. (2012).

Three key positioning deliverability criteria should be considered (Keller, 2003):

1. **Is the position feasible?** For a destination this will relate to the ability of the local tourism industry and host community to deliver the promise offered in the value proposition.

2. **Can the position be communicated?** In terms of developing strong, favourable and unique associations, the efficacy of a destination's communications will depend to a large extent on whether the message is reinforcing existing positively held associations of the destination, or whether an attempt is being made to either create awareness or change opinions.

3. **Is the position sustainable?** The ability of the destination to strengthen associations over time will depend on how well the position can be defended against imitating rivals.

The positioning elements

When the value proposition focus has been determined, the elements to represent the public face of the brand must be selected. For destinations the most important positioning elements are the place name, a logo and a slogan. At the core of the brand is the product name (Aaker, 1991). A well-chosen word can trigger meanings in the mind, and so a good brand name can begin the positioning process by communicating the major benefit of the product (Ries and Trout, 1982: 28): 'In this competitive era, the single most important marketing decision you can make is what to name the product. The name is the hook that hangs the consumer brand on the product ladder in the prospect's mind'.

However, there has been little empirical research into the contribution of the destination's name in the development of favourable brand associations. Unlike new product developments, where an attempt can be made to select a name that enhances the positioning process through either memorability or development of associations, a destination will already have a place name, for which a history of associations has been developed over time.

Tricky place names

For all manner of political, economic and practical reasons, it is extremely difficult to change a place name for tourism purposes, even though it might make sense to some marketers. For example, as mentioned in the Preface, in New Zealand during a late 1980s crisis meeting that I attended between Rotorua's civic leaders and leading Japanese tour wholesalers, convened by then Mayor, John Keaney, to discuss the destination's ailing image in that market, one of the key outcomes was the suggestion that Rotorua should change the city name to *Kingstown*. This was a deliberate reference to Queenstown, which was the preferred New Zealand resort area for Japanese visitors at the time. In line with Ries and Trout's (1982) view that brand names need aural qualities, Rotorua, which is an indigenous Maori name that translates as *second lake* in English, did not appeal to the Japanese in the same way as destinations with British sounding names such as Queenstown and Christchurch. The *Kingstown* suggestion was never pursued seriously beyond the meeting for political and cultural reasons and, I might add, was never made public. The likely local reaction to such a proposal does not bear thinking about.

The Rotorua problem is certainly not unique. For example, Ries and Ries (1998) promoted the suggestion for Guatemala to change to Guatemaya, in order to link the Mayan people and their heritage to one of a number of countries where Mayan ruins may be found. While well-received by the business community in a destination struggling to differentiate, the idea is unlikely politically. In Turkey the Ankara Chamber of Trade president put forward a proposal to the country's Minister of Tourism to revise the destination name: 'The name with which our country is known to the world, "Turkey," needs to be changed. This is the name of a bird in English and is used in a derogatory way to reflect the low intelligence of the bird'.

There have been many examples of place name changes in most parts of the world for political reasons. For example, many places in India changed names following independence from Britain, while a number of Australian town names were changed during the First World War due to being Germanic. However, there have been very few reported examples of destination name (re)creation for tourism branding reasons:

- With wonderful foresight during the 1930s the Queensland beach town of Elston was renamed Surfers' Paradise (Pike, 2004a).

- In the Caribbean, Hog Island was changed to Paradise Island to appeal to the cruise tourism market (Ries and Trout, 1982).

- In 1996 the Republic of Cuervo was created by the well-known tequila brand (see Kotler, 1996, in Pike, 2008), following the purchase of an island off the coast of Tortola in the Caribbean. The company unsuccessfully petitioned for country status at the United Nations and for admission of a volleyball team to the Olympics.

Anyway, there are places that owe a lot of their renown to a tricky name, such as Titicaca, Timbuktu, Popocatepetl, Ouarzazate and Gstaad (Anholt, 2002). So there are opportunities for the myriad of unusual place names such as:

- Bum Bum Creek (Australia);

- Beer (England);

- Condom (France);

- Dildo (Newfoundland, Canada);

- Frog Suck (Wyoming, USA);

- Fucking (Austria);

- Hell (Norway);

- Taumatawhakatangihangakoauauotamateapokaiwhenuakitanatahu (New Zealand).

Adding brand associations

If not able or willing to officially change the place name, amendments can be made to the name used to brand the destination by adding a word association with an important attribute in marketing communications. During 2003 the neighbouring Queensland beach towns of Bargara, Moore Park and Woodgate all made moves to add the word *beach* to the destination name in promotions even though they did not appear on official maps. The names Bargara Beach, Moore Park Beach and Woodgate Beach clearly signal an important functional attribute for these small, emerging destinations. Similarly, Florida's Lee County, home of the USA's best-known shell collectors' haven, Sanibel Island, changed the destination name to Lee Island Coast in promotions. In New Zealand's central North Island the official place name of Taupo has long been promoted by destination marketers as Lake Taupo to take advantage of the district's most noticeable natural feature. Likewise, neighbouring district Ruapehu, which features the North Island's major skiing and climbing attractions, is promoted as Mount Ruapehu.

A further opportunity is that of labelling tourism macro regions with tourism-related names. One example is Utah's promotional regions such as Dinosaurland and Canyonlands. Another is Queensland's Gold Coast and Sunshine Coast. Other attempts at establishing emerging macro regions labels within the state include:

- Fraser Coast, in reference to the world heritage listed Fraser Island;

- Coral Coast, in reference to the southern starting point of the Great Barrier Reef;

- Discovery Coast, in reference to Captain James Cook's 1770 voyage of discovery, explicit in the name of the popular beach, The Town of 1770;

- Capricorn Coast, in reference to the Tropic of Capricorn;

- Tropical North Queensland.

By comparison, the names of England's macro destination regions indicate a geographic reference point, such as South East England, and perhaps miss an opportunity to promote a travel benefit.

Logo

Symbols can enhance brand recognition and recall (Aaker, 1996) by serving as a mnemonic device for the target (Aaker, 1991). Since destination names have not usually been designed to reinforce or create associations with a product class, logos and slogans can play important roles as identifiers. A logo and/or slogan can be designed to reflect a desirable functional feature such as nature or an affective benefit such as *relaxing*. Aaker (1996: 205) suggested posing the question: What mental image would you like customers to have of your brand in the future? A symbol can help to identify the brand with the product class as well as reflect the brand personality. For example, Virgin's logo, with its unconventional script and rakish angle support the Virgin personality, which flaunts the rules (Aaker and Joachimsthaler, 2000). In particular, symbols that are metaphors for the brand personality are more meaningful. Ries and Ries (1998: 132) were critical of many efforts in this regard: 'The power of a brand name lies in the meaning of the word in the mind. For most brands, a symbol has little or nothing to do with creating this meaning to the mind'.

Symbols can emerge from a diverse array of sources, such as a sound (Harley Davidson), architecture (Spanish adobe construction), the product's founder (KFC's Colonel Sanders), a colour (Hertz yellow), packaging (Nivea cosmetics), script style (Cadbury chocolate), a programme (Ronald McDonald House), a character (Energizer bunny), a celebrity (Nike's Michael Jordan) or a distinctive logo (Adidas's three stripes). Ownership of such *communication equity* represents a source of competitive advantage (Gilmore, 2002). For some destinations, a symbol represents well-established icons (Ritchie and Ritchie, 1998: 113): 'Such symbols as the Eiffel Tower, the Pyramids of Egypt, and the Great Wall of China are the kinds of unique and enduring symbols that DMOs are prepared to die for'.

DMOs desire stakeholders to reinforce marketing efforts by using brand positioning elements such as the logo, as evidenced by Tourism Australia (2014) for example:

> *From the beginning,* There's nothing like Australia *has been designed for the tourism industry and the focus has been on creating materials which you can adapt for your own business promotions. A new campaign logo has been created for the trade and industry to support the next phase of* There's nothing like Australia *campaign. Please go to www.tourism.australia.com/tnlalogo.*

Slogan

For many destinations a logo will not be sufficient to communicate a differentiated position. The addition of a slogan offers an opportunity to add more meaning to that which could be achieved by the brand name or symbol (Aaker, 1991). A slogan is a short phrase that communicates descriptive or persuasive information about a brand (Keller, 2003). Interestingly, it has been suggested the word *slogan* emanates from the Gaelic term meaning *battle cry* (Boyee and Arens, 1992, in Supphellen and Nygaardsvik, 2002). The term is sometimes substituted with others such as tag line, strap line and seven-word single-minded proposition.

As Sydney prepared for the 2000 Olympics, Ries and Ries (1998: 153–154) proposed a new positioning slogan based on the following criteria:

- It should be a concept positioning Sydney as a world-class city alongside London, Paris, Rome, New York and Hong Kong.

- It should be a concept that has a strong element of believability. People should say, 'Yes, Sydney is like that'.

- It should be a concept that is alliterative with the name Sydney, to enhance memorability.

- It should be a concept that is consistent with the symbol of the city, the Sydney Opera House.

They suggested that only one slogan, *Sydney, the world's most sophisticated city*, met all four criteria. At the time of writing, Sydney's actual positioning slogan was *There's no place in the world like Sydney*.

Too many destination slogans have been less than memorable (see Dann, 2000; Morgan *et al.*, 2003; Ward and Gold, 1994). Best practice in destination promotion has been limited to a few simple slogans, such as the 1970s development of the 'I ♥ New York' campaign (Ward and Gold, 1994: 4): 'The process of imitation, however, demonstrates a general paucity of creative ideas and effectively ensures that the vast majority of place promotional campaigns rarely manage to cross the threshold of ephemeral indifference'.

The slogans used during 2003 by NTOs around the world were tabled by Pike (2008). The approach used was to record the slogan used on the home page of each NTO's consumer website. The rationale was the assumption that since one of the basic tenets of integrated marketing communication is a consistency of message across different media, the slogan used on the DMO home page should represent the destination positioning theme. A content analysis of the NTO slogans identified 14 positioning categories, which are listed below in order of popularity (see Pike, 2004a):

- leadership;
- discovery;
- nature;
- location;
- people;
- water;
- self-expression;
- escape;
- pleasure;
- treasure;
- royal;
- vibrant;
- climate;
- culinary.

Unfortunately, there are few guidelines in the marketing literature for empirically testing brand slogans (Supphellen and Nygaardsvik, 2002). Richardson and Cohen (1993) developed a hierarchy of destination slogans featuring four criteria, based on Reeves's (1961, in Richardson and Cohen, 1993) concept of a unique selling point (USP):

1. The foundation of the hierarchy is that the slogan must be propositional.

2. Propositions should be limited to one or only a few.

3. Propositions should sell benefits of interest to the market.

4. The benefits must be unique.

Richardson and Cohen categorised the slogans of 46 USA state tourism organisations. Commencing at level zero of the hierarchy, two of the state slogans examined, *Yes! Michigan!* and *Utah!*, were deemed not to be propositional. Ascending to level one of the hierarchy, the slogans of six STOs featured propositions, but which were no more than a plea to *buy our product*. Examples included *Discover Idaho* and *Explore Minnesota*. At level two, the proposition is equivalent to stating *our product is good*. Of the 14 slogans at this level, examples included *Discover the spirit! North Dakota*, *The spirit of Massachusetts* and *Vermont makes it special*. Level 3a featured nine slogans where the proposition promoted an attribute that represented a potential benefit, but that almost every other state could claim. These included *Arkansas – the natural state*, *Maine – the way life should be* and *Oregon – things look different here*. At level 3b the propositional benefit attribute used in the slogans of six states could be claimed by many states. These included *Ohio the heart of it all!*, *Oklahoma – native America* and *Texas, like a whole other country*. At level 4a, the proposition features a unique attribute, but one that does not represent a benefit. The three states at this level were *Delaware – the first state*, *Pennsylvania – America starts here* and *Rhode Island – America's first resort*. At level 4b, the pinnacle of the hierarchy, the slogans of only five states were considered to feature a USP:

- Arizona – the Grand Canyon state;
- Florida – coast to coast;
- Louisiana – we're really cookin'!;
- South Dakota – great faces, great places;
- Tennessee – we're playing your song.

Of these five slogans only Arizona's remained the same in March 2015. This is not surprising, given the historical lack of consistency of DMO slogans over time.

Consistency of proposition themes over time

As discussed in Chapter 10, destination image change occurs only slowly over time (see Crompton, 1979; Gartner and Hunt, 1987; Gartner, 1993; Pike, 2010). Gartner and Hunt (1987) found evidence of positive destination image change over a 13-year period, but concluded any change only occurs slowly. Likewise a study by the English Tourist Board (1983, in Jeffries, 2001), which analysed the impact of an advertising campaign to modify Londoners' perceptions of England's North Country [sic] over a three-year period, found only minor changes in destination image. An ongoing study of the perceptions of a competitive set of five short break holiday destinations in Queensland has found almost no changes in the perceptions of any of the destinations between 2003 and 2012 (see Pike 2007b, 2009, 2010).

The key implication is that destination marketers should resist the temptation to regularly change the brand positioning theme too often, such as Tourism Australia has done five times since 2005. Attention is in short supply out there. It is hard work getting noticed in the market, and so the focused value proposition should be consistent over time. Changes can occur through political interference (see Russell, 2008), intermediary interference or new DMO management. With regard to the latter, McKercher and Ritchie (1997) cited the example of an LTA in Australia, which had four managers in six years. This led to the development of four different marketing plans, with each having a different positioning statement, resulting in market place confusion.

Repositioning is difficult, with few success stories published, and so academic researchers should be careful about recommending such strategies. Remember, the easiest route to the mind is to consistently reinforce already positively held perceptions, such as those identified in an IPA. Consumers are dogmatic, and so it is difficult to get them to change their minds without a big budget and a lot of time. Potential advantages of long-term consistency include (Pike, 2004a):

- ownership of a position, such as 'Virginia is for lovers', since 1969;

- ownership of an identity symbol/slogan such as 'I ♥ New York', since 1977;

- assurance for local tourism businesses and travel intermediaries who invest resources in developing sub-brands that are compatible with the destination umbrella brand.

To address the gap in the literature related to destination repositioning, case study 11.1 summarises the 2014 development of a new brand positioning theme for the state of Goa in India, where the researchers aim to track performance over time.

CASE STUDY

11.1 The repositioning of Goa, India

Associate Professor Ian Michael
Associate Professor Filareti Kotsi
Zayed University, Dubai, United Arab Emirates

The state of Goa is situated in western India on the coast of the Arabian Sea. A Portuguese territory from the sixteenth century until 1961, Goa is the smallest state in India, but is the strongest economically with the highest GDP per capita, due mainly to its mining and tourism history. Tourism is now taking centre stage due to the collapse of the mining industry. Goa's main tourism attractions are its beaches, cultural and archaeological heritage and natural biodiversity. In terms of destination marketing, Goa did not become actively involved until the establishment of a DMO during the 1960s. During 2014 the Goa Tourism Department (www.goatourism.gov.in) launched a new tourism strategy to rebrand and reposition the state, away from its image as a hippy beach destination, often associated with drug consumption, which had developed since the 1960s. Goa was synonymous with western hippies, backpackers and charter flights full of budget travellers. The repositioning campaign is part of a broader tourism development strategy by the state government that includes new infrastructure such as a new airport and cruise terminal.

With the introduction of a liberalised Indian economy in the early 1990s by the then Prime Minister, P. V. Narasimha Rao, India's middle class grew considerably and many domestic tourism destinations benefited from this new wealth. Goa has been successful in attracting this Indian middle class travel segment, who perceive Goa as a *cool* destination in a country that has a much more traditional and conservative culture. For example, Indian women can wear short pants and sleeveless tops, which is not usual in other parts of the country. In this regard, Goa is seen to be safe, comfortable and relaxed. However, the Ministry of Tourism, which oversees the Goa Tourism Department, wanted to diversify the image of the destination away from just a hippy beach holiday destination to one featuring more of the rich Portuguese/Indian culture and heritage and nature hinterland.

In conjunction with brand management company, Chlorophyll, the Goa Tourism Department developed the new *Kenna Campaign*. Kenna is a Konkani (official local language of Goa) word that means *sometimes*. The aim is to showcase the destination as being multi-faceted, in that Goa can be many things for visitors. For example, the taglines used with pictorial depictions to support the message include:

Kenna Fast, Kenna Slow

Kenna History, Kenna Mystery

Kenna Sing, Kenna Dance

Kenna Party, Kenna Safari

Kenna Cool, Kenna Hot

Kenna Spicy, Kenna Mild

Kenna Rock, Kenna Roll

In addition to the new repositioning campaign for Goa, the DMO is also conscious of the need to fit under the umbrella brand of *Incredible India*. This is because in some international markets there is either a lack of awareness of where Goa is situated or there have been misconceptions that Goa was an independent state, much like Hong Kong in China.

Further reading

Michael, I. and Kotsi, F. (2015).
Wilson, D. (1997).

Discussion question

Why is it important for the Goa Tourism Board to use the new Kenna positioning consistently over time?

Analysis of the longevity of destination slogans requires access to historical data, which in the tourism literature is limited. Pike (2004b) focused on STOs in the USA and RTOs in New Zealand, for which slogans have been documented at previous points in time. USA state slogans used in 2003 were compared to those categorised by Richardson and Cohen (1993) and Pritchard (1982). It was felt these timeframes provide an indication of the consistency of use over the short to medium term. Of the 47 slogans used in 1982, only 6 were still in use in 1993, and of the 46 slogans used in 1993, only 13 were still being used in 2003. Over a 21-year period, only 6 of the 1982 slogans remained in use in 2003: Arkansas, Delaware, Massachusetts, New Mexico, New York and Virginia. The New Zealand RTO slogans used in 2003 were compared to those recorded by Pike (1998). Of the 15 slogans listed in 1998, 9 of the RTOs had retained the same message over the 5-year period. A follow-up check of the USA STO slogans undertaken in 2012 and 2015 revealed more consistency over the shorter term, with 30 STO slogans remaining the same over the 3-year period.

CHAPTER SUMMARY

Key point 1: Positioning as a source of competitive advantage

While consumers have an almost limitless number of destinations to choose from, they will only consider the merits of a small number in the actual decision process. The small number of destinations positioned in this competitive set have an advantage over rival destinations that are not salient in decision making.

Key point 2: Positioning as the attempt to enhance congruence between brand identity and brand image

Destination brand identity (Chapter 9) is the self-image aspired to in the market place. Destination brand image (Chapter 10) is the actual image held by consumers and may or may not be reflective of the brand identity. Brand positioning is the attempt to enhance congruence between the brand image and the brand identity. To gain cut-through in crowded markets, the position must represent a focused proposition that is meaningful to the target market and effectively differentiates.

Key point 3: The challenges involved in developing a narrow positioning focus for multi-attributed destinations in multiple markets

Effective positioning requires a succinct, focused and consistent message tailored to meet the wants of target segments, to gain *cut-through* in crowded, heterogeneous and dynamic markets. Key challenges for DMOs are: having to make trade-offs in designing a succinct proposition, from a myriad of place attributes, which encapsulates the brand identity, will be supported by stakeholders, effectively differentiates against rival places and is noticed as being meaningful to consumers in multiple target markets.

REVIEW QUESTIONS

1. Why is positioning mutually beneficial for destination marketers and consumers?

2. What does a DMO risk by not having a positioning theme?

3. Critique the potential of your destination's slogan to effectively differentiate against rivals.

REFERENCES

Aaker, D. A. (1991). *Managing Brand Equity*. New York: Free Press.

Aaker, D. A. (1996). *Building Strong Brands*. New York: Free Press.

Aaker, D. A. and Joachimsthaler, E. (2000). *Brand Leadership*. New York: Free Press.

Aaker, D. A. and Shansby, J. G. (1982). Positioning your product. *Business Horizons* May/June: 56–62.

Anholt, S. (2002). Nation brands: The value of 'provenance' in branding. In Morgan, N., Pritchard, A. and Pride, R. (eds) *Destination Branding*. Oxford: Butterworth-Heinemann, pp. 42–56.

Axelrod, J. N. (1968). Attitude measures that predict purchase. *Journal of Advertising Research* 8(1): 3–17.

Calantone, R. J. and Mazanec, J. A. (1991). Marketing management and tourism. *Annals of Tourism Research* 18(1): 101–119.

Chacko, H. E. (1997). Positioning a tourism destination to gain a competitive edge. *Asia Pacific Journal of Tourism Research* 1(2): 69–75.

Cohen, E. (1972). Toward a sociology of international tourism. *Social Research* 39: 164–182.

Coyne, K. P. (1986). Sustainable competitive advantage: What it is, what it isn't. *Business Horizons* January/February: 54–61.

Crockett, S. R. and Wood, L. J. (1999). Brand Western Australia: A totally integrated approach to destination branding. *Journal of Vacation Marketing* 5(3): 276–289.

Crompton, J. L. (1979). An assessment of the image of Mexico as a vacation destination and the influence of geographical location upon that image. *Journal of Travel Research* Spring: 18–23.

Crompton, J. L., Fakeye, P. C. and Lue, C. (1992). Positioning: The example of the Lower Rio Grande Valley in the winter long stay destination market. *Journal of Travel Research* Fall: 20–26.

Dann, G. M. S. (2000). Differentiating destination in the language of tourism: Harmless hype or promotional irresponsibility. *Tourism Recreation Research* 25(2): 63–72.

DiMingo, E. (1988). The fine art of positioning. *The Journal of Business Strategy* March/April: 34–38.

Fakeye, P. C. and Crompton, J. L. (1991). Image differences between prospective, first time, and repeat visitors to the Lower Rio Grande Valley. *Journal of Travel Research* 30(1): 10–16.

Formica, S. and Littlefield, J. (2000). National tourism organizations: A promotional plans framework. *Journal of Hospitality & Leisure Marketing* 7(1): 103–119.

Gartner, W. C. (1993). Image information process. *Journal of Travel & Tourism Marketing* 2(2/3): 191–215.

Gartner, W. C. and Hunt, J. D. (1987). An analysis of state image change over a twelve-year period (1971–1983). *Journal of Travel Research* Fall: 15–19.

Gee, C. Y. and Makens, J. C. (1985). The tourism board: Doing it right. *The Cornell Quarterly* 26(3): 25–33.

Gilmore, F. (2002). Branding for success. In Morgan, N., Pritchard, A. and Pride, R. (eds) *Destination Branding: Creating the Unique Destination Proposition*. Oxford: Butterworth-Heinemann, pp. 57–65.

Goodrich, J. N. (1978). The relationship between preferences for and perceptions of vacation destinations: Application of a choice model. *Journal of Travel Research* Fall: 8–13.

Henshall, B. D., Roberts, R. and Leighton, A. (1985). Fly-drive tourists: Motivation and destination choice factors. *Journal of Travel Research* 24(1): 23–27.

Hooley, G. J. and Saunders, J. (1993). *Competitive Positioning: The Key to Market Success*. Hertfordshire, UK: Prentice Hall International.

Hunt, J. D. (1975). Image as a factor in tourism development. *Journal of Travel Research* 13(3): 1–7.

Jeffries, D. (2001). *Governments and Tourism*. Oxford: Butterworth-Heinemann.

Johnson, G. and Scholes, K. (2002). *Exploring Corporate Strategy* (6th edition). Harlow, UK: Pearson Education.

Keller, K. L. (2003). *Strategic Brand Management*. Upper Saddle River, NJ: Prentice Hall.

Kendall, K. W. and Gursoy, D. (2007). A managerial approach to positioning and branding: Eponymous or efficient? *Tourism Analysis* 12(5/6): 473–484.

Kozak, M. and Martin, D. (2012). Tourism life cycle and sustainability analysis: Profit-focused strategies for mature destinations. *Tourism Management* 33: 188–194.

Lovelock, C. (1991). *Services Marketing*. Englewood Cliffs, NJ: Prentice Hall.

Lundberg, D. E. (1990). *The Tourist Business*. New York: Van Nostrand Reinhold.

Martilla, J. A. and James, J. C. (1977). Importance–performance analysis. *Journal of Marketing* 41(1): 77–79.

Mazanec, J. A. (1997). Satisfaction tracking for city tourists. In Mazanec, J. A. (ed.) *International City Tourism*. London: Pinter, pp. 75–100.

McKercher, B. (1995). The destination–market matrix: A tourism market portfolio analysis model. *Journal of Travel & Tourism Marketing* 4(2): 23–40.

McKercher, B. and Ritchie, M. (1997). The third tier of public sector tourism: A profile of local government tourism officers in Australia. *Journal of Travel Research* 36(1): 66–72.

Michael, I. and Kotsi, F. (2015). Re-branding the state of Goa, India: The 'Kenna' campaign. *International Interdisciplinary Business-Economics Advancement Conference Proceedings*. Fort Lauderdale, FL. March/April.

Morgan, M. (1991). Dressing up to survive: Marketing Majorca anew. *Tourism Management* March: 15–20.

Morgan, N. J., Pritchard, A. and Piggott, R. (2003). Destination branding and the role of stakeholders: The case of New Zealand. *Journal of Vacation Marketing* 9(3): 285–299.

Morley, P. and Stolz, G. (2003). Gold Coast blunders by promoting wrong beach. *The Courier Mail*. Brisbane. 3. Hard copy newspaper article.

Myers, J. H. (1992). Positioning products/services in attitude space. *Marketing Research* March: 46–51.

Myers, J. H. and Alpert, M. I. (1968). Determinant buying attitudes: Meaning and measurement. *Journal of Marketing* 32(October): 13–20.

Nickerson, N. P. and Moisey, R. N. (1999). Branding a state from features to positioning: Making it simple. *Journal of Vacation Marketing* 5(3): 217–226.

Okumus, F. and Karamustafa, K. (2005). Impact of an economic crisis: Evidence from Turkey. *Annals of Tourism Research* 32(4): 942–961.

Ozturk, A. B. and Van Niekerk, M. (2014). Volume or value: A policy decision for Turkey's tourism industry. *Journal of Destination Marketing & Management* 3(4): 193–197.

Pan, B. and Crotts, J. C. (2012). Theoretical models of social media, marketing implications, and future research directions. In Sigala, M., Christou, E. and Gretzel, U. (eds) *Social Media in Travel, Tourism and Hospitality: Theory, Practice and Cases*. Farnham, UK: Ashgate Publishing Limited, pp. 73–86.

Phelps, A. (1986). Holiday destination image: The problem of assessment. *Tourism Management* September: 168–180.

Pike, S. (1998). Destination positioning: Too many fingers in the pie? *NZ Tourism and Hospitality Research Conference Proceedings*. Christchurch, NZ: Lincoln University.

Pike, S. (2002). Destination image analysis: A review of 142 papers from 1973–2000. *Tourism Management* 23(5): 541–549.

Pike, S. (2003). The use of repertory grid analysis to elicit salient short break holiday attributes. *Journal of Travel Research* 41(3): 326–330.

Pike, S. (2004a). *Destination Marketing Organisations*. Oxford: Elsevier Science.

Pike, S. (2004b). Destination brand positioning slogans: Towards the development of a set of accountability criteria. *Acta Turistica* 16(2): 102–124.

Pike, S. (2007a). Destination image literature: 2001–2007. *Acta Turistica* 19(2): 107–125.

Pike, S. (2007b). Consumer-based brand equity for destinations: Practical DMO performance measures. *Journal of Travel & Tourism Marketing* 22(1): 51–61.

Pike, S. (2008). *Destination Marketing: An Integrated Marketing Communication Approach*. Burlington, MA: Butterworth-Heinemann.

Pike, S. (2009). Destination brand positions of a competitive set of near-home destinations. *Tourism Management* 30(6): 857–866.

Pike, S. (2010). Destination branding: Tracking brand equity for an emerging destination between 2003 and 2007. *Journal of Hospitality & Tourism Research* 34(1): 124–139.

Pike, S. (2012). Destination positioning opportunities using personal values elicited through the repertory test and laddering analysis. *Tourism Management* 33(1): 100–107.

Pike, S. and Ryan, C. (2004). Destination positioning analysis through a comparison of cognitive, affective and conative perceptions. *Journal of Travel Research* 42(4): 333–342.

Plog, S. T. (2000). Thirty years that changed travel: Changes to expect over the next ten. *Keynote Address at the 31st Travel and Tourism Research Association Conference*. Burbank, CA. June. Available at: www.ttra.com

Porter, M. E. (1980). *Competitive Strategy*. New York: The Free Press.

Pritchard, G. (1982). Tourism promotion: Big business for the states. *HRA Quarterly* 23(2): 48–57.

Richardson, J. and Cohen, J. (1993). State slogans: The case of the missing USP. *Journal of Travel & Tourism Marketing* 2(2/3): 91–109.

Ries, A. (1992). The discipline of the narrow focus. *Journal of Business Strategy* November/December: 3–9.

Ries, A. and Trout, J. (1982). The enormous competitive power of a selling product name. *Marketing Times* 29(5): 28–38.

Ries, A. and Trout, J. (1986). *Positioning: The Battle for Your Mind*. New York: McGraw-Hill.

Ries, A. and Ries, L. (1998). *The 22 Immutable Laws of Branding*. New York: HarperCollins.

Ritchie, J. R. B. and Ritchie, R. J. B. (1998).The branding of tourism destinations: Past achievements and future challenges. In Keller, P. (ed.) *Destination Marketing: Reports of the 48th AIEST Congress, Marrakech*, pp. 89–116.

Ritchie, J. R. B. and Zins, M. (1978). Culture as determinant of the attractiveness of a tourism region. *Annals of Tourism Research* 5(2): 252–267.

Russell, S. (2008). Selling down under. *B & T*. 1 August, p. 13. Hard copy magazine article.

Shanka, T. (2001). Tourist destination slogans as unique selling propositions: The case of African tourism. *Tourism Analysis* 6(1): 53–60.

Supphellen, M. and Nygaardsvik, I. (2002). Testing country brand slogans: Conceptual development and empirical illustration of a simple normative model. *Journal of Brand Management* 9(4/5): 385–395.

Tourism Australia. (2014). *Working with Tourism Australia: Global Marketing Prospectus 2014/2015*. Available at: http://www.tourism.australia.com/documents/Markets/Report_WorkingwithTA_May14.pdf

Travelindustrywire (2015). *Study Shows Web Has Transformed Consumers into More Selective Travel Buyers*. Available at: http://www.travelindustrywire.com/article81708.html

Trout, J. and Ries, A. (1979). Positioning: Ten years later. *Industrial Marketing* 64(7): 32–42.

Trout, J. and Rivkin, S. (1995). *The New Positioning*. New York: McGraw-Hill.

Wahab, S., Crampon, L. J. and Rothfield, L. M. (1976). *Tourism Marketing*. London: Tourism International Press.

Ward, S. V. and Gold, J. R. (1994). *The Use of Publicity and Marketing to Sell Towns and Regions*. Chichester, UK: John Wiley & Sons Ltd.

Wilson, C. E. (1981). A procedure for the analysis of consumer decision making. *Journal of Advertising Research* 21(2): 31–36.

Wilson, D. (1997). Paradoxes of tourism in Goa. *Annals of Tourism Research* 24(1): 52–75.

Wind, Y. and Robinson, P. J. (1972). Product positioning: An application of multidimensional scaling. *Attitude Research in Transition*. American Marketing Association, pp. 155–175.

Woodside, A. G. (1982). Positioning a province using travel research. *Journal of Travel Research* 20(Winter): 2–6.

Woodside, A. G. and Wilson, E. J. (1985). Effects of consumer awareness of brand advertising on preference. *Journal of Advertising Research* 25(4): 41–48.

Destination consumer-marketing communications

AIMS

To enhance understanding of:

- opportunities and challenges for relationship marketing by DMOs;
- the DMO's role in stimulating stakeholder collaboration;
- the need for synergy of marketing communications by DMOs and stakeholders.

ABSTRACT

There is no shortage of ways in which a destination can be promoted, and in every destination community there will be a diverse range of opinions on the tactics that should be employed. Therefore the focus of the chapter is highlighting the key principles guiding the development of marketing communications, rather than prescribing technical aspects such as advertising design. Local tourism operators' views on promotional priorities will vary for a range of reasons including: differing levels of professional experience in marketing and tourism; vested business interests in specific types of products and target markets; access to financial resources; and their position within local industry politics. To provide a structure for stakeholders, the chapter discusses the ways in which the DMO communicates the brand position in the market place, based on the tenets of integrated marketing communications: stimulating profitable customer relationships; enhancing stakeholder relationships and cross-functional processes; stimulating purposeful dialogue with consumers; and message synergy.

Stakeholders' 'advice'

The advertising and promotion program is the most visible activity of a tourism board and is certain to be received with mixed reviews by the community. Criticism is likely, and board members should develop thick skins.

(Gee and Makens, 1985: 29)

Anyone who has worked within a DMO for any length of time will almost certainly have experienced the frustration of being surrounded by many different stakeholders offering conflicting advice. Criticism can emerge at any time and from many quarters, including the media, tourism operators, travel intermediaries, government officials and elected representatives, local residents and even other DMOs. Occasionally, the feedback is made public, such as in the criticism by local government and tourism operators in Edinburgh aimed at VisitBritain for their *ludicrous* non-promotion of the city's famous arts festivals (see Ferguson, 2003). Critics claimed VisitBritain advertising focused on fringe festivals instead of major attractions such as the Edinburgh International Festival and Edinburgh Military Tattoo. However, the NTO argued that given the city is always *booked up* during major events, advertising funds were better directed elsewhere.

IN PRACTICE

12.1 'We really need to sell the destination harder'

In Australia Grimaux (2014: 65) reported a typical example of a wealthy businessman from another industry making an investment in tourism and then criticising the DMO for not selling the destination well enough. Peter Bond, an energy company CEO and one of the state of Queensland's wealthiest people, had purchased Dunk Island Resort (www.dunk-island.com) in the Great Barrier Reef and was quoted criticising the STO and RTO for not featuring the island in promotions of the state, and that Tourism and Events Queensland's campaigns like *The Best Job in the World* had missed the mark:

> I can remember 20 years ago seeing the ads for Dunk Island . . . in the middle of winter you'd be getting on a train and there'd be a picture with a crystal blue sky, with a pool and you'd be thinking: 'Gee, I'd rather be there than here'. And I think that sort of push needs to happen again.

Bond bought the iconic resort in 2011 after it was destroyed by cyclone Yasi. The rebuilding was estimated to cost AUD$20 million, hence Bond having a vested interest in DMO promotions featuring the island. Bond's public criticism of the STO's efforts, without any constructive suggestions, is typical of the type of self-interest flak faced by destination marketers on a regular basis: 'We need to sell (Queensland) a lot harder. We really need to sell Queensland much more than we have'.

So it is absolutely essential that stakeholders understand the rationale for the DMO's marketing communications and how they can participate for mutual benefit. The focus of the chapter, therefore, is highlighting the key principles guiding the development of marketing communications, rather than prescribing technical aspects such as advertising design.

Integrated marketing communications

Clearly, dialogue is required with the business community and host population during marketing planning, and yet the DMO must be careful to avoid the trap of trying to please everyone. The shift in thinking towards destinations as brands, along with the rising influence of user-generated content on social media, requires a management approach that focuses on developing relationships with consumers and stakeholders. A structured approach is IMC, which has emerged relatively recently in the marketing literature. The first IMC texts appeared in the early 1990s (see, for example, Schultz *et al.*, 1993). However, the topic has received little academic research attention to date in the destination marketing field, even though the issue was raised in the 1970s by Wahab *et al.* (1976: 182). IMC has been defined as:

> *[a] process of managing the customer relationships that drive brand value. More specifically, it is a cross-functional process from creating and nourishing profitable relationships with customers and other stakeholders by strategically controlling or influencing all messages sent to these groups and encouraging data-driven, purposeful dialogue with them.*
>
> *(Duncan, 2002)*

Inherent in this description are five fundamental tenets that provide both opportunities and challenges for DMOs:

1. profitable customer relationships;

2. enhancing stakeholder relationships;

3. cross-functional process;

4. stimulating purposeful dialogue with consumers;

5. message synergy.

Relationship marketing

Repeat purchase behaviour was introduced in the marketing literature during the 1940s (Howard and Sheth, 1969). For any given travel situation, consumers are spoilt for choice with available destinations offering similar benefits. As a result, many if not most, places will be substitutable during the decision making process. That is, individuals will switch between destinations they are considering as a result of a better deal, a recommendation from a friend, awareness of a special event or other stimuli. Therefore, successfully gaining the attention of consumers, with a meaningful message, at the time a travel decision is being made, is arguably the greatest challenge faced by DMOs (Pike, 2008). Underpinned by the proposition that communicating with previous visitors will be a more efficient use of resources than traditional advertising, the concept of relationship marketing represents one way forward in meeting this challenge. The rationale for investing in relationship marketing is that it costs five times as much to attract a new consumer than to retain an existing customer. A widely accepted definition of customer relationship management (CRM) is that provided by Gronroos (1990: 5): 'a process of identifying and establishing, maintaining, enhancing, and when necessary terminating relationships with customers and other stakeholders, at a profit, so that the objectives of all parties involved are met'.

It must be acknowledged that one potential inhibiting factor is the human need to explore. The need for novelty seeking therefore might preclude re-visitation, although there has been little research to date.

However, one of the recent tourism megatrends has been the rise of repeat visitation to destinations in many parts of the world, due to the advent of low-cost airlines, the trend towards travellers taking more frequent shorter breaks, the demise of communism and the increasing growth in Asia Pacific intra-regional travel. Increasing levels of repeat visitation to many destinations around the world present DMOs with relationship marketing opportunities. In 2015 Tourism New Zealand's vision is 'to motivate our target market to come now, do more and come back' (see http://traveltrade.newzealand.com/en/about). Almost all (93 per cent) of visitors from New Zealand had previously visited Australia (Tourism Queensland, 2006), while already half (47 per cent) of Chinese visitors to Australia were repeat visitors (Allen, 2015). Strong levels of repeat visitation to the Australian state of Victoria from international markets such as New Zealand (over 90 per cent repeaters), Singapore (60 per cent) and Japan (10 per cent) were reported by Harris *et al.* (2005).

In an early study of repeat visitation, Gitelson and Crompton (1984) found five factors that contributed to a return to a familiar destination:

1. reduced risk of an unsatisfactory experience;

2. knowledge that they would find their own kind of people there;

3. emotional or childhood attachment to experience;

4. opportunities to visit aspects of the destination not previously experienced;

5. to expose others to a previously satisfying experience.

Short breaks

The term *short break* is firmly entrenched in the travel industry vernacular and has regularly been the topic of articles in trade publications and in the popular press. However, in the tourism literature it was as recent as 1990 that Fache (1990: 5) referred to short breaks as a 'new form of recreation'. Short breaks emerged relatively recently as a significant holiday trend in Europe (Euromonitor, 1987; Fache, 1990), Australasia (Pike, 2002a, 2007a), North America (Kotler *et al.*, 1999; Plog, 2000) and the UK (see, for example, Middleton and O'Brien, 1987; Teare *et al.*, 1989; Davies, 1990; Edgar *et al.*, 1994; Edgar, 1997). Domestic weekend-break packages by UK hotels was one of a range of initiatives to counter static domestic and international visitor growth during the late 1970s. By the 1990s commercial short breaks in the UK had evolved from an off-season contribution towards fixed costs, to an all-year growth market (Edgar *et al.*, 1994). In Europe it has been claimed that short breaks were growing at a faster rate than other holiday types Lohmann (1990, 1991) and generated the highest per day spend (Gratton, 1990). Gratton suggested increases in the number of short breaks taken each year had reversed the decline in domestic tourism experienced in many European countries during the 1970s.

Increases in leisure time and disposable income have led to one or more shorter holidays being taken each year, which supplemented the annual holiday (Euromonitor, 1987). Euromonitor also estimated that almost one-third of people took more than one such break per year, and that 40 per cent of all holidays taken were short breaks. More recently, my own research in Australia (Pike, 2006, 2007b, 2010; Pike and Mason, 2011) and in New Zealand (Pike, 2002a; Pike and Ryan, 2004) found participants averaged three to four short break holidays each year, often returning to familiar places. Qualitative comments from participants indicate that the short break is now a psychological necessity to temporarily escape daily pressures.

A short break holiday is a non-business trip of between one and four nights away from home. Despite the clear significance of the short break market, relatively few published market perceptions studies have focused on this travel context. Indeed, only 9 of 262 destination image papers published in the literature between 1973 and 2007 indicated an interest in short break holidays (see Pike, 2002b, 2007c). Case study 12.1 summarises an initiative of a Croatian RTO targeting the short break market to address seasonality problems. As discussed in Chapter 1, the issue of how DMOs address seasonality represents a major gap in the tourism literature (see Spencer and Holecek, 2007; Pike and Page, 2014).

CASE STUDY

12.1 Low-cost airlines as promoters of tourism destinations: The case of Zadar County, Croatia

Professor Nevenka Čavlek, University of Zagreb
Assistant Professor Božena Krce Miočić, University of Zadar

Seasonality is one of the GREATEST challenges in the development of tourist destinations. Zadar County, as one of the most typical family seaside destinations, is known for having a strong tourist season lasting from mid-June to early September. Although Zadar County has 2,530 hours of sunshine and an average annual temperature of 14.9°C, this 3,000-year-old city is poorly visited outside the peak season. The Zadar County Tourist Board recognised that the introduction of better air connections with outbound markets would be one of the opportunities for a reduction in seasonality. The goal was to extend the season from early May and increase the number of visitors from the UK and Scandinavian markets. The tourist board decided to make the airport, which is located 7 km from the centre of Zadar, the base for the low-cost airlines/carriers (LCC). The LCCs recognised that the implementation of ICT technologies in their business would not only serve as a new sales channel but also as a powerful marketing tool. This would be advantageous in reaching the target population through promotional activities and achieving a higher response level. Eventually, they could optimise their capacity. The destination recognised the potential for implementing the phrase *value for time* in their business through the use of fast and inexpensive transportation, which improved accessibility to the destination for more remote outbound Croatian markets. At the same time, plans were devised to harness the power of new technology, which had already been developed by the LCCs to achieve competitive advantage. While implementing this strategy, the destination was faced with numerous challenges. First of all, it was necessary to change the domestic perception of tourism development based along the road to the airport. This perception was founded on the fact that Zadar County is the closest coastal destination to the highway that connects the Croatian coast with central Europe, its primary outbound market. In order to achieve these objectives, the destination had to answer the following important questions:

- How is it going to cover the required promotion costs owed to the LCC?
- Who are the visitors that use this kind of transport (guest profile)?
- Is the destination ready for this kind of visitor and how is it going to adapt?

Zadar County decided to cover the relatively high cost of its promotion on the LCC's website (€1.14 million in 2014), which was the prerequisite for signing the contract. The funds were collected from the joint advertising of the national tourist board and from contributions from local government units and the whole tourism industry, based on the number of nights spent in each tourist destination. Zadar County decided to sign a contract with Ryanair, the biggest European airline company with 86.3 million passengers in 2014, according to the IATA statistics. Given that this airline company is exclusively e-business orientated, their website records several million visits per month and it therefore covers a much bigger potential tourism market than any other media. In the process of booking an airline ticket, each user was exposed to the promotion of Zadar County as a tourist destination. The data from the ITB reports show that online bookings continued to grow in 2014, reaching 66 per cent of all tourist reservations worldwide. This very fact reflects the basic advantage of promoting a destination in such a way. The airport at Zadar recorded an increase in the number of air passengers from 68,658 in 2006 to 472,572 in 2014, of which over 60 per cent were Ryanair passengers.

Ongoing research into the LCC passenger profile has been conducted in the locality for several years. Initially, these passengers mostly received information about Zadar from the internet (63 per cent) and the LCC website. This in many ways justified the initial decision to invest in this type of promotion. In 2014 only 15 per cent of passengers found out about Zadar on the internet, while the largest part of them heard about it from their friends and relatives. It was this change that brought into question the need for further investment in such promotions. But it is necessary to emphasise that, unlike the average tourists who have loyally visited Zadar more than three times, about two-thirds of the LCC passengers have visited it only once. At the same time, over the course of five years, a change within the demographic profile of visitors has occurred. Nowadays, they are mainly older and arrive with their families, which has affected the choice of accommodation, with a growing preference for hotel accommodation.

Since the users of LCC services are showing a trend towards shorter stays during the year, this model provides additional benefits for business people in the city of Zadar and its surroundings. The reduced price and time of transport leaves more money for visitors, which has resulted in an above-average tourist spend in the destination. The tourists who use LCCs, as well as other tourists, claim that their primary motives for visiting are sun and sea, but the trends show that these motives are in decline. Significantly, they are choosing new experiences and favourable offers more often as their primary motives. As secondary motives they point to gastronomy and wine offers, together with trips to beauty spots. Actually, the wine and olive oil tours, as well as visits to rural households, are the most requested, but they are not sufficiently promoted as tourist products.

At the same time, other changes in the structure and location of accommodation have occurred in Zadar, the focal point of attraction in the destination. Before the arrival of LCC tourists, the largest share of accommodation in Zadar used to be located in hotel resorts and households close to the beaches. The increase in the number of tourists using the LCC has resulted in displacing accommodation towards the historical city centre, dominated by high quality hotels and private apartments. The level of satisfaction of the tourists who use this kind of accommodation is best reflected in their above-average assessments from 4.2 to 5.0. The largest proportion of visitors (81 per cent) would recommend Zadar as a destination to their friends and relatives. However, at the same time, only a relatively small number of visitors say that they would like to come again, which speaks volumes about the lack of additional facilities that would motivate them to come again. The facilities should be extended to include the organisation of entertainment and cultural events, which are the main reason for arrivals in low season. Only then should a reduction in accommodation prices in the destination follow.

Further reading

Bieger, T. and Wittmer, A. (2006).
Francis, G. *et al.* (2006).

Krce Miočić, B. *et al.* (2012).

Rey, B. *et al.* (2011).

IATA World Air Transport Statistics (WATS), 58th Edition.

ITB World Travel Trends Report 2014/2015.

UNWTO Tourism Highlights, Edition 2013. Available at: http://www.e-unwto.org/doi/pdf/10.18111/9789284415427

Discussion question

What key market opportunity has the destination's strategy of partnering with low-cost air carriers provided?

Visiting friends and relatives (VFR)

Travel to visit friends and relatives generates repeat visitors to a destination (see Gitelson and Crompton, 1984) and represents a significant component of travel patterns. With strong bonds to a destination's residents, the VFR market is generally more resilient than other segments (Godfrey and Clarke, 2000). Chon and Singh (1995) cited research by the US Travel Data Center, which estimated almost half of leisure travel in the USA involved VFR. Clearly this presents opportunities for DMOs. For example, Stephenville in Newfoundland effectively developed a visitor market out of VFR links from marriages between US military personnel and local women (Butler and Baum, 1999). Over 25,000 servicemen served in Newfoundland from the 1940s to the 1960s. VFR tourism also offers opportunities for regions that have been characterised by high migration levels. These range from small rural areas that have experienced urban drift to countries such as Ireland, New Zealand and Samoa, which have disproportionately large percentages of expatriates living abroad. The latter in particular enjoys seasonal influxes of visiting expatriates from the USA, Australia and New Zealand, whose regular trips provide valuable cash injections to the fragile economy.

The VFR market also presents a number of challenges for DMOs, not least of which is that it is not viewed positively by all in the tourism industry, particularly accommodation operators, and DMOs must take due care to investigate its feasibility. Critics argue that the market often ties up valuable aircraft capacity, particularly at peak holiday periods, but at the same time makes relatively little use of accommodation and tourist attractions. For the first text to be published about VFR travel research see Backer and King (2015).

IN PRACTICE

12.2 Invite the world

Invite the world was implemented by Tourism Vancouver in 2002 to urge residents to invite friends and relatives from around the world to visit the destination. The CVB encouraged residents to send an e-postcard from tourismvancouver.com to contacts outside Vancouver and British Columbia. In doing so, the resident was automatically entered into a weekly prize draw. The campaign ran from March to November 2002 at a cost of over CAD$400,000, three-quarters of which was generated from sponsors. Key results included:

- 14,098 e-postcards sent from tourismvancouver.com compared to 4,122 sent over the same time period in 2001, an increase of 242 per cent.
- 1,539,573 unique visits to tourismvancouver.com compared to 976,390 over the same time period in 2001, an increase of 58 per cent.
- 7,966 qualified names collected by permission data capture for future e-marketing efforts.

DMO challenges in relationship marketing

DMOs have faced a unique set of challenges and impediments relative to marketers of other products and services, not least of which is the difficulty in obtaining quality customer data from service providers over which they have no direct control. Since the DMO rarely comes into contact with actual visitors, except through their visitor information offices, how are they to obtain contact details to be able to keep in touch? Therefore, the development of a database by DMOs has been rare (see Truman, 2006). Even with access to contact details, another challenging question has been how is it possible for the DMO to engage with so many visitors with meaningful messages? So the traditional DMO paradigm has been one of not being able to develop relationships with consumers or previous visitors.

Woodside and Sakai's (2001: 378) meta-analysis of government tourism marketing strategies concluded the dominant paradigm in use was transactional and not relational. Marketing activities were designed to attract new visitors, which might not necessarily be appropriate for potential repeat visitors: 'No efforts or budget is planned for development of an ongoing relationship . . . database marketing is rarely being practised'. Periodic destination marketing newsletter *Eclipse* devoted a 2003 special issue to relationship marketing by destinations, where it was estimated at that time that only one NTO employed a specialist relationship marketer (Pike, 2004). During 2006 there were strong calls from the government opposition in Bermuda for that country's NTO to move away from traditional advertising campaigns and invest more in CRM: 'We don't need to reach out to 90 million people on the eastern seaboard of the US, we need to get to them one by one'.

In highlighting the limited degree of destination relationship marketing in practice, Fyall *et al.* (2003) reported two case studies. The first, Project Stockholm, was an example of an introductory attempt to engender more loyalty towards a destination, albeit without loyalty-building tools. The project was a cooperative initiative by the Stockholm RTO, Scandic Hotels and SAS airlines, specifically targeting European weekend tourists. A benefit card was designed for the project, offering added value in the form of free local transport and discounts at shops and restaurants. The second was the Club Program developed to reward repeat visits to Barbados. The programme boasted 1,700 members who had visited the island at least 25 times. Rewards included luncheons hosted by the Barbados Tourism Authority and unofficial ambassador status. One of the key problems highlighted for DMOs was the expense of retaining single visitors in comparison to the predominant transactional marketing activities (Fyall *et al.*, 2003: 654): 'What thus appears sound in theory and operational in practice, particularly as a weapon to achieve sustainable competitive advantage in the market place, is likely to remain in its implementation infancy for destinations for some time'.

Pike (2007a) reported an exploratory investigation into the extent to which RTOs in Queensland, Australia, were encouraging repeat visitors from the state capital of Brisbane, which was the largest source of visitors for each of the destinations. The research highlighted some of the issues hindering relationship marketing development by the RTOs. A mixture of personal, paired and group interviews were conducted with 17 management staff at 11 RTOs. The key findings were:

- an inability of any of the RTOs to track repeat visitation;

- almost no targeting of repeat visitation through communication with previous visitors;

- the assumption that the local accommodation businesses might be engaging in relationship marketing with their previous guests;

- while there was a general recognition of the potential for relationship marketing, none of the RTOs had been able to develop a formal approach to stay in touch with previous visitors;

- a general acknowledgement of the need for a destination-level relationship marketing system in the future.

As summarised in the research snapshot below, a follow-up investigation by Murdy and Pike (2012) in relation to these opportunities and challenges with a small sample of DMOs around the world found a general lack of strategic intent to engage in relationship marketing.

RESEARCH SNAPSHOT

12.1 DMO perceptions of relationship marketing

In a 2008 survey of 65 DMOs around the world, importance–performance analysis was used to analyse perceptions of relationship marketing held by DMOs. Participants were first asked to indicate the *importance* of a battery of 23 relationship marketing attributes and then to rate their own organisation's *performance* across the same list of attributes, using a Likert-type scale. Since there had been a lack of research published about relationship marketing activities of DMOs (Fyall *et al.*, 2003), the questionnaire items were developed from a review of the wider CRM literature. The survey was emailed to a database of 1,435 DMOs in the USA, Canada, UK, Australia and New Zealand, and the 5.3 per cent response rate highlights a problem that has also been encountered by other researchers trying to survey perceptions of destination marketers (see Blain *et al.*, 2005; Park and Petrick, 2006). Feedback from follow-up emails led to the impression that the low response rate might have been indicative of a general lack of relationship marketing orientation by most DMOs at that time. For example, one non-participant suggested the survey would be relevant only to visitor centres. Another advised they did not have the mandate or the funding for relationship marketing and deemed it the responsibility of the tourism operators. Of the DMOs, 15 had a full-time relationship marketing specialist, 2 had a part-time specialist, while 48 had none. For each of the 23 items the mean importance score was higher than that for DMO performance, indicating acknowledgement of the need to be more proactive in engagement with previous visitors. The DMO activities rated most important were related to:

- staff being willing to help visitors in a responsive manner;
- responding to visitor requests promptly;
- understanding the needs of key visitors;
- treating all key visitors with great care;
- having clear goals for visitor acquisition and retention, with support from senior management.

Source

Murdy, S. and Pike, S. (2012).

Digital relationship marketing opportunities

For the first time in history, Web 2.0 presents unprecedented and almost unlimited prospects for DMOs to overcome major barriers to RM, through increased opportunities to directly engage with internet users. For marketers, social media not only offers the benefits of lower costs and higher levels of efficiency than traditional media (Kaplan and Haenlein, 2010) but also increased opportunities to develop a long-term relationship with consumer-travellers. The Web 2.0 era will result in a paradigm shift in destination marketing, as inferred in this assessment by the Queensland Tourism Industry Council in 2015:

> *New technologies have started to considerably disrupt the traditional business model and the economy, particularly in the tourism industry. This is creating challenges and putting increased pressure on business to raise competitiveness and be responsive to new innovations in a rapidly changing business environment.*

Cobos *et al.* (2009) assessed the web-based activities of 260 CVBs in the USA from a relationship marketing perspective, which, from a review of the literature, they promoted as a hierarchy of four stages:

1. timely and accurate *information* provision;

2. effective and constant *communication* with consumers;

3. reliable and seamless electronic *transactions*;

4. effective and lasting relationship-building mechanisms that enhance *assurance*.

Their survey instrument contained multiple items to analyse the level of activity of CVBs at each stage. Results clearly indicated most CVBs were at the level of information provision. Few of these DMOs had evolved into providing functions related to communication, transactions or assurances. The key factors inhibiting high-level web activities were small organisation size and lack of financial resources and managerial technology expertise. Cobos *et al.* suggested that since these issues were likely to continue to make relationship marketing a major challenge, a practical step might be to work collaboratively with other nearby CVBs.

Enhancing stakeholder relationships/cross-functional process

Most CVBs in the USA have membership programmes, even with government room tax funding. Many DMOs are reliant on member subscriptions for funding, which can be a double-edged sword. On the one hand more members generate increased funding, while on the other they generate more responsibility in providing benefits. CVBs do not usually want members unless they are able to help them to secure business. So membership should make sense, and Walters (2005) provided an insightful guide to membership development, retention and dismissal. The major benefits of CVB membership promoted by Walters (2005: 169–170) are summarised in Table 12.1.

Multiplicity of stakeholders

> *The tourism industry (in New Zealand) is so fragmented, diverse, unfocused, self seeking and disorganised that Ph.D. theses have been written on its structural complexities. It's got more separate working parts than a 747's Rolls Royce engine and only some of them are vaguely headed in the same direction.*
>
> *(Chamberlain, 1992)*

Table 12.1 Potential benefits deliverable to CVB members

1. Member events (mixers, annual dinner, marketing updates)
2. Convention and meeting planner sales leads
3. Group tour or motor coach sales leads
4. Convention service sales leads (after a meeting is booked, the planner may be looking for caterers, audio-visual services, speakers, etc.)
5. Listings in publications and on a bureau's website
6. Ability to place brochures in a visitor centre
7. Referrals from a visitor centre
8. Discounts on health insurance, shipping or long-distance calling
9. Ability to advertise in the CVB's publications or on its website
10. Ability to participate in bureau-sponsored coop ads
11. Ability to participate in bureau-led sales missions or trade shows
12. Chance to host news media and travel writers
13. Ability to participate in bureau familiarisation show and events
14. Chance to expose one's business to other bureau members
15. Membership plaque of window decal showing membership status
16. Bureau publications in quantity, usually at no charge
17. Complimentary links from a bureau's website
18. Subscription to the bureau's newsletter and other insider information
19. Benefit from the bureau's lobbying efforts or access to elected officials
20. Access to and ability to influence the bureau's marketing plan

Source: Adapted from Walters (2005).

While Chamberlain's (1992) observation was made in the context of the New Zealand tourism industry, there will be few if any countries where a multiplicity of divergent tourism interests and, therefore, potential for fragmentation to occur, does not exist. For example, at the RTO level, the Kansas City CVB boasted over 2,000 member businesses in 2015 (www.visitkc.com/about-visit-kc), the Philadelphia CVB serves more than 1,300 member businesses (see Walters, 2005), while Tourism Vancouver has over 1,000 members (see Vallee, 2005). At the state level, Pennsylvania has more RTOs than any other in the USA, with 59 agencies in 67 counties (Goeldner *et al.*, 2000), while in the Australian state of Queensland there are an estimated 55,000 tourism businesses (QTIC, 2015). At an NTO level, it has been suggested that there are around 800 DMOs in Austria (Fuchs *et al.*, 2010).

The key tenet of this theme is that a DMO usually has no direct control over the products they represent, nor the packaged offerings of intermediaries such as airlines, tour wholesalers and travel agencies. From the supply perspective, the often eclectic collection of destination features must somehow be presented to the market in a way that not only cuts through the clutter of crowded markets to offer benefits desired by travellers but also satisfies the interests of the host community, local businesses and travel intermediaries. DMO and stakeholder opinions on how this can be achieved are rarely congruent. It is not being cynical to suggest the natural self-interest of many businesses will instinctively be to expect their market of interest to be the target of promotions, which in turn feature their product. The politics of DMO decision making can, and does, inhibit implementation of marketing theory. As indicated in the Preface, implementation is often *easier said than done*. In this respect, destination marketing requires a certain amount of courage, for while it can be richly rewarding it can also feel like life in a goldfish bowl where every move seems to be watched and judged by a multitude of masters, such as those who contribute to funding (e.g. taxpayers), those inconvenienced by congestion (e.g. retirees) and those seeking to profit from increased visitor levels.

Destination collaboration

Even though destination promotion from its very beginning has been collaborative in practice, this is a relatively emergent stream of research (Pike and Page, 2014), much of it based on stakeholder theory (see Freeman, 1984). Research to date has included: modelling collaborative marketing (Palmer and Bejou, 1995; Beldona *et al.*, 2003; Wang and Xiang, 2012), benefits of collaboration (Naipaul *et al.*, 2009; Wang *et al.*, 2013), social inclusion (d'Angella and Go, 2009), intergovernmental collaboration (Wong *et al.*, 2010), stakeholder influence (Park *et al.*, 2008; Wang and Krakover, 2008; Cooper *et al.*, 2009), stakeholder interdependencies (Sheehan *et al.*, 2007) and collaborative innovation (Zach, 2012).

Destinations are an eclectic and diverse mix of businesses and individuals, who might or might not have a vested interest in the success of their destination. Research has indicated that not all stakeholders are necessarily interested in the prosperity of their destination, when their principal motive for operating a business is lifestyle (see Thomas *et al.*, 2011). Regardless, the success of tourism businesses will depend to some extent on the competitiveness of their destination (Pike, 2004). So, given the main driver of marketing leadership of a destination is the DMO, a critical understanding of the factors and circumstances that may constrain or facilitate the effective execution of their destination marketing function is necessary (Pike and Page, 2014). Interdependency of stakeholders is such that the network of tourism businesses could not operate successfully without the DMO, and the DMO could not be competitive without a strong network. In this regard, a DMO is essentially a *network management organisation* (see Wang, 2008). Tourism destination collaboration has been defined as 'formal institutionalized relationships among existing networks of institutions, interests and/or individual stakeholders' (d'Angella and Go, 2009). 'Formal' indicates the need for network participation to be guided by clear boundaries within which to act. In this regard they pointed to five basic challenges faced by any network coordinator, which are applicable to DMOs (see Prahalad and Ramaswamy, 2004: 229):

1. the complexity of network relationships;

2. managing multiple modes of collaboration;

3. coping with rapid change in a competitive environment;

4. the need for centralisation;

5. the need to find a balance between flexibility and accountability.

Zehrer *et al.*'s (2013: 63) literature review found the following tourism network success factors:

- established trust culture among the actors involved and a shared collective representative identity;

- active participation and intern-organisational learning, along with mutual assistance and a willingness by actors to provide input without the expectation of a tangible return;

- variety of competences and resources;

- resource and competence bundling;

- engagement and commitment to common goals;

- a commitment to implementing long-term interests of actors in an efficient and sustainable manner.

Their survey of stakeholders in tourism networks at five destinations in Austria found the most important characteristics to be: (1) mutual trust among the actors involved; and (2) mutual assistance. D'Angella and Go's (2009) case studies of Barcelona and Vienna identified the significant role of *social inclusion* in coordinating networks.

Cooperating to compete

Competition within a destination is positive when it leads to innovation, quality and efficiency (Porter, 1991). The *one-industry* concept recognises that while businesses pursue individual goals, the success of the tourism industry relies on effective interrelationships between stakeholders to produce traveller satisfaction (Collier, 1997). The assumption is that the traveller's perspective of a holiday, while made up of a composite of service encounters, is judged as a total experience (Medlik and Middleton, 1973). At a destination level the implication is that poor service provision by one or more sections of the community, which may or may not be directly involved in the tourism industry, may ultimately impact on the success of other suppliers. Clearly, developing a cooperative approach towards quality assurance, as well as stimulating a *cooperating to compete* marketing philosophy, requires a champion with a holistic perspective. This is a challenge, since while there may be good vertical integration in the travel industry, there has been a general lack of horizontal coordination (Lickorish, 1991). Individual businesses tend to consider the costs first, rather than the benefits of collaboration.

The responsibilities of destination brand management should not rest solely with the DMO. One of the greatest marketing challenges faced by DMOs, certainly in the implementation of IMC, is stimulating a coordinated approach among all those stakeholders who have a vested interest in, and will come into contact with, the target visitors. Ideally, what is required is an understanding by all stakeholders of what the brand identity is, what the brand image is and what the brand positioning strategy is. The more stakeholders have an understanding of the rationale behind the brand strategy, the more effectively they will be able to integrate their own marketing and customer interactions. Clearly, it is too much to expect all stakeholders to do so and yet, in theory, the approach represents a powerful opportunity to enhance the destination brand.

There are essentially four main reasons for DMOs coordinating a *cooperate to compete* approach among tourism operators. The first has been driven out of necessity to stretch the promotional budget. DMOs and tourism operators have recognised the value in pooling limited financial resources to create a bigger bang in the market place, crowded with global corporate brands with far greater budgets promoting substitute products. The second major driver in developing a cooperative destination marketing approach has been a greater awareness that the traveller's experience of a destination can be marred by one bad service encounter. So, it makes little long-term sense for a small group of large visitor attractions to work on marketing and quality issues independently, if the mass of remaining small businesses become the weak link in the visitor's destination experience by failing to deliver. Third, it has only been relatively recently that the concept of brand synergy has become the third key rationale for a destination's cooperative marketing approach. Fourth, the mass of user-generated content on social media swamps the marketing communications of DMOs, which are now facing a future of declining influence over the destination brand image unless there is meaningful collaborative engagement between the DMO, stakeholders and consumers.

> **IN PRACTICE**
>
> ### 12.3 Working with Tourism Australia
>
> *Working with Tourism Australia* is a succinct annual online marketing prospectus designed to support the country's estimated 280,000 tourism businesses with information, advice and contacts for international marketing activities. The prospectus provides a brief overview of the NTO's strategic goals, key markets and major promotional campaigns, along with clear details about how individual businesses can participate. To enable businesses to stay updated on trade marketing opportunities, the prospectus also advises readers to subscribe to the weekly newsletter *Essentials*, follow the NTO on Twitter and LinkedIn and attend the regular industry briefings held around the country.
>
> ### Source
>
> Tourism Australia. (2014).

Stimulating purposeful dialogue with consumers

That the 2007 *Journal of Travel Research* special issue on destination promotion (46(1)) attracted 75 submitted manuscripts (see Fesenmaier, 2007) is an indication of the growing interest in the topic. Anholt (2002) likened marketing to chatting someone up in a crowded bar:

> *In effect, you walk up to somebody you have never met, and have a few seconds in which to convince them you are worth getting to know better, and to win the chance of a longer conversation. Often a joke will do the trick, but if the bar is in Finland or Iraq (unlikely), where making strangers laugh is both difficult and unwelcome, a different opening gambit might be preferable. Either way, there are few countries and few people who will fall in love with a stranger who kicks off the conversation with a long list of his natural advantages, impressive family tree and key historical achievement.*
>
> *(Anholt, 2002: 53)*

All marketing communications should be about purposeful dialogue with the target market. Marketing communications is the marketing element over which the DMO is able to exert the most control and is therefore the focus of DMO activities. The purpose of marketing communications should be to enhance the brand identity, with the communication objective being to inform, persuade or remind consumers about the destination. DMOs use promotion to either pull consumers to the destination or push them through travel intermediaries. In the competitive markets in which DMOs operate, innovative promotional ideas can very quickly be adopted by rival destinations, and so there tends to be a commonality of DMO activity. Until DMOs are able to develop the means to communicate meaningfully with consumers on an individual basis, the emphasis must be on consistent communication of the value proposition representing the brand identity.

Image formation agents

Gartner (1993) proposed a typology of image formation agents, with practical implications that continue to apply in the Web 2.0 era. These ranged in a continuum from overt induced advertising through to organic sources such as visitation, as shown in Table 12.2. Marketers could use such agents

Table 12.2 Image change agents

Image change agent	Examples
Overt induced 1	Traditional advertising
Overt induced 2	Information received from tour operators
Covert induced 1	Second-party endorsement through traditional advertising
Covert induced 2	Second-party endorsement through seemingly unbiased reports, such as newspaper articles
Autonomous	News and popular culture
Unsolicited organic	Unsolicited information received from friends
Solicited organic	Solicited information from friends
Organic	Actual visitation

Source: Adapted from Gartner (1993).

independently, or in some combination, depending on the marketing objectives. Due to increasing use of public relations, organic and induced images may not necessarily be mutually exclusive (Selby and Morgan, 1996), since broadcast news and social media are far more voluminous than advertising and have higher credibility.

Message synergy

The purpose of all DMO marketing communications is to reinforce the brand identity across different mediums. The UNWTO (1999) estimated the breakdown of promotional budgets for NTOs was: advertising (47.1 per cent), public relations (11.5 per cent), promotional activities (28.9 per cent), public information (3.7 per cent), research (3.5 per cent) and 'other' (5.2 per cent). More recently, a survey of 10 NTOs by Dore and Crouch (2003) also found consumer advertising (35 per cent) represented the largest item in the promotional budget. This was followed by personal selling to the trade (23 per cent), publicity and public relations (17 per cent), trade advertising (12 per cent), direct marketing (7 per cent), sales promotion partnerships (5 per cent) and personal selling to consumers (1 per cent). IMC does not use any different marketing communication tools. Ideally, the five key promotional tools of advertising, public relations, direct marketing, sales promotions and personal selling should be integrated to provide a consistency of message.

Travel trade promotions

The DMO acts as an information broker in the tourism distribution system, liaising between their destination service providers and travel intermediaries. Interactions occur at a range of travel trade events and educational initiatives, which are discussed in Chapter 14.

Public relations and publicity

Tourism has been relatively slow to adopt public relations, and there still remains a lack of published research in relation to the development of public relations. It is important to recognise public relations more than the attempt to gain free media publicity. This is the topic of Chapter 13.

Consumer advertising

Advertising is paid, non-personal promotion of ideas or products by an identifiable sponsor (Kotler *et al.*, 1999). The role of advertising is to stimulate the desired images of the brand in the mind of the consumer in such a way that leads to action. There are four generally accepted stages in the design and implementation of any advertising campaign:

1. setting the objectives, which include those relating to sales targets and communication purpose;
2. budget allocation decisions, for which methods include the affordable approach, percentage of sales, competitive parity and objective and task;
3. message decisions, including both the content of the messages and the type of medium;
4. campaign evaluation, including the communication impact and resultant sales.

Of these, it is arguably the message decisions that are most problematic for DMOs. Ward and Gold (1994) suggested that up to that time many destination advertising efforts lacked professionalism. In particular they pointed to a tendency towards wordiness in advertisements, which is better suited to direct mail communications, as well as a lack of identification of a USP. These criticisms reflect one of the themes of this text, which is the difficulty in promoting multi-attributed places to dynamic and heterogeneous markets, with a succinct and focused value proposition. Morgan (2000) cited this comment from an interview with the editor of *Advertising Age*:

> *When you look at the ads . . . you can see transcripts of the arguments at the tourist boards . . . the membership of which all wanted their own interests served . . . you can see the destruction of the advertising message as a result of the politics.*
>
> *(Morgan, 2000: 345)*

IN PRACTICE

12.4 The Super Bowl

In 2015 Ecuador made history by becoming the first overseas country to place a tourism commercial during the US Super Bowl, at a cost of US$3.8 million. The advertising was part of a concerted effort by the nation to enhance competitiveness, which involved billions being spent on improving travel infrastructure. The USA is Ecuador's second largest tourism market after Colombia, and the NTO was aiming to double visitors from there by 2025. It was estimated that a 1 per cent increase in US visitors would pay for the Super Bowl commercial.

Source

http://skift.com/2015/01/26

Brochures

There has been little published about the role and influence of destination brochures, particularly in the digital era. Since the establishment of the first DMOs, brochures have been a common form of destination advertising. Jeffries (2001: 72) suggested this may have been as much to do with providing tangible evidence to the local tourism industry of *fair* exposure: 'It may be the projection of a political and administrative entity and only coincidentally meaningful from the consumers' point of view, offering too much information in some respects and not enough in others'.

A survey by Wicks and Shuett (1991) of tourism brochure producers in the USA, which included CVBs, found the majority reported the sales aid was produced without any specific target market in mind. Likewise, Alford (1998) cited research commissioned by the English Tourist Board, which found consumers were most likely to be influenced by the type of holiday or activity, whereas RTBs were promoting regions or towns. RTBs generally still produced the regional brochure as if trying to be all things to all people.

A key decision in the design of a destination brochure is its purpose, of which there are two main categories. The first role is to attract visitors to the destination. The design focus is on developing the image of the destination, and the brochure usually has the style and quality of a magazine, often with no advertising content. Distribution is external to the destination since they are expensive to produce and will often be the primary sales aids used to service travel exhibitions and direct consumer enquiries. The second role is a *visitors' guide* designed as a directory of facilities and attractions to aid trip planning. This provides an opportunity for local advertisers to pick up a share of business from travellers at the destination. Distribution may take place both externally, such as in ticket wallets, and locally through the VIC and accommodation outlets. Often for smaller RTOs the purpose will be to achieve both functions with one brochure due to a lack of funds and reliance on advertising revenue.

Destination visitor guides that are reliant on advertising are often controlled by private sector interests, saving the RTO time and money. However, in other cases ownership by the RTO can raise valuable promotional funds, which can be used in additional marketing communications, featuring the brochure as an incentive for advertisers. For example, we used this approach for over 20 years at Tourism Rotorua to raise over NZ$100,000 annually to fund a television advertising campaign. The visitors' guide then became the official destination brochure, used to service campaign responses, which made it easier for local operators to prioritise the multitude of advertising opportunities presented to them. The initiative also enabled the RTO to demonstrate to council funders the direct financial contribution of the private sector towards destination marketing.

Davidson and Rogers (2006: 119) cited the innovative practice of the Glasgow City Marketing Bureau (www.seaglasgow.com), which was printing visitor guides on a daily basis, with a printed *best before* date: 'The premise for doing so is that DMOs own nothing but information: if they provide out of date information via their brochures, this compromises their services'. Online downloadable brochures have been introduced by many DMOs since the mid-2000s.

CHAPTER SUMMARY

Key point 1: Opportunities and challenges for relationship marketing

The shift in thinking towards destinations as brands, along with the rising influence of user-generated content on social media, requires a management approach that focuses on developing relationships with customers. This is underpinned by the realisation that it is a far more efficient use of resources to stay in contact with current customers than it is to attract new ones. This is particularly opportunistic with the potential for increased repeat visitation through short breaks. However, since DMOs rarely come into direct contact with visitors to their destination, they have to date lacked visitor data and contact details with which to make meaningful contact.

Key point 2: The DMO's role in stimulating stakeholder collaboration

Destinations are a mix of a diverse and eclectic range of businesses and individuals, who may or may not have a vested interest in the success of their destination. However, the success of tourism businesses will depend to some extent on the competitiveness of their destination. Interdependency of stakeholders is such that the network of tourism businesses could not operate successfully without the DMO, and the DMO would rarely be competitive without a strong, collaborative network of stakeholders.

Key point 3: The need for message synergy

The purpose of all DMO marketing communications is to reinforce the brand identity. To do so effectively requires consistency of message across all mediums, by as many stakeholders as possible. It is particularly advantageous for all stakeholders to support the brand identity theme in their own marketing communications. The crowded nature of marketing by competing places and substitute products necessitates message synergy in order to be noticed more effectively by busy consumers.

REVIEW QUESTIONS

1. Summarise the concept of IMC and the rationale for its adoption. What are the key challenges faced by DMOs in implementing IMC?

2. What are the potential benefits for your DMO to engage in relationship marketing? What practical steps could your RTO undertake to engage in visitor relationship marketing?

3. What is meant by synergy of marketing communication messages, and why is this so important?

REFERENCES

Alford, P. (1998). Positioning the destination product: Can regional tourist boards learn from private sector practice? *Journal of Travel & Tourism Marketing* 7(2): 53–68.

Allen, L. (2015). Islands pin hopes on China tourism. *The Australian* 11–12 April, p. 25. Hard copy newspaper article.

Anholt, S. (2002). Nation brands: The value of 'provenance' in branding. In Morgan, N., Pritchard, A. and Pride, R. (eds) *Destination Branding*. Oxford: Butterworth-Heinemann, pp. 42–56.

Backer, E. and King, B. (2015). *VFR Travel Research: International Perspectives*. Clevedon, UK: Channel View Publications.

Beldona, S., Morrison, A. M. and Anderson, D. J. (2003). Information exchange between Convention and Visitor Bureaus and hotels in destination marketing: A proposed model. *Journal of Convention & Exhibition Management* 5(1): 41–56.

Bieger, T. and Wittmer, A. (2006). Air transport and tourism: Perspectives and challenges for destinations, airlines and governments. *Journal of Air Transport Management* 12(1): 40–46.

Blain, C., Levy, S. E. and Ritchie, J. R. B. (2005). Destination branding: Insights and practices from destination management organizations. *Journal of Travel Research* 43(May): 328–338.

Butler, R. W. and Baum, T. (1999). The tourism potential of the peace dividend. *Journal of Travel Research* 38(1): 24–29.

Chamberlain, J. (1992). On the tourism trail: A nice little earner, but what about the cost? *North & South* September: 88–97.

Chon, K. S. and Singh, A. (1995). Marketing resorts to 2000: Review of trends in the USA. *Tourism Management* 16(6): 463–469.

Cobos, L., Wang, Y. C. and Okumus, F. (2009). Assessing the web-based destination marketing activities: A relationship marketing perspective. *Journal of Hospitality Marketing and Management* 18(4): 421–444.

Collier, A. (1997). *Principles of Tourism: A New Zealand Perspective* (4th edition). Auckland, NZ: Addison Wesley Longman.

Cooper, C., Scott, N. and Baggio, R. (2009). Network position and perceptions of destination stakeholder importance. *Anatolia* 20(1): 33–45.

D'Angella, F. and Go, F. M. (2009). Tale of two cities' collaborative marketing: Towards a theory of destination stakeholder assessment. *Tourism Management* 30(3): 429–440.

Davidson, R. and Rogers, T. (2006). *Marketing Destinations & Venues for Conferences, Conventions and Business Events*. Oxford: Elsevier.

Davies, B. (1990). The economics of short breaks. *International Journal of Hospitality Management* 9(2): 103–109.

Dore, L. and Crouch, G. I. (2003). Promoting destinations: An exploratory study of publicity programmes used by national tourism organizations. *Journal of Vacation Marketing* 9(2): 137–151.

Duncan, T. (2002). *IMC: Using Advertising and Promotion to Build Brands*. New York: McGraw-Hill.

Edgar, D. A. (1997). Capacity management in the short break market. *International Journal of Contemporary Hospitality Management* 9(2): 55–59.

Edgar, D. A., Litteljohn, D. L., Allardyce, M. L. and Wanhill, S. (1994). Commercial short break holiday breaks: The relationship between market structure, competitive advantage and performance. In Seaton, A. V. (ed.) *Tourism: The State of the Art*. Chichester, UK: John Wiley & Sons Ltd.

Euromonitor. (1987). *Weekend Breaks and Day Trips: The UK Market for Short Break Holidays and Day Trips*. London: Euromonitor.

Fache, W. (1990). (ed.) *Shortbreak Holidays*. Rotterdam, The Netherlands: Center Parcs.

Ferguson, B. (2003). Tourism chiefs under fire for festivals snub. *Evening News*. Edinburgh. 15 August. Hard copy newspaper article.

Fesenmaier, D. (2007). Introduction: Challenging destination promotion. *Journal of Travel Research* 46(1): 3–4.

Francis, G., Humphreys, I., Ison, S. and Aicken, M. (2006). Where next for low-cost airlines? A spatial and temporal comparative study. *Journal of Transport Geography* 14(2): 83–94.

Freeman, R. E. (1984). *Strategic Management: A Stakeholder Approach*. Boston, MA: Pitman.

Fuchs, M., Hopken, W., Foger, A. and Kunz, M. (2010). E-business readiness, intensity, and impact: An Austrian destination management organization study. *Journal of Travel Research* 49(2): 165–178.

Fyall, A., Callod, C. and Edwards, B. (2003). Relationship marketing: The challenge for destinations. *Annals of Tourism Research* 30(3): 644–659.

Gartner, W. C. (1993). Image information process. *Journal of Travel & Tourism Marketing* 2(2/3): 191–215.

Gee, C. Y. and Makens, J. C. (1985). The tourism board: Doing it right. *The Cornell Quarterly* 26(3): 25–33.

Gitelson, R. J. and Crompton, J. L. (1984). Insights into the repeat vacation phenomenon. *Annals of Tourism Research* 11(2): 199–217.

Godfrey, K. and Clarke, J. (2000). *The Tourism Development Handbook*. London: Continuum.

Goeldner, R. C., Ritchie, J. R. B. and McIntosh, R. W. (2000). *Tourism: Principles, Practices, Philosophies* (8th edition). New York: John Wiley & Sons.

Gratton, C. (1990). The economics of shortbreak holidays. In Fache, W. (ed.) *Shortbreak Holidays*. Rotterdam, The Netherlands: Center Parcs.

Grimaux, A. (2014). Bond urges tourism makeover. *The Courier–Mail*. 13 September, p. 65. Hard copy newspaper article.

Gronroos, C. (1990). Service management: A management focus for service competition. *Service Industry Management* 1(1): 5–14.

Harris, R., Jago, L. and King, B. (2005). *Case Studies in Tourism & Hospitality Marketing*. Frenchs Forest, NSW: Pearson.

Howard, J. A. and Sheth, J. N. (1969). *The Theory of Buyer Behavior*. New York: John Wiley & Sons.

IATA World Air Transport Statistics (WATS), 58th Edition. Available at: https://www.iata.org/publications/pages/wats-passenger-carried.aspx

ITB World Travel Trends Report 2014/2015. Available at: http://www.itb-berlin.de/media/itb/itb_dl_de/itb_itb_berlin/itb_itb_academy/ITB_2015_WTTR_Report_A4_4.pdf

Jeffries, D. (2001). *Governments and Tourism*. Oxford: Butterworth-Heinemann.

Kaplan, A. M. and Haenlein, M. (2010). Users of the world unite! The challenges and opportunities of social media. *Business Horizons* 53(1): 59–68.

Kotler, P., Bowen, J. and Makens, J. (1999). *Marketing for Hospitality and Tourism* (2nd edition). Upper Saddle River, NJ: Prentice Hall.

Krce Miočić, B., Sušac, V. and Milković, T. (2012). Interaction between low-cost airlines and the development of tourist destination. *2nd Advances in Hospitality and Tourism Marketing and Management Conference.* Corfu. Available at: http://www.ahtmm.com/proceedings/2012/2ndahtmmc_submission_162.pdf

Lickorish, L. J. (1991). *Developing Tourism Destinations: Policies and Perspectives.* Harlow, UK: Longman.

Lohmann, M. (1990). Evolution of shortbreak holidays in Western Europe. In Fache, W. (ed.) *Shortbreak Holidays.* Rotterdam, The Netherlands: Center Parcs.

Lohmann, M. (1991). Evolution of shortbreak holidays. *The Tourist Review* 46(2): 14–23.

Medlik, S. and Middleton, V. T. C. (1973). The tourist product and its marketing implications. *International Tourism Quarterly* 3(1): 28–35.

Middleton, V. T. C. and O'Brien, K. (1987). Short break holidays in the UK. *Travel & Tourism Analyst* May: 45–54.

Morgan, N. J. (2000). Creating supra-brand Australia: Answering the challenges of contemporary destination marketing. In Robinson, M., Evans, N., Long, P., Sharpley, R. and Swarbroke, J. (eds) *Management, Marketing and the Political Economy of Travel and Tourism.* Sunderland, UK: Business Education Publishers, pp. 352–365.

Murdy, S. and Pike, S. (2012). Perceptions of visitor relationship marketing opportunities by destination marketers: An importance–performance analysis. *Tourism Management* 33(5): 1281–1285.

Naipaul, S., Wang, Y. and Okumus, F. (2009). Regional destination marketing: A collaborative approach. *Journal of Travel & Tourism Marketing* 26(5/6): 462–481.

Palmer, A. and Bejou, D. (1995). Tourism destination marketing alliances. *Annals of Tourism Research* 22(3): 616–629.

Park, O. J., Lehto, X. Y. and Morrison, A. M. (2008). Collaboration between CVB and local community in destination marketing: CVB executives' perspective. *Journal of Hospitality & Leisure Marketing* 17(3/4): 395–417.

Park, S. Y. and Petrick, J. F. (2006). Destinations' perspectives of branding. *Annals of Tourism Research* 33(1): 262–265.

Pike, S. (2002a). *Positioning as a Source of Competitive Advantage: Benchmarking Rotorua's Position as a Domestic Short Break Holiday Destination.* PhD Thesis. University of Waikato. November. Hard copy only.

Pike, S. (2002b). Destination image analysis: A review of 142 papers from 1973–2000. *Tourism Management* 23(5): 541–549.

Pike, S. (2004). *Destination Marketing Organisations.* Oxford: Elsevier Science.

Pike, S. (2006). Destination decision sets: A longitudinal comparison of stated destination preferences and actual travel. *Journal of Vacation Marketing* 12(4): 319–328.

Pike, S. (2007a). Repeat visitors – An exploratory investigation of RTO responses. *Journal of Travel & Tourism Research* Spring: 1–13.

Pike, S. (2007b). Consumer-based brand equity for destinations: Practical DMO performance measures. *Journal of Travel & Tourism Marketing* 22(1): 51–61.

Pike, S. (2007c). Destination image literature: 2001–2007. *Acta Turistica* 19(2): 107–125.

Pike, S. (2008). *Destination Marketing: An Integrated Marketing Communication Approach.* Burlington, MA: Butterworth-Heinemann.

Pike, S. (2010). Destination branding: Tracking brand equity for an emerging destination between 2003 and 2007. *Journal of Hospitality & Tourism Research* 34(1): 124–139.

Pike, S. and Mason, R. (2011). Destination competitiveness through the lens of brand positioning. *Current Issues in Tourism* 14(2): 169–182.

Pike, S. and Page, S. (2014). Destination marketing organizations and destination marketing: A narrative analysis of the literature. *Tourism Management* 41: 202–227.

Pike, S. and Ryan, C. (2004). Destination positioning analysis through a comparison of cognitive, affective and conative perceptions. *Journal of Travel Research* 42(4): 333–342.

Plog, S. T. (2000). Thirty years that changed travel: Changes to expect over the next ten. *Keynote Address at the 31st Travel and Tourism Research Association Conference.* Burbank, CA. June. Available at: www.ttra.com

Porter, M. E. (1991). Towards a dynamic theory of strategy. *Strategic Management Journal* 12: 95–117.

Prahalad, C. K. and Ramaswamy, V. (2004). Co-creation experiences: The next practice in value creation. *Journal of Interactive Marketing* 18(3): 5–14.

QTIC. (2015). *2015 Queensland Election: Priorities for Tourism.* Brisbane, QLD: Queensland Tourism Industry Council. January.

Rey, B., Myro, R. L. and Galera, A. (2011). Effect of low-cost airlines on tourism in Spain: A dynamic panel data model. *Journal of Air Transport Management* 17(3): 163–167.

Schultz, D., Tannenbaum, S. and Lauterborn, R. (1993). *Integrated Marketing Communications*. Lincolnwood, IL: NTC Publishing.

Selby, M. and Morgan, N. J. (1996). Reconstruing place image: A case study of its role in destination market research. *Tourism Management* 17(4): 287–294.

Sheehan, L., Ritchie, J. R. B. and Hudson, S. (2007). The destination promotion triad: Understanding asymmetric stakeholder interdependencies among the city, hotels, and DMO. *Journal of Travel Research* 46(1): 64–74.

Spencer, D. M. and Holecek, D. F. (2007). Basic characteristics of the fall tourism market. *Tourism Management* 28(2): 491–504.

Teare, R., Davies, M. and McGeary, B. (1989). The operational challenge of hotel short breaks. *International Journal of Contemporary Hospitality Management* 1(1): 22–24.

Thomas, R., Shaw, G. and Page, S. J. (2011). Understanding small firms in tourism: A perspective on research trends and challenges. *Tourism Management* 32(5): 963–976.

Tourism Australia. (2014). *Working with Tourism Australia: Global Marketing Prospectus 2014/2015*. Available at: http://www.tourism.australia.com/documents/Markets/Report_WorkingwithTA_May14.pdf

Tourism Queensland. (2006). Why do Kiwis come to Queensland? *T.Q. News* 7(Winter): 45–47.

Truman, R. (2006). Tourism WA innovates its interactive. *B&T*. March 10, p. 22. Hard copy magazine.

UNWTO. (1999). *Budgets of National Tourism Administrations*. Madrid, Spain: UNWTO.

Vallee, P. (2005). Destination management in Canada. In Harrill, R. (ed.) *Fundamentals of Destination Management and Marketing*. Washington: IACVB, pp. 229–244.

Wahab, S., Crampon, L. J. and Rothfield, L. M. (1976). *Tourism Marketing*. London: Tourism International Press.

Walters, J. (2005). Member care. In Harrill, R. (ed.) *Fundamentals of Destination Management and Marketing*. Washington: IACVB, pp. 161–172.

Wang, Y. (2008). Examining the level of sophistication and success of destination marketing systems: Impacts of organizational factors. *Journal of Travel & Tourism Marketing* 24(1): 81–98.

Wang, Y. and Krakover, S. (2008). Destination marketing: Competition, cooperation or coopetition. *International Journal of Contemporary Hospitality Management* 20(2): 126–141.

Wang, Y. and Xiang, Z. (2012). Toward a theoretical framework of collaborative destination marketing. *Journal of Travel Research* 46(1): 75–85.

Wang, Y., Hutchinson, J., Okumus, F. and Naipaul, S. (2013). Collaborative marketing in a regional destination: Evidence from Central Florida. *International Journal of Tourism Research* 15(3): 285–297.

Ward, S. V. and Gold, J. R. (1994). *The Use of Publicity and Marketing to Sell Towns and Regions*. Chichester, UK: John Wiley & Sons Ltd.

Wicks, B. E. and Schuett, M. A. (1991). Examining the role of tourism promotion through the use of brochures. *Tourism Management* December: 301–312.

Wong, E. P. Y., Mistilis, N. and Dwyer, L. (2010). Understanding ASEAN tourism collaboration: The preconditions and policy framework formulation. *International Journal of Tourism Research* 12(3): 291–302.

Woodside, A. G. and Sakai, M. (2001). Evaluating performance audits of implemented tourism marketing strategies. *Journal of Travel Research* 39(4): 369–379.

Zach, F. (2012). Partners and innovation in American destination marketing organizations. *Journal of Travel Research* 51(4): 412–425.

Zehrer, A., Raich, F., Siller, H. and Tschiderer, F. (2013). Leadership networks in destinations. *Tourism Review* 69(1): 59–73.

13

The destination marketing organisation (DMO), public relations (PR) and publicity

AIMS

To enhance understanding of:

• the importance of managing DMO relationships with stakeholders (publics);

• the advantages of media publicity for DMOs;

• publicity opportunities for DMOs.

ABSTRACT

For destinations, publicity represents a cost-efficient means to gain market exposure. Publicity can appear from many sources over which the DMO may or may not have had any control, involvement or even knowledge, and may or may not be positive. The cost-efficiency, along with the relatively high credibility of media editorial coverage, is attractive to DMOs with limited resources, and so publicity-seeking initiatives are a key aspect of any destination marketing plan. However, it is important to recognise publicity is not the only aspect of PR. PR is more than publicity-seeking in that it represents working with stakeholders (publics) in a concerted effort to develop favourable impressions of a destination. This involves both the generation of positive publicity by the DMO as well as the stimulation of positive relations between internal and external stakeholders, to mitigate potentially negative issues before they become public. Since DMOs are essentially in the business of communication, the process of communication management should not be left to chance. Therefore, the DMO needs to carefully manage relationships with key stakeholders such as politicians, media, tourism businesses and the host community as part of their programme to enhance positive publicity for the destination and enhance the reputation of the tourism industry.

PR (aka relationships with stakeholders)

Since DMOs are essentially in the business of communication to manage the image of the destination and the reputation of the tourism industry, the process of communications management, otherwise known as PR, should not be left to chance. PR has been attempted to be defined for over a century without a clear consensus (Tench and Yeomans, 2014). For example Tench and Yeomans cited a study by Harlow (1976), which identified 476 different definitions coined between 1900 and 1976. One of the most cited definitions in the academic literature is by Broom (2009: 25): 'Public relations is the management function that establishes and maintains mutually beneficial relationships between an organization and the publics on whom its success or failure depends'.

Inherent in this description is the notion of relationships with stakeholders (publics), in addition to consumers in target markets, who are important to the organisation. However, there has been relatively little published in the literature about PR in tourism to date, which is surprising given the economic scale of the sector. In this regard L'Etang et al. (2007) promoted three major characteristics of tourism to argue the case that tourism warrants more attention from PR researchers. These three characteristics have been discussed in this text and repeatedly in the tourism literature, and so they are not new. However, their point is well made in relation to the need for more tourism PR research. First is the scale of the tourism industry's impact on the environment and society. For example, L'Etang et al. cited an annual travel issue of *Newsweek* that concluded that the world's greatest monuments were crumbling and endangered from over-visitation, in their call for PR to engage with the issue of social responsibility in the relationship between guests and hosts. Second is the vulnerability of tourism, partly due to intangibility, to risk and disasters, and the resultant dependence on media imagery, which needs to be managed to avert exaggerated speculation by the media. Third is the scale of the special events sector, which necessitates a hybrid of organising and financing between the private sector and government. The prevalent use of taxpayers' money, along with social and environmental impacts, necessitates PR stakeholder research.

It is surprising that there has been such a lack of specialist tourism journals, books and academic conferences related to PR, and so this is a major gap in the literature. PR in tourism includes a wide spectrum of functions, including:

- engaging with key stakeholders (publics) to attempt to manage perceptions;
- striving to achieve positive media editorial coverage;
- active management of communications;
- brand reputation management;
- networking with potential customers at seminars, exhibitions and events;
- wining and dining important customers.

Academic models of PR are generally based on the hierarchy shown in Table 13.1. While PR is a communication process, publicity is a communication medium. Effective PR requires the organisation to reinforce the brand identity, monitor stakeholders' perceptions, be prepared to adjust to change and/or convince others to change. PR may be viewed as a two-pronged approach to communication management for DMOs. On the one hand, the focus of most PR initiatives by DMOs will be *press agentry*, attempting to generate editorial media publicity for the destination. After all, 'advertising is what you pay for . . . editorial is what you pray for!' (Trout and Rivkin, 1995). On the other hand, there is a need to manage relations, using *two-way symmetrical PR*, with stakeholders who represent a much broader group than consumers in target markets.

An important first step in the PR programme is prioritising groups of stakeholders and identifying potential negative issues and opportunities for dialogue. A stakeholder is any individual or group who can impact on, or be impacted by, the organisation. The range of different types of potential stakeholders of interest to a DMO, both internal and external to the destination, is listed in Table 13.2. Some stakeholders

Table 13.1 PR models

Function	Philosophy
Press agentry	Striving for media publicity
Public information	Disseminating objective, but positive information only
One-way asymmetrical PR	Utilising research to design messages that will stimulate stakeholders to behave the way the organisation desires
Two-way symmetrical PR	Using research and open communication to enhance relationships, where both the organisation and publics can be convinced of the need for change

Table 13.2 DMO stakeholders

Internal
Politicians
Government policy advisers
The media
The host community, including taxpayers and other residents
The tourism community and other local businesses
Educators
Conservationists
Financiers

External to the destination
Visitors and target consumers
Politicians
Government policy advisers
The media
Travel intermediaries
Event promoters
Property developers
Conservationists
Financiers

will be active, while others will be passive. The latter might, however, become active when a topical issue of interest to them arises and so should not be neglected.

Other than visitors, particularly active stakeholders are usually:

- politicians and government policy advisors;
- the host community, including residents, taxpayers, conservationists and businesses;
- the media;
- travel trade intermediaries (see Chapter 14).

Political relations

Political relations are important for DMOs at all levels, for two primary reasons, both of which have the wider tourism community interests at heart. First is the need for long-term government funding security to avoid market failure and ensure a holistic destination marketing approach (see Chapter 3). Second is influencing policies that have the potential to impact on the many factors related to sustainable tourism development and destination competitiveness (see Chapter 2). Importantly, DMOs not only need to develop relationships with the current governing administration but also with leading opposition political parties. Governments and their policies change over time, and a term of political office is a relatively short period in the development of a destination. However, there has been little published research about political lobbying at tourism destinations (Pillmayer and Scherle, 2014).

Pritchard (1982) reported an interesting political PR initiative in the USA by Wisconsin's STO. For the constituency of every elected government representative, the STO had its research department prepare a breakdown of the number of tourism businesses, tourism employees, tourism tax revenue and the total value of tourism to the area. The STO then sent this information to each legislator to improve the case for tourism marketing funding. This initiative resulted in 240 press releases being generated by the legislators to their local media around the state. The end results were two-fold. The first was an increased public awareness of the value of tourism, and the second was an increased awareness of tourism as a re-election vehicle for legislators.

McGehee et al. (2006) undertook a comparative analysis of the attitudes of state legislators in North Carolina (USA) towards tourism in 1990 and 2003. They found that while legislators viewed tourism more positively in 2003, their knowledge of tourism remained limited. This aspect was disappointing given the extent to which the STO had employed lobbying strategies. In the limited research related to such lobbying, White (1991, in McGehee et al., 2006) analysed four types of lobbying commonly used by non-profit organisations:

1. constituency-based, where initiatives include forming coalitions with other organisations and stimulating influential constituents to lobby government;
2. classic-direct techniques, which include asking government officials to express an opinion on an issue, serving on advisory committees and alerting legislators to the effect of a particular bill;
3. electronic lobbying by email;
4. schmoozing techniques, which involve providing favours for political officials, filing lawsuits, attempts to influence public appointments and making contributions to political campaigns.

Arguably the most effective technique in the long term is the constituency-based approach. McGehee *et al.* (2006) concluded that while the North Carolina STO was employing some classic-direct and constituency-based initiatives, a more aggressive approach was required.

IN PRACTICE

13.1 Economic impact research

Brand USA commissioned Oxford Economics to research the economic impact of a future without the NTO's marketing activities. The research was part of the successful lobby to the federal government's consideration of 2014 legislation to renew Brand USA for a further five years. The research report claimed that with no NTO during 2016–2020 the USA would lose US$54 billion in business sales, which would have created 53,000 new jobs (Travelindustrywire, 2014).

Host community relations

Interestingly, in Denmark, there has been a long tradition of involvement with RTOs by local citizens, through membership subscriptions (see Halkier, 2014). Even though for most DMOs their host community will not be actively involved as members, they remain a potentially powerful group on two levels. On the one hand local residents can help tell the destination's story to their visiting friends and relatives, as well as during their own travels. For example, a survey of @Australia Instagram followers found 69 per cent of Australian respondents thought posting their photos could help promote more travel to Australia, while 88 per cent indicated the page influenced an increased desire to travel more around their country (Tourism Australia, 2014). An expatriate Australian respondent living in London posted: 'Love your page!. . . I use your page to showcase Australia to my English friends'.

On the other hand, residents can be a negative influence on local politics if they are not supportive of tourism development. In many communities there are some well-known and active prolific *letters to the editor* antagonists. However, there are others who are passive until an issue motivates them to speak out. This is particularly so with proposed tourism developments in pristine ecological areas, as well as events and developments that might be perceived to impact negatively on the lifestyle of residents. The tourism industry should, therefore, be seen as being part of the local community and not some separate entity. Open and ongoing communication needs to take place between the DMO and the host community for a number of reasons. Examples of inclusiveness are:

- The destination brand should encapsulate local residents' sense of place, and so their views need to be canvassed at the brand identity development phase, the rationale being that support and understanding of the brand leads to more residents being enthusiastic ambassadors for the destination.

- Residents need to be made aware of plans for new tourism-related events, products and infrastructure developments as early as possible in the process, to identify any potential perceived negative impacts.

- Following the previous point, there should be ongoing communications to ensure local taxpayers are made aware of the purpose of DMO funding by government, in terms of the wider and longer-term socio-cultural and economic benefits for the community.

- Residents and other business sectors should have a forum for communicating tourism-related problems at an early stage, rather than approaching the media with negative issues. It might be that social media offers opportunities in this regard in the future. However, as discussed in Chapter 4, there is little evidence of successful online community engagement by DMOs to date.

- Residents interact with visitors in a variety of situations, such as on public transport, in traffic and at airports, gas/petrol stations, supermarkets, shopping malls and beaches. Support for tourism will hopefully manifest in friendly encounters if locals understand and accept the value of visitors. DMOs therefore need to consider initiatives involving communication forums and research to track community acceptance of visitors. In terms of developing a community relations programme, the Centre for Regional Tourism Research in Australia developed an excellent kit for RTOs during 2000 (see Rosemann *et al.*, 2000). The kit provided suggested tactics, along with cases from practice around Australia. A brief selection of examples is shown in Table 13.3.

Table 13.3 Communicating the benefits of tourism to the host community

Community initiatives	The small island state of Tasmania developed a 'Tourism awareness week' to overcome misconceptions and complacency in the community. Initiatives included an advertising campaign, a positioning slogan ('tourism means jobs') and logo, targeting key opinion leaders, emails to businesses, news releases and a question in Parliament for the Tourism Minister about activities to boost tourism. The initial campaign won a 1999 Pacific Asia Travel Association Gold Award. Similar campaigns have been organised in New South Wales and the Australian Capital Territory
• Information expos • Programmes to engage visitor interest in local culture • Targeting visiting friends and relatives tourism • Encourage locals to experience local tours • Provide residents with familiarisations of businesses indirectly involved in tourism • Reduced admission prices for locals accompanying visitors • Local attraction loyalty cards • Encourage community involvement in the visitor information centre • Voluntary ambassador programmes • Direct mail initiatives • Regular visits to local services clubs • Visits to high schools	
Business initiatives • Promote information availability as a community resource • Service award programmes • Create a membership level for businesses indirectly involved in tourism	Members of the Capricorn Tourism & Development organisation were encouraged to stamp their cheque payments with 'It was only possible to pay this account because of tourism'. Recipients are also encouraged to join the organisation
Local government initiatives • Lobby local government elected representatives • Educate local government	The Country Victoria Tourism Council produces two booklets for local governments in the state: *Why Should Local Government Invest in Tourism* and *Local Government and Tourism: The Partnerships*

(continued)

Table 13.3 *(continued)*

Media initiatives	Townsville Enterprise Limited developed a range of activities including: weekly staff meetings to develop story ideas, two newspaper columns sponsored by media members, an annual briefing for all media and a two-weekly news flash. Over AUD$100,000 in airtime and space has been provided by media sponsors annually
<ul><li>Build strong media relationships</li><li>Find ways to make tourism newsworthy</li><li>Host media open days</li><li>Regular press releases and newspaper columns</li><li>Invite media to local tourism meetings</li></ul>	
Research initiatives	
<ul><li>Engage in local research fund by local government</li><li>Publish tourism statistics regularly</li><li>Survey tourism dependent workers to feed back to the community</li></ul>	

Source: Adapted from Rosemann *et al.* (2000).

To enhance credibility of a CVB in the community, Gartrell (1994: 281) recommended a strategy of consistently using messages that repeat key terms: 'Telling the bureau's story may seem mundane or repetitious, but the message must be stated again and again'. Examples of key repetitive terms include those related to *economic development* and *tax benefits*. After all, in many cases a large proportion of residents are taxpayers and therefore indirectly funding the DMO, and so it is critical that their perceptions of tourism are monitored. The issue of analysing the perceptions of the host community towards tourism is discussed as a DMO performance measure in Chapter 15. For a review of the literature related to host community perceptions of tourism see Sharpley (2014).

Local tourism operators

The underlying purpose of the DMO, which is to enhance destination competitiveness for holistic community benefits, might not always be obvious to some local tourism operators. After all, many are entrepreneurs, risking their own equity in the pursuit of tomorrow's cash flow and capital gain, and some will see a DMO's role as only being to solely focus on increasing numbers of visitors who will be interested in their business. Others might have a short-term *promotion orientation* rather than a longer-term *marketing orientation* (see Chapter 1). If tourism operators have not been informed, it is dangerous to assume they will automatically understand the need for a wider, sustainable community perspective from destination marketers. The DMO should, therefore, initiate regular measures to identify the extent to which the ever-changing tourism community understands the organisation's purpose and role and to undertake initiatives to enhance dialogue. In this regard, common initiatives include newsletters, meetings with sector group representatives and public forums.

Local businesses also need to be briefed on DMO strategies, such as the rationale for the brand identity and positioning theme, and on tactics such as joint venture promotional opportunities. Again, a forum for two-way participative communication is necessary so that: (1) promotional opportunities are maximised; and (2) potential problems are handled before the issue is brought to the attention of the media. Initiatives include market briefings, networking functions, an annual conference, user-friendly marketing plans and an annual report. A dedicated website for members can also be used effectively to disseminate information and seek feedback. Most DMO sites remain one-directional (top-down), with little opportunity for the wider community of stakeholders to contribute content or public feedback, which is representative of a one-way asymmetrical PR approach listed in Table 13.1.

Media relations

Traditional broadcast media has undergone a radical restructuring in the past decade. The effect of free content available via Web 2.0 technologies impacted on the revenues of traditional media, who were forced to downsize, particularly in the number of investigative journalists employed, in order to remain financially viable. Instead, there is increasing reliance by media on news from syndicated sources and corporate media releases, of which the latter clearly presents opportunities for DMOs. For local issues the implication for DMOs is a proactive programme of communications to local media and the need for a recognised tourism spokesperson the media can go to when required. When a topical tourism issue arises, it is important the right people are involved in any public debate to ensure fairness of reporting. Initiatives to establish credibility by the DMO in this regard can include regular newspaper columns and TV/radio segments.

DMOs need a proactive approach to developing relations with the media. Such relationships develop through a mix of positive human traits such as trust, honesty, perseverance, humour, reliability and consistency. Further, the relationship is not one-way only. That is, it is not always about sending story ideas to the journalist. As discussed, there will be times when the journalist contacts the DMO for comment, often about a negative issue the organisation or destination might be facing. Clearly the DMO needs to be prepared to handle such a cold call. One 'no comment' about a tricky situation might jeopardise how the same media will react to the DMO's next media release. Barry (2002, in Pike, 2004) promoted the three *Ws* of media relations:

- **Why is what we have to say of interest?** Is it news? It is the job of the communicator to ensure the needs of the journalist are met. Is it relevant to their audience?

- **When is their deadline for accepting information?** Expecting the media to revolve around the communicator's timetable is arrogant.

- **What format does the media require?** The journalist's preference will dictate whether your message is actually noticed.

IN PRACTICE

13.2 How to work with the media

To assist tourism businesses to increase their chances of generating media interest and positive editorial coverage, Tourism Australia provides an online *How to work with the media* guide at www.tourism.australia.com. The NTO's annual online marketing prospectus (see Tourism Australia, 2014) also advises how individual businesses can participate in Tourism Australia's PR initiatives, such as the *Australian Stories* newsletter, which is emailed to over 4,000 international media each week. Businesses that participate are able to track any resultant media publicity through the NTO site.

Negative publicity

Images held of a destination will be either positive or negative, but will usually consist of both. Effective corrective marketing is difficult and, as discussed in Chapters 10 and 11, once a negative image has become established, marketing activities will struggle to reverse it. Meler and Ruzic (1999), discussing the negative image of post-war Croatia, found one or a few negative attributes could stimulate the creation of a negative image of the destination. In the case of Ireland, Ehemann (1977) found an overwhelmingly negative image portrayed in the general media as a result of *the troubles* related to the violent republican movement. Ehemann was interested in the evaluative vocabulary used in the media about the destination and the nature of the image that might be developed by an individual with no direct experience of a destination. As well as the negative publicity in relation to the demise of Rotorua, New Zealand, which was highlighted in the Preface (see also Ateljevic, 1998; Ateljevic and Doorne, 2000; Horn *et al.*, 2000; Pike, 2002, 2007; Pike *et al.*, 2011), a number of examples concerning this issue have been reported in the literature including: Benidorm, Spain (Amor *et al.*, 1994); Bradford, England (Bramwell and Rawding, 1996); Wales (Selby and Morgan, 1996; Pride, 2002) and Vietnam (Laderman, 2009).

At a local community level, negative media issues can relate to a diverse range of issues such as: crime against visitors, unruly visitor behaviour, natural disasters, DMO funding, impacts of tourism growth and controversial building developments. As was discussed in Chapter 7, the DMO should not leave response to chance. Handling negative publicity requires patience and a long-term consistency of message. However, attempts to place a positive spin on events led former magazine editor, Warwick Roger, to offer this reflection on the PR industry: 'Journalists, for the most part, still work in the interests of the public. PR and advertising people . . . operate only in the interests of money and bullshit' (*Inside Tourism* 246, in Pike, 2008).

From the DMO perspective it is worth remembering that *people aren't stupid, silly* (P.A.S.S.), so always remain open and truthful and avoid the temptation for continual positive *spin* (propaganda).

IN PRACTICE

13.3 The John Cleese effect

British comedian, John Cleese, caused great offence in Palmerston North in 2006, when he labelled the city 'the suicide capital of New Zealand' (NZPA, 2006). Cleese suggested: 'if you want to kill yourself but lack the courage to, I think a visit to Palmerston North will do the trick . . . we had a thoroughly miserable time there and were so happy to get out'. The city increased exposure to the issue by developing a *Passionate about Palmerston North* competition in New Zealand and Australia, which invited people to write about why they would like to visit. Palmerston North claimed the last laugh by naming a local rubbish tip after Cleese.

Attracting positive publicity

There has been a lack of research reported in the literature on the use of positive publicity as a promotional tool by DMOs (Dore and Crouch, 2003). Editorial media coverage offers DMOs three key benefits. First, publicity campaigns have the potential to be more economical and cost-effective than paid advertising. Second, news generally has higher credibility than paid advertising. In the mid-1990s Trout and Rivkin (1995) suggested six times as many people read an average news article as read the average advertisement and attributed this to editors being better communicators than advertising agencies at the time. While there is increasing scepticism towards claims made in advertisements, consumer suspicion about paid advertising is not a new phenomenon, as evidenced by the view of Wahab *et al.* in the mid-1970s:

To obtain a buying decision means overcoming the buyer's resistance to yet one more sales message. There are so many, and life has taught him that they promise so much more than they achieve, that the buyer acquires a built-in suspicion and hostility, which we know as sales resistance.

(Wahab et al., 1976: 73)

Third, the results of campaigns to generate publicity represent a visible aspect of destination marketing and therefore provide tangible evidence of DMO effectiveness to stakeholders. This issue is discussed as a performance indicator in Chapter 15.

As discussed in Chapter 12, the DMO's marketing communications should aim for message synergy across all media platforms. The publicity programme should, therefore, integrate the messages being used in other marketing communications, to reinforce the brand identity. To do so requires similar planning with clear objectives, target audience, message proposition and tactics. However, this is not advertising where space is being purchased for the desired message. In this field there is not the same level of control over: (1) whether there will be any resultant publicity; (2) when the publicity might occur; and (3) whether or not the publicity will be positive. A DMO's publicity programme commonly focuses on the following tactics:

- visiting media programme;
- capitalising on television programmes, movies, literary tourism and photogenic icons;
- capitalising on the power of celebrity visitors.

Visiting media programme

The DMO's visiting media programme is the proactive targeting and hosting of media at the destination, with the aim of generating positive editorial content in target markets. Such programmes are heavily reliant on the cooperative support of transport, accommodation and attraction operators to host the visiting media's travel arrangements. Travel articles in newspaper and magazine travel columns are commonly positive about destinations, given the writer has usually been sponsored by the DMO, airline, accommodation and attractions. However, many travel writers tell it as they find it, so hosting the media is not without some risk.

IN PRACTICE

13.4 Let me see the real thing

A personal friend, who has been a travel writer for over 20 years, lamented to me how it is sometimes difficult for him to experience *the real thing* when invited to a destination. He explained that such visits are usually brief and so he prefers to get out and about exploring the destination on his own as quickly as possible to get a feel for the place, as a basis for constructing a story. He, of course, understands that such trips are sponsored, and so there are always obligations to visit certain attractions. However, he laments that on more than one occasion he has been met at the airport with a chauffeur limousine and driven to meetings with either the mayor or other high-ranking officials who want to spend time singing their destination's praises. His message to destination marketers is to give travel writers freedom during their stay to explore by themselves and find interesting story angles that are not scripted by the DMO. The travel writer knows more about what their audience will be interested in, and often these can be aspects of a place that the local DMO takes for granted.

An essential element of any publicity programme is a database of travel writers and other news media. For larger DMOs, such databases are becoming more sophisticated and capture individual journalists' previous articles, travel preferences and personal information. The Society of American Travel Writers (www.satw.org) was established over 50 years ago as a professional association to raise standards in the travel writers' profession. The British Guild of Travel Writers (see www.bgtw.metronet.co.uk) was established in 1960. The guild's 220 mostly freelance members contribute to 38 national and provincial daily newspapers, 56 magazines, 86 general interest publications, 37 trade journals, 42 in-flight magazines and travel guidebooks.

IN PRACTICE

13.5 Journalist VIP passport

To more effectively assist journalists, the Orlando/Orange County CVB developed a Journalist VIP passport (Courtenay, 2005). CVB members offered pre-qualified (rather than scammers) journalists complimentary services, accommodation and meals. The passports permit visiting journalists to plan flexible itineraries, to which the CVB can tailor specific information and other items to fit a particular story angle.

In a survey of the publicity practice of ten NTOs from Europe, Africa and Asia/Pacific, Dore and Crouch (2003) found the largest budget item within the PR budget was the visiting media programme. While the PR allocation was the third highest in the promotional budget, behind advertising and personal selling, it was rated as the highest in importance (in this pre-Web 2.0 era) by NTOs due to the cost-effectiveness. Key problems with visiting media programmes identified by NTOs include: limited funds and staff resources, lack of industry support, short notice arrival of media, quality control of ensuing publicity and results not meeting expectations.

The demise of the travel writer?

In the pre-Web 2.0 era, Courtenay (2005) cited research estimating around one-third of travellers acknowledged the travel media influenced their travel plans. Cincotta (2006) provided similar sentiments by publishers of *Gourmet Traveller*, *Travel and Leisure* and *Cruise*, who argued such publications are trusted and authoritative sources of information for discerning travellers. Sandra Hook, publisher of *Vogue Entertaining and Travel*, argued magazines' point of difference is an obvious one: 'Magazines provide inspiration with their editorial and pictorial coverage of destinations. Readers are presented with new destinations and travel opportunities. The net basically provides up-to-date information on destinations that the potential traveller has already selected'.

While much publicity about destinations occurs in the general news and entertainment media without the influence of DMOs or the travel industry, travel writers have been a primary target of DMO PR managers in the visiting media programme. However, as discussed, with the rise in influence of user-generated content on social media, newspapers have been downsizing to compete. This has resulted in fewer numbers of investigative journalists and travel writers and more reliance on syndicated news sources. With so much online content available, for how long will the traditional newspaper travel section and travel magazines be relevant?

Ironically, in one of my previous books (see Pike, 2008), I lauded Travelwriters.com (www.travelwriters.com) as an example of one of the many resources available to current and aspiring travel writers, providing advice for PR agents, DMOs and tourism operators, such as: a writer database, travel publications directory and a press release forum. A community of 10,000+ professional travel writers, Travelwriters.com was based on a simple principle: to connect top-tier travel writers with editors, PR agencies, tourism professionals, CVBs and tour operators, nurturing the important link that so heavily influences the travel media. Ominously, a cursory visit to check the website in May 2015 revealed this post: 'Due to unforeseen circumstances, a management decision was made to close TravelWriters.com. We appreciate the opportunity we had to serve you and apologize for any inconvenience this may cause you'.

At this stage there is a lack of research published investigating this aspect of travel planning. This is particularly topical given the rise of user-generated content on social media and the rise of professional Instagrammers, as discussed in Chapter 4.

IN PRACTICE

13.6 Who needs travel writers?

In March 2015 Australian daily newspaper *MX*, which is delivered free to commuters in the state capital cities, commenced an initiative to enlist readers to contribute the bulk of the content to the weekly *Wanderlust* travel section (*MX*, 2015): 'Our boss is too tight to send us anywhere good, but we know our *MX* tribe are intrepid travellers. You are going to be our travel guides'. *MX* announces what the feature destination will be the following week and invites readers to send their photos and travel tips to their Instagram page: @mxsnaps.

Digital media resource library

It is good practice for DMOs to maintain a digital resource library to service the needs of the media and travel trade. Resources typically include story ideas, photos and video clips of local attractions. These are useful, for example, for travel writers who are not equipped to replicate professional images that may have been obtained in perfect weather conditions and by special means such as a helicopter. Limited time, resources and inclement weather can inhibit the travel writer's ability to record suitable images during a brief visit. Also, as discussed in Chapter 9, images provide a pre-test of what to expect and therefore help sell the destination's story ideas to the media. Requests for destination imagery by media and tourism operators, including photos and brand logos, are usually vetted to ensure appropriate representation. In the case of Tourism Australia's images and videos, the NTO advises that use is free if it is used to promote tourism to Australia. To access both the gallery websites (www.images.australia.com and www.video.australia.com) registration, which is free, is required.

Capitalising on television programmes, movies, literary tourism and photogenic icons

TV programmes

In the UK the first TV travel programme to be broadcast was the BBC's *Holiday* in 1969 (Yeoman, 2008). Such programmes are now common around the world and clearly present a wealth of opportunities for DMOs.

IN PRACTICE

13.7 What have you got that I can't get anywhere else?

The media rely on interesting story angles. At the 2005 Tourism and Travel Research Association conference in New Orleans, keynote speaker, Peter Greenberg, well-known to Americans as the *Travel Detective* on one of the national television networks, challenged the audience with the same question he poses to DMOs that lobby him to film a segment at their destination: 'Tell me what experience you offer me that I can't find anywhere else'. This gets to the heart of the challenge of destination marketing, which is differentiating amid an almost endless list of competitors. Greenberg argued that from his experience most destinations struggle to answer this question effectively.

One small Australian LTA with a small limited budget that has been successful in attracting national publicity for the destination is Queensland's Burnett Shire Council. The Burnett Shire is located 350 km north of Brisbane, the state capital. The local government provides a relatively modest financial allocation to destination promotion. However, council staff, who have other roles but work part-time on tourism initiatives, have been very proactive in terms of targeting high-profile media and coordinating industry support for the visits through their work with a Tourism Industry Advisory Committee (TIAC). In October 2003 the shire hosted the weather segment of Australia's leading national breakfast television programme. Presenter, Sami Lucas, broadcast a series of 12 × 5-minute segments live from Bargara Beach, Moore Park Beach and Bundaberg over 3 days. Equivalent advertising value of the airtime was estimated at AUD$600,000. The total cost of hosting the film crew was approximately AUD$20,000, of which almost all was provided by tourism industry sponsorship.

Readers will also be aware of the plethora of television programmes that have generated publicity in various parts of the world for destinations such as the cases of *Coronation Street* and *Queer as Folk* (Manchester), *Sea Change* (Australia, see Beeton, 2001) *Neighbours* (Australia), *Bergerac* (Jersey, see Tooke and Baker, 1996) and *Rome* and *Las Vegas*, to name but a few. Movie- and television-induced tourism is not a new phenomenon. For example, Davidson and Maitland (1997) reported how the West Yorkshire village of Holmfirth became a tourism destination overnight in 1972 following the airing of the BBC TV series *Last of the Summer Wine*. Similarly, Bradford made use of its television and film history to promote short break packages based on *Wuthering Heights*, *Emmerdale Farm* and *The Last of the Summer Wine* (Buckley and Witt, 1985). Case 13.1 summarises how Tourism Australia worked with Oprah Winfrey to stimulate television-induced tourism.

CASE STUDY

13.1 *Oprah's Ultimate Australian Adventure*

In 2010 The Oprah Winfrey Show attracted a weekly audience of 40 million in the USA and a further 40 million in 147 countries around the world. In December of that year the show travelled to Australia and the following month broadcast 4 episodes from the 700 hours of footage filmed during the 8-day visit. Each of the 4 episodes had a mostly Australian audience of 6,000, who were selected from a ballot that attracted 350,000 people. *Oprah's Ultimate Australian*

Adventure was announced on air by Oprah in dramatic fashion at the start of her 25th and final season. At the invitation of Tourism Australia and Qantas, Oprah, 200 of her staff and the 302 audience members that day, would all be travelling to Australia. The objective was to use Oprah's star power to demonstrate to the world why *There's nothing like Australia*, the new NTO branding. As well as the contributions made by the NTO and corporate sponsors, Oprah's Harpo Productions spent US$7 million on the visit.

Oprah visited Queensland's Great Barrier Reef, the Northern Territory's Uluru National Park, Melbourne and Sydney. The 302 audience members accompanying her from the US hailed from 38 states as well as 13 from Canada and 1 from Jamaica, ranging in age from 18 to 75. They attended two of the taped episodes and travelled in different groups that visited all eight Australian states and territories.

In January 2011 when the episodes aired there was a 66 per cent increase in visits to the Tourism Australia website. By February 2011 the initiative had generated 86,000 news stories with an equivalent advertising value of AUD$368 million. Tourism Australia and 16 partners invested AUD$5.4 million in a US marketing campaign associated with the initiative, which generated almost AUD$20 million in travel bookings. Marketing research undertaken in the USA during 2011 in February, June, September and November to track perceptions of consumers who had read, seen or heard about *Oprah's Ultimate Australian Adventure*, identified very strong sentiment and travel intentions towards Australia (see Chapter 15). Tourism Australia reported the consumer research and feedback from the tourism industry suggested the *Oprah effect* was working for the country.

Further reading/viewing

https://www.youtube.com/watch?v=HWyP1PeIgPY
https://www.youtube.com/watch?v=qd5_m3GIFS8
http://www.tourism.australia.com/media/media-oprah-ultimate-australian-adventure.aspx
Johns, R. and Weir, B. (2014).
Tourism Australia. (2011).

Discussion question

Of all the famous TV show hosts, what was it about the *Oprah effect* that made her the key target for Tourism Australia?

An example of combining movie and TV tourism . . . at the invitation of Tourism Ireland, French current affairs television programme *Envoyé Spécial* in 2015 filmed segments in Northern Ireland at sites that featured in the *Game of Thrones* series (TravelandTourWorld, 2015). The episode was expected to be watched by over 4 million French viewers.

Movies

Voase (2002) cited research indicating the main reason for visiting Austria for three out of every four international visitors was the film *The Sound of Music*, while Tourism New Zealand (2013, in Hoppen *et al.*, 2014) found 1 per cent of all visitors to New Zealand during 2004 attributed *The Lord of the Rings* as their main or sole reason for travelling there. A year after the 1977 movie *Close Encounters of the Third*

Kind was released, the level of visitors to the Devil's Tower National Monument increased by 74 per cent (Riley *et al.*, 1992). Other examples of movie-induced tourism discussed by Riley and Van Doren (1998) included: *Deliverance* (Rayburn County, Georgia), *Dances with Wolves* (Fort Hayes, Kansas), *Thelma and Louise* (Arches National Monument, Georgia), *Field of Dreams* (Iowa), *The Piano* (New Zealand), *Steel Magnolias* (Natchitoches, Louisiana) and *Crocodile Dundee* (Australia). For a review of the wealth of literature related to movie-induced tourism, see Connell (2012).

In terms of proactive DMO initiatives, Petersburg in Virginia took advantage of the 2003 release of the movie *Cold Mountain* to promote tours of the scene of the 1864 civil war's Battle of the Crater, which is relived in the opening scenes of the movie (Bergman, 2004). The New Zealand government allocated a special fund of NZ$10.4 million in 2001–2002 and NZ$4.4 million in 2002–2003 towards promotion of *The Lord of the Rings* trilogy (Foreman, 2003). The state of North Carolina provides a website discussing the importance of the movie industry (see www.nccommerce.com/film). Since 1980, North Carolina has attracted over 600 feature films. A number of case studies of movie-induced tourism have been reported in the tourism literature, including: Nottingham and *Robin Hood: Prince of Thieves* (see Holloway and Robinson, 1995), New Zealand and *The Lord of the Rings* trilogy (see Croy, 2004), Australia and *Ned Kelly* (see Frost, 2003).

IN PRACTICE

13.8 Bollywood beckons

As well as Hollywood, Bollywood is now a key target for many NTOs, and movie tourism trade events have been initiated to bring producers and destinations together. For example, the Indian International Film Tourism Conclave, established in 2013, is an annual series of one-day exhibition events for destinations in the major film centres of Chennai, Hyderabad and Mumbai (see http://www.iiftc.in). The events attract over 100 of India's top film makers. To entice producers, incentives offered by NTOs include expedited permission turnarounds and sales tax concessions while on location.

While there is evidence to suggest movies do improve perceptions of a destination (see Hudson *et al.*, 2011) and increase visitors to the location (see Tooke and Baker, 1996), movie-induced tourism does have its critics. For example, the director of Natural History New Zealand, a documentary producer owned by Fox Television Studios, described the tourism focus on *The Lord of the Rings* as 'tacky . . . it's just extraordinary to listen to boring little people trying to quantify it in value (to) tourism. It is sickening'. There was also criticism in Wales that it was the landscape in that country that inspired Tolkien's Middle Earth and not New Zealand. While *The Lord of the Rings* movie trilogy generated enormous publicity for New Zealand, there was initial resistance from the producers to permit Tourism New Zealand to promote areas where filming took place. Producers were reluctant to have Middle Earth associated with New Zealand for fear of damaging the first film's mystery. Ultimately, Tourism New Zealand was able to demonstrate that an association between New Zealand and the movie franchise would be beneficial. Tourism New Zealand was required to seek the producers' permission before any aspect of the movies could be used in promotions.

In examining the tourism impact of the Australian TV series *Sea Change* on the seaside village of Barwon, Beeton (2001) lamented a change in the visitor mix, which may have long-term impacts on the destination's traditional holiday market. DMOs interested in this emerging area of research will find a rich resource of examples of the positive and negative impacts of film locations in the papers of Riley *et al.* (1992), Tooke and Baker (1996) and Riley and Van Doren (1998). In a rare investigation of host community attitudes towards movie tourism during the pre-production stage of filming *Glastonbury: Isle of Light*, Semley and Busby (2014) encountered concerns over costs, uncertainty, lack of knowledge and scepticism about film content. Their paper is a case study of some of the impacts of Visit Somerset's attempt to enhance local economic development through movie tourism. The findings pointed to the need for DMOs to engage with the local community to identify potential concerns of the impact of movie-induced tourism, not only in terms of logistical issues such as congestion but also in terms of perceived commercialisation of the local culture.

Movie-induced tourism is also not without some risk of damaging perceptions in the market place. In this regard, Redondo (2012) identified the movie genres that would be most interesting to potential travellers and proposed guidelines for DMOs to systematically evaluate proposed movie projects. Stein (2006) suggested a large part of the success of controversial film *Borat* was inadvertently created by the government of Kazakhstan first threatening legal action and then taking out an unsuccessful four-page tourism ad in the *New York Times*.

Most research related to movie-induced tourism has relied on secondary data (Quintal and Phau, 2014). Therefore, the research snapshot below provides a rare insight into how movies might be an important information source about travel destinations.

RESEARCH SNAPSHOT

13.1 The effect of a romantic comedy on New York's image

Using Kim and Richardson's (2003) research model, Quintal and Phau (2014) used an experimental design to examine how a romantic comedy as an information source can shape perceptions of, and intent to visit, New York. A survey of visitors at a large cinema complex in Australia found the group of participants who had just watched the New York-based romantic comedy *Friends with Benefits* (n = 228) differed significantly in their attitude to New York in comparison to those in the control group who had just watched the romantic comedy *Dezi Boy* that was set in London and India (n = 230). Empathy, past experience, familiarity, perceptions and intent to visit New York were significantly higher for the experimental group. Also, perceived financial risk was significantly lower for the experimental group.

Further reading

Quintal, V. and Phau, I. (2014).

Literary tourism

The extent to which DMOs have maximised the potential for literary tourism, which includes author-related places, fiction-related places, literary festivals and bookshop tourism (see Hoppen *et al.*, 2014), has not been widely reported in the academic literature, even though there is evidence of novels as promotional tools dating back to the nineteenth century. For example, since the publication of Bram Stoker's novel *Dracula* in 1897, there has been a continued fascination by travellers with Romania's Transylvania (see Light, 2012). Likewise, but on a smaller scale, over a century ago *The Mystery of a Hansom Cab* by Fergus Hume is said to have attracted many tourists to Melbourne, Australia, where the murder-mystery was set (Richardson, 1999).

There exists a tourism sector based on visits to the areas where famous literary figures once lived. This is particularly evident in the UK, where the NTO actively promotes sites that offer a glimpse of the lives of Britain's authors, playwrights and poets (see www.visitbritain.com). For example, in 2015 the NTO was promoting the *Literary Tour of England with the National Trust*. The National Trust Pass offers access to over 300 historic homes and gardens throughout the UK, with residences once occupied or visited by literary figures such as George Bernard Shaw, Virginia Woolf, Charlotte Bronte, Beatrix Potter, William Wordsworth, Rudyard Kipling and Agatha Christie. Examples of regional destinations that lay claim to the home of Britain's finest wordsmiths include:

1. Emily Bronte's West Yorkshire (www.brontecountry.info);

2. William Shakespeare's Stratford-upon-Avon (www.shakespeare-country.co.uk);

3. Jane Austen's Hampshire (www.visitsouthwest.co.uk);

4. William Wordsworth's Lake District (www.lakedistrict.gov.uk);

5. Charles Dickens's London (www.hidden-london.com).

IN PRACTICE

13.9 *Alice in Wonderland* and Mary Poppins

The village of Lyndhurst in the UK's New Forest and the town of Maryborough in Queensland, Australia, are examples of how destinations off the traditional tourism trail have been able to capitalise on literary and movie tourism. Lyndhurst was the home of Alice Liddell, who is said to have inspired the novel *Alice in Wonderland* by Lewis Carroll. Lyndhurst offers fans of the novel the chance to see an exhibition based on the looking glass theme, a Mad Hatter's tea party and Alice's memorial. Maryborough was the birthplace in 1899 of author P. L. Travers, whose novels about Mary Poppins were adapted for films and musicals. The town commemorates the life of the author with a Mary Poppins statue outside the heritage listed building where the author was born and each year stages a Mary Poppins Festival.

Further information

http://www.thenewforest.co.uk/alice-in-wonderland.aspx
http://www.marypoppinsfestival.com.au

Theme parks that take advantage of literary figures have also emerged since the mid-2000s. May 2007 saw the opening of Dickens World in Kent, UK, themed around the life, times and books of the author; while in July 2014, Universal Orlando Resort officially opened the Wizarding World of Harry Potter theme park in Florida, based on the writings of author J. K. Rowling. For a review of the literature related to literary tourism, and the opportunities and challenges faced by destination marketers, see Hoppen *et al.* (2014).

Capitalising on photogenic icons

Walk along Hollywood Boulevard on any day of the week and you will see people taking photos of the bronze stars embedded in the footpath, an example of which is shown in Figure 13.1. My own excuse for taking this photo was a random chance encounter with the actor as he officiated the placement of the plaque. The popularity of the Hollywood walk of fame is a masterstroke in the creation of photo opportunities, given that visitors are only actually looking at, and photographing, the names of entertainment stars . . . just the name of a person embedded in the pavement! The area learned early on of the power of an iconic photo opportunity of course, with its famous Hollywood sign on the hill above the city. Originally erected as *Hollywoodland* to temporarily promote a real estate development in the 1920s, the sign has been protected ever since for its photogenic quality.

Photo opportunities *tangible-ise* otherwise intangible travel experiences. For example in Figure 13.2, the author's son, Jesse, is pictured in front of the iconic Notre Dame Cathedral in Paris, as it appeared on Facebook in 2014. The square in which he is standing is one of the most popular places for tourist photos in the city and is free of any commercial development, such as shops and cafes for that very reason. Clearly, every destination needs to maximise photo opportunities for visitors, particularly in the Web 2.0 era when user-generated content overwhelms marketing communications by DMOs and the tourism industry. For example, for a list of the 20 most photographed places on Instagram, headed by the Teacups ride at Disneyland, see http://www.traveller.com.au/the-top-ten-most-popular-places-on-instagram-in-2014-11zg0q. For a list of the top 25 landmarks in the world in 2015, headed by Cambodia's Angkor Wat, see http://www.tripadvisor.com.au/TravelersChoice-Landmarks-cTop-g1-a_Mode.expanded.

A popular form of photo opportunity publicity for destinations is *Big Things*. One of the most outrageous of these, and possibly from the *Only in America* category, is an eight-storey office building built in the shape of a basket, headquarters of the Longaberger Basket Company in Newark, Ohio. Man-made icons have long been popular in small towns, where eye-catching roadside figures can become *must see* photo opportunities for some travellers. Some Australian examples are listed in Table 13.4. In 2007 five of the icons were featured in a special set of Australian postage stamps, entitled *Big Things*.

Figure 13.1 Hollywood walk of fame

Figure 13.2 Photo opportunity at the iconic Notre Dame Cathedral, Paris

Table 13.4 Examples of Australian small town icons

Icon	Town
The Big Apple	Stanthorpe, Queensland
The Big Avocado	Byron Bay, New South Wales
The Big Banana	Coffs Harbour, New South Wales
The Big Cheese	Bega, New South Wales
The Big Cow	Nambour, Queensland
The Big Guitar	Tamworth, New South Wales
The Big Lobster	Kingston, South Australia
The Big Merino	Goulburn, New South Wales
The Big Oyster	Taree, New South Wales
The Big Peanut	North Tolga, Queensland
The Big Pineapple	Nambour, Queensland
The Big Pie	Yatala, Queensland
The Big Prawn	Ballina, New South Wales

Capitalising on the power of celebrity visitors

The following is the start of a post made on Facebook by Hollywood actor, Vin Diesel, on 1 February 2011:

> *I have long dreamed of going to a place as sacred as Egypt, I was always, like everyone, fascinated by its rich history . . . one that both predates and has shaped our collective history.*
>
> *A year ago I was blessed with the opportunity to travel to Egypt . . . the experience changed me.*

Could this have been Diesel's own personal initiative, or was it more likely an example of a covert organic image development tactic by Egypt's NTO? Regardless, the actor has over 90 million Facebook followers and so the power of celebrity is one that cannot be ignored by DMOs. For a review of the literature related to the positives and negatives of celebrity endorsements, see Johns and Weir (2014). What is critical with any celebrity endorsement, whether it be in advertising or on a Facebook page, is that the consumer's self-image is congruent with the destination's image and the celebrity's image (see Glover, 2009). For destination branding, an *association* might be formed in the consumer's mind between the celebrity and the destination. As discussed in Chapter 10, associative network theory sees memory as consisting of nodes (neurons) with links to other nodes (see Anderson and Bower, 1979; Anderson, 1983). A node represents stored information about a particular concept and is part of a network of links to other nodes. Activation between nodes occurs either through the action of processing external information or when information is retrieved from memory. When a node concept is recalled, the strength of association will dictate the range of other nodes that will be activated from memory. A destination brand is conceptualised as representing a node with which a number of associations with other node concepts (wants, attributes and benefits) are linked. So, in the case of *Oprah's Ultimate Australian Adventure*, viewers would not have been influenced unless Oprah and/or Australia matched their own self-image (Johns and Weir, 2014: 120): 'Oprah Winfrey's "Rags to Riches" story makes Oprah seem even more believable; that is, she is someone viewers can aspire to become. Furthermore, because of their apparent lack of agenda, celebrities such as Oprah are trusted by the public'.

Johns and Weir (2014: 127) observed that on a number of occasions during the Australian episodes Oprah made reference to her difficult childhood and how she never dreamed she would ever visit Australia; it is this accessibility to her audience that makes her popular: 'she fit in well with the Australian environment . . . her use of common slang had her fitting in with the Australian audience and offering a comedic relief to the international audience'.

In addition to inviting celebrity visits, another approach is to maximise the opportunity to enhance brand associations presented by unsolicited visitation. For example, the 2014 visit of China's President, XI, and his wife, Madame Peng, to Australia for the G20 summit presented a unique opportunity for Tourism Australia to tap into the saturated media coverage covering every move of the well-respected couple (see Tourism Australia, 2015). The NTO's *#Dada's Visit to Australia* on Instagram delivered over 120 million views in just 6 days. Dada is a term of affection Chinese citizens have given to the President. The NTO's social media campaign was based on the public welcome the famous couple received on the streets from the local Chinese community. The patriotic scenes were captured and shared on Sina Weibo (the China equivalent to Facebook/Twitter) to kick off the campaign. This was followed by imagery of a state banquet held in Tasmania, which centred on the President's comments about fresh food quality (an important attribute for Chinese travellers). One of the most *shared* stories of the campaign was Madame Peng's visit to Brisbane's Lone Pine Koala Sanctuary, which resulted in numerous fan enquiries to the NTO. The 41 posts in 6 days led to an increase of 30,000 fans on the NTO's Sina Weibo site. The most popular single post, an interview with the President's executive chef about Tasmanian food, generated 30 million views, 3,000 likes, 300 comments and 3,500 re-tweets.

13.10 #20yearsofinlove

During 2015 a joint venture between Tourism New Zealand, Air New Zealand and three RTOs brought Chinese actor, director and singer, Huang Lei, and his wife to New Zealand for an 8-day visit to mark the couple's 20 years together. During the holiday, Huang Lei's two posts to his social media Weibo account attracted 90,000 likes, and the freshly created #20yearsofinlove attracted 1.6 million views. The couple's visit was a follow-on from Huang Lei's 2014 visit to New Zealand to film two episodes of China's top-rated television show *Dad, Where Are We Going?* The episodes were watched by over 400 million Chinese viewers. Huang Lei's first publicity visit to New Zealand was in 2008, when his family took part in Air New Zealand's inaugural flight between Shanghai and Auckland. News of the 2015 visit generated over 500 media articles, with an equivalent advertising value of at least NZ$2.7 million. The joint venture partners claimed the visit demonstrated their 'phenomenal run in attracting China's biggest celebrity names to showcase the country despite increasing competition from other destinations'.

Other initiatives

Other DMO initiatives that fall under the label *publicity* include:

- celebrations of place anniversaries, such as Quebec City's 400th anniversary in 2008, and Germany's Dresden, which celebrated its 800th anniversary in 2006 by presenting over 400 special events;

- celebrations of anniversaries of famous people, such as in Spain during 2006–2007 to mark the 125th anniversary of Picasso's birth;

- stimulation of the use of locations in corporate brochures, such as by Canada in Porsche's magazine;

- contra prizes for game shows;

- contra prizes for consumer goods retail competitions;

- sponsorship of media competitions;

- encouraging department stores to use destination themes;

- public 'film' evenings;

- use of celebrities as tourism ambassadors, such as the Tourism Australia's use of world surfing champion, Lane Beachley; model, Megan Gale; and swimmer, Ian Thorpe. Maison France used actor, Woody Allen, in the trade promotion video *Let's Fall in Love Again*. The Queen and the royal family participated in the promotion of British Tourism Day, 2003.

CHAPTER SUMMARY

Key point 1: Managing relationships with stakeholders

PR is more than publicity-seeking, in that it represents working with stakeholders (publics) in a concerted effort to develop favourable impressions of a destination. This involves both the generation of positive publicity by the DMO, as well as the stimulation of positive relations between internal and external stakeholders, to mitigate potentially negative issues before they become public. Since DMOs are essentially in the business of communication, to manage the image of the destination and the reputation of the tourism industry, the process of communication management should not be left to chance. Therefore the DMO needs to carefully manage relationships with key stakeholders such as politicians, the media and the host community.

Key point 2: Advantages of media publicity

For destinations, publicity represents a cost-efficient and effective means to gain market exposure. Publicity can appear from many sources, over which the DMO may or may not have had any control, involvement or even knowledge and may or may not be positive. The cost-efficiency and relatively high credibility of media editorial coverage are attractive to destination marketers with limited resources, and so publicity-seeking initiatives are a key aspect of any destination marketing plan.

Key point 3: Publicity opportunities for DMOs

As well as stimulating media editorial through media releases and visiting media programmes, other popular publicity-seeking initiatives by DMOs include capitalising on movies, television programmes, literary figures, iconic photo opportunities and celebrity visits.

REVIEW QUESTIONS

1. Imagine you have been asked by a television network to provide a photo of an icon that best represents your local destination. This photo will be used briefly alongside those from other centres during the evening weather update. Explain why. Share your views with others and gauge the level of agreement.

2. What experience does your city offer that is truly unique? Use this unique selling point to prepare a release to the travel media.

3. Do professional travel writers have a future in the digital age? Explain.

REFERENCES

Amor, F., Calabug, C., Abellan, J. and Montfort, V. R. (1994). Barriers found in repositioning a Mediterranean 'sun and beach' product: The Valencian case. In Seaton, A. V., Jenkins, C. L., Wood, R. C., Dieke, P. U. C., Bennett, M. M., MacLellan, L. R. and Smith, R. (eds) *Tourism the State of the Art*. Chichester, UK: John Wiley & Sons Ltd.

Anderson, J. R. (1983). *The Architecture of Cognition*. Cambridge, MA: Harvard University Press.

Anderson, J. R. and Bower, G. H. (1979). *Human Associative Memory*. Hillsdale, NJ: Lawrence Erlbaum.

Ateljevic, I. (1998). *Circuits of Tourism: (Re)Producing the Place of Rotorua, New Zealand*. Unpublished PhD Thesis. University of Auckland. Hard copy only.

Ateljevic, I. and Doorne, S. (2000). Local government and tourism development: Issues and constraints of public sector entrepreneurship. *New Zealand Geographer* 56(2): 25–31.

Beeton, S. (2001). Smiling for the camera: The influence of film audiences on a budget tourism destination. *Tourism, Culture & Communication* 3(1): 15–25.

Bergman, J. (2004). A peek into hell's pit. *The Sunday Mail*. Brisbane. 22 February, p. 6. Hard copy newspaper article.

Bramwell, B. and Rawding, L. (1996). Tourism marketing images of industrial cities. *Annals of Tourism Research* 23(1): 201–221.

Broom, G. (2009). *Effective Public Relations* (10th edition). Upper Saddle River, NJ: Pearson Prentice Hall.

Buckley, P. J. and Witt, S. F. (1985). Tourism in difficult areas: Case studies of Bradford, Bristol, Glasgow and Hamm. *Tourism Management* September: 205–213.

Cincotta, K. (2006). Web content, glossy editorial: A happy co-existence. B & T. 31 March, p. 15. Hard copy magazine article.

Connell, J. (2012). Film tourism: Evolution, progress and prospects. *Tourism Management* 33(5): 1007–1029.

Courtenay, D. (2005). Communications. In Harrill, R. (ed.) *Fundamentals of Destination Management and Marketing*. Lansing, MI: The Educational Institute of the American Hotel & Lodging Association, pp. 77–98.

Croy, G. (2004). The Lord of the Rings, Middle Earth, New Zealand and tourism. *14th International Research Conference of the Council for Australian University Tourism and Hospitality Education*. Brisbane, QLD: The University of Queensland.

Davidson, R. and Maitland, R. (1997). *Tourism Destinations*. London: Hodder & Stoughton.

Dore, L. and Crouch, G. I. (2003). Promoting destinations: An exploratory study of publicity programmes used by national tourism organizations. *Journal of Vacation Marketing* 9(2): 137–151.

Ehemann, J. (1977). What kind of place is Ireland: An image perceived through the American media. *Journal of Travel Research* 16(1): 28–30.

Foreman, M. (2003). Tourism chomping through old grants. *The Independent*. 17 July. Hard copy newspaper article.

Frost, W. (2003). Braveheart-ed Ned Kelly: Destination image and historic films. *Taking Tourism to the Limits: An International Interdisciplinary Conference in the Waikato*. University of Waikato.

Gartrell, R. B. (1994). *Destination Marketing for Convention and Visitor Bureaus*. Dubuque, IA: Kendall/Hunt.

Glover, P. (2009). Celebrity endorsement in tourism advertising: Effects on destination image. *Journal of Hospitality and Tourism Management* 61(1): 16–23.

Halkier, H. (2014). Innovation and destination governance in Denmark: Tourism, policy networks and spatial development. *European Planning Studies* 22(8): 1659–1670.

Harlow, R. F. (1976). Building a definition of public relations. *Public Relations Review* 2(4): 34–42.

Holloway, J. C. and Robinson, C. (1995). *Marketing for Tourism* (3rd edition). Harlow, UK: Addison Wesley Longman.

Hoppen, A., Brown, L. and Fyall. A. (2014). Literary tourism: Opportunities and challenges for the marketing and branding of destinations. *Journal of Destination Marketing & Management* 3(1): 37–47.

Horn, C., Fairweather, J. R. and Simmons, D. C. (2000). *Evolving Community Response to Tourism and Change in Rotorua*. Rotorua Case Study Report No. 14. Christchurch, NZ: Lincoln University. Hard copy report.

Hudson, S., Wang, Y. and Gil, S. M. (2011). The influence of a film on destination image and the desire to travel: A cross-cultural comparison. *International Journal of Tourism Research* 13(2): 177–190.

Johns, R. and Weir, B. (2014). The power of celebrity: Exploring the basis for Oprah's successful endorsement of Australia as a vacation destination. *Journal of Vacation Marketing* 21(2): 117–130.

Kim, H. and Richardson, S. L. (2003). Motion picture impacts on destination images. *Annals of Tourism Research* 30(1): 216–237.

Laderman, S. (2009). *Tours of Vietnam: War, Travel Guides, and Memory*. Durham, NC: Duke University Press.

L'Etang, J., Falkheimer, J. and Lugo, J. (2007). Public relations and tourism: Critical reflections and a research agenda. *Public Relations Review* 33(1): 68–76.

Light, D. (2012). *The Dracula Dilemma: Tourism, identity and the state of Romania*. Farnham, UK: Ashgate Publishing.

McGehee, N. G., Meng, F. and Tepanon, Y. (2006). Understanding legislators and their perceptions of the tourism industry: The case of North Carolina, USA, 1990 and 2003. *Tourism Management* 27(2): 684–694.

Meler, M. and Ruzic, D. (1999). Marketing identity of the tourist product of the Republic of Croatia. *Tourism Management* 20(1): 635–643.

NZPA. (2006). City fights Cleese's Fawlty claims. *The Courier-Mail*. 22 March, p. 40. Hard copy newspaper article.

Pike, S. (2002). *Positioning as a Source of Competitive Advantage: Benchmarking Rotorua's Position as a Domestic Short Break Holiday Destination*. PhD Thesis. University of Waikato. November. Hard copy only.

Pike, S. (2004). *Destination Marketing Organisations*. Oxford: Elsevier Science.

Pike, S. (2007). A cautionary tale of a resort destination's self-inflicted crisis. *Journal of Travel & Tourism Marketing* 23(2/3/4): 73–82.

Pike, S. (2008). *Destination Marketing: An Integrated Marketing Communication Approach*. Burlington, MA: Butterworth-Heinemann.

Pike, S., May, T. and Bolton, R. (2011). RTO governance: Reflections from a former marketing team. *Journal of Travel & Tourism Research* Fall: 117–133.

Pillmayer, M. and Scherle, N. (2014). Tourism lobbying in Bavaria: Between ignorance, parochialism and opportunism. *European Planning Studies* 22(8): 1671–1692.

Pride, R. (2002). Brand Wales: 'Natural revival'. In Morgan, N., Prichard, A. and Pride, R. (eds) *Destination Branding*. Oxford: Butterworth-Heinemann, pp. 109–123.

Pritchard, G. (1982). Tourism promotion: Big business for the states. *HRA Quarterly* 23(2): 48–57.

Quintal, V. and Phau, I. (2014). Romancing 'friends with benefits': Does it benefit New York as a travel destination? *Tourism Analysis* 19(1): 51–67.

Redondo, I. (2012). Assessing the appropriateness of movies as vehicles for promoting tourist destinations. *Journal of Travel & Tourism Marketing* 29(7): 714–729.

Richardson, J. I. (1999). *A History of Australian Travel and Tourism*. Elsternwick, VIC: Hospitality Press.

Riley, R. and Van Doren, C. (1998). Movies as tourism promotion: A push factor in a pull location. *Tourism Management* 13(3): 267–274.

Riley, R., Baker, D. and Van Doren, C. S. (1992). Movie induced tourism. *Annals of Tourism Research* 25(4): 919–933.

Rosemann, I., Prosser, G., Hunt, S. and Benecke, K. (2000). *Promoting Awareness of the Value of Tourism: A Resource Kit*. Lismore, NSW: Centre for Regional Tourism Research.

Selby, M. and Morgan, N. J. (1996). Reconstruing place image: A case study of its role in destination market research. *Tourism Management* 17(4): 287–294.

Semley, N. and Busby, G. (2014). Film tourism: The pre-production perspective. A case study of Visit Somerset and the Hollywood story of Glastonbury. *Journal of Tourism Consumption and Practice* 6(2): 23–53.

Sharpley, R. (2014). Host perceptions of tourism: A review of the research. *Tourism Management* 42(1): 37–49.

Stein, J. (2006). Borat make funny joke on idiot Americans! High-Five! *Time*. 13 Nov: p. 60.

Tench, R. and Yeomans, L. (2014). *Exploring Public Relations* (3rd edition). Harlow, UK: Pearson Education Limited. Hard copy newspaper article.

Tooke, N. and Baker, M. (1996). Seeing is believing: The effect of film on visitor numbers to screened locations. *Tourism Management* 17(2): 87–94.

Tourism Australia. (2011). *Oprah in Australia*. Available at: http://www.tourism.australia.com/documents/corporate/The_Oprah_Effect.pdf

Tourism Australia. (2014). *Working with Tourism Australia: Global Marketing Prospectus 2014/2015*. Available at: http://www.tourism.australia.com/documents/Markets/Report_WorkingwithTA_May14.pdf

Tourism Australia. (2015). *President Xi's Visit to Australia*. Available at: http://www.tourism.australia.com/documents/corporate/President-XI-Visit-Social-Media-Recap.pdf

TravelandTourWorld.com. (2015). *Northern Ireland to Reach 4.5 Million French Viewers through Famous TV Series*. Available at: http://www.travelandtourworld.com/news/article/4-5-million-french-tv-viewers-see-northern-ireland

Travelindustrywire.com. (2014). *Travel Leaders Applaud Bipartisan Effort to Extend Travel Promotion Program in Omnibus Bill*. Available at: http://www.travelindustrywire.com/article81260.html

Trout, J. and Rivkin, S. (1995). *The New Positioning*. New York: McGraw-Hill.

Voase, R. (2002). *Tourism in Western Europe: A Collection of Case Histories*. Wallingford, UK: CABI Publishing.

Wahab, S., Crampon, L. J. and Rothfield, L. M. (1976). *Tourism Marketing*. London: Tourism International Press.

Yeoman, I. (2008). *Tomorrow's Tourist: Scenarios and Trends*. Oxford: Elsevier.

Chapter **14**

Destination marketing organisations (DMOs) and the travel trade

AIMS

To enhance understanding of:

- the DMO's role as an information broker in the tourism distribution system;
- the need for collaboration with travel intermediaries;
- the range of travel trade events.

ABSTRACT

For the product marketer, distribution refers to the logistics involved in the physical movement of goods from the place of manufacture through various channels to the point of sale. In services marketing, however, distribution clearly does not involve the physical transportation of a tangible product. The concepts of immovability and inseparability generally mean the destination service is consumed at the place of production, and the tourism provider and the consumer must be present for the service to be delivered. In tourism, distribution represents the cost of getting a sale through commissioned travel intermediaries. While some of the earlier DMOs were directly involved in the selling of destination travel packages as wholesalers and/or retailers, this is rarely the case today except for visitor information centres. Instead, the DMO acts as an information broker in the tourism distribution system, liaising between their destination service providers and external travel intermediaries through a range of travel trade events and educational initiatives. Currently the power balance in the tourism distribution system is again undergoing change through the democratisation of the internet for consumers and the resultant disintermediation in the supply chain through the rise of online bookings. This is providing opportunities as well as challenges to DMOs and their service providers.

Tourism distribution

For the product marketer, distribution refers to the logistics involved in the physical movement of goods from the place of manufacture through various channels to the point of sale. In services marketing, however, distribution clearly does not involve the physical transportation of a tangible product. The concepts of immovability and inseparability generally mean the destination service is consumed at the place of production, and the tourism provider and the consumer must be present for the service to be delivered. In tourism, distribution represents the cost of getting a sale through commissioned travel intermediaries. Distribution channel intermediaries for tourism services often represent the most effective means of reaching travellers, but at the same time can incur high costs in the form of commission fees paid to travel intermediaries. For a review of the literature relating to studies of tourism distribution prior to Web 2.0, see Pearce and Schott (2005). There is a need for more published research about the extent to which digital technologies are shaping the tourism distribution system.

Some of the early DMOs were directly involved in the selling of travel services for their destination. For example, in Australia, the Queensland Tourism and Travel Corporation operated retail travel services through its government tourist bureaus until the 1990s and, as a wholesaler, through its leading Sunlover Holidays brand until licensing it out to the private sector in 2007. Also, as discussed in the Prologue, the world's first NTO, the New Zealand Department of Tourist and Health Resorts, was from the outset involved in many aspects of the distribution system for decades, including the operation of (Pike, 2002):

- a network of overseas travel offices that served as: (1) a wholesaler facilitating reservations for travel agents; and (2) as a travel agent selling direct to the public, until the 1980s;

- a leading coach touring company, Tiki Tours, until the 1980s;

- a network of domestic tourism bureaus that sold domestic travel and local sightseeing, until 1990;

- a hunting and fishing advisory office that arranged high-yield tailor-made itineraries, until the 1980s.

Apart from operating local visitor information centres (VICs), most DMOs now leave reservation systems to the private sector. DMOs have moved away from operating a wholesale business to focus efforts on marketing. One exception to this is Tourism Northern Territory in Australia, which provides a direct booking portal for travellers and the travel trade (see http://www.territorydiscoveries.com). Operating a wholesale business has political implications relating to the selection of businesses included in the packages. In Scotland the NTO licensed a private operator to use the name VisitScotland.com for a travel booking site. The company posted a loss of over £2 million in 2004, when bed and breakfast operators boycotted the site. The operators refused to pay a 10 per cent commission, as they were under the impression the site was owned by the NTO, to which they already paid memberships levies.

RESEARCH SNAPSHOT

14.1 Tourism distribution situation analysis

In 2013 there was a comprehensive situation analysis of tourism distribution by Australia's NTO and STOs. The aims of the study were two-fold. The first was to understand the relevance of different tourism distribution approaches across Australia's key holiday markets, and the second was to review the structure and activities of Tourism Australia and the STOs. In addition to reviewing the DMOs' distribution activities, the research also included stakeholder interviews and a consumer survey. The key findings included:

1. Consumer identification of Australia as a destination, along with travel planning, was increasingly undertaken online. However, levels of digital planning and booking were low in developing markets and long haul markets and had plateaued in mature markets. Therefore traditional distribution channels, such as retail travel agents, remain important.

2. Greater cooperation was needed to ensure Australia went to market under one banner, instead of duplicating resources. In this regard there was friction in the relationship between the NTO and some STOs. The STO was perceived by some to have a coercive and controlling attitude. Of the NTO's marketing budget, 61 per cent was spent on consumer promotion, 11 per cent on PR, 19 per cent on trade cooperative campaigns and 9 per cent on travel trade training and familiarisation trips. For the STOs, an average of 7 per cent was spent on consumer promotion, 20 per cent on PR, 49 per cent on travel cooperative campaigns, 17 per cent on travel trade training and familiarisations and 7 per cent on events and travel missions.

3. While there was agreement that the Australian Travel Exchange (ATE) was a valuable mechanism for stakeholders to connect with overseas channels, there was a need to reduce participation costs and the length of the event.

4. While the Aussie Specialist Programme (ASP) was generally viewed as a valuable means of attracting more visitors, the training programme was expensive for STOs to maintain, and there were concerns over the lack of performance metrics. In particular, there were limited metrics relating to the volume of sales generated by individual ASP members.

The federal system of government in Australia was responsible for creating difficulties in delineating each government's role to be played in international tourism. As a result, a key recommendation from the situation analysis was for a more coordinated national distribution strategy, with the NTO taking a more proactive role in facilitating STO, RTO and industry activities.

Further reading

PWC. (2013).

The power of travel intermediaries

As discussed in Chapter 9, the history of branding over the centuries has been inextricably linked with the shifting balance of power between suppliers, distributors and consumers. Currently, the power balance in the tourism distribution system is again undergoing change through the democratisation of the internet for consumers, and the resultant disintermediation in the supply chain with the rise of online bookings. For example, Tripadvisor.com now wields considerable influence in the travel distribution system through ownership of major online travel agents expedia.com, orbitzworldwide.com and wotif.com. Nevertheless, in many tourism markets, a small number of powerful intermediaries control considerable amounts of visitor traffic and are therefore a primary stakeholder for DMOs. For example, in Brazil, 90 per cent of trips sold are by members of the Brazil Tour Operators Association (http://braztoa.com.br/eng, 20 March 2015).

At the opening session of the International Tourism Conference held in Alanya, Turkey during November 2006, the rector of the host university shared his views on the local tourism industry's problems. Clearly passionate about Alanya, he nevertheless lamented his destination had gone 'from heaven to hell', because of the control exerted by European package wholesalers:

In terms of economy, productivity is decreasing not increasing. The competition of the foreign tour monopolists is kept on by decreasing the price and marketing all-inclusive packets, which causes the best hotels to be marketed at very low prices. Only about 25 per cent of this income stays in Antalya and 75 per cent of it goes out of the city.

(Pike, 2008)

Ozturk and van Niekerk (2014) cited a report estimating only 10 per cent of spending by all-inclusive package visitors to Turkey directly benefited the local resort area economies, and that the immediate area surrounding the hotels received little economic benefit. This problem in Turkey has also been investigated by Okumus and Karamustafa (2005). A study of a similar overreliance on all-inclusive packages on mature, small island destinations was reported by Parra-López *et al.* (2006, in Pike, 2008). Vial (1997, in Morgan and Pritchard, 1998) cited the example of the *Feast for the senses* brand developed by Publicis for the Morocco Tourist Board, which was derailed by resistance from overseas tour wholesalers who viewed the campaign as promoting cultural tourism when they were in the business of catering to the need for sun and sea packages.

The DMO as information broker

Other than the operation of VICs by some DMOs, mostly at RTO level, the role played by destination marketers in the tourism distribution system is one of information broker. That is, serving as a conduit between constituent service providers and the range of external travel intermediaries. Tourism operators need access to intermediary decision makers, while travel intermediaries are always looking for new, innovative or more efficient products to offer their customers. The aim of information brokering for the DMO is the stimulation of travel packages to the destination.

> ### IN PRACTICE
>
> #### 14.1 Tourism data warehouse
>
> The Australian Tourism Data Warehouse (ATDW) (www.atdw.com.au) is a trade digital platform designed to provide intermediaries with access to product and destination information from a single source in a common format. The site was created in 2001 as a joint venture between the country's NTO and STOs. By 2014 the database featured 35,000 listings (see Tourism Australia, 2014). On the supply side, the database provides all tourism businesses with cost-effective online information distribution. The database has a search function enabling any intermediary from around the world to seek out desired services. The ATDW also provides a highly regarded Tourism eKit to help service providers improve their online presence. The eKit consists of a series of printed and video tutorials for registered Australian businesses.

Types of travel intermediaries

There is a diverse range of travel intermediaries of potential interest to DMOs, including:

- VICs;
- retail travel agents;
- travel wholesalers;

- inbound tour operators;

- incentive travel planners;

- professional conference organisers;

- corporate travel offices;

- general sales agents;

- airlines;

- cruise lines.

VICs

It has been common for DMOs at the RTO level to operate a VIC, as a means of distributing information about local tourism services to visitors. Cooperation between regions also enables RTOs to distribute their destination information to other centres around the country, in either a formal or an informal visitor information network. Given the nature of operations, these offices are rarely profitable and often rely on volunteer labour and government grants to remain viable. The future of visitor information offices in their traditional format is currently unclear given the rise of the use of mobile technologies by travellers.

Retail travel agents

Travel agents are the public face of travel distribution, with a presence on every high street and in every shopping mall. Agents earn commission from travel service providers, and the commissions are tiered depending on the level of *preferred* status that has been negotiated with suppliers.

Travel wholesalers

Travel wholesalers usually do not sell direct to the public, rather they assemble packages that are offered for sale by travel agents. As discussed, in many countries distribution of packages to travel agents has traditionally been controlled by only a handful of wholesalers. This power has necessitated attempts by DMOs to influence decisions that will favour their destination and constituent service providers.

Inbound tour operators

As specialists in inbound tourism, inbound tour operators (ITO) promote and sell travel packages to offshore trade such as wholesalers and travel agency chains. The expertise of these businesses has been central to the distribution system in many countries, probably more so in developing markets and emerging destinations than in mature markets and established destinations. Key advantages of dealing with an ITO for overseas travel wholesalers include: local destination knowledge, better negotiated tariffs, better time management than dealing with multiple suppliers and a local contact on the ground for tour problems. Advantages for the DMO and tourism operators in dealing with ITOs include market knowledge and improved market access. Therefore, establishing working relationships with local ITOs is an essential part of the DMO's marketing plan.

IN PRACTICE

14.2 ITO licensing

To be officially recognised in Australia, ITOs must obtain a licence from the federal government's Office of Fair Trading, under the Travel Agents Act of Parliament. ITOs must be licensed to become members of the Australian Tourism Export Council (ATEC) (www.atec.net.au). ATEC is the peak national umbrella association representing the tourism industry in Australia. ITOs must also be audited every year to ensure they meet the criteria of the Travel Compensation Fund, which ultimately protects overseas wholesalers, travel agents and visitors.

Incentive travel planners

Incentive travel programmes were introduced by corporations as a means of motivating staff to achieve targets. Targets are related to business objectives and commonly involve either sales increases or cost reductions. Rewards might include individual travel and commonly involve large groups, which are a lucrative target for destinations. For the global peak body for incentive travel companies see www.siteglobal.com. The tailored nature of reward packages also tends to generate a higher than average yield for the destination's participating businesses. Incentive travel planning is a highly specialised business, and destinations need to carefully consider the resources required to effectively cater to this segment. Itineraries are custom-made to suit the needs of the group and tend to be creative in terms of venues and activities. Witt and Gammon (1994) suggested only destinations at the mature stage of the lifecycle need apply, since there needs to be a well-developed infrastructure, good accessibility and a sufficient mix of attractions. For the incentive to appeal to staff, the itinerary needs to be attractive and the destination needs to be well-known and have *brag value*. Distance and travel time to the destination are also important, given incentive group travel is commonly in the form of a short break. Promotion is clearly very targeted, usually involving personal selling to incentive travel specialists who are contracted by the corporation.

Professional conference organisers (PCOs)

Clearly, all conferences must be organised. PCOs are contracted by organisations, associations and DMOs to take care of the logistical arrangements such as registration, venue hire, AV equipment, functions, pre and post conference tours and, in some cases, travel arrangements/discounts. While PCOs are a major target for hoteliers in particular, DMOs develop relationships with PCOs for their involvement with destinations bidding for the rights to host conferences.

Corporate travel offices

Very large corporations often employ their own travel planners to provide travel arrangements for official staff business. For example, 90 per cent of international and domestic travel by employees of the Northern Territory government in Australia must now be booked through a central corporate system (TravelandTourWorld.com, 2015a). The system requires travel management firms to compare quotes and to also track potential cost savings in the reporting. In other cases, such as with many universities, for example, there will be a *preferred* arrangement with one travel agency chain, where all staff business travel will be channelled.

General sales agents

A general sales agent (GSA) undertakes representation of a group of independent tourism service providers and DMOs in given markets and can be domiciled in the host country or in the market. In this operation it is more affordable for the DMO and tourism businesses to employ part of a GSA's time than to employ sales staff in the market. A GSA might provide representation at trade events and sales calls, organise familiarisation tours for travel intermediaries and provide market updates to clients.

Airlines

Airlines have increased their influence in the distribution system dramatically in the post-1990s internet era. This has occurred through: drastic reductions of air fare commissions to travel agents; inducements for consumers to book flights directly online; and opportunities to purchase land arrangements such as accommodation, theme parks, rental cars and travel insurance. The rise of low-cost carriers since the 1980s, in an increasingly deregulated market, has presented unprecedented opportunities for destinations not previously serviced by the traditional carriers, and so there is much lobbying by DMOs to lure more carriers to their region. A successful example of this was highlighted in case study 12.1 in Chapter 12.

Cruise lines

The phenomenal rise in cruise tourism in recent years has had positive and negative impacts on destination marketing. On the one hand, there is the lure of the potential for a destination to receive thousands of visitors in a day to contribute to the local economy. On the other hand, cruises are essentially a destination in their own right, competing with a destination's accommodation suppliers. Not only are visitors only disembarking at destinations for around eight hours or less but in some cases the destination might be a private island owned by the cruise line, as is common in the Caribbean. A cruise ship appeals to many travellers as being safer than many destinations, with almost everything conveniently organised for the traveller.

Cruise holidays are perceived by some to be one of the worst types of mass tourism, for the negative environmental and socio-cultural impacts. These impacts are more noticeable in the more established cruise regions such as the Caribbean and Mediterranean, but not as public in fledgling areas such as the South Pacific. Many passengers and destination stakeholders seeking cruise ship patronage are not aware of these impacts, which might include:

- ship registration in a nation with lower human resource management requirements than most, resulting in low wages for staff who work long hours, seven days a week for months at a time;

- direct emission of sewerage and grey water into the ocean;

- import leakage through the mark-up made on shore excursions, where the ship profits more than the destination's tour operators;

- the impact on the destination experience of non-cruise visitors when the ships' masses disembark at the port.

Joint venture (JV) marketing campaigns

Few people are better qualified to discuss the tangled web of DMO/intermediary relationships than Owen Eagles, Managing Director of ANZCRO (www.anzcro.com.au), a travel wholesaler with offices in Australia, New Zealand, England and the USA. With 28 years' DMO experience with New Zealand's NTO in Australia, New Zealand, Japan and the USA, and 20 years at ANZCRO, Eagles understands only too well the dynamics of the relationship between DMOs and those within the tourism distribution system: 'It's a real mess, and not well understood by all the players themselves who end up protecting their jobs with populist decisions promoting apparent success through a scenario of smoke and mirrors'.

As is discussed in Chapter 15, it is very difficult to quantify the return on investment for DMO initiatives with intermediaries and consumers. Eagles argues one way to do so is through JV projects between DMOs and intermediaries, a scenario where investment return can ultimately be measured by bookings. Such a JV between ANZCRO, an NTO, three RTOs and four travel agency chains, is an example of effectively steering through the politics to achieve a vertically integrated JV. Eagles' summary of the positives and negatives of JV marketing are summarised in Table 14.1.

Table 14.1 Positives and negatives of joint venture marketing

Positives	Negatives
• Ability to measure results through the origin and timing of sales • Ability to budget for, and control, costs • Ability to choose appropriate supplier constituents who contribute towards the marketing programme with special product offers (very measurable by their unique and coded nature) and cash • Choice of a wholesaler whose distribution system is clear and concise, e.g. one that may have preferred relationships with 2,500 retail travel agents in Australia • Ability to leverage the campaign by increasing resources with contributions from suppliers and airline, wholesaler and travel agent chain	• Negotiating the clutter available to the consumer at travel agent outlets (often overcome with educational incentives and productivity rewards) • Choosing the right wholesaler and suppliers – both should have a working relationship in place • Managing the compromises necessary with a number of project partners, particularly in the production of visual material • Maintaining the destination product offer over a substantial period of time, say three years, so that it has time to become established • The accusation, by suppliers not selected, that the DMO is biased and unfairly leaning towards those suppliers chosen for the product offer

---

IN PRACTICE

14.3 NTO/RTO/wholesaler/travel agent JV

ANZCRO (www.anzcro.com.au) is a leading wholesaler of New Zealand tourism services in Australia. The company has built a strong niche position in the Australian travel market with expertise in planning New Zealand travel itineraries. Whereas many competing South Pacific destinations promote *stay put* sun and beach resort holidays to Australians, New Zealand is well-known as a touring destination. This requires itinerary planning that is more intensive, for travel agents as well as consumers, than for *stay put* resort holidays. ANZCRO's business model was developed on the basis of being a one-stop-shop for travel agents dealing with customers wanting individual touring itineraries. CEO, Owen Eagles, recognises the importance of creating JVs with New Zealand regions as a way of increasing market exposure for their products that will be of interest to Australian consumers. In this particular case, the JV partners included the NTO, Tourism New Zealand and three RTOs in New Zealand's South Island: Queenstown, Dunedin and Christchurch/Canterbury. The impetus for linking with the NTO in the JVs was that the major RTOs committed all the JV funding in Australia to Tourism New Zealand's high-profile television and newspaper campaign *What's on in New Zealand*, promoting travel in the autumn season. The advertising referred consumers to a Tourism New Zealand website promoting, in this case, ANZCRO's autumn travel packages, to the participating regions, with four Australian retail travel agent chains. ANZCRO sponsored a page in the travel catalogue of Flight Centres, one of Australia's largest travel agency chains, which distributes over 300,000 copies each month. ANZCRO's month-long participation in the campaign's performance was monitored through the company's reservation call centre. Web traffic data was also provided by Tourism New Zealand.

During 2015, examples of JV marketing campaigns between Tourism Australia and travel intermediaries around the world included a five-year AUD\$30 million JV with Etihad Airways and a five-year AUD\$50 million JV with Virgin Australia. Around 20 per cent of the NTO's marketing spend is on JV campaigns (PWC, 2013). Case study 14.1 describes an example of an effective JV between an RTO and a major online travel agent.

> **CASE STUDY**
>
> ### 14.1 DMO collaboration with an online travel agent
>
> **Kim Stockham**
> **Head of Public Relations, Wotif Group, Australia**
> **As at February 2015**
>
> Destination marketing, at its best, is a collaborative journey between a DMO and its stakeholders, including their strategic partners. Before marketing a destination, DMOs must endeavour to understand the needs of key stakeholders, which can include tourist attractions in-market, hotels, travel agents and marketing channel partners. Of course, they also need to understand what travellers want to experience, or expect to gain, from a visit to the destination they plan to promote. This helps tap into compelling destination images and messaging later in the process.
>
> Destination marketing, conducted in partnership with an online travel agent (OTA), can have many advantages for DMOs, which include the opportunity to gain insights into traveller booking behaviour and online trends through the sharing of *rich digital data*, which they may not be able to access otherwise. OTAs may also provide insights about compelling times and ways to position the destination to their unique audience of travellers, particularly geared to an online-savvy audience.
>
> Consumers visit an OTA site at various stages of the purchase funnel, from being inspired about a destination, to actively searching for a deal, or comparing pricing and value for money between sites and destinations. The ideal, final step would be in the booking of a trip to the promoted destination. Marketing a destination with OTAs can help build brand/destination awareness and focus attention on key attributes of the destination and promote reasons to book.
>
> OTAs like those in the Wotif Group portfolio, including wotif.com and lastminute.com.au, work very closely with many DMOs to promote their destination. In our experience, great OTA destination campaigns tend to have common elements: compelling design and images, unique *content* for each channel targeted to the key audience using that distribution channel, amplified through PR and social media and orchestrated to build a positive *image* of, and interest in, the destination. A common promotional path is for the DMO to utilise the OTA's *owned channels* (these predominantly being the OTA's website, as well as re-marketing via the OTA's customer relationship management communication channels, most commonly via email). At times, promotional campaigns also utilise *paid* channels (which include joint search engine marketing investment and *above the line* advertising activities). When combined, these marketing channels can provide the DMO with huge audience *reach* into key source markets for a destination. Incorporating the OTA embeds a connected path between promotions and the booking channel.
>
> In the online environment, there is a highly measurable component to marketing campaigns, including the evaluation of the number of *clicks* to a landing page, or to destination travel products, or content on the OTA site. The ability to attract *clicks* confirms target audience interest in the destination and/or confirms that the destination deal on the OTA site is compelling. And ultimately, campaign

success can be evaluated directly on consumer purchase behaviour, which occurs when online bookings of travel-related products in the promoted destination occur via the OTA site.

DMOs, travel suppliers (hotels, etc.) and the partner OTA can all benefit from destination campaigns where sales are generated, but travellers are the ultimate winners in this type of destination marketing approach, as OTAs often negotiate special product pricing in the promoted destination to support the marketing activity during the campaign period.

Additional elements in a compelling destination campaign can include social media and PR activities by the DMO, as well as by its OTA partner, which in turn can drive audience *reach*, and at times drive audience *engagement*, as well as potentially driving search engine optimisation (SEO) benefits for the DMO, OTA and for the campaign/destination. The OTA's *owned* social media channels (i.e. the OTA's social media sites such as Facebook, Google+, Instagram and Twitter) can work to support images and messages shared via the OTA's *earned* communication methods, such as PR (particularly any resulting media coverage) and *social sharing* by online audiences. These are often referred to as *below the line* promotions.

A recent example of how public relations helped fuel awareness and build a positive destination image for Melbourne in media coverage (as part of a coordinated destination campaign on lastminute.com.au) can be seen below. This type of aligned approach across multiple channels, including PR activity, takes a great deal of forward planning, creative thinking and an acknowledgement that news media rarely run a story about marketing campaigns, but can be interested in trends, statistics and data on a destination or traveller habits. As such, the PR team can source and position destination-related *news* and share this news with media outlets, ideally at the same time as the campaign is running on *owned* and perhaps *paid* channels.

For the *Play up in Melbourne* campaign on lastminute.com.au, the PR team surveyed the OTA's audience of travellers some weeks before the start of the campaign and then shared the supporting survey results with media, along with images. The resulting media coverage was directly attributable to lastminute.com.au's PR efforts as part of a broader destination marketing campaign. The *News Ltd* Escape.com.au article reached a wide Australian audience as a result of syndication of the story (into *The Daily Telegraph*, *The Herald Sun*, *The Courier Mail*, *Perth Now* and *Adelaide Now*, for example http://www.dailytelegraph.com.au/travel/australia/this-is-the-city-aussies-most-want-to-visit-in-2015/story-fnjjv1f2-1227208777517). The journalist utilised the PR angle shared by the lastminute.com.au PR team around Melbourne being the Australian city most people want to visit in 2015, as based on lastminute.com.au survey results.

Even broader audience awareness and geographic reach was gained for the same proactive PR outreach in additional media coverage in *The Daily Mail*, which utilised the same survey data, in a different way, to support an *Aussie City Wish List* story, also promoting Melbourne: http://www.dailymail.co.uk/news/article-2940573/Sydney-Melbourne-Hobart-Perth-Darwin-make-wish-list-Aussie-cities-capital-city-Australians-want-visit.html

Media coverage drives reach and builds awareness, but as occurred in this example, it can also be an important channel to foster online sharing of the marketing campaign through social media reach (the sharing of the story via social networks). In this same example, further online reach was driven by the sharing of the stories on Escape.com.au's social channels, which the DMO may then choose to share with its network of followers via their own *social* channels.
https://www.facebook.com/escape.com.au?fref=nf
https://twitter.com/Escape_team

Embedded *links* in the online version of stories not only help to drive SEO benefits for the campaign, but they play an important role in helping people interested in travelling to Melbourne to find a great travel deal on, you guessed it, lastminute.com.au. In short: mutual benefits for the OTA, the DMO and the destination. Together, all channels work to drive visitors to (and therefore *clicks*) the lastminute.com.au *Play up in Melbourne* campaign *landing page*, which featured Melbourne travel deals, completing the purchase cycle:

http://www.lastminute.com.au/dms/site/play-melbourne/index.html?intcmp=l:home:pod4:visualnav:
   play_melbourne

Discussion question

What are the main advantages for a DMO partnering with an OTA?

Travel trade events

The most effective means of stimulating meaningful dialogue with customers is personal selling. Travel trade events provide an opportunity to use personal selling to launch new products, services, brands and facilities to the travel trade. The first DMO involvement in travel trade events shows arguably started over a century ago, with the Honolulu Chamber of Commerce and Merchants Association's tourism promotional visits to the US mainland in 1901 and 1902 (see Choy, 1993) and the fledging New Zealand NTO's sales mission to the 1904 St Louis Exposition in the USA (see NZTPD, 1976).

IN PRACTICE

14.4 Advice from a tourism industry practitioner

Trish May
Principal at May Communications and Marketing Ltd.

Despite the rapid diversification of the channels of business in the tourism industry, one channel that continues to remain relevant is the travel trade. The travel trade is by its very nature commercial. They are the converters of business. The role they perform is one of creating and booking the travellers' itineraries for which they receive a commission, provided by the included accommodation, transport, activity or attraction. So, is there a role for the destination marketer to interact with the travel trade? Yes. Even though the destination marketing entity is not commercial (they do not have a bookable product to sell themselves), they do have important roles with the travel trade.

Creating a destination platform

For a destination marketer, a fundamental function is to create and position your location as an attractive 'must visit' destination. Making your destination appealing is attractive for the travel trade too, as it helps create demand and ultimately drives business, through them, to your destination. The easier the destination makes this task the more likely the trade will develop not only multiple itineraries, which include the region, but they are likely to have more nights included in that region. Destination marketers can use the trade to help communicate your brand and positioning. The trade are using destination marketers' communication tools to help make sales.

Here are a few tactics that can help in communicating your destination easily to the trade:

Create a database

Create and maintain a database of key travel trade who you know bring business to your region/ state and those who have potential to do so. The selection of who to include on this database will be an accumulation of knowledge about the trade.

This knowledge may be gained through hosting agent familiarisation visits: Are the attendees wholesalers or retailers? Were they decision makers/product managers or junior staff? Are they airline staff or representatives from the national tourism authority?

Dip into information from umbrella organisations that represent the travel trade. In New Zealand the travel trade is generally referred to as the *inbound industry* and many are members of the Tourism Export Council of New Zealand (TECNZ). Reviewing their membership lists and their company profiles will help make the decision about whether a particular inbound operator should be on your database.

With reference to the travel trade events section below, gather the business cards from those meetings and add them to your database.

Remember to adhere to your own legislation regarding the creation and use of databases. In New Zealand the obligation is to ensure you have a direct or implied relationship with the subject. The family visit is definitely a direct relationship, as are the contacts from travel trade events. The implied relationship would be one where you are interrogating an association database, such as TECNZ. To be on the safe side, permission should be sought before including those names, even though an implied relationship could be argued.

Create destination editorial

Create and provide free destination editorial. Having well-written editorial, of various copy lengths, allows the travel trade to include destination information according to their needs, whether this is in a traditional glossy A4 brochure or online. OTAs actively seek content as it helps with their own search engine optimisation.

As a complement to the editorial copy, provide a high-resolution photo gallery of destination images that can be easily downloaded. They need to be copyright-free so that there are no restrictions on their use.

Create destination videos

Increasingly video is critical in communicating your destination and its positioning. So, as with photos, make copyright-free video content available to the travel trade. Lake Wanaka Tourism, the RTO for the southern region of Wanaka, is a good example. They have invested, produced and circulated a series of seasonally themed 90-second videos (see https://www.youtube.com/playlist?list=PLtQDir__hYe_KwKOgU3Ff-YnbPMaNerOF).

These videos have the dual purpose of providing content for Lake Wanaka Tourism's own active digital activities, especially through social media.

Create suggested itineraries

You are conversant with your destination, you know the geography and distances, the products and the seasons. So share this knowledge via the creation of suggested itineraries for the trade. This is enormously helpful to them as they are not as knowledgeable about your region.

All of these resources can be accumulated in a dedicated trade zone on your destination website. By creating a resource hub, you are providing a convenient location for the trade to find this relevant information. Two examples from New Zealand RTOs are:

http://www.queenstownnz.co.nz/trade
http://marlboroughnz.com/about/working-with-us/travel-trade

Be a conduit for your local operators

Destination marketers are well-placed to be a conduit for connecting the travel trade with their local accommodation, transport, attraction and activity operators. As awareness of your destination grows and you develop relationships with the trade, they are likely to make contact and seek the latest, relevant information about your destination.

Know who your operators are: know what they offer in terms of their product and, importantly, whether they are 'export-ready'. Are they interested in business from the travel trade (which will mainly be international business)? Which countries of origin are they interested in or most suited to? Perhaps they have foreign language staff, if so what languages are available? Is their product of a good enough quality to provide consumer satisfaction? Do they have an independent quality assurance grading? Most importantly, does their pricing structure allow enough money to be paid as a commission, which is usually between 20 per cent and 30 per cent, to the travel trade? It has been known for operators to add on 20 per cent to their existing retail price. No! That will be the end of the business from the travel trade FOREVER, as it makes them uncompetitive and the consumer has the potential to find out if they are paying more than they would have if they had come direct to the door of the operator concerned. Export-ready operators have commission integrated into their pricing structure, and that structure needs to cover pricing up to two years ahead. Commission is a cost of distribution.

Developing an inventory of your export-ready operators, whether this is a printed manual or an online listing, gives the travel trade an easy way of sourcing relevant products for their itineraries. Although this should be unbiased, it should also be a list of integrity. Putting forward an operator who may be a member, but who is not export-ready, is a disservice to all concerned.

Regional Tourism Organisation of New Zealand (RTONZ) – Inbound trade event: An exercise in being a conduit

RTONZ is the umbrella body for all 30 of New Zealand's RTOs. Each year RTONZ facilitates an event for the RTOs to showcase their export-ready product to the inbound travel industry. This is held over two days in Auckland, which is where most of the travel trade is based, and provides the opportunity for RTOs to meet one-on-one with travel trade.

In this environment the RTOs have an opportunity to enhance relationships with the trade, share the latest trade-related information and introduce and update information on export-ready product.

Figure 14.1 Christchurch and Canterbury Convention Bureau

Figure 14.2 Marketing *The Lord of the Rings* destinations

Marketing partnership with the trade

A mature destination marketing entity may well enter into a marketing partnership with selected travel trade. This can be as simple as participating in brochure support fees to ensure more of your editorial/photos/video are covered in the travel trade outlets, to a significant online marketing campaign with, for example, an OTA.

Travel trade events

Although we have many ways of communicating with the travel trade, travel trade events continue to flourish. Nothing beats the value of establishing a personal, direct relationship with the travel trade. Fundamentally, the travel trade will do business first with people they know and trust, who make their lives easier (by furnishing the items as mentioned above) and, importantly, follow up on requests.

Tourism Rendezvous New Zealand (TRENZ)

In New Zealand the premier travel trade business-to-business event is TRENZ, which is held in May of each year. In these situations the in-country sellers (who are accommodation, transport, attractions, activities and RTOs) all take up a booth and undertake pre-scheduled appointments with visiting international travel agents.

At events like TRENZ the role of the RTOs includes:

1. Coordinating a regional presence. Before the event, work with your attending operators, who have bought their own booth, to agree on a common theming. A shared appearance across the booths and through uniforms helps create an impact.

2. While the operator's meeting is primarily about their business, knowing about other complementary operators can help elongate the stay in the region.

3. If an operator is new to the event, even set up some mock appointments and coach them through possible scenarios.

At TRENZ Destination Marlborough chose to take away the interior booth walls and created an open Marlborough-themed appearance. Each business had their own appointment streams.

Figure 14.3 It's brilliant every day at Marlborough

Consider hosting additional functions. Most events will have 'free' evenings, which are specifically free so that buyers can organise dinners or events to host travel trade of importance. This is at your own expense, but sharing with your participating operators can keep the costs down. Well in advance of the event, thoroughly research your potential appointments and follow the steps in the pre-appointment scheduling process accurately to ensure the best possible appointment schedule. Preparation is the key. Ensure you have well-trained staff to undertake appointments at your booth, as well as additional staff available to seize the opportunity to meet with other industry colleagues. In New Zealand's example it is quite important to connect with Tourism New Zealand and Air New Zealand at TRENZ. There is likely to be a visiting media programme, so ensure your media specialist is taking the opportunity to furnish the media with great stories. In the instance of one TRENZ, each morning there were breakfast briefings of only half an hour's duration with a variety of speakers. Ensure you attend similar events and disseminate information to your operators thereafter.

Pre- and post-famils: Around these large events there will be an active programme of hosted agent familiarisation visits. Ensure you work closely with the organisers of that programme and host agents to your region. After all, having them in your region is the best possible outcome.

KIWILINK's Tourism New Zealand has created a series of events in their key markets known as *Kiwilink*, for example, Kiwilink China, Kiwilink South East Asia, etc. This is their brand name for what is essentially TRENZ in-market. The New Zealand tourism industry is invited to these events, for which they pay a participation fee, while Tourism New Zealand sources venues and secures the agents from that particular market. The events are generally held over 2–3 days where you can see up to 100 agents in pre-arranged appointments.

The tactics as outlined for TRENZ generally apply to offshore events too. It may be a little impractical to get too elaborate with regional theming (due to the cost of shipping elements to the market), but it is critical to research the agents you will be seeing. Consideration should be given as to whether there is a need to translate information, but this will differ by market. There may be an opportunity to have an additional function in-market, and there will be media opportunities too. However, an additional aspect of Kiwilinks, which are particularly relevant to RTOs, is *frontliner training*. While the core event will attract senior agents who are decision makers, frontliner training is designed for their junior staff. Unlike the core event, where appointments are one-on-one, frontliner training can often be delivered to a group of agents, and these frontliners may have little or no knowledge of the destination and so it can be quite rudimentary.

Independent sales calls

With the accumulation of these activities, as the destination matures and your relationships with the travel trade are enhanced, there is an opportunity to visit them at their offices. This gives an additional point of contact, but importantly may allow you to access other office staff, staff that normally may not be in direct contact (at a travel trade event), or who may not have had an opportunity to visit your destination (on a famil).

The conversation is adapted to suit, but is within the framework of:

• what the destination can do to help;
• what opportunities are there to help develop new itineraries;
• provision of your resources such as images, editorial, etc.

> In this scenario the destination marketer should be careful to schedule calls well in advance, at times when the travel trade is not as busy. It will take more time to visit their offices, as compared to a travel trade event. So careful planning of the sequence of calls is important. Independent sales calls can be a part of the mix of interacting with the trade, but are likely to be more meaningful for a more mature relationship between the destination and the trade concerned.

Calendars of major travel trade events and conferences around the world are maintained by the UNWTO (see www.unwto.org/calendar/index.php?t=99and), Pacific Area Travel Association (see www.pata.org) and World Travel and Tourism Council (see www.wttc.org). Key trade events comprise travel exhibitions, tourism exchanges, sales missions and trade education programmes.

Travel exhibitions

The world's largest travel trade event is ITB in Berlin (www.itb-berlin.com), which started in 1966. Even with an overall display area of 170,000 square metres, space is so tight in the fully booked event that an increasing number of displays feature two storeys. Key figures for the five-day 2015 event included (TravelandTourWorld.com, 2015b):

- 10,096 exhibitors from 186 countries;
- 175,000 total visitors;
- 115 travel trade visitors;
- 2.4 days average duration of visit to ITB;
- resultant sales estimated at €6.7 billion;
- 23,000 ITB convention visitors.

For some emerging destinations, hosting inbound travel trade events has only commenced since the mid-2000s.

- The World Travel Market Latin America and World Travel Market Africa are recent spin offs from the parent WTM event that has been held in London since 1980 (see http://www.wtmlatinamerica.com/ and http://www.wtmafrica.com). WTM is also to enter Asia and China in 2016. The WTM portfolio of eight international travel marts now facilitates over US$7 billion in travel industry deals (TravelandTourWorld.com, 2015c).
- The first travel exhibition in Eastern Africa took place in Arusha, Tanzania, in 2006.
- China, the emerging powerhouse of world tourism, opened its first World Travel Fair (WTF) in February 2004.
- The first Turkish inbound travel exhibition took place in 2004.

Since the 1990s, DMO participation at travel trade events has shifted towards cooperative promotions with tourism businesses. In this role the DMO underwrites the often substantial cost of the display space and sells on participation space to constituent tourism businesses. The cooperative funding approach enables the DMO to stretch resources further, while controlling message synergy. The tourism businesses would otherwise find the participation cost-prohibitive. Often, at the larger international events, the NTO will be supported by STOs and RTOs rather than individual businesses. The high costs of participation sometimes necessitate the pragmatic sharing of display space by competing NTOs, as has been the case with Australia and New Zealand at ITB.

Tourism exchanges

Tourism exchange meetings can be an effective means of reaching key travel decisions, by providing tourism suppliers with individual meetings with a limited number of retailers and wholesalers selected by the NTO and major airlines. These exchanges are similar in concept to speed dating. The local product supplier hires booth space to gain access to international travel intermediaries in the form of short meetings of around 15 minutes. Logistically, it is usually not possible for the supplier to schedule appointments with all buyers during a typical two-day event and so a ballot system might be used. Suppliers must, therefore, not only be targeted in their appointment preferences but also take advantage of social networking opportunities to meet other contacts they were unable to schedule appointments with. Commonly the NTO invites key international buyers to the destination for a two- or three-day meeting and offers pre- and post-familiarisation tours to different parts of the country, hosted by participating STOs, RTOs and transport, accommodation and attraction operators. Considerable organisation is required, along with sponsorship by airlines and other tourism businesses.

- The Australian Tourism Exchange (www.tradeevents.australia.com) attracted 1,500 seller representatives from 500 companies, 700 buyer delegates from 36 countries, and 50 international and Australian media to the 36th annual event in 2015.

- The British Travel Trade Fair (www.britishtraveltradefair.com) attracted 300 exhibitors and 3,000 domestic and international buyers in 2015.

- In 2014 China Outbound Travel and Tourism Market (see www.cottm.com) attracted 3,298 Chinese outbound travel buyers and 400 exhibitors from 65 countries.

- In 2015 International Pow Wow, USA (see https://www.ipw.com) attracted 6,500 delegates from 73 counties in its 47th year. Deals initiated at the 2015 IPW are expected to attract 8.8 million visitors and US$28 billion in spending over the following three years (see TravelandTourWorld.com, 2015d).

- PATA Travel Mart (see www.PATA.org).

- South Pacific Tourism (see www.spto.org).

- In 2015 TRENZ (see www.trenz.co.nz) attracted 300 exhibitors and 260 buyers.

The increasing numbers of international tourism exchanges is forcing competition for the limited numbers of key travel decision makers. Unfortunately, in 2004, competition for key global travel intermediaries by neighbouring Australia and New Zealand led to the cancellation of the South Pacific Tourism Exchange, organised by a collective of small Pacific Island nations (see Pike, 2008).

Sales missions

The reverse of the tourism exchange format is for a DMO-led delegation of tourism suppliers to key markets to meet with influential travel intermediaries. A DMO-led delegation will usually provide participating suppliers with improved opportunities to meet key decision makers than would otherwise be possible for them individually. This has been increasingly popular since the 1980s for NTOs, STOs and RTOs. Sales missions are often a roadshow of educational seminars for travel agents and more personal meetings with wholesalers. However, the latter is losing favour with time-poor agents. For example, the chair of the Association of National Tourism Office Representatives (ANTOR) in the UK observed that there was declining interest from agents in destination road shows: 'ANTOR members accept that the day of the travel agent road show is probably dying on its feet. Agents have made it pretty clear they are not interested'.

Therefore DMOs need to make the educational seminars attractive to time-poor travel agents, and the use of incentives, such as travel prizes, is common practice. Also, the larger and better known the participating brands, the more appeal to the travel trade. For example, Brand USA's educational seminar Discover America, in New Delhi, India during March 2015 attracted 180 travel agents (TravelandTourWorld.com, 2015e). Participants joining the NTO were STOs from California, Florida, Massachusetts and Oregon, along with CVBs from Los Angeles, Philadelphia and New York. In addition, officials from the US Embassy in New Delhi were also present during the seminar.

Trade education programmes

In an effort to improve distribution effectiveness, many NTOs have established formal training programmes for selected travel agents in key markets. The most common initiative involves the accreditation of specialist agents. In the USA, for example, where there are over 20,000 travel agents, an international NTO can direct consumer advertising responses to the specialist agent nearest the enquirers' postcode area. The NTO has the benefit of knowing the specialist agent has the resources to service the enquiry, the agent benefits from the lead generation and the risk of uncertainty is alleviated for the consumer. Examples of specialist destination agent programmes include:

* Brand USA's *USA Discovery Program* (http://usadiscoveryprogram.com), which was launched in 2015;

* Go Scandinavia's *Scandinavia Specialist Program* (http://www.goscandinavia.com/scandinavia/go-scandinavia);

* Tourism Australia's *Aussie Specialists Program* had over 12,000 qualified travel agents across more than 100 countries before it was relaunched in June 2015 (see http://www.tourism.australia.com/programs/aussie-specialists-program.aspx). The NTO provides advice for how individual tourism businesses can participate in the programme in its annual online marketing prospectus (see Tourism Australia, 2014);

* Tourism Ireland's *Ireland Specialists* (www.irelandspecialists.com);

* Tourism New Zealand's *100% Pure NZ Specialists* (www.traveltrade.newzealand.com/en/training-resources-help).

Another form of travel trade training is familiarisation (also referred to as famils and educationals) tours to the destination. Services are usually provided free of charge by participating businesses. These events are usually by invitation only to tourism operators due to the nature of the itineraries, and so the politics of decision making about the itineraries can be challenging for the DMO and for new and small businesses.

Disintermediation

Disintermediation refers to a lessening of control of traditional intermediaries due to the advent of the internet as both a platform for information and direct bookings by the consumer with the service provider. This is particularly relevant in the travel and tourism sector, where intangible service providers do not require physical distribution of goods. There is a lot of uncertainty facing tradition travel intermediaries in this new era, resulting in considerable change in the travel agency sector. Key arguments for the continued survival of travel agents include: provision of professional advice, which adds value and reduces risk; expertise and contacts that results in saving itinerary search time for the consumer; access to bulk pricing discounts; security of financial transactions; and travel agency legislative protection such as compensation funds. Arguments against travel agents include: agents add to the cost of travel due to commissions they earn; agents are biased towards *preferred* suppliers who pay higher commissions; many older travellers are now more experienced than the average travel agent, due to the high turnover of staff, poor training and low wages; the emergence of do-it-yourself booking technologies; and the power of OTAs. There is a difficulty in assessing how the number of travel agents has declined in many parts of the world, partly because of the rise of small independent agents operating from their homes who are not listed on any official register.

A 2015 survey of millennials (18- to 34-year-olds) by skift.com in the USA found that only 10 per cent had used the services of a travel agent in the previous year (Ali, 2015). The study also reported 84 per cent of those surveyed had never ever used a travel agent to book leisure travel. Research commissioned by Tourism Australia (2013) found that 46 per cent of international travellers to Australia booked some of their travel arrangements online prior to arrival.

IN PRACTICE

14.5 Strong reliance on travel agents

As discussed, a comprehensive distribution situation analysis for Tourism Australia identified consumer identification of Australia as a destination, along with travel planning, was increasingly undertaken online (see PWC, 2013). However, levels of digital planning and booking were low in developing markets and long haul markets and had plateaued in mature markets. Therefore, traditional distribution channels, such as retail travel agents, remain important. While almost half (46 per cent) of holiday travellers to Australia were booking some aspect of their trip online, traditional travel intermediaries still played a key role in converting the other 54 per cent. In emerging markets it was estimated that up to 90 per cent of travellers were using travel agents. Stakeholder interviews indicated the expectation that little would change in this regard through to 2016. Some organisations that had enjoyed rapid growth through a total online presence and booking system were expanding into traditional retail channels.

CHAPTER SUMMARY

Key point 1: The DMO's role as information broker in the tourism distribution system

The distribution (place) element of the marketing mix is vastly different for marketers of tourism services than for consumer goods. Tourism distribution traditionally concerns the development and communication of package offerings through travel trade intermediaries, such as tour wholesalers, airlines and travel agents. Usually having no products to sell, the DMO's role is one of information broker, connecting and liaising between constituent tourism service providers and travel trade intermediaries.

Key point 2: The need for collaboration with travel intermediaries

It is critical that there is strong collaboration between destination stakeholders when engaging in travel trade initiatives, in order to ensure consistency of message, share of the high costs and share of information. Many travel trade events are cost-prohibitive for individual tourism businesses, and so the DMO acts as the umbrella organisation to bring interested stakeholders together.

Key point 3: Travel trade events

Arguably the most effective means of stimulating meaningful dialogue with customers is personal selling. Travel trade events provide an opportunity to use personal selling to launch new products, services, brands and facilities. DMOs with small budgets tend to favour such push strategies as they cost less than consumer advertising. Opportunities include trade exhibitions, special interest travel trade exhibitions, tourism exchanges and trade education seminars.

REVIEW QUESTIONS

1. Why have DMOs moved away from operating wholesale and/or retail travel services?

2. Describe what is meant by the role of the DMO being an information broker.

3. Summarise the main types of travel trade initiatives DMOs are typically involved with.

REFERENCES

Ali, R. (2015). *Travel Habits of Millennials: Only 10 Per Cent Used a Travel Agent Last Year.* Available at: http://skift.com/2015/03/16/travel-habits-of-millennials-only-10-percent-used-a-travel-agent-last-year

Choy, D. J. L. (1993). Alternative roles of national tourism organizations. *Tourism Management* 14(5): 357–365.

Morgan, N. and Pritchard, A. (1998). *Tourism Promotion and Power: Creating Images, Creating Identities.* Chichester, UK: John Wiley & Sons Ltd.

NZTPD. (1976). *75 Years of Tourism.* Wellington, NZ: New Zealand Tourist & Publicity Department.

Okumus, F. and Karamustafa, K. (2005). Impact of an economic crisis: Evidence from Turkey. *Annals of Tourism Research* 32(4): 942–961.

Ozturk, A. B. and Van Niekerk, M. (2014). Volume or value: A policy decision for Turkey's tourism industry. *Journal of Destination Marketing & Management* 3(4): 193–197.

Pearce, D. and Schott, C. (2005). Tourism distribution channels: The visitor's perspective. *Journal of Travel Research* 44(1): 50–63.

Pike, S. (2002). *Positioning as a Source of Competitive Advantage: Benchmarking Rotorua's Position as a Domestic Short Break Holiday Destination.* PhD Thesis. University of Waikato. November. Hard copy only.

Pike, S. (2008). *Destination Marketing: An Integrated Marketing Communication Approach.* Burlington, MA: Butterworth-Heinemann.

PWC. (2013). *Distribution 2020: Situational Analysis.* Sydney, Australia: PWC. March.

Tourism Australia. (2013). *Distribution in Australia's International Markets: Situational Analysis.* Sydney, Australia: Tourism Australia. March. Hard copy report.

Tourism Australia. (2014). *Working with Tourism Australia: Global Marketing Prospectus 2014/2015.* Available at: http://www.tourism.australia.com/documents/Markets/Report_WorkingwithTA_May14.pdf

TravelandTourWorld.com. (2015a). *Travel Companies to Compare Quotes for NT Government Travel Management.* Available at: http://www.travelandtourworld.com/news/article/travel-companies-compare-quotes-government-travel-management

TravelandTourWorld.com. (2015b). *ITB Berlin Sets New Records with Increased Trade Visitors and Business.* 9 March. Available at: http://www.travelandtourworld.com/news/article/itb-berlin-sets-new-records-increased-trade-visitors-business

TravelandTourWorld.com. (2015c). *WTM Portfolio to Enter Asia and China in 2016.* 16 June. Available at: http://www.travelandtourworld.com/news/article/wtm-portfolio-enter-asia-china-2016

TravelandTourWorld.com. (2015d). *U.S. Travel's 2015 IPW Sets Business Meeting Record.* 5 June. Available at: http://www.travelandtourworld.com/news/article/u-s-travels-2015-ipw-sets-business-meeting-record

TravelandTourWorld.com. (2015e). *Brand USA Conducts Educational Seminar 'Discover America' in New Delhi.* 9 March. Available at: http://www.travelandtourworld.com/news/article/brand-usa-conducts-educational-seminar-discoveramerica-new-delhi

Witt, S. F. and Gammon, S. (1994). Incentive travel. In Witt, S. F. and Moutinho, L. (eds) *Tourism Marketing and Management Handbook* (2nd edition). Hertfordshire, UK: Prentice Hall.

15

Destination marketing organisation (DMO) performance measurement

AIMS

To enhance understanding of:

- the challenge of quantifying the DMO's contribution to destination competitiveness;
- evaluations of DMO market performance;
- evaluations of DMO organisational effectiveness.

ABSTRACT

Measuring performance is one of the most challenging aspects of destination marketing, which probably explains why it is one of the least reported topics in the tourism literature. The DMO is but one of many agents responsible for attracting visitors to a destination, and so it is difficult to quantify return on investment (ROI), both in terms of short-term measures of market performance and longer-term destination competitiveness. It has been suggested that due to this complexity, DMOs use performance indicators that measure what *can* be measured as opposed to what *should* be measured. However, following the 2008–2009 global financial crisis, the pressure for DMOs to demonstrate their value in the face of government austerity measures has intensified. The challenge of demonstrating value will only increase as DMOs lose control of their destination's brand image to user-generated content on social media. Instead of receiving income from sales, DMOs rely predominantly on grants provided by government and are not, therefore, accountable to shareholders in the same manner as a commercial enterprise. DMO staff find themselves accountable to multiple masters, such as the board of directors, tourism businesses, travel intermediaries, local taxpayers and government funding agencies. DMO effectiveness is, therefore, partly subject to the perspective of the stakeholder and so needs to be evaluated based on a combination of indicators relating to market performance, stakeholders' satisfaction and organisational effectiveness.

Evaluating DMO effectiveness

A critical gap in the tourism literature is research investigating the extent to which the DMO enhances destination competitiveness (Pike and Page, 2014). This is underpinned by the proposition that the success of individual businesses is reliant on the competitiveness of the destination. As discussed in Chapter 2, sustained destination competitiveness is the mission of DMOs. However, the construct comprises economic, social, cultural and environmental dimensions, over which the DMO has minimal direct control. The main role of DMOs is to market the destination's resources, and yet there has been a surprising lack of published research related to the evaluation of destination marketing effectiveness.

A number of studies have highlighted the lack of marketing research undertaken to monitor the outcome of destination marketing objectives around the world, including Australia (see Prosser *et al.*, 2000; Carson *et al.*, 2003), North America (Sheehan and Ritchie, 1997; Masberg, 1999) and Europe (Dolnicar and Schoesser, 2003). Morgan *et al.* (2012) cited research by the UNWTO and ETC indicating that while 82 per cent of NTOs had an official brand strategy, one-third of these DMOs had no plans to evaluate the success of the initiative. The challenges inherent in measuring performance are not unique to the field of destination marketing research. For example, the topic of brand metrics has also been rare in the wider services marketing literature (Kim *et al.*, 2003). Australian Marketing Institute (AMI) president Roger James (2007: 29) lamented the lack of mainstream media coverage about the marketing effectiveness of corporate Australia: 'We see many examples of outstanding strategic marketing, yet few boards receive comprehensive information about marketing performance'.

The theme of the 2004 conference of the Travel and Tourism Research Association (TTRA), one of the most influential tourism research collectives, was *Measuring the tourism experience: When experience rules, what is the metric of success?* (see www.ttra.com). Seven years later, the theme remained topical and challenging. A survey of academic and practitioner members and roundtable discussions at the TTRA's 2011 conference, which sought to prioritise research issues for the next decade, identified *validating marketing programmes and standardising return-on-investment (ROI) performance measures* as the most important research method issue, and *the performance of destination marketing/management strategies* as the second most important management research issue (see Williams *et al.*, 2012). The following key questions were raised to address critical research gaps (Williams *et al.*, 2012: 9):

- What types of ROI indicators and assessment methods are credible and relevant to DMOs and their stakeholders?
- How can non-economic indicators of destination performance (e.g. human and social capital, ecological capital and reputational capital) be incorporated into a standardised form of triple-bottom-line performance reporting?
- How can emerging interactive technologies help identify the impacts of marketing strategies at different stages in the product purchase lifecycle?

Celebrating success is important for public agencies such as DMOs, to enhance the organisation's credibility in the minds of stakeholders and to acknowledge the hard work undertaken by staff. Therefore, DMOs will almost certainly claim credit when things go well (Craik, 1991: 24): 'In boom times, tourist bodies typically take the credit for increased visitation and infrastructure development, while, in downturns, the same bodies blame the lack of government funding and seek increases to budgets'.

The following is a range of examples of typical success claims that have been made over the years:

- In 2015 Visit California claimed the STO's marketing efforts attracted 4 million additional visitors to the state in 2014, who spent approximately US$8.1 billion, representing an ROI of US$327 for each marketing dollar spent (Travelindustrywire.com, 2015).

- Tourism and Events Queensland's AUD$100 million 2014–2015 budget achieved AUD$17 billion in visitor spending (QTIC, 2015).

- Brand USA suggested that every US$1 spent on international promotion in the NTO's 2013 marketing campaign generated a return of US$47 for the nation (Travelindustrywire.com, 2014).

- Visit Florida celebrated ten years of operation as a public–private partnership in 2006 with the following results achieved since 1996: visitor numbers up 78 per cent, visitor spending and tourism taxes up 51 per cent and tourism jobs up 18 per cent (www.travelindustryreview.com, 1 March 2006, in Pike, 2008).

- The April 2003 internet newsletter of the Colorado Tourism Office reported results of a 2002 advertising effectiveness study, designed to measure the ROI for tourism advertising (see Pike, 2004). The report claimed 1.86 million visitors, who spent US$522 million, visited Colorado as a 'direct result' of the STO's US$2.5 million advertising campaign. On this basis, it was claimed that every advertising dollar generated US$205 in visitor spending and US$12.74 in tax revenue.

- Slater (2002: 155) cited the Louisiana cabinet secretary to the Department of Culture, Recreation and Tourism: 'The more money we spend, the more visitors we get'.

- The introduction of the 'I ♥ New York' promotion was so successful it generated an increase of almost 12 per cent in tourism receipts over the previous year (Holcolmb, 1999). Between 1977 and 1981 the US$32 million campaign was estimated to have generated at least eight times that amount in additional tax revenues and US$2 billion in extra tourism revenue for the state (Pritchard, 1982).

However, readers should be aware of the complexities in measuring a destination's market performance when interpreting such claims. The problem is, of course, that the DMO never knows the long-term effect of individual marketing campaigns on future visitor arrivals, including those visitors who purchased travel independent of campaign sponsors. Therefore, it has been suggested DMOs generally use performance indicators that evaluate what *can* be measured, as opposed to what *should* be measured, by failing to address four critical issues (Morgan *et al.*, 2012: 75):

1. How has additional visitor spending been increased through above-the-line advertising?

2. DMOs are not evaluating the increasingly significant online marketing activities.

3. DMOs are not investigating the effect of branding on consumer behaviour.

4. DMOs do not evaluate the growing emphasis on PR management and social media engagement.

Monitoring destination marketing effectiveness is a necessary, but immensely challenging, undertaking and, currently, there is no model to quantify the relationship between the work of DMOs and: (1) short-term market performance; and (2) longer-term destination competitiveness. The issue is only going to become more challenging in future as DMOs increasingly lose control of destination brand image to user-generated content on social media. Reflect for a moment on the tens of thousands of visitors who are in London, for example, on the day you are reading this and consider these questions:

- To what extent are the visitors there as a result of initiatives by DMOs such as the former NTOs, the British Tourist Authority and English Tourist Commission; the current NTOs, VisitBritain and Visit England; the RTO Visit London; or by promotional activities of airlines, travel intermediaries or individual tourism businesses?

- To what extent are the visitors there as a result of their own organic attitude development through a previous visit, word-of-mouth referrals, social media user-generated content, movies, novels, media editorials or even school history lessons?

- To what extent are the visitors there for a non-tourism primary reason, such as visiting friends or relatives, or for business or medical appointments?

- If visitor numbers are up or down this year, to what extent can this be attributed to destination marketing relative to external forces such as the global economy, international exchange rates, domestic interest rates, the weather, hallmark events such as the Chelsea Flower Show or disasters?

Consider the destination you are likely to visit next. Are you able to recall what initially stimulated your interest and what role the DMO has played, either directly or indirectly, in shaping your image of the destination and intent to travel there? The extent to which DMOs are able to monitor the effectiveness of their activities is a key destination marketing management function, not only for improving future promotional efforts but also for accountability, funding purposes and, as discussed in Chapter 3, in some cases their very survival as an entity. See, for example, Morgan *et al.* (2012):

> *This pressure is likely to be exacerbated further by the continuing economic crisis in more economically developed countries, its impact on their public spending resource allocation, and the subsequent drive for value for money. If DMOs cannot demonstrate this added value, they will face further budget reductions and the curtailment of their activities.*
>
> *(Morgan et al., 2012: 74)*

To reiterate from Chapter 2, a competitive destination is one that features a balance between at least nine critical success factors: effective market position, profitable tourism businesses, ease of access, attractive physical environment, positive visitor experiences, ongoing investment in new product development, cooperative tourism community, supportive local residents and effective DMO organisation. Remembering the DMO is responsible for *marketing* the destination's resources and not *managing* them, the three main categories of indicators to address in the evaluation of effectiveness, as shown in Figure 15.1, are: market performance, organisational effectiveness and stakeholder satisfaction.

Evaluating market performance

The first 40 years of destination marketing literature has been surprisingly devoid of research that addresses the question: To what extent are DMOs responsible for increases in visitor arrivals, length of stay, spending and other performance metrics? related to destination competitiveness (Pike and Page, 2014: 211). Visitor metrics provide a degree of DMO accountability and, apart from counting visitor arrivals, have been attempted by measuring the ratio of DMO marketing spend and spending by visitors from those markets (see Hunt, 1990; Crouch *et al.*, 1992; Kulendran and Dwyer, 2009), visitor spending (Aguilo *et al.*, 2005), tourism expenditure growth and employment growth (Deskins and Seevers, 2011) and length of stay (Pearce, 1977; Silberman, 1985; Fakeye and Crompton, 1991; Gokovali *et al.*, 2006; Martinez-Garcia and Raya, 2008; Menezes *et al.*, 2008; Barros and Machado, 2010). Despite the obvious weaknesses in isolating cause and effect relationships in these metrics, marketing alone is not the sole

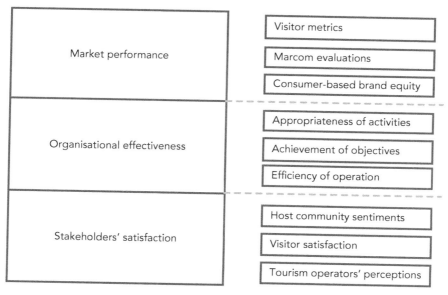

Figure 15.1 DMO performance measures

determinant of arrivals in a destination, as many established econometric studies of arrivals demonstrate (Pike and Page, 2014). For more details on destination econometrics, such as tourism satellite accounts and employment multipliers, see, for example, Vanhove (2005), Dwyer and Forsyth (2006), Dwyer *et al.* (2014) and the academic journal *Tourism Economics*.

The topic of tourism marketing performance measurement appeared relatively recently in the academic literature, particularly for DMOs. For example, Pizam (1990) cited research indicating only a minority of STOs actually bothered to evaluate the effectiveness of their promotions. Likewise, Hawes *et al.* (1991) found only 7 out of 37 STOs in the USA used measurable objectives and performance measures. Sheehan and Ritchie's (1997) review found very little interest in DMO market performance measures up to that point in time, while Faulkner (1997) suggested most evaluations reported by DMOs had been *ad hoc*. In an examination of the Italian NTOs' promotional plans, Formica and Littlefield (2000: 113) discovered the entire section on evaluation of the plan was missing: 'Instead, spurious correlations often led to subjective evaluations of promotional performances'. The major barriers to measuring DMO marketing performance identified in Sheehan and Ritchie's survey of CVBs remain relevant (Sheehan and Ritchie, 1997: 113):

1. subjectivity of measures, and the difficulty in proving their importance to sceptics;

2. the lack of ability to measure tourism activity;

3. lack of research funds;

4. inconsistency in the collection or reporting of data;

5. lack of cooperation from stakeholders.

The next section discusses three categories of market performance measurement: visitor monitors, marketing communication evaluations and consumer-based brand equity (CBBE).

Visitor monitors

The most effective, but not common, method for capturing metrics such as numbers, length of stay, reason for visit and market origin of visitors is through a visitor monitor programme. Counting the number of visitor arrivals has long been a measure of the health of a destination's tourism industry. NTOs have access to international visitor arrivals data through collection by immigration officials at arrival gateways. However, the collection of visitor data can be more difficult for STOs and RTOs. It was as recent as 2000, in a keynote address at the Tourism and Travel Research Association conference in Hollywood, that the director of the Los Angeles CVB asked delegates for assistance in developing a valid method for tracking visitor flows to this region of 88 cities. At that time the CVB did not have an accurate measure of visitors, who arrive at different parts of the region by plane, train, bus and private car.

The emergence of visitor monitor programmes has provided STOs and RTOs with a valuable vehicle for tracking arrivals, but has occurred only recently for most DMOs. Indeed, there are still many RTOs that do not operate a visitor monitor and rely on data captured from NTO and STO intercept survey samples (see, for example, Gitelson and Crompton, 1984; Gyte and Phelps, 1989; Oppermann, 1996; Pyo *et al.*, 1998). A March 2015 discussion on TRINET, an online list serve forum for over 2,000 tourism researchers, identified a lack of standardised visitor monitors in many parts of the world including, for example, the USA, UK, Europe and Australia.

One country that has had a national standard commercial accommodation monitor since the 1990s is New Zealand. Now undertaken by the government's Ministry of Business, Innovation and Employment (see http://www.med.govt.nz/sectors-industries/tourism/tourism-research-data/other-research-and-reports/regional-visitor-monitor), it is a requirement that accommodation operators participate in the scheme. Statistics New Zealand publishes monthly data on capacity, occupancy rates, visitor nights, length of stay and employee numbers. Among the benefits of such a national standard visitor monitor is the ability for regions to undertake market share analysis. RTOs have access to month-on-month data for all competing regions. This enables benchmarking of performance by each RTO in comparison to previous points in time and relative to competing destinations. Also, accommodation operators are able to compare their visitor mix, length of stay and occupancy rate with the local and national averages. The first regional visitor monitors, which were the catalyst for the national programme, were developed in Queenstown and Rotorua in 1990 (Pike, 2002b). A notable addition to the Rotorua visitor monitor was a monthly survey of local households to provide an additional estimate of visitors staying privately with friends or relatives (known as VFRs). The VFR segment is important to many destinations, but is often neglected in research related to visitor metrics.

Critics of visitor monitor programmes argue that they are flawed, due to a reliance on individual accommodation operators completing the monthly forms accurately and honestly. In this regard, it is important to acknowledge the key challenge in the development of a visitor monitor is gaining the confidence of accommodation operators, convincing them that their individual data will be treated confidentially, pooled in aggregated data and not accessible by a third-party. In the Rotorua case, it took months of sometimes heated debate with accommodation representatives to gain acceptance of the need for, and benefits of, a visitor monitor. The end result was a tracking system, with a simple form that was not onerous for accommodation operators, which became a key element of the RTO's reporting to the local government that funded destination marketing.

Marketing communication evaluations

The primary marketing communication mediums necessitating evaluations are social media, advertising, public relations and publicity and travel trade events. Other less reported performance effectiveness evaluations reported in the literature have included: the use of coupons (Woodside, 1981), direct response marketing (Burke and Lindblom, 1989), destination brochures (Zhou, 1997) and promotional videos (Shani *et al.*, 2010; Alvarez and Campo, 2011).

Social media

Leung *et al.*'s (2013) review of the 2007–2011 literature concluded that there was little evidence of financial ROI for social media initiatives in tourism. In spite of the increasing dominance of online marketing communications by DMOs, there has been little empirical research published to date in relation to the effects of social media marketing on destination brands (Munro and Richards, 2011; Oliveira and Panyik, 2015). However, it must be recognised this is also the case in the wider market-ing literature (see Laroche *et al.*, 2013). It is difficult for companies in the early stages of social media development to measure ROI. Indeed, ROI has been, and is likely to continue to be, disputed due to the overwhelming speed of social media usage and savage budget cuts following the 2008 global financial crisis (Fisher, 2009, in Hays *et al.*, 2013). There are three key measures DMOs are using to evaluate their social media activities:

1. **Audience size.** Commonly this is measured by tracking the number of followers, such as Facebook *likes*. For example, according to Tourism Australia's social media campaign surrounding the 2014 visit of China's President to the country for the G20 summit (see Chapter 13), the most popular single post, an interview with the President's executive chef about Tasmanian food, generated 30 million views, 3,000 likes, 300 comments and 3,500 re-tweets (Tourism Australia, 2015).

2. **Degree of consumer engagement.** For example, Hays *et al.* (2013) reported that users visiting the VisitBritainshop.com via a link on Facebook were 28 per cent more likely to purchase and had 58 per cent larger shopping baskets than other visitors to the shop. Tourism Queensland's local fans engaged with the STO's Facebook page during the 2010 floods by posting pics showing most tourist areas were unaffected. As discussed in Chapter 4, key results tracked by Tourism and Events Queensland for the 2009 online *Best Job in the World* campaign included:

   - 8.7 million website hits at an average of 8.25 minutes each, with 55 million page views;
   - an estimated 3 billion people were reached through the media;
   - media coverage worth over AUD$400 million in equivalent advertising value;
   - from a creative perspective, the campaign won over 35 international advertising awards.

3. **Consumer sentiment.** This involves interpreting what social media users are saying about the desti-nation in user-generated content, as was discussed in detail in Chapter 4.

Advertising

Despite the prevalence of advertising, the topic of the medium's effectiveness has not been widely reported in the tourism literature. Early studies concluded the link between destination advertising and tourist receipts was tenuous (see, for example, Faulkner, 1997; McWilliams and Crompton, 1997). As an example of this, Hughes (2002) discussed the difficulties in measuring the effectiveness of Manchester's gay tourism advertising campaign:

> *The campaign is ongoing and its success since 1999 has been difficult to assess given that, for obvious reasons, no record is kept of the number of gay and lesbian tourists, and even if there was it would be difficult to attribute any increase to any one cause.*

> *(Hughes, 2002: 158)*

Indeed, a common adage in the advertising industry is *we know half of our advertising is working . . . we just don't know which half*. The main problem is the difficulty in controlling for the range of extraneous variables, over which the advertiser has no control, but which will be in play at the time of the advertising. This has led to the extraordinary claim that the relationship between advertising and sales has yet to be established in the marketing literature (see, for example, Schultz and Schultz, 2004). Consider, for example, the challenge of measuring the effectiveness of one of the highest profile forms of advertising: outdoor media, such as the ubiquitous roadside billboard. In Australia outdoor media attracts only 4 per cent of advertising spend due to the difficulty in monitoring effectiveness.

Arguably the most widely used method of tracking advertising effectiveness is a conversion study, which estimates how many enquiries generated from advertising are converted to visitors and what the characteristics are of the converted visitors. To do so involves surveying a sample of consumers who have responded to a DMO promotion during the year. Perdue and Pitegoff (1990) proposed four major benefits of conversion studies for DMOs:

1. the ability to monitor changes that result from advertising campaigns over time;

2. the ability to assess how well the advertising is reaching the target segment;

3. the opportunity to assess the quality of the information package and its contribution to visitor satisfaction;

4. the opportunity to undertake pre- and post-campaign surveys.

However, a number of authors have been critical of tourism conversion studies, and there remain few studies published. Key criticisms of conversion studies are that they are usually only a snapshot survey at one point in time, they inflate the ROI (see Kim *et al.*, 2005), they do not consider non-response bias as those who visit a destination are more likely to respond to such a survey (see Faulkner, 1997) and they fail to take into account the effect of digital channels and social media engagement (Morgan *et al.*, 2012: 76): 'Unlike the traditional brochure requester, the journey of the web researcher is untraceable and therefore not measurable in a typical conversion model'.

Woodside (1990) proposed the most effective means of examining the relationship between advertising and sales is through field experiments. Separate groups can be exposed to different advertising in what are termed split-run techniques. A famous example of this approach used by Budweiser Beer in the USA was reported by Ackoff and Emshoff (1975, in Keller, 2003). The experiment, which tested seven advertising levels in different sales regions, ranging from no advertising at all through to 200+ per cent advertising spend, ran for a full year. Interestingly, the *no advertising* market achieved the same level of sales as the *same level of advertising* market, and the *−50 per cent advertising* market achieved an increase in sales. The researchers concluded that strong brands do not require the same level of advertising as lesser known or liked brands. An example of a split-market variation used to analyse destination advertising was reported by Schoenbachler *et al.* (1995) in an analysis of the effectiveness of an advertising campaign run by a US STO. They used three geographic markets, two of which were exposed to the same advertising, while a control group received no advertising. Following the advertising campaign, a mail questionnaire was sent to 3,000 consumers in each of the three markets to measure unaided recall, awareness of destination features, image and intent to visit. It was found that intent to visit and awareness of destination features was much higher in the two test markets, compared to the control group that received no advertising.

IN PRACTICE

15.1 Visit Wales new evaluation framework

Morgan *et al.* (2012) provided a detailed analysis of the process of developing a new marketing evaluation framework for the NTO. The rationale for the development was acknowledgement that traditional key performance indicators (KPI) used by DMOs were unsuitable in the digital age and disintermediated marketing environment. The new framework was developed through a practitioner/academic collaboration involving extensive stakeholder engagement, which began with the establishment of a taskforce in 2007. Key limitations of the existing KPIs, which were based on the 1998 publication *Tourism Marketing: A Practical Guide to Evaluation* (produced for NTOs of England, Scotland, Northern Ireland and Wales) were the failure to address the following questions:

1. How effective is advertising in changing perceptions?

2. Does changing perceptions lead to a change in behaviour?

3. How does the effectiveness of communications vary by channel?

4. What is the longer-term impact on the Visit Wales brand?

5. Which messages of the advertising campaign have been effective?

6. Which messages are leading to action?

7. Which elements of the marketing mix have had the greatest long-/short-term impact?

To address these questions a new evaluation framework was developed, and piloted in 2009. The four key measurement elements, which assessed performance of Wales relative to leading UK competitors such as Ireland and Scotland, were:

1. a weekly panel survey to track awareness of campaigns and the effects on visitation intentions;

2. a survey to consumers who had contact with the NTO via direct marketing, at different times during the year, to monitor the effect of engagement on visitation intentions;

3. a re-contact survey of those who participated in the initial contact survey, to correlate visitation with engagement with the NTO, including questions to identify why non-visitation occurred;

4. a *slide in* survey invitation to users of the NTO website, to identify how they became aware of the site, for example, through marketing campaigns.

Morgan *et al.* provided detailed explanations about what the eight new KPIs capture and how they benefit the NTO: destination awareness, total campaign awareness, claimed campaign response, known campaign response, emotional proximity (brand engagement), conviction to visit, conversion through decision making process and value per respondent.

Further reading

Morgan *et al.* (2012).

PR and publicity

PR performance measurement is also problematic. For example, Barry (2002, in Pike, 2008) reported the finding of a survey of UK PR consultants, where one in five revealed they did not believe the success of their PR efforts could be accurately measured. Barry suggested that the golden rule is about knowing where you started from. What is the current position and what is the publicity campaign objective? Trout and Rivkin (1995) argued that most PR activities were *name in the press* tactics, which are measured in the same way you measure chopped liver – by the pound! Content seemed to be largely irrelevant. Rather, weight is all that counts. DMOs have tended to focus on this publicity aspect of PR measurement. Equivalent advertising value (EAV) has been a popular means for DMOs to monitor the results of their media publicity results: first, because it is relatively easy to track and second, because of the absence of more comprehensive evaluation methods. EAV is a simplistic measure of the amount of advertising dollars required to purchase the equivalent amount of air time or column centimetre generated by the PR initiative. Examples reported have included:

- Tourism New Zealand claimed EAV of NZ$2.7 million in 2015 as a result of 530 media articles related to the visit of famous Chinese actor, director and singer, Huang Lei (Backpackertradenews.com, 2015).

- VisitBritain estimated that hosting the London 2012 Olympic Games yielded £3.3 billion in positive EAV in print and on television between January and June 2012 (Pike and Page, 2014).

- The 2010 *Oprah's Ultimate Australian Adventure* generated 86,000 news stories with an EAV of AUD$368 million (Tourism Australia, 2011).

- Tourism Queensland's 2009 *Best Job in the World* social media campaign reached an estimated 3 billion people, with media coverage worth over AUD$400 million in EAV (Belch *et al.*, 2009).

- The British Tourist Authority's (BTA) 2001 publicity campaign during the foot-and-mouth disease outbreak generated EAV of £1.9 million (Frisby, 2002). Corporate press officer for the BTA, Frisby, indicated the results of the NTO's PR campaign during the foot-and-mouth outbreak included: 600 articles and broadcast features, 151,000 square centimetres of print and 2,700 seconds of broadcast coverage of Britain as a tourism destination.

In Australia tourism businesses that have been involved in the NTOs' media hosting programme are able to track any publicity that mentions their product, at www.publicity.australia.com. While EAV can be a useful PR tool in a DMO's efforts to enhance credibility among stakeholders, there are a number of problems that should be factored into reporting:

- EAV figures do not provide any indication of who actually read the article or viewed the screening.

- EAV figures do not measure whether readers were part of the DMO's target segment(s).

- The old adage *any publicity is good publicity* should be considered in terms of how the publicity reinforced the destination brand identity.

- Not all media articles included in EAV figures can be directly attributed to DMO initiatives.

- EAV can include negative editorial.

- There can be a significant time lag between organising and hosting a media visit and subsequent publication, which can skew reporting of year-on-year activities and results.

Qualitative analyses of editorial coverage should also be used to supplement EAV measures (see Castelltort and Mader, 2010; Stepchenkova and Eales, 2011). For example, Frisby (2002) advised the results were measured using both qualitative and quantitative assessment of media coverage:

The media evaluation system measures individual items of overseas print and broadcast coverage, incorporating the type of publication, content, story angle, audience and readership and impact – scoring each. Other information is also recorded to develop data and aid customer relationship management with individual journalists.

As discussed in Chapter 13, Tourism Australia commissioned marketing research in the USA during 2011 in February, June, September and November, to track perceptions of consumers who had read, seen or heard about *Oprah's Ultimate Australian Adventure*, which took place in December 2010. Table 15.1 lists some of the results that showed strong sentiment and travel intentions towards Australia. Tourism Australia reported the consumer research and feedback from the tourism industry suggested the *Oprah effect* was working for the country.

Travel trade events

It is in the interests of travel trade event organisers to monitor the performance of their events, in order to sell participation space for the following year. For example, as discussed in Chapter 14, the world's largest

Table 15.1 USA consumer perceptions following *Oprah's Ultimate Australian Adventure*

June 2011

As a result of seeing, reading or hearing about Oprah's visit:

- 39% wanted to find out more about a holiday in Australia
- 27% said they wanted to visit in the next 12 months
- 85% perceived Australia as a welcoming/friendly destination
- 67% would consider going to Australia for a vacation

September 2011

- 73% said the show influenced their decision to visit Australia
- 49% of those who had visited Australia in the previous six months said their decision was influenced by Oprah
- 38% of those who had booked a visit to Australia over the next 12 months said their decision was influenced by Oprah

November 2011

Of those who had seen, read or heard about *Oprah's Ultimate Australian Adventure* and had visited Australia in the previous six months:

- 59% agreed the show had made them visit places outside the main cities they had not previously considered
- 64% were prepared to spend more time on their trip than they originally thought they would
- 59% were prepared to spend more money on their trip than they originally thought they would

Of those who had seen, read or heard about *Oprah's Ultimate Australian Adventure* and had booked a trip to Australia in the next 12 months:

- 69% agreed the show made them want to explore more outside the main cities
- 50% plan to spend more time on their trip than they originally thought they would
- 43% planned to spend more money on their trip than they originally thought they would

Source: Adapted from Tourism Australia (2011).

travel trade event, ITB Berlin, boasted resultant sales estimated at €6.7 billion from the 2015 event, along with the following metrics (TravelandTourWorld.com, 2015):

- 10,096 exhibitors from 186 countries;
- 175,000 total visitors;
- 115,000 travel trade visitors;
- 2.4 days average duration of visit to ITB;
- 23,000 ITB convention visitors.

However, the success of participation by DMOs at travel trade events is more difficult to evaluate, given that the role of the destination marketer is as a broker of information between constituent tourism businesses and travel intermediaries. Little has been reported in the tourism literature to date on measuring success of DMO participation in trade expos, travel exchanges and familiarisation tours. For example, as discussed in Chapter 14, while Tourism Australia's Aussie Specialist Programme (ASP) (training programme for overseas travel agents) was generally viewed as a valuable means to attract more visitors, the training programme was expensive for STOs to maintain, and there were concerns over the lack of performance metrics (PWC, 2013). In particular, there were limited metrics relating to volume of sales generated by individual ASP members.

One useful example of travel trade metrics was provided by Eagles (2008, in Pike, 2008) who summarised a joint venture campaign between a travel wholesaler and an NTO that sought to get results the old-fashioned way, through a 12-month travelling road show of rural communities. The initiative also involved local travel agents in each community. The case clearly demonstrated how it is possible to directly track the effectiveness of such a joint venture destination promotion from enquiries through to actual bookings.

The influence of consumer travel expo participation on actual travel is also problematic to measure. It is even difficult at consumer travel expos to screen genuine enquirers from brochure collectors and identify those with a propensity to visit the destination. However, most consumer expos now charge admission fees, which does provide an element of screening compared to setting up a display in a shopping mall. DMOs often distribute coupons, for which the redemption rate can be measured, or attempt to collect database listings through competitions. Pizam (1990) reported USA STOs had generally used *rough* estimates of travel show effectiveness. The most common methods included: numbers of enquiries, numbers of contacts, amount of literature distributed, staff evaluations, conversion studies, number of group bookings and surveys. The topic of evaluating travel trade event effectiveness remains an important gap in the tourism literature.

CBBE

Generally, there has been a tendency in tourism marketing to focus on short-run measures of marketing communication effectiveness. This is a reflection of the short-term focus that pervades many boardrooms. Relatively few current DMO decision makers are likely to still be in office in ten years' time, since the high profile and political nature of DMOs' management inhibits long periods in governance and senior management. While short-run performance measures are important, they should also be supplemented with indicators addressing a longer-term view of destination branding performance. However, given the time consuming, costly and subjective nature of marketing research, it is perhaps not surprising that this has been a relatively new activity for DMOs at STO and RTO levels. For example, in evaluating the initial effects of the Brand Oregon campaign, Curtis (2001) lamented the lack of perceptions research:

In terms of evaluation of the initial campaign, the Tourism Commission essentially took account of two factors; first the number of visitor enquiries received, and second, the number of awards won from the advertising industry for the campaign. Unfortunately, no consumer evaluation of the image campaign, nor a critical analysis of the campaign's effectiveness was ever conducted.

(Curtis, 2001: 76)

As discussed in Chapter 9, the branding literature commenced during the 1940s, but the first publications related to destination branding did not appear until half a century later. Pike's (2009) review of 74 destination branding publications by 102 authors from the first decade of destination branding literature (1998–2007) identified 9 research gaps warranting attention. In particular, there has been a lack of research reported about the extent to which DMOs have been successful in enhancing destination brand equity in the manner intended in the brand identity. Little research has been undertaken to track destination branding performance over time, and Pike argued the need to address this gap in the tourism literature, given:

1. the increasing levels of competition between destinations and the need for differentiation;

2. the increasing investment in branding by DMOs since the 1990s;

3. the complex political nature of DMO brand decision making and accountability to stakeholders (see Pike, 2005);

4. the long-term nature of repositioning a destination's image (see Gartner and Hunt, 1987).

The relatively recent emergence of user-generated content on social media presents a further compelling reason. As discussed in the introduction, Morgan *et al.* (2012) cited research showing that, while 82 per cent of NTOs had an official brand strategy, one-third of these DMOs had no plans to evaluate the success of the initiative due to the complex challenges involved.

An emerging concept for monitoring branding performance is CBBE. Initially promoted by Aaker (1991, 1996) and Keller (1993, 2003), CBBE offers the potential to supplement the more traditional financial balance sheet measures of brand equity. As discussed in Chapter 9, for example, the world's most valuable brand in 2014 was Apple with a worth of US$118.9 billion. The rationale underpinning CBBE as a brand performance measure is that consumer perceptions form the pillar of any financial measure of brand equity, which is essentially an estimate of future earnings potential. Such a financial balance sheet brand equity measure is of no practical value to a destination's stakeholders, and so the concept of CBBE is worthy of attention from DMOs. There are three key advantages for DMOs using this approach, with CBBE providing the opportunity for:

1. practical branding performance tracking with measures of the effectiveness of past marketing communications;

2. indicators of future performance;

3. more transparent accountability to stakeholders through clear linkages between the rationale for marketing objectives and the resultant performance measures.

The first destination CBBE journal articles were published only in the mid-2000s (see Konecnik, 2006; Konecnik and Gartner, 2007; Pike 2007a). In the decade since then the concept has attracted increasing interest from destination marketing researchers, as highlighted by the range of destination CBBE studies at NTO, STO and RTO levels in Table 15.2.

Table 15.2 Destination CBBE studies

Destinations	Authors
Slovenia	Konecnik (2006); Konecnik and Gartner (2007); Gartner and Konecnik Ruzzier (2011)
Gold Coast, Sunshine Coast, Coral Coast, Fraser Coast, Northern New South Wales (Australia)	Pike (2007, 2009, 2010)
Las Vegas, Atlantic City (USA)	Boo et al. (2009)
Australia	Pike et al. (2010); Bianchi and Pike (2011); Pike and Bianchi (2014)
Mongolia	Chen and Myagmarsuren (2010)
Taiwan	Horng et al. (2012)
Georgia, South Carolina, Florida (USA)	Lim and Weaver (2012)
Sweden	Fuchs et al. (2012)
South Tyrol, Italy	Sartori et al. (2012)
Korea	Im et al. (2012)
Brazil, Argentina, Chile	Bianchi et al. (2014)

While different researchers have varied in the dimensions they have used to measure CBBE, the three core elements are brand salience, brand image and brand loyalty. Figure 15.2 visually highlights how these different levels of CBBE align with common DMO goals and the traditional *hierarchy of effects* of advertising effectiveness (see Lavidge and Steiner, 1961). This hierarchy has been adapted in the advertising industry

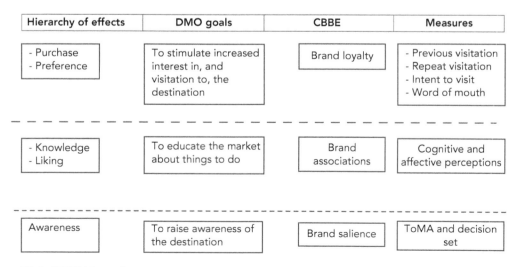

Figure 15.2 CBBE hierarchy

Source: Adapted from Pike (2007a); Pike and Page (2014).

as the AIDA model, with which communications seek to guide the target consumer through the levels of Awareness, Interest and Desire, to Action. A summary of measurement indicators for each level of the hierarchy also aligns with the DMO goals.

Brand salience

The first goal of marketing communications is to enhance awareness of the brand. The foundation of the CBBE hierarchy is brand salience, which is more than simply awareness in that it represents the strength of the brand's presence in the mind of the consumer. Therefore, the DMO objective should be more than improving general awareness per se, but to be remembered for the right reasons (Aaker, 1996). As discussed in Chapter 10, investigating the number of destinations in a consumer's awareness set is largely pointless, given the sheer number of destinations consumers are likely to be aware of. Salience concerns those brands that come to mind during travel planning decision making. Of particular interest are top of mind awareness (ToMA) and decision set composition (see, for example, Pike, 2002a), as discussed in Chapter 10. Identification of the decision set composition is important in understanding the competitive set of destinations, which is critical in brand positioning analysis.

Brand associations

Once awareness has been achieved, the aim should be to increase familiarity with the brand through development of strong associations with the product category (Keller, 2003). Brand associations held in the mind about a product aid consumer information processing: 'A brand association is anything "linked" in memory to a brand' (Aaker, 1991: 109), also referred to as destination image and which was discussed in Chapter 10, has been the most popular topic in the destination marketing literature. What is most critical is that brand associations are strong, favourable and unique, in that order (Keller, 2003). Destination brand associations are a mix of tangible features (cognitive attributes), measured by Likert-type scales and the benefits they offer (affective images), measured by semantic differential scales.

Brand loyalty

The quintessential goal of marketing and, therefore, the dependent variable in any CBBE model, is brand loyalty. Given the increasing substitutability of destinations, the key advantages of brand loyalty for destinations include lower marketing costs, increased travel trade leverage and word-of-mouth referrals. For a review of the literature relating to destination loyalty see Gursoy et al. (2014). For destinations, important measurement variables are: previous visitation, intent to visit in the future and propensity for word-of-mouth recommendations to others.

As discussed, there has been little research published in relation to tracking destination branding performance over time. Case study 15.1 describes the use of the CBBE hierarchy to track the branding performance of an emerging destination, along with key competing destinations, from 2003 to 2012. While some aspects of the project have previously been reported (see Pike, 2006, 2007a, 2009, 2010), at the time of writing the 2012 data had not been published. The key finding to date is that there has been little change in CBBE, in terms of brand salience, brand image and brand loyalty in the first ten years of the branding campaign. Furthermore, there was almost no change in brand salience rankings and brand image for any of the five destinations in the competitive set, supporting the proposition that destination image change will only occur over a long period of time. The project is ongoing with further data being collected in 2015.

CASE STUDY

15.1 Tracking CBBE for a destination from 2003 to 2012

In the state of Queensland, Australia, 13 RTOs are officially recognised by the STO, Tourism and Events Queensland (see www.tq.com.au). The STO provides financial and human resource assistance to the RTOs, much of which has been invested in the development of destination brand campaigns in recent years. Brisbane, the Queensland state capital, is the most important market in terms of visitor arrivals for all the RTOs, with the 2.1 million residents representing almost half of the state's 4.3 million census population in 2011 (www.censusdata.abs.gov.au).

At the start of this research project, the new brand name of the destination of interest was *Bundaberg – Coral Isles and Country*, which was categorized by the STO as an *emerging destination*. The name was chosen to reflect the diversity of a region covering 26,000 square kilometres and 11 local government areas who were asked to form an RTO region in return for STO funding. Located a four-hour drive north of the Brisbane city centre, the region encompasses a large rural hinterland, for which Bundaberg (population 45,000) is the largest city, and a lengthy coastline that includes the southern starting point of the iconic Great Barrier Reef. In recognition of this world renowned feature, the destination brand name was recently changed to *Bundaberg – Southern Great Barrier Reef* (see http://teq.queensland.com/en-AU/Destinations/Bundaberg).

During 2002, the STO undertook a series of focus groups with Brisbane residents to investigate perceptions of the Bundaberg region. The study found awareness of the town of Bundaberg was strong due to the manufacture of Australia's most famous brand of rum (see http://www.bundabergrum.com.au), but the area lacked a clear identity as a tourism destination (Tourism Queensland, 2003, in Pike, 2007a). To address this problem, a new destination brand, developed by the RTO and STO, was launched in 2003 with three objectives:

1. to raise awareness of the destination;

2. to educate the market about things to do;

3. to stimulate increased interest in, and visitation to, the region.

As suggested in Figure 15.2, these objectives are the most commonly used by DMOs around the world. Therefore, while this project focuses on destinations in Australia, the real world problem, the method, the results and the implications will be of interest to destination marketing researchers in other countries.

The new brand positioning theme was *Take Time to Discover Bundaberg, Coral Isles and Country*. In 2003 this research project started to benchmark perceptions of the destination, relative to four key competing regions in the Brisbane market, immediately prior to the campaign launch. The aim was to monitor perceptions over time, relative to the three objectives. Four studies were undertaken between 2003 and 2012 during the first decade of the brand's existence. The research focus was limited to the analysis of market perceptions over time. Resources did not enable individual case studies of the competing destinations' marketing communication tactics during the time period to be undertaken.

The travel situation of interest for this project was short break holidays by car, defined as a non-business trip of between one and four nights away from home. Domestic short break drive tourism is an important aspect of Australian travel patterns. BTR (2002) estimated 76 per cent of domestic travel is undertaken by car, 70 per cent of which is intrastate. Short breaks of 1 to 3 nights represented 68 per cent of the Queensland self-drive market. Brisbane residents are spoilt for choice with over 100 short break destinations within a four-hour drive.

Study 1: 2003

The initial 2003 study was a longitudinal design involving two stages, using a systematic random sample drawn from the Brisbane telephone directory. The stage 1 paper-based mail questionnaire contained questions about recent and intended short break holiday activity, ToMA/decision set preferences and importance ratings of a battery of destination attributes. The second paper-based mail questionnaire, distributed to the same participants three months later, involved questions about actual travel undertaken since the first questionnaire and perceptions of the competitive set of five destinations (Gold Coast, Sunshine Coast, Fraser Coast, Northern New South Wales and Bundaberg and the Coral Coast) across the same battery of destination attributes, as well as intent to visit.

Study 2: 2007

The 2007 study used a new sample, randomly drawn from an updated Brisbane telephone directory, and again a paper-based mail questionnaire was used with the same structure of the 2003 second stage questions, in order to track any changes in brand salience, image and loyalty over the four years.

Study 3: 2012

The 2012 study used a new sample invited from the panel of a commercial marketing research firm, and the questionnaire was administered online. Again, the same question structure was used to track any changes in brand salience, image and loyalty since the Bundaberg branding campaign commenced in 2003.

Key results

The useable sample sizes were 521 in 2003, 444 in 2007 and 541 in 2012. The characteristics of the participants were generally similar to the wider Brisbane census population. Participants indicated a strong familiarity with short break holidays, with a mean of three such trips by car per year in 2003 and 2007, and 2.5 in 2012.

Destination brand salience

The mean number of destinations listed in decision sets was 3.8 in 2003, 3.1 in 2007 and 2.6 in 2012, all within the theorised range of 4 +/− 2. The decision set size and composition has serious implications for those destinations not listed, since these destinations are less likely to be considered in the selection process. Bundaberg region destinations were listed in only 58 (11 per cent) of participants' decision sets in the 2003 study, 25 (6 per cent) in 2007 and 20 (4 per cent) in 2012. The ranking of each destination was consistent between 2003, 2007 and 2012. The ToMA and decision set findings highlight a lack of improvement in *brand salience* for the region between 2003 and 2012. This is important given that brand salience is the foundation of the CBBE hierarchy and was the RTO's first objective for the new brand campaign. The destination brand salience results for the five destinations were consistent between 2003, 2007 and 2012.

Destination brand associations

In relation to the RTO's second objective, the brand associations of Bundaberg region did not improve across any of the destination attributes over the ten-year period. From a positioning perspective, the Coral Coast consistently rated lowest on half of the cognitive items and both affective items, but highest on three attributes. Two of these, *friendly locals* and *uncrowded*, represent an as yet unused market position that the RTO could better exploit to improve other measures of CBBE. The destination attribute importance means were consistent between 2003, 2007 and 2012.

A *don't know* option was provided alongside each of the attribute scale items. See Pike (2007b) for a discussion on the rationale for this approach. For the attribute importance items, the maximum rate of *don't know* usage was 1.3 per cent, which indicated participants were familiar with the attributes. However, every Bundaberg region attribute performance item attracted a *don't know* response rate of between 30 per cent and 50 per cent. For the RTO, the implication is that more work is needed to improve cognition of what the destination has to offer, as per the second objective of the brand campaign.

Destination brand loyalty

Over 90 per cent of participants had previously visited their unaided ToMA destination in 2003, 2007 and 2012. The implication that there is a low likelihood of ToMA selection without previous visitation in the short break travel context of this project is important, given the link between stated intent and actual travel identified in the first study. While around 40 per cent of participants indicated having previously visited the Bundaberg region, the mean likelihood in the 2012 study of visiting the region within the next year was 2.7, which showed no improvement from 2003 or 2007. An indicator of possible future performance, this was the lowest of the competitive set of destinations, as it was in 2003 and 2007. Participants were asked to rate the extent to which they would recommend each destination to friends. On this 7-point scale (1 = definitely not, 7 = definitely) the mean for the Coral Coast was 3.9 in 2007 and 3.7 in 2012. This result was the lowest of the five destinations.

Discussion

The research identified minimal changes in perceptions of the competitive set of five destinations, over a decade, in their closest and most important visitor market. It is evident that such induced efforts have only served to maintain market positions. Therefore, academics and marketing researchers need to understand the ramifications of any recommendation to reposition a destination. As discussed, there has been limited evidence in the literature of any successful destination repositioning. While this project was undertaken in Australia, the research approach provides DMOs in other parts of the world with a practical tool for evaluating brand performance over time, in terms of measures of effectiveness of past marketing communications, as well as indicators of future performance.

Further reading

Pike, S. (2006, 2007a, 2007b, 2009, 2010).

Discussion question

How does this case highlight the need for consistency of the brand positioning theme over time?

Evaluating organisational effectiveness

Good management starts with good measurement.

(Aaker, 1996: 316)

Few DMOs are forced to bid for government funding against other prospective organisations in a tender situation. Therefore, it is important to consider that while destinations must compete, DMOs are not actually in a competitive position as an entity, and this has implications for organisational performance measurement (Pike and Page, 2014):

> *Destinations compete against other destinations in competitive markets but the DMO is not competing. Rather, they are like a regional hospital that is the only such organisation in town. In the private sector, poorly managed firms go out of business. We suggest the paucity of research into DMO best practice is related to the lack of agreement, within academia and in practice, as to what is the dependent variable in modelling of DMO performance.*
>
> *(Pike and Page, 2014: 218)*

Organisation performance evaluation is concerned with the degree to which a firm has achieved its objectives, the appropriateness of those objectives and the efficiency of implementation. For investigations of DMO technical efficiency reported in the tourism literature, see Pestana *et al.* (2011) and Medina *et al.* (2012). Akehurst *et al.* (1993: 59) found the main performance indicators for European NTOs to be:

1. the amount of activity of the NTO, such as the number of trade fairs attended;

2. promotion cost per tourist or per additional tourist, or per dollar of expenditure;

3. grants per job created.

Elliott (1997: 12–14) proposed the following questions to address organisational efficiency:

• Have objectives been achieved for the lowest cost?

• Have resources been used efficiently?

• Has the return on public investment been reasonable?

Heath and Wall (1992: 185) offered the following questions:

• Is the mission of the DMO for the region clearly stated in market-oriented terms? Is the mission feasible in terms of the region's opportunities and resources? Is the mission cognizant of tourist, environmental, business and community interests in a balanced way?

• Are the various goals for the region clearly stated, communicated to, and understood by the major tourism businesses in the region?

• Are the goals appropriate, given the region's competitive position, resources and opportunities?

• Is information available for the review of progress towards objectives, and are the reviews conducted on a regular basis?

An independent marketing audit is recommended as a systematic process for evaluating marketing practice. For destination marketing audits reported in the tourism literature, see Faulkner (1997), Go *et al.* (1992) and Woodside and Sakai (2001, 2009). An audit would be expected to examine the following (Hooley and Saunders, 1993, in Pike, 2004):

- marketing environment audit – to assess changes in the macro and operating environments;

- strategy audit – to assess the appropriateness and clarity of corporate and marketing objectives and the appropriateness of the resource allocation;

- analysis of the structure, efficiency and interface efficiency of the marketing department;

- analysis of marketing systems such as information system, planning system and control system;

- cost-effectiveness analysis;

- analysis of marketing mix.

Destination marketing awards: The opportunity to celebrate success

An academic reviewer of one of my previous destination marketing texts questioned the relevance of having a section on destination marketing awards. However, anyone with any practical marketing experience will appreciate that awards represent rare, tangible (albeit subjective) recognition and an opportunity to celebrate success. Destination marketers are usually hard working, creative and highly competitive and so enjoy the recognition from their peers. For example, in 2005 the then Tourism Australia Managing Director, Scott Morrison, welcomed the news that the country was the first ever to have been awarded *cool brand* status in the annual Cool Brand Leaders list in the UK (Pike, 2008): 'We are thrilled that The Brand Council in the UK has named Australia as one of the world's Cool Brand Leaders, especially as this is the first time that a country has been included on its annual list'.

Remember that DMOs must demonstrate value to stakeholders. Destination marketing awards do help the cause.

Evaluating stakeholder satisfaction

DMOs rely predominantly on grants provided by government, and are not therefore accountable to shareholders in the same manner as a commercial enterprise. DMO staff find themselves accountable to multiple masters, such as the board of directors, tourism businesses, travel intermediaries, local taxpayers and government funding agencies. DMO effectiveness is, therefore, partly subjective to the perspective of the stakeholder. As discussed, a DMO will usually have a diverse and eclectic range of individual stakeholders who have differing values, expectations, tourism experience and market interests from destination marketing. Even perceptions held by DMO staff themselves should be investigated (see, for example, Illum and Schaefer, 1995; Bramwell and Rawding, 1996). The three primary groups of stakeholders to be considered are the tourism industry, visitors and the host community.

Tourism industry perceptions

Clearly it is critical to monitor perceptions of tourism operators within the DMO's jurisdiction, to maximise the collaborative partnership approach required for effective destination marketing. This is particularly important for membership-based DMOs. In this regard, Donnelly and Vaske (1997) investigated factors influencing membership of a DMO. Tourism Vancouver management has long recognised the need to report performance tracking to stakeholders. In 1993 the CVB introduced monthly tracking of around 70 measures and quarterly reporting to the industry (Vallee, 2005). Of particular interest to DMOs will be the stakeholders' perceptions of:

- leadership;

- networking capability;

- stakeholder relationship management;

- knowledge sharing;

- operational effectiveness;

- governance, transparency and accountability;

- professionalism of staff;

- appropriateness of the brand identity and strategy.

Regarding the last issue, Sartori *et al.* (2012) used the CBBE hierarchy to examine stakeholders' perceptions of the branding of South Tyrol, Italy. Other studies examining local tourism operators' perceptions of DMO effectiveness include: Evans and Chon (1989); Sheehan and Ritchie (2005); d'Angella and Go (2009); Wagner and Peters (2009) and Bornhorst *et al.* (2010).

As discussed in Chapter 10, one research technique that is particularly useful for communicating research data in a graphical format that is easily understood by practitioners with little statistical knowledge is importance–performance analysis (IPA). Introduced by Martilla and James (1977), IPA was first used to assess stakeholder satisfaction with a DMO by Evans and Chon (1989), as summarised in research snapshot 15.1.

RESEARCH SNAPSHOT

15.1 DMO stakeholder satisfaction using IPA

Evans and Chon (1989) trialled the applicability of IPA in the formulation and evaluation of tourism policy at two USA destinations. The first destination was at the *maturity* stage and had a number of community conflicts regarding tourism policy. The second destination was classified *immature*, in that the small rural community did not have an established tourism industry and was exploring the possibility of developing tourism. IPA requires participants to first rate the importance of a series of attributes and then to rate the performance of the destination of interest across the same range of attributes. In addition to the tourism policy research objectives, local business operators at the *mature* destination were surveyed in relation to the perceived performance of the local DMO:

1. Did members of the business community feel that the DMO was performing well?

2. Was the DMO mission clear?

The results indicated that the DMO was not perceived to be performing well in relation to community expectations. Also, the mission was not clear for most participants. The IPA results were helpful to the DMO in resolving a community conflict and in clarifying the organisation's mission. Evans and Chon recommended that the DMO repeats the IPA each year to monitor the business community's perceptions of performance.

Further reading

Evans, M. R. and Chon, K. (1989).
Martilla, J. A. and James, J. C. (1977).

A second stakeholder group of interest to DMOs is travel trade intermediaries. There is a wealth of research published about the role of intermediaries and their perceptions of destinations and DMOs (see Gearing *et al.*, 1974; Var *et al.*, 1977; Ritchie and Zins, 1978; McLellan and Foushee, 1983; Teye, 1989; Roehl, 1990; Tang and Rochananond, 1990; Walmsley and Jenkins, 1993; Gartner and Bachri, 1994; Illum and Schaefer, 1995; Oppermann, 1996; Go and Zhang, 1997; Grabler, 1997; Dimanche and Moody, 1998; Lubbe, 1998; Mohsin and Ryan, 1999; Shanka and Frost, 1999; Chacko and Fenich, 2000; Baloglu and Mangaloglu, 2001; Morgan *et al.*, 2003; Hankinson, 2004; Baloglu and Love, 2005; Konecnik, 2005; Grosspietsch, 2006; Woodland and Acott, 2007; Sartori *et al.*, 2012).

Another perspective is that of the satisfaction of members of an alliance (see Selin and Myers, 1998). St Hill and Lewis (2015) interviewed marketing representatives from 12 of the 30 NTO members of the Caribbean Tourism Organization (CTO) to assess the effectiveness of the organisation's collaborative marketing efforts. The study found that the CTO's initiatives were deemed to be effective in that member NTOs were committed to the organisation, but ineffective over issues such as questionable governance and imbalance and inequity in terms of reciprocity. The participants agreed the CTO propels a regional image that heightens visibility of the Caribbean. However, smaller NTOs believed they were overshadowed by the larger nations and 'pegged to receive lesser benefits' (St Hill and Lewis, 2015: 81), to the extent the CTO was perceived as an 'elite club' (St Hill and Lewis, 2015: 82). While they might be provided with equal opportunities to participate in initiatives, the smaller NTOs simply did not have the resources.

Visitors' satisfaction

The quality of the visitor experience and perceptions of value for money are paramount to sustained destination competitiveness, due to the effect of word-of-mouth referrals, social media user-generated content and repeat visitation intentions. The seminal text in this regard was Ryan (1995). There is a wealth of literature in this field. For example, 105 of the 262 destination image studies tabled by Pike (2002a, 2007a) intercepted visitors at the destination to survey them on their perceptions of the place. For a literature review on destination visitor satisfaction see Chen *et al.* (2010).

Host community perceptions

One of the key pillars of destination competitiveness is a supportive host community (Pike and Page, 2014). The host community plays a major role at many destinations in helping deliver the brand promise to visitors. Engagement between local residents and visitors occurs at many levels other than only tourism service delivery. Encounters can occur in service delivery at non-tourism businesses, as well as such

Table 15.3 Studies of host community perceptions

Destination branding	Henderson (2000a, 2000b, 2007); Donald and Gammack (2007); Merrilees *et al.* (2007); Wagner and Peters (2009); Kotsi *et al.* (2014)
Host community consumer-based brand equity	Pike and Scott (2009)
Influence of the destination brand on host community behaviour	Choo *et al.* (2011)
Support for tourism and perceptions of tourism impacts	Schroeder (1996); Gu and Ryan (2008); Kang *et al.* (2008)
Destination image	Witter (1985); Jutla (2000); Phillips and Schofield (2007)

diverse situations as in traffic and in recreation areas. It is clearly in the best interests of the DMO to have supportive local residents who appreciate the value that visitors can bring to their community and therefore support taxpayer funded destination marketing and the ensuing increases in visitor levels. Table 15.3 summarises aspects of host community perceptions of interest to the DMO, along with a selection of publications addressing these issues. For a review of the literature related to host community perceptions of tourism see Sharpley (2014).

CHAPTER SUMMARY

Key point 1: The challenge of quantifying the DMO contribution to destination competitiveness

One of the most challenging, but least reported, aspects of destination marketing is that of measuring DMO performance. Isolating and quantifying a DMO's contribution to destination competitiveness is currently an almost impossible task. Ultimately, the success of a destination will be as a result of a combination of factors, many of which will be external to the DMO's control. Examples include the global economy, hallmark events, government visa policies, the weather, disasters and the marketing activities of tourism businesses and travel intermediaries. DMOs at all levels should be wary of staking claims to overall credit for the success of a tourism season, in exactly the same way they should not accept sole responsibility for a poor industry performance.

Key point 2: Evaluations of market performance

Since the 1970s destination marketing literature has been surprisingly devoid of research investigating the extent to which DMOs are responsible for increases in visitor arrivals, length of stay, spending and other performance metrics. The reliance on short-run ROI measures of effectiveness misses the DMO's full contribution to destination competitiveness. Efforts should also be made to model and measure consumer-based destination brand equity over time. This requires market research to estimate levels of destination salience, brand associations and destination loyalty.

Key point 3: Evaluations of DMO organisation effectiveness

There are three dimensions in modelling measures of DMO effectiveness. The first two are internal organisation measures: the appropriateness of activities and the efficiency of the plan in relation to stakeholder expectations. The third is monitoring stakeholders' satisfaction, since DMOs must continually demonstrate value to multiple masters, particularly in the new digital era and during times of economic uncertainty.

REVIEW QUESTIONS

1. Explain why it is so difficult to quantify a DMO's contribution to destination competitiveness.

2. Why is it important to measure stakeholders' perceptions of DMO performance?

3. How is CBBE an indicator of future performance?

REFERENCES

Aaker, D. A. (1991). *Managing Brand Equity*. New York: Free Press.
Aaker, D. A. (1996). *Building Strong Brands*. New York: Free Press.
Aguilo, E., Riera, A. and Rossello, J. (2005). The short-term price effect of a tourist tax through a dynamic demand model: The case of the Balearic Islands. *Tourism Management* 26(3): 359–365.

Akehurst, G., Bland, N. and Nevin, M. (1993). Tourism policies in the European Community member states. *International Journal of Hospitality Management* 12(1): 33–66.

Alvarez, M. D. and Campo, S. (2011). Controllable versus uncontrollable information sources: Effects on the image of Turkey. *International Journal of Tourism Research* 13(4): 310–323.

Backpackertradenews.com. (2015). *Chinese Mega-Star Picks Aotearoa*. Available at: http://www.backpackertradenews.com.au/chinese-mega-star-picks-aotearoa

Baloglu, S. and Love, C. (2005). A cognitive-affective positioning analysis of convention cities: An extension of the circumplex model of affect. *Tourism Analysis* 9(4): 299–308.

Baloglu, S. and Mangaloglu, M. (2001). Tourism destination images of Turkey, Egypt, Greece, and Italy as perceived by US-based tour operators and travel agents. *Tourism Management* 22(1): 1–9.

Barros, C. P. and Machado, L. P. (2010). The length of stay in tourism. *Annals of Tourism Research* 37(3): 692–706.

Belch, G., Belch, M., Kerr, G. and Powell, I. (2009). *Advertising and IMC*. Sydney, Australia: McGraw-Hill.

Bianchi, C. and Pike, S. (2011). Antecedents of attitudinal destination loyalty in a long-haul market: Australia's brand equity among Chilean consumers. *Journal of Travel & Tourism Marketing* 28(7): 736–750.

Bianchi, C., Pike, S. and Lings, I. (2014). Investigating attitudes towards three South American destinations in an emerging long haul market using a model of consumer-based brand equity (CBBE). *Tourism Management* 42(1): 215–223.

Boo, S., Busser, J. and Baloglu, S. (2009). A model of customer-based brand equity and its application to multiple destinations. *Tourism Management* 30(2): 219–231.

Bornhorst, T., Ritchie, J. R. B. and Sheehan, L. (2010). Determinants of tourism success for DMOs & destinations: An empirical examination of stakeholders' perspectives. *Tourism Management* 31(5): 572–589.

Bramwell, B. and Rawding, L. (1996). Tourism marketing images of industrial cities. *Annals of Tourism Research* 23(1): 201–221.

BTR. (2002). *Travel by Australians, 2001: Annual Results of the National Visitor Survey 2001*. Canberra, Australia: Bureau of Travel Research.

Burke, J. F. and Lindblom, L. A. (1989). Strategies for evaluating direct response tourism marketing. *Journal of Travel Research* Fall: 33–37.

Carson, D., Beattie, S. and Gove, B. (2003). Tourism management capacity of local government: An analysis of Victorian local government. In Braithwaite, R. W. and Braithwaite, R. L. (eds) *Riding the Wave of Tourism and Hospitality Research: Proceedings of the Council of Australian University Tourism and Hospitality Education Conference*. Coffs Harbour, NSW: Southern Cross University, Lismore. CD-ROM.

Castelltort, M. and Mader, G. (2010). Press media coverage effects on destinations: A monetary public value (MPV) analysis. *Tourism Management* 31(6): 724–738.

Chacko, H. E. and Fenich, G. G. (2000). Determining the importance of US convention destination attributes. *Journal of Vacation Marketing* 6(3): 211–220.

Chen, C.F. and Myagmarsuren, O. (2010). Exploring relationships between Mongolian destination brand equity, satisfaction and destination loyalty. *Tourism Economics* 16(4): 981–994.

Chen, Y., Zhang, H. and Qiu, L. (2010). A review on tourist satisfaction of tourism destinations. In Zhang, Z., Zhang, R. and Zhang, J. (eds) *LISS 2012 Conference Proceedings*. Berlin, Germany: Springer, pp. 593–604.

Choo, H., Park, S. Y. and Petrick, J. F. (2011). The influence of the resident's identification with a tourism destination brand on their behaviour. *Journal of Hospitality Marketing & Management* 20(2): 198–216.

Craik, J. (1991). *Government Promotion of Tourism: The Role of the Queensland Tourist and Travel Corporation*. Brisbane, QLD: The Centre for Australian Public Sector Management, Griffith University.

Crouch, G. I., Schultz, L. and Valerio, P. (1992). Marketing international tourism to Australia: A regression analysis. *Tourism Management* 13(2): 196–208.

Curtis, J. (2001). Branding a state: The evolution of Brand Oregon. *Journal of Vacation Marketing* 7(1): 75–81.

D'Angella, F. and Go, F. M. (2009). Tale of two cities' collaborative marketing: Towards a theory of destination stakeholder assessment. *Tourism Management* 30(3): 429–440.

Deskins, J. and Seevers, M. T. (2011). Are state expenditures to promote tourism effective? *Journal of Travel Research* 50(2): 154–170.

Dimanche, F. and Moody, M. (1998). Perceptions of destination image: A study of Latin American intermediary travel buyers. *Tourism Analysis* 3: 173–180.

Dolnicar, S. and Schoesser, C. M. (2003). Market research in Austrian NTO and RTOs: Is the research homework done before spending millions? In Braithwaite, R. W. and Braithwaite, R. L. (eds) *Riding the Wave of Tourism and Hospitality Research: Proceedings of the Council of Australian University Tourism and Hospitality Education Conference.* Coffs Harbour, NSW: Southern Cross University. CD-ROM.

Donald, S. H. and Gammack, J. G. (2007). *Tourism and the Branded City: Film and Identity on the Pacific Rim.* Aldershot, UK: Ashgate.

Donnelly, M. P. and Vaske, J. J. (1997). Factors affecting membership in a tourism promotion authority. *Journal of Travel Research* Spring: 50–55.

Dwyer, L. and Forsyth, P. (2006). *International Handbook on Tourism Economics.* London: Elgar Publishing.

Dwyer, L., Pham, T., Forsyth, P. and Spurr, R. (2014). Destination marketing of Australia: Return on investment. *Journal of Travel Research* 53(3): 281–295.

Elliott, J. (1997). *Tourism: Politics and Public Sector Management.* London: Routledge.

Evans, M. R. and Chon, K. (1989). Formulating and evaluating tourism policy using importance–performance analysis. *Hospitality Education & Research* 13(2): 203–213.

Fakeye, P. C. and Crompton, J. L. (1991). Image differences between prospective, first time, and repeat visitors to the Lower Rio Grande Valley. *Journal of Travel Research* 30(1): 10–16.

Faulkner, B. (1997). A model for evaluation of national tourism destination marketing programs. *Journal of Travel Research* Winter: 23–32.

Formica, S. and Littlefield, J. (2000). National tourism organizations: A promotional plans framework. *Journal of Hospitality & Leisure Marketing* 7(1): 103–119.

Frisby, E. (2002). Communicating in a crisis: The British Tourist Authority's responses to the foot-and-mouth outbreak and 11th September, 2001. *Journal of Vacation Marketing* 9(1): 89–100.

Fuchs, M., Chekalina, T. and Lexahagen, M. (2012). Destination brand equity modelling and measurement: A summer tourism case from Sweden. In Tsiotsou, R. H. and Goldsmith, R. E. (eds) *Strategic Marketing in Tourism Services.* Bingley, UK: Emerald, pp. 95–115.

Gartner, W. C. and Bachri, T. (1994). Tour operators' role in the tourism distribution system: An Indonesian case study. *Journal of International Consumer Marketing* 6(3/4): 161–179.

Gartner, W. C. and Hunt, J. D. (1987). An analysis of state image change over a twelve-year period (1971–1983). *Journal of Travel Research* Fall: 15–19.

Gartner, W. C. and Konecnik Ruzzier, M. (2011). Tourism destination brand equity dimensions: Renewal versus repeat market. *Journal of Travel Research* 50(5): 471–481.

Gearing, C. E., Swart, W. W. and Var, T. (1974). Establishing a measure of touristic attractiveness. *Journal of Travel Research* 12(4): 1–8.

Gitelson, R. J. and Crompton, J. L. (1984). Insights into the repeat vacation phenomenon. *Annals of Tourism Research* 11(2): 199–217.

Go, F. M. and Zhang, W. (1997). Applying importance–performance analysis to Beijing as an international meeting destination. *Journal of Travel Research* Spring: 42–49.

Go, F. M., Milne, D. and Whittles, L. J. R. (1992). Communities as destinations: A marketing taxonomy for the effective implementation of the tourism action plan. *Journal of Travel Research* 30(4): 31–40.

Gokovali, U., Bahar, O. and Kozak, M. (2006). Determinants of length of stay: A practical use of survival analysis. *Tourism Management* 28(4): 736–746.

Grabler, K. (1997). Perceptual mapping and positioning of tourist cities. In Mazanec, J. A. (ed.) *International City Tourism.* London: Pinter, pp. 101–113.

Grosspietsch, M. (2006). Perceived and projected images of Rwanda: Visitor and international tour operator perspectives. *Tourism Management* 27(2): 225–234.

Gu, H. and Ryan, C. (2008). Place attachment, identity and community impacts of tourism: The case of Beijing hutong. *Tourism Management* 29(4): 637–647.

Gursoy, D., Chen, J. S. and Chi, C. G. (2014). Theoretical examination of destination loyalty formation. *International Journal of Contemporary Hospitality Management* 26(5): 809–827.

Gyte, D. M. and Phelps, A. (1989). Patterns of destination repeat business: British tourists in Mallorca, Spain. *Journal of Travel Research* Summer: 24–28.

Hankinson, G. (2004). The brand images of tourism destinations: A study of the saliency of organic images. *Journal of Product & Brand Management* 13(1): 6–14.

Hawes, D. K., Taylor, D. T. and Hampe, G. D. (1991). Destination marketing by states. *Journal of Travel Research* Summer: 11–17.

Hays, S., Page, S. J. and Buhalis, D. (2013). Social media as a destination marketing tool: Its use by national tourism organisations. *Current Issues in Tourism* 16(3): 211–239.

Heath, E. and Wall, G. (1992). *Marketing Tourism Destinations: A Strategic Planning Approach*. New York: John Wiley & Sons.

Henderson, J. C. (2000a). Selling places: The new Asia-Singapore brand. In Robinson, M., Evans, N., Long, P., Sharpley, R. and Swarbrooke, J. (eds) *Management, Marketing and the Political Economy of Travel and Tourism*. Sunderland, UK: The Centre for Travel & Tourism, pp. 207–218.

Henderson, J. C. (2000b). Selling places: The new Asia-Singapore brand. *The Journal of Tourism Studies* 11(1): 36–44.

Henderson, J. C. (2007). Uniquely Singapore? A case study in destination branding. *Journal of Vacation Marketing* 13(3): 261–274.

Holcolmb, B. (1999). Marketing cities for tourism. In Judd, D. R. and Fainstein, S. S. (eds) *The Tourist City*. Newhaven, CT: Yale University Press, pp. 54–70.

Hooley, G. J. and Saunders, J. (1993). *Competitive Positioning: The Key to Market Success*. Hertfordshire, UK: Prentice Hall International.

Horng, J., Liu, C., Chou, H. and Tsai, C. (2012). Understanding the impact of culinary brand equity and destination familiarity on travel intentions. *Tourism Management* 33(4): 815–824.

Hughes, H. L. (2002). Marketing gay tourism in Manchester: New market for urban tourism or destruction of 'gay space'? *Journal of Vacation Marketing* 9(2): 152–163.

Hunt, J. D. (1990). State tourism offices and their impact on tourist expenditures. *Journal of Travel Research* Winter: 10–13.

Illum, S. and Schaefer, A. (1995). Destination attributes: Perspectives of tour operators and destination marketers. *Journal of Travel & Tourism Marketing* 4(4): 1–14.

Im, H. H., Kim, S. S., Elliot, S. and Han, H. (2012). Conceptualizing destination brand equity dimensions from a consumer-based brand equity perspective. *Journal of Travel & Tourism Marketing* 29(4): 385–403.

James, R. (2007). Brand valuation: A global initiative. *Professional Marketing* June/July, p. 59.

Jutla, R. S. (2000). Visual image of the city: Tourists' versus residents' perceptions of Simla, a hill station in northern India. *Tourism Geographies* 2(4): 404–420.

Kang, S. K., Leeb, C., Yoon, Y. and Long, P. T. (2008). Resident perception of the impact of limited-stakes community-based gaming in mature gaming communities. *Tourism Management* 29(4): 681–694.

Keller, K. L. (1993). Conceptualizing, measuring, and managing customer-based brand equity. *Journal of Marketing* 57(January): 1–22.

Keller, K. L. (2003). *Strategic Brand Management*. Upper Saddle River, NJ: Prentice Hall.

Kim, D., Hwang, Y. and Fesenmaier, D. (2005). Modelling tourism advertising effectiveness. *Journal of Travel Research* 44(1): 42–49.

Kim, H., Kim, W. G. and An, J. A. (2003). The effect of consumer-based brand equity on firms' financial performance. *The Journal of Consumer Marketing* 20(4/5): 335–351.

Konecnik, M. (2005). Slovenia as a tourism destination: Differences in image evaluations perceived by tourism representatives from closer and more distant markets. *Economic and Business Review* 7(3): 261–282.

Konecnik, M. (2006). Croatian-based brand equity for Slovenia as a tourism destination. *Economic and Business Review* 8(1): 83–108.

Konecnik, M. and Gartner, W. C. (2007). Customer-based brand equity for a destination. *Annals of Tourism Research* 34(2): 400–421.

Kotsi, F., Michael, I., Stephens Balakrishnan, M. and Zoëga Ramsøy, T. (2014). Place branding: Perception mapping of visual and auditory communication elements. Implications for brand U.A.E. *Proceedings of the 5th Destination Marketing & Branding Conference*. Macau: IFT. December.

Kulendran, N. and Dwyer, L. (2009). Measuring the return from Australian tourism marketing expenditure. *Journal of Travel Research* 47(3): 275–284.

Laroche, M., Habibi, M. R. and Richard, M. (2013). To be or not to be in social media: How brand loyalty is affected by social media? *International Journal of Information Management* 33(1): 76–82.

Lavidge, R. E. and Steiner, G. A. (1961). A model for predictive measurements of advertising effectiveness. *Journal of Marketing* 25(1): 59–62.

Leung, D., Law, R., van Hoof, H. and Buhalis, D. (2013). Social media in tourism and hospitality: A literature review. *Journal of Travel & Tourism Marketing* 30(1/2): 3–22.

Lim, Y. and Weaver, P. (2012). Customer-based brand equity for a destination: The effect of destination image on preference for products associated with a destination brand. *International Journal of Tourism Research* 16(3): 223–231.

Lubbe, B. (1998). Primary image as a dimension of destination image: An empirical assessment. *Journal of Travel & Tourism Marketing* 7(4): 21–43.

Martilla, J. A. and James, J. C. (1977). Importance–performance analysis. *Journal of Marketing* 41(1): 77–79.

Martinez-Garcia, E. and Raya, J. M. (2008). Length of stay for low-cost tourism. *Tourism Management* 29(6): 1064–1075.

Masberg, B. A. (1999). What is the priority of research in the marketing and promotional efforts of convention and visitors bureaus in the United States? *Journal of Travel & Tourism Marketing* 8(2): 29–40.

McLellan, R. W. and Foushee, K. D. (1983). Negative images of the United States as expressed by tour operators from other countries. *Journal of Travel Research* 22(1): 2–5.

McWilliams, E. G. and Crompton, J. L. (1997). An expanded framework for measuring the effectiveness of destination advertising. *Tourism Management* 18(3): 127–137.

Medina, L. F., Gomez, I. G. and Marrero, S. M. (2012). Measuring efficiency of sun and beach tourism destinations. *Annals of Tourism Research* 39(2): 1248–1251.

Menezes, A. G., Moniz, A. and Vieira, J. C. (2008). The determinants of length of stay of tourists in the Azores. *Tourism Economics* 14(2): 205–222.

Merrilees, B., Miller, D., Herington, C. and Smith, C. (2007). Brand Cairns: An insider (resident) stakeholder perspective. *Tourism Analysis* 12(5/6): 409–418.

Mohsin, A. and Ryan, C. (1999). Perceptions of the Northern Territory by travel agents in Kuala Lumpur. *Asia Pacific Journal of Tourism Research* 3(2): 41–46.

Morgan, N. J., Pritchard, A. and Piggott, R. (2003). Destination branding and the role of stakeholders: The case of New Zealand. *Journal of Vacation Marketing* 9(3): 285–299.

Morgan, N. J., Hastings, E. and Pritchard, A. (2012). Developing a new DMO evaluation framework: The case of Visit Wales. *Journal of Vacation Marketing* 18(1): 73–89.

Munro, J. and Richards, B. (2011). The digital challenge. In Morgan, N., Pritchard, A. and Pride, R. (eds) *Destination Brands: Managing Place Reputation* (3rd edition). Oxford: Butterworth-Heinemann, pp. 142–154.

Oliveira, E. and Panyik, E. (2015). Content, context and co-creation: Digital challenges in destination branding with references to Portugal as a tourist destination. *Journal of Vacation Marketing* 21(1): 53–74.

Oppermann, M. (1996). Convention destination images: Analysis of association meeting planners' perceptions. *Tourism Management* 17(3): 175–182.

Pearce, P. L. (1977). Mental souvenirs: A study of tourists and their city maps. *Australian Journal of Psychology* 29(3): 203–210.

Perdue, R. R. and Pitegoff, B. E. (1990). Methods of accountability research for destination marketing. *Journal of Travel Research* Spring: 44–49.

Pestana, B. C., Laurent, B., Nicholas, P., Elisabeth, R., Bernardin, S. and Assaf, A. G. (2011). Performance of French destinations: Tourism attraction perspectives. *Tourism Management* 32(1): 141–146.

Phillips, L. and Schofield, P. (2007). Pottery, pride and prejudice: Assessing resident images for city branding. *Tourism Analysis* 12(5/6): 397–407.

Pike, S. (2002a). ToMA as a measure of competitive advantage for short break holiday destinations. *Journal of Tourism Studies* 13(1): 9–19.

Pike, S. (2002b). *Positioning as a Source of Competitive Advantage: Benchmarking Rotorua's Position as a Domestic Short Break Holiday Destination*. PhD Thesis. University of Waikato. November. Hard copy only.

Pike, S. (2004). *Destination Marketing Organisations*. Oxford: Elsevier Science.

Pike, S. (2005). Tourism destination branding complexity. *Journal of Product & Brand Management* 14(4): 258–259.

Pike, S. (2006). Destination decision sets: A longitudinal comparison of stated destination preferences and actual travel. *Journal of Vacation Marketing* 12(4): 319–328.

Pike, S. (2007a). Consumer-based brand equity for destinations: Practical DMO performance measures. *Journal of Travel & Tourism Marketing* 22(1): 51–61.

Pike, S. (2007b). Destination image questionnaires: Avoiding uninformed responses. *Journal of Travel & Tourism Research* 2(Fall): 151–160.

Pike, S. (2008). *Destination Marketing: An Integrated Marketing Communication Approach*. Burlington, MA: Butterworth-Heinemann.

Pike, S. (2009). Destination brand positions of a competitive set of near-home destinations. *Tourism Management* 30(6): 857–866.

Pike, S. (2010). Destination branding: Tracking brand equity for an emerging destination between 2003 and 2007. *Journal of Hospitality & Tourism Research* 34(1): 124–139.

Pike, S. and Bianchi, C. (2014). Destination brand equity for Australia: Testing a model of CBBE in short haul and long haul markets. *Journal of Hospitality & Tourism Research*. Available at: http://jht.sagepub.com/content/early/2013/06/19/1096348013491604.full.pdf+html

Pike, S. and Page, S. (2014). Destination marketing organizations and destination marketing: A narrative analysis of the literature. *Tourism Management* 41: 202–227.

Pike, S. and Scott, N. (2009). Destination brand equity among the host community: A potential source of competitive advantage for DMOs: The case of Brisbane, Australia. *Acta Turistica* 21(2): 160–183.

Pike, S., Bianchi, C., Kerr, G. and Patti, C. (2010). Consumer-based brand equity for Australia as a long haul tourism destination in an emerging market. *International Marketing Review* 27(4): 434–449.

Pizam, A. (1990). Evaluating the effectiveness of travel trade shows and other tourism sales-promotion techniques. *Journal of Travel Research* Summer: 3–8.

Pritchard, G. (1982). Tourism promotion: Big business for the states. *HRA Quarterly* 23(2): 48–57.

Prosser, G., Hunt, S., Braithwaite, D. and Rosemann, I. (2000). *The Significance of Regional Tourism: A Preliminary Report*. Lismore, NSW: Centre for Regional Tourism Research.

PWC. (2013). *Distribution 2020: Situational Analysis*. Sydney, Australia: PWC.

Pyo, S., Song, S. and Chang, H. (1998). Implications of repeat visitor patterns: The Cheju Island case. *Tourism Analysis* 3: 181–187.

QTIC. (2015). *2015 Queensland Election: Priorities for Tourism*. Brisbane, QLD: Queensland Tourism Industry Council.

Ritchie, J. R. B. and Zins, M. (1978). Culture as determinant of the attractiveness of a tourism region. *Annals of Tourism Research* 5(2): 252–267.

Roehl, W. S. (1990). Travel agent attitudes toward China after Tiananmen Square. *Journal of Travel Research* Fall: 16–22.

Ryan, C. (1995). *Researching Tourist Satisfaction: Issues, Concepts, Problems*. London: Routledge.

Sartori, A., Mottironi, C. and Corigliano, M.A. (2012). Tourist destination brand equity and internal stakeholders: Empirical research. *Journal of Vacation Marketing* 18(4): 327–340.

Schoenbachler, C., di Benetto, A., Gordon, G. L. and Kaminski, P. F. (1995). Destination advertising: Assessing effectiveness with the split-run technique. *Journal of Travel & Tourism Marketing* 4(2): 1–21.

Schroeder, T. (1996). The relationship of residents' image of their state as a tourism destination and their support for tourism. *Journal of Travel Research* 34: 71–73.

Schultz, D. and Schultz, H. (2004). *Brand Babble: Sense and Nonsense about Branding*. Mason, OH: South-Western.

Selin, S. W. and Myers, N. A. (1998). Tourism marketing alliances: Member satisfaction and effectiveness attributes of a regional initiative. *Journal of Travel & Tourism Marketing* 7(3): 79–94.

Shani, A., Chen, P. J., Wang, Y. and Hua, N. (2010). Testing the impact of a promotional video on destination image change: Application of China as a tourism destination. *International Journal of Tourism Research* 12(2): 116–133.

Shanka, T. and Frost, F. A. (1999). The perception of Ethiopia as a tourist destination: An Australian perspective. *Asia Pacific Journal of Tourism Research* 4(1): 1–11.

Sharpley, R. (2014). Host perceptions of tourism: A review of the research. *Tourism Management* 42(1): 37–49.

Sheehan, L. R. and Ritchie, J. R. B. (1997). Financial management in tourism: A destination perspective. *Tourism Economics* 3(2): 93–118.

Sheehan, L. R. and Ritchie, J. R. B. (2005). Destination stakeholders: Exploring identity and salience. *Annals of Tourism Research* 32(3): 711–734.

Silberman, J. (1985). A demand function for length of stay: The evidence from Virginia Beach. *Journal of Travel Research* Spring: 16–23.

Slater, J. (2002). Brand Louisiana: 'Come as you are. Leave different.' In Morgan, N., Pritchard, A. and Pride, R. (eds) *Destination Branding*. Oxford: Butterworth-Heinemann, pp. 148–162.

St Hill, N. and Lewis, A. (2015). An assessment of the Caribbean tourism organization's collaborative marketing efforts: A member nation perspective. *Journal of Vacation Marketing* 21(1): 75–85.

Stepchenkova, S. and Eales, J. S. (2011). Destination image as quantified media messages: The effect of new on tourism demand. *Journal of Travel Research* 50(2): 198–212.

Tang, J. C. S. and Rochananond, N. (1990). Attractiveness as a tourist destination: A comparative study of Thailand and selected countries. *Socio-Economic Planning Sciences* 24(3): 229–236.

Teye, V. B. (1989). Marketing an emerging international tourist destination: The case of Arizona. *Journal of Travel Research* Spring: 23–28.

Tourism Australia. (2011). *Oprah in Australia*. November. Available at: http://www.tourism.australia.com/documents/corporate/The_Oprah_Effect.pdf

Tourism Australia. (2015). *President Xi's Visit to Australia*. January. Available at: http://www.tourism.australia.com/documents/corporate/President-XI-Visit-Social-Media-Recap.pdf

TravelandTourWorld.com. (2015). *ITB Berlin Sets New Records with Increased Trade Visitors and Business*. 9 March. Available at: http://www.travelandtourworld.com/news/article/itb-berlin-sets-new-records-increased-trade-visitors-business

Travelindustrywire.com. (2014). *Travel Leaders Applaud Bipartisan Effort to Extend Travel Promotion Program in Omnibus Bill*. 15 December. Available at: http://www.travelindustrywire.com/article81260.html

Travelindustrywire.com. (2015). *Record-Breaking Year for California's Travel Economy*. 5 May. Available at: http://www.travelindustrywire.com/article83447.html

Trout, J. and Rivkin, S. (1995). *The New Positioning*. New York: McGraw-Hill.

Vallee, P. (2005). Destination management in Canada. In Harrill, R. (ed.) *Fundamentals of Destination Management and Marketing*. Washington, DC: IACVB, pp. 229–244.

Vanhove, N. (2005). *The Economics of Tourism Destinations*. Oxford: Elsevier.

Var, T., Beck, R. A. D. and Loftus, P. (1977). Determination of touristic attractiveness of the touristic areas in British Columbia. *Journal of Travel Research* 15(1): 23–29.

Wagner, O. and Peters, M. (2009). Can association methods reveal the effects of internal branding on tourism destination stakeholders. *Journal of Place Management & Development* 2(1): 52–69.

Walmsley, D. J. and Jenkins, J. M. (1993). Appraisive images of tourist areas: Application of personal constructs. *Australian Geographer* 24(2): 1–13.

Williams, P. W., Stewart, K. and Larsen, D. (2012). Toward an agenda of high-priority tourism research. *Journal of Travel Research* 51(1): 3–11.

Witter, B. S. (1985). Attitudes about a resort area: A comparison of tourists and local retailers. *Journal of Travel Research* 3(Summer): 14–19.

Woodland, M. and Acott, T. G. (2007). Sustainability and local tourism branding in England's South Downs. *Journal of Sustainable Tourism* 15(6): 715–734.

Woodside, A. G. (1981). Measuring the conversion of advertising coupon inquirers into visitors. *Journal of Travel Research* Spring: 38–41.

Woodside, A. G. (1990). Measuring advertising effectiveness in destination marketing strategies. *Journal of Travel Research* 29(2): 3–38.

Woodside, A. G. and Sakai, M. (2001). Evaluating performance audits of implemented tourism marketing strategies. *Journal of Travel Research* 39(4): 369–379.

Woodside, A. G. and Sakai, M. (2009). Analyzing performance audit reports of destination management organizations' actions and outcomes. *Journal of Travel & Tourism Marketing* 26(3): 303–328.

Zhou, Z. (1997). Destination marketing: Measuring the effectiveness of brochures. *Journal of Travel & Tourism Marketing* 6(3/4): 143–158.

Index